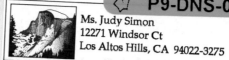

More praise for *The Best and the Brightest*

"Most impressive, superb—perceptive, literary, multidimensional."
—*The New York Times Book Review*

"Eloquent, witty, perceptive . . . Important not only because of its fascinating subject matter, but because of its high intellectual and literary qualities."

—*The New Leader*

"I predict that this brilliant and unsparing book will stir the conscience of the next generation if not of this."
—*The New York Post*

"Superior history, superbly researched and wonderfully written."
—John Kenneth Galbraith

"A brilliant, angry, funny book about the men who led us into the Vietnam war. . . . It is all here: Johnson's passion for secrecy, the marvelous flow of language, vulgar, brilliant, shrewd, ferocious."
—*Business Week*

The Best and the Brightest

The Best and the Brightest

TWENTIETH-ANNIVERSARY EDITION

David Halberstam

BALLANTINE BOOKS · NEW YORK

A Fawcett Book
Published by The Random House Publishing Group

Published in the United States by Fawcett Books, an imprint of
The Random House Publishing Group, a division of Random
House, Inc., New York, and simultaneously in Canada by
Random House of Canada Limited, Toronto. This work was
originally published in different form by Random House, Inc.,
in 1972. This edition published by arrangement with Random
House, Inc.

Grateful acknowledgment is made to the following for
permission to reprint previously published material: *ATLANTA
Magazine:* Excerpts from "Notes of a Native Son" by Ray
Moore (interview with Dean Rusk originally for WSV-TV) from
the October 1965 issue of ATLANTA Magazine. Copyright ©
1965 by ATLANTA Magazine. Reprinted by permission of
ATLANTA Magazine, Ray Moore, and WSB-TV.

www.ballantinebooks.com

Library of Congress Catalog Card Number: 93-90154

ISBN 0-449-90870-4

Cover design by Susan Grube

Manufactured in the United States of America
First Ballantine Books Edition: November 1993

29 28 27 26 25 24 23 22 21 20

For Dorothy deSantillana

I REMEMBER THE MOMENT WHEN I FIRST BEGAN TO UNDER-
stand why I felt so driven on this particular book. I was one year into the
legwork and had gone to a party for a friend's book. Teddy White, who had been
an important role model for me—his *Fire in the Ashes* had come out when I
was a sophomore in college—was off in a corner, I had joined him, and we were
talking about American politics. Suddenly another colleague wandered over,
turned to Teddy, and asked—I was stunned by the bluntness of the question,
it was the kind of thing you might think but did not dare *ask*—"What is it that
makes a bestseller, anyway?"

Teddy, whose first book about the collapse of China *(Thunder Out of China)*,
had reflected much of his pessimism about Chiang's forces which had been
suppressed by his employer, Harry Luce, had surprised us both with his answer:
"A book that burns in your belly—something that has to be written before you
can go on to anything else." He had, I realized in the weeks and months to
come, defined not just one of his earlier books, but the one I was working on
as well, an account of the origins of the war in Vietnam.

That book had its roots in a trip I made to Vietnam for *Harper's Magazine*
in the fall of 1967. I had been appalled and disillusioned by what I found in my
three months there. The war, despite the optimism of the Saigon command, was
a stalemate: our total military superiority checked by their total political superiority. In effect this meant we could win any set-piece battle we wanted, but the
other side could easily replenish their battlefield losses whenever *they* wanted.

What was even more depressing was the optimism I found among the top Americans in Saigon, which struck me as essentially self-deception. There was much heady talk implying that we were on the very edge of a final victory and that the other side was ready to crack. Invitations were even sent out that December by some high-ranking diplomats asking friends to come to the light-at-the-end-of-the-tunnel Christmas party.

It was the same old false optimism I had first witnessed there five years earlier as a young reporter for the *Times,* when the stakes were so much smaller. It reflected once again the immense difference between what people in the field thought was happening and what people in the Saigon command, responding to intense political pressure from Washington, wanted to think was happening. One night near the end of my tour in 1967 I was invited to Ambassador Ellsworth Bunker's house for dinner. At the end of the dinner, Barry Zorthian, then the chief public affairs officer, who was himself in the process of turning from hawk to dove and who was trying to dampen Bunker's seemingly unshakable optimism about the progress of events, had set me up with a planted question.

"Mister Ambassador," he had said near the end of the evening, "David Halberstam has been away from Vietnam for four years, and he's been back traveling around the countryside for the last three months. Perhaps he would share some of his impressions with us."

Thus cued, I suggested that we were fighting the birthrate of the nation, that the war was essentially a stalemate—but a stalemate which favored the other side, since eventually we would have to go home. What our military did not understand, I added, was that Hanoi controlled the pace of the war, and it could either initiate contact and raise the level of violence or hold back, lick its wounds, and lower it, depending on its needs at a given moment.

Bunker was considered one of the ablest and least conventional men in the foreign service at that moment, although his years in Vietnam did not add luster to his reputation. His was a graceful and courteous presence, and I think this last assignment, with the steadily mounting bitterness which it provoked, must have been one of diminishing pleasure for him. He listened politely to what I said (which was more than one of his predecessors had done—four years earlier an American ambassador had literally thrown me out of his office when I had expressed reservations about an extremely dubious ARVN success). He had, Bunker said, spoken with his generals—he named several of them—all fine men, and they had assured him that, contrary to what I said, everything was on schedule and that there was an inevitability to the victory we sought, given the awesome force we had mounted against the North Vietnamese army and the Vietcong.

That evening was not the place for a confrontation, and Ellsworth Bunker, with his old-fashioned, almost courtly New England manner, was certainly not a man anyone wanted to be in a confrontation with. As such, what followed was rather mild. His generals, I suggested, were like all Western generals before them, starting with the French: not so much in the wrong war, but on the wrong planet. Their ability to calibrate this war was limited, their skills were tied to other wars in other places, and with very few exceptions they, like the French before them, tended to underestimate the bravery, strength, resilience, *and the political dynamic which fed the indigenous force* they were fighting. In addition, the briefings they received from subordinates were always tied to career and promotion.

As I spoke I thought of one of my favorite generals, Bob York, a rugged, craggy-faced ex-boxer whom I had known in my earlier tour and who had always gotten things right—had gotten them right because when he went into the countryside he unpinned his stars; with his rough looks he seemed more like an enlisted man than the West Pointer he was, and people told him the truth. At the dinner Ambassador Bunker reiterated his confidence, Zorthian, having hit a wall—and not for the first time, one suspected—changed the subject and the party soon ended. I left the ambassador's residence more depressed than ever; the embassy was isolated, it still did not understand the roots and therefore the strength of its adversary, it was once again telling Washington what Washington wanted to hear without even knowing. A few months later the Tet offensive caught the American mission, both military and civilian, largely by surprise and undermined the legitimacy of almost everything it was reporting about Vietnam, most particularly its relentless military optimism. What the American army at the highest levels lost in Vietnam, my close friend and colleague Charlie Mohr told me years later, in the best summation of that time, was its intellectual integrity.

I returned back from Vietnam to America properly depressed. A war which was not winnable was going to play itself out, with, I thought, terrible consequences for both America and Vietnam. I had little time to ruminate on this, for I spent the coming year covering the growing domestic turbulence caused by the war. 1968 was one of those landmark years in which everything came to a head—or, as in this case, seemed to come apart, marked as it was by the withdrawal of the sitting President from the race, by two tragic assassinations, and by a political process which began in the snows of New Hampshire just as the Tet offensive took place and ended in violence in the streets of Chicago. That year I covered many of those events, and in addition I wrote a small book about Robert Kennedy's campaign. When the year was over, I felt like someone who had been living for too long on the edge of events. I was exhausted, and I had no sense of what I wanted to do next. What about an article on McGeorge Bundy? suggested our executive editor at *Harper's*, Midge Decter (not yet identifiably in her neoconservative incarnation) an article on McGeorge Bundy? A light went on immediately. It was a chance to look at perhaps the most luminescent of the Kennedy people, all of whom had seemed so dazzling when they had first taken office, a chance to look at the Kennedy years themselves from a certain distance, and finally, and perhaps most important, a chance to look at the decision making on the war itself. Suddenly all my energies were fused. It was exactly what I wanted to do, and I spent the next three months working on it. The article, "The Very Expensive Education of McGeorge Bundy," ran three times the normal magazine length and caused something of a storm. The general power of print and of a magazine like *Harper's* was a good deal greater twenty years ago in relationship to television than it is today, and this was regarded as an important article. It marked the first time anyone in any major centrist magazine, let alone a presumably liberal one, had been so critical of a member of the Kennedy Administration; far more important, it was the first time a writer in the liberal center had suggested that the Kennedy Administration might be overrated and that its decision making on Vietnam was significantly flawed. Up to then there had been something of a gentleman's agreement among those who might be called The Good Journalists of Washington that the Kennedy Administration was one of excellence, that it was for good things and against bad things, and that when it did lesser things it was only in self-defense, and in order that it might do other good things. The Kennedy charm and skill and ability to manipulate events was not inconsiderable. I had been viewed by some in the inner Kennedy circle as a hostile journalist because of the pessimistic quality of my early reporting from Saigon, and had angered some people even more when I had told in an earlier book of the President's frustration with me, and his attempts to have the publisher of the *Times* transfer me from my Saigon beat.

Now with the publication of the Bundy article the stakes were about to go up. Bundy was a dual icon. He had been a dean of Harvard at an unspeakably young age, portrayed constantly in the press as the most cerebral member of the Kennedy Administration other than the President himself, and at the same time the leader of the next generation of the American Establishment. "You have begun," my friend Tom Wicker, who still lived in Washington, told me when the article was published, "to take on most of the icons in a city that does not like to see its icons criticized." The outcry upon publication was immediate. My clearest memory of the many attacks on me, some overt, some covert, is of that by Archibald MacLeish, the poet and former librarian of Congress, and an absolute paragon of the Establishment. MacLeish was a man with very close ties to the Bundy family, and to Dean Acheson, and to the Cowles family, which by chance then happened to own *Harper's*. He wrote a long, very angry letter (albeit not for publication) taking great umbrage at what I had done, and wondering how I dared do it. He sent one copy to Cass Canfield, then the head of Harper Brothers publishing house who wisely simply passed it on without comment to Willie Morris our editor, and another to John Cowles, Jr., who was the overall owner of *Harper's Magazine*. John Cowles, not by a long shot as good at this game as Cass Canfield, not only sent it on to Willie, but unwisely added his own letter, addressed not to me, but to Willie, and far more sympathetic, it seemed to me and my colleagues, to Bundy than to me. Cowles seemed to be suggesting that a considerable injustice had been done. His letter was not without its clubby overtones—he constantly referred to me as Halberstam and to Bundy as Mac. Those were edgy times. Cowles and I had a heated exchange of letters in which I suggested that if he did not like what I wrote, he could call me up, or he could write me directly.

That article, however, gave me not merely a book idea, but a sense of purpose. I would do a book about how and why we had gone to war in Vietnam, and about the men who were the architects of the war. The basic question behind the book was why men who were said to be the ablest to serve in government in this century had been the architects of what struck me as likely to be the worst tragedy since the Civil War. In another time I might have hesitated before setting out on a task so ambitious. It was a major jump in terms of what I had attempted in the past—my previous books were an extension of the daily and monthly journalism I had already completed, and this was a book more likely to fall into the category of contemporary history. But from the moment I thought of extending the magazine article into a book, I had no doubts. Done properly, it would take four years, and if I gave roughly two and a half years to the legwork and a year and a half to the writing, I could do it. In fact that proved to be a surprisingly close approximation of what was required. Looking back, I think of myself as working on it in a kind of prolonged fever. If there was a formula to doing the book, I thought, it would be one of input. If I went out and did two interviews each day, I was sure I would not fail. I did the two a day with ease. Sometimes I did three. If I found someone who was helpful, I would see him not once, but two or three or four or five times. There was, I found, always more to learn.

My years at *Harper's,* after I had gone there in 1967 after twelve years of working for daily newspapers, had been eye-opening: In the past, the greatest limitations placed on a daily journalist were those of space (the average story in those days ran about 800 words) and time: a reporter usually had only one day to work on a story. By contrast, at *Harper's* I had some six to eight weeks to do a piece, and virtually as much space as I wanted. That had been a quantum leap not merely in terms of time and space, but, more important, in terms of freedom. Now I intended to take another leap from the *Harper's* freedom, and expand it even more, from eight weeks to 200 weeks, from 10,000 words to as many words as I needed. The only failings would be my own. So it was that I signed a contract with Jim Silberman at Random House. If I could stick with my schedule, I was sure I could come up with a portrait of the time, of the men, the era, and the process which had led to this war.

I was thirty-five years old when I started; I had left the *Times* two years earlier to become a contract writer for Willie Morris at *Harper's* and he had treated me and my colleagues with the greatest of care; now, though I retained my connection to *Harper's,* I cut my base salary, which had been all of about $20,000, to a much smaller retainer. My financial dilemma was fairly typical of that of many a young writer trying to branch out from magazines while doing a major project: how to devote some 80 percent of my energy to one all-consuming project, while making only about 25 or 30 percent of my income from it. Though I did have the retainer from *Harper's,* in truth for the first time in my life I was effectively self-employed. The advance from Random House was hardly grand even for those days of more limited advances, and reflected the somewhat limited view of the commercial possibilities inherent in my topic. A book on the origins of the Vietnam War was not considered a hot topic. The total, after commissions, was $41,000, and it was to cover the four projected years of work. It was not a bad sum in those pre-inflation days, but if amortized over four years, it was less than a news clerk at the *Times* was making. Whatever else I had in mind when I took on the book, it was not money.

The hardest thing I had to do at the start was to take leave of my byline for the next four years. Ours is a profession built upon the immediacy of reward: We graduate from college, and our peers go off to law school and graduate school and medical school. They have barely started their first-year classes, and our names are bannered across the front pages of the nation's leading newspapers. They get their medical or law degrees, and start out in their residencies or as the lowest hirelings in a law office, and we are old-timers, covering the statehouse, or on our way to Washington, by now, we believe, the possessors of a well-known brand name. The byline is a replacement for many other things, not the least of them money. If someone ever does a great psychological profile of journalism as a profession, what will be apparent will be the need for gratification—if not instant, then certainly relatively immediate. Reporters take sustenance from their bylines; they are a reflection of who you are, what you do, and why, to an uncommon degree, you exist. It was hard enough to give so much of it up when I went to *Harper's,* where I would get only five or six bylines a year. But to go from the world of easy recognition, from the world of The *Times* and *Harper's,* to a world where I might get only one byline in four years, was a great risk. A journalist always wonders: If my byline disappears, have I disappeared as well? My friends, knowing my compulsions, my innate impatience, wondered if I could do it. Would I be able to resist assignments and stay with my project? It was, as much to my surprise as theirs, the easiest thing I had ever done. I had replaced the need for immediacy with something far more powerful, an obsession. Teddy White had been absolutely correct about the drive that the right book topic would create in me. I never regretted the deadlines, never missed the office. In a way I simply disappeared from journalism. When I was at parties and people asked what I was doing, I would talk about the book, but it seemed so vague an idea for most people that I would notice their eyes glaze over.

It was in some ways an opportune time to be doing a book like this. The failure of a major policy—and Vietnam, no matter what the highest officials were saying, was a failed policy—is, if nothing else, a marvelous lever with which to open a debate. At the time I began the book, no larger debate on the origins of Vietnam was going on in Congress, but in 1969 and 1970 and 1971 how and why it had all happened was very much in the minds of many of the people who had been a part of it. Therefore I was interviewing people of all ranks at precisely the same moment many of them were examining not merely the failure of so tragic a policy, but their own participation in it. Thus, as I interviewed them, they were able to air their own doubts about what had happened in a way that often struck me as oddly cathartic.

It was, of course, far more than obsession which carried me—it was a profound curiosity as well. I had seen the war from the Saigon side but not from the Washington one; I had no idea why many decisions had been made, how policy had evolved, or what the effect of the Cold War and the McCarthy period had on the decision makers, long after McCarthy himself had been condemned by the Senate.

Some twenty years later I have come to think of each of the major books I have written, books which often took four or five or six years out of my life, as the first of one of many universities, that I entered, one with courses on how policy is made, and what the effects of the McCarthy era were on policy making. I began to enjoy doing the book, not just because it was an obsession, but because it offered me a chance to ask broader questions and to take more time answering them. And, sometimes against my will, it forced me to grow.

Journalists by and large, like people in other professions, mirror the form of their work. If they are always asked to write in 800-word takes, they will end up thinking in 800-word takes; if they are always asked to report on the evening news in bites of one minute, fifteen seconds, they will end up thinking in bites of 1:15. The great liberation for me, in doing a book like this, was the ability to escape the limits of form. So it was that the interviews became more than mere source material, they became part of an education. I had been a poor student in college: I was not ready to learn, or to delve into the past. As a journalist I had on several occasions been excited by the pull of dramatic events, in Vietnam and in the early Civil Rights movement. Now something more complicated was happening to me—I was becoming caught up in the excitement of history, in the pull of the past.

Nothing about it bored me. I could hardly wait to go to work each day. Interviews for daily newspapers are rarely long; interviews for magazines at *Harper's* tended to last an hour to an hour and a half. The interviews for this book were different; they might last three or four hours. Very early on I went to visit Daniel Ellsberg in Los Angeles. We had known each other in college, and I had given him an early briefing in 1964, when I had just come back from Vietnam and he was on his way out there. Now we held a series of marathon interviews at his home on the beach. When I typed up my notes on them—the typing took several days as well—they came to some twenty-five single-spaced pages. Two and a half years later, after *The Pentagon Papers*—the documented history of the war—came out, I realized that the notes I had taken were like a concentrate of *The Papers,* that Ellsberg had already studied *The Papers,* knew the bureaucratic history brilliantly, and understood what the documents meant. I was doubly lucky: He had in effect given me a valuable road map. Had I been given *The Papers* themselves that early, I would probably have become a prisoner of them—as it was, I had a good sense of the bureaucratic history as related by an expert, but I was also free to do several hundred interviews, not merely to flesh out the bureaucratic history, but to balance the pure paper history with a human history, and to relate secret decisions as they were not always set down on paper.

One of the things which surprised me was how thin most of the newspaper and magazine reporting of the period was, the degree to which journalists accepted the norms of the government and, particularly in the glamorous Kennedy era, the reputation of these new stars at face value. Credit was given more readily for educational prowess and for academic achievement than for accomplishment in governance. The one member of the Administration who had deigned to enter pluralistic politics was the President himself. Being verbal seemed to be an end in itself. Among those dazzled by the Administration team was Vice-President Lyndon Johnson. After attending his first Cabinet meeting he went back to his mentor Sam Rayburn and told him with great enthusiasm how extraordinary they were, each brighter than the next, and that the smartest of them all was that fellow with the Stacomb on his hair from the Ford Motor Company, McNamara. "Well, Lyndon," Mister Sam answered, "you may be right and they may be every bit as intelligent as you say, but I'd feel a whole lot better about them if just one of them had run for sheriff once." It is my favorite story in the book, for it underlines the weakness of the Kennedy team, the difference between intelligence and wisdom, between the abstract quickness and verbal facility which the team exuded, and true wisdom, which is the product of hard-won, often bitter experience. Wisdom for a few of them came *after* Vietnam.

But that doubt about the Administration and its members and their abilities did not exist in the early years under Kennedy, when they had first come to power. Rarely had a new Administration received such a sympathetic hearing at a personal level from the more serious and respected journalists of the city. The good reporters of that era, those who were well educated and who were enlightened themselves and worked for enlightened organizations, *liked* the

Kennedys and were for the same things the Kennedys were for. In addition, the particular nature of the President's personal style, his ease and confidence with reporters, his considerable skill in utilizing television, and the terrible manner in which he was killed had created a remarkable myth about him. The fact that a number of men in his Cabinet were skillful writers themselves and that in the profound sadness after his murder they wrote their own eloquent (and on occasion self-serving) versions of his presidency had strengthened that myth.

At the time it was somewhat fashionable to compare this Administration with its lineal predecessors, those who had served under Truman and who had fashioned the basic elements of the Containment policy. But even here the comparisons were hardly flattering. The men who had made those early hard decisions of the Cold War had served a much longer, much more complete apprenticeship in their professions. The decisions on how to handle the Soviet Union were made as a result of carefully weighing the advice of accomplished men like Kennan, Bohlen, and Harriman, who had in different ways devoted much of their lives to the study of the Soviet Union. Clearly, the new terms of apprenticeship in modern America as the nation ascended so quickly to superpower status were to be much briefer. On the issue which was to prove so critical to them, Vietnam, and which so greatly undermined any positive accomplishments of the Administration, and to the question of extending the logic of the Cold War in Europe to the underdeveloped world, and to a spot where nationalism was clearly at stake, they brought no comparable expertise at all. There is no small irony here: An administration which flaunted its intellectual superiority and its superior academic credentials made the most critical of decisions with virtually no input from anyone who had any expertise on the recent history of that part of the world, and it in no way factored in the entire experience of the French Indochina War. Part of the reason for this were the upheavals of the McCarthy period, but in part it was also the arrogance of men of the Atlantic; it was as if these men did not need to know about such a distant and somewhat less worthy part of the world. Lesser parts of the world attracted lesser men; years later I came upon a story which illustrated this theory perfectly. Jack Langguth, a writer and college classmate of mine, mentioned to a member of that Administration that he was thinking of going on to study Latin American history. The man had turned to him, his contempt barely concealed, and said, "Second-rate parts of the world for second-rate minds."

Mine, though I did not think of it this way at the time, was probably the first Kennedy revisionist book, though on the increasingly harsh scale of what was to come later it was rather mild. I did not see Kennedy as a romantic figure (although, later, I saw his younger brother Robert that way) but rather as a cool, skillful, modern politician, skeptical, ironic, and graceful. The best thing about him, I thought, was his modernity, his lack of being burdened by myths of the past. Because I saw him as cool and skeptical it always struck me that he would not have sent combat troops into Vietnam. He was too skeptical, I think, for that: I believe that, in the last few months of his life, he had come to dislike the war, it was messy and our policy there was flawed and going nowhere, and he was wary of the optimism of his generals. In 1964 I think he wanted to put it on the back burner, run against Goldwater, beat him handily (which I think he expected to do) and then negotiate his way out. His first term had been burdened by his narrow victory over Nixon and the ghosts of the McCarthy period; with luck he would be free of both these burdens in his second term, and I do not believe he intended to lose in the rice paddies of Indochina what he considered this most precious chance for historic accomplishment. But that having been said, it should be noted that he significantly escalated the number of Americans there, and the number of American deaths; that his public rhetoric was often considerably more aggressive than his more private doubts; and that he gave over to Lyndon Johnson that famous can-do aggressive team of top advisers.

The other thing I learned about the Kennedy–Johnson team was that for all their considerable reputations as brilliant, rational managers they were in fact very poor managers. They thought they were very good, and they were always talking about keeping their options open, even as, day by day and week by week, events closed off those options. The truth was that history—and in Indochina we were on the wrong side of it—was a hard taskmaster and from the early to the middle sixties, when we were making those fateful decisions, we had almost no choices left. Our options had been steadily closing down since 1946, when the French Indochina War began. That was when we had the most options, and the greatest element of choice. But we had granted, however reluctantly, the French the right to return and impose their will on the Vietnamese by force; and by 1950, caught up increasingly in our own global vision of anti-Communism, we chose not to see this war as primarily a colonial/anticolonial war, and we had begun to underwrite most of the French costs. Where our money went our rhetoric soon followed. We adjusted our public statements, and much of our journalism, to make it seem as if this was a war of Communists against anti-Communists, instead, as the people of Vietnam might have seen it, a war of a colonial power against an indigenous nationalist force. By the time the Kennedy–Johnson team arrived and started talking about all their options, like it or not (and they did not even want to think about it) they had in fact almost no options at all. In fact, for a team of Democratic politicians they were sooner or later going to be faced with the most unpalatable of choices: getting out, and then being accused of losing a freedom-loving country to the Communists, or sending in combat troops to fight an unwinnable war. "Events," wrote George Ball, paraphrasing Emerson "are in the saddle, and ride mankind." In addition the Kennedy–Johnson team never defined the war, what our roles and missions were, how many troops we were going to send and, most important of all, what we were going to do if the North Vietnamese matched our escalation with their escalation, as they were likely to. It was an ill-defined commitment, one made in stealth and in considerable secrecy, because those making it were uneasy about their path and feared an open debate, feared exposing the policy to any serious scrutiny.

Of the things I had not known when I started out, I think the most important was the degree to which the legacy of the McCarthy period still lived. It had been almost seven years since Joe McCarthy had been censured when John Kennedy took office, and most people believed that his hold on Washington was over. The people comprising the body politic of America might not in general, particularly if things were honestly explained to them, be that frightened of the Communists (making legitimate claims to nationalism) taking over a small country some 12,000 miles away, or for that matter frightened or very impressed by Joe McCarthy himself. But among the top *Democrats,* against whom the issue of being soft on Communism might be used, and among the Republicans, who might well use the charge, it was still live ammunition.

If the Kennedy people privately mocked the bombast and rigidity of the Eisenhower and Dulles years (years in which Dulles had made his own separate peace with the Republican right) they did not lightly reverse Dulles's policies, particularly where they were most irrational and dangerous, in an emerging post-colonial Asia. McCarthyism still lingered: a McCarthyism that was broader than the wild outrages of the Senator himself, something that even men as fine as Bob Taft were caught up in. The real McCarthyism went deeper in the American grain than most people wanted to admit: it was an odd amalgam of the traditional isolationism of the Midwest (cheered on greatly by Colonel McCormick of Chicago); McCarthy's own personal recklessness and cruelty; the anxiety of a nation living in a period of new and edgy atomic tensions and no longer protected from adversaries by the buffer of its two adjoining oceans; and the fact that the Republican party had been out of power for so long—twenty years, until Dwight Eisenhower, a kind of hired Republican, was finally elected. The Republicans' long, arid period out of office, accentuated by Truman's 1948 defeat of Dewey, had permitted the out-party in its desperation, to accuse the leaders of the governing party of treason. The Democrats, in the wake of the relentless sustained attacks on Truman and Acheson over their policies in Asia, came to believe that they had lost the White House when they lost China. Long after McCarthy himself was gone, the fear of being accused of being soft on Communism lingered among the Democratic leaders. The Republicans had, of course, offered no alternative policy on China (the last thing they had wanted to do was suggest sending American boys to fight for China) and indeed there was no policy to offer, for China was never ours, events there were well outside our control, and our feudal proxies had been swept away by the forces of history. But in the political darkness of the time it had been easy to blame the Democrats for the ebb and flow of history.

The fear generaled in those days lasted a long time, and Vietnam was to be something of an instant replay after China. The memory of the fall of China and what it did to the Democrats, was, I think, more bitter for Lyndon Johnson than it was for John Kennedy. Johnson, taking over after Kennedy was murdered and after the Kennedy patched-up advisory commitment had failed, vowed that he was not going to be the President of the United States who lost the Great Society because he lost Saigon. In the end it would take the tragedy of the Vietnam War and the election of Richard Nixon (the only political figure who could probably go to China without being Red-baited by Richard Nixon) to exorcise those demons, and to open the door to China.

That was the terrible shadow of the McCarthy period. It hung heavily albeit secretly over the internal calculation of Democratic leaders of the period. But of course it was never discussed in the major newspapers and magazine articles that analyzed policy making in Vietnam. It was a secret subject, reflecting secret fears. Nor did the men who made the policy have any regional expertise as they made their estimates about what the other side would do if we escalated and sent American combat troops. All of the China experts, the Asia hands who were the counterparts of Bohlen and Kennan, had had their careers destroyed with the fall of China. The men who gave advice on Asia were either European-ists or men transferred from the Pentagon. When my book was finally done and accepted by my publisher, I realized I had not made this point strongly enough. So I added another chapter, the story of John Paton Davies, one of the most distinguished of the China hands who had had his career savaged during the McCarthy years. The section reflected my belief that in a better and healthier society he or someone like him might have been sitting in as Assistant Secretary of State during the Vietnam decisions. I think adding the chapter strengthened the book, but years later as I ponder the importance of the McCarthy era on both our domestic and foreign policy, I am convinced that this flaw in the society was even greater than I portrayed it, and that if I were to do the book over, I might expand the entire section. It was one of the great myths of that time that foreign policy was this pure and uncontaminated area which was never touched by domestic politics, and that domestic politics ended at the water's edge. The truth, in sharp contrast, was that all those critical decisions were primarily driven by considerations of domestic politics, and by political fears of the consequences of looking weak in a forthcoming domestic election.

WRITING THE BOOK WAS THE MOST INTELLECTUALLY EXCITING quest of my life. Each day for the three and a half years the book took to write, I simply could not wait to get to work. Most journalists are impatient to get their legwork done and to start the actual writing, but I was caught up in something else, the actual doing. The legwork became for me infinitely more interesting than the writing, and in fact for a time that became something of a problem in my work, a tendency to pursue certain aspects of a book for too long and to seek too much detail. Some two years into the project, I became convinced that I was on to something special, not necessarily something special commercially, for it never really occurred to me that the book would have a particularly large audience, but something special in terms of its validity, its truth, and that to the degree I could bring a moment alive, I was doing so. (That was something else I owed Teddy White. I and others of my generation, who went from newspaper and magazine reporting to writing books, owed him a far greater debt of gratitude than most people realized. As much as anyone he changed the nature of nonfiction political reporting. By taking the 1960 campaign, a subject about which everyone knew the outcome, and writing a book which proved wondrously exciting to read, he had given a younger generation a marvelous example of the expanded possibilities of writing nonfiction journalism. As I worked on my own book, I remembered his example and tried to write it as a detective novel.)

In 1972, as I was finishing the book, I became unusually nervous. I kept a duplicate set of notes and a duplicate manuscript outside my apartment. (These were, after all, days when strange things were taking place on orders from the White House.)

Right up until publication we were unsure about the title. I had liked the phrase "best and brightest," which I had used in the original *Harper's* piece on Bundy to describe the entire group as it swept so confidently into Washington. But others did not like it. Ken Galbraith, who was unusually generous to me in those years, offering advice and guidance, did not like it. "Call it *The Establishment's War*, Halberstam," he said. I was not excited by that. My backup title was *Guardians at the Gate*, which came from a speech of Johnson's saying that we had not chosen to be the guardians at the gate but that, if need be, we would honor that role. But I still liked *The Best and the Brightest*, and in the end I went with it.

Most people who liked the book liked the title, except the writer Mary McCarthy, who seemed not to like me, the book, or the title. I could not even get the title right, she claimed in a violent attack on me and the book in *The New York Review of Books*. In the Protestant hymn, she pointed out, the phrase is "brightest and best." I was never very strong on hymns and knew nothing of the one she cited. I was much cheered by a letter from Graham Greene, who thanked me for sending him a copy and said that he was quite puzzled by the vicious attack Mary McCarthy had written in *The New York Review*: "I couldn't understand the ferocious attack by Mary McCarthy, who is not one of my favourite writers," he wrote to me. "I suppose she resented your not having quoted anything from her account of a weekend in Hanoi," he said. As for the title, she was wrong about that; hymn or no, it went into the language, although it is often misused, failing to carry the tone or irony that the original intended.

It did not occur to me that the book would be a major commercial success. For years others had assured me that I was wasting my time, that no one was interested in a book about the origins of the Vietnam War, and that it would have little commercial appeal. My editor Jim Silberman and I agreed that if it cleared 50,000 in hard cover, it would be a significant success. The print order for the book was originally 25,000, by far the largest for anything I had ever written. A few weeks before publication we began to have a sense that the book was going to move. Excerpts in both *Harper's* and *Esquire* had helped greatly. The publishing order was increased to 50,000. By the date of publication it was 75,000. In the first two weeks it sold some 60,000 copies, almost unheard-of for a book that serious. Eventually it sold around 180,000 copies in hard cover, which was considered astonishing, and an estimated 1.5 million in paperback. The reviews were almost uniformly good; it was that rarest of successes, a book which was both a critical success and a commercial success. More, it got out there. It did not just sit on coffee tables. People read it and took it seriously; to this day I still hear from people who like to tell me how old they were and where they were when they read it and the name of the person who encouraged them to read it, and how it reshaped their thinking on Vietnam.

The great pleasure for me was an inner pleasure: it was very simply the best I could do. In my own mind, I had reached above myself. There were no skills I possessed which were wasted, and there were skills which I found in doing it which I had never known of before, of patience and endurance. If a reporter's life is, at its best, an ongoing education, then this had been in the personal sense a stunning experience, and it had changed the way I looked not just at Vietnam, but at every other subject I took on from then on. I had loved working away from the pack, enjoyed the solitude of this more different, lonelier kind of journalism which I was now doing. I had gotten not just a book which I greatly valued from the experience, but a chance to grow.

The Best and the Brightest

Chapter One

A COLD DAY IN DECEMBER. LONG AFTERWARD, AFTER THE assassination and all the pain, the older man would remember with great clarity the young man's grace, his good manners, his capacity to put a visitor at ease. He was concerned about the weather, that the old man not be exposed to the cold or to the probing questions of freezing newspapermen, that he not have to wait for a cab. Instead he had guided his guest to his own car and driver. The older man would remember the young man's good manners almost as clearly as the substance of their talk, though it was an important meeting.

In just a few weeks the young man would become President of the United States, and to the newspapermen standing outside his Georgetown house, there was an air of excitement about every small act, every gesture, every word, every visitor to his temporary headquarters. They complained less than usual, the bitter cold notwithstanding; they felt themselves a part of history: the old was going out and the new was coming in, and the new seemed exciting, promising.

On the threshold of great power and great office, the young man seemed to have everything. He was handsome, rich, charming, candid. The candor was part of the charm: he could beguile a visitor by admitting that everything the visitor proposed was right, rational, proper—but he couldn't do it, not this week, this month, this term. Now he was trying to put together a government, and the candor showed again. He was self-deprecating with the older man.

He had spent the last five years, he said ruefully, running for office, and he did not know any real public officials, people to run a government, serious men. The only ones he knew, he admitted, were politicians, and if this seemed a denigration of his own kind, it was not altogether displeasing to the older man. Politicians *did* need men to serve, to run the government. The implication was obvious. Politicians could run Pennsylvania and Ohio, and if they could not run Chicago they could at least deliver it. But politicians run the world? What did they know about the Germans, the French, the Chinese? He needed experts for that, and now he was summoning them.

The old man was Robert A. Lovett, the symbolic expert, representative of the best of the breed, a great surviving link to a then unquestioned past, to the wartime and postwar successes of the Stimson-Marshall-Acheson years. He was the very embodiment of the Establishment, a man who had a sense of country rather than party. He was above petty divisions, so he could say of his friends, as so many of that group could, that he did not even know to which political party they belonged. He was a man of impeccable credentials, indeed he passed on other people's credentials, deciding who was safe and sound, who was ready for advancement and who was not. He was so much a part of that atmosphere that he was immortalized even in the fiction of his class. Louis Auchincloss, who was the unofficial laureate of that particular world, would have one of his great fictional lawyers say: "I've got that Washington bug. Ever since I had that job with Bob Lovett . . ."

He had the confidence of both the financial community and the Congress. He had been good, very good, going up on the Hill in the old days and soothing things over with recalcitrant Midwestern senators; and he was soft on nothing, that above all—no one would accuse Robert Lovett of being soft. He was a witty and graceful man himself, a friend not just of the powerful, the giants of politics and industry, but of people like Robert Benchley and Lillian Hellman and John O'Hara. He had wit and charm. Even in those tense moments in 1950 when he had been at Defense and MacArthur was being MacArthur, Lovett had amused his colleagues at high-level meetings with great imitations of MacArthur's vanities, MacArthur in Korea trying to comb his few strands of hair from side to side over his pate to hide his baldness, while standing in the blast of prop-plane engines at Kimpo Airfield.

They got along well, these two men who had barely known each other before. Jack Kennedy the President-elect, who in his campaign had summoned the nation's idealism, but who was at least as skeptical as he was idealistic, curiously ill at ease with other people's overt idealism, preferring in private the tart and darker view of the world and of mankind of a skeptic like Lovett.

In addition to his own misgivings he had constantly been warned by one of his more senior advisers that in order to deal with State effectively, he had to have a real man there, that State was filled with sissies in striped pants and worse. That senior adviser was Joseph Kennedy, Sr., and he had consistently pushed, in discussions with his son, the name of Robert Lovett, who he felt was the best of those old-time Wall Street people. For Robert Lovett understood power, where it resided, how to exercise it. He had exercised it all his life, yet he was curiously little known to the general public. The anonymity was not entirely by chance, for he was the embodiment of the public servant— financier who is so secure in his job, the value of it, his right to do it, that he does not need to seek publicity, to see his face on the cover of a magazine or on television, to feel reassured. Discretion is better, anonymity is safer: his peers know him, know his role, know that he can get things done. Publicity sometimes frightens your superiors, annoys congressional adversaries (when Lovett was at Defense, the senior members of the Armed Services committees never had to read in newspapers and magazines how brilliant Lovett was, how well he handled the Congress; rather they read how much he admired the Congress). He was the private man in the public society *par excellence.* He did not need to impress people with false images. He knew the rules of the game: to whom you talked, what you said, to whom you did not talk, which journalists were your kind, would, without being told, know what to print for the greater good, which questions to ask, and which questions not to ask. He lived in a world where young men made their way up the ladder by virtue not just of their own brilliance and ability but also of who their parents were, which phone calls from which old friends had preceded their appearance in an office. In a world like this he knew that those whose names were always in print, who were always on the radio and television, were there precisely because they did *not* have power, that those who did hold or had access to power tried to keep out of sight. He was a twentieth-century man who did not hold press conferences, who never ran for anything. The classic insider's man.

He was born in Huntsville, Texas, in 1895, the son of Robert Scott Lovett, a general counsel for Harriman's Union Pacific Railway, a railroad lawyer, a power man in those rough and heady days, who then became a judge, very much a part of the power structure, the Texas arm of it, and eventually a member of the Union Pacific board of directors and president of the railway. His son Bob would do all the right Eastern things, go to the right schools, join the right clubs (Hill School, Yale, Skull and Bones). He helped form the Yale unit of pilots which flew in World War I, and he commanded the first U.S. Naval Air Squadron. He married well, Adele Brown, the beautiful daughter of James Brown, a senior partner in the great banking firm of Brown Brothers.

Since those post-college years were a bad time for the railways, he went to work for Brown Brothers, starting at $1,080 a year, a fumbling-fingered young clerk who eventually rose to become a partner and finally helped to arrange the merger of Brown Brothers with the Harriman banking house to form the powerful firm of Brown Bros., Harriman & Co. So he came naturally to power, to running things, to knowing people, and his own marriage had connected him to the great families. His view of the world was a banker's view, the right men making the right decisions, stability to be preserved. The status quo was good, one did not question it.

He served overseas in London, gaining experience in foreign affairs, though like most influential Americans who would play a key role in foreign affairs entering government through the auspices of the Council on Foreign Relations, the group which served as the Establishment's unofficial club, it was with the eyes of a man with a vested interest in the static world, where business could take place as usual, where the existing order could and should be preserved. He saw the rise of Hitler and the coming military importance of air power; when he returned to America he played a major role in speeding up America's almost nonexistent air defenses. He served with great distinction during World War II, a member of that small inner group which worked for Secretary of War Henry Stimson and Chief of Staff George C. Marshall ("There are three people I cannot say no to," Lovett would say when asked back into government in the late forties, "Colonel Stimson, General Marshall and my wife"). That small group of policy makers came from the great banking houses and law firms of New York and Boston. They knew one another, were linked to one another, and they guided America's national security in those years, men like James Forrestal, Douglas Dillon and Allen Dulles. Stimson and then Marshall had been their great leaders, and although they had worked for Roosevelt, it was not because of him, but almost in spite of him; they had been linked more to Stimson than to Roosevelt. And they were linked more to Acheson and Lovett than to Truman; though Acheson was always quick to praise Truman, there were those who believed that there was something unconsciously patronizing in Acheson's tones, his description of Truman as a great little man, and a sense that Acheson felt that much of Truman's greatness came from his willingness to listen to Acheson. They were men linked more to one another, their schools, their own social class and their own concerns than they were linked to the country. Indeed, about one of them, Averell Harriman, there would always be a certain taint, as if somehow Averell were a little too partisan and too ambitious (Averell had wanted to be President whereas the rest of them knew that the real power lay in letting the President come to them; the President could take care of rail strikes, minimum wages and farm prices, and they would take care of national security). Averell had, after all—there was no getting around it—run for public office and won; he seemed too much the politician and too much the intriguer for them. Perhaps not as bad as Roosevelt, but not exactly one of them, either.

In 1947, after Acheson had resigned as Undersecretary of State, Marshall (who was then head of State) chose Robert Lovett as his successor, and in

1950 he became Secretary of Defense. If the torch had been passed in earlier years to Elihu Root and Teddy Roosevelt and then to Stimson and Marshall, by 1960 Lovett was next. He had become, now as the sixties were about to begin, the great link to the Stimson-Marshall era. Acheson was a link too, but somehow Acheson had been scarred during the McCarthy era; it was not so much that he had done anything wrong as the fact that he had been forced to defend himself. By that very defense, by all the publicity, he had become controversial. He had been in print too often, it was somehow indiscreet of Dean to be attacked by McCarthy. Lovett was cleaner and he seemed to represent a particularly proud and, more important, successful tradition. For the private men felt they had succeeded admirably: they had taken a great dormant democracy, tuned it up for victory over Japan and Germany, stopped the Russian advance in Europe after the war and rebuilt Western Europe under the plan whose very name was more meaningful to them than to most others. The Marshall Plan had stopped the Communists, had brought the European nations back from destruction and decay, had performed an economic miracle; and there was, given the can-do nature of Americans, a tendency on their part to take perhaps more credit than might be proper for the actual operation of the Marshall Plan, a belief that *they* had done it and controlled it, rather than an admission that it had been the proper prescription for an economically weakened Europe and that it was the Europeans themselves who had worked the wonders. Yet it seemed as if history had come their way: just as they had predicted, the Russians proved untrustworthy and ungentlemanly (by 1944 there had been growing tensions between Roosevelt and some of his national security people over Soviet postwar aims; the national security people had held a view more parallel to that of Churchill) and had tried to expand in Europe, but Western democratic leadership had turned them back. They were not surprised that a cold war ensued; its very existence made their role, their guidance more necessary than ever. Without the Cold War—its dangers, tensions and threats—there might have been considerably less need of them and their wisdom and respectability. The lesson of history from Munich to Berlin was basic, they decided: one had to stand up, to be stern, to be tough. Lovett himself would talk of those years in the late forties as almost miraculous ones, when the American executive branch and the Congress were as one, when the Marshall Plan, the Point Four program and NATO had come about and been approved.

The men of that era believed, to an uncommon degree, that their view of history had been confirmed; only a very few questioned it. One of their eggheads, George F. Kennan, became in the fifties increasingly disillusioned with the thrust of American policy, believing that those men had exaggerated Soviet intentions in Western Europe, and had similarly exaggerated their own role and NATO's role in stopping them. But Kennan was too much of an intellectual; he had been useful to them in the early part of the Cold War, but he became less useful as his own doubts grew; besides, he was not a central member of their group—Lovett was.

SO THAT COLD DECEMBER DAY KENNEDY WAS LUNCHING WITH A MAN who not only symbolized a group, the Establishment, and was a power broker who carried the proxies for the great law firms and financial institutions, but was also tied to a great and seemingly awesome era. If Kennedy, as he always did in that period, complained that he knew no experts, that was no problem; the Establishment had long lists and it would be delighted to co-operate with this young President, help him along. It was of course above politics. It feared the right (the Goldwater campaign of 1964 was an assault on the entrenched powerful Eastern money by the new and powerless Southern and Western money; it was not by chance that the principal villain for them at San Francisco had been Nelson Rockefeller), and it feared the left; it held what was proclaimed to be the center. More often than not it was Republican, though it hedged its bets. A few members were nominal if cautious Democrats, and some families were very good about it—the Bundy family had produced William for the Democrats, and McGeorge for the Republicans—and it was believed that every major law firm should have at least one partner who was a Democrat. In fact, on the question of Kennedy and Nixon there had been an element of indecision in the Establishment world. One had a sense of the Establishment in an election year being like a professional athletic scout watching a championship match, emotionally uninvolved with either competitor, waiting until it was over and then descending to the locker room of the winner, to sign him on, to offer him the club's facilities—in this case the trusted, respectable, sound men of the Establishment.

Kennedy believed in the Establishment mystique; there had, after all, been little debunking of it in early 1960. Rarely had there been such a political consensus on foreign affairs: containment was good, Communism was dangerous, there was of course the problem of getting foreign aid bills through Congress, bills which would help us keep the Third World from the Communists. Besides, he was young, and since his victory over Nixon was slimmer than he had expected, he needed the backing of this club, the elitists of the national security people. And he felt at ease with them: after Chester Bowles and Adlai Stevenson and all the other Democratic eggheads pushing their favorite causes, Lovett, who seemingly pushed no causes and had no ideology, was a relief.

The two took to each other immediately. When Kennedy asked Lovett what the financial community thought of John Kenneth Galbraith's economic views (Galbraith being one of the President's earliest and strongest supporters), he was much amused when Lovett answered that the community thought he was a fine novelist. And when Lovett told Kennedy that he had not voted for him, Kennedy just grinned at the news, though he might have grinned somewhat less at Lovett's reason, which was Lovett's reservation about old Joe Kennedy. In a way, of course, this would have made Lovett all the more attractive, since much of the Kennedy family's thrust was motivated by the Irish desire to make these patricians, who had snubbed Joe Kennedy, reckon with his sons; this meeting was, if anything, part of the reckoning. ("Tell me," Rose Kennedy once asked a young and somewhat shocked aristocratic college classmate of Jack Kennedy's back in 1939 as she drove him from Hyannisport to Boston, "when are the good people of Boston going to accept us Irish?")

The meeting continued pleasantly, Caroline darting in and out, carrying a football, emphasizing to Lovett the youth and the enormity of the task before this man. Lovett had a feeling that he was taking too much of the President-elect's time, but he found that just the opposite was true. Kennedy tried hard to bring Lovett into the government, to take a job, any job (earlier Kennedy had sent Clark Clifford as a messenger with the offer to serve as Secretary of the Treasury, which Lovett had turned down). Lovett, who had not voted for Kennedy, could have State, Defense or Treasury ("I think because I had been in both State and Defense he thought he was getting two men for the price of one," Lovett would later say). Lovett declined regretfully again, explaining that he had been ill, bothered by severe ulcers, and each time after his last three government tours he had gone to the hospital. Now they had taken out part of his stomach, and he did not feel he was well enough to take on any of these jobs. Again Kennedy complained about his lack of knowledge of the right people, but Lovett told him not to worry, he and his friends would supply him with lists. Take Treasury, for instance—there Kennedy would want a man of national reputation, a skilled professional, well known and respected by the banking houses. There were Henry Alexander at Morgan, and Jack McCloy at Chase, and Gene Black at the World Bank. Doug Dillon too. Lovett said he didn't know their politics. Well, he reconsidered, he knew McCloy was an independent Republican, and Dillon had served in a Republican Administration, but, he added, he did not know the politics of Black and Alexander at all (their real politics of course being business). At State, Kennedy wanted someone who would reassure European governments: they discussed names and Lovett pushed, as would Dean Acheson, the name of someone little known to the voters, a young fellow who had been a particular favorite of General Marshall's—Dean Rusk over at Rockefeller. He handled himself there very well, said Lovett. The atmosphere was not unlike a college faculty, but Rusk had stayed above it, handled the various cliques very well. A very sound man. Then a brief, gentle and perhaps prophetic warning about State:

the relations between a Secretary of State and his President are largely dependent upon the President. Acheson, Lovett said, had been very good because Truman gave him complete confidence.

Then they spoke of Defense. A glandular thing, Lovett said, a monstrosity. Even talking about it damaged a man's stomach. In Lovett's day there had been 150 staffmen, now there were—oh, how many?—20,000; there were fourteen people behind every man. An empire too great for any emperor. Kennedy asked what makes a good Secretary of Defense. "A healthy skepticism, a sense of values, and a sense of priorities," Lovett answered. "That and a good President, and he can't do much damage. Not that he can do much good, but he can't do that much damage." They discussed men of intelligence, men of hardware, men of the financial community, men of driving ambition. The best of them, said Lovett, was this young man at Ford, Robert McNamara, the best of the new group. The others, people like Tom Gates, Eisenhower's Secretary of Defense, were getting older. Lovett had worked with McNamara in government during the war, and he had been terrific: disciplined, with a great analytical ability, a great hunger for facts.

Then the meeting was over, and the young man guided the older man through the throng of waiting reporters, saying that he had asked Mr. Lovett to come down and have lunch with him to see if he could get him for State, Defense or Treasury. (That night Lovett's old friend Arthur Krock, the *New York Times* columnist, called him to ask, "My God, is there any truth in it— it's going all over town," and Lovett answered, "Oh, I think he was just trying to make me feel good.") Since it was cold and there were no taxis, Kennedy gave Lovett his own car and driver, having failed to give him State, Defense or Treasury.

Chapter Two

I F LOWER MANHATTAN ISLAND AND STATE STREET, BOSTON, and the rest of the world of both Louis Auchincloss and John O'Hara read of the Kennedy-Lovett meeting with considerable reassurance, the first sign that the man in the White House, though young, Irish and a Democrat, knew his shortcomings and that they could deal with him, then there was at least one man who learned of it with a haunting sense of confirmation of what he had always feared. This was not someone who had run against Kennedy or opposed his nomination, but curiously enough someone who had worked very hard for Kennedy's election and was technically his chief foreign policy adviser—Chester Bowles of Connecticut, liberal icon, whom Kennedy had so assiduously cultivated and pursued just one year earlier, and whose views on all matters of foreign policy Kennedy had seemed, at that moment, to share with such great devotion. Now Bowles watched from a distance what was happening as Kennedy prepared to take office; his phone did not ring often, and what he knew about the Kennedy-Lovett meeting was largely what he read in the *New York Times*. He sensed that the young President-elect was flashing his very considerable charms at Robert Lovett, just as he once had done with Bowles himself.

It had been very different in 1959. Then Jack Kennedy had readied himself to run in his party's primaries, and he had done this as a good liberal Democrat. He was by no means the most obvious of liberals, being closer to the center of his party, with lines put to both the main wings. He knew from the start that if he was going to win the nomination, his problem would not be with the professional politicians, but with the liberal-intellectual wing of the party, influential far beyond its numbers because of its relations with, and impact upon, the media. It was a section of the party not only dubious of him but staunchly loyal to Adlai Stevenson after those two gallant and exhilarating defeats. That very exhilaration had left the Kennedys, particularly Robert Kennedy, with a vague suspicion that liberals would rather lose gallantly than win pragmatically, that they valued the irony and charm of Stevenson's election-night concessions more than they valued the power and patronage of victory. That feeling of suspicion was by no means unreciprocated; the New Republic liberals were well aware who had fought their wars during the fifties and who had sat on the sidelines.

The true liberals, those derivative of Eleanor Roosevelt and Adlai Stevenson, were at least as uneasy about Kennedy as he was about them, sensing that he was too cool, too hard-line in his foreign policies, too devoid of commitment. To them, Kennedy seemed so much the new breed, so devoted to rationalism instead of belief that even his first biographer, James MacGregor Burns, had angered the Kennedy Senate staff, particularly Theodore Sorensen, by suggesting that Kennedy would never risk political defeat on behalf of a great moral issue. They felt he had made too many accommodations in deference to the Cold War climate and adjusted his beliefs; he in turn thought them more than a little naïve and unrealistic about what was then considered a real Soviet threat. As a young congressman, then very much his father's son, he had been capable of being pleased by Richard Nixon's defeat of Helen Gahagan Douglas in California, a race marked by the shabbiest kind of Red-baiting. In Massachusetts, where McCarthyism was a particularly emotional issue, dividing the Catholic mass and the intellectual elite, he had carefully avoided taking a stand. He was in the hospital in December 1954 at the time of the Senate vote on McCarthy, but it was said that he had intended to vote for the censure; his evasion of the issue, however, combined with liberal suspicion of both his father's wartime beliefs and his own Catholicism, did not endear him to traditional liberals. As he moved toward becoming a presidential candidate, he had decided first to ease liberal doubts. He wanted Stevenson's support, but that would not come. Since he sensed that Stevenson, though playing Hamlet, rather badly wanted the nomination, Kennedy moved after the next-best thing, the support of Chester Bowles, a hero of the liberal left.

Bowles seemed so attractive a figure that even in 1958, when Kennedy talked with friends about his own future and candidly admitted that he planned to run for the Presidency, Chester Bowles's name hung over the conversation. Kennedy thought he had a very good chance at the nomination,

certainly better than Symington, Humphrey or Johnson, he said, citing the political liabilities of each. At the moment it looked very good, he confided, and
the only real problem was that 1958 was likely to be a good Democratic year
and might produce new candidates who could become instant national
figures. Two men in particular might pose a real threat: Richardson Dilworth
of Pennsylvania, an aristocratic liberal, and Bowles, then contending for a
Connecticut Senate seat. Both, he said, could carry the New Republic crowd,
the intellectuals and the liberals, and they had as good or better a claim on
the constituency which he sought; but unlike him they were Protestants, and
thus might serve the purpose of his enemies, many of whom were uneasy
about his Catholicism. It was a revealing conversation, about the way he saw
the road to the nomination, and the cold and tough-minded appraisal of the
problems he faced.

The twin threat did not materialize. Bowles was unsuccessful in securing
the nomination; he was not particularly good at dealing with professional politicians like John Bailey, head of the Connecticut party, who was deeply committed to Kennedy, and Dilworth made the mistake of declaring that Red
China ought to be admitted to the United Nations, a statement which contributed mightily to his defeat in Pennsylvania. Dilworth's brand of candor
was somewhat different from the Kennedy candor, which was private rather
than public, in that he would freely admit in private what he could not afford
to admit publicly (such as telling Bowles and Stevenson after the election that
he agreed completely with their positions, that our own policy on China was
irrational, but that he could not talk about it then—perhaps in the second
term).

Bowles's standing with the party's liberals was not diminished after his set-
back, since defeat was never a liberal dishonor; if anything, it was more of a
decoration. Kennedy had gone after Bowles early in 1959, but first he ro-
manced one of Bowles's chief aides, Harris Wofford, then a law school professor at Notre Dame and a long-time protégé of Bowles's. He was a young man
deeply committed to racial progress both at home and overseas (it would be
Wofford's suggestion during the campaign that resulted in the Kennedy
phone call to the family of the imprisoned Martin Luther King, Jr.). Kennedy
approached Wofford both for his own availability and as a bridge to Bowles.
There was a major staff position open for Wofford, Kennedy said, as a speech
writer right next to Sorensen himself. Their meetings were impressive; Kennedy, Wofford later reflected, knew exactly which issues would touch
Wofford. Much ideological sympathy was expressed, and eventually Wofford
went to work for him. The Democratic party had to get away from the Cold
War policies of the past, not just of Dulles, but of Acheson as well, Kennedy
said. It needed new, fresher leadership. It desperately needed a new China

policy. It needed to encourage anticolonial feeling. Of course, all these things echoed Wofford's own sentiments, and he helped remove some of the doubts held by Bowles.

Kennedy himself worked hard on Bowles and used all his charm in stressing the vast areas they agreed on, philosophically if not tactically (a difference which seemed small then, though perhaps not so small as time passed). Finally Bowles came around, with grave reservations. He was not really comfortable with Kennedy, with the brashness and self-assurance of this younger man. He had an old and abiding loyalty to Hubert Humphrey, with whom he had fought so many battles all those lonely years—for civil rights, for foreign aid, for disarmament—but as a professional politician he was able to look coolly at the field and decide that Kennedy might be able to go all the way and beat Nixon, while Humphrey might fall by the wayside. It was a crucial switch within the competing factions of the Democratic party, an institution severely damaged by the McCarthy years and by Republican charges of twenty years of treason. Here was Bowles, if not moving from the Stevenson–Humphrey–Eleanor Roosevelt–Bowles wing to the more centrist camp of John Kennedy, and if not actually leaving his old group, at least conferring an ideological acceptance on the Kennedy camp, easing liberal-intellectual doubts, for no less a liberal institution than the New Republic had listed Bowles as its own dark-horse candidate. Now it was done: Chester Bowles would become Jack Kennedy's chief foreign policy adviser. Through countless liberal psyches would flash the idea, precisely as Kennedy intended it to: Bowles as Secretary of State. Or better still, Bowles as a holding action for a couple of months, and Adlai as Secretary of State.

It was a very good liberal name to have, Chester Bowles. In the eyes of the liberals, he was one of the few who was without a stain. He was, in fact, the definitive liberal-humanist at a time when those particular values had been on the defensive and had been made to seem naïve. Politicians who professed the old liberalism of the thirties in this harsher postwar era were considered too trusting and unrealistic, men who did not understand the dangers of the contemporary world, where Communists constantly lurked to exploit any and all do-good organizations and intentions. This Cold War realism had touched many of the liberal politicians, who had been put on the defensive about their past, but it had not necessarily touched the liberal voters, and in 1960 Bowles was unique among politicians in that he refused to adapt to contemporary pressures. To him, it was as if the Cold War had never taken place. He was markedly untouched by it; he believed that the problems America encountered were its own, what it did at home and in the world, not what the Soviet Union did. He was, it seemed at the moment, somewhat behind the times; a few long years later it would seem that he had been ahead of them.

CHESTER BOWLES'S ORIGINS WERE SOMEWHAT INCONGRUOUS FOR SUCH a good card-carrying liberal. He was the classic New England Yankee, whose people were almost all Republicans, and yet some of his friends thought that his entire political career reflected his background, that he truly believed in the idea of the Republic, with an expanded town-hall concept of politics, of political leaders consulting with their constituency, hearing them out, reasoning with them, coming to terms with them, government old-fashioned and unmanipulative. Such governments truly had to reflect their constituencies. It was his view not just of America, but of the whole world. Bowles was fascinated by the political process in which people of various countries expressed themselves politically instead of following orders imposed by an imperious leadership. In a modern world where most politicians tended to see the world divided in a death struggle between Communism and free-world democracies, it was an old-fashioned view of politics; it meant that Bowles was less likely to judge a country on whether or not it was Communist, but on whether or not its government seemed to reflect genuine indigenous feeling. (If he was critical of the Soviet leadership, he was more sympathetic to Communist governments in the underdeveloped world.) He was less impressed by the form of a government than by his own impression of its sense of legitimacy.

Born in 1901, he was the grandson of a famed liberal editor of the Springfield (Mass.) *Republican,* and the editorials that Samuel Bowles wrote at the time of the Civil War had made a deep impression on him. Even as a boy he was something of a maverick liberal in his family, and when he was in his twenties his heroes were Norman Thomas and Robert La Follette rather than the chosen Republican and Democratic presidential candidates of the period. Although he went to Yale, he did not go to the regular college, but to Yale's engineering school at Sheffield, and this, thought friends, accounted for a certain inferiority complex as far as his own intellectual ability went. He was, in his own mind, virtually self-educated. He was unsure of himself intellectually, and in contrast to the crisp, sharp style of the Kennedy people, his manner would seem slow and ponderous. (Uneasy in their presence, his insecurity showing, he tended to become something of a caricature of himself, speaking too much and too long as a means of trying to cover up his deficiencies.)

After college he worked briefly on the family newspaper, where he proved too liberal. He almost went to China as a foreign service officer, and at the last minute he turned to advertising. Eventually, with Bill Benton, he opened up the firm of Benton & Bowles. They started in July 1929 with very meager resources, but the Depression helped rather than hurt them. The big companies, Bowles noted, were ready for a change, any change, in the early days of the Depression, so the firm of Benton & Bowles prospered. While he was still

in his early thirties, Bowles became a self-made millionaire, but an unusual
one. He did not particularly value money (indeed, he was ill at ease with it),
he did not share the usual political ideas of the rich, and he was extremely
aware of the hardships with which most Americans lived. Instead of hiring
highly paid consultants and pollsters to conduct market research, Bowles did
his own canvassing, going from door to door to hundreds of middle- and
lower-class homes. That became a crucial part of his education; his theoretical liberalism became reinforced by what he learned about people's lives during the Depression.

Advertising was not the real love of either partner in Benton & Bowles, and
both were anxious to get into other fields, preferably politics. Benton went
first, and Bowles soon followed. From then on his career was well known, the
classical, good liberal career. Liberal director of the Office of Price Administration during World War II, liberal and successful governor of Connecticut a
few years later. Liberal ambassador to India in the fifties, eventually liberal
congressman from Connecticut. His following among liberals had continued
to grow during this time, and by the end of the decade he was something of a
hero for two major reasons. First, because more than most liberal politicians,
his internationalism seemed to be a reflection and an extension of his domestic
political ideals. Second, and perhaps even more important, at a time when so
many liberals seemed to be on the defensive about their past and had taken
refuge in the new liberal anti-Communism, Bowles had been particularly unflinching; he had never changed from his original precepts or accommodated
very much. That his ideas seemed to be a little unfashionable did not bother
him. He simply did not take the Russian threat that seriously; he thought the
real dangers in the world were those of poverty and hunger. To many liberals
he was a comforting throwback to the Roosevelt era; he still stood for things
that they believed in but which had recently come under considerable attack.

It was, however, this very quality which would tend to hurt him with his
new allies, the Kennedy team. What the liberals liked about Bowles was his
predictability, which was precisely what the Kennedys came to dislike. The
liberals liked him because he kept saying the old enduring things that had
bound them together in the thirties; the Kennedy people did not like the old
slogans and ideas and wanted to get on with the more modern world. So in
their eyes he would become a curiously heavy figure, and knowing that he
was not as facile as they were, he became even more awkward. While they
were so obviously intellectual, he was more visceral in his instincts; while
they were all men of great and towering accomplishment and proud of them,
he was curiously ashamed of his own successes, of having made it as an advertising man, of being a millionaire. He spoke in terms which were not flashy
and which plain people could understand, but which seemed out of place in
their new style. Even though he sensed the differences between himself and

the Kennedy team, he signed on—serious, ponderous Chester Bowles, given to long answers to short questions, reeking of good intentions and good thoughts, sermons really, among lean, swift young men who thought it quite acceptable to have idealistic thoughts and dreams just so long as you never admitted them.

The relationship never really worked, not from the start. Even in the best of days, at the beginning, the suspicions which had separated them in the past still remained. The differences in style were really differences in substance, and there was no way of getting around it. Bowles had retained his misgivings about Kennedy, more than he realized. This became clear in April of 1960 in Wisconsin, and it was Wisconsin which began the decline of Chester Bowles. This, the second primary was a crucial test for Kennedy on his way to the nomination. Kennedy's liberal credentials were still anything but assured; his only victory as the Wisconsin campaign began was in friendly Catholic New Hampshire. Now he was running in the Midwestern state which was a Humphrey stronghold, more Protestant than Catholic, more tuned to Humphrey's genial Midwestern liberalism. Here Kennedy needed all the liberal support he could muster, and he needed every liberal face to appear on his behalf. In his hour of need he turned to his chief foreign policy adviser. Who balked. Bowles said that when he joined forces, he had specifically ruled out campaigning against his old friend Hubert Humphrey, so he could not go into Wisconsin against Hubert. Robert and Jack Kennedy were appalled by this refusal, and the pressure began to build. They prevailed upon Ted Sorensen, then considered a link to the liberals, to be the persuader. It was terribly important, Sorensen argued, Bowles must come to their aid; if he went in now and fought, many good things would come his way. At first the warnings were gentlemanly, but as time passed, as the heat of the campaign mounted—after all, one primary defeat and it might all be over—the tone became harsher and more demanding. If he did not comply, Sorensen said, there would be dire consequences. Not only would the good things not happen, but bad things might. If he was for them, he was for them, and that was the only thing they understood. And as they became irritated, so too did Bowles; he felt he was having his arm twisted. In a sense the Kennedys were right: he could, after all, campaign for Jack without necessarily being anti-Humphrey. But Bowles felt that although Kennedy might be the best way of beating Nixon, there were old loyalties to Humphrey, and old suspicions: touches of liberal anti-Catholicism remaining in him as well; any liberal governor of Connecticut had had to struggle against the conservative political power of the Church in the past. So Bowles refused to go in, and Harris Wofford, his aide, replaced him in Wisconsin. The Kennedys would later decide, when they cut up their spoils, that they were not that beholden to Bowles or to the liberals who had not been there when they were needed. From then on the balance changed, and as primary victory followed primary victory, Bowles's role and value diminished except as an occasional useful bit of window dressing. He was made chairman of the party platform committee, on which he worked relentlessly, though becoming increasingly aware as the campaign progressed that he had less and less contact and influence with the candidate. In July, at convention time, when he worked very hard for a Kennedy-style platform, he discovered that among the people least interested in the platform was his candidate. Indeed, even as Kennedy was accepting the convention's nomination, an act which should have gladdened Bowles after this long, arduous uphill struggle, Bowles had a feeling that he was far from the action and the decisions, that the link between him and his candidate was weak and growing weaker.

He could not have been more right, for at that very moment Joseph P. Kennedy, Sr., was having dinner in New York at the apartment of Henry Luce, the publisher of magazines which had long specialized in the tormenting of just such people as Chester Bowles and promoting such archenemies as John Foster Dulles, leaving some people with the suspicion that Dulles was *Time* magazine sprung to life (inspiring the liberal poet Marya Mannes to write the short verse: "Foster Dulles/Henry Luce/GOP Hypotenuse"). At the dinner Joe Kennedy gave his word to Luce that his son, while a Democratic presidential nominee, was nonetheless reliable. Joe Kennedy and Henry Luce were old friends in the best sense of many hands scratching many backs, Luce having written an introduction to the first book by Kennedy's son Jack, a book entitled *Why England Slept*, while Joe Kennedy, not to be outdone, had arranged to get Luce's son Hank his first job after college, as special assistant to the chairman of the Securities and Exchange Commission—the chairman, of course, being Joseph P. Kennedy, Sr.

What Luce and Kennedy were discussing was in effect what it would take to neutralize *Time* and *Life* during the forthcoming campaign. It turned into something of a heated discussion because Luce tried to divide the issues between foreign and domestic affairs and implied that he would not be upset by Jack Kennedy's liberalism on domestic issues, and Joe Kennedy took this personally. No son of mine is going to be a goddamn liberal, Kennedy interjected. Now, now Joe, Luce answered, of course he's got to run as a liberal. A Democrat has to run left of center to get the vote in the big northern cities, so don't hold it against him if he's left of center, because we won't. We know his problems and what he has to do. So we won't fight him there. But on foreign affairs, Luce continued, if he shows any sign of weakness toward the anti-Communist cause—or, as Luce decided to put it more positively—if he shows any weakness in defending the cause of the free world, we'll turn on him. There's no chance of that, Joe Kennedy had guaranteed; no son of mine is going to be soft on Communism. Well, if he is, Luce answered, we'll have to tear him apart.

Then they went back to watching the acceptance speech, and Kennedy, the sire of a great political family, his own driving ambitions now close to realization, thanked Luce for all he had done for the Kennedys in the past, a gesture Luce accepted cordially at the time. Later, however, as the campaign progressed, he would wonder if *Time* and *Life* were doing too much for young Jack Kennedy—had they been too favorable, too straight in their reporting? It was, he realized, a hard line to draw, and made more difficult not so much by personal obligations to the Kennedy family, but by the difficulty in finding real differences between the Nixon and the Kennedy foreign policies. In fact, during the fall, when *Life* was geared up to run a major editorial praising Nixon's foreign policy, the editors, at Luce's suggestion, held off a week because Nixon had not made his stand any noticeably more anti-Communist than Kennedy. Later, when the election was over and the narrowness of Kennedy's margin became clear, Luce's good Republican conscience would bother him: perhaps, if he had been truer to his party, Nixon would be in the White House. But it did not bother him so much that he turned down a chance to attend the Kennedy inaugural ball, and sit, just by chance, in the box with the Joseph P. Kennedys.

Which was far from where Chester Bowles sat that night. He sat with some of his boys, that special group of talented young men which he regularly seemed to discover and propel into public life, some of whom (like Jim Thomson, Abe Chayes, Tom Hughes and Harris Wofford) would do particularly well in the new Administration. That night he was with Wofford, who was to be a White House Special Assistant for Civil Rights, and Tom Hughes, who would become Director of Intelligence and Research (INR) at the State Department. Hughes was one of the few genuine intellectuals of the era, a funny, skeptical, almost cynical man who had worked earlier for Bowles, then for Humphrey(who in 1959 was a hotter political figure), and finding Humphrey a less interesting man, had returned to Bowles. Wofford had been Bowles's main link to the Kennedys, the man who had worked hard to bring him into the Kennedy campaign. Replacing Bowles during the Wisconsin primary, Wofford had said in Madison, a hotbed of liberalism, "There is a Stevenson-Humphrey-Bowles view of the world, and Jack Kennedy is the most likely man to carry it out." Later, when Kennedy was elected and his first two announcements were the reappointment of the heads of both the FBI and the CIA, Hughes sent Wofford a postcard saying: "I want you to know that I finally voted for your Stevenson–Humphrey–Bowles–Kennedy–Hoover–Allen Dulles view of the world . . ."

For ever since he gained the nomination in Los Angeles, Kennedy had changed: he did not need the liberals that much; they had nowhere else to go. It was no longer Kennedy versus Humphrey or Stevenson; it was Kennedy versus Nixon. He turned to face different doubts and different suspicions. On the way to the nomination the question had been whether or not he was sufficiently liberal; then it became a question of whether he was sufficiently mature, tough and anti-Communist. He was facing a candidate who had been catapulted into American life on the issue of anti-Communism, and who had been the hatchet man against the Democrats in previous campaigns on the issue of softness on Communism, to such a degree that his superior, Dwight Eisenhower, was sometimes made uneasy (not so uneasy as to make him stop; Eisenhower was not uneasy when that rhetoric benefited Dwight Eisenhower, simply dubious whether a man who depended upon it was worthy of succeeding him in that lofty office). No doubt he would use that same issue once more against the Democrats, should they show any small sign of weakness. So Kennedy moved toward the right to reassure America that he was just as tough as Nixon, that he wanted a firm foreign policy, that he cared as much for Quemoy and Matsu as Nixon did, and in fact charging that the Eisenhower Administration was, yes, soft on Cuba. Since Cuba was a Democratic issue in 1960, Lyndon Johnson, working the South for Kennedy, said he knew what to do. First he'd take that Castro fellow and wash him. (Cheers.) And then shave him. (Cheers.) And then spank him. (Wild cheers.) And as Kennedy worked this issue he moved away from the positions of his principal foreign policy adviser and the Stevenson wing of the party, and the Stevenson imprimatur became increasingly suspect inside the Kennedy camp after Los Angeles. After the campaign was over, the Stevenson people were assigned to work up a series of foreign policy papers. George W. Ball, a Chicago lawyer who was originally a Stevenson man, had prepared them, and they were really Ball papers, not Stevenson papers; nevertheless, Ball was so uneasy about the Stevenson taint that he let a deputy take the papers to Palm Beach for Kennedy's perusal.

Bowles's influence had diminished steadily during the campaign. Early during the race the question had arisen of whether he should seek re-election to his Connecticut congressional seat, and something of an Alphonse-Gaston charade took place. Kennedy asked Bowles to run. Bowles deferred, saying that if he was not going to serve out his full term it would not be fair to the good voters of Connecticut's Second Congressional District, nor to his protégé William St. Onge, who wanted the seat. Then Kennedy argued that if Bowles dropped out of the race, the Stevenson supporters would think a deal had been made that Bowles was to be Secretary of State; hence they would not work as hard for the cause. Bowles then insisted that the Stevenson people were made of sterner stuff, and pushed very hard for Kennedy's permission not to run. Implicit in all this, of course, was the idea that if Bowles did not run, the Administration was committed to giving him something very high, perhaps even State. Kennedy did not like to be crowded and he was uneasy with Bowles's request, and he did not give his approval to the Bowles withdrawal. Bowles, who did not like the House of Representatives, dropped out of the race anyway. This irritated Kennedy, who felt Bowles had gone around him, and whatever chance Bowles had to be Secretary of State, which had never been great, diminished appreciably.

The real problem of course was that the mix between the two was not very good, either personally or professionally. Bowles spoke in long, quasi-theological terms and the Kennedy people spoke in shorthand, almost a code, the fewer words the better, for tartness and brevity showed that you understood the code, were on the inside. Bowles spoke in terms of idealism, of world opinion, of political morality, wearing his high hopes for mankind right there on his sleeve, and the Kennedy people, if they thought that way—and some did and some did not—thought the worst thing you could do was confess openly to high idealism. Bowles, though wealthy, lacked the aristocratic style one might find at the dinner party of an Alsop or a Harriman, and at the Bowles' one was likely to find Indians, Africans, American Negroes and others; in an Administration which placed great emphasis on style and, ironically, would be remembered more for its style than its achievements, there was a feeling that Bowles had the wrong style; his wife, after all, was given to wearing Indian saris. All this was a problem, and so too was the fact that his basic view of the world, which had remained unchanged despite the pressures of the McCarthy years and the Cold War, had given him an image of being fuzzy and woolly-headed, and had made a convenient target for hard-liners in the press and in Congress. Part of this was Bowles's own fault; he was marvelous at long-range thinking, at seeing the dangers inherent in policies, but he was a weak infighter. He lacked an ability to dissemble, he had no instinct for the jugular, he did not maneuver well at close hand. Thus, while Averell Harriman might stand for the same policy as Bowles, Harriman was not a good target; he was a vicious, almost joyous, brutal infighter, and anyone who tangled with him would do so in the full knowledge that Harriman would remember and strike back, and for a hard-line columnist like Joe Alsop, who had more than a little of a bully in him, Bowles made a much better target. His career in government thus was limited by the knowledge of potential adversaries that they could strike at him and he would not strike back.

Actually there was precious little chance for Bowles, anyway, for it was one thing to use a liberal name to woo back the eggheads, but it was quite another to reassure the financial establishment, and the Democratic party was bitterly divided on questions of foreign policy, with two main chords running through it. One followed a harder line on foreign affairs, with a certain amount of cool acceptance of the New Deal issues. It was exemplified in foreign policy by the traditionalists like Dean Acheson, who had broken with Roosevelt in the New Deal over financial questions, whose entourage included the Alsop brothers as columnists and, to a degree, William Fulbright in the Senate. These men were committed to a view of manifest U.S. destiny in the world, where America re-placed the British throughout the world as the guarantor of the existing order. It was a group linked to the Eastern establishment, that nebulous yet very real conglomerate of businessmen, lawyers and financiers who had largely been determining American foreign policy in this century. They believed that the great threat to the world was Communist, an enemy at once totalitarian, antidemocratic and antibusiness, that the Communists must be stopped and that the Communists understood only one thing, force. This group was above all realistic. It understood power; it was, in a favorite word of the era, hard-nosed. Some of its principal members had, for all their anti-Communism, been badly burned during the McCarthy years and they would never want to look soft again. The Cold War had not surprised them and they had rallied gladly to its banner. This wing had called for greater defense spending, and in the fifties and in general, the Democratic party espoused that cause, with only Hubert Humphrey of its congressional leaders speaking for disarmament. In fact, the Democratic party had been more committed to military spending than the Republicans. It was the Democrats who wanted a larger and larger defense establishment, and although Kennedy was not one of the great lead-ers at the time, he had been a part of it. (In 1960, at the start of the campaign, slightly worried about Kennedy's lack of credentials in this area, a young Ken-nedy staff member named Deirdre Henderson had called one of the Defense intellectuals to summon his help on the problem. Kennedy, she said, needed a weapon. Everyone else had a weapon: Scoop Jackson had the Polaris, and Lyndon had Space, and Symington had the B-52. What could they get for a weapon for Kennedy? Well, said the young Defense intellectual, whose name was Daniel Ellsberg, "What about the infantryman?")

Former Secretary of State Acheson, the leader of this group, was uneasy with the Dulles years, not because of Dulles' bombast, but because Acheson sensed weakness in Dulles. Acheson was afraid there was too little will to sacrifice, to spend for military might. In the late fifties, when the Democratic party's Advisory Council met periodically to criticize the Eisenhower policies, some of the liberals like Kenneth Galbraith, Arthur Schlesinger and Bowles would later try and tone down the foreign policy statements, which they had come to refer to as "Acheson's declarations of war."

The second wing of the party had its roots in the Roosevelt era, and its chief proponent was Eleanor Roosevelt. (The *grande dame* of the party had retained her suspicions of Jack Kennedy despite his attempts to convince her that he was committed to the same ideals. Shortly after his election he made one last journey to see her at Hyde Park and found her once again filled with suspicion. You don't really trust me entirely, he said. No, that's right, she an-swered. "What can I do to ease your suspicions?" he asked. "Make Adlai Secretary of State," she answered. Later he left, shaking his head and smiling, impressed by her for the first time: "She's really tough, isn't she?") During the fifties, this wing had found its principal spokesman in Stevenson, with his elegant prose, his self-deprecating wit. It felt that the United States must take more initiatives to end the arms race, that if America did not recognize Red China it should at least begin to move toward that goal, that nationalism was the new and most potent force in the underdeveloped world, that the United States must support it even at the expense of weakening ties with NATO allies, and finally that the greatest threat in the world might prove to be not Communism, but the combination of the arms race plus hunger and poverty in the Third World. To the Acheson group, the members of this wing, particularly Stevenson, seemed soft; they were do-gooders who did not understand power and force, who were too quick to believe in the UN. Adlai became a ready target—he was depicted as being too quick to talk and too slow to act; he was indecisive. In the great drawing rooms of Georgetown such as the Harrimans', they would tell their Stevenson jokes (Stevenson about to give a speech and being told that he would go on in five minutes, asking an aide, "Do I have time to go to the bathroom?" Being assured that he did, then asking, "Do I want to go to the bathroom?"). The Stevenson group was seen as too committed to some vague idea of morality in world affairs and too committed to the search for world opinion, willing to waste real relationships with solid European nations in return for vague promises from untrustworthy little wog nations that would probably vote against us in the UN, anyway.

In this party division Kennedy had managed very well to straddle the factions. Since his own sense of style and presence was akin to the Stevenson group's, he had attracted some of its members, having made speeches critical of French colonialism and French colonial wars, as well as the U.S. policy supporting the French. By the same token, in 1959 he had told Harris Wofford (knowing full well that this was exactly what moved Wofford) that the most important thing about the coming election was to change America's foreign policy, to get away not just from the Dulles years but from the equally inflexible views of Acheson, which were so dominant within one section of the Democratic party; that we had to have new policies on China and on the underdeveloped world; and that we had to get away from the rigidity of the Cold War.

Kennedy's speeches on Algeria and French colonialism had angered Acheson and the French in approximately that order. Acheson subsequently wrote a book called *Power and Diplomacy*, which cited the Kennedy Algerian speech as a classic example of how not to make foreign policy, "this impatient snapping of our fingers." This was not the way to treat our oldest ally, which was still smarting over the defeats of World War II and which bore an inferiority complex. Acheson was obviously angered that a United States senator should take the liberty of being critical of American foreign policy, no matter how, as in this case, dubious and ill-conceived it was; if nothing else, Acheson's wrath was a reflection of how centrist that policy was, and how little real criticism was permitted. Some of the antipathy lingered on, with Acheson in 1960 telling a Washington luncheon club that Kennedy was an "unformed young man" (a comment ironically not particularly different from Mrs. Roosevelt's), and with Acheson's son-in-law William P. Bundy, who often reflected the Achesonian viewpoint, expressing his doubts about Kennedy's toughness.

If Kennedy was not exactly in the Acheson group, there was nonetheless an element of the hard-liner in him, as there was to almost everyone in politics at that point; at best he was cool and cautious and not about to rush ahead of events or the current political climate by calling for changes in the almost glacierlike quality of the Cold War. He was the epitome of the contemporary man in a cool, pragmatic age, more admiring of the old, shrewd, almost cynical Establishment breed (he was quite capable of telling John McCloy, another senior statesman of the Establishment, after trying to get him to take a high post, that the trouble was that the younger breed wasn't as good, they lacked the guts and toughness of the McCloy generation) than of the ponderous do-good types like Bowles, who talked too much and might lose you countries (even in the business world Bowles's success by Establishment lights was judged dubious; he had made millions, to be sure, but he had made them in advertising, which was not a serious profession, was in fact a noisy, splashy profession given to arousing people's emotions rather than soothing them, a craft to be watched circumspectly). So if Kennedy straddled the two positions, it was not surprising—given the era, the Cold War still a major part of our life—that in January 1960 when he announced his candidacy for the Presidency his friend Joseph Alsop, the liberal hard-line columnist and journalistically a purveyor of the Acheson line, watched him and said enthusiastically to Earl Mazo, another reporter, "Isn't he marvelous! A Stevenson with balls."

Chapter Three

KENNEDY HAD DECIDED EARLY ON TO BE HIS OWN SEC-
retary of State, a decision which was much applauded, since he was obviously
well read (followers of newspapers and magazines were regularly apprised of
what he and Jacqueline were reading that week, and when Jacqueline, meeting Ian Fleming, the British suspense writer, inquired if he was *the* Ian Fleming, the latter's position as a major culture figure was assured, doubly so because it soon became apparent that the young President himself wanted to
meet Fleming); he had served on the Senate Foreign Relations Committee
(largely thanks to Lyndon Johnson, who did not so much want to put Kennedy on the committee as he wanted to keep Estes Kefauver *off*, and needed
someone with a party following in order to justify the exclusion of Kefauver);
and he was, in Washington terms, considered conversant with the great problems of the world.

This confidence in his ability had not always existed; indeed, Kennedy had
not been a towering figure in Washington prior to his 1960 race, one main
reason being that since 1956 he had almost never been there, always dashing
out of town, meeting delegates, in preparation for the 1960 campaign. Lyndon Johnson was considered a more formidable force in Washington, in part
because he was highly visible, a definitive man of Washington who reveled in
the city, its intrigues, its power, whereas during much of the late fifties Jack
Kennedy was a figure darting into the airport, sending an aide to the paper-
back-book counter to buy something for the trip, preferably history. There

was a great Trevor-Roper phase in 1958, an aide remembered; one learned too little from fiction. But the 1960 campaign had changed his reputation in Washington. He had won the nomination, and had been given the chance to run for the Presidency, perhaps a more bully pulpit than the bully pulpit itself, Americans liking competitions as much as the end results of them.

Sometime in the middle of the campaign he had hit his stride. Suddenly there was a new confidence in his speeches, even the timbre of his voice seemed to change. That harsh New England tone, which at first had jarred others, seemed to soften a little at the very same time that the nation began to find it distinctive and began to listen for it. He seemed to project a sense of destiny for himself and for his nation: he knew where he as a politician and we as a nation were going. Even Walter Lippmann sensed it, Lippmann, who more than any other man determined critical Washington's taste buds. Lippmann influenced Reston, and Reston influenced the writing press and the television commentators, who influenced the television reporters. Lippmann began to hail this young man, who as no one since Franklin Roosevelt had caught and stirred and held the imagination of the American people. Day after day, columns in this vein appeared until finally, later in the campaign, the *other* venerable columnist, Arthur Krock, stomped out of his office, smoke belching from his cigar, saying, "Well, I may be getting old, and I may be getting senile, but at least I don't fall in love with young boys like Walter Lippmann." But Lippmann and the rest of the Washington community had watched the 1960 campaign and had approved; the feel, the texture of it was very good, and Richard Nixon had never been a particular favorite of critical Washington, to say the least. In Kennedy they had found a man worthy of the city, of the job, of the decade ahead. So when it became clear that he wanted to be his own Secretary of State, Washington did not dissent. This was a strong, well-educated, well-prepared young man. The idea was appealing: a strong President towering over his Secretary of State, whoever he might be. But to an extraordinary degree the very process of that choice would mark what the Administration was, and what many of its more basic attitudes and compromises were.

Whoever else the Secretary was, it would not be Adlai Ewing Stevenson, a prophet with too much honor in his own party. Stevenson wanted the job, wanted it almost too much. He had played a historic role for his party, twice its presidential candidate, the first time running against impossible odds in 1952, at the height of the Korean War and McCarthyism, with the party already decaying from the scandals of twenty years in power. Running against the great hero of an era, Dwight Eisenhower, Stevenson had lost, of course, but his voice had seemed special in that moment, a voice of rationality and elegance. In the process of defeat he had helped salvage the party, giving it a new vitality and bringing to its fold a whole new generation of educated

Americans, volunteers now in the political process, some very professional amateurs who would be masterly used by the Kennedys in 1960. If Jack and Robert Kennedy seemed to symbolize style in politics, much of that was derived directly from Stevenson. He had, at what should have been a particularly low point for the party, managed to keep it vibrant and vital, and to involve a new kind of people in politics. The sense of Kennedy gratitude for these offerings was limited; the Kennedy brothers regarded him as indecisive and almost prissy, and somewhat disingenuous in the way that he seemed to like to portray himself being above politics and yet accepting the support of the Daley machine. It was all right, they thought, to present an image as the citizen-leader rather than the politician who made deals, but it was dangerous to believe it yourself. The Kennedys regarded him as weak and lacking in toughness, despite the fact that the races against great odds in 1952 and 1956 might historically be viewed as acts of courage (similarly, Kennedy would regard him as soft during the Cuban missile crisis, although Stevenson consistently stood alone against an enormous onslaught of the hard-line detractors). Stevenson, of course, had not named Jack Kennedy his running mate in 1956, but worse, he had opened the choice to the convention, which had made him seem indecisive.

Yet for all this, there were many times in 1960 when he could have been chosen Secretary of State. There were overtures, made largely through Stevenson's friends, letting him know that if he came aboard, State was his; the Kennedys still respected him, knew he had a powerful hold over many articulate elements in the party, and though the primaries were going well, the nomination was not locked up by a long shot. Stevenson seemed crucial. He might block them at Los Angeles, and the Kennedy people knew that Lyndon Johnson was counting on Stevenson to stay alive and stay open to the draft. Even as late as the day after the Oregon primary in May, the idea of State was still open, and Kennedy himself, visiting with Stevenson in Libertyville, Illinois, on his way back East from Portland, asked friends of Stevenson's if he should make the offer right then and there. The aides said no, they thought it would offend the governor at that moment. The next day, when Stevenson was apprised of the offer, he seemed more reluctant than ever to join the team; the previous day's meeting had not gone well. If the Kennedys thought him weak and indecisive, he in turn thought them arrogant and aggressive ("That young man," he would tell friends of Jack Kennedy's, "he never says please, he never says thank you, he never asks for things, he demands them"). Yet the offer stayed open through Los Angeles, though it closed there; the Kennedys found they could do without him, and his due bills evaporated overnight. As for Stevenson, though he desperately wanted to be Secretary of State, he could not make the deal, in part because he thought it wrong to barter an office of this import, but also because he still dreamed the impossible dream. He still wanted the Presidency himself and could not shed that haunting dream, which for several hours at Los Angeles threatened once more to come to life.

Even though he had not played their game, he was hoping, long after the convention was over, that he would get State; he believed himself best qualified. So when Kennedy offered him the post as Ambassador to the United Nations, Stevenson was appalled. He would not take it, he said privately, it was an insult, he had had that job before. "What will you do if you don't come aboard?" an old friend asked him. "I'll do what I've been doing all along," he answered. "And have your speeches printed on page forty-seven of the *New York Times?*" the friend said.

Kennedy, who was annoyed by Stevenson's refusal to accept the offer immediately, and who had decided upon Rusk as Secretary, asked Rusk to call Stevenson. Kennedy took no small amount of pleasure in recounting to friends how Rusk had hooked Stevenson. "Adlai," Rusk had said, "the President has asked me to take this job and it is a sacrifice, but I have given it careful consideration, despite the element of sacrifice, and I have decided I cannot refuse. I cannot say no. I feel all of us have a loyalty greater than our own interests. I'm going to be a soldier. I think this is necessary. We need you, the country needs you. I hope you will serve as he has asked you to serve." In retelling the story to friends, Kennedy would chuckle and say, "I think old Adlai was really impressed."

There was an aura of thinly veiled contempt toward Stevenson at the White House; he was someone to take Jackie to the theater. It was all a humiliating experience. During the Cuban missile crisis, when Stewart Alsop and Charles Bartlett, both good friends of the President's and disciples of Acheson's, wrote a semiofficial account of the events, they quoted one high official as saying that Stevenson wanted a Munich. The article was published in the *Saturday Evening Post* and there was a great storm over those particular quotes; most Washington insiders suspected McGeorge Bundy, the sharp, caustic Bundy who had so frequently been critical of Stevenson. Only later, after the death of Kennedy and the end of the *Saturday Evening Post*, did one of the editors admit that the statements had come from Kennedy himself and that he had insisted that they be published. He had, however, been careful to ask the authors to exclude a part which showed Ted Sorensen being potentially soft; Kennedy would take care of his own, and Stevenson was not his own. (It was not surprising that in early 1964, when Stevenson showed up in Washington and had lunch with an old friend, he began to praise Lyndon Johnson extravagantly. "We have a great President now," he said. The friend was somewhat surprised, since the Stevenson-Johnson friendship had never been that close, but as Stevenson described his meeting with the President, it soon became clear why he was so enthusiastic: as soon as he had walked into

Johnson's office, the latter had risen, pointed to his chair and said, "Governor, by all rights you should be sitting in this chair and in this office.")

But Kennedy wanted to be his own Secretary of State, and above all he did not want a Secretary who already had a constituency worthy of a President, rather he wanted Stevenson's constituency, both here and abroad. Kennedy knew that he could not really perform as a President until he had taken Stevenson's people away from him. This he proceeded to do with stunning quickness, depending more on style and grace than policies; nonetheless, when Stevenson died in 1965, a year and a half after Kennedy, he seemed a forlorn and forgotten figure, humiliated by his final years; his people mourned the loss of Kennedy more than of Stevenson. It would only be later, as the full tragedy of the Vietnam war unfolded and a Stevenson disciple named Eugene McCarthy challenged Johnson, as humanist values seemed to be resurgent and regenerative against the rationalist values, and the liberal community looked back to see where it had gone wrong, that Stevenson would regain his constituency. Posthumously.

So it would not be Bowles or Stevenson. Nor J. William Fulbright, whom Kennedy had worked with on the Senate Foreign Relations Committee. Fulbright impressed him—the intelligence, the range, the respect he commanded on the Hill as the resident intellectual. Kennedy was not as close to Fulbright as he was to Mike Mansfield or even Humphrey, but they had worked well together, even though Kennedy had not been the most diligent member of the committee. He was often absent, and on the rare occasions when he was present, he seemed to spend much of his time autographing photos of himself which were to be sent out to fervent young admirers. To Fulbright's credit was the fact that his constituency was the Hill rather than the New York intellectual world, so that his coming aboard would be an asset rather than a liability, as in the case of Stevenson. But Fulbright was not without his critics; the Acheson group now regarded him with some suspicion (Fulbright was unfortunately something of a dilettante, Acheson had told Kennedy at a tea in late November 1960, given to making speeches calling for bold, brave new ideas, and yet always lacking in bold, brave new ideas.) He was not an entirely serious man. Besides, there was the problem of his position; he was chairman of the committee, and thus could do Kennedy and his policies a great deal of good sitting right where he was.

Yet, for all this, Kennedy was inclined toward him. He was anxious to have a Democratic Secretary of State, and Fulbright seemed to be the ablest man around. His problem, finally, was similar to that of Bowles: he made too many speeches, had too many public positions and eventually too many enemies. He had signed the Southern Manifesto, an antidesegregation statement by Southern congressmen, he had voted against civil rights bills (indeed, elevating him to State would open a seat in Arkansas, and wasn't Orval Faubus, the man who had become nationally known with his defiance at Little Rock, the likely candidate for his seat? Would a new Administration want that on its hands?). He had made speeches which the Jews, well organized, vocal, influential, regarded as suspiciously pro-Arab. In fact, when Harris Wofford, who was a liaison man with liberal groups during the talent-search period, heard that it might be Fulbright, he got on the phone and called Negro and Jewish groups imploring them to send telegrams criticizing Fulbright. Their wires made a profound impression on Robert Kennedy, who was already uneasy about how the underdeveloped world would regard a new Administration with a Secretary of State from Arkansas. Thus was Bill Fulbright vetoed by the left as Bowles had been from the right. (Later, when Fulbright visited Palm Beach, Joe Kennedy took him aside and said it was a great shame about his not becoming Secretary of State, but the NAACP, the Zionists and the liberals had all screamed bloody murder about the appointment. The senior Kennedy decided that a man with enemies like that could not be all bad, and when Fulbright returned to Washington he found a case of Scotch waiting for him, a gift of the ambassador.) Six years later, when there were several hundred thousand Americans in Vietnam, and Fulbright had become the Good Fulbright, he was at a cocktail party where he ran into Joe Rauh, the ADA man who had opposed his nomination as Secretary of State and had helped muster lobby groups against him. "Joe," asked Fulbright, "do you admit now that I was right on my stand on civil rights so that I could stay up here and do this?" Rauh, somewhat stunned by the statement, could only mumble that it was an unanswerable proposition, "to do wrong in order to do right."

NOR WOULD IT BE McGEORGE BUNDY. WALTER LIPPMANN AND others were pushing him very hard for high jobs, perhaps not State but something good, and Kennedy, listening to their recommendations, had thought, well, if he was that good, why not State itself? Kennedy liked Bundy and had been impressed by Bundy's willingness to criticize the appointment of Lewis Strauss by Eisenhower, the kind of unpredictable response that Kennedy particularly valued. Bundy's credentials were impeccable; he had support from the intellectual community, if not by dint of articles or books, at least by virtue of standing. He had taken no wrong positions, he was not soft, and though he was a Republican, even this could be dealt with. For a time Kennedy considered him for State, and flying down to Palm Beach right after John, Jr., was born, he told a group of trusted reporters that State was still a problem. He didn't know what he was going to do, but he wished he could make Bundy Secretary of State; Bundy was now his personal choice. "Why can't you?" asked Sander Vanocur, one of the pool reporters. "Because he's too young. It's bad enough that I'm that young, but if there's a Secretary of State that young it'll be too much. Besides, he's a Republican and Adlai will never serve under him." Which was true. Stevenson might bury his disappointment about not getting State and might serve in the Department, but he had demanded at least some say in the choice of his boss. (It was typical of the political subtleties of the selection process that before Kennedy decided on who his Secretary would be, he had decided on who it would not be, and had already chosen some of the key assistants at State, as well as Stevenson for the UN, Soapy Williams for Africa, Harriman as ambassador-at-large. It was as if, knowing that it would not go to a real party enthusiast, he had balanced it by giving lower-echelon jobs to major party figures.) So Stevenson, unable to attain what he wanted, had retained, if nothing else, something of a veto power. This he used against McGeorge Bundy, brilliant intellectual, great liberal, who had voted for Tom Dewey over Harry Truman, and twice for Dwight Eisenhower over Adlai Stevenson. If there were limits to Bundy's liberalism, there were also limits to Stevenson's tolerance.

Nor, finally, David K. E. Bruce—rich, patrician, the classic diplomat, smooth, intelligent, his assets including a very wealthy wife. He had haunted the great chambers of Europe for two decades, a man with a great sense of where power was and how to deal with it, the proper ambassador, the very American model of the British diplomat. He was well connected in the Democratic party hierarchy, in part because of many generous past contributions. Against Bruce was his age, sixty-two, which made him almost twenty years older than the President he would serve. There was a feeling that he would not be good going up on the Hill, that this was not a role he would enjoy. Nor was he helped by his own close ties with Stevenson; Kennedy had heard that Bruce's wife had burst into tears when Kennedy had been nominated at Los Angeles. Yet if there was no great enthusiasm for David Bruce, there were at least few objections, and at one time it hung in the balance: a little passion for Bruce on the part of one or two people around Kennedy, and the job might have been his.

What it came down to was a search not for the most talent, the greatest brilliance, but for the fewest black marks, the fewest objections. The man who had made the fewest enemies in an era when forceful men espousing good causes had made many enemies: the Kennedys were looking for someone who made very small waves. They were looking for a man to fill the most important Cabinet post, a job requiring infinite qualities of intelligence, wisdom and sophistication, a knowledge of both this country and the world, and they were going at it as presidential candidates had often filled that other most crucial post, the Vice-Presidency, by choosing someone who had offended the fewest people. Everybody's number-two choice. Thus their choice would be determined by neither talent nor brilliance, but to a degree by mediocrity. It was a sign of the extent to which the power of the Presidency had grown that this was applauded in many quarters. That the man they turned to was virtually unknown was revealing in itself, for if he had really done anything significant in his career, then he would have a record, for better or for worse.

DEAN RUSK. HE WAS EVERYBODY'S NUMBER TWO.

At the height of the selection process, Kennedy had turned to Bowles and said, "If you were Secretary of State, what kind of organization would you set up?" Bowles, who was on the board of the Rockefeller Foundation, being the Foundation's opening to the left, had answered that he would begin by naming Dean Rusk Undersecretary. "Dean Rusk?" Kennedy said. "Isn't he the head of the Rockefeller Foundation?"

Everyone spoke well of him. Good qualities. Hard-working. Patient. Balanced. Steady. A good diplomat. Lovett admired him. Acheson, the Secretary of State emeritus, put in a strong word: Rusk had been loyal and reliable. Fulbright spoke well of him, a fellow Southerner and a fellow Rhodes scholar. He also got support from Paul Nitze, another Establishment figure who was much honored within the group and rarely seen outside it. (Nitze was the real Acheson candidate for Secretary of State, but eventually he went to Defense as Assistant Secretary for International Security Affairs, where his deputy would be Bill Bundy, Acheson's son-in-law.) Everyone spoke well of Rusk, even the old Dulles people, for Dean Rusk left few men with a bad impression. He was always courteous, hard-working and thoughtful. Only one person, McGeorge Bundy, was strongly opposed to Rusk. They had met several times when Bundy was the dean of Harvard and Rusk ran the Rockefeller Foundation and held the purse strings. Bundy did not like Rusk (the Rusks of the world do not, except under extreme provocation, permit themselves the luxury of liking or disliking; God did not create public servants for the purposes of liking or disliking) and had decided that there was something missing. Bundy was an elitist, flashing out his prejudices, partial to first-rate people, to a considerable degree a Semitophile because he believed Jews were bright, and like himself, combative, his mind drawn to combat with other first-rate minds but intolerant of second-rate minds, and sensing in Rusk something second-rate. Kennedy's future adviser on national security affairs cast a vote against Rusk, but it was not that important, anyway, since he would be working in the White House and not at State.

And so Dean Rusk slowly sidled into the prime position. Rusk was a quiet man of enormous self-control, his ambition carefully masked. It did not flash naked for all to see like a Bundy's or McNamara's, but it was there nonetheless. He had campaigned for the job cautiously and consciously in his own veiled way; through the Establishment's channels he had sent up a few cautious signals to acknowledge that he was, well, available. He had taken Bowles aside so that Bowles could tell the Kennedys that Rusk had been working for them up there in Scarsdale. Though he was not known for his published work, he had published an article, a rare act indeed, in *Foreign Affairs*, the official journal of the Council on Foreign Relations, which was not given to turning down articles by heads of major foundations. The article, which was not entirely by chance published in the spring of 1960, dealt with the role of the Secretary of State. It called for the President to make a lot of decisions in foreign affairs and for the Secretary to travel less (no Secretary would travel as widely as Rusk). Similarly, Rusk had, just by chance, a willing citizen duly concerned, written a letter to the President-elect, dated November 22, 1960, on the subject of the electoral college, which also said that the President should work to heal racial scars ("As a Georgia-born citizen who believes that the Supreme Court decision on integration was long overdue . . ." the letter began). No Southern Manifesto for Dean Rusk, no Orval Faubus to take his place at the Foundation. Indeed, there seemed to be a mild element of lobbying, for on the same day that Rusk's letter on the South and the electoral college arrived, the prominent Harvard government professor William Yandell Elliott (who, like Rusk, had close ties to the past Republican Administration) weighed in with a letter recommending Rusk: "But I hope he [the President] will not neglect the possibility that Dean Rusk could be attracted from his important duties at the Rockefeller Foundation to the post that may be the most critical for the success not only of the next President but of the American nation in confronting the world we presently live in . . . Dean combines a thorough knowledge of not only the military, but of political strategy . . ."

Thus the coming of Dean Rusk. One pictures the process. The Establishment peers sit around and ponder who its candidates should be. Slowly varying possibilities are checked off. Most of the best-known are too old. The young President seems to want a Democrat and that eliminates a good many other names. And finally the name that comes to the fore is Dean Rusk, a man who is nominally a Democrat (he holds his job at the Foundation not so much through the courtesy of the Rockefellers as through John Foster Dulles, who got it for him). Knows the military, knows strategy, plays the game. So, quietly, the campaign for Rusk was put together and his qualifications tallied: not too young, not too old; a Democrat, but not too much of one; a Southerner but not too much so; an intellectual, but not too much so; worked on China, but no problems on that—in fact, good marks from the Luce people, who watch the China thing carefully. The acceptable man.

The Kennedy investigation into Rusk was marginal. There were a few phone calls, one from Richard Goodwin, a bright young man on the White House staff, to a reporter who had served in the China-Burma-India theater, a vast area which had contained the then Colonel Rusk. What about Rusk? Well, he was considered a good guy out there, not making enemies with the British like Stilwell, soothing tempers when Stilwell ruffled them, but he disapproved of the way the British treated the wogs. And he had a slight reputation as a ladies' man. "Great," said the New Frontiersman, "Kennedy will love that." The first and last hint of Dean Rusk the swinger. "What about the China thing," Goodwin asked, "was he involved in any of that?" "They never laid a glove on him," answered the reporter, which delighted Goodwin, though later, in a very different era, he would note upon reflection that this should have been a tip-off, the fact that Rusk could have lived through those years and not be touched by the great events. An enigmatic figure before entering the government, he was an enigmatic figure during it (not surprisingly, the best article ever to appear about him was written late in his second term, by Milton Viorst in *Esquire* under the title "Incidentally, Who *Is* Dean Rusk?"). Luckily for Rusk, the Kennedy people did not check all of Rusk's speeches made when he was Assistant Secretary of State for Far Eastern Affairs in 1950, for that might have jarred them slightly. There was one which, even given the temper of that particularly rigid time, was a horror, the blood virtually dripping off the teeth of the Chinese-Russian aggressor. It was a speech which might have made the cool Kennedy wince, an affront to his distaste for zealotry.

By chance, Rusk happened to be with Bowles at a Rockefeller Foundation meeting in Williamsburg when he got his first call from Kennedy.

"What do you think he wants to talk to me about?" he asked Bowles in a note.

"He's going to ask you to become Secretary of State," Bowles wrote in answer.

Rusk met with Kennedy the next day and later phoned Bowles.

"How did it go?" asked Bowles.

"Forget it," said Rusk. "We couldn't communicate. If the idea of my being Secretary of State ever entered his mind, it's dead now. We couldn't talk to each other. It's all over."

"I doubt it," said Bowles.

They were both right.

After Rusk had been offered the post as Secretary of State, he retained one doubt about accepting, which was financial. Unlike most good Establishment candidates, he had no resources of his own, neither by inheritance nor by dint of working in a great law firm for six figures a year. (This was a recurrent theme, the financial burden caused by serving in government, and some men, like McNamara's deputy, Roswell Gilpatric, though not lacking in resources from their New York firms, had to put a sharp limit on the amount of time they spent in Washington in each tour. In Gilpatric's case the problem was the enormity of alimony caused by two previous marriages.) Rusk, who had just bought a new house in Riverdale, mentioned this problem to Averell Harriman, and while it was not a situation which Harriman had ever faced personally, he enjoined Rusk not to worry. "For God's sake, man, when you leave State you'll be overwhelmed with offers, you'll be rich," he said. But Lovett was aware of the financial problem, of Rusk's limited resources, and he moved quickly to bolster Rusk's position. Rusk, he said, was entitled to some termination allowance in view of accrued pension rights which he would abandon by leaving the Foundation. A very generous settlement was made, and sped by both the Establishment's connections and resources, Rusk left for Washington.

On being told that Chester Bowles would be his Undersecretary, Rusk had said again and again how pleased he was with the news. They would, he said, have a Marshall-Lovett relationship—Rusk as the Old Man, Bowles as Bob Lovett. It was an odd idea, for although there were a lot of things in this world that Chester Bowles was guilty of, few would accuse him of being in style, thought or outlook like Bob Lovett. Not surprisingly, the Rusk-Bowles relationship never became a reality, since Rusk worked under a President with whom he could not communicate, and above an Undersecretary who made the President uneasy; none of the three was on the same wavelength as the others. When Rusk and Bowles did communicate it was not always happily (when Bowles returned from Southeast Asia in 1962 and suggested the neutralization of Vietnam, Rusk turned to him, quite surprised, and said, "You realize, of course, you're spouting the Communist line"). It ended very badly, with Bowles being driven from the Department with no small amount of humiliation involved, after one attempt to fire him failed and after Bowles staved off another himself, much to the annoyance of Joseph Alsop, one of his headhunters. In his column, Alsop said that this proved that Bowles was a eunuch, since he did not know when he was fired. The second attempt to fire him, in the reorganization of the State Department late in 1961 which subsequently became known as the "Thanksgiving Day Massacre," was a bit more successful, though just as messy, Rusk telling Bowles that he hated to do it, but that Kennedy was behind it, and Kennedy telling Bowles he hated to do it, but Rusk was behind it. Bowles was shifted to a meaningless post at the White House and eventually to his second tour as ambassador to India, an ideal place in the eyes of the Kennedys, since he could listen to the Indians and they to him. He served once again with distinction, and when he retired in 1969 a small group of old friends and enemies gathered at the State Department to bid him farewell. The last toast was proposed by Dean Rusk, in a speech of extraordinary grace in which he talked about Bowles's constant, relentless youth, the freshness of his mind, and the fact that he had more ideas in a day than most people have in a year.

The Kennedy years, which were so glittering for everyone else, were a time of considerable pain for Rusk; more than any other senior official he was not on the Kennedy wavelength. There was no intimacy; the President never called him by his first name as he did the other senior officials. The Washington rumormongers, who sensed these nuances with their own special radar, soon turned on him. They claimed that Rusk would go, a rumor mill fed by Kennedy's own private remarks reflecting doubt upon the Secretary. Even today the photographs of that era bear testimony to the incompatibility: the Kennedy people standing at attention waiting for some foreign visitors, all young and flashy, and Rusk—surprisingly tall—and his wife, both dowdy and older and more tired, looking like the representatives of a previous Administration, or perhaps simply the chaperons at the party. Rusk's own description of himself, voiced not without some pride, was that he looked like the neighborhood bartender. He knew that Georgetown cut him up, that he did not fit in, and occasionally, when he was relaxed and far from Washington on a trip, a fierce populism would surface against the silky world of Georgetown, the columnists and the writers and the lovely women who did not know the difference between the editorial page and the society page and all of these people who made their living destroying a man's reputation. There was other, subtler evidence too: Jackie Kennedy's intimate, graceful letter to Ros Gilpatric, thanking him for a book of beautiful poems and mocking the idea that a gift of such rare sensitivity might have come from "Antonio Celebrezze or Dean Rusk."

The Kennedy-Rusk relationship failed on more serious levels. Rusk, who always did things through channels and by the book, was never able to adjust to the freewheeling, deliberately disorganized Kennedy system, and was more formal in his view of the world than Kennedy. In almost every sense the relationship was exactly what Lovett had warned Kennedy that it should not be. Years later, as the war progressed and Rusk seemed to many of the Kennedy people a symbolic figure, a betrayer of the Kennedy dream, he would be attacked by the very people who had praised the brilliance of the Kennedy selection process. There could be no one to blame but the President himself, and those who had applauded the idea of the weak Secretary of State had gotten what they wanted and deserved. Those years would show, in the American system, how when a question of the use of force arose in government, the advocates of force were always better organized, seemed more numerous and seemed to have both logic and fear on their side, and that in fending them off in his own government, a President would need all the help he possibly could get, not the least of which should be a powerful Secretary of State.

Thus had the liberals lost the important job in the Administration, though of course they could never admit this. Rather, the main literature of the era was liberal (Schlesinger, Sorensen), and in it there is no note of how Kennedy manipulated the liberals and moved for the center, partly because of a reluctance to admit that it happened, a desire to see the Kennedy Administration as they would have it, and partly to claim Kennedy for history as liberal. Curiously, the closest thing to an admission for the liberals of the era can be found in a novel by John Kenneth Galbraith called *The Triumph*, in which, describing Worth Campbell, a character based on Dean Rusk, Galbraith wrote:

And when the Democrats returned, his old friends mentioned him as a man who should be used. He could serve a function but little understood in liberal administrations. These administrations need liberals for domestic tasks—not even a moderate conservative can be Secretary of Labor or of Health, Education and Welfare. But for foreign policy it is essential to have men who inspire confidence. This liberals do not do. Unless immediately on taking office they allay suspicion by taking an exceptionally strong stand in the Cold War, they will be suspected of a tendency, however subjective, towards appeasement of the Communists. The smallest gesture of conciliation will confirm this mistrust. Accordingly liberal administrations must place conservatives in charge of foreign policy or best of all, nonpolitical experts. Thus their need for men like Worth Campbell . . .

Chapter Four

Iᴛ ᴡᴀs ᴀ ɢʟɪᴛᴛᴇʀɪɴɢ ᴛɪᴍᴇ. Tʜᴇʏ ʟɪᴛᴇʀᴀʟʟʏ sᴡᴇᴘᴛ ɪɴᴛᴏ ᴏғғɪᴄᴇ, ready, moving, generating their style, their confidence—they were going to get America moving again. There was a sense that these were brilliant men, men of force, not cruel, not harsh, but men who acted rather than waited. There was no time to wait, history did not permit that luxury; if we waited it would all be past us. Everyone was going to Washington, and the word went out quickly around the Eastern seacoast, at the universities and in the political clubs, that the best men were going to Washington. Things were going to be done and it was going to be great fun; the challenge awaited and these men did not doubt their capacity to answer that challenge. Even the campaign quote of Jack Kennedy seemed to keynote it. He had used it again and again, moving swiftly through small towns in the New Hampshire winter, closing each speech with the quote from Robert Frost: ". . . But I have promises to keep,/And miles to go before I sleep,/And miles to go before I sleep." History summoned them, it summoned us: there was little time to lose.

We seemed about to enter an Olympian age in this country, brains and intellect harnessed to great force, the better to define a common good. Robert Frost, who had occasionally dropped by the Eisenhower White House to complain about the lack of leadership, sensed it. At the inaugural he said that a great new Augustan age was upon us, though he also challenged the new President to be more Irish than Harvard (not realizing that Harvard would

THE BEST AND THE BRIGHTEST

produce a fine new breed of aggressive policy makers). It seems long ago now, that excitement which swept through the country, or at least the intellectual reaches of it, that feeling that America was going to change, that the government had been handed down from the tired, flabby chamber-of-commerce mentality of the Eisenhower years to the best and brightest of a generation.

The Eisenhower stock could not have been lower; the country, which had taken reassurance from him at the beginning and relaxed in his easy presence, and which after the Korean War tensions had been ready for a father figure, was now restless. In Eisenhower's last year in office, James Reston wrote a column in the *Times* which reflected the disappointment with Ike. Interviewing his friend Uniquack, Reston asked, "Who's going to win the election?" Uniquack answered that Kennedy would win because "every President in this century has a double letter in his name. William McKinley—two *l*'s in William, Theodore Roosevelt—two *o*'s. Then there were Woodrow Wilson, Warren Harding, Calvin Coolidge, Herbert Hoover, Franklin Roosevelt, and of course, Harry."

"What about Eisenhower? Wasn't he President?"

Uniquack: "We must await the judgment of history on that."

Golf had long symbolized the Eisenhower years—played by soft, boring men with ample waistlines who went around rich men's country-club courses in the company of wealthy businessmen and were tended by white-haired, dutiful Negroes. (Although almost everything John Kennedy did, thought, read, believed, liked was described and examined in minute detail by the public, one thing which was little known and deliberately obscured about the new President was that he was an excellent golfer, a far better player than the outgoing General.)

In contrast, the new men were tough—"hard-nosed realists" was a phrase often used to define them, a description they themselves had selected. They had good war records; they were fond of pointing out that they were the generation which had fought the war, that they had been the company commanders, had borne the brunt of the war and lost their comrades. This gave them special preparation for the job ahead, it was the company commanders replacing the generals, and even here was seen virtue. Actually, most of it was a myth. It was Walt W. Rostow, Bundy's deputy, who had made this point, and typically, he had not been a company commander—he had picked bombing targets in Europe. While there were men in the Kennedy Administration who had been company commanders, they had little power in foreign policy. Rusk had been in the service but had been a staff colonel; Robert McNamara had been a semi-civilian doing statistics in the War Department; McGeorge Bundy had been an aide to a family friend who was an admiral; John McCone, head of the CIA, had made millions in shipbuilding (of the top people in national security, only the President had a distinguished war record).

But their image was of virility; they played squash and handball to stay in shape, wrote books and won prizes (even the President had won a Pulitzer prize), climbed mountains to clear their minds. Many of them read poetry and some were said to be able to quote it.

Day after day we read about them, each new man more brilliant than the last. They were not just an all-star first team, but an all-star second team as well. There were counts kept on how many Rhodes scholars there were in the Administration, how many books by members of the new Administration (even the Postmaster, J. Edward Day, had written a novel, albeit a bad one). There was a sense of involvement even for those who were not a part of the excitement; the social columns of the major newspapers were closely read to find out who went to which cocktail and dinner party. We soon found out, however, that they did not go to many cocktail parties. They didn't have time for that, for the idle chitchat. There were too many outsiders; they preferred, instead, dinner parties among their own, drinking a limited amount of good wine instead of too much hard liquor. The bright, quick repartee was reported, who had said what to whom.

The President himself was of course the object of the greatest fascination, and we craved details on what he read, what he ate, where he and Jackie went; all of that was news, and started, or ended, trends. It caused James MacGregor Burns to write with some irritation:

He is not only the handsomest, the best dressed, the most articulate, and graceful as a gazelle. He is omniscient; he swallows and digests whole books in minutes; his eye seizes instantly on the crucial point of a long memorandum; he confounds experts with superior knowledge of their field. He is omnipresent; no sleepy staff member can be sure that he will not telephone—or pop in; every hostess at a party can hope that he will. He is omnipotent; he personally bosses and spurs the whole shop; he has no need of Ike's staff apparatus; he is more than a lion, more than a fox. He's Superman!

McNamara, Bundy (who had been too powerful for Pusey at Harvard), Rostow, Arthur Schlesinger, Sargent Shriver. Did they need a Texan? Everyone who met Bill Moyers came away impressed—a Kennedy-style Texan, with perhaps too much of the Bible in him, but that would change. A general? They had Maxwell Taylor, a *good* general, soldier-statesman, an intellectual who read books avidly and had even written one. They said he had resigned in the Eisenhower years in protest against the archaic defense policies, but they were wrong—he had not resigned, he had retired after serving the full four years, and then he had written his book. But the book was so critical that it seemed as if he had resigned—a small but very important difference which went unnoticed at the time. Still, he was their general; if Harvard produced generals it would have produced Max Taylor.

It was an extraordinary confluence of time and men, and many people in the know quoted Lyndon Johnson's reaction to them at the first Cabinet meeting. He, the outsider, like us, looked at them with a certain awe, which was no wonder, since they had forgotten to invite him to the meeting, and only at the last minute, when the others were arriving, did someone remember the Vice-President and a desperate telephone search went on to find him. They were all so glamorous and bright that it was hard to tell who was the most brilliant, but the one who impressed him the most was "the fellow from Ford with the Stacomb on his hair." The fellow from Ford with the Stacomb on his hair! A terrific line, because it once again delineated Johnson, who, Vice-President or no, seemed more a part of the Eisenhower era than this one. What was not so widely quoted in Washington (which was a shame because it was a far more prophetic comment) was the reaction of Lyndon's great friend Sam Rayburn to Johnson's enthusiasm about the new men. Stunned by their glamour and intellect, he had rushed back to tell Rayburn, his great and crafty mentor, about them, about how brilliant each was, that fellow Bundy from Harvard, Rusk from Rockefeller, McNamara from Ford. On he went, naming them all. "Well, Lyndon, you may be right and they may be every bit as intelligent as you say," said Rayburn, "but I'd feel a whole lot better about them if just one of them had run for sheriff once."

So THEY CARRIED WITH THEM AN EXCITING SENSE OF AMERICAN elitism, a sense that the best men had been summoned forth from the country to harness this dream to a new American nationalism, bringing a new, strong, dynamic spirit to our historic role in world affairs, not necessarily to bring the American dream to reality here at home, but to bring it to reality elsewhere in the world. It was heady stuff, defining the American dream and giving it a new sense of purpose, taking American life, which had grown too materialistic and complacent, and giving it a new and grander mission. (That special hubris about the American age remained with some of the Kennedy people long after it had all gone sour and indeed come apart. In 1968, when the horror of the war and Gene McCarthy's success in New Hampshire had finally driven Robert Kennedy from his role of Hamlet to announcing that he would become a candidate, Theodore Sorensen wrote for his announcement speech: "At stake is not simply the leadership of our party, and even our own country, it is our right to the moral leadership of this planet." The sentence absolutely appalled all the younger Robert Kennedy advisers, who felt it smacked of just the kind of attitude which had gotten us into Vietnam. Nonetheless, despite their protests, it stayed in the speech.) The United States playing a new role, mighty and yet good. Not everyone, of course, was stirred by it. If there was a lack of modesty in the Kennedy beginnings, there were intellectuals who felt a more modest, limited sense about their own nation and its possibilities. In

1957, at a special symposium of American scholars, Walt Rostow, who would come to symbolize during both the Kennedy and the Johnson years the aggressive, combative liberal nationalism of the era, had made his case for an American national interest earlier in the symposium. Then David Riesman, the Harvard sociologist, quietly warned against the dangers implicit in much of what Rostow had suggested (the Rostow idea that the American perspective of the world had not kept pace with American power in it and over it), which struck Riesman as jingoism. The Civil War, Riesman said, was "deadly serious as an omen of bellicosity and bigotry," and he thought a humbler and more modest view of American society and its potential role in a diverse world was called for, as well as recognition of the failure of American culture here at home, the failure of the quality of American life, an understanding that not all indices of American life could be found in the booming statistics of the GNP. He felt that something was desperately missing. Commenting on "a kind of blandness that I somehow see as inhuman," he noted that "when I see a French or Italian movie, the faces seem more alive and expressive than American faces in equivalent films. The very rich are perhaps unhappy in all countries. Their faces are often sour, fearful and suspicious. In America, millions are among the very rich in international terms, while the white-collar workers and many of the factory workers seem to me to be unhappy also—ill at ease in Zion."

It would not be the last time Riesman was prophetic: in 1961, when the Kennedy team was already on board and there was great enthusiasm over the new theories of counterinsurgency (Rostow, his antagonist in the 1957 symposium, became one of the great propagators of antiguerrilla warfare) and Vietnam had been chosen as a testing ground, Riesman remained uneasy. In mid-1961 he had lunch with two of the more distinguished social scientists in the Kennedy government. On the subject of Vietnam the others talked about limited war with the combativeness which marked that particular era, about the possibilities of it, about the American right to practice it, about the very excitement of participating in it. All of this smacked strongly of the arrogance and hubris of the era, and Riesman became more and more upset with the tone and the direction of the conversation, until finally he stopped them and asked if they had ever been to Utah. *Utah!* No, they said, not Utah, but why Utah, had Riesman ever been there? No, Riesman answered, but he had read a great deal about the Church of the Latter-day Saints, and it occurred to him that his friends did not know much about America, about how deep the evangelical streak was. "You all think you can manage limited wars and that you're dealing with an elite society which is just waiting for your leadership. It's not that way at all," he said. "It's not an Eastern elite society run for Harvard and the Council on Foreign Relations."

He left them after lunch, uneasy about the direction the country was taking. He had made a hobby of studying the American Civil War and he had always been disturbed by the passions which it had unleashed in the country, the tensions and angers just below the surface, the thin fabric of the society which held it all together, so easy to rend. They were, he thought, provincials. Brilliant Atlantic provincials.

It was only natural that the intellectuals who questioned the necessity of American purpose did not rush from Cambridge and New Haven to inflict their doubts about American power and goals upon the nation's policies. So people like Riesman, classic intellectuals, stayed where they were while the new breed of thinkers-doers, half of academe, half of the nation's think tanks and of policy planning, would make the trip, not doubting for a moment the validity of their right to serve, the quality of their experience. They were men who reflected the post-Munich, post-McCarthy pragmatism of the age. One had to stop totalitarianism, and since the only thing the totalitarians understood was force, one had to be willing to use force. They justified each decision to use power by their own conviction that the Communists were worse, which justified our dirty tricks, our toughness.

Among those who felt that way was Riesman's opponent in the debate, Walt Whitman Rostow, who had authored one of the best of the campaign phrases—"Let's get this country moving again"—and he was now safely ensconced in the White House. Kennedy had intended to funnel him to State, but Rusk, who had accepted most of Kennedy's other appointees, and half the former Democratic governors of America, had finally put his foot down. He found Rostow particularly irritating—this verbose, theoretical man who intended to make all his theories work. So Rostow was shifted to the White House, under McGeorge Bundy, who was already installed in a better slot than he had expected.

At first there had been some talk about Bundy getting a position at State, but he had quickly turned down an offer to become Deputy Undersecretary of State for Administration, saying that he did not feel it was worthwhile to leave Cambridge, where he was a dean, to come to Washington to be a dean. Kennedy thereupon offered him the position of Assistant Secretary of Defense for International Security Affairs, but since Bundy did not appear to know much about it, the job not carrying with it the power and prestige that the McNamara years would bring to it (prestige in part due to McNamara's tendency, conscious or unconscious, to usurp the powers of the Secretary of State, and Rusk's tendency to let him do it), he turned it down. He was then made Special Assistant to the President for National Security Affairs, where by the force of his personality, intelligence, and great and almost relentless instinct for power, he was to create a domain which by the end of the decade would first rival and then surpass the State Department in influence. Since he ended up with a job far better than he had expected, his support of Kennedy during the campaign having been somewhat less active than other professors', and though he was not a great admirer of Rostow and shared some of the doubts of Rostow's colleagues, he quickly paid a debt to Kennedy by adding Rostow to the White House staff, sure that he could handle him there.

For there was no doubt in Bundy's mind about his ability to handle not just Rostow, and the job, but the world. The job was not just a happenstance thing; he had, literally and figuratively, been bred for it, or failing this, Secretary of State. He was the brightest light in that glittering constellation around the President, for if those years had any central theme, if there was anything that bound the men, their followers and their subordinates together, it was the belief that sheer intelligence and rationality could answer and solve anything. If this was the quality of the young President, then no one else exemplified it more than Bundy, who seemed on the surface to be the sharpest intellect of a generation, a repository of national intelligence. Even Kennedy talked of Bundy with a certain awe: what a pleasure it was to work with him all day, he could sense what you wanted before you ever knew it yourself. "You can't beat brains," Kennedy said of Bundy. He was young and vigorous, and besides intelligence, he had style too. He was an egghead, but he was safe. Although he was a Republican, he had been for the Kennedy candidacy —was there any greater guarantee that he would rise above petty partisanship to serve the nation, the right idea of nation? He was not committed to the myths of the past, he was committed only to the existence of a strong, free, democratic America in a stable world.

Bundy was a man of applied intelligence, a man who would not land us in trouble by passion and emotion. He was an aristocrat and a Brahmin, and yet, more than that, not a prisoner of the Brahmin world; he had gone beyond that closed little arena to play in a larger sphere. He was admired for his cool, lucid mind, the honed-down intelligence, the brilliance of the mathematician, the insight of the political-science scholar at Harvard. He had been a legend in his time at Groton, the brightest boy at Yale, dean of Harvard College at a precocious age and perilously close to being president of it (*"Sic transit gloria Bundy,"* quipped the classicist John Finley when Nathan Pusey was chosen). The early Washington years seemed to confirm the Bundy legend. He was at the center of things, darting in and out of the President's office ("Goddammit, Mac," someone heard Kennedy say, "I've been arguing with you about this all week long," and *that* was power—being able to argue with the President all week long). He was a Kennedy favorite, that was clear, and in 1962, when he was offered the presidency of Yale (a job which might have tempted him in another time, and which eventually went to his close friend Kingman Brewster), Kennedy was, there is no other word for it, effusive about not losing him. In a rare show of emotion, Kennedy declared that the possibility of Bundy's leaving the White House was *out of the question.*

He was above self-interest, as others, politicians, labor leaders, Negro leaders, were not ("Bundy's devotion to duty is consonant with his upbringing," said the *Saturday Evening Post* in 1962). In contrast to the austere quality of his work style, he was considered charming at dinner parties, engaging and witty, and people marveled at the difference between the professional Bundy and the social Bundy. While the latter seemed almost gay and irreverent—if not warm, at least open—the professional Bundy was all steel and work and drive; the smile was hard, almost frozen. There was also a lack of willingness to resist a put-down when someone was inept or slowed him down, and at times there seemed to be a certain cruelty about him, the rich, bright kid putting down the inferior. "Stop whining," he told one high State Department official, and the official upon reflection decided that he had, in fact, been whining, though the put-down did not make him like Bundy any more. When in 1961 Daniel Ellsberg at Defense discovered that the Joint Chiefs of Staff had a War Plan, which told how they would go to war, and more important, that they had carefully hidden this fact from civilians, including among others the Secretary of Defense, he was dispatched to the White House by his superiors to inform Bundy. Feeling that the manner in which he had uncovered the plan and the secrecy around it were almost as significant as the plan itself, Ellsberg began by trying to explain how he had come across it. Bundy quickly interrupted him. "Is this a briefing or is it a confessional?" he snapped. It was the kind of put-down that many others in the government would feel, and thus in later years, when Bundy began to develop his problems and his reputation slipped, there was a surprising number of people who took no small pleasure in it. He had left more scars than he intended, in contrast to McNamara, who tended to retain a far higher degree of personal loyalty from his subordinates.

Yet these stories would surface later; if one was put down by Mac Bundy in those days, he did not boast about it. That would have been a sign of being on the outside, for Bundy was a favorite, if not *the* favorite of the taste makers, a man who had nevertheless entered the White House with Walter Lippmann promoting him for Secretary of State. That is to say, he was not the favorite man of Capitol Hill and the bureaucracy, which he treated with an icy disdain, the former as if it did not exist, the latter as if it existed to be circumvented, telling friends that he was a traffic cop on the job, trying to short-circuit the government machine. Rather, he was the favorite of that predominantly liberal part of Washington which sets the tone of the city, deciding who is good and who is bad, who is in and who is out, what is legitimate and what is not, who has power and who does not. He made himself accessible to the right elements of the press, columnists linked with the establishment such as James Reston or Joseph Alsop, or Henry Brandon, a reporter for the London *Sunday Times* who sometimes seemed almost a part of the high level of government. That this small segment of the press did not constitute the press itself did not bother him, and some of the newer journalists such as Sander Vanocur, the White House correspondent for NBC, complained regularly that Bundy snubbed reporters representing such proletarian outlets as the National Broadcasting Company. (His feelings about the press, its uses and values were probably best illustrated by a note he sent to Pierre Salinger on the occasion of the latter's communiqué at the time of Diem's death: "Pierre, Champion! Excellent prose. No surprise. A communiqué should say nothing in such a way as to feed the press without deceiving them." Later there was some question about whether he had said "feed the press" or "fool the press," and Bundy insisted he only wanted to feed the reporters.)

Men like Vanocur and James Deakin, a highly respected reporter for the St. Louis *Post-Disptach* who, interviewing Bundy, heard him say, "This is very boring," did not come to love Bundy at all, and there was a feeling of many in Washington that Bundy was in all his dealings too much the elitist. But even here he worked successfully, he was a cool operator who held most of the press at bay, and yet at the same time saw his reputation grow, so that at the height of those years, just before it all began to sour, Joseph Kraft, one of the best political writers in America, a taste maker himself and the kind of columnist a Bundy would talk to, wrote of him:

The central fact, what I want most to say, is that Bundy is the leading candidate, perhaps the only candidate for the statesman's mantle to emerge in the generation that is coming to power—the generation which reached maturity in the war and postwar period. His capacity to read the riddle of multiple confusions, to consider a wide variety of possibilities, to develop lines of action, to articulate and execute public purposes, to impart quickened energies to men of the highest ability, seems to me unmatched. To me, anyhow, he seems almost alone among contemporaries, a figure of true consequence, a fit subject for Milton's words:

> A Pillar of State; deep on his
> Front engraven
> Deliberation sat, and publick care;
> And princely counsel in his face . . .

That, of course, was the high point. It was written in the summer of 1965 and published in the fall, and by then the war was deepening, and the doyens of the Establishment were already losing control; only two and a half years later, in 1968, after the assassination of Robert Kennedy, some key figures in the Establishment were looking for a candidate who would be both respectable and against the war, and they narrowed it down to Eugene McCarthy or Nelson Rockefeller. They decided to put together as many blue-chip names as they could on an important list and thus begin sending out waves of dovish respectability. The man originating the idea was Kingman Brewster, Bundy's closest friend, the president of Yale, a cool and skillful politician, caught between the enormously conflicting pressures of his ties to the Establishment and of the growing anger and rebelliousness of his students, the sons of the Establishment. So when Brewster called one of the top officials in the McCarthy campaign to see if the idea was acceptable, he was told the idea sounded all right and they should go ahead. Brewster then asked for names for the list. "Well, what about your friend Mac Bundy?" the McCarthy official asked.

"Mac," said Brewster, "is going to spend the rest of his life trying to justify his mistakes on Vietnam."

BUNDY IS FROM BOSTON. THE REST OF THE WORLD WHICH IS NOT FROM Boston thinks of him as being very Boston and the name as being very Boston. This is not true, since the Bundys are from Grand Rapids, Michigan, and the name by itself means very little in Boston history, a view corroborated by Shreve's, a famous jewelry store in Boston. In 1966, when Bundy was leaving government, a group of his aides in the White House decided to give him something better than the traditional silver ashtray and came up with the idea of silver dice on a silver tray, something to roll as a means of determining foreign policy. In Washington several jewelry stores said it couldn't be done, but since most of his people were from Cambridge in the first place, they remembered Shreve's, and one of them was dispatched to arrange it. Silver dice on a silver tray? Yes, said a proper old gentleman at the shop. He thought it could be done. And what name would go on it?

"McGeorge Bundy," said the White House aide.

"McGeorge Bundy . . . McGeorge Bundy . . . Bundy . . . oh, yes, isn't he the boy who married Mary Lothrop?"

Bundy is by Boston standards not a Bundy but a Lowell (on his mother's side. "His father is from Michigan someplace," a Bostonian noted). Katharine Bundy is also a Putnam, which by Boston standards is very good too, but the pedigree is on the Lowell side, as is much of the determination and the drive. The family descended from Percival Lowle, who came to America in 1639 and sired a great family which became noted for its inventiveness, its shrewdness, its industry, its success and, by the nineteenth century, its dominance of Harvard College and the New England textile mills. The problem of a labor force for these mills had always been a serious one, but the Lowells came up with a brilliant solution, the hiring of what came to be known as Lowell Mill girls. All the good young country girls of New England came to the mill towns, where in return for chaperoning, religious training and proper housing they worked in the mills, a solution which at once satisfied both religious and economic drives, a happy Calvinist ending indeed. Although much was made at the time of what a good and virtuous idea this was, a showpiece, in fact, for foreign visitors, the working hours were long and the pay was small.

It was against this backdrop that the great fortunes were made, fortunes which allowed the first families to dominate the society of that era. Theodore Parker, a crusading minister in the 1840s, wrote of the Lowells and these other great families: "This class is the controlling one in politics. It mainly enacts the laws of this state and the nation; makes them serve its turn . . . It can manufacture governors, senators, judges to suit its purposes as easily as it can manufacture cotton cloth. This class owns the machinery of society . . . ships, factories, shops, water privileges." They were also families which had a fine sense of protecting their own position, and they were notorious for giving large grants to Harvard College, which was *their* college, and just as notorious for doing very little for public education.

John Amory Lowell, the great-great-grandfather of McGeorge Bundy, was a towering figure of his era in Boston, having picked no fewer than six presidents of Harvard; Augustus Lowell, his son, increased his share of the family inheritance six or seven times, and in addition produced a remarkable family even by the standards of a Lowell: Amy Lowell the poet, A. Lawrence Lowell the educator, and Percival Lowell the astronomer. The fourth child was Elizabeth Lowell, who married William Putnam and gave birth to Katharine Lawrence Putnam, who later married Harvey Hollister Bundy.

A. Lawrence Lowell had married a cousin, and since they had no children, Kay Putnam, his favorite niece, became something of an unofficial hostess at Lawrence Lowell's gatherings. She was a vivacious, bright, intense, argumentative woman, with a strong sense of her own rightness, aware of who she was, where their tradition had come from and where it was going next, an intellectual heiress letting others know that she had accomplished something intellectually, a woman known by her contemporaries for force of mind and a capacity to dominate a conversation. "Mother never forgot for a minute that she was a Lowell. She was one of those people who believed that there are three classes in society—upper, middle and lower—and you know which one she belonged to. We sometimes kidded her about it, but it was assumed in the family that none of us would want to become bus drivers. Mother took this position that you have this tradition, so why not use it, and I suppose we did," her daughter and Bundy's sister Mrs. G. Andelot Belin, wife of a Boston lawyer, said to reporter Milton Viorst. "We were," Mrs. Belin added, "a noisy family, and Mother was the noisiest among us. For her, things were black and white. It's an outlook that descends directly from the Puritans and we all have it. But Mac has it more than the rest of us."

By contrast Harvey Hollister Bundy was a mild, reserved figure. "Most of us remember the evening we celebrated the election to honorary membership of Henry Lewis Stimson," says a yearbook of the Century Association, an exclusive New York club for upper-class gentlemen, primarily white and Protestant, interested in letters, "the occasion was no less moving because it was also gay. The speakers were Stimson's friends and associates: Dwight Eisenhower, John Davis, and Harvey Bundy. Bundy told some stories about the Secretary fishing for trout in Europe in the wartime; stories that made some of us say to one another, 'Is this the man that has been called "dry and stiff"?' " Surely that warm evening at the Century he was anything but, and those who met him then for the first time found him responsive and engaging. But a Centurian who knew him well for a long time has explained that Harvey could be extremely dry and stiff to those who tried to persuade him to compromise with his principles or betray a confidence. This same friend speaks of him as a "Bostonian not born in Boston. Coming from the Midwest, he surprised those who supposed that rigid adherence to principle is an exclusive Boston characteristic . . ."

Harvey Bundy graduated from Yale in 1909 with high honors, and was later first in his class at Harvard Law, an achievement which brought him an appointment as law clerk to Oliver Wendell Holmes. He returned to Boston in 1915 and here the Lowell connections did not hurt. In Boston in those days one of the chief industries was taking the vast fortunes of the great families and turning them into trust funds in order to avoid taxes, and Harvey Bundy became the lawyer for many of them. A few years later he also became a close friend and confidant of Henry Stimson's, "Colonel Stimson" as he liked to be known, after he reached that rank in World War I. Stimson had been very close to Teddy Roosevelt, and at Roosevelt's urging even ran (unsuccessfully) for governor of New York in 1910, served under Taft as Secretary of War in 1911 as a Taft gesture to the Roosevelt wing, though when the 1912 split came, he stayed loyal to Taft. Stimson was firmly linked to the tradition of Teddy Roosevelt: an aristocracy come to power, convinced of its own disinterested quality, believing itself above both petty partisan interest and material greed. The suggestion that this also meant the holding and wielding of power was judged offensive by these same people, who preferred to view their role as service, though in fact this was typical of an era when many of the great rich families withdrew from the new restless grab for money of a modernizing America, and having already made their particular fortunes, turned to the public arena as a means of exercising power. They were viewed as reformers, though the reforms would be aimed more at the newer seekers of wealth than at those who already held it. ("First-generation millionaires," Garry Wills wrote in *Nixon Agonistes*, "give us libraries, second-generation millionaires give us themselves.")

Harvey Bundy was typical of this era. He served Stimson loyally as an aide when he was Hoover's Secretary of State. ("There was no dearth of men who wanted to be Assistant Secretary of State," according to Stimson's biography, "but in one of Stimson's favorite phrases, the men who made themselves applicants were usually men who were thinking 'what the job would do for them' and he was hunting for men whose first interest was 'what they could do for the job'!"). In Stimson's opinion Franklin Roosevelt, running for the Presidency in 1932, was an untried and untested figure, and Stimson found the general public antagonism toward Hoover surprising, though he noted that "the people of sobriety and intelligence and responsibility" were on Hoover's side. He wrote at the time: "The people of this country are in a humor where they don't want to hear any reason . . . they want a change and I think they are going to get it, but if they get it, in less than a year they will be the sickest country that ever walked the face of this earth or else I miss my guess." Though he missed that guess, he would eventually meet with Roosevelt and find to his surprise that the new President was intelligent and competent, and a few years later, when Roosevelt was in the subtle process of preparing the country for European intervention, he brought Stimson back to the government as Secretary of War, since Stimson was a strong and forceful advocate of preparedness. ("In our house," Bill Bundy, Mac's brother, once noted, referring to the Stimson tie, "the State Department and the Pentagon were interchangeable," a comment not just about his family but about an era, which he himself would confirm in 1964 by moving from a job as Assistant Secretary of Defense and taking a comparable one at State.)

As Secretary of War, Stimson worked with Frank Knox, who was Secretary of the Navy, a man who had been a friend for more than twenty-five years, since he had first shown up in Stimson's office with an introductory note from Teddy Roosevelt saying: "He is just our type!" At War, his first assistant was Robert Patterson, and after him, his assistants were John McCloy, Robert Lovett and Harvey Bundy. "All," says the Stimson biography, "were men in the prime of their life, the forties and fifties, but all were so much younger than Stimson that none ever called him by his first name. All four had been conspicuously successful in private life, three as lawyers, and one as a banker; all of them had come to Washington at serious financial sacrifice. None of them had ever been politically active, and none had any consuming political ambition. All four were men of absolute integrity and none was small-minded about credit for his labors. All but one were Republicans, but not one of them ever aroused partisan opposition . . ."

The Stimsonian tradition of public service and power, and the Stimsonian philosophy of preparedness and force, had made a deep mark on the Bundy household; it is Stimson's photograph which sits on Bundy's desk to this day. After the war, when Stimson decided to publish his memoirs and wanted some help, he naturally chose as his literary aide McGeorge Bundy, the bright and ambitious son of his friend Harvey Bundy; together they produced his biography, *On Active Service in Peace and War.*

THE BUNDY YOUTH WAS NOT UNLIKE THAT OF THE KENNEDYS IN some respects; lots of children everywhere, lots of intellectual and physical competition, lots of energy and lots of confidence. There were violent games of their own lawn sport, a somewhat more physical form of croquet, with Mrs. Bundy leading the pack. According to friends of the family, she seemed to center her hopes on Bill, two years older than Mac; in fact, some of Mac's old friends attribute his intense drive and competitiveness, the combination of what they feel is calm on the surface and considerable seething tension underneath, to boyhood competition with an older and slightly favored brother.

Mac Bundy was born in 1919. He attended Groton, the greatest prep school in the nation, where the American upper class sends its sons to instill the classic values: discipline, honor, a belief in the existing values and the rightness of them. Coincidentally it is at Groton that one starts to meet the right people, and where connections which will serve well later on—be it Wall Street or Washington—are first forged; one learns, at Groton, above all, the rules of the game, and even a special language: what washes and what does not wash. (In 1967 John Marquand, the writer and son of the great chronicler of the Boston aristocracy, was part of a group which ran an advertisement in the Martha's Vineyard newspaper protesting congressional testimony by Undersecretary of State Nicholas Katzenbach that the President could do what he wanted to under the terms of the Tonkin Gulf Resolution. Why, Johnny, why, asked Bundy, weekending at the Vineyard, did he help ruin Lydie Katzenbach's summer? "Well, her husband helped ruin my whole year," answered Marquand. Bundy looked at him. The small smile. "It won't wash, Johnny, it just won't wash.") *Cui servire est regnare* is Groton's motto. "To serve is to rule." The overt teaching was that the finest life is service to God, your family and your state, but the covert teaching, far more subtle and insidious, was somewhat different: ultimately, strength is more important; there is a ruling clique; there is a thing called privilege and you might as well use it. That is the real world and it is going to remain that way, so you might as well get used to it. If not, you can rebel, but only within the prescribed rules. Groton is a school more than a little short on Catholics, Negroes, Jews and hyphenated Americans, and it reflected in its real values what some students there called "a muscular Christianity." Bundy was of course part of this and has always accepted the special privilege that his advantages offered, working perhaps discreetly to change it from within (but never so much as to be tabbed as something odd, like a reformer), but accepting it nonetheless, an acceptance which has made some outsiders a little suspicious. If he is really that egalitarian, what is he doing in all those clubs? At Yale, for instance, where his friend Kingman Brewster turned down the secret societies, Bundy joined (the best, naturally) Skull and Bones, and later, in Washington, he would similarly resist requests from friends that he resign from the Metropolitan Club, which ten years after the great storm about its membership in 1961 was not noticeably more egalitarian.

At Groton, Bundy was something of a legend in his time, as he would be everywhere he went. Besides capturing every available honor, he could have been a good second-team quarterback—excellent play calling—but he thought that athletics took too much time, so he played club football instead. He was a brilliant debater when debating still meant something, and won the Franklin D. Roosevelt Debating Trophy three times, a prize named for an old boy. Louis Auchincloss, a contemporary at Groton, has said that Bundy was ready to be dean of the school at the age of twelve. Richard Irons, the school's best history teacher, said that even then it was astonishing to read Bundy's essays, they were always better than the books he had used as reference. The story is told of a group of outstanding students asked to prepare a paper on the Duke of Marlborough. The next day Bundy was called upon to read his composition in class. As he started to read, his classmates began to giggle and continued all the way through his reading of a perfectly excellent paper. The teacher, pleased by the essay but puzzled by the giggles, later asked one of the students what it was all about. "Didn't you know?" said the student. "He was unprepared. He was reading from a blank piece of paper."

After Bundy graduated from Groton when he was sixteen—summa cum laude, of course, just as Bill had before him—he took the college board exam. He refused to answer either of two English essay questions: "How did you spend your summer vacation?" and "My favorite pet." Instead he wrote an essay attacking the themes as meaningless and the college board people for having chosen such foolish and irrelevant subjects when there were so many great issues before Americans in today's world. The first grader read the essay, and annoyed by the arrogance, failed him. A second reader was called in, because of the incredible discrepancy between this mark and all the others Bundy had made. He was delighted, believing himself that the college boards should stop this inanity. A third grader, the head of the English section, was called over. Having read about too many pets and vacations, he marked down Bundy's English score: 100.

From Groton he went to Yale. The very choice of Yale was somewhat unorthodox, since Bostonians usually sent their children to Harvard after Groton, but the Bundys had decided that after both Boston and Groton, Yale might be somewhat broadening. On arrival, the freshmen were summoned to a mass meeting where the dean announced that there were two distinguishing features about the class: first, it comprised 850 students, which was the desired number; second, one member of the class was the first Yale student to get three perfect scores on his college entrance exams. Bundy of course. (Bundy recalled this thirty years later with a certain annoyance: "I thought it was a very improper thing to do—I don't think you should talk about grades that way, either good ones or bad ones.") And he continued to excel; his Groton history teacher, Richard Irons, afraid that Bundy and a few contemporaries might be ahead of themselves and the normal curriculum at Yale, had arranged for some special advanced standing freshman courses for them there. In one of them, which was taught by David Owen, a distinguished historian, Bundy wrote an essay entitled "Is Lenin a Marxist?" and the product so staggered Owen that he later told Irons he did not think there were two men on the Yale faculty who could have written it.

Bundy was class orator and also became a columnist for the *Yale Daily News*, refusing to try out for the paper, as most young men did, because it was too time-consuming, but because of his special abilities, he was allowed to write for it, anyway. And he was a member of Phi Beta Kappa. Altogether he was a formidable figure on the campus, so much intelligence harnessed to so much breeding, all that and the competitive urge as well. The Yale yearbook for 1940 noted: "This week passed without Mahatma Bundy making a speech." He was—not surprisingly, given his background, the ties of his family to Stimson—already deeply involved in foreign affairs, a committed internationalist and interventionist. In 1940 in a book called *Zero Hour*, in which young writers discussed the threat to the United States, Bundy, writing in a style which reflects the sureness of his upbringing and the values instilled in him, said: "Let me put my whole proposition in one sentence. I believe in the dignity of the individual, in government by law, in respect for the truth, and in a good God; these beliefs are worth my life and more; they are not shared by Adolf Hitler."

From Yale, Bundy went to Harvard, but hardly as a struggling graduate student. Rather, he was a Junior Fellow, a member of the select Society of Fellows, the chosen of the chosen. The Society had been founded by his great-uncle A. Lawrence Lowell, who set aside millions of his own money to endow the program and who told each new Fellow, "You will practice the virtues and avoid the snares of the scholar. You will be courteous to your elders, who have explored to the point from which you may advance; and helpful to your juniors, who will progress farther by reason of your labors. Your aim will be knowledge and wisdom, not the reflected glamour of fame. You will not accept credit that is due another, or harbor jealousy of an explorer who is more fortunate . . ." The Society was a special program at Harvard designed to spare supremely talented people the drudgery of normal doctoral work. (It means, among other things, that Bundy is not Dr. Bundy. Of course, anyone can get a Ph.D., but very few can be Junior Fellows.) The fact is that he has in his lifetime done almost no serious scholarly work. Of his two major books, the first is the collaboration with Stimson on his memoirs, the second is the edited speeches of his brother's father-in-law, Dean Acheson. The Stimson biography is a good and serious book, and perhaps in a way more reflective of that elitist viewpoint than it intended to be, but it is hardly pioneer work. It is a subject about which Bundy retains some sensitivity, and recently, when a magazine article hinted that perhaps the Stimson book was not exactly brilliant, he was able to quote verbatim what Walter Lippmann had said about it (and Bundy's role in it) some twenty years earlier. The important thing is how easy it all was for him; very few young men in their twenties, with no previous literary credentials, are offered the job to share in the writing of the memoirs of such a distinguished public servant. He was bright, but he was also so incredibly well connected that things came to him much more readily than to his contemporaries (like a girl who is both prettier than the other bright girls and brighter than the other pretty girls, it was almost unfair), and along the way he picked up less wisdom, less scar tissue than other men.

While he was a Junior Fellow at Harvard, Bundy made his one attempt to run for elective office, and the way in which he became involved is somewhat revealing about the way things are done for those who have a certain head start in life. "Henry Shattuck, who was a very powerful and important figure in Boston in those days, called me and asked me if I wanted to run for his place on the Boston City Council," he once told a reporter. "He told me that for a young man with an interest in public life it was a splendid way to begin. He assured me that the election was a formality, no one but a Republican had ever won before, and he would assure the support of the Republican Ward Committee, and since it was a very heavy Republican area, I agreed. I had an opponent, he did his work and I did not, and I got licked and I deserved to be beaten." Bundy never ran for public office again, nor did he ever make himself answerable to public controls and public checks again (until belatedly, when as head of the Ford Foundation he felt the enormous pressure brought on by the New York school strike against both the Foundation and himself and he suddenly became available and friendly both to reporters and congressional leaders).

This foray into Boston politics was important in the shaping of his political outlook. Although American elective politics is often an imperfect thing, sometimes cheap and degrading, perhaps too much for men who lack the fiber, it is at the same time a great humanizing force, particularly for the strong, for those who already have advantages and resources. These men can manage to overcome the tawdry and cheapening aspects, and absorb, sometimes almost in spite of themselves, a feeling for the country, a certain respect and almost affection for its foibles. Those who knew Jack Kennedy well felt he was a different man after the West Virginia primary in 1960; similarly, Robert Kennedy was a changed man as he went from running a campaign to becoming a candidate himself. But Bundy gave it up, and instead turned to using power in the private, elitist sense, ignoring public pressures. (When he finally decided to talk about his role in Vietnam he did it, significantly, at the

Council on Foreign Relations, off the record, with no question-and-answer period.)

He left Harvard for the war. Although he had been rejected by his draft board because of weak eyes, he managed to memorize the eye charts, and he ended up serving as an aide to Vice-Admiral Alan Kirk, a family friend. (When Bundy went to the White House in 1961, one of the few people he wanted to get a job for was Admiral Kirk, who became ambassador to Taiwan; Kirk's son-in-law Peter Solbert became a deputy to William Bundy at Defense, and Kirk's son Roger moved up in the State Department under William Bundy.) On board the *Augusta*, Admiral Kirk's flagship, he participated in much of the planning for the D-Day landings. He was remembered for his intelligence and audacity, and those who were aboard said he was not afraid to correct General Omar Bradley on minor matters. The brashness was clearly there; on June 9, when Bradley was leaving the ship, Bundy reminded the general that when he was gone, Captain Bundy would once again become the ranking Army officer aboard the *Augusta*.

Restless with Army staff work, he managed to get himself transferred to the infantry and was on orders to participate in the invasion of Japan when the war ended. When he returned to civilian life he worked for a time on some of the postwar planning that went into the Marshall Plan, became a political analyst for the Council on Foreign Relations, wrote speeches for John Foster Dulles in his New York Senate campaign, and eventually ended up at Harvard as a lecturer in government, where he also did some discreet recruiting for the CIA. (This was not surprising—brother Bill being in the Agency and Allen Dulles being a good friend of the family's—since the CIA needed the right people on the right campuses to find the right young men with both muscular Christianity and brains who also knew the rules of the game.) In those years you had a feeling, as one friend said, that he was not so much changing jobs as working for the same people and simply changing offices.

He spent the fifties at Harvard and they were happy years for him. He was immensely popular with the undergraduates, he was very accessible and not at all pompous; rather, he was considered open and challenging. In an atmosphere sometimes distinguished by the narrowness of professional discipline, Bundy was a generalist, in touch with the world at large, and he brought a sense of engagement of energy and vitality to his work. He loved taking on students, combating them and their ideas, challenging them, bright wits flashing back and forth, debate almost an end in itself. In the world of the Harvard government department, where towering figures like Carl Friedrich and William Yandell Elliott seemed distant and unapproachable, men who belonged more to the graduate students than the undergraduates, Bundy was quite a contrast. He particularly liked teaching freshmen, he was a spectacularly good Government 1 section man, a role that few other bright instructors cherished, and he held on to his freshman sections as long as he could.

His major undergraduate course, Government 180: The U.S. in World Affairs (his successor in teaching it was, fittingly enough, a young German émigré intellectual named Henry Kissinger), was taught with great style and enthusiasm. His Munich lecture was legendary at Harvard, and when word got out that it was on the day's schedule, he played to standing room only. It was done with great verve, Bundy imitating the various participants, his voice cracking with emotion as little Czechoslovakia fell, the German tanks rolling in just as the bells from Memorial Hall sounded. The lesson was of course interventionism, and the wise use of force. He was already surfacing with a commitment to force which would be important in his own make-up years later and which was quite fashionable in the Harvard government department—and government departments of other Eastern universities—of those days. This was known as the ultrarealism school. Its proponents believed that they were tough, that they knew what the world was really like, and that force must be accepted as a basic element of diplomacy. Toughness bred toughness; Stalin had been tough in Eastern Europe, so the West would be tough somewhere else. The Communists legitimized us; force met force. John Kenneth Galbraith, a friend and colleague of Bundy's but far more a Stevenson disciple, later remembered that he and Bundy always argued at Harvard and later in Administration days about the use of force, and Bundy would tell Galbraith with a certain element of disappointment, "Ken, you always advise against the use of force—do you realize that?" Galbraith would reflect on that and then note that Bundy was right, he always *did* recommend against force, in the belief that there were very few occasions when force can be used successfully.

Though Bundy was a good teacher, he was not in the classic sense a great expert in foreign affairs, since he had not come up through the discipline. He was not particularly at ease with Ph.D. candidates, those men who might be more specialized in their knowledge than he. Yet, he was such a star of the government department that it was quickly decided that tenure must be awarded. The idea was advanced to President James Bryant Conant, who had been a distinguished member of the chemistry department before he took over the university. Conant was a little uneasy about endorsing the recommendations; Bundy, it seemed, had never taken any graduate or undergraduate courses in government. Was that correct?

"That's right," the representative of the government department said.

"Are you sure that's right?" asked the puzzled Conant.

"I'm sure," the professor answered.

"Well," Conant sighed. "all I can say is that it couldn't have happened in Chemistry."

BUNDY WAS A GENUINELY POPULAR FIGURE AT HARVARD. DESPITE HIS breeding and traditions he was not pompous and not a blue blood in style. If he did not rebel against that which produced him, he seemed not to take it too seriously, he did not rely on it; it did certain things for him, and he was sure enough of its authenticity and value not to flaunt it. When in 1953 James Conant left Harvard to become U.S. High Commissioner to Germany, there was considerable talk that Bundy, at the advanced age of thirty-four, might succeed him. If ever there was a faculty candidate for the job, it was Bundy. Instead, Harvard chose Nathan Pusey, since the university was under severe attack from McCarthy and since the prospect of a deeply religious figure from the Midwestern heartland was somehow reassuring to alumni. Bundy became merely dean of the College, inspiring a Yale colleague to pen this doggerel:

> A proper young prig, McGeorge Bundy,
> Graduated from Yale on a Monday
>   But he shortly was seen
>   As Establishment Dean
> Up at Harvard the following Sunday.

The faculty of Harvard came quickly to dislike Nathan Marsh Pusey (when he wrote letters to John Kenneth Galbraith which began "Dear John," Ken Galbraith would reciprocate by answering with "Dear Marsh" letters). No sooner had Pusey arrived at Harvard than he announced that the first piece of business would be the renovation and modernization of the Harvard Divinity School, a subject as far from the hearts of that secular faculty as anything could be. The faculty's misgivings about Pusey soon came to match what would later be the intellectual community's feelings about Dean Rusk, a suspicion that there was simply too little flexibility for a first-rate mind. Pusey was bland and cautious, and looking, in the words of Sir Isaiah Berlin, like a retouched photograph; Bundy was dashing, bright, brittle, the antibureaucratic man, the anticonventional man. Bundy, playing on a field where he had grown enormously sure of himself and living in his own environment, seemed to dominate Pusey, who appeared to prefer the background spot to which Bundy relegated him. After Bundy left Harvard, however, Pusey took more than a year to name a successor and was heard to say that he wanted the pleasure of running the university himself for a while. With that particular style of his, Bundy seemed to denigrate Pusey's role without ever having to say anything (years later, after the great bust at Harvard in 1970, Bundy

wrote a long article about the university in which he paid homage to Conant
seven times and mentioned Pusey once; for Bundy-watchers it was a revealing document: it showed that he felt about Pusey as they had always suspected).

By the standards of very tough critics, Bundy was a magnificent dean. It
was a virtuoso performance, designed as much as possible to open up the university, to bring it greatness despite the usual bureaucratic restrictions. David
Riesman (social sciences), Erik Erikson (psychiatry), Laurence Wylie (French
civilization)—all were brought in by Bundy despite the opposition of the departments to which they would be assigned; Bundy had, for instance, been
impressed because Wylie, a Romance-languages professor, had retooled himself in middle age, learned about cultural anthropology and gone on to co-
author a landmark book called *Village in the Vaucluse*. And Lillian Hellman,
the playwright and a good friend of Bundy's, remembers being with Bundy in
Cambridge one night when he suddenly said to her, "Why don't you come up
here and teach?"

"Oh," she said, "the English department wouldn't want me."

"We'll see about that," he said. Off he went and in about an hour he called
her. "It's all set."

"But I don't know how to teach," she protested.

"But you know something about writing," he answered. "Give them some
real work. Teach them how to take from what's really around them and how
to use it."

Even the slight nastiness, which has from time to time been a Bundy trade-
mark, was an advantage; he had the ability to be unfair, to go after special
men and give them special privileges, people like Riesman and Erikson who
did not teach as much as other members of the faculty. Perhaps a less aristocratic, less arrogant man with a greater sense of fairness and a greater sense of
risk (the name Rusk comes to mind, Rusk would never have broken the rules)
might not have done it. Bundy took the complex Harvard faculty—diverse,
egomaniacal—and played with it, in the words of a critic, like a cat with
mice. This feat was partly due to the very structure of his mind. Although he
was not a great reader (there were a surprising number of books one would
have imagined that he had read which he had not), he was brilliant at learning
things in conversation, in absorbing. The great skill of his mind, the training in
classics and math, allowed him to see and understand how other people's intellectual processes work; he was considered better at understanding how the
minds of the scientists worked than any nonscientist in Cambridge. He was a
deft bureaucratic politician; he knew the men around him, whom to flatter,
whom not to. Later his successor, Franklin Ford, gave long statistic-crammed
reports to the faculty, which would not be impressed, whereas Bundy had
told very little in his reports, but deftly, with the Bundy style. He used such

understated eloquence that if the performance was not satisfactory, there was a lingering feeling that it was somehow the fault of the listener rather than Bundy. "He was so good," said one of his friends who knew his strengths as well as his weaknesses, "that when he left I grieved for Harvard and grieved for the nation; for Harvard because he was the perfect dean, for the nation because I thought that very same arrogance and hubris might be very dangerous."

Mac Bundy was a good and true Republican (Bill was the family Democrat) and had voted twice for Eisenhower, but in the late fifties he began to forge a relationship with Jack Kennedy, a relationship in which Arthur Schlesinger served as the main intermediary. Bundy and Kennedy got on well from the start, both were quick and bright, both hating to be bored and to bore, that was almost the worst offense a man could commit, to bore. Rationalists, both of them, one the old Boston Brahmin, the other the new Irish Brahmin, each anxious to show to the other that he was just a little different from the knee-jerk reactions of both his background and his party. Whereas a generation before, the gap between them might have been far greater than the common ground (the thought of Harvey Bundy getting on easily with Joe Kennedy does not, to use their word, wash), now they seemed to be free of the prejudice of the past. Indeed, the achievement of a close relationship between his son and a Lowell-Bundy was what it had been all about for Joe Kennedy. If they had much in common, Jack Kennedy still had some advantages; though he was a new kind of Brahmin he was nonetheless a product of outsiders, he knew the difference between theory and practice in the society, the little things about America that the history books never tell. He had traveled a far longer and harder road than Bundy; he had triumphed in electoral politics and had thus created a real base for himself, whereas Bundy had no personal base. If he was to play a role in American policy making he would have to be dependent upon someone like Kennedy. He had to sense Kennedy's moves, his whims, his nuances. To an uncommon degree, Bundy possessed that capacity to sense what others wanted and what they were thinking, and it would serve him well.

And so he joined the new Administration. He came full-blown, a man of definite characteristics. By a curious irony he arrived, in Washington's mind, a full-scale intellectual, though in Harvard's mind the super administrator, a man who often took the side of the individual against the bureaucracy (though eventually in Washington some of the men around him would realize that he was, above all, the administrator, the supreme mover of papers. "Clerk of the world," said Mark Raskin, a disenchanted man who once worked for him on disarmament. Raskin had been hired as an opening to the far left, but it never worked, Raskin leaving early as a bitter critic of the government's directions, firing off letters and documents critical of the Administration. "Please stop identifying yourself as a former White House aide," Bundy enjoined him). He was bright and he was quick, but even this bothered people around him. They seemed to sense a lack of reflection, a lack of depth, a tendency to look at things tactically, functionally and operationally rather than intellectually; they believed Bundy thought that there was always a straight line between two points. He carried with himself not so much an intellectual tradition as a blood-intellectual tradition, a self-confirming belief in his origins and thus himself, all of this above partisanship. "I was brought up in a home where the American Secretary of State is not the subject of partisan debate," he once said during the McCarthy period when Acheson was under attack. It was the Establishment's conviction that it knew what was right and what was wrong for the country. In Bundy this was a particularly strong strain, as if his own talent and the nation's talent were all wrapped up together, producing a curious amalgam of public interest and self-interest, his destiny and the nation's destiny; a strong conscious moral sense of propriety, which he was not adverse to flashing at others, and a driving, almost naked thrust for power all at once. Partly as a result, he had what one friend called a "pugnacious morality." McGeorge Bundy, then, was the finest example of a special elite, a certain breed of men whose continuity is among themselves. They are linked to one another rather than to the country; in their minds they become responsible for the country but not responsive to it.

Thus, foreign policy was not a chord running through the country and reflecting the changes, and in 1964 and 1965 when Martin Luther King, Jr., began to make public speeches criticizing the war, the entire Establishment turned on him to silence him. They assured him that he knew about civil rights, but not about foreign policy; he was not an expert and they were. He remained bitter about this put-down to the day he died, feeling that he had in effect been told that, Nobel Prize or not, there were certain things that were not his business. Others who were in the Administration felt similarly excluded. "Those of us who had worked for the Kennedy election were tolerated in the government for that reason and had a say, but foreign policy was still with the Council on Foreign Relations people," Galbraith would recall years later. "We knew that their expertise was nothing, and that it was mostly a product of social background and a certain kind of education, and that they were men who had not traveled around the world and knew nothing of this country and the world. All they knew was the difference between a Communist and an anti-Communist. But that made no difference; they had this mystique and it still worked and those of us who doubted it, Goodwin, Schlesinger, myself and a few others, were like Indians firing occasional arrows into the campsite from the outside."

The other strain running through Bundy, not surprisingly, given the first strain, was a hard-line attitude which was very much a product of the fifties and the Cold War, the ultrarealist view. That this attitude also made one less vulnerable to attacks from the right about softness on Communism did not hurt; it dealt at once with totalitarians abroad and wild men at home. Force was justified by what the Communists did; the times justified the kind of acts which decent men did not seek, but which the historic responsibilities made necessary. This was very much a part of Bundy, a willingness to accept the use of force and to concentrate his energies on operational tactical questions.

As Special Assistant for National Security Affairs, Bundy soon became the invaluable man in the Kennedy Administration. Keeping the papers moving, reminding the President when a decision was coming up, occasionally helping to channel a promising young man in State who might give a slightly different viewpoint to the President, protecting the President against people who wanted his time but were not worthy of it, making sure that people who needed his time got it, learning quickly what the President's tastes, needs, reservations were, always moving things. In his own words, the traffic cop. Doing it with style, which would show at an early press conference. Kennedy usually did well on these occasions, but this time he was hampered by a lack of news to reveal. Someone suggested that Kennedy's decision to reverse the last Eisenhower decision—to bring home the dependents of U.S. troops overseas—would be a dramatic announcement. But the Kennedy decision had not yet been cleared through the bureaucracy, and normally something like that takes weeks and weeks. While others were talking about whether it could be done, Bundy was on the phone, calling Douglas Dillon at Treasury and then the Pentagon and then State, saying, "The President would like to announce today that . . . Do you see any objections?" In five minutes he was back, it was all cleared, all very nifty. So he was busy, protecting the President against the bureaucracy, cutting through the red tape where he could. Being above the petty factional and emotional fights of the bureaucracy, being of course neither a man of the right or of the left but disinterested and realistic, which meant that all things being equal, he was more a man of the status quo than anything else. The changes he would bring, the openings, would be very small, more tactical than anything else. He was not, for example, a great help on the question of disarmament; he stood aside on that one, as did Rusk, while the Defense Department, with John McNaughton and McNamara, was far more helpful.

He was invaluable, functioning very easily. At meetings the President would ask him to sum up, and then, looking for all the world as if he had not even paid attention, Bundy would instantly give the quickest, most incisive, most complete summing up imaginable. He was a great list man, too. They always needed prospective names, and Mac of course had the list, a job here, a committee there. Mac knew who should go on it, how far left or right it could go, who was acceptable, who was not. Mac was a terrific memo writer, facile, brief and incisive. It was not, as publication of documents would later prove, exactly something which would make the literary world envious, but to be a good memo writer in government was a very real form of power. Suddenly everyone would be working off Bundy's memos, and thus his memos guided the action, guided what the President would see. For example, friends think that he killed the ill-conceived, ill-fated plan for a multilateral nuclear force, first by determining the crucial bit of evidence, and then by a memo. It was a major policy decision and it was done in typical Bundy fashion. He was against the MLF from the start, it jarred the cleanliness of his mind, and he bided his time as the evidence on the proposal came in; then he dispatched Richard Neustadt of Columbia to make a special investigation, knowing that Neustadt, a specialist in operational procedure, would be appalled by it, which Neustadt was, and thus Bundy summed up the case pro-MLF and anti-MLF, which left the MLF bleeding to death on the floor, speared, as it were, by a memo.

State was of course large and unwieldy (Acheson liked to tell of how much it had grown; when he became Secretary he had gone by to see Cordell Hull and had suggested that that venerable gentleman come by and meet the Assistant Secretaries. "Well, Dean, you don't mind if I refuse," Hull answered, "I never was very much good in a crowd . . ."). This natural clumsiness, coupled with Rusk's cautiousness, soon created a problem in the bureaucracy. Kennedy was quickly dissatisfied with State, and Bundy, sensing the vacuum, moved deftly to fill it. He began to build his own power, looking for his own elite staff, a mini State Department of very special experts who could protect the President and give alternative answers. They could move papers quickly, something State could never do, and through an informal network at Defense and CIA, they could exploit sympathetic friends and thus create an informal inner network in the government. State, after all, was given to missing deadlines with papers and then answering with last year's myths. Bundy created an extraordinary staff, bright young men summoned from all areas of the government and academe. They were Robert Komer and Chester Cooper from CIA, Carl Kaysen from Harvard, Jim Thomson from Bowles's staff, Michael Forrestal, Francis Bator. He worked well with them, and exhibited the rare quality in Washington, in Thomson's words, "of being able to evoke whatever excellent existed in a person. Every encounter was like a mini Ph.D. exam."

Bundy tried to hide his disdain for Rusk as best he could, though in rare moments it would slip through. (It was said that Rusk held his counsel so closely that no one, including the President, was privileged to hear it, and sometimes Bundy would tell the story about a meeting of the six top officials, with Rusk asking all the others to leave so he could talk to the President. When they were alone, the President asked Rusk what it was, and Rusk said, "Well, if there weren't so many of us in the room . . .") Rusk, the least incandescent member of the group, bore it well. He resisted the impulse to react to stories being told about him, but at times the anger and irritation would flash through. "It isn't worth being Secretary of State," he once told Dick Goodwin, "if you have a Carl Kaysen at the White House." Substitute for the name Kaysen the name Bundy.

The latter, of course, did not worry about the rumors of his growing power and influence; he delighted in them, knowing that the reputation that you are the man to see feeds on itself, and makes you even more so. He loved power and did not shrink from it, rather the opposite was true, there was an enormous thrust for it; it sometimes seemed almost naked; the knowledge that he had this reputation bothered him some, yet his own instinct carried him forward. He was known at the White House as a tough infighter; at the beginning of the Administration, Schlesinger and some of the other intellectuals had pushed for Bundy's Harvard colleague Henry Kissinger to serve as a special consultant on European questions, since Kissinger was said to be very good on the Germans and the Germans always needed reassuring. For a time Kissinger traveled from Cambridge to Washington, though he was not entirely sure whether he wanted to be in or out, and Bundy did not, to say the least, encourage Kissinger's visits. Eventually they stopped. In 1969, when Kissinger arrived permanently in Washington under Nixon to take the same seat that Bundy had held, it was also announced that Dr. Richard V. Allen, a right-wing figure of some renown, would be Kissinger's assistant. Asked by friends how he would treat Dr. Allen, who was considered somewhat warlike (in those days Kissinger was not considered warlike), Kissinger answered, "I will handle him the way Mac Bundy handled me."

The early White House years were golden years for Bundy. He seemed to gloss over the problems of the world, it was a dream realized, the better for him, the better for the nation. Some of those who knew him felt that although he was not a negative figure, there was something lacking: his thinking and performance were too functional and operational, he was not considering the proper long-range perspective, instead he was too much the problem solver, the man who did not want to wait, who believed in action. He always had a single pragmatic answer to a single question, and he was wary of philosophies, almost too wary (during the great Vietnam debates of 1965 he would call George Ball, a more philosophic man, "the theologian"). But pragmatic thinking is also short-range thinking, and too often panic thinking. A government is collapsing. How do we prop it up? Something is happening; therefore we must move. Thus, in 1965 Bundy was for getting the country into the Dominican mess, because *something* had to be done, and then very good at extricating us when he realized that extrication had become the problem, though as he and the men around him would learn, not all countries were as easy to get out of as the Dominican Republic.

Chapter Five

FOR ALL THE STYLE AND EXCITEMENT OF THE NEW TEAM, AND all the great promise, 1961 was a terrible year for the Kennedy Administration. The young President had arrived in the White House with a far slimmer margin of victory than he hoped, a mere 100,000 votes. It was not one of the great mandates, rather a margin which seemed to strengthen his enemies more than his friends, and the mandate of getting America moving again was questionable. America might move at his demand, but in which direction? And in what way could he move it? By building more and heavier missiles? Turning around an irrational policy on China? Bringing the nation together by accelerating long-neglected commitments to American Negroes? His nomination, his campaign, his election had meant many things to many people; now they waited, and many would find themselves disappointed in that first year. He was the first of a new kind of media candidate flashed daily into our consciousness by television during the campaign, and as such he had managed to stir the aspirations and excited millions of people. It had all been deliberately done; he had understood television and used it well, knowing that it was his medium, but it was done at a price. Millions of people watching this driving, handsome young man believed that he *could* change things, move things, that their personal problems would somehow be different, lighter, easier with his election. As President, Kennedy was faced with that great gap of any modern politician, but perhaps greatest in contemporary America: the gap between the new unbelievable velocity of modern life which can send information and images hurtling through the air onto the television screen, exciting desires and appetites, changing mores almost overnight, and the slowness of traditional governmental institutions produced by ideas and laws of another era, bound in normal bureaucratic red tape and traditional seniority. After all, although he had said in his campaign that he wanted to get America moving again, he had not mentioned that the people must allow for the conservatism of Judge Howard Smith of the House Rules Committee; he had implied that he could do it, it would move. In many ways he was as modern and contemporary as an American politician can be, more practiced at the new means of campaigning than any other major figure (he was frankly bored by the traditional power struggles of the Senate; it was not where the action was, or at least the action he sought). So, elected, he was charged with action against a bureaucracy and a Congress which regarded him and his programs with suspicion, the suspicion varying in direct proportion to the freshness and progressiveness of his ideas. In his first major struggle, the great battle to expand the House Rules Committee, a classic conflict of the two forces, Kennedy finally won. But his victory was more Pyrrhic than anything else; it exposed the essential weakness of his legislative position, the divisions in his party, and as such, enemies on the Hill would feel encouraged in their opposition. The lesson, not immediately discernible in the early part of the decade but increasingly important as Americans came to terms with the complexity of their society, was that it was easier to stir the new America by media than it was to tackle institutions which reflected vested interests and existing compromises of the old order. In a new, modern, industrial, demographically young society, this was symbolized by nothing so much as congressional control by very old men from small Southern towns, many of them already deeply committed, personally and financially, to existing interests; to a large degree they were the enemies of the very people who had elected John F. Kennedy. He was caught in that particular bind.

But there were other problems too. The Administration came in committed to greater defense spending, to ending the missile gap, and the first year would see an intensification of the Cold War as the Administration and the Soviets tried to gauge each other. In terms of the Cold War, 1961 would be a difficult year: there was the Bay of Pigs in April, followed by the escalation in the arms race, the bullying by Khrushchev in Vienna, the growing tensions in Laos, the outbreak of violence in the Congo, the almost daily conflicts over the Berlin Wall, the preliminary reports that Vietnam might be a problem. All this took some of the edge off the excitement of the job, and Kennedy's oft-quoted comment was that the most surprising thing about coming to office was that everything was just as bad as they had said in the campaign. A less quoted remark, underscoring the difficulties inherent in events outside his control, came when Carl Kaysen, a White House expert on disarmament, brought in the news that the Soviets had resumed atmospheric testing. The President's reaction was simple and basic and reflected the frustrations of that year. "Fucked again," he said.

All the setbacks would seem minor compared to the Bay of Pigs, which was a shattering event, both within the Administration and outside. It would seriously disturb the balance of the first two years of the Kennedy Administration; it would almost surely necessitate a harder line both to prove to domestic critics that he was as tough-willed as the next man, and to prove to the Russians that despite the paramount foolishness of this adventure, his hand was strong and steady. By necessity now, an Administration which had entered almost jaunty, sure of itself, a touch of aggressiveness and combativeness to it, a touch of wanting to ease tensions in the world, would now have to be more belligerent both for internal and external reasons, and it would not be for another eighteen months, when the Kennedy Administration had already deepened the involvement in Vietnam, that it would begin to retrieve a semblance of its earlier balance.

In a way it was a test run for the Vietnam escalations of 1965, and it would be said of John Kennedy and Lyndon Johnson that both had their Bay of Pigs, that the former's lasted four days and the latter's lasted four years. But the component parts were there: serious misreading of aspirations of a nonwhite nation; bringing Western, Caucasian anti-Communism to a place where it was less applicable; institutions pushing forward with their own momentum, ideas and programs which tended to justify and advance the cause of the institution at the expense of the nation; too much secrecy with too many experts who knew remarkably little either about the country involved or about their own country; too many decisions by the private men of the Administration as opposed to the public ones; and too little moral reference. And finally, too little common sense. How a President who seemed so contemporary could agree to a plan so obviously doomed to failure, a plan based on so little understanding of the situation, was astounding.

There were men who opposed the invasion or at the very least were uneasy with it, and to a degree, they were the same men who would later oppose the Vietnam commitment. One was General David M. Shoup, Commandant of the Marine Corps. When talk about invading Cuba was becoming fashionable, General Shoup did a remarkable display with maps. First he took an overlay of Cuba and placed it over the map of the United States. To everybody's surprise, Cuba was not a small island along the lines of, say, Long Island at best. It was about 800 miles long and seemed to stretch from New York to Chicago. Then he took another overlay, with a red dot, and placed it over the map of Cuba. "What's that?" someone asked him. "That, gentlemen, represents the size of the island of Tarawa," said Shoup, who had won a Medal of

Honor there, "and it took us three days and eighteen thousand Marines to take it." He eventually became Kennedy's favorite general.

Significantly, two of the men who might have been Secretary of State knew of the plan and were opposed (a third, Stevenson, did not know of it, but presumably would have opposed it), and both were Democratic party professionals who also knew something of foreign affairs. Senator J. William Fulbright and Undersecretary of State Chester Bowles, public men with a sense of public responsibility, were objecting to a clandestine operation organized by private men who seemed to be responsible to no one but their own organizations, with even that responsibility so secret that it was difficult to define whether it existed. (In secret organizations, a subordinate's failure reflects badly upon his superior as well, so there is a very strong instinct on the part of both to cover it up; it is only when knowledge about such failure is out in the open that a superior himself becomes responsible.) Bowles heard of the plan at the last minute, agonized over it, and wrote Rusk suggesting he fight it, noting:

. . . Those most familiar with the Cuban operation seem to agree that, as the venture is now planned, the chances of success are not greater than one out of three. This makes it a highly risky operation. If it fails, Castro's prestige and strength will be greatly enhanced. . . . I realize that this operation has been put together over a period of months. A great deal of time and money has been spent and many individuals have become emotionally involved in its success. We should not, however, proceed with the adventure simply because we are wound up and cannot stop.

If you agree that this operation would be a mistake, I suggest that you personally and privately communicate your views to the President. It is my guess that your voice will be decisive.

The man who had been chosen as Secretary of State, Dean Rusk, a Democrat but a private man, was against the invasion but did not really oppose it; he expressed doubts but not really strong opposition.

In the aftermath, the crux of the matter was not whether the United States should have provided the counterinsurgents with air power or not (the air cover would only have prolonged and deepened the tragedy without changing its outcome); the crux was how the U.S. government could have so misread the Cuban people. Had there been even the beginning of serious anti-Castro feeling in the country, nothing would have rallied the average Cuban more quickly to the cause of Fidel than to have an invasion sponsored by the United States. The least of the mistakes were the ones most frequently commented on, the tactical ones, the question of the air power (attaching the United States in the eyes of the world to a slow death of a terrible political mistake instead of, happily, a quick one). But these were the mistakes which were fastened on. General Maxwell D. Taylor was called in to conduct a special review which centered on the tactical faults (too few men in the Brigade assembled in Guatemala, too few pilots in the air arm, too few men prepared and ready to relieve commanders, too few reserves, too little knowledge about uncharted reefs).

There was far too little questioning of the moral right to launch the attack: after all, the Communists did things like this all the time, that was the way it was, the way power was used. A vast number of people felt it had failed because too little force had been used (this indeed appeared to be the problem for the President; the right was noisier in those days). The President himself probably, in some of the far reaches of his mind, began to learn important lessons about institutional wisdom, but among his advisers there seemed to be little learned. Nothing very important, nothing very serious. "A brick through the window," McGeorge Bundy would tell friends. Part of the fault, the Administration believed, was that the advice had come from relics of the Eisenhower years, Allen Dulles at CIA and General Lyman L. Lemnitzer, Chairman of the Joint Chiefs of Staff, and the departure of both would be precipitated, the idea being that people more loyal to the President should head those institutions and thus make them more Kennedy-like. Bundy seemed preoccupied with the tactical aspects of the failure; when he met with his staff the day after the debacle, he seemed very much in control. The Bay of Pigs, he told his staff, showed that Che had learned more from Guatemala than the United States had (apparently a reference to the importance of air power). As for the members of the Brigade (many of them still strung out on the beaches), he said that these counterrevolutionaries were very much like assistant professors at Harvard, who were always being reminded about the possibility of not getting tenure but who never really believed your warnings until tenure failed to arrive.

Rusk's weak stand left the Kennedy people in retrospect more frustrated by his performance than anything else, and left both Kennedy and Rusk wishing that he had spoken up more clearly. But as soon became apparent, it was consistent with both his character and his view of the job; Rusk had, after all, not been chosen because Kennedy wanted a strong man, but because he would be a low-profile Secretary of State. Thus a voice which might predictably have been strongly opposed to this kind of military adventure was muted. On the other hand, the overt opposition of Bowles and Fulbright did not do them much good. Although in Fulbright's case it strengthened his reputation in Washington as the chief Hill intellectual, it did not bring him any closer to the Kennedy circle, in part because of his own growing doubts about the men now in the executive branch.

For Bowles it would be a good deal worse. Somehow the word got out that he had been against the invasion. Soon there was a story going around Washington that Bobby Kennedy had come out of a meeting, jammed his fingers into Bowles's stomach and told him, that he, Bowles, was for the invasion, remember that, he was for it, they were all for it (the story did not originate with the Bowles people, either). The Bay of Pigs debacle seemed to symbolize the futility of Bowles and to seal his end; he was talky, a do-gooder, had probably been against the venture for the wrong reasons. He was too ideological, while they, of course, were all pragmatists. In the early days of the Administration that particular word had been used so frequently that David Brinkley, writing the introduction of an early book of portraits of the Kennedy people, would dwell on that single word, and note that at an early Washington cocktail party a woman had gone around the room asking each of the hundred people there if he was a pragmatist.

In May, a month after the Bay of Pigs, when a variety of lessons might have been sinking in, Bowles, who was considered so good at spotting long-range problems and so bad at handling immediate ones, wrote one of the most prophetic analyses of the new Administration in his private diary:

The question which concerns me most about this new Administration is whether it lacks a genuine sense of conviction about what is right and what is wrong. I realize in posing the question I am raising an extremely serious point. Nevertheless I feel it must be faced.

Anyone in public life who has strong convictions about the rights and wrongs of public morality, both domestic and international, has a very great advantage in times of strain, since his instincts on what to do are clear and immediate. Lacking such a framework of moral conviction or sense of what is right and what is wrong, he is forced to lean almost entirely upon his mental processes; he adds up the plusses and minuses of any question and comes up with a conclusion. Under normal conditions, when he is not tired or frustrated, this pragmatic approach should successfully bring him out on the right side of the question.

What worries me are the conclusions that such an individual may reach when he is tired, angry, frustrated, or emotionally affected. The Cuban fiasco demonstrates how far astray a man as brilliant and well intentioned as Kennedy can go who lacks a basic moral reference point.

The problem for Bowles would soon become somewhat personal. He had entered the Administration with powerful enemies, some on the Hill, some in the entrenched wing of the foreign service, and some in the Democratic party–Acheson hard-line group. His enemies had not decreased in the early months of the Kennedy Administration. He had added Bobby Kennedy to them, a most formidable person indeed in those days, the ramrod of the Administration. At the end of May an incident occurred which certainly contributed to Bowles's downfall. While both the President and Rusk were in Europe with De Gaulle, there was a crisis in the Dominican Republic following General Rafael Trujillo's assassination. A group headed by Bobby Kennedy, but including McNamara and a few others (with Rusk, Kennedy and Bundy out of town, they represented the highest officials in the government), wanted to effect an immediate, though somewhat limited American intervention. They had some CIA contacts who promised that the right kind of Dominicans would rally and thus save the republic. Bowles, acting as Secretary, held the line against intervention because he doubted the legality of what they wanted to do. The others argued that speed was of the essence. Bowles suggested they find out a little more about which way events were moving. At that point Bobby Kennedy, still in his hard-nosed incarnation, the tough guy of the Administration, unleashed a cascade of insults about Bowles's being a gutless bastard, which made some of the others in the room wince. Later in the day Bowles went on the phone to the President in Paris, explaining what the activists wanted to do and why he objected. Kennedy concurred in the objections.

"Well, I'm glad to hear it," said Bowles, "and in that case, would you clarify who's in charge here?"

"You are," the President said.

"Good," said Bowles. "Would you mind explaining it to your brother?"

In addition to everything else, the functioning of the State Department just wasn't working out well. At a dinner party in the spring of 1961 after the Bay of Pigs, Bundy would tell friends, "Something has to be changed at State and you can't fire the Secretary of State. Particularly," he added, "if you hired him after only one meeting," a reference to the fact that if you have made a snap judgment you dare not admit that it is wrong. By early July 1961 a somewhat embarrassed Rusk was offering Bowles a job as roving ambassador, preferably to rove out of town, and admitting that it was Kennedy's idea. A few days later Charles Bartlett, a close friend of Kennedy's, wrote in his syndicated column that Bowles was on his way out. Bowles called up Kennedy and asked for a meeting. A curious conversation ensued. Kennedy began by saying that perhaps it had been a mistake not to make Bowles Secretary of State and that if so, things might have been different. But Rusk *was* Secretary of State, and the Department had not come up with new policies, and changes had to be made. Would Bowles like Chile? No, Bowles would not like Chile. As far as new ideas were concerned, he told Kennedy he had spent a great deal of time coming up with them, but they did not seem to go beyond Rusk's desk. They decided to meet together in a few days, on July 17.

In the meantime Washington seethed with rumors that Bowles was on his way out. He had become the perfect target for the conservatives, while the liberals, uneasy about the direction of the Kennedy Administration, began to rally round Bowles. For the first time the split personality of the Kennedy Administration seemed to show itself. Stevenson, Walter Reuther, Soapy Williams all rallied and told Bowles not to leave without a fight. He had become, in spite of himself, a litmus paper of the Administration. At the July 17 meeting he showed up armed with his memos on Cuba, China and related issues, memos which incorporated far more new ideas than the Kennedy Administration was prepared to handle. He told Kennedy he did not intend to take Chile. Later that day Press Secretary Pierre Salinger held a briefing and said no, Bowles's resignation was not currently expected, but he added that off the record, for background, he was not expected to be around very long.

There were others in the Kennedy circle uneasy with the direction of the Administration and particularly with the decision-making processes used in the Bay of Pigs. Shortly afterward Arthur Goldberg, the new Secretary of Labor (a labor negotiator who had been a particular favorite of the Kennedy people, having worked for them when much of labor's hierarchy was anti-Kennedy because of the rackets committee investigation), asked the President why he hadn't consulted more widely, why he had taken such a narrow spectrum of advice, much of it so predictable. Kennedy said that he meant no offense, but although Goldberg was a good man, a friend, he *was* in labor, not in foreign policy.

"You're wrong," Goldberg replied, "you're making the mistake of compartmentalizing your Cabinet. There are two people in the Cabinet you should have consulted on this one, men who know some things, and who are loyal to you and your interests."

"Who?" Kennedy asked.

"Orville Freeman and me."

"Why Orville?"

"Because he's been a Marine, because he's made amphibious landings and because he knows how tough they can be even under the very best circumstances. He could have helped you."

"And why you?"

"Because I was in OSS during the war and I ran guerrilla operations and I know something about guerrillas. That they're terrific at certain things. Sabotage and intelligence, nothing like them at that. But they're no good at all in confronting regular units. Whenever we used them like that, we'd always lose all our people. They can do small things very well, but it's a very delicate, limited thing. But you didn't think of that—and you put me in the category of just a Secretary of Labor."

"A BRICK THROUGH THE WINDOW." WINDOWS ARE EASY TO REPLACE, and the Bay of Pigs did not change the basic direction of the Kennedy Administration in foreign affairs. It was still activist, anxious to show its muscles, perhaps more anxious than before. At Defense, McNamara was an activist, pledged to end a missile gap which did not exist, and whose own immediate instincts, once he was in government, were if anything to add to the arms race; he was, at first, very much the hardware man. In early 1961 some of the White House people like Science Adviser Jerome Wiesner and Carl Kaysen of the National Security Council were trying to slow down the arms race, or at least were in favor of a good deal more talking with the Soviets before speeding ahead. At that point the United States had 450 missiles; McNamara was asking for 950, and the Joint Chiefs of Staff were asking for 3,000. The White House people had quietly checked around and found that in effectiveness, in sheer military terms, the 450 were the same as McNamara's 950. Thus a rare moment existed, a chance to make a new start, if not turn around the arms race, at least to give it a temporary freeze.

"What about it, Bob?" Kennedy asked.

"Well, they're right," McNamara answered.

"Well, then, why the nine hundred and fifty, Bob?" Kennedy asked.

"Because that's the smallest number we can take up on the Hill without getting murdered," he answered.

Perhaps, thought one of the White House aides, by holding back we might have slowed the cycle rather than accelerated it. But in 1961 the advocates of disarmament encountered an Administration which considered the issue a little peripheral, not something that could be taken up immediately, something that would have to wait. Of the high officials, the President himself seemed the most receptive to the idea, though he was in no rush to lead the parade. McNamara appeared to be surprisingly educable, and if not an ally, at least open-minded, a man who could be brought around. Bundy was of little help; in the early days this was something he simply stayed out of. And Rusk, whose job at State it really was to create a disarmament lobby, seemed the least interested in the subject.

If anything, the Bay of Pigs had made the Kennedy Administration acutely aware of its vulnerability and determined to show that it was worthy, that this was not a weak young President unable to cope with the Soviets, but that he was just as tough as they were, just as fast on the draw. In the Administration, those who were the tough-minded realists were strengthened; those less inclined to use force were weakened. Kennedy would soon have a chance to show whether he was worthy of his mandate, at the upcoming conference with Nikita Khrushchev in Vienna in early June, a meeting scheduled so soon after the Bay of Pigs that the very holding of it was dubious. But he went through with it, and the outcome, rather than lowering tensions, increased them. The President left Khrushchev in Vienna feeling that he had been bullied, more determined than ever to show Khrushchev that despite his youth, despite the Bay of Pigs, he was someone to conjure with. He would call up the reserves, and flex American muscle in many ways.

PERHAPS, JUST PERHAPS, IT NEED NOT HAVE BEEN THAT WAY. AVERELL Harriman had long felt that a meeting between Khrushchev and Kennedy was inevitable, and he had carefully prepared himself for it. He was then sixty-nine years old, and a supreme party warhorse. Although something of a failure in domestic politics (in 1958 he was beaten badly by Nelson Rockefeller in the New York gubernatorial race; and he had wanted his party's presidential nomination but never came close to it), he was one of the most forceful players at governmental politics of a generation, relentless, restless and ruthless, expert in the care and feeding of Presidents of the United States. In 1960, after his defeat in New York, the low point in his career, close friends like Michael Forrestal and Pat Moynihan would meet and discuss what they could possibly do to ease Harriman's pain and the prolonged humiliation which now seemed to be his fate for the rest of his life. He had fallen from grace and activity as only a defeated American politician can. Gay Talese, then a young *New York Times* reporter, later recalled being assigned to cover a Harriman press conference in 1960. The ex-governor, having just returned from a trip abroad, had deigned to announce that he would reveal his version of it; since in those days the *Times* covered *everything,* Talese was dispatched to the Harrimans' magnificent East Side town house, with its great bust of Roosevelt by Jo Davidson and the accompanying Matisse, Cézanne and Rousseau paintings. Among these great objects he waited; he waited for a very long time alone, because he was the only reporter to show up, and after about forty minutes the press conference was mercifully called off.

Even at this low point, Harriman had been thinking ahead, projecting a future role for himself. Sensing that there was a good chance of a Democratic President's being elected in the fall, and wanting to specialize in Soviet affairs, exploiting the most personal kind of expertise that went back to his boyhood, he had written to Khrushchev suggesting that the Premier invite him to Moscow (which would be a marvelous piece of wampum to barter with a new President). Khrushchev, who understood the game, of course, and who knew what Americans did not know, that a Harriman was just as much a Harriman out of office as in office, indeed that the office was marginal, more of a lark than anything else, immediately responded, and invited him. They spent two days together, twelve good long hours, and at the beginning Khrushchev, as was his wont, bullied Harriman, threatened, stomped, the voice rising: if the Americans did not move out of Berlin the rockets would fly, the tanks would roll, and he, Citizen N. Khrushchev, could not be responsible for all the terrible things which would happen. Harriman listened and then quietly rejoined that rocketry was a two-way avenue, that there were now few shelters left on either side, that the Soviet industrial might was just as vulnerable as American might and had been built up at just as high a national price. That done with, they had subsided into long and profitable talks about other subjects, the possibility of coexistence, the aims of the Chinese, a very pleasant exchange which had lasted the two days.

Harriman came back from that trip believing that there was a possibility of a deal with the Soviets, that history had finally converged to a point where both nations were ready, that the Soviet fear of the Chinese radically changed their national security problems. He felt in this winter of a long career that this was the special contribution he could make, particularly to a young President. He told friends that every man wants to contribute what he knows best, and since Soviet-American relations were his specialty, he had a special belief that he could give a new President the legacy of this special knowledge of the Soviets.   Harriman had come over to the Kennedy side rather belatedly, the reason of course being doubts about Joe Kennedy, *that man*. He had not been a great aid during the campaign, and to the Kennedys he was someone who had once been Democratic governor of New York, someone they ought to do something for. He had a serious hearing problem, which would not have been a problem except that he also had a serious vanity problem, which precluded a hearing aid. At the first meeting with Kennedy after November 1960, he had been at his worst; asked what he thought about a complicated question of Soviet intentions, he had answered "Yes." Later Kennedy had taken Michael Forrestal, Harriman's protégé, aside and asked if there was someplace they might talk privately. Forrestal suggested the bathroom, and they went in there, locking the door, Forrestal delighted, sure that his own big job was coming, at State. Or perhaps, like his father, at Defense. At least an Assistant Secretaryship. "Do you think," asked Kennedy, "that you can get Averell to wear a hearing aid?"

But Harriman's friends continued to push his case to the Kennedys, trying to overcome their doubts. Arthur Schlesinger, for example, pressed his case very hard, saying that they should try Harriman at State, even in a lower capacity; they would be surprised by his ability. "You're sure you're not just being sentimental?" Bobby Kennedy asked him.

In February 1961 Harriman was made roving ambassador, a particularly low level in the governmental hierarchy when one considers the many distinguished posts he had held in the past. But he accepted with good grace; asked how it was going, in the early months of the Administration, he answered, "Oh, you know, all these Presidents are the same. You start at the bottom and work your way up." His stock rose steadily in the Administration. His style was more than adequate; he gave the best dinner parties in town; and in tough sessions with other Kremlinologists, he more than held his own. But he was furious at the time of the Vienna meeting because he had not been consulted on the planning. That had been left to people like Charles Bohlen, Llewellyn Thompson and George Kennan, kids really, boys that he had trained, but nonetheless men very much his junior. So with the intrusive, audacious style which makes him unique in government ("What makes Averell different from other men?" a reporter once asked one of his very young aides in 1969. "Well, he's the only *ambitious* seventy-seven-year-old I've ever met," the aide answered), Harriman just happened to show up in Paris as Kennedy was visiting De Gaulle, and just happened to see the President's sister Eunice Shriver to let her know that he desperately had to talk to the President. He just happened to get himself invited to a state dinner, just happened to sit one sister and one person away from the President, and just happened to hear the sister say to the President, "Look, Averell is here and I think he has something to say about Khrushchev and Vienna," and Kennedy, well primed, said, "Yes, I hear there is something you want to say to me." Harriman, of course, had practiced what he wanted to say. He had taught all his protégés always to be brief when talking to a President; they have so little time, everyone is always telling them things, keep it short and simple, and brevity above all. One idea, a few brief sentences. Having determined to put the lessons of his long sessions with Khrushchev and forty years together in a few sentences, the gist of what he said was: Go to Vienna. Don't be too serious, have some fun, get to know him a little, don't let him rattle you, he'll try to rattle you and frighten you, but don't pay any attention to that. Turn him aside, gently. And don't try for too much. Remember that he's just as scared as you are, his previous excursion to the Western world in Europe did not go too well, he is very aware of his peasant origins, of the contrast between Mrs. Khrushchev and Jackie, and there will be tension. His style will be to attack and then see if he can get away with it. Laugh about it, don't get into a fight. Rise above it. Have some fun.

That was the sum of the Harriman advice, though the contrary advice had been just as explicit. Stand up to him, show him that you're not young, that you're just as tough as he is, that the Bay of Pigs was an accident and not a reflection of your will. Indeed there were those who felt that a confrontation was needed, that we had to test our will, and the sooner the better. So Kennedy had gone to Vienna, and the meeting was a disaster, harsh and tense; the tensions of the world, centering over Berlin, had seemed to intensify rather than ebb with the meeting; Khrushchev had attacked, and Kennedy, surprised, had finally rejoined. Vienna, like the Bay of Pigs, had increased the tensions in the world.

The Vienna meeting made a powerful impact on Kennedy. James Reston, the *New York Times* columnist and Washington bureau chief, and the most powerful and influential journalist in the capital, had asked for a private meeting with the President after the final encounter. Because of his unique position, it had been granted. Knowing that such a session would enrage his colleagues, Reston spent the day in Vienna hiding from fellow journalists and was smuggled into a special room at the embassy. The blinds were drawn lest anyone see him, he waited there for several hours in the darkness. When Kennedy finally arrived, he could not see Reston at first because of the dark. Finally he spotted Reston and as the journalist began to rise the President waved him down, came over and sat down on a couch next to him. He was wearing a hat; Reston remembered that because it was only the second time he had seen Kennedy with a hat on; the first time was at the inaugural. Kennedy sank into the couch, pushed the hat over his eyes like a beaten man, and breathed a great sigh.

"Pretty rough?" Reston asked.

"Roughest thing in my life," the President answered. He was, Reston thought, genuinely shaken.

Kennedy told Reston that he had studied Khrushchev carefully beforehand, and he knew that the Russian had great contempt for Eisenhower; whenever they had met and a serious question was asked, Ike would turn to Dulles for the answer. So Kennedy had decided to go it alone, to show his equality with Khrushchev, to show that he had done his homework. Just the two of them would meet, and the interpreters. He had gone in and, he felt, held out his hand, saying that the two of them had very special responsibilities for peace in the world. "I propose to tell you what I can do, and what I can't do, what my problems and possibilities are and then you can do the same." The reaction was astonishing, a violent attack on the United States, on its international imperialism, but particularly on its presence in Berlin. As he had threatened Harriman before, he now threatened Kennedy on Berlin: the missiles would fly, the tanks would roll, they must not doubt his word. He had kept the pressure on all week, and Kennedy had finally answered in kind. So Kennedy had told Reston, "I've got two problems. First, to figure out why he did it, and in such a hostile way. And second, to figure out what we can do about it. I think the first part is pretty easy to explain. I think he did it because of the Bay of Pigs. I think he thought that anyone who was so young and inexperienced as to get into that mess could be taken, and anyone who got into it, and didn't see it through, had no guts. So he just beat hell out of me. So I've got a terrible problem. If he thinks I'm inexperienced and have no guts, until we remove those ideas we won't get anywhere with him. So we have to act." Then he told Reston that he would increase the military budget (which he did) and send another division to Germany (which he also did). He turned to Reston and said that the only place in the world where there was a real challenge was in Vietnam, and "now we have a problem in trying to make our power credible, and Vietnam looks like the place." (Ironically, a year later, after the Americans had begun their limited commitment to Vietnam, Khrushchev would tell Ambassador Llewellyn Thompson that the Americans were making a major mistake in Vietnam. "In South Vietnam," he said, according to

Thompson's cable back to Washington, "the U.S. has stumbled into a bog. It will be mired there for a long time.")

In retrospect, Reston was convinced that the Vienna bullying became a crucial factor in the subsequent decision to send 18,000 advisory and support troops to Vietnam, and though others around Kennedy retained some doubts about this, it appeared to be part of a derivative link, one more in a chain of events which saw the escalation of the Cold War in Kennedy's first year. Reston in particular would see these events as a study in irony, believing that by October 1962, after the Cuban missile crisis, Kennedy had made good his need to show Khrushchev his fiber, but by that time it was too late as far as Southeast Asia was concerned; there were already more than 15,000 Americans in South Vietnam. For the Cold War was still quite real in 1961, on both sides of the Atlantic, and the men who had come to power in Washington were very much a part of it. They had been fashioned out of it, and now in their first year they were getting regular reminders that it had not yet crested, and their own very eagerness to be tested would in fact accelerate it.

Berlin, of course, had dominated their thoughts for some time. They believed that the hopes for war and peace somehow centered around that divided city, and its access routes. Could we maintain our access? Would the Soviets block it? They were the men in power, preoccupied with the tiniest details; it was as if the President were the desk officer, and the Secretary of State his assistant. There was no event too small for their concern, as if one little misplay would somehow start a chain of events which they might not be able to control. When someone questioned the President about spending too much time on Berlin, he answered, better too much than too little, and he did not mind checking too closely on military convoys; he did not, after all, want the world to be blown up because some young captain had a hangover on a given morning. If Berlin had seemed central in early 1961, Vietnam had loomed somehow very distant. Around that time a knowledgeable Far Eastern correspondent named Stanley Karnow had dropped by the Justice Department to talk with the President's brother. In the course of the conversation Karnow began to single out Vietnam as probably the most serious problem there, the one which bore the greatest long-range potential for danger. "Vietnam," said Robert Kennedy, "Vietnam . . . We have thirty Vietnams a day here."

THIRTY VIETNAMS. FROM THE BEGINNING IT HAD BEEN THAT WAY, A tiny issue overclouded by the great issues. It had risen to pre-eminence partly because of neglect and omission, a policy which had evolved not because a group of Westerners had sat down years before and determined what the future should be, but precisely because they had not. Vietnam had begun as the most peripheral of problems to the United States, a new Western power sprung suddenly to superpower proportions and facing a prolonged confrontation with the Communists. There had been time only for the great decisions, and Vietnam had been part of the price, something small which grew into something large. Who, in 1945, when decisions were being made, had time for Indochina? Nineteen forty-five was a time when the problems of Europe were pre-eminent, when the question of the atomic weapon and the atomic balance with the Soviet Union was next, when even China was on the periphery; Vietnam was on the periphery of the periphery.

But it began to go sour for this country as early as July 1945, when the new and uncertain President of the United States, Harry Truman, made his first major trip abroad, to Potsdam, to come to terms with the enormous problems that seemed to come hurtling at him, great decisions which would decide the immediate wartime and postwar future. He was not particularly concerned with Indochina, as it was then called; but because some of the issues arising at Potsdam might touch on China, Truman had brought along, as part of his State Department team, a China and Asian expert, John Carter Vincent, chief of the China division of the State Department.

Because later his career, along with those of many of his colleagues, would be destroyed during the post-China Red-baiting, John Carter Vincent would gain a kind of fame that he had neither expected nor desired. And somehow, because those men were attacked for what were alleged to be left-wing sympathies, the idea would grow that John Carter Vincent was a radical. The truth could hardly have been more different. He was a charming, social, pleasant, nominally conservative man who had unusually good connections on the Hill, came from a good Georgia family and was called, in that gracious Southern tradition, John Carter by almost everyone. Having spent a large part of his career in Asia, he felt a distinct empathy for Asian nationalism, and had a rather realistic view of the future. By early 1945 he had come to the conclusion that the President in particular believed in indigenous nationalism in Asia and was moving in that direction. Those days, in fact, would be the highwater mark of American support for nationalism in Vietnam, with Roosevelt talking about a trusteeship for the area. It would end with the trip Vincent was on at that moment, the trip to Potsdam. He did not think a great deal about Vietnam at Potsdam because it was not on the agenda, and because it was not supposed to be discussed at all.

But a decision was made at Potsdam on Vietnam, without any real consultation. It concerned the surrender; the British would accept the Japanese surrender below the 16th parallel, the Chinese above it. It appeared quite inconsequential at the time, but the matter of who accepts a surrender is a vital one; it determines who will control the turf and who will decide future legitimacy. The British, uneasy about questions that Roosevelt had raised in the past about independence in Asia, worried about what it might mean for Burma and Malaya, since they were anxious to control future colonial questions in Asia; the British, after all, were not eager to see the dissolution of their empire. Truman, pushed by his military advisers who were wary of what anticolonialism might mean as far as the future of U.S. naval and air bases in Asia was concerned, urged that we go along with the British. There had been no prior discussion among the Americans (though later evidence would show that there had been a good deal of collusion beforehand between the French and the British on this issue). Having accepted the surrender, the British would permit the French to return, and all subsequent events would flow from this: the French would reassert their authority, they would smile politely at all American requests to deal with the indigenous population, but they would pay no attention; the Americans, after all, had given away the leverage, the French Indochina war would begin, and the Vietnamese would gain their freedom by force of arms.

It was, of course, a minor point clouded over by great issues at the time, and the responsible political officer, John Carter Vincent, did not participate; in fact, he learned of it after the conference was over. A fateful decision unfatefully arrived at. It was, he would acknowledge many sad years later, the turning point, the moment at which it all began to go wrong.

VIETNAM UP TO THEN HAD ONLY COME INTO THE PUBLIC'S EYE through articles in the *National Geographic*, or old newsreels. It was filled with exotic but dutiful natives, whom the French were helping to become modern. In Washington it was viewed as a land with vital resources—vital, but not that vital. In 1941, when the United States learned from radio intercepts that the Japanese planned to move against southern Indochina, its reaction had been modest. The military argued against any action which might take us to war with Japan, because of our lack of preparedness (General Marshall and Admiral Harold Stark noted that America should go to war "only if Japan attacked or directly threatened territories whose security to the United States is of very great importance," which included Indonesia, and British and American possessions in Asia). What became clear as events progressed in 1941 and during the war was that Vietnam was important not in itself, but to the extent that the Japanese used it as a gateway to move toward other areas ("We must let them [the Japanese] see the seriousness of this step they have taken and let them know that such constitutes an unfriendly act because it helps Hitler to conquer Britain," Secretary of State Cordell Hull told Sumner Welles in 1941). But at a time when resources were limited and needs were crucial, there was no arrogance of American power, every resource was carefully weighed, and a young general named Dwight Eisenhower wrote in February 1942: "We must differentiate sharply and definitely between those things whose current accomplishment in the several theaters over the world are *necessary* to the ultimate defeat of the Axis powers, as opposed to those which are merely *desirable* because of their effect in facilitating such defeat." Thus Europe was the prime theater, Asia was the second one. It would be nice to stop Japanese expansion, but it was not that vital. "The defeat of Germany," Roosevelt wrote to Harry Hopkins, George Marshall and Admiral Ernest King in July 1942, "means the defeat of Japan, probably without firing a shot or losing a life." So American wartime policy was set. Prime effort in Europe, little effort in Asia, as little engagement of the Japanese mainland as possible, indeed a maximum use of technology, and a war which reflected that faith in technology—island hopping, moving from island to island securing bases for American air power to be aimed at Japan, rather than the more painful (and postwar politically more profitable) crawling up the mainland.

In Indochina itself, the collapse of the French had given enormous new momentum to political stirrings among the Vietnamese, and there was a belief that somehow the great war was being fought for them as well, a view shared by some Americans, notably their President. Franklin D. Roosevelt was a man before his time: anticolonialism had not surfaced yet as the great global movement (though the very war which he was helping to mastermind would speed the collapse of the old order and the end of colonialism), but Roosevelt had strong ideas about colonialism that were a reflection of his own—and his wife's—domestic political egalitarianism. He was instinctively on the side of the little man, and anticolonialism seemed consistent with his own domestic political style; indeed his national security advisers thought him very soft on the dangers of world Communism. He saw a role for the United States as a symbol of the new freedoms, and he was intuitively receptive to the idea that the many poor of the world would turn against the few rich. If Roosevelt did not like colonialism in general, he did not like French colonialism in particular. Part of this was due to his general annoyance with France as an ally during the war, part of it to his special pique with Charles de Gaulle, Roosevelt's failure to understand the unique role which that particular leader had chosen to play, grandeur *in absentia.* The French, Roosevelt was fond of telling people, had been in Indochina for fifty years and the people were worse off than when they had arrived. He had determined that the French would not automatically come back and reassert their control over Indochina; there would be some kind of international trusteeship, and if the French came back at all, it would be as some sort of partner in the trusteeship. But though this idea was real and he talked of it with a few close advisers, Roosevelt was, as the war progressed, an overburdened, exhausted man who was preoccupied with too many decisions of greater immediacy. There were no plans on Indochina, no inner workings of the bureaucracy set in motion on a post-war philosophy of colonial policy. On January 1, 1945, Roosevelt wrote a note to Edward Stettinius, his Secretary of State, saying: "I still do not want to get mixed up in any Indochina decision. It is a matter for post-war. By the same token I do not want to get mixed in any military effort towards the liberation of Indochina from the Japanese. . . ."

At the Yalta meeting between Stalin, Churchill and Roosevelt in February, the question of Indochina was discussed. Charles Bohlen's notes record that Roosevelt had a trusteeship in mind; further that the British did not like the idea because of its implications for Burma. The notes also reveal the ingenu-ousness of Western leaders talking about Asians in that period, and a first hint of the French desire to return:

The President said that the Indochinese were people of small stature like the Javanese and Burmese and were not warlike. . . . he said that General de Gaulle had asked for ships to transport French forces to Indochina. Marshal Stalin inquired where de Gaulle was going to get the troops. The President replied that de Gaulle said he was going to find the troops when the President could find the ships, but the President added that up to the present he had been unable to find the ships.

Less than a month later, on March 15, 1945, Roosevelt asked Charles Taussig, a State Department adviser on Caribbean affairs, to give him guidance on colonial questions for the forthcoming United Nations meeting. The conversa-tion reflected more clearly than anything else the crystallizing of Roosevelt's feeling about both the French and the area. Taussig recorded the conversa-tion for the Department:

The President said he is much concerned about the brown people in the East. He said that there are 1,100,000,000 brown people. In many eastern countries they are ruled by a handful of whites and they resent it. Our goal must be to help them achieve indepen-dence—1,100,000,000 potential enemies are dangerous. He said he included the 450,000,-000 Chinese in that. He then added, Churchill doesn't understand this. The President said he thought we might have some difficulties with France in the matter of colonies. I said that I thought that was quite probable and it was also probable that the British would use the French as a "stalking horse." I asked the President if he had changed his ideas on French Indochina as he had expressed them to us at the luncheon with Stanley [Colonel Oliver Stanley, the British Secretary of State for the Colonies, who had lunched with Roosevelt and Taussig on January 16]. He said no, he had not changed his ideas: that French Indochina and New Caledonia should be taken from France and put under a trusteeship. The President hesitated a moment and then said—Well if we can get the proper pledge from France to assume for herself the obligations of a trustee, then I would agree to France retaining these colonies with the proviso that independence was the ultimate goal. I asked the President if he would settle for dominion status. He said no—it must be independence. He said that is to be the policy, and you can quote it in the State Department.

This was to be the high-water mark of American governmental interest in pure anticolonialism in Indochina. Roosevelt's interest was strictly personal. He was supported neither by his bureaucracy (even at State the dominant force was the European desk, which reflected the views of the existing colonial powers), nor by his national security people (who were more sympathetic to the old allies, and who held to the military view that broad anticolonialism might threaten U.S. rights to its own Pacific possessions), nor by his traditional European allies. To bring the bureaucracy with him would have been a considerable struggle, something he could have done, but there was not enough time. By the same token, it would have taken a considerable amount of political effort to withstand the pressure from old traditional allies, anxious to reassert their colonial control, to go back to business as usual in areas they claimed to know best, particularly if the threat of Communism were entwined with the new Asian nationalism.

That this latter was the case became clear in March 1945 when de Gaulle summoned the American ambassador to France, Jefferson Caffery, to discuss U.S. aid for French troops to return to Indochina. The French had appealed for American aid and had been told none would be forthcoming. Now De Gaulle told Caffery that there was an expeditionary force ready to go, but promised British transport had failed to materialize, largely, he gathered, because of American pressure. "This worries me a great deal," De Gaulle said, "and it comes at a particularly inopportune time. As I told Mr. [Harry] Hopkins when he was here, we do not understand your policy. What are you driving at? Do you want us to become, for example, one of the federated states under the Russian aegis? The Russians are advancing apace, as you well know. When Germany falls, they will be upon us. If the public here comes to realize that you are against us in Indochina, there will be terrific disappointment and nobody knows to what that will lead. We do not want to become Communist; we do not want to fall into the Russian orbit, but I hope you will not push us into it." It was a significant response; it reflected not only the intention of the French to return to Indochina, but it also, for the first time, raised the question of Communism in the context of Vietnam; those who did not help the colonialists would be helping the Communists.

A few short weeks later Roosevelt was dead, and with him any hope for a genuine declared policy of anticolonialism for Vietnam. He was the only high player truly committed to the idea of keeping the French out. The other principals would reflect their own bureaucratic weight: State the pressure from the European allies, the military the pressure to keep bases. Indeed, Roosevelt's death was a signal to the Europeanists in the State Department that the road was cleared, and since the one high official who might have been a real enemy was out of the way, they moved immediately to present Truman with a *fait accompli* policy in Indochina. Within a week the Europeanists in the

Department acted: they quietly prepared a paper on Indochina saying that U.S. policy was to support the French position, and to work through the French in that region. Before handing it to superiors, they needed the concurrence of their colleagues in Southeast Asia, and so at five o'clock the paper was handed to Abbott Low Moffatt, the Department officer responsible for Southeast Asia, with a note that it was to go to the White House at nine the next morning. Moffatt, who was deeply committed to the cause of Asian nationalism, immediately understood what the game was and blocked the memo. But it signified to him that with Roosevelt gone, it was all going to be much tougher, that the French desk would be more aggressive.

The very organization of the Department in those days was the basic problem for the Asian officers. Asia was not a separate area; instead the colonies were handled through the European nations, and concurrent jurisdiction was required for policy changes. That meant that on any serious question involving a territory supposedly emerging from colonialism, both the European and Asian divisions had to agree before the question could go to a higher official. Effectively this meant that the French people would concur with the French policy of returning to Indochina, the Asian people would oppose it vigorously and the question would go to the next level, where officials would bounce it back down, suggesting that everyone get together on this. The result, of course, was that this favored the status quo, and the European division. A neutral policy was no policy: the French would do as they pleased. They were important, Asians were not. France was weak, its pride hurt; it had to be coddled. American policy in Indochina would begin, rooted not so much in anti-Communism—that was secondary—as in indifference. John Carter Vincent, then Director of Far Eastern Affairs (comparable to the later Assistant Secretary of State for Far Eastern Affairs), would recall fighting for a different policy, warning what so indifferent an attitude would mean in the long run, and being told by George Kennan: "John Carter, your views on Asian policy are quite sound from the traditional U.S. standpoint, but the immediate problem is to maintain the morale of Europe and its will to resist the Communist challenge."

The U.S. government knew what was going to happen in Vietnam, but committed to its European allies, it could not or would not use any leverage to change the course. The division in the government between its instincts for global power and its brain—a split which would haunt us right through 1965—was spelled out in June 1945 when Colonel Stimson asked the State Department to prepare a paper on the future of Asia. The paper clearly reflected the split between the European peoples and the Asian peoples ("The United States government may properly continue to state the political principle which it has frequently announced, that dependent peoples should be given the opportunity, if necessary after an adequate period of preparation, to achieve an increased measure of self-government, but it should avoid any course of action which would seriously impair the unity of the major United Nations . . ."). The paper then forecast quite accurately that Vietnamese political aspirations and consciousness, which had been increasing sharply in the nineteen-thirties and were more heightened than ever, would lead the Vietnamese to fight the French, and that the French would have "serious difficulty in overcoming this opposition and re-establishing French control." Knowing this, the U.S. government did nothing; it already feared French weakness in Europe and it was not about to pressure a weak and proud ally.

The intelligence people at State were not the only ones who knew the French would have trouble. In Vietnam, General Jacques Philippe Leclerc, De Gaulle's favorite general, landed to take charge of French forces. After a tour of the country he was fully aware of the political-military problems that lay ahead. Turning to his political adviser, Paul Mus, he said, "It would take five hundred thousand men to do it, and even then, it could not be done."

In France no one listened to either Leclerc or Mus, and in Washington no one listened to the young American political officers warning of the coming struggle. The idea of Asian rebels standing up to a powerful Western army was preposterous at the time. No one had yet heard of political war, of Mao's concept of fish swimming in the ocean of the people, of Asian guerrillas giving the European country the cities and strangling them by holding the countryside; of an army losing battle after battle but winning the people and thus the war. Instead the important thing in Washington was to strengthen France, and in Paris the important thing was to regain France's tarnished greatness. One did not restore greatness by giving in to Asian bandits. One restored greatness by force. And so in 1945 and 1946 it became increasingly clear that negotiations between France and the Vietminh would fail; France was too proud to deal with these little yellow men. The Asian-oriented officers in the State Department desperately pleaded with their superiors to pressure France to have real negotiations, to give the Vietnamese some sort of independence, warning that war was on its way and that it would do no one any good, least of all France. These pleas evoked much condescension among the European experts, who scorned this emotionalism, this panic. When Moffatt warned of the rising tide of anger and resentment in Vietnam, of the willingness and capacity of the Vietminh to fight, he was told by his colleagues and superiors not to be so emotional. This talk about nationalism was all Japanese propaganda, he was told; they had heard it before, they knew what the Japanese had been up to out there, trying to stir up these people. It would all pass. The Vietnamese wanted it the old way, they knew their limitations. And when Moffatt and his aides continued to argue and fight, he was told that it might not be a bad idea for certain Americans who had spent a few weeks in

Asia to spend a little time with some old-timers out there, some Frenchmen who had been there all their lives and *knew* these people. Charlton Ogburn, one of Moffatt's field people, would also report on the growing pressure for independence, of the need to pressure the French to come to terms with it, and would be told by the French desk that he listened too much to the pitter-patter of naked little brown feet.

Again and again it was the same thing, and men like Moffatt and Ogburn were told that they had to be serious about these things. First things first. They had to see the world in perspective and not become emotional. And so their efforts had precious little effect. Occasionally a cable would go out to Paris calling for the American ambassador to pressure the French to do something about negotiations, but even then they knew it was toned down by Ambassador Caffery. It was all becoming hopeless, they thought, as 1946 passed and the tensions mounted on both sides. While traveling in Indochina in December, Moffatt sensed the desperation of the Vietnamese, saw that no one was talking to anyone any more and that war was imminent. He cabled Washington, describing the explosive feeling in Vietnam and offering his good offices as a negotiator to serve between the French and the Vietminh. The French immediately turned down the offer. Before the week was out, fighting started. The war was on, and though the Americans began by standing on the sidelines, neutral but somewhat sympathetic to the Vietminh but being realistic about Europe, they would soon find themselves slowly drawn into the conflict, first to support the French, eventually to replace them. But the policy began in indifference, and even in the early years Lauriston Sharpe, a Cornell anthropologist who had served in the area during the war and who remained to work for the State Department, would complain bitterly about the lack of American leadership, about the vacuum which the United States had helped create. One telegram from the United States, he told Ogburn, and it could all have been avoided, all this bloodshed. If in March 1946, when the French had signed a preliminary accord with the Vietminh recognizing them as a legitimate authority—an agreement from which they quickly reneged—if then the United States had been wise enough to send a telegram congratulating Paris on its forward-looking leadership and announcing that the United States was sending a minister to Hanoi, all this could have been avoided, all the heartache erased. Perhaps that was too strong, one telegram would have meant little, but the truth was that during the crucial months and years, the U.S. policy, despite all its commitments to freedom, independence and anti-colonialism, had permitted an ally to start a bitter and foolish colonial war. Without raising a finger or sending any real telegrams.

Chapter Six

In Asia, the first confrontation would take place over
Laos. Even before Kennedy took office he had met with President Eisenhower, whose proudest boast for his term of office would be that no shooting
war had started during his two-term Presidency; and that man of peace had
shocked Kennedy by saying that it looked like we might have to go to war
over Laos. It was the day before the Kennedy inauguration, and each man
had been surrounded by members of his team, Kennedy guided through the
rituals by Clark Clifford, the skilled Democratic link to the past who had handled Kennedy's part of the transition period. It was a somber meeting. The
great crisis, Eisenhower said, was in Southeast Asia, Laos was the key to it. If
we let Laos fall, we have to write off the whole area. We must not, Eisenhower said with considerable emotion, permit a Communist takeover. We
should get the South-East Asia Treaty Organization or perhaps the International Control Commission for Laos to help us defend the freedom of the
country. We should get allies, perhaps the British, but failing that, we must
do it unilaterally, a last desperate measure if necessary, he said. Both his
outgoing secretaries, Christian Herter at State and Thomas Gates at Defense,
supported this intervention. Kennedy asked quietly how long it would take to
get troops into Laos. Gates said twelve to seventeen days, less time if they
were already in the Pacific. It was not an encouraging answer. Kennedy left
the meeting profoundly shaken; the old President, who had come to symbol-

ize peace, was now offering his young successor a war in Southeast Asia over Laos, and was of course offering his support from the farm in Gettysburg. But go to war over Laos? This from Eisenhower, the fumbling, placid man whose lack of will and lack of national purpose the Democrats and Kennedy had just finished decrying.

At that point Laos seemed a dubious proposition; if ever anything was an invention of the Cold War and its crisis psychology, it was the illusion of Laos. It was a landlocked country, a part of the Indochina nation, and the Laotians, a peaceful people living on the China border, had managed to participate as little as possible in the French Indochina war. Of the Indochinese peoples it was the Vietnamese and particularly the North Vietnamese who were considered warriors, but Dulles had decided to turn Laos into what he called "a bastion of the free world." It was the least likely bastion imaginable; it seemed like a country created by Peter Ustinov for one of his plays. The best writing about its military and political turmoil was found not on the front pages of the great newspapers, but rather in the satire of Russell Baker and Art Buchwald. Its people were sleepy, unwarlike, uninterested in the great issues of ideology; yet unlikely or not, it bore the imprimatur of American foreign policy of that era: the search for an Asian leader who told us what we wanted to hear, the creation of an army in our image, the injection of Cold War competition rather than an attempt to reduce tension and concentrate on legitimate local grievances or an attempt to identify with nationalist stirrings, no matter how faint. Since there was neither a hot nor a cold war in Laos, the problem fell between State and Defense—the very small war, semicovert—and thus it was a CIA show, the country perilously close to being a CIA colony (in the sense that the local airline was run by the CIA, and a good many of the bureaucratic jobs were financed by the CIA).

Our man there, so to speak, was a general named Phoumi Nosavan, a right-wing strong man, to use the phrase of that era, but more of a comic-strip figure. Meeting him in Washington for the first time, Kennedy said, "If that's our strong man, we're in trouble." On a more practical level, he found Phoumi so small that he, assuming that generals are bigger than privates, called for an immediate check on weapons carried by Laotians, knowing instantly that the basic American infantry weapon, the M-1, was too large for them. Since 1958, Phoumi had lived well off the Cold War, like many a strong man, but there were additional benefits to being a Laotian military leader: he was also in the opium trade, from which he profited considerably. He had an army handsomely paid, but worthless in battle. "Your chief of staff couldn't lead a platoon around a corner to buy a newspaper," the American ambassador, Winthrop Brown, once told him. "I know," Phoumi answered, "but he's loyal." When once, by mistake and by lack of opposition, his troops captured

Vientiane, the Laotian capital, Phoumi refused to go there for the swearing in of his government because his soothsayer had warned that he would die a violent death.

While American policy might have worked to diminish international tensions, and indeed the very importance of Laos, it had done quite the opposite. During the Dulles years, when neutralism was considered somewhat sinful, the Americans had deliberately sabotaged indigenous Laotian attempts, led by their ruler, Prince Souvanna Phouma, at neutralism and a coalition government between the various factions. Graham Parsons, ambassador to Laos during the latter Dulles years, when American ambassadors in Asia were particularly rigid in their anti-Communism, later testified before a congressional committee: "I struggled for sixteen months to prevent a coalition." With our money, our CIA men and our control of the Royal Laotian Army, we had in fact systematically destroyed the neutralist government of Souvanna, eventually forcing the neutralists to the side of the Communist Pathet Lao (though in 1962 we would spend millions and millions of dollars to re-create the very neutralist government we had toppled). One month before Kennedy entered office in 1961 Souvanna had fled to Thailand, and Kong Le, the military leader of the neutralist forces who wanted above all to be left alone, had joined the Pathet Lao to fight against General Phoumi's army. In the next two months, skirmishes took place (the Laotian civil war, which flared up periodically, was distinguished by considerable journalistic coverage, troops moving through on sweeps, maps on the front pages of American newspapers, and the fact that there were almost never any casualties). When the two sides finally met in early February on the strategically important Plain of Jars, General Phoumi's army, better equipped, better paid, predictably broke and ran. As they ran, the Kennedy Administration had its first Asian crisis.

IT WAS THE CLASSIC CRISIS, THE KIND THAT THE POLICY MAKERS OF the Kennedy era enjoyed, taking an event and making it greater by their determination to handle it, the attention focused on the White House. During the next two months, officials were photographed briskly walking (almost trotting) as they came and went with their attaché cases, giving their No comment's, the blending of drama and power, everything made a little bigger and more important by their very touching it. Power and excitement come to Washington. There were intense conferences, great tensions, chances for grace under pressure. Being in on the action. At the first meeting McNamara forcefully advocated arming half a dozen AT6s (obsolete World War II fighter planes) with 100-lb. bombs, and letting them go after the bad Laotians. It was a strong advocacy; the other side had no air power. Thus we would certainly win; technology and power could do it all. ("When a newcomer enters the field [of foreign policy]," Chester Bowles wrote in a note to himself at the time, "and finds himself confronted by the nuances of international questions he becomes an easy target for the military-CIA-paramilitary-type answers which can be added, subtracted, multiplied or divided. . . .") Rusk, who had seen the considerable limits of air power in jungle terrain when he was in the China-Burma-India theater during the war, gently dampened the idea; in addition, given the size of the Plain of Jars, the effectiveness of six small fighter-bombers was bound to be limited.

There were other ideas; some of the civilians were interested in the possibility of a quick strike at the Plain of Jars, an airborne landing. Could we get them in there? Kennedy asked the Chairman of the Joint Chiefs. "We can get them in there, all right," General Lemnitzer answered. "It's getting them out that worries me." What quickly became clear was that the military, particularly the Army, were in no rush to fight a ground war in Laos. The Army still felt itself badly burned by its experience in Korea, where it had fought a war which was immensely frustrating for commanders who felt they were sacrificing their men for limited political objectives, a kind of rationing of men for politics, which was difficult for officers to come to terms with. In addition, the impact of the Eisenhower years on the Army, years of cutback and depletion, had left the strategic reserve seriously reduced. "If we put as many as one hundred and twenty-five thousand into Southeast Asia, we wouldn't be able to fight a war in Florida," one general told the President. Yet the Chiefs of Staff did not recommend against the Laotian commitment; rather, they said that if we were to get involved, we should go in with a large force, and the use of force should be open-ended—thus the possible use of nuclear weapons was implicit. They wanted 250,000 men for the invasion. At one of the National Security Council meetings someone asked what would happen if the Chinese came in—in that case a quarter of a million Americans would not be enough. "We'll take care of that," Lemnitzer answered somewhat vaguely. But when the civilians pursued the questioning, it became clear that if the Chinese or the Soviets moved in combat troops, the main military contingency plan would be the use of nuclear weapons.

Kennedy in particular was annoyed because he felt the Chiefs were not being candid; that they were building a record against him, covering themselves against an invasion and putting the onus on him; that they were hiding behind the nuclear weapons, and yet not stating the case explicitly. (The same ambiguity would recur without fail as the Laotian crisis resurfaced from time to time, usually in the rainy seasons, when the Pathet Lao could move with greater protection. A year later there was a new Laotian crisis, and after a NATO conference in Europe, McNamara went back via Saigon to meet with top U.S. officials. He asked each one in turn what the United States should do. First was Admiral Harry Felt, commander of all American forces in the

Pacific. "We have the Seventh Fleet and we have the planes to wipe Tche-pone off the face of the earth." Then McNamara turned to Lemnitzer. "Well, Lem, what do you think?" "I don't think air power alone will do it. We need to challenge them on the ground. Secure the Mekong. Use SEATO Plan Five . . . Put some men in there." Then to General Paul Harkins, commander of Military Assistance in Vietnam: "Paul, you're the theater commander, what do you think?" "I think the situation is very serious. Naturally we have to respond. We have to impress the Communists with the seriousness of our intention. And yet we must act within our capabilities." McNamara then turned to Ambassador Frederick Nolting, who replied, "I look upon our Asian policy having two pillars, South Vietnam and Thailand. Laos is the keystone supporting them. If the keystone falls, the pillars will collapse." It was all fairly chilling, and McNamara, a little better informed than the year before when he lived in a world of AT6s, said, "Let me play the devil's advocate: if we intervene in Laos, if we overfly North Vietnam, will the Chinese let us do it? Lem, you want to use the SEATO plan. What will Hanoi do? Will they just sit there or will they come in?" Then he leaned back. "Now let us get down to it." He waited. Their staffs had long since left the room. What ensued was one of the longest and most appalling silences McNamara had ever sat through. They had all been pushing hard, willing to commit troops, in effect go to war if necessary, but they had given little or no thought to what the other side might do. Now they had no answers, nothing to say.)

IT WAS AT THIS POINT IN THE FIRST LAOTIAN CRISIS THAT HARRIMAN entered the picture, in April 1961. He was a man who had lived through most of the past Cold War policies and had helped create them, but he was not tied to them; above all, he was not an ideologue. He was a man of power, but he knew that power was always changing, also that the most dangerous thing about power is to employ it where it is not applicable, and he had serious doubts about the value of an American commitment to Laos. He differed from the other high officials in understanding that the pluralism of the Communist world was a real thing, that it had changed, that the Communist world was in flux. As it was changing, genuine new opportunities would present themselves and he was determined that this Administration take advantage of them, and that he play a part. It was something in the darker days of 1961 that he never lost sight of and he would see to it that the chance for progress was interrupted as little as possible. As roving ambassador he had talked with Khrushchev, who had not thought Laos was worth war ("Why take the risk?" Khrushchev told Ambassador Llewellyn Thompson. "It will fall into our lap like a rotten apple"). In March, Harriman had arranged to see Souvanna Phouma, the neutralist leader the United States had succeeded in ousting.

They met at an airport in New Delhi, and although they shared no common language, Harriman had broken through. He came away convinced that this was a man you could deal with, that he represented something viable in Laos.

He had returned to Washington, and knowing the importance of repetition within a government, he had started repeating a litany whenever he could at Washington meetings, at dinner parties—Souvanna Phouma, Souvanna Phouma, Souvanna Phouma—until at a certain point close friends were somewhat alarmed; perhaps this time Averell really was showing his age. It was not long after that Kennedy assigned him the job of getting a Laotian settlement at the conference in Geneva in May; it was not something he particularly wanted, and it was distant from the area of his prime concern. He did not think a decent settlement was really possible, but it was a job; he was underemployed and he needed to show these young people that he could run with them. He was willing to work for an accord, however, not just because he had a high opinion of Souvanna but because he had also formed a low opinion of the right-wing forces there (arriving in Vientiane, he sensed that the right-wing forces had no legitimacy, were an American creation; when CIA agents gave him carefully prepared briefings on the Laotian desires for freedom, they were annoyed to find Harriman simply turning off his hearing aid. They had no answers he was interested in). Indeed, the way he carried out what he himself would describe as a "good bad deal" so impressed the President that Harriman started an upward journey which might have brought him the Secretary's job itself were it not for the assassination.

Harriman himself did not have great hopes for the mission, but he went at it doggedly. At one point a friend asked how it was going, and he answered, "Just about as unsatisfactorily as we expected." He was appalled by the size of the mission he took over in Geneva, and by the amount of deadwood. He did, however, like one member of the staff, Bill Sullivan, a thirty-eight-year-old officer way down the list in seniority. Bill Sullivan had served in Asia as a young man and did not seem to spout the clichés of most of the mission, and Harriman immediately offered him a job as his deputy. Sullivan declined, noting there were a dozen people senior to himself in the mission. Several days later Harriman called Sullivan in again and offered him the same job; by this time he had sent home everyone senior to Sullivan. This did not endear him to some of the departed who were connected with the Department's traditionalists, and as he continued to negotiate with the Soviet delegate, G. M. Pushkin, there were mutterings that he was giving away too much of Laos, that great bastion. "I think the next cable will be signed 'Pushkin,'" said one high-level official. Harriman's reaction when he heard of the remark was swift and devastating (he was not called "The Crocodile" for nothing), he decided that the man be transferred to . . . he thought for a minute and then chose . . . Afghanistan.

In Geneva he worked single-handedly toward the neutral settlement, trying to convince the Soviets that they had little to lose, that the real problem for them was the Chinese, and that neutralism was more of a problem for the Chinese than for the Russians. At one point during the negotiations Pat Moynihan, who had worked for him during the Albany days, ran into him in Geneva.

"What are you doing now?" he asked Harriman.

"Oh, I'm just waiting. We've done all the talking we can do. And the Russians are making up their minds and I'm waiting for them. That's all, waiting."

Eventually a neutralist agreement met with all the delegates' approval, much to the anger of the hard-liners such as Alsop, who said it reminded him of the White Queen in *Alice in Wonderland* teaching herself to believe six impossible things before breakfast. So the Kennedy Administration had moved away from force in Laos, but not without first a show of force, by stationing U.S. Marines on Okinawa and in Japan for possible forays into the Mekong Valley, and not without a grand *son et lumière* show, a television spectacular starring Kennedy himself, with maps, charts, clichés about Laotian freedom being tied to American freedom. "The security of all Southeast Asia will be endangered if Laos loses its neutral independence. Its own safety runs with the safety of us all. I know that every American will want his country to honor its obligations to the point that freedom and security of the free world and ourselves may be achieved," he said on television, while telling Arthur Schlesinger at lunch of the discrepancy between what he thought he could say and what he believed: "We cannot accept a visible humiliation." The opposition to the use of force at the high levels of the U.S. government was remarkably frail; the President himself, wiser now (he would say later that the Bay of Pigs had saved us from going to war in Laos), still felt that he could not be candid about the stakes or lack thereof in Laos.

So the Laotian crisis had been brought to a successful negotiated settlement, but it was an eerie and unsettling experience to the men in Washington, for they had come far too close to involvement within a country where the faction they supported lacked any chance of success. What really saved the United States from confrontation in Laos was not the Bay of Pigs, or even Harriman, but the Laotians themselves. For the Pathet Lao were not a classic guerrilla force. If Phoumi was a foolish figure, Souphanuvong, leader of the Pathet Lao, was a Communist counterpart. Neither he nor his people had invested the kind of sacrifice and commitment to the struggle that the Vietcong had in South Vietnam; the force and dynamism of the Indochinese guerrilla movement had never really touched Laos. A major Communist power, such as the Soviet Union, could in fact serve as a broker for an agreement, which it could not do in Vietnam, where the indigenous Communist force was all that mattered. (This led to a misconception in Washington: a belief that the Russians, if they wanted to, could control and negotiate events in Vietnam as they did in Laos, and that eventually the Russians would help us out.) In Vietnam, however, the Americans would learn that the indigenous force was far more real, far tougher (the very quality of the fiber of the Vietnamese people which encouraged Washington to make a stand in Vietnam instead of in Laos would work against us there as well). In Vietnam a dynamic, relentless guerrilla movement was in the fifteenth year of an endless struggle to take over and unify the whole country, and for the leaders of that movement what the United States did or did not do was irrelevant. They would continue at their own pace. In addition, if the Communist investment in Laos was marginal, so was the American one, compared to Vietnam. Phoumi may have been a strong man, but no one would ever accuse him of being a Miracle Man, as Diem was called, for in Vietnam we had committed more, made more speeches, trained more troops. There was the beginning of a Vietnam lobby in the United States, and in fact both the President and his father had in some way been part of it.

With luck the United States had managed to stay out of Laos, and though there were protests from the hard-liners, most of the country greeted the decision not to fight either with boredom and indifference or with relief. There was one small footnote to the Geneva agreement, and though it did not seem important at the time, in retrospect it would take on considerable significance. After the agreement had been reached, Kennedy assigned his own liaison man with Harriman, the young Wall Street lawyer Michael Forrestal, to brief Lyndon Johnson on the settlement. Johnson, of course, already knew of the accords, and Forrestal arrived to find that the meeting had been arranged so that Forrestal would get there about ten minutes after Johnson's masseur had arrived. Forrestal began to discuss the accords, only to find himself blocked again and again by the masseur. Forrestal spoke, the masseur chopped, Forrestal spoke, the masseur rubbed. For ten minutes Forrestal tried to explain the agreement and found no way of getting Johnson's attention; it was, Forrestal thought at the time, and even more so later, Johnson's way of showing contempt for the Laotian accords.

OF ALL THE MEMBERS OF THE NEW ADMINISTRATION ONLY ONE MAN besides Bowles had ever shown much interest in the underdeveloped world, or much feel for it. It was not McNamara, for whom it might have factored in as a potential future market for the 1980s, or Rusk, who felt himself more sympathetic to the colored of the world than Acheson, but had managed to deliver some of the State Department's best speeches in defense of the French position in Indochina; nor Bundy, who was classically a man of the

Atlantic. It was, oddly enough, John F. Kennedy. He had been to Indochina twice, in 1951 and 1953, once as a congressman and once as a senator: the first time he was met at the airport by half the French army ready to brief him, to convince him of victory, to introduce him to a few Vietnamese officers bursting from their paratroop uniforms to prove to him how committed the natives were to a French type of freedom. He went to the official briefings, but he also jumped the traces, got the names of the best reporters in town and showed up unannounced at their apartments, looking so young and innocent that they had trouble believing that he was really a member of the Congress of the United States. There he asked his own questions and got very different briefings from the official ones: the pessimism was considerable, the Vietminh were winning the war, and the French were not giving any real form of independence to the Vietnamese (ironically, a dozen years later in exactly the same situation, on the same soil, Kennedy would rage at the reporters for their pessimism, while at the same time occasionally confiding in Schlesinger that he learned more from their dispatches than he could from his generals and ambassadors. In 1952 he was particularly impressed with the work of one reporter, Homer Bigart, then of the New York *Herald Tribune,* and wrote him a personal letter of congratulation, while a decade later his embassy in Saigon singled out the same skeptical and pessimistic Bigart, by then with the *New York Times,* as the major problem in winning the war). He also met at length with Edmund A. Gullion, a young foreign service officer who was the leader of the dissenters at the mission (starting a friendship which would continue for ten years, with Gullion eventually becoming his ambassador to the Congo). He finally told Gullion that he was right, there had to be more pressure on the French to give independence ("This is going to cost me some votes with my French Catholic constituents, but it seems like the right thing to do").

Those trips to Vietnam had begun Kennedy's education on the underdeveloped world and colonialism. Later he spoke twice against the French position in Indochina (there was a third speech on Vietnam, which was pro-Diem) and continued with a major address against the French position in Algeria. It was not an expression of great passion, rather it was a reflection of his almost Anglicized nature, his distaste for colonial callousness and vulgarity. He did not like the French colonial officials; they seemed stupid and insensitive, trying to hold on to something in a world which had already changed. In addition, he felt a distaste for the harshness that their particular role apparently brought about. They were bad politicians and they were living in the past; by contrast, he was impressed with what the British had done in India, leaving when they should, with none of the worst predicted consequences taking place.

Kennedy's understanding of Indochina was not, aides would recall, particularly sophisticated; it was more an intuitive feeling, and he was less than anxious to see the countless Vietnamese exiles who headed for his office. But having sensed which way the wind was blowing in Vietnam, he continued with much the same feeling about the French colonial war in Algeria, and his Algerian speech became one of his best known. In June 1957 he talked casually with his staff about the connection between Vietnam and Algeria and suggested that Fred Holborn, a young speech writer and former Harvard government instructor, write the outline of a speech. Holborn came up with what was essentially a critique of the colonial position; Kennedy thereupon surprised Holborn by sharpening the arguments rather than softening them, as he usually did. The speech was a good one, and it went against the traditional foreign policy of supporting the French blindly no matter what they did, on the grounds that our oldest ally was also a weak oldest ally, given to great internal division and lack of fiber, and thus might come apart at the slightest prod of an American finger. Just how rigid and centrist American foreign policy was at that moment could be judged by the vehemence of the reaction to so mild a speech. It was hardly a radical speech; yet it was criticized not only by Eisenhower and Dulles' allies in the Republican party, but by the *New York Times,* by Adlai Stevenson, and of course by Dean Acheson. How could he do this, he was damaging an ally; he was young and inexperienced, he lacked expertise, this was a serious business, criticizing your own country and an ally over foreign policy. Hervé Alphand, the French ambassador in Washington, went to see him to present an official complaint. Kennedy deliberately kept Alphand waiting, then again, deliberately, served him a terrible lunch, and did not back down a bit. Instead he went right at Alphand, reminding him how little support the war really had in France.

It was the first major speech for Kennedy on an international issue, and the first time a speech brought him serious criticism. Later he would recall that it was also the only speech he had made which helped him after he became President; it gave him an identification with independence movements throughout the world. But he was, he told aides, wary of being known as the Senator from Algeria and immediately looked around for another country to give a speech on, choosing Poland this time, a reasonably safe and secure topic, since he could be for freedom without offending his constituents. Yet his overall view on colonialism was now clearly stated, it was above all rational and fatalistic. It wasn't that he liked Algerians or Vietnamese. He was bored by them; their intensity and parochial views did not much interest him. He was intrigued by some of the revolutionary figures; they, unlike some of the bureaucratic figures in the underdeveloped world, caught his imagination.

It was almost as if the colonialists' lack of style offended him the most, and this was not surprising, because the thirty-fifth President of the United States paid great attention to style; style for him and for those around him came perilously close to substance. He did not like people who were messy and caused problems, nor did he like issues that were messy and caused problems. He would make his own limited commitment to Vietnam in a few short months, not so much to embrace the issue as to get rid of it, to push it away. He was the new American breed, not ideological, and wary of those who were; among the most frequently quoted remarks of the 1960 campaign was the fact that he did not like the doctrinaire liberals of the Americans for Democratic Action, he did not feel comfortable with them.

Kennedy was committed only to rationality and brains, nothing more. Rational decisions were to be welcomed; presumably the other side, the Soviets, would be as rational as we were; they would, despite a different language and a different system, have the same basic symmetry of survival and thus the same basic symmetry of rationality: they would no more want Moscow destroyed by a nuclear attack over a squabble about the access routes to Berlin than we would want Washington blown up.

Kennedy was almost British in his style. Grace under pressure was that much-quoted phrase describing a quality which Kennedy so admired, and so wanted as a description of his own behavior. It was very much a British quality: to undergo great hardship and stress and never flinch, never show emotion. Weaker, less worthy Mediterranean peoples showed emotion when pressure was applied, but the British kept both their upper and lower lips stiff. The British were loath to show their emotions, and so was Jack Kennedy. He could forgive his opponent Richard Nixon for many of the egregious slurs Nixon had cast upon the Democratic party in the 1950s, but he could not forgive him for his lack of style and class in permitting Pat Nixon to be shown on Election Night 1960 as she seemed to be close to a breakdown. Kennedy himself was always uneasy with emotion; James MacGregor Burns would note that when, as President, Kennedy visited Ireland and thousands upon thousands of Irishmen wildly cheered, his reaction was to tug self-consciously at his tie and straighten it. His style and speeches were restrained, as if to contrast them with the exhibitionism which had been identified with the Irish politicians of another era, most notably his own grandfather, Honey Fitz Fitzgerald.

He did not like people who pushed and crowded him, who told him of their cause or their problems. He wanted in his career no one's problems but his own. He had come to the Presidency at an important time in American history, when many of the forces which had produced the worst and most emotional tensions of the Cold War were fast ebbing, but when American political rhetoric had not yet adapted to those changes. As a political figure his perceptions were particularly good, and he was more sensitive to changes in the world than most of his contemporaries; but as a political figure he was cautious and almost timid. If the world was changing and the Cold War tensions were abating, he did not intend to accelerate those changes at the risk of his own career; he wanted to keep up with them, but not to be either ahead of the changes or behind them.

For the thirty-fifth President of the United States was a classic expression of the democratic-elitist society which had produced him in the middle part of the twentieth century. As the country expanded, the old elites in the East had opened up their universities to the best qualified of the new elites, and his education had been superb. As the Democratic party had been the natural home of the newer immigrant groups of America, so he and his family had made their way to that refuge, though by economic impulse their more natural home would have been the Republican party. As money was important in American egalitarian politics, he was at once very rich without seeming rich or snobbish and he spent his money wisely and judiciously, allowing it to make his political way easier, yet using it in ways which were carefully designed not to offend his more egalitarian constituency. So it was not surprising that many of his fellow citizens found reassurance in the fact that he was President ("Superman in the Supermarket," Norman Mailer once wrote of him). In a country which prized men who were successful and got ahead, he had always been marvelously successful, and he had gotten ahead. He had made no false moves, no votes had been cast in the heat of idealism to be regretted later. Each move had always been weighed with the future in mind. Better no step than a false step. Never would he be too far ahead of his own constituency, even when that Massachusetts constituency was wallowing in the worst part of the McCarthy period.

With television emerging in American politics as the main arbiter of candidates, his looks were striking on the screen, and he was catapulted forward in his career by his capacity to handle the new medium, thus to be projected into millions of Protestant homes without looking like a Catholic. And he was, despite all the advantages, still very hungry; he had all the advantages of the rich, with none of the disadvantages. The Kennedys had not grown soft, they still wanted almost desperately those prizes which were available. It was not by chance that Nelson Rockefeller, the one candidate who probably could have beaten him in 1960, the Brahmin WASP Republican with all the advantages of Kennedy, just as photogenic, just as rich, perhaps not quite as bright, was above all a Rockefeller and thus lacked the particular hunger, the edge, the requisite totality of desire for the office, and so even before the primaries had allowed himself to be bluffed out by Richard Nixon. Lack of hunger was a problem which might affect subsequent generations of Kennedys, but in 1960 the edge was there. Nelson Rockefeller's father had never had to leave one city and move to another because he felt there was too little social acceptance of his children, but Joseph Kennedy had moved from Boston to Bronxville for precisely that reason when his sons were teen-agers.

Yet if many politicians are propelled forward and fed by the tensions and deprivations of their youth, Kennedy was again different. Being Irish may have been an incentive; Jack Kennedy felt no insecurity about it. The drive was there, mixed in with the fatalism about it all. Lyndon Johnson, product of a poor and maligned section of the country, may never have lost his feeling of insecurity about his Texas background; Richard Nixon, poor and graceless and unaccepted as a young man, the classic grind, became the most private and hidden of politicians, always afraid to reveal himself, but Kennedy bore no scars. He had been excluded from the top Boston social circles as a young man, but he felt no great insecurity about it. His social friends at the White House tended to be the very people who had ruled those social sets, and he clearly enjoyed having them come to him. But he was unabashedly proud and sure of himself. Someone like John Kenneth Galbraith could note that he had never met a man who took such a great pleasure in simply being himself and had as little insecurity as Kennedy (which allowed him to accept the failure of the Bay of Pigs, without trying to pass the blame). Once during the 1960 campaign against Nixon someone had asked Kennedy if he was exhausted, and he answered no, he was not, but he felt sorry for Nixon, he was sure Nixon was tired. "Why?" the friend asked. "Because I know who I am and I don't have to worry about adapting and changing. All I have to do at each stop is be myself. But Nixon doesn't know who he is, and so each time he makes a speech he has to decide which Nixon he is, and that will be very exhausting."

If John Kennedy was cool and above the fray, detached, seeing no irrationality in the awesome Kennedy family thrust for power, he could well afford that luxury, for the rage, the rough edges, the totality of commitment bordering on irrationality belonged to his father. If John Kennedy was fatalistic about life, Joseph Kennedy was not. You did not accept what life handed you and then just tried to make the best of it; instead you fought ferociously for your chance, you pushed aside what stood in your way, the civilized law of the jungle prevailed. Joe Kennedy was a restless, rough genius anxious to shed his semi-immigrant status, anxious to avenge old snubs and hurts; having failed to do so despite his enormous wealth, he was determined to gain his final acceptance through his sons. What better proof of Americanization than a son in the White House, a son running the Justice Department, and a son in the Senate (the last triumph would become somewhat unsettling to the elder boys, who thought perhaps the family was overdoing it, though the patriarch himself knew the code better than they—there was no way of overdoing it). If Joe Kennedy's daughters had been sent to the very best Catholic schools, the better to retain the parochialism and tradition in order to pass it on to his grandchildren, his sons had been educated exactly for the opposite reasons— to shed it. There would be no Holy Cross, or Fordham, or Georgetown Law School in their lives. They were sent instead to the best Eastern Protestant schools, where the British upper-class values were still in vogue. For Jack it had been Choate, not Groton or St. Paul's perhaps, but still a school for proper Christian gentlemen, who understand duty and obligation, and then Harvard. Eventually, after the service in World War II, a political career; the thrust at the beginning was certainly Joseph Kennedy's rather than that of his son, who seemed to be merely pursuing the obligatory career. Later, of course, there was no absence of his own ambition, and he became a remarkable American specimen, carrying in him an immigrant family's rage to get their due, but carefully concealed behind a cool and elegant façade: in the prime of his career in the late fifties as he prepared to run for President, he did not seem an upstart and an outsider raging to get his due, but rather a very fine, well brought up young man dealing with an outmoded unfortunate prejudice. The perfect John O'Hara candidate for President. Once during his Administration a scandal broke out over the fact that the Metropolitan Club, Washington's most elite social and political meeting place, did not encourage Jewish or Negro membership. Many of Kennedy's friends resigned, but not McGeorge Bundy. Kennedy was amused by this and began to tease Bundy, who became irritated and lashed back. Kennedy, he said testily, belonged to clubs which did not have many Jews and Negroes, such as the Links in New York. "Jews and Negroes," laughed Kennedy. "Hell, they don't even allow Catholics!"

HE HAD, BOTH AS CONGRESSMAN AND SENATOR, AVOIDED ATTACHMENT to particular programs, issues or causes; the one issue on which he used the full force of his intellectual powers during the senatorial period was labor-reform legislation, a curious passion for a Democratic politician. He symbolized that entire era—post-Depression, postwar, post-McCarthy America. Ideology seemed finished, humanism was on the decline as a political force; rationality and intelligence and analysis were the answers. There was no limit to what brilliant men, untrammeled by ideology and prejudice and partisanship, could do with their minds in solving the world's problems. Indeed, making the case for Kennedy in a 1960 campaign tract, Arthur Schlesinger wrote:

It should be evident that Kennedy is an exceptionally cerebral figure. By this I mean that his attitudes proceed to an unusual degree from dispassionate rational analysis. If elected he will be the most purely cerebral President we have had since Woodrow Wilson. "Purely cerebral" is in this case a relative term. Wilson's rationalism masked deep passions, and Kennedy has the normal human quota of sympathy and prejudice . . .

Good intelligent men could go beyond their own prejudices and escape the rhetoric of the past. George Kennan, Kennedy's ambassador to Yugoslavia, and the most cerebral member of the foreign service himself, would never be so impressed as when Koča Popovic, the Yugoslav foreign minister, visited Washington and met with Kennedy. Instead of being filled with the usual East-West rhetoric and debate, the conversation began with Kennedy leaning over toward Popovic and asking in a particularly disarming way, "Mr. Minister, you are a Marxist and the Marxist doctrine has had certain clear ideas about how things were to develop in this world. When you look over things that have happened in the years since the Russian Revolution, does it seem to you that the way the world has been developing is the way that Marx envisaged it or do you see variations here or any divergencies from Marxist predictions . . . ?"

It was also symbolic of the era that Kennedy wanted to be his own Secretary of State, not Secretary of Health, Education and Welfare, not Secretary of Labor, not Attorney General. It was symbolic because in the universities, in the journals and in the intellectual circles it was generally held that the real action was in determining the role America played in the world, rather than redefining America domestically. It was where the excitement was, this competition with the Soviet Union, a competition of politics and of economics and ideas. Kennedy believed in it, and so did other men of power and ambition in that era. Bright young men off the Eastern campuses went to Mississippi to redefine America in 1964, but in the 1950s they had gone into the CIA and into the State Department, and even in 1961 they went into the Peace Corps and the Defense Department. Even as a congressman Kennedy had asked Ted Sorensen what Cabinet post he wanted. Sorensen had talked about HEW, but Kennedy was different, Jack Kennedy as Cabinet officer wanted only State or Defense, that was where the power was. The real power and resources and energies, financial and intellectual, of the United States were committed to the cause of the new American empire, in bringing proof that our system was better than theirs. Neither Kennedy nor very much of the country, including the press, was particularly interested in domestic reform. In his inaugural address Kennedy gave short shrift to domestic issues, and no one criticized him. Joseph Swidler, chairman of the Federal Power Commission, a man strongly committed to regulating the big power and utility interest, found his first year with the Kennedy Administration immensely frustrating. He had gone to Washington because he had been promised a strong anti-interest commission. That commission, he soon found out, would not be forthcoming. It was bogged down in the pluralism of American politics and by the President's primary concern with foreign affairs: in order to get his key foreign aid bills through Congress, Kennedy needed the co-operation of men like Sam Rayburn and Senator Robert Kerr. The price they exacted from the President was at the expense of the Federal Power Commission; they wanted and received men sympathetic to their and the big interests' views. This left

Swidler angry, and with a feeling that he was being betrayed by the Administration. He would tell friends of how he set out from his office for the White House to let the President know just how bitter he felt, with thoughts of resignation flashing through his mind. On the way he would think of the President's problems: Berlin. Laos. The Congo. Disarmament. The Middle East. The foreign aid bill. Khrushchev. All those burdens. And minute by minute as he approached the office Swidler felt his anger lessen, until by the time the President's door opened, he heard his own voice saying: "What can I do for you, Mr. President?"

Chapter Seven

Yet if there was a problem with the pragmatism of the period, it was that there were simply too many foreign policy problems, too many crises, each crowding the others, demanding to be taken care of in that instant. There was too little time to plan, to think; one could only confront the most immediate problems and get rid of them piecemeal but as quickly as possible, or at least postpone any action. Long-range solutions, thoughtful changes, would have to wait, at least until the second term. And thus it was the irony of the Kennedy Administration that John Kennedy, rationalist, pledged above all to rationality, should continue the most irrational of all major American foreign policies, that policy toward China and the rest of Asia. He was aware of the change in the Communist world, he was aware of the split between the Chinese and the Russians; it was, he realized, something very important. But he would deal with it later.

Early on, when Stevenson and Bowles repeatedly mentioned China to Kennedy, saying that the policy was absurd and that it was urgent to try to change it, Kennedy would smile and agree and say yes, it was a stupid policy, but it would all have to wait. Until the second term. It could not be changed now. There was a limit to the things he could do. Nor was anyone other than Bowles at the State Department eager to look ahead; Rusk believed in the demonology of China, the yellow giant inhaling her neighbors. At State's Policy Planning Council, the one organ of government which was charged with long-range thinking on foreign policy issues, there was no change. George

McGhee, Rusk's hand-picked man there, called in his staff very early in the Administration and made it clear that he wanted no new ideas on China. The Policy Planning Council, he told a meeting of its staff, was a sacrosanct place. It had never been investigated by the Congress, and he did not want it to be. "Now," he said, pausing and looking around the room, "I'm sure no one in this room is in favor of recognizing Red China and now that we're all agreed, we can go ahead . . ." At virtually the same time, at a meeting of the Committee of Principals (the Secretary of Defense, the Secretary of State, the head of the CIA), Jerome Wiesner, the President's Science Adviser, suggested that there be a major review of America's China policy. He was met by total silence. If discussed at all, he learned, China must be discussed in private, not even at the most secret meetings, for fear that the idea that the Administration was even *thinking* of China might somehow leak out to the press and arouse the primitives.

Even at a personnel level there could be no change or re-examination. A number of people had already begun to push for another look into the case of John Paton Davies, Jr., one of the most grievously wronged China officers. The new Administration was well stocked with friends and admirers of Davies' who thought that rehabilitating him was long overdue, and more, would be a sign, albeit a small one, that the new Administration was going to make amends for old wrongs, and also to take a new and more rational look at China and Asia. Harriman, Bowles, Kennan, Schlesinger and McGeorge Bundy all brought up the issue of John Davies at various points (Harriman was the most vociferous, feeling that it was one of the major injustices of the Eisenhower years), but nothing came of their efforts. Rusk, though an old friend of Davies', did not push the idea, and Kennedy was in no rush to take the political heat for what might be a peripheral issue. Not that he thought Davies was a victim of anything but gross misjustice. He told White House aides that he wanted, while in office, to clear two people, J. Robert Oppenheimer and John Paton Davies, and he wanted Charlie Chaplin to perform once more in this country. He got only as far as Oppenheimer, whom he gave the Fermi Award; Davies and Chaplin would have to wait. When the issue of Davies was brought before him he said yes, it was a terrible injustice, but it would have to be postponed until the second term.

All of this was part of one of the great illusions of the country and the Administration in 1961, the belief that the McCarthy period had come and gone without the country paying any real price, that the Administration and the nation could continue without challenging or coming to terms with the political and policy aberrations of that period. If there were problems, the Administration would somehow glide around them, letting time rather than political candor or courage do the healing. It was a belief that if there were scars from the period (and both the Democratic party and the Department of State were deeply scarred), they were by now secret scars, and if there were victims, they were invisible victims. If one looked away and did not talk about them, somehow they would go away. Yet the truth was altogether different: the scars and the victims were real, and the McCarthy period had frozen American policies on China and Asia. The Kennedy Administration would in no way come to terms with the aberrations of those policies; it had not created them, as its advocates pointed out, but it did not undo them, either. It would take no new stands on China (the one Kennedy Administration speech on China, by Roger Hilsman, was not given until after the President's assassination), and Davies was finally cleared by the State Department in the last few months of the *Johnson* Administration.

The failure to come to terms with China and with the McCarthy period was costly, because without looking realistically at China, the Administration could not look realistically at the rest of Southeast Asia. It was failures and frustrations over China which had involved the United States in Vietnam and changed American policy there in 1949; now, because it was not coming to terms with China, the Kennedy Administration would soon expand the Eisenhower Administration policy and commitment in Vietnam. Above all, John Kennedy did not want to revise America's Asia policy (even in October 1963, with Vietnam falling apart, he told television interviewers that he did not want to cut off aid to Vietnam because that might start events comparable to those preceding the fall of China, and that was the last thing he wanted). Thus, because he did not look back on America's China policy, it was easier for him, in 1961, to move forward in Vietnam.

AMERICAN POLICY IN THE IMMEDIATE POSTWAR YEARS HAD BEEN marked by uncertainty and ambivalence. Although the French were allowed to return to Indochina, they were not given the arms they wanted, the transport they said they needed, the economic assistance they sought. The United States was traditionally anticolonial, and anti-Communism as a major issue had not yet arisen, though there were already some disturbing signs; the 1944 Dewey-Roosevelt race had seen the first use of major Republican Red-baiting. In Indochina, American sympathy for nationalism was muted, not so much for fear of Communism as by a kind of inertia, a preoccupation with other areas, an unwillingness to go against an old and threatened ally. But an even-handed approach, if such was the case, obviously worked in favor of the French; a status quo attitude meant they would reassert their control of Indochina, perhaps not as readily as with U.S. aid, but a reassertion nonetheless. What was most striking about this first failure of American policy was that it took place before the Cold War had hardened, before the Iron Curtain descended, at a time when there was still some residual influence from Roosevelt, essentially anticolonial in his viewpoint, and when the Secretary of State was George Catlett Marshall, who was more dubious about an American order, a man of some modesty in his view of what the U.S. role in the world should be, a representative of an older and more modest generation, a pre–American-empire generation. (Thus in 1947 Secretary of the Navy James V. Forrestal, the first of the militant Cold Warriors, would write of Marshall: "The only areas where I am not sure of his equipment are, first, the economic background, and second, awareness of the nature of Communist philosophy. However, he learns fast.") Marshall, as Roosevelt before him, saw a more diverse and pluralistic world, but their successors in the world of national security would not be quite so tolerant of the world's instincts to go its own way. The Cold War was coming and the American empire would be part of it.

Yet even in the years of Secretary of State Marshall, the policy was a particularly unsatisfactory one, and in 1946 he cabled Paris instructions which noted both the injustices of the colonial regime and Ho Chi Minh's Communist associations. The cable concluded: "Frankly we have no solution of the problem to suggest." If the State Department did not apply adequate pressure on the French to negotiate (it applied pressure without leverage, knowing full well the limits of its position), by the same token it did not accept the French tenet that this was a free-world fight against Communism, an idea close to the hearts of the French government. Though the American press did not delve with great insight into the struggle between the Vietminh and the French, it did not accept the assumptions of the French that this was a great Western crusade against Communist hordes. The war was, in fact, viewed as a colonial war.

Two events would change the American perceptions, and equally important in this case, the disposition to perceive nuances. (Many things, after all, were perceptible, if one wanted to see them, but the seeing involved increasing risk. It became better not to see the shades of difference—the fact, for instance, that Ho, although a Communist, might also be primarily Vietnamese and under no orders from Moscow.) The first event was the hardening of the Cold War as tensions in Europe grew; the second was the fall of China, which sent deep psychic shock waves into the American political structure. These events, coupled with the Korean War and the coming of Senator Joseph McCarthy, would markedly change the American perceptions of international Communism, and more important, change the disposition of high political figures to discern subtleties within the Communist world. The spectrum of American political attitudes would sharply narrow, and there would be an enormous two-party consensus of anti-Communism. The only main difference was on how to implement it, one centrist group believing in subtle anti-Communism, using economic aid as a weapon, using nationalism as a weapon; the other believing more in sheer military force. A major party would find itself on the defensive on the charge of having lost a major country to the Communists; and most remarkable of all, the key architect of an entire era of militant anti-Communism, Dean Acheson, would find himself the center of a national political campaign, the charge being not that he was too harsh in his anti-Communism, but that he had been too soft.

It was an unreal time. The events in Europe, the postwar drawing of lines between the Communists and the Western powers, probably had a historical inevitability to it. Two great and uncertain powers were coming to terms with each other, a task made more difficult by their ideological differences (each believed its own myth about itself and its adversary) and by the additional frightening factor of the atomic weapon. Long-range historical analysis will probably show that in those years they were like two blind dinosaurs wrestling in a very small pit. Each thought its own policies basically defensive, and the policies of its adversary basically aggressive. Out of this would come new tensions and new fears for a new world power like the United States. But the China issue, even more emotional, and the coming of the Korean War, would legitimatize the fringe viewpoints, would limit rational discussion and rational political activity. China would help freeze American policy toward Communism. A kind of demonology about a vast part of the world would become enshrined as accepted gospel. One major political party would be too frightened to challenge it, the other delighted to reap the benefits from it. All of this would affect Indochina.

NINETEEN FORTY-SEVEN AND FORTY-EIGHT WERE THE WATERSHED years. The lines of a hard peace were becoming apparent; the foreign ministers' meeting had failed. Czechoslovakia went Communist in a coup, and Foreign Minister Jan Masaryk jumped or was pushed to his death. A few months later the Berlin blockade took place.

In 1947 Marshall had announced the Marshall Plan for European economic recovery, a move which the Soviet Union regarded as a gesture of economic warfare. In May of 1947 the Truman Doctrine was announced. The American policy was now clearly one of containment. The Soviet Union had become an adversary and the national security planners were committed to total and constant conflict. *The Forrestal Diaries*, which provide poignant insights into the thinking of one of the most forceful and persuasive architects of that period, are filled with references, first, to the dangers and vulnerability of the American public and the American press to Communist propaganda, and second, to the old post-Munich fear of the democracies of competition with a totalitarian dictator (in October 1947, during a lunch with Robert Lovett, Walter Bedell Smith, Robert Murphy and General Lucius Clay, Forrestal asked Smith, our ambassador to the USSR, if the Russians wanted war. Smith an-

swered by quoting Stalin as saying the Russians did not want war, "but the
Americans want it even less than we do and that makes our position
stronger"). It would be this fear that the American public might be soft plus
the parallel need to make decisions for it in this most difficult and complex
struggle, which would become a basic tenet of faith for national security planning in this era; a belief that by its nature the competition was simply unfair.
There was a certain irony here; it was as if the national security people in
1947 under Forrestal and Acheson had worked so hard to gear up a campaign
of anti-Communism that some eighteen years later their lineal descendants
could not escape the rhythms they helped create; having once mounted the
tiger's back, they found it difficult to descend.

But they were worried less about descending than about motivating this
country to the threat they perceived. These men were all from the big investment and banking houses, or lawyers for them; they and their class had long
harbored an abiding suspicion not so much of Russia as of *Communism*. Their
tendency was to see the growing American-Soviet conflict in their terms and
definitions, fulfilling their long suspicions. To them it was an ism, not just two
new great powers struggling to find their balance. Thus the men who defined
postwar American policy defined it in ideological, not national terms. Forrestal, who was particularly suspicious of Communist designs, was delighted to
find a brilliant young diplomat-intellectual named George F. Kennan at the
U.S. embassy in Moscow, and Kennan's warnings about Soviet intentions
were immediately seized upon by Forrestal as intellectual and historical evidence of the great struggle ahead. Forrestal made the Kennan reports available to friends throughout Washington, and Kennan's career took off overnight. His reporting was eventually published both in *Foreign Affairs* (under
the byline *X*) and as a book which became the primer of postwar American
diplomacy and was read by almost every college student at every great university, one of the most influential books of an entire generation. Kennan became known as the author of the containment policy, but he had been talking
more about *Russia* than about Communists. He would eventually find his
ideas being exploited, as it were, by his superiors, used as a justification for an
increasing militarization of American foreign policy. He eventually broke
with the other foreign policy architects because he thought they were too ideological and too military-oriented in their policies. He felt that the Communist world was much more nationalist in its origins than it was monolithic, and
that we were creating our own demonology. His opinions in the early fifties
represented the first truly major dissent within a largely consensus view of a
nonconsensus world.

The Kennan experience was not to be the last time that the national security principals would take the intelligence reporting of their own experts and
exploit it out of context, de-emphasizing the issue of nationalism and exploi-

ting the issue of Communism. The same thing happened during the Korean War, when the China experts predicted accurately what China would do, not based on Communist intentions but on *Chinese* history, and the last time would be during the Vietnam war, when again the experts predicted accurately Hanoi's responses to American escalation. But these were distinctions few were interested in twenty years ago; what was needed was a unity of national purpose against the Communists. Nothing else would suffice.

It was an ideological and bipartisan movement; it enjoyed the support of the press, of the churches, of Hollywood. There was stunningly little debate or sophistication of the levels of anti-Communism. It was totally centrist and politically very safe; anything else was politically dangerous. Acheson would note that in 1947, when Truman was discussing his proposals for American aid to Greece and Turkey with congressional leaders,

he stressed that these attacks and pressures upon these countries were not, as surface appearances might suggest, merely due to border rows originating with their neighbors, but were part of a series of Soviet moves, which included stepped-up Communist party activity in Italy, France and Germany. I can see Senator Vandenberg now, suddenly leaning forward on the sofa in the President's office and saying, "If you will say that to the whole country, I will support you." The presentation was put in this way, to the surprise and disapproval of some commentators.

Among those who were surprised was Acheson's boss, George Marshall, who thought the statement a little rash and too broad. He misunderstood the coming need to overlook certain subtleties as the Cold War developed. Thus were Greece and Turkey the first dominoes, and thus did a Democratic Administration offer up as justification for its foreign policies something far closer to what the Republican minority wanted, which reflected the interests and prejudices of the most influential bankers and lawyers. In order to get the job done, the Administration was willing to see the conflict in ideological rather than nationalist terms. The Democrats, feeling themselves vulnerable on this question (liberals often associated with reform causes which were tainted with domestic Communism), were increasingly willing to trim their own sails and accept the assumptions of their more conservative domestic adversaries.

There were the first stirrings of domestic anti-Communism as an issue. Senators elected in 1946 were markedly both more conservative and anti-Communist as a group than the men defeated. In 1946 Richard Nixon had won a California house seat by comparing the voting record of his opponent to that of Vito Marcantonio, the left-wing New York congressman. The smell was in the air. In 1947, even as he was pronouncing the Truman Doctrine in foreign affairs, the President issued an executive order creating a Loyalty Security program which became the opening wedge for the security cases of the following years. Under the Truman decree the Attorney General drew up lists of subversive and front organizations; when questioned by friends who were uneasy about the direction and about this order, Truman replied that he had done it to take the play away from J. Parnell Thomas, who headed the House Un-American Activities Committee. When Truman's friend Clifford Durr, a member of the Federal Communications Commission, asked the President about it, Truman replied that if there were injustices he could modify the order or repeal it.

Rather than combating the irrationality of charges of softness on Communism and subversion, the Truman Administration, sure that it was the lesser of two evils, moved to expropriate the issue, as in a more subtle way it was already doing in foreign affairs. So the issue was legitimized; rather than being the property of the far right, which the centrist Republicans tolerated for obvious political benefits, it had even been picked up by the incumbent Democratic party. The first of the China security cases, that of John Stewart Service, took place in the Truman years. Yet in comparison to what was to come, this was all still quite mild.

In 1948, NORMAL DOMESTIC ISSUES DOMINATED THE PRESIDENTIAL campaign. Foreign policy did not become a major point because the Republicans did not choose to make it one, for a very good reason. They were very much a part of the existing policies, and more important, they did not think they needed the issue. Out of power for sixteen years, they were now confident, indeed overconfident, of victory; they felt themselves rich in Democratic scandals, and they overestimated the degree of unhappiness in the country. They also underestimated Truman as a political figure. He was so different from the graceful, attractive Roosevelt, patrician, the perfect voice for the radio age, generating through the airwaves a marvelous self-assurance that was politically contagious, his confidence becoming the nation's confidence. After four defeats by Roosevelt, the Republicans were glad of the difference. In underestimating the political attractiveness of Truman, jaunty, unpretentious, decisive, his faults so obvious, they failed to realize that these were the faults of the common man and that the voter identified every bit as much with Truman's faults as with his virtues. It was a campaign where the common man versus big-business interests was still a credible one, and Truman was a marvelous symbol of the average American, the little man. Every bit the consummate politician, he made the issue of anti-Communism partly his own, and shrewdly seized the liberal center, isolating both Henry Wallace and Strom Thurmond's Dixiecrats. The Republicans mounted a frail campaign, in substance a me-too campaign, and they lost. They would learn their lesson and become less scrupulous the next time; by 1952, foreign policy and alleged softness of the State Department would be major issues.

None of this had yet affected American policy toward Indochina, mainly because precious little policy toward it existed. What effect the rising domestic issue of anti-Communism had could not be good, but it was not yet bad. Then a major event took place in 1949 which meant that a French victory in Indochina was impossible, and yet, ironically and tragically, also meant that American support of the French was inevitable and that eventual U.S. entry into the war was a real possibility. The event was the fall of China and it was, again, produced by great historical forces outside our control; Barbara Tuchman would write in her book on General Joseph Stilwell in China: "In the end China went her own way as if the Americans had never come."

As World War I had taken a decaying feudal Russian regime and finally destroyed it, bringing on the Communists, so Japan's aggression against China, the first step in what was to become World War II, did the same thing to China: a fledgling semidemocratic government was trying to emerge from a dark and feudal past and was pushed beyond the point of cohesion, the Japanese catching Chiang Kai-shek when he might have moved into the modern era and frightening him back into the past, revealing more his weaknesses than his strengths. The embryo China of Chiang came apart, and the new China would not be that of Chiang and the Western powers, but of Mao Tsetung and the Communists, a powerful modern antifeudal force touching the peasants and the age-old resentment against foreign intrusion, liberating powerful latent feelings in that great country. American policy had been to support Chiang, to try and use him as a force against the Japanese; later, as Chiang's forces began to collapse and the Communists became a more viable force, we tried as best we could to reconcile the irreconcilable and get them to work together. The young American foreign service officers in China warned that we had to come to terms with the failure of Chiang's order. It was a story which would repeat itself in Vietnam: of Chiang, as would later be true for many years of Diem, it would be said that he was too weak to rule and too strong to be overthrown. His forces were corrupt, his generals held title on the basis of nepotism and loyalty, his best troops never fought; faced by mounting terrible pressures, he turned inward to listen to the gentle words of trusted family and sycophants. It was the sign of a dying order.

If the decay and erosion of Chiang's forces were a historical force, so too was the rise of the new China. Produced in reaction to all the political sickness around, it reflected a new and harsh attempt to harness the resources of that huge and unharnessed land. The Communists were rising from the ashes of the old China, and they were in stark contrast to what had existed before. They were powerfully motivated, almost prim and puritan in their attitudes to the world, their view of corruption. On the mainland itself a brilliant group of young State Department officers were reporting the events with great insight, warning of the coming collapse of Chiang. The word "courageous" comes to mind to describe their reporting; but it was not applicable at the time. They were simply doing their job, reporting and forecasting as accurately as they could, which was very accurately indeed.

BY LATE 1944 AND EARLY 1945 IT HAD BECOME CLEAR TO SOME people high in the government and a few people in China that a major struggle was going to take place. Theodore H. White, then a young *Time* reporter, experienced both in American politics and Chinese affairs, had a dark and foreboding sense of the future (as well he might; his own excellent reporting on China would drive him from the Luce publications; White might have his China, but Mr. Luce had *his* China and he was not going to accept White's version). By 1945 White knew that real civil war was inevitable, and when it came, Chiang would collapse and the Communists would win. White realized that this might affect the careers of some of his far-sighted friends in the foreign service when they reported developments as they saw them. He mentioned this to Raymond Ludden, one of the ablest of the young foreign service officers (they were so outstanding that Stilwell had simply taken the best of them from the embassy and attached them to his own staff): "You know something may happen because of this—a lot of people back home aren't going to like the way it's going." And Ludden answered, "The duty of a foreign service officer is to report the truth as he sees it without adjusting it to American domestic considerations." It was, White thought at the time, a wonderful answer. The sheer honesty and integrity of it moved him, but he was also made uneasy by it; wasn't there a touch of innocence too? (There was: Ludden spent the rest of his career regarded by his superiors as being contaminated, and was moved around from different non-Asian post to post.)

What White had begun to foresee in 1945 very quickly came true. As the China tragedy unfolded, many foreign service officers would have their careers destroyed, but of the group, John Paton Davies and John Stewart Service were the most distinguished, and as such they would suffer the most. Younger men a rank or two below them might quietly leave the Asian bureau and go to another area, their careers damaged but not entirely destroyed, but for Davies and Service, it was the end of two brilliant careers. For the country they served it would have even darker implications because they were the best of an era, and the foreign service does not produce that many men of rare excellence. They were the Asian counterparts of George Kennan, Chip Bohlen and Llewellyn Thompson; under normal conditions they might have stayed in, and by the time the Kennedy Administration arrived, become senior State Department officials, perhaps Assistant Secretary of State for Far

Eastern Affairs. They might have been able to provide that rarest of contributions in government: real expertise at a high operational level.

By 1945 and 1946 it was clear that China would become something of a domestic political problem; the first glimmerings of a right-wing pro-Chiang force began to surface as a domestic political threat. The China officers were particularly vulnerable because of charges by Patrick Hurley, who had resigned as ambassador, that they had consciously and deliberately undermined him and that their sympathies were with the Communists. Hurley, unable to come to terms with the failure of his mission, the inability to reconcile the irreconcilable, had turned on his own staff—he was of course extremely influential with the Republican right, and now it seemed as if there were expert testimony against the State Department officials. In particular, the pressure against some of the younger officials increased, motivated by the belief of one faction of the military that it could all be done on the cheap, China might have been saved with air power, without the Americans having to pay any real price (again the divisions would be remarkably similar to those which later followed in Vietnam). The case for air power had always been made by General Claire Chennault, and his side was prosecuted with considerable skill in the inner chambers of the Administration by a young staff officer named Joseph Alsop, well connected in Washington with Harry Hopkins, and a distant cousin of Eleanor Roosevelt. Captain Alsop was intoxicated both by China and his own role in it, and he had turned out to be a very shrewd and forceful bureaucratic politician, playing a crucial role in the decision to recall Stilwell in 1944. (Service remembered years later that Alsop used to show up at the embassy in Chungking and say of Stilwell, "He should be drawn and quartered and flogged." It was amazing, Service mused, when you consider that Stilwell was a four-star general and Alsop a captain, and although Stilwell had the embassy staff working for him, Alsop still outmaneuvered him.) Stilwell was replaced by General Albert Wedemeyer, who with Chennault formed the pro-Chiang group in Asia which had powerful ties with Republicans in this country. Stilwell was called back because he was blunt and open about Chiang's failures; Wedemeyer made it a policy to get along with Chiang, which was fine except that it meant nothing, nothing moved, nothing happened. It was a good relationship, which went only one way, and soon Wedemeyer too began to complain to Marshall about the lack of co-operation he received from the Chinese.

By 1947 the pressure on China began to mount. Giving in to the increasing opposition, Secretary of State Marshall lifted the embargo on shipment of munitions to China in May. When the U.S. Marines withdrew from China at the same time, they turned over their ammunition to the Nationalists. In July, General Wedemeyer was sent on a fact-finding mission, a small gesture to the opposition. In September, John Carter Vincent was relieved as Chief of the

Office of Far Eastern Affairs, to appease the Republicans and to protect him from the rising wave of Republican criticism. The contamination was reaching higher and higher; Vincent had been the foremost bureaucratic protector of the China and Asian experts, and the highest-level advocate at State of the colonized, pleading their case with fervor. (When he sat down to a dinner sometime in the late forties, he found himself introduced by the wife of the Dutch ambassador as "Mr. Vincent—you know, darling, the man who lost Indonesia for us.") Vincent, though a senior State Department official, was sent overseas, but not as an ambassador, because that would require Senate approval. He was replaced by W. Walton Butterworth, a man specifically selected because he had no ties with Asia. He had handled U.S. economic interests in the Iberian Peninsula during the war and thus had unusually good credentials for handling a delicate political issue. Marshall trusted him as a steady and responsible man and seemingly immune from attacks from the right, since his Iberian work had made him a target for considerable abuse from the left, for having worked with those Fascist nations. Butterworth was clean and he intended to stay that way; he knew his orders from Marshall, which were that the United States was not to be dragged into a war in China. "Butterworth," Marshall said to him, "we must not get sucked in. I would need five hundred thousand men to begin with, and it would be just the beginning." Butterworth later remembered Marshall, the set of the face, like the M-G-M lion, adding, "And how would I extricate them?"

Butterworth had been chosen because he was straight and conservative, but it was not the man who was contaminated, it was the issue; as pleasant, somewhat conservative Vincent was almost unemployable at the end of his tour, so was pleasant, conservative Butterworth. In 1950 he would be unable to take any job which required Senate confirmation (by that time Vincent was ticketed to be ambassador to Costa Rica, a seemingly safe spot, but his enemies still lurked, it was too risky, and he ended up in Tangier, where again confirmation was not necessary). When Butterworth took over, Vincent was already being questioned for loyalty. He was saved by family contacts with two powerful senators, Walter George of Georgia and Burnett Maybank of South Carolina, and the fact that Acheson knew him personally and vouched for him. "I know John Carter Vincent and there is no substance to this," Acheson said at the time. (A few years later, when McCarthy brought loyalty charges against Vincent, by then in Switzerland, his defense counsel would have a good deal of difficulty getting Vincent to prepare his case. "He took the attitude that if things had reached this point, if even *he* could be considered a Communist, the hell with it; the world was going to the dogs and there was nothing to be done about it. So all he wanted to do was go off and play golf," recalled his counsel, Bernard Fensterwald, Jr.)

If Acheson felt a sense of personal commitment to Vincent, Dulles was hardly eager to maintain it. These China people, after all, were causing him problems, and there was no doubt about it in his mind, they had been naïve. Once when Dulles was with Vincent, he pulled down a copy of Stalin's *Problems of Leninism,* and asked if Vincent had read it. Vincent said he had not. "If you had read it, you would not have advocated the policies you did in China," Dulles said. So it was that almost as soon as Dulles took over, he made sure Vincent was removed from the profession. A special review board created by Truman and headed by Judge Learned Hand was studying Vincent's loyalty case at the time Dulles took office. Dulles told Judge Hand that his services were not needed, and ruled himself that while there was no "reasonable doubt as to the loyalty" of Vincent, he had demonstrated "a failure to meet the standard which is demanded of a Foreign Service Officer of his experience and responsibility at this critical time. I do not think he can usefully continue to serve the U.S. as a Foreign Service Officer." Dulles offered him the choice of being fired or retiring, and Vincent applied for retirement.

Service was not as lucky, if that is the word, as Vincent. He was not as well connected, and he did not know Acheson personally, which was vital in determining the Secretary's attitude, so when a security board recommended against Service on what were extremely dubious charges, which the courts later overruled, Acheson separated Service by sundown. It was a decision made by the Truman Administration, though there is no reference to it in Acheson's long treatment of the McCarthy period in his *Present at the Creation.*

MUCH OF THE HEAT HAD BEEN MOUNTING EVEN BEFORE CHINA FELL, but when Chiang collapsed completely in 1949 and the Communists took over, the impact really began to be felt. To America, China was a special country, different from other countries. India could have fallen, or an African nation, and the reaction would not have been the same. For the American missionaries loved China; it was, by and large, more exciting than Peoria, had a better life style and did not lack for worthy pagans to be converted; add to that the special quality of China, a great culture, great food, great charm, and the special relationship was cemented. The Chinese were puritanical, clean, hard-working, reverent, cheerful, all the virtues Americans most admired. And so a myth had grown up, a myth not necessarily supported by the facts, of the very special U.S.-China relationship. We helped them and led them, and in turn they loved us. A myth fed by millions of pennies put in thousands of church plates by little children to support the missionaries in their work in this exotic land which was lusting for Christianity. China was good; the Chinese were very different from us, and yet they were like us; what could be at once more romantic, yet safer. The Japanese were bad, more suspicious and could not be trusted. The Chinese were good and could be trusted.

Thus, after a war filled with intensified propaganda, movies showing Japanese raping China, American fighting units saving Chinese, Chinese nurses saving wounded American pilots and, of course, falling in love with them, the fall of China was a shock. What had happened to the Chinese who loved us? It certified, as it were, an even harder peace, it necessitated the reorientation of our demonology (from the wartime of Good Russians, Bad Germans and Good Chinese, Bad Japanese to the postwar period of Good Germans, Bad Russians, Good Japanese, Bad Chinese). It caught this country psychologically unprepared. It was natural for a confused country to look for scapegoats and conspiracies; it was easier than admitting that there were things outside your control and that the world was an imperfect place in which to live.

THE STATE DEPARTMENT KNEW THE CRUNCH WAS COMING; IN AUGUST 1949 it published its White Paper on China, a document designed to show that the fall of China was the fault of Chiang and that the United States had gone as far as an ally could go. What is remarkable about the White Paper in retrospect is the intelligence and quality of the reporting. It was written by very bright young men putting their assessments on the line; in that sense it would be a high-water mark for the Department. From then on young foreign service officers would learn their lessons and hedge their bets, and muddle their reporting.

The first assault on the Department came early in 1950, and it came in the Republican *Saturday Evening Post* in a series of articles which provided that material for the ensuing Republican attacks upon the Department and the Democrats. Rather than trying to hold the line for sane and thoughtful assessments, an important organ like the *Post* was looking for conspiratorial answers, and it had exactly the right author, former Captain Joseph Alsop, now back in America, bitter over our failure to support Chiang and the full Chiang line, anxious to get even. The title of the three-part series was "Why We Lost China," and it was not a serious bit of journalism, a view of a decaying feudal society, but rather a re-creation of the Chennault-Chiang line. It set the tone, though slightly loftier than some successors, for the conspiracy view of the fall of China: the blame was placed on the State Department. The title is worth remembering: *"Why We Lost China."* China was ours, and it was something to lose; it was an assumption which was to haunt foreign policy makers for years to come. Countries were ours, we could lose them; a President was faced with the blackmail of losing a country.

In those days the *Post* was a powerful and respectable if somewhat conservative magazine; the Alsop articles were on the borderline of respectability.

They were not particularly thoughtful or deep, for that is not his style, and they did not charge conspiracy; they only implied it, as is also his style ("The origin of this venture must be traced as far back as the 1930s when General Stilwell was military attaché to China and his political adviser John Davies, was vice-consul there. Among Whittaker Chambers' celebrated pumpkin papers is a Stilwell intelligence report of this period, revealing that even in the 30s he was already strongly prejudiced against the Chinese Nationalists and in favor of the Chinese Communists. Davies' viewpoint was approximately similar. Essentially Stilwell and Davies were victims of the then fashionable liberalism which idyllically pictured the Communists as 'democratic agrarian reformers' . . ."). The Alsop articles emphasized the conspiratorial nature of events; they did not really raise the issue of treason, and they were all right if no one went further.

Someone else would go further. The Alsop articles began the process of legitimizing the issue: twenty years later, both Davies and Service could single out the articles as a key to the turning point; the *Post* articles took the issue from the radical fringe and gave it a respectability where it would be adopted by a Republican party badly in need of issues. It would be valuable to the Republicans, but it would also be material for McCarthyism, and one of the darker chapters of this American century. McCarthy would exploit the charges to such an extent that even Alsop would be appalled. It was one thing to get even with a few of the younger and more foolish boys in the State Department, but it was another when McCarthy went after old and trusted friends like Dean—Dean Acheson. There was a memorable moment in Wisconsin when McCarthy had been making his charges, reckless as usual, against the top boys, and Alsop, a member of the press corps, stood up and angrily challenged him, shouting that this simply was not true; Alsop could vouch for men like Acheson, he knew them personally. Yet as the pressures against the China officers grew, Alsop became outraged and behaved well, testifying in their behalf and working to get lawyers for them, though not behaving so well that he was not unwilling to try some of the same tactics twenty years later when Vietnam arose as an issue, telling people in Washington that dovish reporters were traitors (and of course letting people know that he had behaved well, telling a reporter years later on the subject of Owen Lattimore, a distinguished Sinologist who had been particularly abused in those years: "Lattimore was a perfect fool, of course. It's awful to have to defend fools and knaves, but sometimes you do have to . . . And there *is* a difference between foolishness and treason"). Years later he would sit in Saigon bars and tell reporters there that they were fools, that they would be investigated by congressional committees for their mistakes, but that he would testify in their behalf.

Not everybody made the distinction between foolishness and treason. It

was not a particularly propitious time for distinctions, even those as unsubtle
as this. For it was 1950 now. We had lost China, the Republicans were hungry, the Democrats were clearly on the defensive. Had they been too soft on
the Communists? Too muddled? They would rally now. To make sure that
they did, to take the last measure of flexibility out of an increasingly inflexible
foreign policy, there was the coming of Joseph R. McCarthy, Republican of
Wisconsin. Tail gunner Joe. The accidental demagogue. How quickly he
came and how quickly he disappeared, and how much he left behind. He had
been elected to the Senate in 1946, beating a too liberal and too confident
Bob La Follette in the Republican primary, capitalizing on and vastly exaggerating his own war record in the election. "He and millions of other guys
kept you from talking Japanese . . . Congress needs a tail gunner . . .Amer-
ica needs Fighting Men . . . These Men who fought upon foreign soil to Save
America have earned the right to Serve America in times of peace . . ." He
had gone on to win the general election; he was a good candidate, forceful,
physical, he was part Populist in a state where Populist roots went deep.
There was a sense of shrewdness to him, a sense of the jugular on an issue, yet
also a lack of seriousness, and an attention span of marked limitations. But the
physical energy was there, it was part of him. There was a certain pathos too.
Though he was playing this role, Joe the rugged fighter against all those sinister forces and effete Easterners, there was a feeling that more than anything
he wanted to be accepted as one of the boys, to be good old Joe, to be the
outsider welcomed in.

Four years after he was elected he was looking for an issue; he could not,
after all, keep running against the Japanese. In January 1950 he found it. On
January 7 he had dinner with some friends, all Catholics: William Roberts, an
ex-Marine and a liberal adviser of Drew Pearson; Professor Charles Kraus, a
political science instructor at Georgetown, also an ex-Marine; and Father Edmund Walsh, vice-president of Georgetown, regent of its very conservative
school of foreign service, a man who had been at war with Communism for
three decades and had just written a book on the Communists entitled *Total
Power.* At the dinner in the Colony Restaurant, McCarthy outlined his problem; he needed an issue that would catch attention and excite the voters.
What about the St. Lawrence Seaway, Roberts suggested. No sex appeal, said
McCarthy. Then McCarthy talked about a national pension plan, $100 a
month to everyone over sixty-five. Too utopian, the others argued (the mind
boggles for a moment; suppose he had gone to pension plans instead of Communists. Would history have been different?). After dinner they moved from
the restaurant to Roberts' office. Father Walsh began to talk about his favorite subject, Communism. It was, he said, a major issue, and it would be increasingly important. As Walsh spoke, McCarthy picked him up on it. It
sounded right; he had done a little of it himself once or twice, and the feed-

back had always been good. As McCarthy thought about it, he became excited; it was a real issue, and it could be used. The government, he said, was full of Communists: "The thing to do is hammer away at them." Some of the others warned him that he would have to be careful; he would have to do his homework and be very accurate (later they would all disown him). But it was too late, McCarthy was already on his way.

On February 9, 1950, McCarthy flew into Wheeling, West Virginia, where he made the first of his major Red-baiting Communist-conspiracy charges: "While I cannot take the time to name all the men in the State Department who have been named as members of the Communist party and members of a spy ring, I have here in my hand a list of two hundred and five that were known to the Secretary of State as being members of the Communist party and who, nevertheless, are still working and shaping policy in the State Department . . ." His timing could not have been better; in four months the Korean War began, and because the China experts were already in disrepute, the State Department did not heed their warnings on what American moves might bring the Chinese into the war. The warnings unheeded, the Chinese entered, and the anti-Communist passions against the China experts mounted. It was a Greek thing.

It had really begun. The issues were drawn, false issues; the real issues were postwar fear and uncertainty. Around the country he flew, reckless and audacious, stopping long enough to make a new charge, to exhibit a new list, a good newsworthy press conference at the airport, hail-fellow well met with the reporters, and then on to the next stop, the emptiness of the charge never catching up with him, the American press exploited in its false sense of objectivity (if a high official said something, then it was news, if not fact, and the role of the reporter was to print it straight without commenting, without assaulting the credibility of the incredulous; that was objectivity). It was like a circus; he was always on the move, his figures varied, his work was erratic and sloppy, he seemed to have no genuine interest in any true nature of security. It sometimes seemed as if he too were surprised by the whole thing, how easy it was, how little resistance he met, and so he hurtled forward to newer, larger charges. But if they did not actually stick, and they did not, his charges had an equally damaging effect: they poisoned. Where there was smoke, there must be fire. He wouldn't be saying those things unless there was something to it. And so the contamination remained after the facts, or lack of them, evaporated; long after the specifics had faded into obscurity, the stain remained. Not just of lowly people, but of Acheson, and even Marshall. Even the figure of the stature of Marshall, the most distinguished soldier-servant of an entire era, was stained by it. So was the Democratic party, and the State Department. He knew no bounds—he was attacking the very government officials who thought that they themselves would determine the scope and limits of anti-Communism.

All of which did not displease the Republican party. The real strength of McCarthy was not his own force or brilliance, it was the acquiescence of those who should have known better. Very few performed well in that period. The press was willingly exploited by him; very few stood and fought (even the much-heralded Edward R. Murrow documentary of McCarthy was shown in March 1954 after McCarthy had attacked the Army, four years after the Wheeling speech). It was as if the press too felt guilty, haunted by its past. The Democratic party did not combat McCarthy or the bases of his charges. A few individuals did, but the congressional leadership did not confront him. It decided to let him spend himself, run his course. When he had gone too far, then they would turn on him, which they did—by going too far they meant of course that he had begun to attack the Republicans themselves. So the Democratic party, victim of his charges, did not fight as an institution, nor use its real force, but the Republicans were worse. They welcomed him; the more he assaulted the Democrats, the better for them; the Democrats were on the defensive, and the Republicans were the beneficiaries. He was, in the words of one observer, "like a pig in a minefield for them." "Joe," said John Bricker, one of the more traditional Republican conservatives, a candidate for Vice-President in 1944, "you're a real SOB. But sometimes it's useful to have SOBs around to do the dirty work."

Bricker was not the only one to acquiesce; the awesome Robert Taft, Mr. Integrity, also played the game, and made this the darkest chapter of his career. He would tell McCarthy that if one case did not pan out, he should drop it and try another (part of Taft's odd relationship with McCarthy was personal; McCarthy had done a particularly shrewd job of playing up to Taft's invalid wife, visiting her regularly and ingratiating himself greatly). A young and ambitious senator from California named Richard Nixon would play the role of bridge between McCarthy and the more respectable center of the Republican party. Taft, though, was the fallen idol of that period; in his eagerness to get at the Democrats he had been a willing party to the most reckless kind of political charges, against men whose loyalty was unassailable. Had he stood and confronted the recklessness of McCarthy's charges, the Republican party would have stood with him. Of him the epitaph for this chapter in his life was that he knew better but the temptation was too great.

What rises must converge; what goes up quickly comes down even more quickly. Eisenhower allowed McCarthy to destroy himself. By 1954 McCarthy was finished, he had gone too far, he had long since been repudiated by his early advisers from that Colony dinner, he had shed himself of advisers who urged restraint. He was censured by the Senate, he began to drink heavily; by 1957 he was dead; but the fears he left behind would live long after him. He had contributed a word to the language, "McCarthyism"; and he had, by his presence and by the fears that he had found in the country and exploited, helped damage two major organs of government, the State Department and the Democratic party. He had also made the foreign policy of the United States even more rigid, both then and later. The country would in particular pay the price for this in Vietnam. The legacy of it all was poison.

THE CONFLUENCE AND THE MIXING OF THESE THREE EVENTS, THE FALL of China, the rise of McCarthy and the outbreak of the Korean War, would have a profound effect on American domestic politics, and consequently an equally significant effect on foreign policy. The Democratic Administration was on the defensive; a country could not be lost without serious political consequences; each new Administration became increasingly susceptible to blackmail from any small oligarchy which proclaimed itself anti-Communist. The anti-Communist rhetoric of the Truman Doctrine had come rather easily in 1947, now even more; succeeding U.S. governments would find themselves prisoners of that rhetoric. There would be, and this was a subtle thing, a disposition to see the world somewhat differently, and this was particularly true in Indochina. There was now less of a disposition to see the French war as a colonial war, more of a disposition to see it as a Western war against the Communists, a war which sought to bestow freedom upon Vietnam. Bao Dai, the emperor the Japanese had installed in 1940, became a respectable figure in late 1949. The element of nationalism which Ho Chi Minh held began to diminish in State Department accounts, and with the coming of the Korean War, in journalistic accounts as well. There was an even greater disposition to see Communism as a universal force; the war in Korea and the war in Indochina were linked as one (Eisenhower said in his inaugural in January 1953 that the French soldier in Indochina and the American soldier in Korea were fighting the same thing). Similarly Acheson, testifying at the MacArthur hearings, and wanting to hold off Republican criticism against our allies, would make this same point. By prior arrangement Senator Lyndon Johnson asked: "Mr. Secretary, some Republicans are attacking our allies for not helping us in the Korean War. Mr. Secretary, can you comment here where our allies are helping us elsewhere? I mean Indochina."

"That's an excellent point," Acheson answered. "The French have been fighting that battle since World War II." This was a reverse of his earlier position, which was that it was a stupid colonial war but there was no alternative to it. Thus the policies of the 1950s in Asia were poisoned.

Chapter Eight

THE ESSENCE OF GOOD FOREIGN POLICY IS CONSTANT RE-EX-amination. The world changes, and both domestic perceptions of the world and domestic perceptions of national political possibilities change. It was one thing to base a policy in Southeast Asia on total anti-Communism in the early 1950s when the Korean War was being fought and when the French Indochina war was still at its height, when there was, on the surface at least, some evidence of a Communist monolith, and when the United States at home was becoming locked into the harshest of the McCarthy tensions. But it was another thing to accept these policies quite so casually in 1961 (although McCarthy was gone and the atmosphere in which the policies had been set had changed, the policies remained much the same), when both the world and the United States were very different. By 1961 the schism in the Communist world was clearly apparent: Khrushchev had removed his technicians and engineers from China.

It was seven years since the United States Senate had censured McCarthy. Not only was he gone but many of his colleagues of that era, Kem, Knowland, Jenner, McCarran—his fellow travelers all—were gone too, and the new Republicans who entered the Senate in the late fifties and early sixties would tend to be far more moderate and modern men. But the Kennedy Administration did not re-evaluate any of the Eisenhower conceptions in Asia (conceptions which Dulles had tailored carefully to the disposition of the McCarthy group in the Senate); if anything, the Kennedy people would set out to upgrade and modernize the means of carrying out those policies. Later, as their policies floundered in Vietnam, they would lash out in frustration at their own personnel there, at the reporters, at the incompetence of the client government. What they did not realize was that the problem was not just American personnel, which was often incompetent, nor the governmental reporting, which was highly dishonest, nor the client government, which was just as bad as its worst critics claimed—the real problem was the failure to reexamine the assumptions of the era, particularly in Southeast Asia. There was no real attempt, when the new Administration came in, to analyze Ho Chi Minh's position in terms of the Vietnamese people and in terms of the larger Communist world, to establish what Diem represented, to determine whether the domino theory was in fact valid. Each time the question of the domino theory was sent to intelligence experts for evaluation, they would send back answers which reflected their doubts about its validity, but the highest level of government left the domino theory alone. It was as if, by questioning it, they might have revealed its emptiness, and would then have been forced to act on their new discovery. In fact, the President's own public statements on Laos and on Vietnam, right through to the time of the assassination, reflected if not his endorsement of the domino theory, then his belief that he could not yet challenge it, and by his failure to challenge it, the necessity to go along with it.

So it was not surprising that the Administration's attitude toward Southeast Asia in general and Vietnam in particular remained being activist, aggressive, hard-line anti-Communism. If the Eisenhower Administration followed an anti-Communism dependent on the nuclear threat and bombastic words, the Kennedy Administration—liberal, modern, lacking above all in self-doubt, with a high proportion of academics—would be pragmatic and assertive in its anti-Communism. At almost the same moment that the Kennedy Administration was coming into office, Khrushchev had given a major speech giving legitimacy to wars of national liberation. The Kennedy Administration immediately interpreted this as a challenge (years later very high Soviet officials would tell their counterparts in the Kennedy Administration that it was all a mistake, the speech had been aimed not at the Americans, but at the Chinese), and suddenly the stopping of guerrilla warfare became a great fad. High officials were inveighed to study Mao and Lin Piao. The President's personal interest in fighting guerrillas was well publicized, and the reading and writing of books on antiguerrilla warfare was encouraged ("I urge all officers and men of the Marine Corps to read and digest this fine work . . ." he wrote in the introduction to a particularly mediocre collection of articles on the subject).

The fascination with guerrilla warfare reflected the men and the era: aggressive, self-confident men ready to play their role, believing in themselves, in their careers, in their right to make decisions here and overseas, supremely confident in what they represented in terms of excellence. The nation was still locked in an endless struggle with the Communists: Europe was stabilized, and there would be no border-crossing wars after Korea, so the new theater of activity would have to be guerrilla warfare. Everyone joined in. Robert Kennedy, afraid that America was growing soft, afraid that we did not have ideas that caught the imagination of the young of the world, was one of the leaders, but others were equally part of the faddism. General Maxwell Taylor, the President's military adviser, was a regular member of the counterinsurgency meetings and was regarded with some awe whenever he spoke, having once parachuted into France. Roger Hilsman's fighting behind the lines in Burma received no small amount of attention, and it was known that Kennedy had questioned him at length about his days as a guerrilla (both of them oblivious to the fact that Hilsman had been a commando, not a guerrilla. He had not been part of any indigenous political organization).

A remarkable hubris permeated this entire time. Nine years earlier Denis Brogan had written: "Probably the only people who have the historical sense of inevitable victory are the Americans." Never had that statement seemed more true; the Kennedy group regarded the Eisenhower people as having shrunk from the challenge set before them. Walt Rostow, Bundy's deputy, thought the old Administration had overlooked the possibilities in the underdeveloped world, the rich potential for conflict and thus a rich potential for victory. It was not surprising, for the Eisenhower people were men of the past who had never been too strong on ideas; one could not imagine Sherman Adams inspiring the youth of Indonesia or even being concerned about it. But this new Administration understood ideas and understood the historic link-up between our traditions and those in the underveloped world; we too were heirs to a great revolution, we too had fought a colonial power. Were we much richer than they, and more technological? No problem, no gap in outlook, we would use our technology *for* them. Common cause with transistors (inherent in all this was the assumption that the more we gave them of our technology, the less they would notice the gap between their life style and ours). Rostow in particular was fascinated by the possibility of television sets in the thatch hutches of the world, believing that somehow this could be the breakthrough. This did not mean that we did not understand the hard poisonous core of the enemy, that we were too weak and democratic to combat it. "The scavengers of revolution" Rostow called those guerrilla leaders, like Ho and Che, whom he did not approve of.

All of this helped send the Kennedy Administration into dizzying heights of antiguerrilla activity and discussion; instead of looking behind them, the Kennedy people were looking ahead, ready for a new and more subtle kind of conflict. The other side, Rostow's scavengers of revolution, would soon be met by the new American breed, a romantic group indeed, the U.S. Army Special Forces. They were all uncommon men, extraordinary physical specimens and intellectual Ph.D.s swinging from trees, speaking Russian and Chinese, eating snake meat and other fauna at night, springing counterambushes on unwary Asian ambushers who had read Mao and Giap, but not Hilsman and Rostow. It was all going to be very exciting, and even better, great gains would be made at little cost.

In October 1961 the entire White House press corps was transported to Fort Bragg to watch a special demonstration put on by Kennedy's favored Special Forces (after his death the special warfare school would become the John F. Kennedy Special Warfare School), and it turned into a real whiz-bang day. There were ambushes, counterambushes and demonstrations in snake-meat eating, all topped off by a Buck Rogers show: a soldier with a rocket on his back who flew over water to land on the other side. It was quite a show, and it was only as they were leaving Fort Bragg that Francis Lara, the Agence France-Presse correspondent who had covered the Indochina war, sidled over to his friend Tom Wicker of the *New York Times*. "All of this looks very impressive, doesn't it?" he said. Wicker allowed as how it did. "Funny," Lara said, "none of it worked for us when we tried it in 1951."

THE FIRST WARNING ON VIETNAM HAD BEEN SOUNDED IN JANUARY 1961, by one of the most unusual members of the United States government. It was as if Brigadier General Edward Lansdale had been invented with the Kennedy Administration in mind. He was a former advertising man, a former Air Force officer, a CIA agent now, a man deeply interested in doing things in Asia the right way, the modern way. He had risen to fame within the government as an antibureaucratic figure of no small dimension, and State, Defense and the CIA were well stocked with his enemies. In the early fifties he had helped Ramón Magsaysay defeat the Huk rebellion in the Philippines, and had become the prototype of the Good American overseas as opposed to the Bad American; he was against big bumbling U.S. government programs run by insensitive, boastful, bureaucratic, materialistic racists, and for small indigenous programs run by folksy, modest American country boys who knew the local mores, culture and language. He was the Good American because in part his own experience had convinced him that Americans were, in fact, good, and that the American experience and American ideals were valid elsewhere. He would write of the early Philippine experience:

One day, while driving on a back road in Pampanga province, I came upon a political meeting in a town plaza. A Huk political officer was haranguing the crowd, enumerating their troubles with crops, debts, and share in life, blaming all ills on "American imperialism." Impetuously, I got out of the jeep from where I had parked it at the edge of the crowd, climbed up on its hood, and when the speaker had paused for breath I shouted, "What's the matter? Didn't you ever have an American friend?" The startled crowd turned around and saw an American in uniform standing up on his jeep. I had a flash of sobering second thoughts. I kicked myself mentally for giving in to such an impulse among hundreds of people living in hostile territory. But the people immediately put me at ease, they grinned and called hello. The speaker and many of the townspeople clustered around me, naming Americans they had known and liked and asking if I was acquainted with them. I teased them with the reminder that these folks they had known were the "American imperialists" they had been denouncing. They assured me that not a single one of them was. It was a long time before I could get away from the gossipy friendliness.

The Philippine experiment had worked and a national best seller had been written about him called *The Ugly American*; Colonel Lansdale was thinly disguised as Colonel Hillandale. (If his role in *The Ugly American* was to show how to be a Good American, some people thought he starred involuntarily in another and far more chilling book of the era, Graham Greene's *The Quiet American*, in which this new Good American, a nice idealistic young man anxious to do good in an older society to save that society from Communism in spite of itself, is a well-intentioned but singularly dangerous man.) Lansdale was the classic Good Guy, modern, just what Kennedy was looking for. He had, what better mark of merit, been languishing out of the action during the latter years of the Eisenhower Administration. He was the median man who understood the new kind of war, and had helped defeat the Communists in a similar (if far different and simpler and far more embryonic) insurgency in the Philippines. He embodied what America had turned into more than anyone realized: the corrosion of the traditional anticolonial instinct had become hard-line anti-Communism. He was the Cold War version of the Good Guy, the American who did understand the local ambience and the local nationalism. For he was a CIA agent, and not just an intelligence officer, he was an operational functional man, a man of programs and a man who was there to manipulate. The real question for men like Lansdale, who allegedly knew and loved Asians, was no longer the pure question of what was good for the local people, but what was good for the United States of America and perhaps acceptable locally. The Asians could have nationalism, but nationalism on *our* terms: nationalism without revolution, or revolution which we would run for them—revolution, it turned out, without revolution.

His view of the recent history of Vietnam was comforting, and managed to minimize the role of the Vietminh and the effect of a prolonged war of independence. The Vietminh had less popular support than they imagined; the population had stayed away from both sides, and the French at the end were pictured as fighting for Vietnamese independence:

Vietnamese told me of their history. In brief, these high-spirited people had been under Chinese rule for a thousand years and under French rule for a hundred years, with nearly every one of those years marked by struggles for independence. At the end of World War II, the Vietnamese had declared their independence from the feeble hold of Vichy French administrators. The Communists under Ho Chi Minh were participants and set about eliminating their political rivals in a bloodbath which the survivors never forgot nor forgave, even though the world at large remained ignorant of it. The Communists held the power when the French Army returned in 1946. Fighting broke out between the Vietnamese and the French, and Ho took his forces to the hills to enter into "protracted conflict" with the French, who captured and held the cities and towns.

The majority of the Vietnamese, still hungering for independence, had no side to join. They were opposed to both the Communist Vietminh and the French. As the war raged around their families and homes, they gave lip service to whichever side was locally dominant, in order to stay alive. When French Union forces ravaged the countryside trying to destroy the Vietminh guerrillas, the resentful people joined the Vietminh to get revenge. Later, when the French increased measures of Vietnamese self-rule and promised an independent Vietnam, nationalists started joining the fight against the Vietminh in ever-mounting numbers. By the time I visited Vietnam in 1953, millions of Vietnamese had taken a definite stand against the Vietminh.

In 1954, in the last dying days of the French presence in Indochina, the Lansdale group had run around Hanoi putting sugar in the gas tanks of Vietminh trucks, a gesture of no small amount of mindlessness. The war was over, an Asian nationalist army had just defeated a powerful Western nation for its independence, and here was the top American expert on guerrilla war employing the pettiest kind of sabotage—mosquito bites, they were, at a historic moment. In Saigon, Lansdale helped sponsor Ngo Dinh Diem in his search for a Vietnamese Magsaysay, and played a key role in convincing a very dubious U.S. government that Diem was worth the risk. He taught Diem some lessons in modern leadership, lessons to which Diem always carefully and faithfully paid lip service. He taught Diem how to campaign against Bao Dai, and Diem, ever the worthy student, insisted upon receiving 98 percent of the vote. Lansdale also sponsored other little gestures which seemed somehow to belong more to the past than the present: hiring soothsayers—symbols of the suspicious feudal Vietnamese past—to predict bad years ahead for Ho Chi Minh, and good years for Ngo Dinh Diem.

Lansdale would become in effect an antirevolutionary figure in Vietnam. There was to be much talk of revolution and of land reform, but the American presence effectively stopped any kind of social change. None of this affected Lansdale's reputation in his own somewhat uncritical country; the legend of him as a semi-underground figure continued to grow, the unconventional man for the unconventional war. He himself stayed in the background, and the legend seemed to thrive on his lack of visibility. In person he sometimes appeared to be a curiously disappointing, almost simplistic man, especially in contrast to the flashing verbalism of others of the Kennedy era. He was a man who talked vague platitudes just one step away from the chamber of commerce. You had to get with the folks, he would say, it was better to let the baby learn to walk on its own rather than try and teach him too much. Part of it was his natural style, part of it was his belief that it did not help to seem too bright. His intimates could watch him speak in private with considerable insight, and then, with the arrival of an outsider, switch to his low-key, folksy approach. Friends thought part of his success (such as it was) in the Philippines and in Vietnam came about because he had always been careful not to try and overpower the Asians he was dealing with; he was the rarest of Americans overseas, a listener.

At the tail end of the Eisenhower years he returned to Vietnam. Having angered powerful figures at Defense, he had experienced trouble in finding a sponsor, but he had finally found a friend in the government who let him make the trip. He found to his dismay, as reporters there were also discovering in 1960, that the new version of the Vietminh, named the Vietcong, were near victory by fighting guerrilla style in the countryside while the American military mission continued to train the Vietnamese army for a Korean-style invasion. President Diem was almost totally isolated from his former friends and allies, and increasingly dependent on his egomaniacal brother, Ngo Dinh Nhu; Diem and the American ambassador, Elbridge Durbrow, virtually did not speak to each other.

Lansdale wrote a lengthy and very pessimistic report critical of both the Americans and of Diem, but particularly of the former. This was important, because Lansdale was one of the men who had invented Diem, and you do not knock your own invention, but more significant, it was indicative of the Lansdale approach and that of other Good Americans, those sympathetic to Asians. They did not feel that it was deeply rooted historic forces pitted against us which were causing the problems, but rather a failure to supply the right people and the right techniques. Implicit in the Lansdale position was the belief that if the right Americans influenced Diem in the right way, Diem would respond. It was a form of limited can-doism. He recommended a new antibureaucratic team in the Lansdale mold: "Our U.S. Team in Vietnam should have a hard core of experienced Americans who know and really like Asians, dedicated people who are willing to risk their lives for the ideals of freedom; and who will try to influence and guide the Vietnamese towards U.S. policy objectives with the warm friendship and affection which our close alliance deserves. We should break the rules of personnel assignment, if necessary, to get such U.S. military and civilians to Vietnam." What Lansdale was recommending was, of course, Lansdale.

The Lansdale report was picked up by a friend, who read it in the final days of the Eisenhower Administration and passed it on to the new Administration. Within days it landed with Rostow, who had been looking for something precisely like this. (Lansdale's effect on Rostow is interesting: in 1954 Lansdale had gone around pouring sugar in the Vietminh gas tanks; in 1962, at the height of the Cuban missile crisis, when the clock was ticking off the minutes and seconds of a massive immediate confrontation, Rostow was going around Washington talking about sabotage against the Cubans, putting sugar in their oil refineries, which would halt their production and transportation . . .) Rostow urged Kennedy to read it, but the President seemed reluctant, he always had too little time. Was it really that important? he asked. Rostow insisted. Kennedy flipped through the pages. "Walt, this is going to be the worst one yet," Rostow recalled him saying, and then adding, "Get to work on this." Which Rostow quickly did.

As for Lansdale, he had made a favorable impression on the President; this was the kind of man Kennedy needed. Shortly afterward Lansdale found himself awakened by a presidential call on a Sunday morning and hastily summoned to a special breakfast meeting at the White House. As he walked in, Kennedy greeted him graciously and said somewhat casually, pointing to Rusk, "Has the Secretary here mentioned that I wanted you to be ambassador to Vietnam?" Lansdale, caught by surprise, mumbled that it was a great honor and a marvelous opportunity. He was deeply touched, and even more surprised, for it was the first he heard of the idea, and also, as it happened, the last. The appointment never came through; Lansdale later thought he had been blocked by Rusk, though he also realized that Defense was less than anxious to have him in Vietnam. He would not return for five more years, and by then antiguerrilla warfare was a thing of the past. Lansdale seemed a particularly futile and failed figure; the author of how to fight guerrilla wars the right way being part of a huge American mission which used massive bombing and artillery fire against Vietnamese villages.

Lansdale's more specific proposals were channeled through to Roswell Gilpatric, the Deputy Secretary for Defense (significantly, Vietnam was already being treated as a military problem). The suggestions were essentially antibureaucratic, with Lansdale opposing what he assumed was the inevitable Americanization of the operation, the creation of a mission based on American bureaucratic needs rather than on Vietnamese realities. In early 1961 Gilpatric was scheduled to head a task force which would oversee the operation in Washington, and Lansdale was to be its chief in Saigon; there would be a minimal increase in personnel, a few specialists in the Lansdale mold, operating of course under Lansdale. These recommendations, eventually made in late April, were soon pushed aside by bureaucratic needs; as soon as the game was opened, each competing agency began to beg for more men. It was like amoebae multiplying: every agency wanted to double itself; one would become two, two would become four. Under the revised recommendations the military mission, then totaling 685 men, would be increased to around 3,000 men in the training group; other agencies would grow proportionately.

The recommendations were brought before Kennedy, who greeted them with the greatest distaste. He was by no means anxious to send that many more Americans to Vietnam; he had just staggered through the Bay of Pigs, and if he was wary of being caught looking soft in a Cold War confrontation, he was also wary of jumping into another confrontation. Years later Gilpatric would remember, more than anything else, Kennedy's reluctance to add anything at that time to Vietnam, particularly men. Even the small number the President finally approved was agreed to as grudgingly as possible. There would be no 3,000-men military group, although on April 29 the President did approve a 400-man Special Forces group for training missions; they were, after all, his special favorites, and they were supposed to be experts on this kind of war. But essentially his attitude was to remain conventional about it; instead of the Vietnam mission being taken over by antibureaucratic specialists, as Lansdale wanted, it would be run by regular career State and Defense officials in the conventional way. There would be no specialists and no Lansdale there.

THE FIRST MOVE TOWARD CONTINUING THE COMMITMENT HAD, however, been taken earlier without the Administration's even being aware of how fateful a step it was taking. It was done in an attempt to avoid a real decision, but it would have long-range repercussions. This was the switching of ambassadors to Vietnam on March 15, 1961, when Elbridge Durbrow was replaced by Frederick E. Nolting, Jr. The Durbrow tour had not been a happy one; he had watched the beginning of the Vietcong pressure against Diem, and simultaneously the accelerated estrangement of Diem from friends, allies and reality. Their discussions had become longer and longer monologues, and then, as Durbrow insisted on interrupting and telling Diem how poorly things were going, their meetings became more and more infrequent. Durbrow was, if anything, a very conservative figure, but he had been told to be candid with Diem, and that candor was now becoming unpleasant; toward the end Durbrow suggested that Ngo Dinh Nhu be sent into exile as an ambassador to a foreign country. His pleas to Diem about governmental reform, about improving the quality of commanders, about broadening the base of the government, resembled nothing so much as the pleas of General Stilwell to Chiang Kai-shek to do the same thing, and they were met with the same lack of appreciation. By the end of his tour, Durbrow was virtually *persona non grata*. When the Administration decided to replace him, it did not change the policy; it did not doubt the accuracy of what Durbrow had been reporting, but it could not afford a serious re-evaluation of the policy, dependent as it was on Diem with all his faults. So the change in policy would go from being honest with Diem to being nice to him, hoping that somehow this would create a new confidence and mutuality of trust. To inspire this confidence the Administration picked Frederick Nolting.

Fritz to his friends, who were numerous. A proper man of proper credentials. He had been a college teacher at one time, he came from a good Virginia family, and he had a good war record, Navy of course. He was part of that special group of relatively conservative Democrats from Virginia who play a major role in the foreign service and control much of its apparatus from the inside, who regard the foreign service as a gentleman's calling, and feel they produce a particularly fine brand of gentleman. He had compiled a very good record, this hard-working, straight, somewhat unquestioning man. He was steady and solid, and he had been sponsored by everyone he had ever worked for. Before coming to Vietnam, he had been at NATO, where he was head of the political section, with rank of minister, thus the first deputy to the NATO ambassador. Vietnam was his first ambassadorial post; he had never been to Asia before, and his ideas of Communism had all been fashioned through his European experience. It was axiomatic that those who knew most about Asian nationalism were not allowed to serve in their chosen area (they were contaminated by their past), and if they had not left the foreign service they had at least switched to another desk. Thus the price of the past was sending Europeanists like Nolting to Asia; the new ambassador, knowing nothing of Asia, soon asked for and received as his deputy chief of mission his prime deputy from NATO, William Trueheart, who had not been to Asia either. Trueheart was Nolting's closest friend; they had been together at the University of Virginia, and it was Trueheart who had talked Nolting into joining the foreign service.

Coming from NATO, Nolting seemed to symbolize the continuity of an American belief that it was American policies and American arms which had held the line against the Communists; that we, with our determination, could in fact make our decisions and then implant them in foreign countries; that the world welcomed our protection and our values; and that NATO and Vietnam were one and the same thing—despite, of course, a war of independence fought in Vietnam against a NATO power. ("NATO," Nolting said shortly after his arrival, "was formed as a barrier against overt attack and it has held up for thirteen years. We haven't found a barrier yet against covert aggression. If we can find such a technique, we'll have bottled up the Communists on another front.")

No one in the Kennedy group knew very much about him; it was an appointment which seemed to slip by them at the time. Only one man seemed to be aware of its potential import, and that was Chester Bowles. He had al-

ready been arguing for a major change of policy toward Asia, and neutralization of Vietnam; he alone at that point seemed to see the inevitability of a
larger conflict, and the dangers of continued support of the Diem regime. As
Undersecretary of State he was responsible for most of the ambassadorial assignments, and he believed strongly that you changed policy by changing personnel. He learned of the Nolting appointment at the last minute and tried to
intercede against it. He felt that Nolting was being pushed by the traditionalists and the hard-liners in the Department, which was not surprising, considering the NATO origins. Bowles had come up with what he thought was a
particularly good man for Vietnam, a foreign service officer named Kenneth
Todd Young who had served there in the past and had maintained a reputation for being unusually sensitive to indigenous problems and nationalism. He
had felt so frustrated that he had left the State Department during the Dulles
years in despair over American policies. Young had returned with the coming
of the Kennedy Administration and was assigned to a task force on Laos,
where he caught Bowles's attention. At that point in early March, Young was
ticketed to be ambassador to Thailand. Bowles, however, was even then convinced that Vietnam rather than Thailand was going to be the main problem
in Southeast Asia, and he wanted his most sensitive man there. Besides, he
thought that Young was politically more in tune with Kennedy than Nolting
was, and he thought this would be very important for an ambassador whose
country was teetering on the brink of survival.

So, after both men had been approved for their respective posts, Nolting
for Saigon, Young for Bangkok, Bowles maneuvered to have them switched.
He talked with Young about it and found him less than eager to accept the
proposition because Young did not want to knock Nolting out of his assigned
post, but more important, because of reservations he had about working with
the Ngo family. He told Bowles he wanted to sleep on it.

Young thought long and hard that night about all the problems. Since the
Vietnamese President was an old friend, Young knew a good deal about
Diem's abilities and liabilities, and he was also a reluctant authority on Mr.
and Mrs. Nhu. He thought they were nothing less than poison, and that nothing could be accomplished in Vietnam as long as they were part of the government. They would have to be split and split quickly from Diem if there
were to be any chance of success. One could not hope to be there and work
against the Nhus if they were still in the country; each night they would destroy each day's work. The new ambassador would have to establish a relationship of total frankness with Diem, a relationship based totally on mutual
professional needs, and not marked by the personal ups and downs of the
past. The next day Young went to Bowles and said that he was willing to give
it a try. Soon there was a phone call from Lansdale representing Gilpatric
saying that Young was to rush over to meetings of the Vietnam Task Force.

Young was puzzled: Why was he needed? "Don't you know?" Lansdale asked. "The President's agreed for you to go to Saigon." So it appeared to go through, and then once again it was stopped, the protocol problems were too complicated and in addition, Nolting had reacted badly, finding the switch insulting, which in a way it was. So Ken Young went to Thailand, where he performed very well under far less pressure than if he had been in Vietnam. From Bangkok he watched Saigon with mounting horror as it became clear from the start that all demands for reform would be dropped and the Nhus would become the dominant figures in the government. And Fritz Nolting in Saigon would find himself under such tension that it finally drove him not just from Vietnam but from the foreign service as well.

Nolting was, above all, a man of the surface. If Diem could have designed an ambassador for his country and his regime, he would have come up with Fritz Nolting. He was a fine example of the foreign service officer who commits himself only to the upper level of the host government and the society, not to the country itself. If you get along with the government and pass on its version of reality, then you are doing your job. It was not his job to ask questions; it was his job to get things done. There was no doubt that Nolting believed in what he was doing and saying. He had looked and listened, and had decided that Diem was the best anti-Communist around (there was, of course, no one else; Diem had systematically removed all other opposition—Communist, neutralist, anti-Communist). People who worried about the regime's lack of appeal, of the growing isolation of the regime, were, in his words, taking their eyes off the ball. Stopping Communism was having your eyes on the ball. If civilians in Saigon discussed growing political resentment and repression he would assure all, including Washington, that he knew nothing of it, which was true, of course; no Vietnamese other than the family trusted him. He had forbidden members of the embassy staff to talk to any Vietnamese dissidents; if one did not hear it, it did not exist; if one did not see it, it never happened.

Duty instead of intelligence motivated Nolting. He was there to hold the line, not to question it. His policy was to build credit with Diem by agreeing to everything Diem wanted, hoping that one day he could cash in the due bills. It necessitated reassuring Diem constantly, by always giving in, always nodding affirmatively. There was a curious irony in this, because Americans always warned that Asians tended to tell you what you wanted to hear; now we had an American ambassador who told Asians what *they* wanted to hear. But the special significance of Fritz Nolting was that in the very choice of him, and his decision that yes, we could make it with Diem, we were binding ourselves into an old and dying commitment, without really coming to terms with what it meant.

THE TIGHTENING OF THE BIND OF THE COMMITMENT WOULD CONTINUE shortly. In late April 1961 Kennedy, deciding against increasing the American mission substantially, thought he would boost Diem's confidence by intangible instead of tangible aid. The means would be the Vice-President of the United States, Lyndon B. Johnson, then somewhat underemployed. Though Johnson was scheduled to visit a number of Asian countries, the key stop would be Vietnam. Curiously enough, it was not a stop that the Vice-President particularly wanted to make. Just as a year later he would balk when the President asked him to make a symbolic trip to Berlin—feeling somehow that he was being used, and that his career (and possibly his life) might be damaged—Johnson was so unenthusiastic about going to Saigon that Kennedy had to coax him into it. "Don't worry, Lyndon," he said. "If anything happens to you, Sam Rayburn and I will give you the biggest funeral Austin, Texas, ever saw."

The trip came nonetheless at an opportune time for Johnson, who was at the lowest point in his career, being neither a Kennedy political insider nor a Kennedy intellectual. To intimates he would occasionally talk about how his chauffeur had advised him not to leave the Senate to become Vice-President, muttering that he wished he had had that chauffeur with him in Los Angeles when Kennedy made the offer. With others, of course, he went to great pains to show that he was deeply involved in the inner decisions of the Administration, that he was the real insider. One day in early 1961 Russell Baker, then a Hill reporter for the *New York Times*, who knew Johnson well, had been coming out of the Senate when he was literally grabbed by Johnson ("*You*, I've been looking for *you*") and pulled into his office. Baker then listened to an hour-and-a-half harangue about Washington, about how busy Lyndon Johnson was, how well things were going. There were these rumors going around that he wasn't on the inside; well, Jackie had said to him just the other night at dinner as she put her hand on his, "Lyndon, you won't desert us, will you?" They wanted him. It was pure Johnson, rich and larger than life, made more wonderful by the fact that if Baker did not believe it all, at least for the moment Johnson did. And in the middle of it, after some forty minutes, Baker noticed Johnson scribble something on a piece of paper; then he pushed a buzzer. A secretary came in, took the paper, disappeared and returned a few minutes later, handing the paper back to Johnson. He looked at it and crumpled it. Then the harangue continued for another fifty minutes. Finally, exhausted by this performance, Baker left and on the way he passed a friend named David Barnett, also a journalist. They nodded and went their separate ways, and the next day when Barnett ran into Baker, he asked whether Baker knew what Johnson had written on that slip of paper. No, Baker admitted, he did not know. " 'Who is this I'm talking to?' " said Barnett.

Now, on the trip all that energy with which he had overwhelmed Washington in his earlier capacity as Senate Majority Leader, the most influential Democrat in Washington, burst loose. He was away from Washington, he had something to do, barnstorming, finding that all people were alike, that he could reach out by being with them, hunkering down with them, discovering what goals they had in common (eradication of disease, food for all, access to electric power). There he was, campaigning among the villagers, the more rural the better, riding in bullock carts, inviting a Pakistani camel driver to the United States. Johnson loved it all ("There is no doubt the villagers liked it," wrote John Kenneth Galbraith, recently appointed ambassador to India, "and their smiles will show in the photographs").

As a gesture of the President's concern, Johnson had brought with him Kennedy's sister and brother-in-law, Jean and Stephen Smith. Being a good campaigner, Lyndon did not neglect to show their symbolic value of traditional American concern for Asians. At every stop they were introduced, their importance heralded, their own positions magnified with typical Johnsonian exaggeration: Jean Smith, who started out being "the President's lovely little sister" soon became his "tiny little baby sister," and then his "itsy-bitsy little baby sister." And Steve Smith, perhaps the only member of the family who was *not* in the government, was introduced as "the President's brother-in-law, one of the closest members of his family," then as "a State Department official," then as "an important State Department official," and finally as "a man who held one of the most important and most sensitive jobs in the State Department."

Johnson had been told to inquire in Vietnam whether Diem wanted troops, but it was not a particularly meaningful query; neither State nor Defense had given much thought to the question of sending troops to Vietnam other than as a symbol, the way American troops stood in West Berlin as a symbol of American intent; these would, if they were accepted, be troops to stand and be seen rather than fight. By their presence they would show the Communists that America was determined to resist; this would give the Communists something to think about. If that did not work there would be other gestures, gestures as much to the American people as to the Communists. Johnson met with Diem and found that Diem was in no rush to have Caucasian troops on his soil. Diem knew, first, that his people would resent seeing any successor to the French there and that it might be counterproductive, and second, that it would be a sign of *personal* weakness as far as the population was concerned if he accepted American troops too readily. He was already too dependent on the Americans as it was.

Johnson was impressed by Diem; yet the entire episode became an example of the gamesmanship of the period. In his final report to the President, Johnson wrote that Diem "is a complex figure beset by many problems. He has admirable qualities, but he is remote from the people, is surrounded by persons less admirable than he . . ." All in all it was a reasonably fair analysis, particularly for that time, when no one tied the problems Diem faced to the problems created by the French Indochina war. But if that was Johnson's private view (which was not much different from what American reporters were writing at the time), what he was saying in public was quite different. In public Diem was hailed as "the Winston Churchill of Southeast Asia." It was a comparison which boggled the mind of everyone except members of the Ngo family, who found it only fitting and proper. On the next leg of the trip Stan Karnow, who was then working for the *Saturday Evening Post*, asked Johnson if he really believed that about Diem. "Shit, man," Johnson answered, "he's the only boy we got out there." (Later there would be some criticism in the Eastern press of his flamboyance in general and his lauding of Diem in particular, the impression that once again the Texas cowboy had overdone it in his exuberance, that he had, unlike the Kennedys, no subtlety, that he did not know foreign affairs. Privately Johnson was quite bitter about that, feeling that he had acted and spouted off under orders, and he would tell aides that he was angry about the charges that he had cut the cards. "Hell," he said, explaining that he was under orders, "they don't even know I took a marked deck out there with me.")

Johnson reported to the President that Communism must be and could be stopped in Southeast Asia ("The battle against Communism must be joined in Southeast Asia with strength and determination to achieve success there") and that even Vietnam could be saved ("if we move quickly and wisely. We must have a coordination of purpose in our country team, diplomatic and military. The most important thing is imaginative, creative American management of our military aid program"). It was a fine example of the hardening American view of the time, looking at Vietnam through the prism of American experience, American needs and American capacities. American purpose with *Americans* doing the right things could affect the destinies of these people. The Vietnamese were secondary, a small and unimportant people waiting to be told what to do by wiser, more subtle foreigners. If it was one more example of the can-do syndrome, it was similarly to stand as an example of the dangers of the game of commitment. Kennedy had sent Johnson to Vietnam as a sign of good will, as a means of reassuring a weak and unsatisfactory government of his commitment; the lasting effect, however, was not on the client state but on the proprietor, and in this case, most importantly, on the messenger himself, Lyndon Johnson; *he* had given *our* word. It not only committed the Kennedy Administration more deeply to Diem and Vietnam, attached Washington a little more firmly to the tar baby of Saigon, escalated the rhetoric, but it committed the person of Lyndon Johnson. To him, a man's word was important. He himself was now committed both to the war and to Diem personally.

There was a special irony to the game of commitment as it was played with South Vietnam, great verbal reassurance in lieu of real military support, for that was exactly how South Vietnam had been created, an attempt to strengthen a military-political position on the cheap. Instead of intervening directly in the French Indochina war, the United States had decided that the benefits were not worth the risks; then, later, after the Geneva Agreement in 1954, the United States had tried to get the same end result, an anti-Communist nation on the border of Asian Communism, again with others doing the real work for us.

THE AMERICANS WHO WERE WARY OF THE FRENCH COLONIAL WAR had seen their reservations pushed aside by the fall of China in 1949 and the coming of increased domestic political pressures against any similar signs of weakness. Gradually the war had in our eyes gone from being a colonial war, to a war fought by the West against international Communism. At the same time the Americans began to underwrite it financially in 1950. But this brought little change. The Vietminh were scarcely affected by Washington's will and dollars, and by 1954 the Americans were more committed to the cause in Indochina than an exhausted France. At that time the question arose of whether to intervene on behalf of the French—only American intervention could keep the French in. President Eisenhower decided against it, saying in effect that Vietnam was not worth the military commitment. The creation of South Vietnam, a fragile country in which few had any real hopes, followed Geneva, more as an afterthought than anything else.

Four years of American aid, half a billion dollars a year, had had little effect on the war. It raised the level of violence, and for a time it raised the hopes of the French military, at precisely the same time that French popular support was dwindling. It had once been a centrist political war in France, but by 1954 both extremes, the left and the right, were gaining in the National Assembly. After eight years it was a dying cause; moral views of the struggle began to follow battlefield failure. The pressure from the French for overt American military aid had been growing in 1953, and it soon became more intense. The French command, frustrated by the hit-and-run engagements with an adversary who was all-too-often invisible, had in early 1954 devised a trap which it intended to spring on an unsuspecting enemy. Since the Vietnamese, as General Marcel Le Carpentier had said, did not have colonels and generals and would not understand a sophisticated war, it would be easy to fool them. The idea was to use a French garrison as bait at an outpost in the highlands, have the Vietminh seize on it for a set-piece battle and mass their forces around it. Then when the Vietminh forces were massed, the French would strike, crush the enemy who had so long eluded them, and gain a major political and psychological victory, just as peace talks were starting in Geneva. The name of the post where the trap was to be sprung was Dienbienphu.

With the kind of arrogance that Western generals could still retain after eight years of fighting a great infantry like the Vietminh, the French built their positions in the valley and left the high ground to the Vietminh, a move which violated the first cardinal rule of warfare: always take the high ground. An American officer who visited the site just before the battle noticed this and asked what would happen if the Vietminh had artillery. Ah, he was assured by a French officer, they had no artillery, and even if they did, they would not know how to use it. But they did have artillery and they did know how to use it. On the first night of the battle the French artillery commander, shouting "It is all my fault, it is all my fault," committed suicide by throwing himself on a grenade. Westerners always learned the hard way in Indochina; respect for the enemy always came when it was too late.

French domestic support had been ebbing daily and this finished it; the garrison, however, was trapped, and day by day as the Vietminh pounded the French defenders, pressure grew for the Americans to enter the war and save the gallant French. Significantly, as was to happen eleven years later, the original idea was only partial intervention, not really to take over the French war and supplant the French on the ground, but simply to rescue the garrison. Use a little air power. Bombing alone would do it. The rationale was made as limited as possible, and again, as would happen later, it was given under crisis-panic conditions. Naturally, the French found allies in the American government anxious to involve this country in their war, a war which over the last three years was no longer seen in the United States as a colonial war, but now, more conveniently, as part of a global struggle against Communism.

In the high levels of the American government there were at least two people who wanted to go and bomb the Vietminh and rescue the garrison. The first was Admiral Arthur W. Radford, Chairman of the Joint Chiefs of Staff, who had become a zealot of air power. Radford was one of the architects, perhaps the chief architect, of the Eisenhower Administration's New Look policies: the bigger bang for the buck, and a belief that air power, and carrier-based air power with nuclear weapons or perhaps simply the threat of nuclear weapons, would determine the global balance. A new and glistening and yet *inexpensive* Pax Americana—what could be better? The other Chiefs thought that it had all come about when Eisenhower made his famed campaign promise to go to Korea. He and Dulles had picked up Radford in Honolulu, where the admiral made the case for the new policies which would bring air power to its zenith at a cut-rate price and which would spare American lives; the kind of dirty war that was being fought in Korea would never have to be fought again, particularly in Asia, where the hordes and hordes of yellow people made a good old-fashioned land war untenable. Under the New Look the budget would be cut, but we would be as powerful, perhaps more powerful than ever. Dulles was of course enthusiastic, it fit in with his view of the U.S. role in the world, particularly of playing a greater role in Asia.

So the New Look became policy; much to the chagrin of the United States Army, West Point's most illustrious graduate was cutting back the Army's roles and missions. Radford, a man of force, conviction and forthrightness, was then a Chief whose military policies had become Administration political policies; they were, some thought, more theoretical than realistic. Now with the garrison trapped at Dienbienphu, Radford was ready; it was his first chance to test the New Look, and he was eager to go. One good solid air strike at the attackers, and that would do it. There was, in his presentation, very little emphasis on what would happen if the air strikes did not work. Like many high Air Force supporters and converts, he believed in the invincibility of his weapon; Army officers were rarely so convinced.

The second figure who ostensibly wanted to go in was Secretary of State John Foster Dulles. The word "ostensibly" is used here because while there was no doubt about Radford's real desire, there is some doubt about Dulles'; the public and the private Dulleses were not always the same thing. He was a moralist, if anything even more Wilsonian than Acheson, a true hard-liner. Despite all the campaign oratory of Democratic failures, he believed that Acheson had succeeded in Europe but that he had failed in two areas: holding the line in Asia and dealing with the Congress. In order to seek an accommodation with the Congress he would, in fact, appease it by opening the doors of his Department to the security people, offering his Asian experts to them, small concessions really, firing John Paton Davies as a minor human sacrifice, though he knew that Davies was above reproach.

Eager to mold history to his whims, Dulles was quick to talk about the evils of Communism, particularly Asian Communism, particularly the evil Chinese Communists. Bedell Smith, his Undersecretary, would tell friends, "Dulles is still dreaming his fancy about reactivating the civil war in China." Yet there was sometimes a degree of flexibility to him in private which contrasted with the soaring arrogant moralism of his public statements (questioned about this, he would smile and tell friends that he had not been the highest paid corporation counsel in New York for nothing; he knew how and when to deal). Just how much he wanted to go into Indochina is still in doubt; perhaps he was more interested in making the case for going in, and thus put the burden for the failure to intervene on allies and the Congress. This would be a division of responsibility (as Acheson had not shared responsibility on China). They did, after all, have to live up to their rhetoric.

Eisenhower himself was more than ambivalent. He had been elected as a peace candidate, for one thing, and he was particularly reluctant to get into a land war in Asia; he had been elected in large part because of national fatigue with just such an enterprise. While considerable evidence exists that some members of his Administration wanted to go in, there is very little evidence that Eisenhower shared their view and used the full force of his personality and the weight of his office to convince legislative and bureaucratic doubters. If anything, the reverse is true: he activated all those around him, let them make their case (their case being destructive to the idea of intervention), and sat like a judge.

When Eisenhower was running for President in 1952, he had moved first to consolidate his position within his newly adopted political party and establish rapport with the more conservative Republicans headed by Taft. Taft was embittered by the Korean War, not because he thought it was the wrong war, but because he felt that Truman had usurped the powers of the Congress. During the 1952 campaign Eisenhower had again and again pledged that he would consult with the legislative branch, that he would return the Congress to its proper place in decision making. In addition, he had been extremely critical of the war itself. "If there must be war," he said during the campaign, "let it be Asians against Asians with our support on the side of freedom." So Eisenhower was committed to genuine consultations and he was also against land wars in Asia. At the same time, he belonged to a party which had come to power exploiting the issue of anti-Communism and the failure to hold the line against the Communists, particularly in Asia. Now, with pressure mounting for intervention in Vietnam, he was caught in something of a dilemma. The party lines were already being drawn; perhaps Red-baiting would be a two-way street. (Thruston Morton, then an Assistant Secretary of State for Congressional Relations, would recall coming out of a House session at the time and overhearing Franklin Roosevelt, Jr., say to James Richards, "The damn Republicans blamed us for losing China and now we can blame them for losing Southeast Asia.")

If early in 1954 Eisenhower had any doubts about the attitude of the Congress toward American intervention, they disappeared in February 1954 when the Department of Defense announced that forty B-26 fighter-bombers and two hundred *American* technicians were being sent to Indochina. This was the first American aid in personnel, and if it was a trial balloon, it worked handily; the Congressional reaction was swift and ferocious. The Administration, somewhat surprised by the vehemence of the response, immediately announced that the technicians would be withdrawn by June 12. But even this was considered too late. Mike Mansfield rose in the Senate to ask whether it was true, as rumored, that the United States planned to send two combat divisions to Indochina. He was assured by Majority Leader William Knowland, speaking for the Administration, that it had no such intention. And Senator

Richard Russell warned that this was a mistake which could bring us piece-meal into the war. The Administration quickly backed down, and in backing down, it showed that it realized just how war-weary the country was.

Nevertheless, the pressure from the French continued to build. With the garrison at Dienbienphu obviously trapped, there was an emotional quality to the crisis, a desire to save the boys. Admiral Radford was sympathetic. Dulles seemed sympathetic. Vice-President Nixon was said to favor intervention. Eisenhower was reported to be ambivalent, not revealing his own feelings. On April 3, 1954, at Eisenhower's suggestion, Dulles met with the Congressional leadership, a group which included Minority Leader Lyndon B. Johnson and the ranking Democrat on the Armed Services Committee, Richard Russell. Significantly, though the idea for the meeting was Eisenhower's, he was not present; he did not put his own feelings and prestige on the line that day. Rather he let his Secretary of State make the case, even though Dulles had far less influence with the Democrats because of partisan statements in the past.

As it turned out, though, Dulles was in effect putting his office on the line; he himself did not make the case. It was Admiral Radford who carried the ball, a man who neither represented a national American position, nor for that matter even an Administration position, nor necessarily the position of the American military. The purpose of the meeting soon became clear: the Administration wanted a congressional resolution to permit the President to use naval and air power in Indochina, particularly a massive air strike to save the garrison at Dienbienphu. Radford made a strong and forceful presentation: the situation was perilous. If Indochina went, then Southeast Asia would go. We would be moved back to Hawaii. The Navy, he assured the senators, was ready to go, two hundred planes were on the carriers *Essex* and *Boxer*.

The senators began to question Radford. Would this be an act of war? Yes, we would be in the war. What would happen if the first air strike did not succeed in relieving the garrison? We would follow it up. What about ground forces? Radford gave an ambivalent answer.

Senator Knowland told his colleagues that he was on board, which was not surprising, since he was a certified hawk, a member of the China Lobby, fond of ending meetings by giving the Nationalist toast, "Back to the mainland." Not everyone else was so euphoric or enthusiastic. Senator Earle Clements of Kentucky asked Radford if all the other Chiefs were on board. Radford said they were not.

"How many of them agree with you?" Radford was asked.

"None," he answered.

"How do you account for that?"

"I have spent more time in the Far East than any of them and I understand the situation better." (Which was not true; all the other Chiefs had spent comparable time in Asia.)

At this point Johnson took over. He had talked with Russell earlier—at this stage of his career he was still quite dependent on Russell for private leadership and advice—and had found that Russell was appalled by the whole thing. Russell had in fact been wary of the gradual expansion of the American empire since World War II. He did not think our power was limitless, and he was worried that our designs would take us beyond our reach, that we would enter places where we were not wanted. Indochina, he thought, was the symbol of it all and might turn into an enormous trap. Now Johnson was disturbed by the implications of the Radford appeal for a variety of reasons. He doubted that the necessary resources existed in a war-weary country which had just come out of Korea, and he did not want the blame for refusing to go to war placed on him and the Democratic leadership in Congress. If Eisenhower went for a congressional resolution, then Johnson would be right smack on the spot, which was exactly where he did not want to be—he was always uneasy about being out front. He certainly did not want the Democrats to be blamed for losing Indochina.

The Democrats, he told Dulles, had been blamed for the Korean War and for having gone in virtually alone without significant allies. Knowland himself, Johnson pointed out, had criticized the Democrats for supplying 90 percent of the men and money in Korea. The patriotism of Democratic officials had been questioned. He was touched now to be considered so worthy and so good a patriot as to be requested to get on board. But first he had some questions, because he did not want to relive the unhappy recent past. What allies did they have who would put up sizable amounts of men for Indochina? Had Dulles consulted with any allies? No, said the Secretary, he had not.

By the time the two-hour meeting was over, Johnson had exposed the frailty of the Administration's position. (This may have been exactly what Eisenhower wanted, to expose his case and have the Congress itself pick apart the weaknesses. Eisenhower was a subtle man, and no fool, though in pursuit of his objectives he did not like to be thought of as brilliant; people of brilliance, he thought, were distrusted. It was not by chance that he had not been present; let Dulles make the case.) The military were far from unanimous about whether to undertake the air strike. In addition, the United States might have to go it alone if it entered a ground war. Dulles was told to sign up allies, though it was known that Anthony Eden was dubious. Thus the burden, which the Administration had ever so gently been trying to shift to the Congress, had now been ever so gently shifted back, if not to the Administration, at least to the British, who were known to be unenthusiastic.

No one, it seemed, was eager to take real responsibility. The President had again used the Congress as a sounding board and had quickly sensed deep reservations. But as Dienbienphu still held, the pressure did not go away.

Again, however, a key individual would help prevent the United States from stumbling into this war which no one wanted, but which the rhetoric seemed to necessitate. This time it was the Army Chief of Staff, General Matthew B. Ridgway. He was an imposing figure, Big Matt Ridgway, hard and flinty. Organizer of the first American airborne division, the 82nd, he led the first American airborne into Sicily, and then jumped again in Normandy, and was the first commander of the 8th Airborne Corps in 1945. When the end of the war was near, he had been chosen to lead all airborne troops in the scheduled invasion of Japan. He had thus ended the war as a general with an enormous reputation, yet his career still very much in bloom, the top commander of elite units. He had been brought to the Pentagon right before the Korean War and was considered a possible Chief of Staff, and when the Korean War broke out, he had been told to keep an eye on General Walton Walker's Eighth Army and be ready to go if anything happened to Walker. When Walker was killed in an accident, he took over the Eighth Army. He made a point of being a dramatic figure, aware that the men were always watching. Even as commander of the Eighth Army in Korea, he wore his paratrooper's jump harness, a reminder to a trooper that he had been airborne, and on that harness his ever-present two grenades. Almost the first thing he did when he took over the Korean command was symbolic: he stopped all troops from riding in closed jeeps because he felt it gave them a false sense of warmth and security and thus made them more vulnerable to the enemy and the cold. When Truman finally fired MacArthur, Ridgway replaced him, and had systematically pulled the U.S. forces back together, and made his reputation even more enviable, both to soldier and civilian. He was by 1954 the most prestigious American still in uniform, an old-fashioned, hard-nosed general of great simplicity and directness.

When Ridgway left for Korea in December 1950, he had been Deputy Chief of Staff for over a year. During that period the State Department had on several occasions asked for increased military aid for the French, and each time Ridgway had bitterly opposed it. To him, it was like throwing money down a rathole, and a bad rathole at that. He did not have much sympathy for the French cause; after all, they had never sent their own draftees to Indochina—just mercenaries, as he called them. Part of his reasoning was very old-fashioned: he thought we were supposed to be an anticolonial power and this was a colonial war, absolutely contrary to the traditions we said we espoused. If Radford believed that politically we had to stop Red China from sweeping over the entire peninsula, then Ridgway was a man of different political convictions; he thought the region was important but not vital, and he believed in diversity; he did not think that the Communists could long hold control over such diverse peoples. They might try, he thought, but it would not work well. It could not be done. He was, in effect, a military extension of Kennan.

Now, in April 1954, with the pressure mounting, and knowing that bombing would lead to ground troops, Ridgway was very uneasy. He knew Radford wanted in, and he suspected Dulles wanted to test the New Look. Ridgway had always thought the New Look both foolish and dangerous. Wars were settled on the ground, and on the ground the losses were always borne by his people, U.S. Army foot soldiers and Marines. It was his job to protect his own men. So he sent an Army survey team to Indochina to determine the requirements for fighting a ground war there. What he wanted was the basic needs and logistics of it. He sent signalmen, medical men, engineers, logistics experts. What were the port facilities, the rail facilities, the road facilities? What was the climate like, which were the endemic diseases? How many men were needed?

The answers were chilling: minimal, five divisions and up to ten divisions if we wanted to clear out the enemy (as opposed to six divisions in Korea), plus fifty-five engineering battalions, between 500,000 and 1,000,000 men, plus enormous construction costs. The country had nothing in the way of port facilities, railroads and highways, telephone lines. We would have to start virtually from scratch, at a tremendous cost. The United States would have to demand greater mobilization than in Korea, draft calls of 100,000 a month. Nor would the war be as easy as Korea, where the South Koreans had been an asset to the troops in the rear guard. It was more than likely that in this political war the population would help the Vietminh (Ridgway was thus willing to make this crucial distinction that everyone glossed over in 1965). Instead of being like the Korean War it would really be more like a larger and more costly version of the Philippine insurrection, a prolonged guerrilla war, native against Caucasian, which lasted from 1899 to 1913 and which had been politically very messy. Nor did the Army permit the White House the luxury of thinking that we could get by only with air power. Radford's plans for an air strike were contingent on seizure of China's Hainan Island, which seemed to guard the Tonkin Gulf, because the Navy did not want to enter the gulf with its carriers and then have Chinese airbases right behind them. But if we captured Hainan, the Chinese would come across with everything they had; then it was not likely to remain a small war very long.

Thus the Ridgway report, which no one had ordered the Chief of Staff to initiate, but Ridgway felt he owed it both to the men he commanded and to the country he served. His conclusion was not that the United States should not intervene, but he outlined very specifically the heavy price required. On April 26 the Geneva Conference opened. On May 7 Dienbienphu fell. On May 11 Ridgway briefed the Secretary of the Army and the Secretary of Defense on his survey team's report. Shortly afterward he briefed the President. Eisenhower did not say much at the time, Ridgway recalled, just listened and asked a few questions. But the impact was formidable. Eisenhower was a professional soldier and an expert in logistics; the implications were obvious. "The idea of intervening," Ridgway would write, "was abandoned." Later Eisenhower himself wrote of his doubts of a Radford air strike; it would be an act of war which might easily fail and then leave the United States in a position of having intervened and failed.

Even after Dienbienphu fell there would be other efforts by Dulles to arrange for American intervention. But the high point of it had passed, the emotional pitch had been reached when there were white men trapped in that garrison, about to be overrun by yellow men. The pressure thereafter would be more abstract. Dulles still talked of going in, and there were even letters from Eisenhower to the British suggesting that common cause be made. The British, more realistic about their resources, wanted no part of it. These subsequent attempts to go in were sincere, and to what degree they represented an attempt to share responsibility for not going is difficult to determine. But Eisenhower was in no mood for unilateral action, and in 1954 his manner of decision making contrasted sharply with that of Lyndon Johnson some eleven years later. Whereas Eisenhower genuinely consulted the Congress, Johnson paid lip service to real consultation and manipulated the Congress. Eisenhower's Chief of Staff had made a tough-minded, detailed estimate of what the cost of the war would be; eleven years later an all-out effort was made by almost everyone concerned to avoid determining and forecasting what the reality of intervention meant. In 1954 the advice of allies was genuinely sought; in 1965 the United States felt itself so powerful that it did not need allies, except as a means of showing more flags and gaining moral legitimacy for the U.S. cause. Eisenhower took the projected costs of a land war to his budget people with startling results; Johnson and McNamara would carefully shield accurate troop projections not only from the press and the Congress but from their own budgetary experts. The illusion of air-power advocates and their political allies that bombing could be separated from combat troops, which was allowed to exist in 1965, was demolished in 1954 by both Ridgway and Eisenhower.

Thanks to Eisenhower and Ridgway, a war that no one wanted was allowed to slip by; responsibility was very pleasantly divided among the Administration, the military, the Congress and the allies. Eisenhower himself deserved the credit, but Ridgway made it easier by giving the President a base of expertise and old-fashioned integrity, a general less than eager for a bad war. Later Ridgway would write that of all the things he had done in his career—the battles fought, units commanded, medals won, honors accorded—there was nothing he was prouder of than helping to keep us from intervening in Indochina. The country was very lucky in having him there; it would not always be so lucky. Eleven years later he watched with mounting horror how we were doing all the things he had managed to prevent. In 1965 he would serve as a source for doubters like columnist Walter Lippmann and Senator Fulbright, but repeated efforts to make him go public with his reservations failed. He did not feel he could go against the men like Westmoreland he had once led.

If Ridgway was not consulted by President Johnson in 1965, perhaps it was because his views were already known. But in February 1968, when the great controversy raged over whether to limit intervention, he was called in by the President to discuss the war. And there was one moment which reflected the simplicity and toughness of mind which he and others had exhibited in 1954, and the fuzziness of the 1965 decision making. Ridgway was sitting talking with Johnson and Vice-President Humphrey when the phone rang. When Johnson picked it up, Ridgway turned to Humphrey and said there was one thing about the war which puzzled him.

"What's that?" Humphrey asked.

"I have never known what the mission for General Westmoreland was," Ridgway said.

"That's a good question," said Humphrey. "Ask the President."

But when Johnson returned, he immediately got into one of his long monologues about his problems, pressures from every side, and the question was never asked.

BUT NOT GOING INTO FRENCH INDOCHINA IN 1954 WAS NOT THE SAME thing as getting out. We decided that we would stay and supplant the French after the Geneva Agreements had been signed in July, calling for a division of the country. Ho Chi Minh established himself in the North, so Dulles decided that the rest of the country, below the 17th parallel, would be a Western bastion against the Communists—exactly, we thought, what the South Vietnamese would want: our protection, our freedoms. There was arrogance, idealism and naïveté to it. We assumed that as Western Europe had welcomed our presence there, the South Vietnamese would want us in their country, despite the fact that we had been on the wrong side of a long and bitter colonial war. We had assumed that we could sit on the sidelines without helping the nationalists in their fight for freedom; we could help the colonial power and somehow not pay a heavy price. Yet this illusion existed; we were different, we were not a colonial power. Dienbienphu, Dulles said at the time, "is a blessing in disguise. Now we enter Vietnam without the taint of colonialism."

Nothing would hold Dulles back; there was an absolute belief in our cause, our innocence and worthiness, also a belief that it was politically better to be in than to be out. It was mostly Dulles' initiative. We would start in South Vietnam, Dulles decided, by sending a couple of hundred advisers there. The foreign aid bill at that time contained a provision which allowed the President to switch 10 percent from one aid program to another. This could be done without congressional approval, so at Dulles' urging, Eisenhower took 10 percent of the money set aside for other countries and ticketed it to Vietnam. In addition, the decision to send advisers was made in late September, when Congress was out of session, but as a courtesy the President and the Secretary of State agreed that the congressional leaders should be notified.

Thruston Morton was assigned to inform Senator Russell of the Armed Services Committee that the President would be sending an estimated 200 men to South Vietnam as well as funding the country. Russell answered that it was a mistake, it would not stay at 200, it would eventually go to 20,000 and perhaps one day even as high as 200,000.

Morton answered that he doubted this, and that the President intended to go ahead; they were just advisers, anyway.

"I think this is the greatest mistake this country's ever made," Russell said. "I could not be more opposed to it."

Morton again answered that the President and the Secretary were determined to go ahead.

"I know," said Russell, "he mentioned that he might do it. Tell him, then, that I think it is a terrible mistake but that if he does it I will never raise my voice." Thus intervention in South Vietnam was sanctioned.

Nothing, however, could have been more naïve than Dulles' statement that the United States would now enter Vietnam without a trace of colonialism, for the sides were already drawn. The Vietminh were supremely confident that they could gain ascendancy in the South either through elections or through subversion and guerrilla warfare. They were a modern force, and the one opposing them in the South was feudal. By now they were the heroes of their people: they had driven out the French and stirred the powerful feelings of nationalism in the country. During the war the Vietminh had done more than expel the French. They had taken Vietnamese society, which under colonial rule had been so fragmented and distrustful, where only loyalty to family counted, and given it a broader cause and meaning, until that which bound them together was more powerful than that which divided them. This, then, had made them a nation in the true sense.

In the South the reverse was true. The men who formed the government in the South were men whom Westerners would deal with, men who were safe precisely because they had done nothing for their country during this war; they had either fought side by side with the French or profiteered on the war, or, as in the case of Ngo Dinh Diem, stayed outside the country, unable to choose between the two sides. In the South the old feudal order still existed, soon to be preserved by the conservative force of American aid; in the South that which divided the various political groups from one another was more powerful than that which bound them together. The tradition of the old Vietnam had been loyalty to family alone; symbolically the Ngo Dinh Diem government was a family government, and by the time of his downfall Diem trusted only his family. From the very start, one Vietnam lived in the past and the other in the present.

This was reflected in the leadership. The North was led by a man who had expelled the foreigners, the South by a man who had been installed by foreigners. Ho Chi Minh had been in exile during the worst years of French colonialism because he could not speak openly and remain in Vietnam; Diem had gone into exile during the most passionate war of liberation because he did not approve of the Vietminh. Ho did not need foreign aid to hold power, his base had deep roots in the peasant society which had driven out foreigners. Diem could not have survived for a week without foreign aid; he was an American creation which fit American political needs and desires, not Vietnamese ones. By Vietnamese standards, there was little legitimacy; Diem was a Catholic in a Buddhist country, a Central Vietnamese in the South, but most important of all, he was a mandarin, a member of the feudal aristocracy in a country swept by revolution.

Yet if he did not meet Vietnamese demands, in 1954 Diem clearly met American needs. He was a devout anti-Communist, yet he was also anti-French and thus technically a nationalist, and he often gave speeches about social reform which soothed American liberal consciences. If the acts of his regime were basically authoritarian, his speeches were not, and in conversations he seemed difficult but not unreasonable. His behavior was proper, correct; a relentless Christian, he did not chase after women the way Sukarno did. Where a true Asian radical or nationalist might have been rude or condescending to American envoys or, worse, to visiting congressmen, Diem was quite the opposite, solicitous, serious, responsible. To an America still in the midst of the McCarthy period he was the ideal representative for a foreign establishment, rigidly and vehemently anti-Communist for the conservatives, yet apparently concerned about social welfare for the liberals, who, on the defensive about the loss of China and about McCarthy's attacks, could rally round Diem without offending their consciences. The perfect coalition candidate. "The kind of Asian we can live with," William O. Douglas, one of Diem's early liberal sponsors, had said when he recommended Diem to Senator Mike Mansfield, who would also become an early supporter.

Diem was a complicated figure, deeply religious, a monk really, who believed completely in his own rectitude; thus if he was correct in his attitudes, it was the obligation of the population to honor and obey him. He was a man of the past, neither Asian nor Western, better than the dying order he was chosen to protect, isolated, rigidly moral, unable to come to terms with a world which had passed him by.

Only a few Americans believed in him from the beginning. Indeed the entire commitment to South Vietnam was almost offhand: there was nothing else to be done there, so why not try it. But from the very start his failings, the righteousness, the rigidity, the dependence on his family were already self-evident. The first American ambassador to Vietnam, J. Lawton Collins, thought him totally incapable, and Edgar Faure, the French premier, told the French National Assembly that "Diem is not only incapable, but mad." Only Lansdale really fought for Diem ("Most of those with whom I talked felt that Diem was a great patriot, probably the best of all the nationalists still living, with an outstanding record as a wise and able administrator; some even asserted that he was far better known among his countrymen than was Ho Chi Minh," Lansdale would later write, in describing how he first heard of Diem). It was Lansdale who sold Diem to his CIA boss, Allen Dulles, and thus to John Foster Dulles, and it was Lansdale who helped guide Diem through early struggles against the religious sects, which solidified Washington's support.

It was a shaky basis on which to found a policy, but it did not seem like a major decision at the time, nor a major policy. The attitude was essentially that there was little to lose, a certain small investment in American money, virtually no investment in American lives. In the beginning there was little illusion about the legitimacy of the government, or the state, or its chances for survival. That illusion would come gradually, later on, for a commitment is a subtle thing, with a life of its own and a rhythm of its own. It may, as in the case of South Vietnam, begin as something desperately frail, when the chances for survival are negligible. For a while, oxygen is breathed in, mouth-to-mouth, at great effort but little cost, and then the very people who have been administering the oxygen, desperate to keep the commitment alive (not because they believe in any hopeful prognosis, but because they do not want to be charged with failing to try and give first aid), look up one day and find that there is indeed a faint pulse, that the patient is more alive than dead. But at this point they are not relieved of their responsibility; instead, for the first time the commitment really begins, and now they are charged with keeping it alive. It is a responsibility, it is real. Its death would mean genuine political repercussions.

In 1954, right after Geneva, no one really believed there was such a thing as South Vietnam. But Diem made it through the next few years largely because Hanoi did not pose a challenge and was busy securing its own base. Despite French and British protestations, Dulles encouraged Diem in his instinct not to hold the requisite elections, and slowly the idea of viability began to grow. Like water turning into ice, the illusion crystallized and became a reality, not because that which existed in South Vietnam was real, but because it became real in powerful men's minds. Thus, what had never truly existed and was so terribly frail became firm, hard. A real country with a real constitution.

An army dressed in fine, tight-fitting uniforms, and officers with lots of med-als. A supreme court. A courageous President. Articles were written. "The Tough Miracle Man of Vietnam," *Life* called him. "The bright spot in Asia," the *Saturday Evening Post* said ("Two years ago at Geneva," read the blurb for the latter, "South Vietnam was virtually sold down the river to the Com-munists. Today the spunky little Asian country is back on its feet thanks to a 'mandarin in a sharkskin suit who's upsetting the Red timetable' "). A lobby for Diem began to emerge. Speeches were made in his honor. In 1956, in the modest words of Walter Robertson, Dulles' Assistant Secretary of State for Far Eastern Affairs: "Among the factors that explain the remarkable rise of Free Vietnam from the shambles created by eight years of murderous civil and international war, the division of the country at Geneva, and the continu-ing menace of predatory Communism, there is in the first place the dedica-tion, courage and resourcefulness of President Diem himself." In all this there is a subtle change; the client state does not really come to life but the illusion does; as such, the proprietor state begins to live slightly at the mercy of the client state.

It was a subtle genesis, and it was not matched by real political changes in South Vietnam, which was still a feudal society. Diem was supposed to be an anti-Communist nationalist, and there was, in fact, no such thing. His political base, always narrow, became over the years narrower than ever. Faced by great political problems, and possessing few political resources, he turned in-ward. Morbidly suspicious, he alienated his few allies in the government and turned more to his scheming, neurotic family, to his police force and to grow-ing U.S. aid. He became more rigid, more isolated than ever, while ironically, the United States was becoming more committed to him. But at the same time year by year the U.S. sense of the futility of the whole enterprise dimin-ished. By 1961 the Americans believed firmly in Diem, believed in his legiti-macy; they saw South Vietnam as a real country, with a real flag. Having in-vented him and his country, we no longer saw our own role; our fingerprints had disappeared. In 1961 Kennedy could ruefully tell White House aides, "I can't afford a 1954 kind of defeat now."

The trouble was that after seven years, none of the American rhetoric, none of the gestures that the Americans were making to reassure Diem, had had any effect on the most important people in South Vietnam, the peasants. Quickly, night after night, the Vietcong, the heirs and linear descendants of the Vietminh, were practicing the same kind of skilled guerrilla warfare and rural recruitment that the Vietminh had used during the French war, growing ever stronger, exploiting the multitude of local grievances against the govern-ment. In the field nothing had changed; the Army of the Republic of Viet-nam, its commanders all former French officers and noncoms, resembled the French troops which had gone through the countryside in the daytime, using far too much fire power, and stealing and looting from the peasants; at night when the ARVN troops were gone, the Vietcong re-entered the villages and spread their skilled political propaganda, against which Diem was particularly impotent. (For a long time he had even refused to concede that a major insurgency was going on, since the very admission would have shown that his government was not perfect. Since he believed in his own rectitude, there could not be an insurgency against him.)

Not surprisingly, though the pressure came from the South Vietnamese, and rural ones at that, Diem turned to white foreigners for help, for more aid, for air power, for a new treaty with the Americans. The idea of Ho Chi Minh needing help or reassurance from the Russians or the Chinese is inconceivable; the idea of Diem being able to understand the needs of the peasants and respond to them in kind is equally inconceivable.

Throughout much of 1961, despite the pessimistic assessments of independent reporters and people like Lansdale, the American mission remained reasonably optimistic. Diem was doing better, went the line, and the ARVN was fighting better. Others, not in the chain of command, were more dubious. Theodore White, visiting Vietnam on his own in August, wrote to the White House of Vietcong control in the lower Mekong Delta, and of the fact that no American wanted to drive outside of Saigon even during the day without military convoy. Remembering what had happened in China, White sensed history about to repeat itself. In September the Vietcong began to use some of the muscle they had accumulated. They tripled the number of incidents, and after seizing a provincial capital fifty-five miles from Saigon, they publicly beheaded the provincial chief. The latter act had a profound effect in Saigon, where issues of morale and confidence were taken very seriously.

By the end of the month there were strong demands in Washington for new military moves. Walt Rostow, ever enthusiastic and ready to use force (and not particularly knowledgeable about the rural realities), recommended that 25,000 SEATO troops be stationed on the border between the demilitarized zone and Cambodia in order to stop infiltration. (The insurgency, intelligence experts were noting, was almost entirely taking place within the South; all Vietcong troops were Southerners; the weapons were captured from government posts. Some Southerners, however, were cadre-trained in the North and then repatriated to the South. It was a small part of the war; 80 to 90 percent of the Vietcong were locally recruited, the National Intelligence Estimate said on October 5, 1961.) The Rostow proposal gave military men studying it a chill. It showed so little understanding of the rugged terrain; the 25,000 men would be completely swallowed up and ineffectual. The choice would be left to the enemy to either by-pass this thin line of men or systematically to eradicate it. Instead, on October 9 the Joint Chiefs of Staff responded to the Rostow proposal with a counterproposal, a commitment of American troops (around 20,000, but it would grow larger) to Vietnam. But the JCS wanted the troops in the Central Highlands and warned that under the Rostow proposal the SEATO troops would quickly be chewed up. Two days later the JCS reported at a National Security Council meeting that it would take only 40,000 American combat troops to clean up the Vietcong; in case the North Vietnamese and the Chinese Communists intervened, then an additional 128,000 troops would be needed.

At almost the same time, as if it were all orchestrated, Diem sent a cable asking for more fighter-bombers, civilian pilots for helicopters, more transport planes, and U.S. combat units for "combat-training" missions near the DMZ. He also asked that the Americans consider a request for a division of Chiang Kai-shek's troops to support his own army. Ambassador Nolting recommended "serious and prompt" attention to all requests. Kennedy would soon have to make his first move on Vietnam.

THUS THE PRESSURES WERE BUILDING ON KENNEDY ALL THE TIME. HE and his people had come to power ready to assert American power and they would find ample tests of it, ample pressures on them. Not just pressures from the Communists, but parallel political pressures at home. Even as he was about to make his first major move in response to the mounting urgency in Vietnam, he was similarly making another crucial appointment at the very top of his government, an appointment which reflected not so much his control of the government, his sureness of step, but his lack of control and his loss of balance. All of these major responses of the Kennedy Administration in the first year were based on two major premises: first, that the Communists were indeed a harsh and formidable enemy (if it was not a monolith, it was still treated as one) and that relaxation of tensions could only come once the Administration had proven its toughness, and second, that Kennedy's political problems at home were primarily from the right and the center, that the left could be handled, indeed that it had nowhere else to go, and that it must accept the Administration's private statements of good will and bide its time for the good liberal things which might one day come. The latter attitude, the belief in the essential political weakness of the liberal-left, encouraged the Administration in some of its harder-line activities and limited its inclination to look for diversity within the Communist world. If there were changes within the Communist world, Washington believed they were certainly not changes immediately apparent to most Americans, and this was politically crucial to the Administration. The Administration still felt itself under pressure to prove its own worth to centrists and conservative Americans, and it believed that liberal-left Americans would simply have to accept the Kennedy proposition that the Administration was by far the best they could hope for. Most of the key moves by Kennedy in 1961 reflected this attitude, including not just the decisions which followed the forthcoming Taylor and Rostow trip to Vietnam, but indeed the very decision to send Taylor and Rostow instead of, say, Schlesinger and Bowles. (He knew Rostow was aggressive on the subject of the war and that Taylor was committed to the idea of counterinsurgency. Thus in effect he was likely to get something along the lines of the report he received. Had he chosen representatives more dubious about the use of force, he would have a different kind of estimate. In fact, shortly after Taylor and Rostow arrived in Saigon, Kennedy dispatched his new ambassador to India, John Kenneth Galbraith, to stop by and give him a personal report. Galbraith did, and in the very first of what was to be a series of trenchant, prophetic estimates on Vietnam, reported almost the opposite of Taylor and Rostow; he noted the decaying quality of the Diem and American operation there and saw enormous danger that the Americans might replace the French. Above all, he pushed for political rather than military solutions to the problem. But people like Galbraith were still on the outer periphery of the Kennedy Administration, there as much for window dressing as anything else, and his reports probably stirred doubts in the President's mind, but that and little else.) That Kennedy still felt that the right was his problem, that he coveted respectable Establishment support as a form of protection from the right and that he felt more comfortable with the traditionalists was evidenced in another crucial appointment which he made.

This was Kennedy's choice, on September 27, 1961, of John McCone, an extremely conservative, almost reactionary California Republican millionaire to head the CIA. Ever since the Bay of Pigs earlier in the year Kennedy had wanted to change personnel in both the JCS and the CIA; he regarded Allen Dulles as a sympathetic man but an icon of the past, a man with too imposing a reputation for the younger men of the Administration to challenge. Now, in September, Kennedy made his move. He had tentatively offered the job to Clark Clifford, who had impressed him during the changeover from the Eisenhower Administration. But Clifford was not interested; perhaps he sensed that there was not enough power at the Agency to lure him away from his own law practice. The next possibility was Fowler Hamilton, a Wall Street lawyer cut classically from the Establishment mold; in fact the White House was close to announcing the Hamilton appointment when a problem developed at the Agency for International Development, and Hamilton was shifted there. Thus Kennedy, urged on by his brother Robert, turned to McCone.

The appointment caught the rest of the Administration by surprise, and the liberals in the Kennedy group were absolutely appalled by it. One reason the President had been so secretive even within his own Administration (he did not, for example, tell the Foreign Intelligence Advisory Board of his intention, nor solicit the views of its members) was that he knew the opposition to

McCone within the government would be so strong as to virtually nullify the appointment. There was a variety of reasons for liberal distaste for McCone. During the Stevenson-Eisenhower campaign in 1956, a group of scientists at the California Institute of Technology had come out in support of Stevenson's proposals for a nuclear test ban; McCone, a trustee of Cal Tech, immediately retaliated. He claimed that the scientists had been "taken in" by Russian propaganda and were guilty of attempting to "create fear in the minds of the uninformed that radioactive fallout from H-bomb tests endangers life." In addition to his words, which seemed quite harsh, the scientists had good reason to believe that McCone tried to have them fired (a charge which McCone not entirely convincingly denied). Nor did the liberals find very much else in McCone's background which was reassuring (including, for instance, the statement of Strom Thurmond during the Senate hearings that he did not know McCone well, "but in looking over this biography to me it epitomizes what has made America great").

McCone came from a wealthy San Francisco family; he had been in steel before the war, but with the coming of World War II he had become the principal figure in a new company which was formed to go into shipbuilding. The business turned out to be an enormous financial success, and there were many contemporaries who felt McCone was nothing less than a war profiteer (in 1946 during a congressional investigation Ralph Casey of the General Accounting Office, a watchdog of the Congress, testified that Mccone and his associates of the California Shipbuilding Corporation had made $44,000,000 on an investment of $100,000. "I daresay that at no time in the history of American business," Casey remarked at the time, "whether in wartime or peacetime have so few men made so much money with so little risk and all at the expense of the taxpayers, not only of his generation but of future generations"). McCone served as a special deputy to James Forrestal, worked with Forrestal in creating the CIA, and later became an Undersecretary of the Air Force under Truman. A convert to Catholicism, he believed that Communism was evil and must be stopped—along with Claire Booth Luce, he represented Eisenhower at Pope Pius' funeral in 1958. During the Eisenhower years he was known as the classic hard-liner, a believer in massive retaliation and nuclear deterrents.

Thus the liberals within the Administration were appalled by the appointment, and if anything, they regarded it as a step back from Allen Dulles. But it was a very calculated appointment. McCone had been pushed by Robert Kennedy, then very much in his hard-line incarnation, who was also trying to get control of the apparatus of government. Bobby Kennedy wanted movers and doers and activists, men who could cut through the flabby bureaucracy, and McCone had precisely that kind of reputation (which Mccone intended to keep—no sooner had he taken over than he called in the various heads of the other intelligence operations and told them to play ball with him, he intended to be the intelligence czar, that if they played his game, he would increase their power in the government). But in particular, McCone was chosen by Kennedy because he offered one more bit of protection for a young President already on the defensive; having McCone at the CIA would deflect right-wing pressure against his Administration. Which McCone did, though the price was not inconsiderable. Though McCone was reasonably straight in reporting what his subordinates were saying from the field, his own views, when volunteered, and he was not bashful about volunteering them, were always extremely hard-line (he would also from time to time use people in his Agency for causes that were not necessarily Administration causes, such as lending CIA people to the Stennis committee to help make the case against the Administration's test ban treaty position). And it was also a gesture by Kennedy of turning over key parts of his government to people who were in no way part of his domestic political constituency. (In the last months of Kennedy's life Kenneth O'Donnell, annoyed by the fact that the most important jobs in the government had gone to people who had not supported the Kennedy political candidacy, or if they had supported it, had been only marginally sympathetic in their commitment, was pushing for a new kind of appointment. He wanted to replace John McCone at CIA with Jack Conway, who had been Walter Reuther's main political lobbyist, a man committed to Kennedy on domestic issues and fully capable of making judgments on foreign affairs as well. Had Kennedy lived and made the appointment it would have been almost unique in the entire history of national security appointments, a break in class and outlook of considerable proportion.)

Chapter Nine

SO THE APPOINTMENT OF MCCONE HAD SHOWN THE POLITICAL center of the Kennedy Administration to be a good deal farther to the right than his original political supporters hoped; now as he moved on Vietnam they would again take minimal confidence. In October 1961 the President decided to send his own special representatives to Vietnam for an on-site fact-finding trip. He and he alone was responsible for the composition of the team, which would to a very real degree reflect the true outlook of the new Administration toward Vietnam and toward what were essentially political problems in that period. No senior official from State went, partly because Rusk did not want to get involved in Vietnam, partly because he did not believe it was particularly State's responsibility. Another reason was that Kennedy himself did not push it, not having any particular respect for anyone at State other than for Averell Harriman, who was still in Geneva trying to neutralize Laos.

The trip was first proposed as a Rostow mission—just Rostow—but Bowles, who had become extremely nervous about Rostow's militancy ("Chester Bowles with machine guns," Arthur Schlesinger said of him), pushed hard for a high representative from State to go along to give the nonmilitary view. It should be someone of genuine rank, perhaps Bowles himself, but if not, at least an Assistant Secretary, perhaps Harriman. But Rusk was resistant; he still saw it as a military, not a political problem. (In this he was fairly typical of a generation of public officials who had come out of World War II and who saw State serving as the lawyers for the Defense Department; if there was a military involvement of some sort, Defense had primacy.) Eventually, however, as something of a concession to the Bowles viewpoint, the President's military adviser, Maxwell Taylor, was added to the mission. Bowles felt reassured; he remembered long talks in Korea in 1953, when Taylor had said with considerable emotion that American troops must never again fight a land war in Asia. Never again. And so Bowles and some of the others were pleased by the Taylor presence and considered it a sop, but a very important sop to them. The resulting Taylor-Rostow report would significantly deepen the American involvement in Vietnam from the low-level (and incompetent) advisory commitment of the Eisenhower years (geared up for a traditional border-crossing war that would never come) to the nearly 20,000 support and advisory troops there at the time President Kennedy was killed. It was one of the crucial turning points in the American involvement, and Kennedy, by his very choice of the two men who had the greatest vested interest in fighting some kind of limited antiguerrilla war, had loaded the dice. In Saigon the American Ambassador to Vietnam first learned the news of the Taylor-Rostow mission over the radio.

ROSTOW WAS BORN IN NEW YORK IN 1916, ONE OF THREE SONS OF A Russian Jewish immigrant. Even their names expressed a radical newcomer's almost naïve love of America. Walt Whitman Rostow, Eugene Victor Rostow, Ralph Waldo Rostow (in 1966 James Thomson, now teaching at Harvard, wrote a satire on the White House in which a figure named Herman Melville Breslau was consistently militant). Walt had always been a prodigy, always the youngest to do something. The youngest to graduate from a school, to be appointed to something. An unusually young graduate of Yale, a young Rhodes scholar. A young man picking bombing targets in World War II. A young assistant to Gunnar Myrdal; indeed, because of his postwar association he was considered something of the State Department's opening to the left in those days. Then a friend of C. D. Jackson's at *Life*, and a thin connection with the Eisenhower Administration; then MIT, part of a department which seemed eager to harness the intellectual resources of this country into the global struggle against the Communists. Rostow came in contact with Kennedy during the mid-fifties, and Kennedy had been impressed.

Rostow was always eager, hard-working, and in contrast to Bundy, extremely considerate of others. Even during the heights of the great struggles of 1968 in the attempt to turn around the war policy, when he was one of the last total defenders of the policy, many of his critics found it hard to dislike him personally. He seemed so ingenuously open and friendly, almost angelic, "a sheep in wolf's clothing," Townsend Hoopes would write. The reason was simple: he was the true believer, so sure of himself, so sure of the rectitude of his ideas that he could afford to be generous to his enemies. What others mistook for magnanimity in defeat was actually, in his own mind, magnanimity in victory; he had triumphed, his policies had come out as he alone had prophesied.

In the fifties he had been something of a star in Cambridge, a man who published and published regularly, whose books were reviewed in the *New York Times*, and who wrote for the Sunday *Times Magazine*, a man who had a reputation not only in Cambridge but in Washington and New York as well, which was not entirely surprising, for the Rostows were considered by some in Cambridge—a very traditional and somewhat stuffy town—as being quite ambitious socially, perhaps too ambitious. When they entertained, they always seemed to have the current political or literary lions among their guests. There was one party which a Cambridge lady remembered well because the Rostows gave it for Joyce Carey, the great English novelist. Everyone was impressed that the Rostows knew Carey so well, an impression which dimmed somewhat for the Cambridge lady when Carey very politely took her aside and said, "And now do tell me a little something about our charming host and hostess—I know so little about them." Not that giving a party for a lion in order to enhance your own standing was particularly unusual or gauche in Cambridge, or, for that matter, New York or Georgetown, though getting caught at it was.

Kennedy, on the make for an intellectual think tank of his own in the late fifties, particularly liked Rostow, liked his openness, his boundless energy, liked the fact that Rostow, unlike most academics, was realistic, seemed to understand something about how Washington really worked, liked the fact that Rostow mixed well, got on with professional politicians. (After Rostow moved to Washington it was something of a point of pride with him that he was a pluralist intellectual. He could get along with the military, play tennis with them, understand their viewpoint, did not have the knee-jerk antimilitary reaction of most Jewish intellectuals. In fact, on the night of the bombing of Pleiku years later, other aides would remember, Rostow wandered around the White House clapping Air Force officers on the back, asking about the weather, reminding them that he had once picked targets, and he knew that weather was important.) During Kennedy's Senate days he was always helpful, a demon for work, always available when summoned by the senator, producing paper, memos, ideas, a great idea man (Open Skies for Ike, New Frontier and Let's Get This Country Moving Again for Kennedy). He was responsive, too, which was a help; when Kennedy wanted a memo on some subject, Rostow did not, as too many academics did, refer him to some piece of paper they had already written, or some testimony before a committee they had given a year before. Instead, Kennedy would receive good, quick, tart, specific responses.

So the early relationship between Kennedy and Rostow was good, and then Rostow went away for the academic year 1958–59 and by the time he came back, Kennedy was running hard and there was less communication between them. There were more people on Kennedy's staff, and thus more filters between the candidate and the free-lance eggheads. There were those who felt that Kennedy was a little less comfortable with Rostow, a little pressed by him ("Walt," Kennedy said in 1961, not entirely to flatter him, "can write faster than I can read"). Kennedy had less time, and now there seemed to be too many memos, too much energy on the part of Rostow. In addition, Kennedy himself had changed. He was no longer the young senator of the fifties who had been so dependent on the Cambridge eggheads for his special postgraduate education and briefings. Now he was beginning to move ahead of them; more and more of what they were telling him he already knew. During the 1960 campaign Rostow remained among the advisers, a willing one, though on the outer periphery, his name to be summoned forth in the pro-Kennedy literature as one more bit of proof that John Kennedy liked intellectuals and was at ease with them.

Nevertheless, Rostow was ready to enter the new Administration with considerable money in the bank with the President-elect, a genuine certified Cambridge intellectual who had done his part for the greater glory. There were, however, some Kennedy people with reservations about him and they were not, curiously enough, the professional pols in the Kennedy group, but rather some of the Cambridge intellectuals themselves. It was not a particularly strong thing and they would, of course, never voice those feelings to outsiders or blow the whistle on Walt, just as the generals would never blow the whistle to an outsider on a fellow general about whom they had doubts. But there was a sense of unease about Walt, part of it personal, part of it professional, a feeling that for all Walt's talent, wit, brilliance, something was missing. In the personal sense it was Rostow's ability to adapt, to change: one of them remembered Rostow, when he had just come back from Oxford, playing the guitar at a Washington party and singing a very clever doggerel. It was enchanting, witty and very British, except that it was not Rostow, not at all. That feeling would deepen as Rostow went from virtual fellow traveler to militant anti-Communist ideologue, an uneasiness at the facility with which he adapted to fashion, without perhaps even knowing that he was doing it. This sense would heighten among some of his colleagues when they noticed, in the days of the Kennedy Administration, that Rostow sounded a little too much like the President, and grew even stronger when during the subsequent Administration he began to sound like Lyndon B. Johnson, employing the rough, tough language of the Ranch. It was, finally, a sense that behind all that bounciness and enthusiasm, perhaps Rostow did not know who he was, that in the eagerness of the poor Jewish immigrant's son to make it, in the big leagues and with the Establishment, he had lost sight of what was Rostow and what was the Establishment, or perhaps knowing what was Rostow, he wanted to forget it. (And make it with the Establishment he did, joyously, a last holdout on Vietnam when even the Establishment had changed. Thus, in 1971, after the *New York Times* had published the Pentagon documents, which made many in those Administrations look very foolish, not the least of them Walt Rostow, who told a *Times* editor yes, he would write an article for the Op-Ed page, and then almost benignly added that he was concerned about one thing. It was not the printing of the Papers [he could understand that], but the split in the Establishment. The Establishment was very small, which was necessary, and it was in charge of a country which was very young and which could not make the right decisions itself, and thus unity within the Establishment was very important. They must stick together, they must not be divided, America needed the *Times* in the Establishment, that was the important point, and now they must work to heal the breach, to bring the *Times* back.)

If there was one other thing that bothered Walt's colleagues on the professional level, it was the firmness of his belief in his own ideas (at a given time), a lack of healthy skepticism about them, a lack of reflectiveness and open-mindedness. His great strength was also his great weakness: a capacity to see patterns where previously none existed, to pull together diverse ideas and acts into patterns and theories. It was this which made him intellectually interesting and challenging but which made him dangerous as well because, some felt, he did not know when he had gone too far, when to stop, when the pattern was flimsier than he thought. If some doubted his wisdom, few doubted his enthusiasm, the energy of both the mind and the body, that Walt really wanted to use his mind. During the early days of his tour as head of the Policy Planning Council at State he went off to Latin America for a brief trip. On his return he announced to the startled assemblage of the Council that he now knew how you get to understand Latin Americans: you begin by understanding that in the first place they are Asians. "Oh, for God's sake, Walt," someone in the room told him, "why are you talking about something you know nothing about?"

But he was a man of ideas, determined that his ideas should live. All those years he was particularly committed to the idea that the United States with its technology and its ideals could play a dominant role in the underdeveloped world and in stopping Communist revolutions, could in fact sponsor our own peaceful revolutions on our own terms. The gap between the life styles of the poor and of the Americans did not faze him. History was on our side if we did it right. Modernization was the key. To him Ho and men like Che Guevara were evil, out to oppress rather than liberate, and his staff would never forget the meeting he called the day Che Guevara was killed. Like a bit of theater,

Walt very dramatic: "Gentlemen." Pause. "I have very important news." Everyone leaning forward. "The Bolivians have executed Che." Another pause to let the satisfaction sink in. "They finally got the SOB. The last of the romantic guerrillas." Rostow was, the staff noticed, excited, almost grateful for the news. This proved it was all right, that history was going according to schedule, just as his own books had predicted. History was good.

AT THE END OF THE PRESIDENTIAL CAMPAIGN KENNEDY HAD PROMISED Rostow the chairmanship of the State Department's Policy Planning Council, a job which seemed ideal for him, a good place for an idea man and not too close to the center of the action. But Rusk put his foot down; since he had already accepted too many of Kennedy's political people and he was bothered by Rostow, who seemed verbose and ideological, he drew the line. Meanwhile, Rostow was in Cambridge waiting for the phone call from Kennedy or Rusk, but that job offer never came. Instead, Rusk wanted George McGhee, his old friend and colleague during the Truman Administration, for the job, and Rostow could be his deputy. The prospect of being deputy did not intrigue Rostow, who called Kennedy; the President-elect said not to worry, something would be worked out. Then in December 1960, when Kennedy went to Harvard to meet with the Overseers, a symbolic and moving occasion in Cambridge, he summoned Rostow alone for breakfast, a momentous occasion which sent great waves surging across Cambridge, then attuned for all bits of Kennedy gossip, showing that Rostow *must* be an insider, after all. Kennedy was particularly good at using the peripheral benefits of his office and position to ease people's hurt. At the meeting he promised Rostow a job as Bundy's deputy, which delighted Rostow, and he immediately accepted.

Since Rostow was known in Cambridge for his enthusiasm, particularly his enthusiasm for his own ideas, there were those in the Harvard-MIT complex who regarded his appointment as something of a mixed blessing. On the day of the announcement Lucian Pye, a professor of political science at MIT, walked into a seminar, shuffled papers for a minute, looked at his class and finally said, "You know, you don't sleep quite so well any more when you know some of the people going to Washington." If Rostow was not known for his modesty in the Cambridge world, he soon showed up in Washington true to form, grandly defining his job to a reporter in terms worthy of his stature (he had entitled his latest book *The Stages of Economic Growth: A Non-Communist Manifesto*, to which the British publisher would modestly add: "It provides the significant links between economic and noneconomic behavior which Karl Marx failed to discern"). Pointing to Suez on a map, Rostow noted that he and Mac had divided the world, Bundy getting everything west of Suez, and Rostow everything east of it. This seemed a fair split, Bundy being totally a man of the Atlantic, a serious theater for a serious man (Robert Komer, the most articulate White House spokesman for the dark of skin, would complain, only partly in jest, that the key to the world was to get Bundy to go from Gibraltar to Tangier, *that* would be a breakthrough), whereas Rostow was fascinated by the underdeveloped world. He felt that this was the main new arena of confrontation, and that Eisenhower had let it all slip away.

Rostow had arrived with a definite and decided view on Vietnam, that the United States must move, that this was the right spot. In the early days he pushed very hard for action, sponsoring General Lansdale, asking for increased commitment of troops, for more covert operations, promoting the idea of the vice-presidential trip to Saigon. He also talked about bombing the North, hitting the supply routes, and though he was combative and aggressive about it, there were jokes among the insiders about Walt's SEATO Plan Six, and later about Air Marshal Rostow. There was a certain touch of amusement about this, about Rostow being a little too zealous, perhaps a little too energetic, a little too anti-Communist; he seemed to *mean* what he said about the guerrillas and the Communists. Kennedy was amused by this, and by the fact that for all his enthusiastic anti-Communism, the right wing and the security people were always picking on Rostow, and there were constant problems of security clearances for him, a throwback to his leftist days. Kennedy would say, half in irritation, half in jest, "Why are they always picking on Walt as soft-headed? Hell, he's the biggest Cold Warrior I've got." In choosing Rostow for the fact-finding trip to Vietnam, Kennedy was picking the one member of the Administration genuinely *enthusiastic* about a guerrilla confrontation there.

There was an additional reason why Rostow did not fear confrontation in Vietnam, and that was an almost mystic belief in air power. He was convinced, indeed he *knew*, that we had an unbeatable weapon, that we could always fall back, even if reluctantly, on our real might, which was the gleaming force and potential of the U.S. Air Force. Perhaps all men tend to be frozen in certain attitudes which have been shaped by important experiences in their formative years; for young Rostow, one of the crucial experiences had been picking bombing targets in Europe. It had been a stirring time, a time when he was of great service to his country. He had believed in strategic bombing, in the vital, all-important role it played in bringing victory during World War II, that it had broken the back of the German war machine. His enthusiasm for bombing and for his own role had allowed him to withstand all the subsequent intelligence of the U.S. *Strategic Bombing Survey* (not by chance were two of that survey's chief members, John Kenneth Galbraith and George Ball, among the leading doves on Vietnam), which proved conclusively that the strategic bombing had not worked; on the contrary, it had intensified the will of the German population to resist (as it would in North Vietnam, binding the population to the Hanoi regime).

Rostow remained uniquely oblivious to counterarguments about bombing; if anything, he believed that we had not used enough of it against the German oil depots and electric grid, and he would later seek to remedy that omission in Vietnam. Only the Air Force itself was more fervent than Rostow in the belief that in this weapon we had a panacea for military problems. Where others might have been hesitant about a real confrontation with Hanoi, Rostow had fewer fears and more confidence; the idea of being able to use bombing as a fall-back weapon was particularly comforting. His faith in bombing persisted through 1967, despite the mounting evidence against its effectiveness. In fact, after one confrontation with Undersecretary of State Nicholas deB. Katzenbach in 1967 over the failure of bombing, Katzenbach walked out shaking his head. He turned to a friend and said, "I finally understand the difference between Walt and me. I was the navigator who was shot down and spent two years in a German prison camp, and Walt was the guy picking my targets." But all this came later, even the failure. It was his confidence about bombing and its magic that gave him a special fervor; almost alone among the Kennedy people, he was a believer.

THE OTHER MEMBER WAS MAXWELL TAYLOR, THE KENNEDY-TYPE general. He was articulate, he was presentable. (You would, said one member of the Administration years later, be impressed with Max even if he were in civies.) Between 1955 and 1959 he had struggled with the Eisenhower Administration as Chief of Staff of the United States Army, during the years when the doctrine was massive retaliation, a doctrine which severely reduced the size and role of the U.S. Army (the Kennedy people, who were always sloppy in their homework, all thought he had resigned in protest. Quite the opposite was true; though he had presented radically different strategies, he had walked the narrow path, thus managing to coexist for four years; then he retired. After his tour was up, he wrote his dissenting book, which was so critical of the Republicans that it left the impression that Taylor had, in fact, resigned).

He was a man of considerable stature, the linear descendant of the greatest American general of that era, Matt Ridgway; he was a man with a good combat record who was a hero to civilians and soldiers alike, and people seemed to think of him as the next Ridgway. In 1960 Taylor left his job as president of the Lincoln Center for the Performing Arts in New York, a position which had added to his laurels—the *cultured* war hero. He was also more than a little vain, not just about his hearing, which was bad, and for which he did not want a hearing aid, but about his title as well. At the beginning of the Administration there had been some trouble over it: should it be *The* Military Representative of the President, a title which he wanted, or Kennedy's choice, Special Military Representative? Kennedy, being President, won.

The general seemed almost invented for the Kennedy years; he was cool, correct, handsome and athletic. As an airborne general, he was more modern in outlook than other generals; he spoke several languages and had written a book. And he was imposing, always in control. Once, while he was Superintendent of West Point, he had attended an assembly of college presidents at which he spoke forcefully and eloquently, all without a note. Afterward another educator congratulated him on such a good impromptu speech. "I never do anything impromptu," he answered. Most important of all, his strategic views coincided exactly with Kennedy's. He thought nuclear weapons an unthinkable instrument of American policy, and he did not think a U.S. President would initiate a nuclear war. Classic conventional war seemed increasingly outmoded; thus he had written that the next generation of wars would be brush-fire wars which the United States, as keeper of world stability and honor, must extinguish. He *seemed* to be talking about guerrilla wars, though it would turn out that he was the most conventional of men in terms of the new kind of warfare; what he was really talking about was apparently limited use of highly mobile conventional forces in very limited wars. This was, of course, a fine point which might develop later but which was not discernible in the early days of the Administration, a time when there was more excitement about guerrilla warfare and small wars than there was knowledge about them.

To the Kennedy people, then, he was a *good* general, different from the Eisenhower generals, who were simply typical of the military establishment. (Kennedy also assumed that all good generals liked one another, and thus that General James Gavin, similarly a *good* general, a romantic, Airborne figure who had written books and also shortened a brilliant career in protest over Ike's policies, and who had also supported Kennedy against Nixon—a prime test for a good general—must be a friend of Taylor's. "Jim, Jim," Kennedy had once yelled to a departing Gavin in the White House, "Max is here! Max is here!," imagining that the two were close friends, but drawing from Gavin the coldest look imaginable. The truth was that the two disliked each other, had long been rivals, had even skirmished over which airborne division would lead the post-World War II parade through Manhattan, and would end up bitterly divided on the Vietnam war.) In addition, the new Administration people believed that Taylor could and would be a Kennedy general, at least as loyal to them as to his uniform and institution—a very real splitting of loyalties, as it would turn out. He had served Kennedy well during the Bay of Pigs, though his reports had been curiously technical in nature and not very astute politically. But Kennedy was inclined to think of Taylor as being dispassionate and rational, indeed more like himself than anyone else in the new Administration, with the possible exception of Bundy. As if that were not enough, Robert Kennedy was enamored of him and constantly promoted him.

So now here was Taylor, chosen for this mission, not necessarily a man of the JCS, but in the Kennedy eyes more independent than that, more modern, less bureaucratic; he was, above all, a man who had been warning for nearly a decade that the great military problem in the world was not nuclear war, but brush-fire wars, and now he was going to a country which contained, if nothing else, the world's most intense brush-fire war.

So they went, Rostow and Taylor; they got on well together. They were both activists, and those who wondered whether America had been taken over by soft, weak men would be reassured by the many photographs sent back from Saigon showing Taylor and Rostow playing vigorous tennis with various Vietnamese. Kennedy had also asked Lansdale to make a special trip to Vietnam, and he had accepted, learning only later that he would be a part of the Taylor mission. Before they left, Taylor had asked each member of the group to make a list of what he would like to look into once they arrived in Vietnam. Lansdale, who was the most professional member of the group, made a fairly long list of things: he wanted to find out more about the relationship of the government to the people, he wanted to know if the government was reaching the people, what the feeling was of people getting drafted, who could become an officer in the South Vietnamese army (ARVN) and who could not, what the local feeling was toward tax officials, how valid the case of the Vietcong was in rural areas. Lansdale was not a particular admirer of Taylor's in the first place; in the 1955–56 period, when Taylor was the Chief of Staff, Lansdale had wanted more emphasis on the development of Special Forces and irregular-warfare units, and had found Taylor unreceptive to the idea, ready, if anything, to cut back the number of men on irregular duty. Now he again found Taylor unreceptive to his list, which was accepted without comment. The two men never discussed it on the trip, and Taylor never asked Lansdale why he wanted to look into these matters.

Thus it came as no surprise to Lansdale that when the protocol list for official functions for the trip was drawn, Taylor drew the cutoff line immediately above Lansdale's name, Lansdale, of course, being well known and popular in Vietnam. What came as a greater surprise was Taylor's view of what this war was all about. He assigned Lansdale the task of looking into the possibility and cost of erecting a huge fence which would run the length of the country and stop infiltration. For years, Lansdale, along with other knowledgeable Americans in Vietnam, had mocked the French Expeditionary Forces for their preoccupation with static outposts, what the Americans considered a Maginot Line mentality; now as he took the assignment from Taylor he thought to himself, Here we are, trying to create our own Maginot Line. It was, he thought as the mission progressed, all like that, trying to refit conventional ideas for an unconventional war. What it would amount to, he thought, was taking an army that was dubious in battle and making it more mobile, avoiding the real social and political causes for its military failures. But he was below the cutoff line in more than protocol, and his feelings would not be reflected in the mission's findings.

THEY WERE NOT ALONE IN MAKING THE TRIP TO VIETNAM. ALSO GOING was one of Washington's most influential columnists (then he was still influential; the war would severely damage his credibility and systematically lessen his influence), a man with an enormous vested interest in Asian anti-Communism, Joseph Alsop. He had never quite forgiven the State Department for allowing the United States to stand idly by while China went Communist. China had fallen despite his warnings, but he was still a forceful advocate of the domino theory, a man skilled in the ways of Washington, well connected politically and socially, and while he would not stoop to the kind of tactics which had marked McCarthyism, he nevertheless could make the case for holding the line in a way which implied that manhood was at stake; this he now did, and what he wrote from Honolulu on October 18 was symbolic of the kind of writing and pressure a President faced in those days:

Is there any real foundation for all the talk about the Kennedy administration "lack of firmness"? The talk disturbs the President so much that he came to within an ace of making his recent North Carolina speech a major answer to his critics. But is there anything to it but political hot air? On the way to troubled South Vietnam where the administration's firmness is once again being tested, the foregoing question looms very large indeed. This reporter's "yes, but" answer begins oddly enough with a typical specimen of modern American academic politics. . . .

All week Alsop encouraged a troop commitment. First at a time when the guerrilla war was at a markedly low level, with the Vietcong rarely striking in company units, never in battalion, and with perhaps no more than an estimated 17,000 Vietcong in the country, Alsop found not one but two North Vietnamese regular regiments, one in the country, the other on the border preparing to enter (some four and a half years before they actually entered the country and battle):

For many months the massive infiltration into South Vietnam, by guerrilla cadres and bands, has been a known fact. But the appearance of regular units of the regular army of Communist North Vietnam is something else again. In plain terms it is an invasion.

He also realized that while this was an "Asian version of Berlin," to be met with steadfastness, the Communists were ill prepared for the kind of long-term struggle the Americans would demand. "This in turn clearly suggests that the Communist high command is now playing a short term game. They are calling in all their assets without regard to the more remote future because they hope to bring the war to a climax in the near future." (Eleven years later, undaunted by the tenacity of the other side, when Hanoi launched a major offensive in 1972, Alsop wrote that it was their "last hurrah." If the enemy proved to be resilient, rising from the ashes, then so did Alsop.)

EARLIER IN THE YEAR, AS THE INSURGENCY IN SOUTH VIETNAM intensified and as the Vietcong moved steadily to larger units and began more and more to join battle (successfully) with the ARVN, there had been talk of combat troops besides Rostow's suggestion about sending a SEATO force of about 25,000 men to guard the border around Laos. The Joint Chiefs wanted to put some troops into South Vietnam, not so much to engage in combat as to show American firmness (not realizing, of course, that in the particular rhythm of the war, if the Americans upped the ante, so would Hanoi and the Vietcong). Presumably the number would be low, though it was not specified. There was surprisingly little discussion of whether or not the troops would go into combat, though the impression was given that they would not, that they would be there to prevent combat rather than join it, to show our intent to Hanoi and to the Communists, thus automatically de-escalating the other side's intentions in the area.

As much as anything else, this proposal reflected JCS needs elsewhere. At that point it wanted to build up forces, particularly in the depleted strategic reserve, and if troops were ticketed, being used, in fact, in Southeast Asia, that fact would be a powerful bit of evidence for more troops needed at home. In addition, the JCS liked the idea of the precedent involved. It wanted to have a foot in the door in Vietnam; just in case the war grew larger, it would be ready. There would be a logistic base in Saigon, and the legal rights would be cleared for more. You could start with a small commitment; it was always easy to increase it. It was a case of an institution automatically wanting to expand and to feed itself. All institutions do their thing; in the case of the military and generals, wanting troops is their thing.

Now in the fall the Chiefs were pushing again; Admiral Felt of CINCPAC had recently toured Vietnam and had been appalled by the deterioration in the countryside. The Vietcong were stepping up their activities in area after area; where they challenged the government forces, the latter were unequal. The Vietcong troops were well led, and believed deeply in their cause; in contrast, the government troops were made of the same raw material but their leadership was bad. They were commanded by division, regimental and even battalion officers who had never heard shots fired in anger, who held their posts only because of loyalty to Diem, and who were under orders not to allow casualties because this would be considered a reflection against Diem himself, a sign that he was not as beloved and respected as he believed. Since the Vietcong leadership was perfectly willing to accept very high casualties for each individual political gain ("It is," wrote one Vietcong soldier in his diary, "the duty of my generation to die for our country"), the outcome again and again was almost predetermined. As in China, it was a modern army against a feudal one, though this was not perceived by Western eyes, particularly Western military eyes, which saw that the ARVN was well equipped, with radios, airplanes, artillery and fighter planes, and that the Vietcong had virtually nothing, except light infantry pieces. Western observers believed the reverse, believed that the ARVN was a legitimate and *real* army, and that the Vietcong, more often than not wearing only black pajamas, not even uniformed, were the fake army, the unreal one—why, they did not even seem to have a chain of command. It was ironic; the United States had created an army in its own image, an army which existed primarily on paper, and which was linked to U.S. aims and ambitions and in no way reflected its own society. We believed in the army, the South Vietnamese did not. We saw it as a real army which needed only a little prodding, an adviser or two, a few people to help the soldiers with map reading; a more vigorous leadership by the better officers, trained by Americans. This illusion about a dynamic new leadership would persist relentlessly through the years, so that in early 1967 Walt Rostow, still upbeat despite the darkening reports from Saigon, confronted an increasingly pessimistic Daniel Ellsberg, just back from a year and a half in Vietnam, and began to expound his new theories. We had to get away from our American liberal distaste for military regimes, Rostow said. The military was the hope in the underdeveloped world, well-educated, idealistic young officers taking over the nationalism, not those tired old civilians who were part of the colonial era, but bright (crew-cut, English-speaking, Fort Bragg–trained) men who knew the modern world. That's what was happening in Vietnam, these young officers taking over. People like Ky. Terrific fellow.

"Well, that may be true elsewhere in the world, Walt," answered Ellsberg, "but there are very few countries in the world where the bright young officer class has the unique distinction of having fought against its own country's independence and alongside the colonial army."

To the demands by the Joint Chiefs had been added a new pressure for more troops, this time from the South Vietnamese, who had been growing ever more nervous by the fall of 1961, and who also sensed a chance to sink the hook of commitment deeper into the Americans. A year earlier

Diem had not even deigned to recognize the Vietcong as a military force. They were bandits and outlaws (the same words Chiang Kai-shek had used to describe the Red Chinese armies, and for the same reasons of vanity and of wanting to have unchallenged legitimacy). As late as May 1961 he had told Johnson he did not want American troops, but by September, as the Vietcong muscle became more obvious, Diem had called in Ambassador Nolting and asked for a bilateral defense treaty, since he felt that SEATO was not an adequate umbrella; he doubted British and French willingness to come to his aid.

Although the question of Laos' neutrality was still being discussed in Geneva, Diem was, significantly, already using it as a weapon against the Americans. He claimed that a neutral Laos would expose him to greater enemy infiltration (which was not really true; the enemy could infiltrate at will, and if anything was incapable of stopping infiltration, it was the Royal Laotian Army). The fact that American visitors had repeatedly been talking to Diem, pushing their own desires, which in this case was combat troops, was bound to have an effect on him, and he now saw an opportunity to tie the Americans more directly to his regime. Besides, he had distrusted American firmness for some time. By October the pressure increased: Nguyen Dinh Thuan, who was the Acting Defense Minister and probably, except for the Ngo family itself, the most important senior official in the government, called Nolting in to ask for combat troops. They would be "combat trainer units," Nolting reported to Washington. There would be a symbolic U.S. strength near the 17th parallel, and U.S. troops also positioned at key provincial capitals in the Central Highlands. Time, Thuan had emphasized, was of the essence.

Despite all these warnings, the request for combat troops came as something of a surprise to the U.S. government. It was different from what Diem had been saying before, and there was some suspicion that perhaps it was a trial balloon on the part of Ngo Dinh Nhu. Nevertheless, when Taylor and Rostow went, they were specifically assigned the job of investigating the possibility of employment of combat troops. There were three specific strategies they were to look into. One was the use of up to three divisions of American troops to defeat the Vietcong. The second was fewer combat troops, not so much to engage in combat as for the purpose of making a symbolic gesture and getting an American foot in the door. And the third, a step short of combat troops, was an acceleration of U.S. assistance and support to the Vietnamese, more equipment, particularly helicopters and light aircraft, to make the ARVN more mobile.

The fact that Taylor had been instructed to investigate the possibility of combat troops was known in Washington; there had been increasing speculation and gossip in preceding weeks. Despite the pressure of the men around him, the President himself did not like the idea. He had a sense of being cornered. If it was clear that Taylor's main concern was to determine whether combat troops should be sent or not, then it followed that in a few weeks, after Taylor's return, it would be John F. Kennedy who either sent or did not send troops. The issue of combat troops had been deliberately clouded in the pre-trip briefings, and a *New York Times* story of the period, coming from high White House sources, stated that the military leaders were reluctant to send troops, which was not true, and that the idea of combat troops was at the bottom of the list of things which Taylor was to consider, which was equally untrue. What was true was that the President was uneasy with the pressure he was already feeling from the men around him.

AFTER THE FACT-FINDING MISSION LEFT VIETNAM, THEY WENT TO THE Philippines, where Taylor worked on the central part of the report. What Taylor wrote is doubly important, not just because it reflected his feelings about action as early as 1961, but as an insight into his own attitudes about Vietnam as the crisis deepened. In 1954 Ridgway, Taylor's predecessor in the Airborne club and as Chief of Staff, had struggled brilliantly to keep American troops out of Indochina. Kennedy had appointed Taylor partly because he wanted someone like Ridgway, but it would be apparent by this trip alone that Ridgway and Taylor were different men.

Because the Taylor-Rostow mission profoundly changed and escalated the American commitment to Vietnam, and because all news reports at the time said that Taylor had recommended against combat troops, it is easy to underestimate the report. The fact is that Taylor, the dominant figure of the trip— he wrote the crucial report to Kennedy himself—did recommend combat troops. He recommended that up to 8,000 be sent, that more be sent if necessary, and most important, that the job could not be done without them. The recommendations shocked Kennedy to such an extent that Taylor's report was closely guarded and in some cases called back (even people as directly concerned with the decision making as Walter McConaughy, the Assistant Seccretary of State for Far Eastern Affairs, did not know that Taylor had recommended troops). What was made public was part of the report, the recommendations for the advisory and support part of the mission, and the recommendations for reform and broadening of Diem's government. In contrast, Taylor's actual cables barely mentioned reform; they dealt primarily with military problems and were extremely conventional in attitude.

Taylor talked in his cables of a "crisis of confidence" because of the growing Vietcong military build-up and because of the U.S. neutralization of Laos. (At this point in the Cold War, one thing was made clear: for every step forward in beginning to contain it, there had to be at least one step backward. A soft Laos, a hard Vietnam. A few months before, Ben Cohen, the New Deal lawyer, and one of the first men in Washington to spot the danger of Vietnam, had taken his old friend Averell Harriman aside and said that what was going on in Vietnam was disastrous and exactly opposite to Harriman's policy in Laos. Harriman, good loyal Administration member, protested that it was not. Five years later Harriman would take Cohen aside at a Georgetown party and say tartly, "You were right about Vietnam, Ben.") Taylor spelled out clearly the mission of the U.S. troops: it would be a task force largely logistical in make-up whose presence would reassure Diem of the American readiness "to join him in a showdown with the Vietcong or Vietminh." The Taylor cables also outlined the dangers: our strategic reserve was already weak and we would be engaging U.S. prestige. If the first increment failed, it would be difficult to "resist the pressure to reinforce," and if the ultimate mission were the closing of the border and the cleaning up of the insurgents, "there is no limit to our possible commitment," unless "we attacked the source in the North." It might increase tensions "and risk escalation into a major war in Asia."

Yet for all these drawbacks, Taylor reported, nothing would be so reassuring to the government and the people of South Vietnam as the introduction of U.S. troops (a crucial departure, the American assumption here, that the government and the people of South Vietnam were as one, that what Diem wanted was what "the people" wanted; a quick assumption which haunted American policy makers throughout the crisis). It would not have to be a large force, but it must be more than a token. It must be significant. It would help morale because it would show resistance to a Communist takeover. It would conduct operations in support of flood relief (given the instinct for tricks and subterfuge of that era, it is not surprising that there was a good deal of thought given to the introduction of the U.S. units as flood-relief crews, to help combat current flooding in the Mekong Delta. Much humanitarian public relations benefit was foreseen). These troops would not be used to clear the jungles and forests of Vietnam, a task still left to ARVN, but they could fight to protect themselves and the areas in which they lived, and they would give CINCPAC an advance party for SEATO planning (something in there for everybody). As part of the general reserve, they could be employed against main-force VC units, so in effect their use would depend on how eager the other side was to contest our presence.

Thus Taylor was recommending something that would also be a constant in Vietnam, a gesture, a move on our part that would open-end the war, leaving the other side to decide how wide to make the war. This attitude was based on an underestimation of the seriousness and intent of the other side, and on the assumption that if we showed our determination, Hanoi would not contest us. (We made this last mistake repeatedly, from the Taylor mission right through to the incursion in 1969 in Cambodia and in 1971 in Laos, and we were always wrong; the enemy was always more serious about his own country than we were about it.) Now the suggestion for a show of firmness appeared for the first time in the Taylor cables, and it was coming from the man the Kennedy Administration believed its foremost strategic planner; a cautious man who would understand wars like this. Taylor's idea was based on the fallacy that in the end the enemy would be less fanatical about the struggle in his own country, which had at that point been going on in various forms for more than two decades. But General Vo Nguyen Giap, the most important military figure in Hanoi and thus Taylor's opposite number, would not, after all, have to worry about Berlin access, or disarmament, or the level of strength in NATO, or getting the missiles out of Cuba: General Giap would continue to do the same thing after General Taylor left *his* country that he had been devoting himself to for the last twenty years—the unification of Vietnam under a Communist regime.

Taylor acknowledged that the risks of backing into a major Asian war were present but (in words that would live longer than he might have wanted) "not impressive." North Vietnam "is extremely vulnerable to conventional bombing, a weakness which should be exploited diplomatically in convincing Hanoi to lay off South Vietnam" (a vulnerability which, if it existed, Hanoi was less aware of than both Taylor and Rostow). Both Hanoi and Peking, he cabled, faced "severe logistical difficulties in trying to maintain strong forces in the field in Southeast Asia, difficulties which we share, but by no means to the same degree." The starvation conditions in China, he found, would keep the Chinese from being militarily venturesome. As for the key question of how American troops would fare, Taylor found South Vietnam "not an excessively difficult or unpleasant place to operate." In perhaps the most significant passage of all, he thought it was comparable to Korea, "where U.S. troops learned to live and work without too much effort. In the High Plateau and in the coastal plain where U.S. troops would probably be stationed, these jungle forest conditions do not exist to any great extent. The most unpleasant feature in the coastal areas would be the heat, and in the Delta, the mud left behind by the flood. The High Plateau offers no particular obstacle to the stationing of U.S. troops."

This part of the Taylor cables is perhaps the most revealing insight into the way the American military—even the best of the American military—regarded Vietnam and the war. This was the time when unconventional warfare was a great fad in Washington, and here was Taylor, who was supposed to be an expert on it, making a comparison with Korea: we had the same problems there, and we overcame them. In searching for the parallel war, Taylor singled out Korea but mentioned only the comparable quality of the terrain (actually, Korea is far more open and has, from a military point of view, a much easier terrain, where tanks and air power can be used to great advantage), without considering the crucial difference between Korea and Vietnam: the very nature of the war. The former was a conventional war with a traditional border crossing by a uniformed enemy massing his troops; the latter was a political war conducted by guerrillas and feeding on subversion. There was no uniformed, massed enemy to use power against; the enemy was first and foremost political, which meant that the support of the population made the guerrillas' way possible. The very presence of Caucasian troops was likely to turn quickly into a political disadvantage, more than canceling out any military benefits. There was a parallel war: the French Indochina war or the Philippine insurrection. But Taylor made the comparison with Korea, and if this general, who was so widely respected, a man who was an intellectual and quoted Thucydides, did not see this crucial nuance, who else would?

In his summing up on November 3, Taylor said that the advantages of sending American troops outweighed the disadvantages, and that this was imperative to the success of saving South Vietnam ("I do not believe that our program to save South Vietnam will succeed without it," he reported). Then he asked the same question which Kennedy had posed earlier, whether the suggested program, minus the U.S. combat task force, could stop further deterioration in the South. He answered that it was very doubtful, that there was no substitute for a military presence to raise morale and to convince the other side of the seriousness of our intent, "to sober the enemy and to discourage escalation . . ."

Taylor then raised the question of when to get the troops out. There were many answers. One was: after obtaining a quick military victory. But a quick victory was unlikely; the Americans would probably have to stay and hold the line while the South Vietnamese built up their forces. For planning purposes, this date could be set at the end of 1962, by which time Diem's army would comprise 200,000 men.

All in all, the Taylor-Rostow report is an extraordinary document and provides a great insight into the era. It shows a complete misunderstanding of the nature of the war (there was no discussion of the serious political problems of the war in Taylor's cables). It was arrogant and contemptuous toward a foe who had a distinguished and impressive record against a previous Western challenger. It was written by a general who had seen the limits of air power in Korea and now said that if things went wrong, air power would handle Hanoi any time we wanted. It assumed that the people and the government of South Vietnam were the same thing; yet it also said that a people allegedly fighting for their survival, already overstocked with American aid and materiel, needed reassurance, that the problem was not one of political origin, but of confidence. When Ridgway in 1954 investigated the possibility of U.S. troops in Indochina, he maximized the risks and minimized the benefits; now Taylor was maximizing the benefits and minimizing the risks.

NOT EVERYONE ON THE TOUR FELT THE SAME WAY. THE TWO STATE
Department officials who had made the trip, Sterling Cottrell and William J.
Jorden, were more dubious about the possibility of success. Cottrell, head of
the interdepartmental Vietnam task force, was pessimistic about the efficacy
of introducing U.S. combat forces. "Since it is an open question whether the
government can succeed even with U.S. assistance, it would be a mistake for
the U.S. to commit itself irrevocably against the Communists in the South,"
he reported. He did recommend moving to the Rostow plan—presumably to
punish the North by bombing it if continued U.S. efforts failed. Jorden, a
former *New York Times* correspondent, reported on explosive anti-Diem political feeling and the near paralysis of the government, and warned against
the United States' becoming too closely identified "with a man or a regime."
Most State Department officials shared this skepticism, and the Taylor recommendations were relayed to Secretary Rusk, who was in Japan for a conference. Rusk cabled back his reluctance to see the American commitment enlarged without any reciprocal agreement for reform on the part of Diem.
Unless his regime broadened its base and took more non-Communist nationalists into the government, Rusk doubted that a "handful" of American troops
could have much effect.

On the whole, opposition to sending troops was frail. On November 8
Secrecretary of Defense Robert McNamara, reflecting the pressures from his
Pentagon constituency, signed on. In an unusually personalized memo ("The
Joint Chiefs, Mr. Gilpatric and I have decided . . .") he said that the fall of
South Vietnam would lead to serious deterioration throughout Southeast Asia,
and he agreed that we were unlikely to prevent the fall without sending U.S.
combat forces. He accepted Taylor's judgment that anything less would fail to
restore Diem's confidence. However, he noted that even Taylor's 8,000 men
would not necessarily impress the other side with the true seriousness of
American intent. Such a conviction would only come with a clear statement
that we would use more force if necessary, and that if Hanoi continued to aid
the Vietcong, we would take punitive action against the North. This, of
course, might mean a long struggle, and looking at the darkest possibility (that
Hanoi and Peking might intervene directly), we would have to consider involving six divisions (the limit of aid McNamara felt we could give without
disturbing the Berlin requirements). "I believe we can safely assume the maximum U.S. forces required on the ground in Southeast Asia will not exceed six
divisions, or about 205,000 men," he wrote. The basic McNamara summary
was in support of the Taylor position.

There were two important men in Washington who had strong misgivings
about sending in combat troops. One was John Kennedy; the other was
George Ball, Undersecretary of State for Economic Affairs, who was about to
be given Bowles's job. His star was rising at the time, but it was not always

thus. He had almost not made the upper level of the Kennedy team, and bearing the Stevenson taint had not helped. Earlier, in January, as the upper levels of the Kennedy Administration were being systematically filled with Republicans, it became fairly obvious that Ball was one more Democrat about to be by-passed. Then Ball heard that Kennedy and Rusk intended to appoint William C. Foster, another Republican, to the job of Undersecretary for Economic Affairs, and decided to do something about it. He enlisted the aid of Stevenson, who had more power and influence with Kennedy than did Ball. Stevenson called Fulbright, adding his own protest about turning the government over to the Republicans, and Fulbright in turn pressured Kennedy, telling him enough was enough, to ease off this particular Republican appointment.

With Foster blocked, Ball became the obvious candidate, a Democrat, a lawyer willing to defend victims of McCarthy at the height of the witch hunt, a man whose specialty was economic affairs, a protégé of Jean Monnet's, a man who had worked long for the European Common Market. He was also a man of considerable pride and ego, the last man in Washington to write his own speeches, and a forcefully independent man. He may have entered the government with a Stevenson label, but once in office he turned out to be a classic Europeanist, in that sense at least in the Acheson tradition, though with less dependence on military force.

The suggestion to use combat troops in Vietnam disturbed him. He had worked closely with the French during the Indochina war, and he had seen it all, the false optimism of the generals, the resiliency and relentlessness of the Vietminh, their capacity to exploit nationalism and to mire down a Western nation, the poisonous domestic effect. He wanted no part of it for America. When he read the Taylor cables calling for a small, oh so small, commitment, 8,000 men only, he immediately told Bundy and McNamara that if they went ahead with the Taylor proposals, the commitment would not stay small. They would have 300,000 men in there within five years (he was slightly off; it was 500,000 men in five-plus years) because sending combat troops would change the nature of the commitment and the nature of the war, and the other side would not let us out easily. Besides, this was exactly what Diem wanted; it would stabilize his regime and we would do his fighting for him. Both Bundy and McNamara argued with Ball; they believed in the capacity of rational men to control irrational commitments, and in the end they decided that even at 300,000, a troop commitment was worth a try. Then, Ball said, they must tell the President that it was worth that much blood and resources, and Bundy and McNamara agreed. When Ball himself made exactly the same point to Kennedy—that he would have 300,000 men there in a few short years—the President laughed and said, "George, you're crazier than hell."

But it had jarred the President, and had made him even more aware of how long and dark the tunnel might be.

Not that he needed that much jarring; the President had plenty of doubts of his own. He was conscious of the danger of the recommendations, of the facility with which they had been contrived. "They want a force of American troops," he told Arthur Schlesinger at the time. "They say it's necessary in order to restore confidence and maintain morale. But it will be just like Berlin. The troops will march in, the bands will play, the crowds will cheer, and in four days everyone will have forgotten. Then we will be told we have to send in more troops. It's like taking a drink. The effect wears off and you have to take another." Instead, he said, it was the Vietnamese's war, it would have to be won by them. He told others that he was skeptical about the whole thing. He had been there when the French had 300,000 men and could not control the country, and he wondered aloud how we could do it any better than the French. Which angered Miss Marguerite Higgins, another hard-line columnist writing in the seemingly centrist New York *Herald Tribune*, who, hearing of the President's doubts, wrote on November 6 that he had "jumped from a false premise to a false conclusion." The French, she explained, had not lost Indochina, they had given it up in a truce.

Within the bureaucracy there were some inklings that a group was being formed which did not think the problem in Vietnam was primarily military (and thus could not be dealt with by military responses). Rusk remained somewhat on the sidelines, caught in his ambivalence between recurring doubts about the regime and its lack of reforms, as well as the dangers that sending troops might incur, and his conviction that the line against Asian Communism should be held and that the problem was the Chinese. If there was anyone whose job it was at this point to make the case against any military commitment, and make it forcefully, it was Rusk, but he tended to limit his dissent; he sensed that the use of a major advisory-support team was the least the President could get away with, so he acquiesced. The others at State were dubious. George Ball, of course, maintained that even sending advisers was the first step, and that the first step would fail and necessitate a second step. Averell Harriman, about to become Assistant Secretary of State for Far Eastern Affairs, was not an expert on Vietnam, in fact he knew precious little about it; but when he heard that here was a government that lacked confidence and had a crisis of morale, he sensed that these were euphemisms for far more serious illnesses. And there was the President himself, reluctant to send combat troops and repeat the French experience, but at the same time afraid of being charged with losing a country and deserting a brave ally, and thus of the domestic implications of not giving greater aid, of not having tried.

On November 11, three days after the McNamara recommendation to introduce combat forces, there was a new McNamara paper, done jointly with Rusk, which reflected the President's position. It was a compromise with the bureaucracy, particularly the military, and a compromise with the unstated, unwritten pressures against losing a country. Kennedy would send American support units and American advisers, but not American combat troops. We would help the South Vietnamese help themselves. If there really was something to South Vietnam as a nation and it really wanted to remain free, as we in the West defined freedom, then we would support it. We would send our best young officers to advise down to battalion level, we would ferry the ARVN into battle against the elusive Vietcong, and we would, being good egalitarians, pressure Diem to reform and broaden the base of a creaky government and modernize his whole society.

For McNamara to have switched on his recommendations was his normal procedure; his papers were always draft recommendations until the President made up his mind. Then they were tailored to the President's decision so that there would be no record for history of any difference between the Secretary of Defense and the President. He was that loyal. And Kennedy, holding the line on combat troops, told the Joint Chiefs of Staff to go ahead with the planning for a combat commitment, which was a typical procedure: if you do not give them what they want, give them a chance to dream of it. After the Bay of Pigs he had told them to go ahead with the plans for an invasion of Cuba. A little something for everybody, a little nothing for everybody, and in this case the chance to plan would give the Chiefs more of a thrust forward on Vietnam, a chance to think of the future rather than the past. There was in the final Kennedy package a good deal of emphasis on nation-building and reform, and a belief that we could somehow trick Diem into coming round. We would do this by by-passing Diem's government, creating strategic hamlets to protect the people from the Vietcong (on the assumption that they wanted to be protected). We would modernize the state not necessarily with Diem, but in spite of him.

This emphasis on reform and liberalization of the South Vietnamese society was in sharp contrast to the Taylor cables, which were primarily military in their view of the problem, but this was not surprising; it was somehow natural for a liberal, anti-Communist Administration to see the world through the prism of its own attitudes, and it was comforting to think in terms of reform, that liberalism and governmental change implanted from the top (the Vietcong were implementing change from the bottom up) could revive a sick society. Not only was it comforting to the Administration itself, but it was comforting to its supporters as well. It seemed a logical extension of that anti-Communism which was also liberal; it was going to do good for the people as well as stop the Communists. (Nothing came of the reforms, however, and a year and a half later when Taylor, the architect of the policy in the public's mind—the public, reading of the commitment, thought him more an architect of reform than of war, which was totally wrong—visited Vietnam, he was asked by reporter Stanley Karnow what had happened to the much discussed and much praised reforms, since there was no visible evidence of them. Taylor answered, with no small irritation, "I don't know. I'm no theoretician.")

There was, of course, no publicity given to the fact that we had almost sent combat troops. The Administration's public position was that Taylor had advised against the troops, and that he believed that the problem was primarily political and social, which, of course, enhanced his reputation in civilian circles, and again gave the impression that he was different and better than other generals. Yet once again a decision of great importance had almost slipped by the Administration. Very few people were called in to discuss it, there was no major intelligence survey on why the Vietcong were so successful and whether we could in fact halt their growth by military means. (In Saigon, Ambassador Nolting, hearing that a major military-assistance command was to be formed, was enraged and fought against it; the problem, he thought, was primarily political and he did not want to see a burgeoning American military commitment created. He thought seriously of resigning and he was disappointed that Rusk did not press his case more forcefully.)

For many reasons the Taylor-Rostow report was far more decisive than anyone realized, not because Kennedy did what they recommended, but because in doing less than it called for, he felt he was being moderate, cautious. There was an illusion that he had held the line, whereas in reality he was steering us far deeper into the quagmire. He had not withdrawn when a contingent of 600 men there had failed, and now he was escalating that commitment to 15,000, which meant that any future decision on withdrawal would be that much more difficult. And he was escalating not just the troop figure but changing a far more subtle thing as well. Whereas there had been a relatively low level of verbal commitment—speeches, press conferences, slogans, fine words—his Administration would now have to escalate the rhetoric considerably to justify the increased aid, and by the same token, he was guaranteeing that an even greater anti-Communist public relations campaign would be needed in Vietnam to justify the greater commitment. He was expanding the cycle of American interest and involvement in ways he did not know.

The aid did not come without American military bodies, and the military bodies did not come without journalistic bodies, so by expanding the number of Americans, Kennedy was in every way expanding the importance of Vietnam, making his own country more aware of it. From two full-time American correspondents, the number jumped to eight, including, most dangerous of all, American reporters with television cameras who roamed around discovering things that Diem did not want revealed. Diem's political enemies, who were numerous, finding no outlet through the constitution of Vietnam nor through the American embassy, would for the first time find sympathetic listeners in American reporters, and thus the expansion of the American commitment also meant that there would be an inevitable rise in the pace of domestic Vietnamese turbulence (Diem, totally removed from reality, and almost psychotic at the end, believed that when the first Buddhist monk burned himself to death, it had been arranged for and paid by NBC, despite the fact that there were no television cameras on the scene). What was true, however, was that the presence of American reporters tended to open up an otherwise closed country; this was the price Diem paid for getting American aid. Similarly, as the American commitment tended to be stalemated on the ground, the Administration, which had a powerful tendency toward media manipulation, would immediately fall back on the public relations aspect of the policy to justify it. If things in Vietnam were not working well, then the answer was to have more people make more speeches and thus get more positive coverage.

The Kennedy commitment changed things in other ways as well. While the President had the illusion that he had held off the military, the reality was that he had let them in. They now began to dominate the official reporting, so that the dispatches which came into Washington were colored through their eyes. Now they were players, men who had a seat at the poker table; they would now, on any potential dovish move, have to be dealt with. He had activated them, and yet at the same time had given them so precious little that they could always tell their friends that they had never been allowed to do what they really wanted. Dealing with the military, once their foot was in the door, both Kennedy and Johnson would learn, was an awesome thing. The failure of their estimates along the way, point by point, meant nothing. It did not follow, as one might expect, that their credibility was diminished and that there was now less pressure from them, but the reverse. It meant that there would be an inexorable pressure for more—more men, more hardware, more targets—and that with the military, short of nuclear weapons, the due bills went only one way, civilian to military. Thus one of the lessons for civilians who thought they could run small wars with great control was that to harness the military, you had to harness them completely; that once in, even partially, everything began to work in their favor. Once activated, even in a small way at first, they would soon dominate the play. Their particular power with the Hill and with hawkish journalists, their stronger hold on patriotic-*machismo* arguments (in decision making they proposed the manhood positions, their opponents the softer, or sissy, positions), their particular certitude, made them far more powerful players than men raising doubts. The illusion would always be of civilian control; the reality would be of a relentlessly growing military domination of policy, intelligence, aims, objectives and means, with the civilians, the very ones who thought they could control the military (and who were often in private quite contemptuous of the military mind), conceding step by step, without even knowing they were losing.

The immediate result of the Kennedy decision in December to send a major advisory and support team to Vietnam was the activation of a new player, a major military player, to run a major American command in Saigon. At first, when Kennedy took office, the pressure had come only from Diem; then, because of his policy to reassure Diem and make him the instrument of our policy, Kennedy had sent over Fritz Nolting, who would soon seem to many to be more Diem's envoy to the United States than vice versa. Now, by appointing Lieutenant General Paul D. Harkins to a new command, Kennedy was sending one more potential player against him, a figure who would represent the primacy of Saigon and the war, as opposed to the primacy of the Kennedy Administration, thus one more major bureaucratic player who might not respond to the same pressures that Kennedy was responding to, thereby feeding a separate and potentially hostile bureaucratic organism.

Harkins began by corrupting the intelligence reports coming in. Up until 1961 they had been reasonably accurate, clear, unclouded by bureaucratic ambition; they had reflected the ambivalence of the American commitment to Diem, and the Diem flaws had been apparent both in CIA and, to a slightly lesser degree, in State reporting. Nolting would change State's reporting, and to that would now be added the military reporting, forceful, detailed and highly erroneous, representing the new commander's belief that his orders were to make sure things looked well on the surface. In turn the Kennedy Administration would waste precious energies debating whether or not the war was being won, wasting time trying to determine the factual basis on which the decisions were being made, because in effect the Administration had created a situation where it lied to itself.

THE MEETING SEEMED AT THE TIME LIKE A FOOTNOTE TO TAYLOR'S trip. On his way back from Vietnam he had stopped off in Hawaii to visit his old friend Paul Harkins, a three-star general, then commander of the U.S. Army in the Pacific (in the marvelous jargon of the military, naturally, USAR-PAC). At that time the Army was considered somewhat weak in lieutenant generals, a level just below the great generals who had made it at the end of World War II and then come on even stronger in Korea. In fact, General Gavin had earlier urged Kennedy, in his search for his top military, to reach farther down in the ranks for younger men for high positions.

How bad is it out there? Harkins asked, and Taylor replied that it was bad, very bad; Harkins had better get ready to put his finger in the dike. A few weeks later, as is their wont in Army circles, Mrs. Taylor chatted on the phone with her friend Mrs. Harkins and suggested ever so casually that they not plan on staying in Hawaii very much longer. And on January 1 the call came through. Harkins would head the new U.S. command in Saigon, the command which was to be different and unconventional. No one, of course, could have been more conventional than Harkins. He knew nothing about guerrilla warfare, in fact he knew remarkably little about basic infantry tactics (if you knew something about small-unit infantry tactics you could at least learn about the war, because you could put yourself in the infantryman's place). He was a cavalry man in the old days, a great polo player, a dashing social figure in the old Army, and then a tanker, a staffman at that. His career was distinguished because he was, in Army terms, diplomatic. He had been a staff officer for George Patton, and softened some of Patton's verbal blows. He was considered very good on logistical planning. Harkins was, in addition to being a protégé of Patton's, a trusted friend of Taylor's. They had known each other well from the days at West Point and had kept in touch. When Max Taylor was Superintendent of the Point, it was not surprising that Paul Harkins turned up as Commandant of Cadets, and later when Max Taylor had the U.S. Eighth Army in Korea, it was not surprising that Paul Harkins was his chief of staff.

Others in the Army and in the bureaucracy were pushing for an officer with a sense of unconventional warfare, like Major General William Yarborough, then heading the Special Warfare School at Fort Bragg, or Colonel Ray Peers, who had served with the OSS during the war. But Taylor did not want an unconventional man. He had a very conventional view of the fighting and what he wanted was his own man, someone who was, above all, loyal to him. So he produced Harkins, a man with no real reputation of his own. His two main distinctions during his years of service in Vietnam would be, first, that his reporting consistently misled the President of the United States, and second, that it brought him to a point of struggle with a vast number of his field officers who tried to file realistic (hence pessimistic) reports. But even here the fault was not necessarily Harkins'. In all those years he felt that he was only doing what Max Taylor wanted, and there was considerable evidence that this was true, that his optimism reflected back-channel directives from Taylor. But it was one more insight into the era, all that talk about unconventional warfare, and then picking the most conventional officer. Even Kennedy knew it; after he met Harkins in Palm Beach, where the President was resting, Kennedy was asked what he thought of the new commander for Vietnam. He answered, somewhat less than enthusiastically, "Well, that's what they're offering me."

Chapter Ten

I N VIETNAM, THE INFLUX OF AMERICAN AID RECOMMENDED
under the Taylor-Rostow report changed nothing. The American intelligence
reports of the last few years had repeatedly warned that war waged by the
Vietcong was basically political, that the Diem regime was sick, perhaps ter-
minally sick. The American agreement to commit support and advisory elements also called for a broad range of social and political changes and reforms, to which Diem had agreed with considerable reluctance. If anything,
he regarded the American insistence on reform as an affront to him personally; the Communists were the enemy, not he and his family. What were the
Americans doing, involving themselves in Vietnamese domestic affairs, pressuring him to accept into his government people who were unreliable, criticizing his family both directly and indirectly?

Almost as soon as the Americans decided to increase their commitment, the
Ngo regime began to renege on the promised reforms; the Americans, as they
had systematically since 1954 in dealing with Diem, quickly acquiesced. Ambassador Nolting had the job of bringing Diem the news that the United
States would not be sending combat troops to Vietnam. Diem had not been
happy, Nolting reported, but he "took our proposals rather better than I expected." Two days later, however, Nolting reported that he had found out,
through high-level channels, that Diem was sulking and was very upset; at the
same time there were virulent attacks in the Nhu-controlled press claiming
that the Americans, rather than helping the country in an hour of need, were

interfering in Vietnamese affairs, and that they were naïve about reforms and about Communism. It was very clear what was happening; exactly as Ken Young and others had predicted, the Nhus were dominating Diem, warning him against the Americans, against their threat to his regime, and Diem, of course, was responding to his family. So, inevitably, on December 7, 1961, less than a month after the decision to make a far greater commitment based in large part on social reform, Washington was sending its embassy new recommendations, softening the demands for political reform. It was one more in a long series of decisions to go it alone with Diem on his terms, to treat the war as primarily a military problem, and to back off from using American leverage for any kind of social or political reform. Reform, given the nature of the regime, was of course impossible; reform meant getting rid of Mr. and Mrs. Nhu, and Diem was unwilling to do this. Washington had backed down again, and the key figure in this was Nolting, who had recommended that we not pressure Diem, that we trust him. We should accept his word and not demand his deeds. At a cocktail party shortly after the Americans backed down on reform, Ngo Dinh Nhu took an American reporter aside and praised Nolting lavishly. "Your ambassador," he said, "is the first one who has ever understood us." To Nolting, viability in South Vietnam meant getting along with the government at the top level in Saigon, not pressuring the government to do something about desperate conditions in the countryside. Washington accepted this; it showed that once more, despite all the talk of guerrilla warfare and political reform, the Americans were ready to be content with the status quo and to downgrade the political side.

Thus the real problems in Vietnam remained unaffected. The problems were political, but the response was military. The most important rural innovation, the strategic hamlet program, designed to give peasants protection and win their allegiance to the government, was given to Nhu to run, whereupon he, predictably, tried to make it his own personal fief and power base. Of course Nhu did not trust the Americans and the Americans did not trust Nhu; indeed the new allies were always uneasy with each other, and whether they had a genuine mutuality of trust and interest was dubious. (In 1961 one of the American experts sent over to help the Saigon government was a specialist in lie detectors; he authored an elaborate program to rid the government of one of its largest problems, high-level officials who were actually Vietcong agents. It looked like an excellent program until it was blocked by the Saigon CIA, whose officials realized that Saigon might also use the lie detectors to find out which government officials were also secretly on the CIA payroll.) But the important thing was the overall impact of the American aid; it was not finally a booster shot which would liberalize the government, but instead a shot of formaldehyde. The Americans were not modernizing Vietnamese society as Rostow had hoped; they were in fact making it more authoritarian and less responsive than ever. It did not change the balance in the countryside; if anything it simply meant that the Vietcong would now capture newer, better American weapons instead of old, used French weapons ("Ngo Dinh Diem will be our supply sergeant," said one highly accurate Vietcong paper of the period).

If this failure to change the political balance was not realized in Washington, it was understood by many in Saigon, particularly among the Vietnamese military, and it was certainly understood in Hanoi. There Bernard Fall, the French historian, was visiting in early 1962 on a rare visa. He was granted an interview with Prime Minister Pham Van Dong, and instead of finding Dong upset by the newest infusion of American aid, Fall saw that he was rather amused by it all. Poor Diem, Dong was saying, he is unpopular. And because he is unpopular, the Americans must give him aid. And because the Americans must give him aid, he is even less popular, and because he is even less popular, the Americans must give him even more aid . . . At which point Fall said he thought it sounded like a vicious circle. "Not a vicious circle," Dong said, "a downward spiral."

What the new major American involvement affected was not Vietnam, but the United States; its function would be based upon the perceptions, attitudes and judgments not of the President who initiated it, John F. Kennedy, but of the President who reluctantly accepted it, Ngo Dinh Diem. The American policy was to trust Diem and not to cross him; thus the American military mission saw its job as getting along with Diem, so his reporting became our reporting, his statistics our statistics, finally his lies our lies. What we did now, was, on a large scale, accept his view of the war, and of the society. Also, because we had gotten in so much deeper, we wanted to see commensurate results to justify the commitment. Since nothing changed, which meant there was little in the way of results, the American Administration would have to justify the decision it had made by manipulating the facts, by press agentry, by trying to manage the news and events, and finally, when that failed, by constant assaults on reporters in Vietnam who continued to report pessimistically. What could not be affected on the ground against the enemy the Administration tried to affect by public relations, with only slightly greater success.

The nature of our new commitment dictated that we could not be any better than our ally. Nolting could not be better than Diem, and Harkins could not be any better than those political hacks whom Diem had appointed as generals solely because they were loyal—which, if nothing else, gave them a certain kinship to Harkins. Loyalty was why he held his position.

GENERAL PAUL DONAL HARKINS, FIFTY-SEVEN, WAS A MAN OF compelling mediocrity. He had mastered one thing, which was how to play the Army game, how to get along, how not to make a superior uncomfortable. It would be hard to think of a man who had fewer credentials for running a guerrilla war in which Asian political injustices were at stake. To understand best what Harkins was like, it is important to understand what he was *not*. He was not, above all, a Joe Stilwell. Twenty years earlier, Stilwell had been in almost exactly the same position. He was tough, blunt and candid, almost joyously abrasive, delighting in getting along with the simplest private and causing problems for the highest civilian, preferably the President of the United States. Defeated by the Japanese, he walked out of Burma in 1942, and interviewed by reporters, said that he and his men had just taken a hell of a beating and had better go back and even things up (the idea of a contemporary American general ever admitting that he had taken a hell of a beating is inconceivable; there would be a battalion of $20,000-a-year government press spokesmen and public affairs officials descending to correct his statement, assuring reporters and the public that the general's words had been taken out of context; he had meant to say that this was certainly a difficult and complex war, that the enemy, while certain to be defeated in the long run, was surprisingly well led, but that the most important thing was how well his own American troops had fought, proving that Americans could fight under difficult Asian conditions). Stilwell loved to be with the grunts, eating at their mess, never cutting in on a chow line, basking in the knowledge that the boys liked feisty old Vinegar Joe. He was one of the boys, sharing every hardship and every heartache. Classically the commander, leading by being there and sharing the worst kind of front-line hardship, contemptuous of staff officers, perfumed dandies in the rear echelon, glorying in getting mud on his boots. (When Harkins first arrived in Saigon he was asked by an AP photographer named Horst Faas when he was going out in the field because the AP wanted some photos of him in fatigues and boots, walking through the paddies. "Forget that kind of picture," Harkins told him, "I'm not that kind of general.") Back in China, Stilwell wanted above all to be well informed, to know his own men's and the enemy's capabilities, and he knew that anything less than the blunt truth and blunt intelligence about the enemy might cost him lives, his boys. So he not only debriefed his own military people carefully, but plucked from the embassy staff in Chungking the brightest young political officers, like John Paton Davies, John Stewart Service and Raymond Ludden, because he wanted the best. It did not matter whether the news was good or bad; the worse the news, the more you needed it. If things were going well you did not need a good intelligence system quite as much, events took care of themselves.

If Stilwell was classically the commander and the old-fashioned kind of officer, then Harkins was just as much the other kind of general, the staffman who responded to superiors rather than to the field, and who was a good new modern man, there to soothe things over, to get along, not to make ripples but to iron out the wrinkles. (If the American public failed at first to acknowledge the dynamism in Harkins, it was no fault of *Time* magazine, which in May 1962, anxious to drum up support for the war in Vietnam, found Harkins "tall, trim, with grey hair, steely blue eyes and a strong nose and chin . . . looks every inch the professional soldier." *Time* even made comparisons with General George Patton, with whom Harkins had once served. "Outwardly the two were totally different: Patton, a shootin' cussin' swashbuckler; Harkins, quiet, firm, invariably polite. But a fellow officer says, 'I really think that inside, he and Patton were the same.' The same, certainly, in their drive for victory.")

Like almost all Americans who arrived in Vietnam, Harkins was ignorant of the past, and ignorant of the special kind of war he was fighting. To him, like so many Americans, the war had begun the moment he arrived; the past had never happened and need not be taken seriously. If the French had lost a war, they had fought it poorly; besides, they had made the mistake of being in a colonial war, fighting in order to stay, while we were fighting in order to go home. This was clear in our minds and it should be clear to the Vietnamese.

Occasionally Harkins would mouth phrases about this being a political war, but he did not really believe them. The American military command thought this was like any other war: you searched out the enemy, fixed him, killed him and went home. The only measure of the war the Americans were interested in was quantitative; and quantitatively, given the immense American fire power, helicopters, fighter-bombers and artillery pieces, it went very well. That the body count might be a misleading indicator did not penetrate the command; large stacks of dead Vietcong were taken as signs of success. That the French statistics had also been very good right up until 1954, when they gave up, made no impression. The French had lost the war because of a lack of will (the French were known for that) and a lack of fire power; Americans lacked neither will nor fire power.

At an early intergovernmental meeting on the importance of psychological warfare, one of Harkins' key staffmen, Brigadier General Gerald Kelleher, quickly dismissed that theory. His job, he said, was to kill Vietcong. But the French, responded a political officer named Douglas Pike, had killed a lot of Vietcong and they had not won. "Didn't kill enough Vietcong," answered Kelleher. Such was the attitude of the American headquarters; despite all the faddishness of counterinsurgency it was all very conventional, with a dominating belief that more and more force was what was really needed. Besides, it was not a serious war or a serious enemy; as the French generals had been overconfident because the enemy did not register in terms they could visualize and understand, so now were the American generals overconfident.

Who could be serious about an enemy who, having assaulted a village and captured it, did not stay around and defend its prize, but snuck off into the night?

When Harkins first arrived in Saigon to head the U.S. Military Advisory Command, Vietnam (MACV), he had told reporters that he was an optimist and that he was going to have optimists on his staff. He kept his word. From the very first, the reports he sent to Washington were titled "The Headway Report," leaving no doubt that things were going to get better. Very quickly his command became a special, almost unreal place, both isolated and eventually insulated from reality: the enemy was small, yellow, did not wear traditional uniforms, never held terrain, never fought in the daytime, and was known to kill innocent schoolteachers. As a worthy enemy, it was clearly overrated. The Saigon command soon reflected Harkins' views, with a flabby, foolish confidence; a staff can be no better than the man it serves, and Harkins was a pleasant, social-minded officer, a polo player. His intelligence was not without its limits ("He wasn't worth a damn, so he was removed," McNamara would say of him later; "you need intelligent people." Of course McNamara failed to explain why Harkins had held his position for almost two and a half years). He was the direct opposite of the other kind of general officer, the brilliant individual man going against the system and triumphing in spite of it (the latter needs wartime to excel, the former needs peacetime to excel, because warfare with all its unpredictability demands excellence and a willingness to go against the grain; only a very unusual general, like Max Taylor, can excel during both peace and wartime).

Rather than reflecting what was happening in the field, Harkins' shop reflected his Washington orders, and the facts would be fitted to Washington's hopes. Normally, for instance, G-2 (intelligence) is kept separate from G-3 (operations), but not in Harkins' shop. There the intelligence reports were edited down by the operations people, and the Vietcong capability was always downgraded and reduced. Battalion-size attacks became company-size attacks, company attacks became platoon attacks; reports from lower headquarters about the Vietcong capacity to replenish its forces were consistently ignored, as were intelligence reports of growing Vietcong resources (all of which, if taken seriously, would have put Harkins in conflict with Diem, as Stilwell had been in conflict with Chiang, and would have caused problems for General Taylor in Washington). It was all part of the game. Harkins was very genial about it, very friendly, except of course if a subordinate insisted on providing bad news. A civilian intelligence officer later recalled trying to warn Harkins in 1962 about the growing Vietcong threat in the Mekong Delta.

"Nonsense, I am going to crush them in the rainy season," Harkins said (the

rainy season, of course, favored the guerrilla, affording him better canal transportation and infinitely more hiding places than the dry season).

When the intelligence officer insisted, saying that the situation was about to
become irreversible, Harkins pushed him aside. This was not what his own intelligence shop was saying—why, Colonel Winterbottom was very optimistic.

"General Harkins," the civilian interrupted, "your intelligence chief
doesn't understand the threat at all. He's an Air Force officer and his specialty
is SAC reconnaissance and I'm sure he's very good at picking nuclear targets,
but he doesn't understand this war and he's not going to give you any feel for
it."

But Harkins was no longer so genial or so pleasant, nor such a good listener,
the civilian found. Harkins assured the visitor that his intelligence chief was
an officer and a good one and a professional, the best they had in Washington,
and he, General Harkins, did not need anyone in civilian clothes to tell him
how to run a war. And so it went. Harkins was comforted by his staff and his
statistics, and he comforted his staff as well; those who comforted him and
gave him what he was looking for had their careers accelerated.

He had no problems, Harkins told Secretary McNamara in July 1962. No
problems? Well, just one problem, he admitted, the American press. All along
he steadfastly brushed aside the growing problems and warnings from the
field in 1962. One particular incident comes to mind. Harkins had gone to Bac
Lieu, in the heart of the Mekong Delta, on one of his field inspections and the
briefing went very well. The Vietnamese officers may have been slow to learn
how to fight the Vietcong, but they were quick to master the art of what
pleased the Americans, not the least of which was the art of briefing. They
were, in fact, great briefers, and this summary had been particularly good,
Fort Bragg–perfect, made even more poignant by the commander's accent—
a reminder that we had exported the art of briefing.

They had, said the Vietnamese commander, planned only X number of
strategic hamlets, but the population so desperately wanted to be part of this
new national revolution that they insisted on coming in. Thus they had already built 3X hamlets. Harkins was very pleased. Proud is a better word, and
the smile grew on his face (no mention of the fact that the more hamlets built,
the more rake-off for the province chief and the division commander). With a
paternal glow, he congratulated the commander for such a fine presentation.
In an aside to an aide he said that this was the best thing about getting out in
the countryside, away from Saigon with all its intrigues and gossip; out there,
where the war really took place and where the people understood the enemy
and the threat, there were fewer problems. It was all healthier. The aide nodded. This was the real Vietnam.

A few minutes later Lieutenant Colonel Fred Ladd, the division adviser, asked to see Harkins for a minute. Ladd was typical of the best of the American officers in Vietnam, picked men, get your ticket punched for Vietnam, the only war we have; a West Pointer, son of a West Pointer, an intelligent, humane, sophisticated officer of whom it was said, get to know Ladd, a hot officer on the way to his first star. Ladd took Harkins aside and somewhat apologetically said he did not mean to upset the general, but the figures for the strategic hamlet program were flagrantly exaggerated, and the real total was about one third of that given by the Vietnamese commander. And then, rather than getting a wink from Harkins, a we-all-know-the-rules-of-the-game smile, the American commander in Vietnam turned on Ladd and upbraided him for challenging the word of a Vietnamese officer. Of course the Vietnamese figures were accurate. Ladd looked at him for a long time and said simply, "I thought we were talking American to American."

Harkins left, but Ladd had seen very clearly that day that there was a collision course ahead, that the marching orders, which had been implied in that conversation, were very clear: Do not make waves. He knew that it was going to be very difficult for him and that it might hurt his chances of becoming General Ladd, and he was right, there was a collision and he did not become General Ladd.

IN LATE OCTOBER 1961 KENNEDY, WANTING TO HOLD THE LINE ON Vietnam, had approved the new major American military commitment. Ironically, just a month later he took a step which would have profound consequences on that very commitment. As part of a major shake-up of the State Department which became known as the Thanksgiving Day Massacre (in which, among other things, Chester Bowles was removed from his post as Undersecretary), he named Averell Harriman Assistant Secretary of State for Far Eastern Affairs (or FE, as it was known at State). By putting Harriman there, Kennedy was in effect starting a chain of events which would lead Harriman onto a collision course with the new military commitment he had just authorized. In Saigon, Nolting and Harkins were committed to a policy of the past; now, in Washington, Harriman was under orders to modernize the Administration's Asian policies and personnel. The result was an inevitable conflict and the most ferocious governmental struggle of the Vietnam war, which left both sides almost totally depleted.

At the time Harriman took over FE, it was the most conservative branch of the State Department. More than any other bureau it had been damaged by the McCarthy period, and had therefore held to the policies of the Dulles years. Just a few months earlier James Thomson, Chester Bowles's young staff aide, had been assigned the job of clearing a major speech that Bowles planned to give on Asia. He went to the appropriate official, the public affairs officer for FE, who, after looking at the speech, pointed to a particular passage and said that it had to go. This was a reference to the great troubles that China had suffered from 1849 to 1949 at the hands of foreigners, and Bowles wanted to express regret for whatever role the United States had played in what the Chinese viewed as a painful and humiliating period.

Thomson, a China expert himself and later a professor of Asian history at Harvard, wondered why it would have to be cut.

"Because it's the Communist line," said the official.

"It's the Chiang Kai-shek line too," said Thomson, and began the awkward business of negotiating the speech through. Bowles would be allowed to keep the offending passage if he referred to the Chinese capital as Peiping, which was the Chinese Nationalist preference, instead of Peking, which was the Chinese government's preference, and thus normally State Department preference as well; eventually the speech was cleared.

The incident was not surprising to Bowles or Thomson because they were by then accustomed to it. The men who might have served at FE, John Davies, Jack Service, Edmund Clubb, had all been destroyed by the McCarthy investigations, and their successors had been men willing to serve in Asia under the terms dictated by Dulles, terms of the most rigid anti-Communism, where viewpoint and rhetoric often had very little to do with the facts. Dulles had wanted to appease the conservative Republicans on the Hill, and he had done it, but the price had been the integrity of the China desk and the Asian bureau. Neutralism was frowned on at FE; neutralists might come to power and be more sympathetic to the Communist side than to the Western side. At FE, loyalty came before intelligence.

"A wasteland," Harriman said. When he took over, he looked around his office, talked to the people, read the cables, and was absolutely appalled by what he found. "It's a disaster area filled with human wreckage," he confided to friends. "Perhaps a few can be saved. Some of them are so beaten down, they can't be saved. Some of those you would want to save are just finished. They try and write a report and nothing comes out. It's a terrible thing."

As Undersecretary of State, Bowles had begun the process of trying to change FE, but Rusk had held the line by putting his old friend Walter McConaughy there, which struck the Bowles people as too much in the Dulles tradition. Bowles had enjoyed more success with ambassadorial appointments in Africa than in Asia (because Asia was considered a more serious continent, with more at stake, where fewer risks could be taken). He had won one notable battle with the older foreign service people in Asia when he wanted Edwin O. Reischauer, the distinguished Harvard professor, to be ambassador to Japan. The traditionalists in the foreign service lobbied for Graham Parsons, the outgoing Assistant Secretary, and had in fact lined up the right wing of the Japanese Foreign Ministry to claim that it would be embarrassing for the Japanese to have Reischauer there, since his wife was Japanese. Even more striking in the Reischauer case, old FBI reports showed up claiming that Reischauer was a security risk because he was linked with John K. Fairbank, another Harvard professor, who according to the FBI reports had been called "a conscious agent" of the Stalin camp by Senator McCarran. At that point Bowles blew up and told the security people, "If you want someone close to Fairbank, why the hell don't you look over at the White House where he has a brother-in-law working?" (at that time Fairbank and Schlesinger were married to sisters). Reischauer eventually got the Japanese post, but it had not been easy.

So FE had remained much the same during the first year of the Kennedy Administration; now Harriman immediately set out to change it. He was the eldest member of the Kennedy group in the State Department, but he soon became the man that most young people in the Department began to turn to for leadership and freshness—for that element which had been so desperately needed at State for so long—an honest airing of new thoughts. All his career he had specialized in reaching out to young people, and he began to do this now. There was, for example, Michael Forrestal, the son of James Forrestal who had virtually been adopted by the Harrimans after the suicide of the father. Michael Forrestal had been brought down from Wall Street by Kennedy at Harriman's request, placed on the White House staff to work on Vietnam, and given these instructions by the President: "You will be my personal envoy to that special sovereignty known as Averell Harriman." And there was Roger Hilsman, the Director of Intelligence and Research, a Bowles man who seemed to be somewhere between Bowles and Rostow in his view of the underdeveloped world (aggressive on counterinsurgency, he believed his own experiences in Burma were more politically meaningful than they were, but he was against bombing and combat troops in Asia and for a more modern view of China). Harriman assigned Michael Forrestal and Jim Thomson to look for former FE men who still had some ability left, and see if they could be rehabilitated—and if they wanted to come back to dealing with Asia. Ed Rice, an older China hand who seemed to deviate from the accepted Chiang line, was summoned from Policy Planning. (Rice had earlier caught the eye of Bowles by sending over a paper from Policy Planning which showed a surprising degree of flexibility on China. Bowles was pleased by the freshness of the outlook and sent his specialist on China to meet with Rice. Jim Thomson was impressed that someone with Rice's background—he had served in China during the worst and most sensitive period of the forties—had managed to survive without being crushed in the Republican purges of the fifties. The answer was simple, Rice explained; for some reason which he did not understand, Patrick Hurley, the leader of much of the witch hunt, had placed a letter of commendation in his file long before China had become sensitive, and this had scared off the head hunters.) Paul Kattenburg, one of the best of the old Indochina hands, was brought back to the Vietnam working group, where he began to have immediate impact. Bob Barnett, another exiled China hand, was transferred to Harriman's office. Allen Whiting, a China expert, came to INR from Rand and had particularly good credentials because he had written with great insight about the Chinese entry into Korea. But Whiting warned Roger Hilsman that he wanted no part of Vietnam because, as he put it, if the policy was (in the words of Homer Bigart) "Sink or swim with Ngo Dinh Diem," then we were going to sink.

Harriman wanted, above all, men who spoke freely and who did not automatically produce the existing mythology of the recent past. He drove those around him relentlessly, he did his homework (when he heard that Whiting's book on China crossing the Yalu was good, he did not ask some young officer to brief him on it; he read it himself and then summoned Whiting to spend an entire Sunday going over it). He was single-minded, wildly ambitious, often thoughtless, sometimes savage, always combative (at one of the tough sessions on Vietnam he called Major General Victor Krulak, the JCS special representative who was spouting the Taylor-Harkins line of pure optimism, "a goddamn fool"). He became one of the foremost figures in the bureaucracy, a restless, bruising figure who never quit.

He was seventy at the time. "Averell looks terrific," a friend told Marie Harriman that year. "You'd look terrific too," she answered, "if you did nothing but play polo until you were forty years old." He was unique in many ways; he brought with him so much history, so many ties to great figures of the past that the young men who had taken office could not imagine that he would be able to function at their level and speed. They soon learned that it was they who were hard pressed to function at his level and speed and intensity. Six years later Robert Kennedy, admitting defeat (he had once doubted Harriman's vitality), would give a surprise birthday party at Hickory Hill for Harriman. The main feature came at the last minute when the curtains were drawn back to show an illuminated porch with huge blowups of figures from Harriman's past: Churchill, Roosevelt and Stalin. There was a special touch of historic irony here: Joe Kennedy's boy, the boy Joe thought most like him, giving a party in honor of Harriman, the man whom Roosevelt had sent to England at the beginning of the war almost to counteract the pessimistic impressions and appraisals of Joe as ambassador. Harriman, the special envoy, who had stood beside Churchill again and again in public as a visible and tangible evidence of American commitment and presence, who in the dark days of North Africa had hand-carried messages from Winston to General Wavell which said that Harriman had Winston's complete confidence, was most intimate with Roosevelt and Hopkins, and "no one can do more for you . . ."

HE HAD NOT BEEN BORN WITH THOSE PARTICULAR LIBERAL PREJ-
udices; if anything, he had been born with a silver railroad in his mouth. He
was the son of E. H. Harriman, the man who built the Union Pacific (a company not known for its dedication to public service), one of the great ruthless
titans of an age, who had himself been born in 1848, which links Harriman
seemingly to another age. Averell was second-generation, still very much tied
to that ruthless first generation, aware of the reputation, stiff and proper in his
public gestures and stances, unable to repudiate the past in public gestures,
still sensitive about his father, as Nelson Rockefeller was not about his grandfather, the Rockefeller image having been deliberately and successfully tempered from the money grabber of the first generation to the blintz-eating,
arm-pumping good fellow of the third generation. Years and years after, when
contemporary America had long ago forgotten it, Harriman still felt the sting
of Teddy Roosevelt's reference to his father as being among the "malefactors
of great wealth," a charge which must have made the switch to the Democratic party easier.

He went to Groton, of course, and then Yale. His father, who believed that
rowing was the right sport for a young gentleman, particularly a very tall
young gentleman, had imported the Syracuse crew coach in the summers to
coach Averell on a special lake in Orange County in the middle of a vast Harriman estate, with the result that when Averell arrived at Groton he easily
made the crew. Going on to Yale, he would have rowed there, except that a
slight heart murmur was discovered, so he had to row in single and double
sculls instead. This was hardly enough for his abnormal energy, and since
rowing seemed to be in great decline at Yale, he volunteered to coach first the
freshman and eventually the varsity crew. ("Most of the rest of Washington
thinks of Dean Acheson as the Secretary of State under Harry Truman and a
great figure of another time. I still think of him as someone I taught rowing to
on the freshman crew at Yale," he has told friends.) Since there was only one
place to learn about rowing in those days, England, Harriman went there for
two months at his own expense to study Oxford rowing; after his return to
Yale, the crews there showed marked improvement. It was a typical Harriman act, both in professional and in personal life: whatever it is you're interested in, find the source and learn all you can, let nothing stand in your way.
At a late date he decided he wanted to learn bowling, thereupon built two
bowling lanes in his home and practiced until he became quite proficient;
similarly, wanting to learn about croquet, he read every book on the subject,
studied the game, and when he played he took as much as twenty minutes to
play a stroke, thus infuriating and upsetting opponents.

His boyhood was spent at the best school, he traveled around the country
in a private Pullman car, and he was elected to the board of Union Pacific as a
college senior. He did not serve in the Great War, though he was twenty-two

when it began and most members of his age group were attracted to it. There was in fact a certain deal of murmuring at the time about his not going. In those days he seemed well on his way to being another powerful businessman. (Interviewed in *Forbes* magazine in 1920, when he was twenty-nine, he said, "It is indefensible for a man who has capital not to apply himself diligently to using it in a way that will be of most benefit for the country as it is for a laborer to refuse to work, or for a revolutionary to resort to bombs in this country. Idle capital or capital misapplied is as destructive economically as the conduct of the loafing worker or the bomb thrower.") He expanded the Harriman empire into shipping and he immediately became the foremost American operator in that field. He was adventurous in his dealings, and in 1924, when the Soviet Union was looking for foreign capital, it made available a twenty-year concession for exploiting manganese in Georgia. It was the kind of arrangement which appalled almost all capitalists at the time; if the Soviet Union seemed the enemy in the nineteen-fifties, this was even more true thirty years earlier. The mutual stereotypes were more pronounced, and there was an almost neurotic capitalist fear of Communist Russia. For Harriman to take up the Russian offer—he put up about $3.5 million for the rights—was deemed disloyal and excessively risky, but it was a good insight into the unpredictability of Harriman, even in his incarnation as a stiff and traditional businessman. The deal never worked out; the Soviets made a comparable agreement with a German group at better rates, and much merriment was made of Averell's folly. Harriman himself went to the Soviet Union and lobbied for better terms; although he did not succeed, he did talk the Russians into announcing that they would pay back his original investment with a certain amount of interest, which they eventually did. The experience left both Soviet officials and Harriman seeing beyond some of the stereotypes of the period, each side believing that the other could be talked to, and dealt with.

Exactly what brought Harriman into the political world and the Democratic-party world in 1928 is hard to say, but a number of factors worked together. One was the pressure from a maverick elder sister, Mary Harriman, who was far more socially concerned, and was a close friend of Frances Perkins. She had entered a world vastly different from her origins, and had a sense of responsibility to do something with her privileges. Another was his close ties with New York Governor Al Smith, who helped bring Harriman into the Democratic party. Their relationship was warm and personal, and there are those who feel that Harriman's special feeling for John Kennedy (Harriman seemed to age twenty years after the assassination) was a way of paying back this young Catholic President for what an earlier Catholic candidate had done for him, for the worlds he had opened up. A large part of it was the worlds to conquer: in the world of business, the son of E. H. Harriman could be little more than the son of E. H. Harriman. The empire was already built, the mountain had been climbed (and in fact literally chopped down on the Harriman estate in order to find a perfect level site for their home). The challenge was more or less gone. Money bored him, he was not interested in it. Though he accepted what money could do for him, he was not motivated to gain more and he did not like to spend it; he was sensitive to the malefactors-of-great-wealth accusations and saw no reason to give his life to amass an even greater fortune. He could find the challenge in the world of international politics and domestic politics, worlds which would produce enough problems to satisfy his restlessness, and let him become totally absorbed in his project and mission of the moment. In his *Memoirs,* George Kennan later wrote of Harriman's single-mindedness, his total lack of affectation and snobbery (as free of it as only the very rich and very aristocratic can be; Averell, says another friend, is a certain kind of snob, a power snob—he's interested only in who has power).

The concentration, the attention to detail became legendary; he delegated nothing. He made his young aides work hard but he was always aware of everything they were doing, and he remained in command, even when they thought his attention was elsewhere. Among those who learned this particular lesson was Daniel Patrick Moynihan, who was offered a campaign job with Harriman in 1954. Moynihan thought the campaign job would be a marvelous chance to learn the ropes of political machinations, to set up studies and develop issues, but he soon found himself announcing over a loudspeaker system for the Harriman entourage, that and nothing else. The last day of the campaign they started early in the morning on Long Island, with Moynihan doing his thing: "Come meet Averell Harriman here at the Grumman works in ten minutes. The next governor of New York, Averell Harriman, will be here in ten minutes. Come meet Averell Harriman . . ." He had done it all day stop after stop just as he had done it for three months, and now at the end of the day, during the rush hour in the middle of the garment center, with Harriman about to make his last appearance, Moynihan had let loose. All the pent-up energy, all the good lines he had intended to put into speeches came out: an attack on the inequitable tax the Republicans planned, on their insensitivity to the workingman, on their opposition to basic New Deal welfare protection —all this, and other sins as well. He was still attacking the Republicans when he felt a tap on his shoulder from the cop riding with them. "Hey, Mac," the cop said, "Mr. Harriman says 'Just announce. Nothing more. Don't make policy.'"

If he, one of the richest men in the world, did not particularly care that much about making money, he was at least cautious about spending it, and stories about Harriman's tightness became legend. Part of it was a real fear which traced back to his childhood, that people were after him for his money, and he was singularly loath to encourage them in that pursuit. At times this hurt him as a politician: where Rockefeller spent lavishly in his own behalf and occasionally for his party in order to sweeten other party relationships, Harriman was far more austere, both to himself and to his party, particularly the latter. As a good Democrat he had of course contributed to the funds for Herbert Lehman when he campaigned in the past, so when Harriman decided to run on his own in 1954, his aides went to see Lehman. They wanted not just any contribution, they soon made clear, but a large one, worthy of Lehman's own considerable wealth. Lehman listened for a while and inquired what they had in mind. The figure they suggested was in the thousands, several thousands. Lehman, who had a long memory, then asked if they would take a contribution which was double what Harriman had given Lehman. Eagerly the aides said yes. Lehman excused himself, went back to his office to go through the files, came back and handed the aides a check for $200.

HARRIMAN HAD BEEN THE PERFECT FIGURE FOR THE DEMOCRATIC party in foreign affairs in the Roosevelt-Truman years, a full-blown true-blue capitalist who had the allegiance of his class and yet was a party partisan on domestic issues as well. He was the party's most legitimate capitalist, and foreign governments, including the Soviet, knew that he spoke not just for an Administration but for the power structure as well. (When Khrushchev came to America in 1959, he asked Harriman to round up the real power structure of America for him, not the paper power structure. Harriman did just that, thus confirming to Khrushchev that his own view of who held power in America, as opposed to that of those who *thought* they held power in America, was correct, which it probably was.)

As governor of New York he was a singularly poor politician, stiff and proud and unbending to the public, and totally compromising in private. What made him so bad in domestic politics was that he was working for himself and thus was ruthless in the pursuit of his own ambition, whereas in Washington his ambition was still great but somehow tempered by a sense of country, thus evoking the best in him, wisdom, patience and a sense of perspective. Yet not only was he a poor governor, and beaten badly by Rockefeller in 1958, but he almost destroyed the Democratic party of New York, as pointed out by Theodore White, one of his admirers, in *The Making of the President, 1960*. After emphasizing that no American had helped exercise his nation's power throughout the world as Harriman had in the previous two decades, White wrote:

Yet brought face to face with the domestic system of American power, no man proved more incapable of understanding; and his performance in 1958 in directing the Democratic Party in New York not only destroyed the pride and honor of both machine and citizen elements of that Party but probably rendered the Party incapable of governing New York again for years.

That was written in 1960, and in 1972 Rockefeller is still governor, there is a Republican senator, and a Conservative senator, and the last two Democratic candidates for mayor of New York City have been defeated.

HE HAD STARTED THE KENNEDY YEARS AT THE BOTTOM RUNG. HE HAD not realized the Kennedy electoral force early enough, and was prejudiced against the candidate not on grounds of religion, but on grounds of heredity, disliking old Joe Kennedy for many reasons. The early indices of his future with the Administration were not good. He was sent on a preinaugural fact-finding tour of Africa, a place far from the center of the action, and when he showed up at Kennedy's Georgetown house to give his report, he was allowed the grand total of five minutes with the President-elect, then was quickly shuttled off to lunch with an aide named Tom Farmer, delegated to hear the entire story of Africa and Harriman. He was given the job of roving ambassador, and the Administration thought that that would be both the beginning and the end of it. But he had moved up quickly, gaining the President's admiration for his handling of the Laotian problem. Later he would tell friends that it was the easiest set of presidential instructions he ever had, a five-minute phone call during which Kennedy said, "A military solution isn't possible. I want a political solution." He was what Kennedy had been looking for all along, a man both of the Establishment and of the Democratic party with a transferable personal loyalty. He got things done; he did not make a good target for enemies; he was not soft. He had of course entered the Administration fully operative, unlike many of the men in the Administration for whom it was their first time in office. And he had diagnosed the Kennedy Administration very ably; he had sensed that they needed him, that there would be a role to play, and now it was coming true. With Rusk vulnerable, there would have to be a new Secretary of State, and only George Ball at State was a potential rival for the job (Bundy was a Republican and too valuable at the White House, and McNamara was good at Defense and not wise or political enough for State). So he began to move into the vacuum at State that Rusk had created.

In late 1962 and 1963 he clearly emerged as a figure in the Department openly challenging Rusk for leadership, obviously a candidate for Secretary of State, a job which he, a man so private about his own feelings, would once admit wistfully was the only job he had ever wanted; the Presidency thing had not been real, but State, *that* was his ambition. Although he had not been a particular fan of Rusk's from the start, he had begun by being extremely correct with him. But Rusk's style soon irritated him, and those who were around him detected a very subtle patronizing of the Secretary. (It showed at one staff meeting of high-level State officials: Rusk, Ball, Harriman, the Assistant Secretaries. Rusk addressed his team, saying that Harold Wilson was in town and that it looked as if he was going to win the election and become Prime Minister, and perhaps they had better do something for him. Did anyone know where he was staying? No one knew, so Rusk dispatched Ball to call the British embassy and find out. Ball left, came back white-faced a few minutes later, and whispered to Rusk, "He's Averell's house guest." Harriman, sitting there, never moved a muscle.) One incident during the Geneva negotiations had particularly enraged Harriman. He had asked Rusk for permission to see the Chinese delegates in Geneva, and Rusk had refused, leaving Harriman furious.

He began to by-pass Rusk more and more, and encouraged others, such as Hilsman, to do the same; he had, he felt, deferred to the Secretary, but if the Secretary was not going to fight, then the time for deference was past. He became more open in his lack of respect for Rusk, finally turning to friends, saying how could you deal with someone like Rusk who was spending all his time protecting his private parts, and at that point Harriman, usually so correct and proper, bent over and imitated his own description.

THE BUREAUCRACY HARRIMAN HAD ENTERED TENDED TO BE ABOUT ten years behind in their views of current events, but he felt that the Administration, more politically sensitive to changes at home and overseas, should react more rapidly. If so, the bureaucracy and its reporting did not serve the President well and should be challenged by younger and bureaucratically unencumbered men. Then the President would have a choice, otherwise the top people would get together and agree among themselves what was the wise and safe, and tailor the reporting to it. Which of course was exactly what was happening. Harriman's feelings about Vietnam were hardly the result of his ideological bias, and unlike Bowles, he did not bring a grand design to foreign affairs. He was a man who was totally divorced from his own class's political viewpoints and prejudices; more important and far more remarkable, he was able to divorce himself from the prejudices of his own political past, from the years of tension with the Soviet Union. No one had been more a part of the Marshall Plan confrontation than Harriman, yet for him Vietnam would never be Germany, Laos never Italy, and SEATO never NATO. In an era when too many of the key figures seemed overly conscious of their own immediate part in the Marshall Plan—those lessons learned being the only lessons learned; having stopped the Communists in Europe, anxious to apply once more the lessons of containment. Harriman was markedly different, yet no one could have had a greater stake in that era. As ambassador to Russia at the end of the war Harriman had, with Kennan, been among the very first to warn of the difficult years ahead. He had also played a crucial role in influencing James Forrestal, who subsequently geared up the Washington machinery for the American half of the Cold War. The entry in the Forrestal *Diaries* for April 20, 1945, reads:

I saw Averell Harriman, the American Ambassador to Russia, last night. He stated his strong apprehensions as to the future of our relations with Russia unless our entire attitude toward them became characterized by much greater firmness. He said that, using the fear of Germany as a stalking horse, they would continue their program of setting up states around their borders which would follow the same ideology as the Russians. He said the outward thrust of Communism was not dead and that we might well have to face an ideological warfare just as vigorous and dangerous as Fascism or Nazism.

If he had warned about Soviet thrust into Europe, he had also been intimately concerned with the Marshall Plan as head of the Economic Cooperation Administration and later as director of Mutual Security, but he always thought of events within their own context. He sensed immediately that what motivated Asian Communists might be very different from what motivated European Communists; thus they might be very different people. So he entered the confrontation on Vietnam with enormous bureaucratic expertise and toughness, little expertise on Asia, but a great capacity to learn and a remarkably fresh mind.

Within weeks of Harriman's taking over at FE, some of his people were questioning the reporting and the optimism from Saigon. But it is crucial in retrospect to see the limits of the challenge. Then and in the months to follow, Harriman and his aides assaulted the accuracy of the military reports, of Nolting's cables and of Diem's viability, but they did not challenge the issue of dominoes upon which the commitment to South Vietnam was based, nor the broader role of America in the world. They were, in effect, asking the smaller questions in lieu of the larger ones. No one, least of all the President, wanted that kind of problem aired now. So it was a challenge within the limited pragmatism of the period: not whether we should be there or not, but whether we were winning, whether Diem, not South Vietnam, was viable. Harriman himself was still very much the anti-Communist in the broader sense, and he was an enthusiastic member of the counterinsurgency group (years later when a friend of his mildly mocked the faddishness and foolishness of the counterinsurgency period, he became very offended. Why, he answered, we did all kinds of good things throughout Latin America . . .). He was in effect challenging the absurdity of the surface, not the absurdity of the root. His job was to modernize the Dulles policies in Asia, but he and his aides were more disadvantaged in that job than they might have been a few months earlier, because the Kennedy Administration had just taken the very Dulles policies in Vietnam and escalated them. The commitment was greater and larger; there was one more American limb fastened to the Vietnamese tar baby.

Chapter Eleven

BY SENDING ITS VAST ADVISORY AND SUPPORT GROUP—WHICH would eventually number some 18,000 men—the Administration had changed the commitment without changing the war, or the problems which had caused it. If it did not improve the war effort, the commitment did affect Washington; it deepened the Administration's involvement in Vietnam, making it a more important country, moving it off the back burner of crisis quotient. It made the Administration dependent on the military reporting and estimates, for the military would dominate the reporting. The question was no longer one of Diem's popularity or effectiveness (the answer to that question was that he was not popular, but he was *respected*); the real question now was the war, whether it was being won. And the answer was yes, it was being won, it was going very well, all the indices were very good. General Harkins was optimistic; he headed what was now a powerful institutional force for optimism. He had been told by his superior, Maxwell Taylor, to be optimistic, to downgrade pessimism, and he would do exactly that. He perceived his role as duty, duty to the President, and more important, to Max Taylor and the U. S. Army, and he did not question what he was doing. Joe Stilwell's ear had been tuned to the field, but Paul Harkins' ear was tuned to Washington and the Pentagon. Everything, he assured his superiors, was right on schedule; everyone was getting with the program. The war was being won. He saw victory shaping up within a year.

The only thing wrong was that the war was not being won; it was, in fact, not even being fought. The ARVN was a replica of the past, was even more arrogant now than ever. All the old mistakes were being repeated in the field; the army still systematically enraged the population by running giant sweeps through peasant villages, with its soldiers stealing chickens and ducks. It still refused to run operations where the Vietcong were known to congregate. It still launched operations with carefully timed preattack artillery shelling so that the Vietcong, thus forewarned, could escape by carefully planned routes. Since Diem was afraid that if his army suffered losses he would lose face, he told his commanders not to risk casualties, so they joined battle as little as possible. They made up for the difference in results by falsifying after-action reports, creating statistics which were soon on their way to Washington bearing Harkins' imprimatur.

After a brief period in early 1962 when the arrival of the helicopters caught the Vietcong by surprise and there were a couple of quick government victories, the American booster shot failed. The Vietcong quickly learned that if helicopters appeared, it was better to stand and fight than run and be slaughtered. Thus they neutralized the new American-given mobility. Soon the only tangible result of the great American build-up was that the Vietcong were capturing better weapons. All the government optimism was being built on faked reports. That in itself was not surprising; what was surprising was that these lies now bore not just the stamp of the government of South Vietnam but that of the United States of America as well. MACV, Harkins' command, accepted the ARVN battlefield reports without checking them out. The American military and propaganda machine uncritically passed on the lies of a dying regime.

But in the field, things were different. There American officers began to respond to the deceit they encountered daily. It was one thing to sit in Saigon in an air-conditioned room and pass on fake reports; it was another to send young American advisers into combat, knowing that they were risking their lives for what was essentially a fraud. An inevitable confrontation of serious proportions took place.

As the war effort began to fall apart in late 1962 and early 1963, the Military Assistance Command in Saigon set out to crush its own best officers in the field on behalf of its superiors in Washington. It was a major institutional crisis, but Washington civilians were unaware of it. It was not as if two different and conflicting kinds of military reporting were being sent to Washington, with the White House able to study the two and arbitrate the difference. The Saigon command systematically crushed all dissent from the field; the military channels did not brook dissent or negativism. If a colonel surfaced in a newspaper by name as a pessimist it was the end of his career (in 1963, as some of the dissenting colonels turned to the press in their frustration, editors in New York would cable their reporters in Saigon saying those pessimistic stories were all right, but couldn't the reporters please use the names of some of the unhappy colonels?). Had there been some high Washington officials who had gone through the China experience and survived the aftermath, they would immediately have recognized it: the collapse of a feudal army confronted by a modern guerrilla army, with a high-level foreign general trying to cover up. But people in the Administration either did not know what had happened in China, or in a few cases, they knew but desperately wanted to avoid a repetition of it. What was happening was identifiable, except that no one was in any rush to identify it.

The conflict between Harkins and his senior advisers in the Mekong Delta, his colonels and lieutenant colonels, was, however, very real. These officers were the fulcrum between the Saigon command, with its illusions about the war and its sense of responsibility to its superiors in the Pentagon, and the reality in the field where the junior officers, the captains and lieutenants, were discovering their ally did not want to fight and that the enemy was winning. At considerable risk to their own careers, the four key officers began to complain, in varying ways and in varying degrees. The four advisers were Colonel Wilbur Wilson, III Corps (the main area around Saigon, and west and north of it); Colonel Dan Porter, IV Corps (the rest of the Mekong Delta); Lieutenant Colonel John Paul Vann, 7th Division (the northern tier of the Delta); and Lieutenant Colonel Fred Ladd, 21st Division (the southern tier of the Delta). They were all combat veterans of other wars, men who had been specially selected for these slots. They were neither hawks nor doves (those terms did not exist at the time), but they wanted to win the war, and at that point they still thought it a possibility. They were in their late thirties and early forties, and they understood at least some of the political forces the Vietcong represented. Finally, they were living where the war was taking place, and they thought it was a serious business, sending young men out to die, and if you were willing to do it, you also had to be willing to fight for their doubts and put your career on the line. To the Saigon command, then and later, Vietnam and the Vietnamese were never really a part of American thinking and plans; Vietnam was at best only an extension of America, of their own careers, their own institutional drives, their own self-image. To the men in the field it was a real war, not just a brief interruption in their careers, something to prevent damaging your career.

Ladd was quickly put down for pessimistic reporting from his area. Vann was even worse; his reporting had caused some problems in the past. Now a major storm would center around him in January 1963 when the division he advised was badly defeated and performed with great cowardice at the battle of Ap Bac, which, being close to Saigon, was well covered journalistically. Harkins was furious, not at the Vietnamese or their commander, but at Vann for having called it a defeat and for having talked with American reporters.

Harkins planned to fire Vann at the time but was talked out of it by staff members who argued that firing him would bring even more adverse publicity; they also warned that advisory morale was low enough as it was. Instead Harkins upbraided Vann, and Vann became a nonperson. Anything he wrote or said thereafter was simply disregarded, and important visitors to the country were steered away from his area.

Porter, Vann's immediate superior, was next. Before he went home after two long years, he had to turn in a final report, and it was brutally frank. Aides suggested that Porter sweeten it by putting in a few positive notes, but he refused. He was angry and bitter over the way *his* subordinates were being treated, and after consulting with Ladd, Vann and Wilson, he handed in the most pessimistic report on the war so far, on the nature of the peasant, the enemy and the ally. Harkins went into a rage over it; normally final reports of senior advisers were circulated for all other top advisers, but Harkins had Porter's report collected. He told other officers that it would be sanitized and that if it contained anything of interest, he might then make it available. It was never seen again, which did not surprise Porter, but enough was enough, he was leaving the Army.

One other man entered the struggle, a general officer named Robert York who had a distinguished record as a regimental commander in World War II. He was in Vietnam doing special evaluation on guerrilla warfare, which he knew something about, having been stationed as an attaché in Malaya during that guerrilla uprising. He quietly went around the countryside, not touring, the way Harkins did, in chief-of-state style, with the seventeen-course lunch at the province chief's house. Instead York unpinned his general's stars and dropped in on unsuspecting ARVN units. Thus he saw the war and the ally as they really were. Typically, while Harkins came in by helicopter to chew out Vann at the battle of Ap Bac, York was still in the field, pinned down by artillery fire from a province chief. In early 1963, though he had just received his first star, York decided to put his career on the line and handed in a detailed and pessimistic report on the war. But he never heard from Harkins about it; his commander's only response was to scribble "Lies," "More lies," "Vann," "Porter," "Vann again," "Porter again" in the margins. It was indicative of the differences between Saigon and the field; the viewpoints of the command were those of men who lived with peacetime attitudes and had a peacetime military integrity; the men in the field were men at war.

Of these men it was Vann, the most intense and dedicated of them, who came to symbolize the struggle against Harkins and his superior, General Taylor. By the time Vann went home in June 1963, he was the most informed American in the country. A statistician by training, he had managed to come up with a new kind of statistic. In contrast to the MACV, whose figures reflected only the greater American fire power and the American willingness to accept inflated ARVN body counts at face value, Vann had managed to compile a different kind of statistical story. Thus he documented the ARVN failure to fight (of the 1,400 government deaths in his sector in one year, only 50 were ARVN). This did not mean that the ARVN was fighting well, as Harkins implied; it confirmed that they were not fighting at all, and that the burden of the war was being borne by ill-equipped local militia who more often than not (Vann proved this too) were being killed asleep in their defensive positions. He was able to prove that commanders got troops from Diem not on the basis of Vietcong pressure, but on the basis of personal ties and their ability to protect Diem against a coup.

Vann went home a very angry man, to find that Saigon had ordered that he not be debriefed in Washington. So he began to give his briefing to friends at the Pentagon. It was a professional presentation indeed, and very different from the usual briefings which were coming in from Saigon. What made it striking was that it was not just impressionistic, it seemed to be based on very hard facts. Vann began to get higher and higher hearings in the Pentagon until finally General Barksdale Hamlett, the Deputy Chief of Staff of the Army, heard the briefing, was impressed and arranged for Vann to meet with the Joint Chiefs. Vann was warned by several high officers that above all he must not appear to be critical of General Harkins, who was the personal choice of Maxwell Taylor (by this time Chairman of the Joint Chiefs), since Taylor seemed to be particularly sensitive and protective of Harkins and his reporting. He was also warned not to show his briefing until the last minute to General Krulak, who was the Secretary of Defense's special adviser on guerrilla warfare, and a person who was already surfacing as a man with a vested interest in the optimism, having just returned from a tour of Saigon and reported to the Chiefs that the war was going very well, every bit as well as Harkins said.

The Vann briefing was set for 2 P.M. on July 8, 1963. At 9:45 he sent a copy to General Krulak's office. A little later Vann, eager, starched, finally getting his hearing, showed up outside the office of General Earle G. Wheeler, the Chief of Staff, to be on hand in case there were any new developments. He was sitting there when a phone call came in to one of Wheeler's aides. "*Who* wants the item removed from the agenda?" the aide asked. The voice at the other end spoke for a few minutes. "Is this the Secretary of Defense's or the Chairman's office?" There was more talk. "Is that an order or a request?" Then more talk. "Let me get this right. The Chairman *requests* that the item be removed." The aide turned to Vann. "Looks like you don't brief today, buddy." He went to Wheeler's office, returned in a minute, picked up the phone and dialed a number and said, "The Chief agrees to remove the item from the agenda."

Thus a major dissenting view was blocked from a hearing at the highest level by Max Taylor, and thus the Army's position on how well the war was going was protected (had Vann briefed, it would have been much harder for the high-level military to go into meetings with the President and claim that the war was going well). This charade was a microcosm of the way the high-level military destroyed dissenters, day after day in countless little ways, slanting the reporting lest the top level lose its antiseptic views, lest any germs of doubt reach the high level. It confirmed to many in the Pentagon that a good deal of the reason for the Harkins optimism and its harshness on doubters was not just Harkins' doing. Rather, Harkins was a puppet controlled by Taylor and reflected Taylor's decision that this should be the key to back-channel messages and the unofficial "word" which is so important in the Army, that the unofficial word for Harkins was coming from Taylor, and that the messenger between them was General Krulak.

SINCE MID-1962 THE AMERICAN MILITARY HAD BEEN TURNING TO THE handful of American journalists in Saigon, using them as an outlet for their complaints. It was not particularly deliberate; but it was also impossible to keep their skepticism hidden. The journalists kept showing up in the countryside, and it was only a matter of time before they saw how hollow the entire operation was, how many lies were being told, and how fraudulent the war was. It was only a matter of time before a version of the war and of the regime, far more pessimistic, began to surface in the American press. Both Washington and Saigon immediately chose to see this as a press controversy; in reality it was a reflection of a major bureaucratic struggle and of a dying policy. But since the policy now depended for its life on the public relations aspect, on the Administration's attempt to sell a frail and failed policy both to itself and to Diem, the reporters became targets of the Administration, both at home and in Vietnam. They were the one element in Saigon that could not be controlled: Diem controlled his press, his military, his legislature; Harkins his reporting channels, and Nolting his. The only people who could be candid were the American reporters. "Get on the team," Admiral Harry Felt told Malcolm Browne of the AP. "Stop looking for the hole in the doughnut," Ambassador Nolting enjoined reporters. John Richardson, the head of the CIA in Saigon, spoke enviously to colleagues of how the Communists controlled their reporters. Nolting, increasingly angry with the journalistic accounts, ordered his press officer, John Mecklin, to write a major report for Washington saying that the policy "has been badly hampered by irresponsible, astigmatic and sensationalized reporting." General Krulak, one of the shrewder political infighters, decided to assault the reporters by assaulting their manhood, and told favored journalistic friends that reporters in Saigon had burst into tears when they saw dead bodies. Favored journals such as *Time* or reporters such as Joseph Alsop and Marguerite Higgins were cranked up to write more positive stories, which they gladly did.

The reporters seemed to make an inviting target: they were young and without established reputations. Because the reporters were young, their views of the world and of war were not set in a World War II philosophy. Because only one of them was married, there was no wifely pull to become part of the Saigon social whirl, to get along with the Noltings or the Harkinses, the kind of insidious pressure which works against journalistic excellence in Washington. Unlike so many colleagues in Washington, they were not dependent on the good wishes of the people who ran the institution they covered; their friends and contemporaries were out in the field, where the war was. Their reporting of the political stagnation in Saigon, of the false promises of Diem, was consistently on target; and their reporting from the field was far more honest and accurate than that of the military (eight years later the Pentagon Papers would confirm this through analysis by the Pentagon's own experts. It was a belated tribute of no small irony).

But the questions they brought up were the smaller ones. They too did not challenge the given, and by accepting it, they too failed (had they challenged the very premise of the war, they would undoubtedly have been shipped out the next day). Only in the latter part of 1963 and in early 1964 did they begin to perceive that the problem was not just Diem, that Diem was simply a symptom of a larger failure and that the real problem had its roots in the French Indochina war. By then it was very late. Fifteen years earlier in China, restless young State Department officials had played the same role as the reporters did, had conveyed what they saw without jeopardy to their jobs. Now that kind of reporting could not be done through State and had to be done through independent newspapers. But the State Department people had been area experts and thus recognized immediately the root causes of what they saw on the surface, which the young American journalists in Vietnam lacked the sophistication to do (unlike the official personnel, they knew that our program did not work, but unlike their State Department predecessors in China they were not able to trace the reason back far enough why it failed. Whereas the State Department officials in China saw their pessimism come to its logical conclusion—that the United States did not belong in China—the reporters in 1962 and early 1963 did not yet see the parallel in Vietnam). Like everything else in Saigon, the American press did not work quite well enough. It did, however, represent the beginning of an end of an era of American omnipotence by challenging the information which supported the policy; the country and the Administration had overreached itself, and this was the DEW-line warning signal.

The Administration countered quickly enough. If the reporters would not write upbeat stories, the Kennedy Administration, facile, particularly good at

public relations, would generate its own positive accounts. Thus optimism
and optimistic statements became a major and deliberate part of the policy;
warfare by public relations, one more reflection of the Kennedy era. High-
level Americans were sent over not to learn about Vietnam, not to see Vietnam or to improve what was privately known as a frail policy, but to pump up
this weak policy. Their speeches and statements had been written for them
before they left, full of praise for Diem, full of talk of a national revolution, of
the end of the long war, of victory in sight. One day at the Saigon airport,
with television cameras focusing on one of them as he descended the plane
and began reading his statement, Neil Sheehan, then a twenty-five-year-old
reporter for UPI, remarked, "Ah, another foolish Westerner come to lose his
reputation to Ho Chi Minh."

But it became increasingly a policy based on appearances; Vietnamese
realities did not matter, but the *appearances* of Vietnamese realities mattered
because they could affect American realities. More and more effort went into
public relations because it was easier to manipulate appearances and statements than it was to affect reality on the ground. In part the controversy with
the American reporters became so bitter because for the first time there was a
threat to the American mission on appearances (significantly, whenever reporters came up with a story showing that something was grievously wrong,
the instinct of the American mission was to assault the reporters and their
credibility, not to find out whether or not in fact the story was right). The
Buddhist crisis would be troubling because it shattered appearances of tran-
quillity, not because it showed that the regime was stupid and cruel. And
Vietnamese elections from the very start, once the original Geneva elections
were avoided, were always aimed not at expressing Vietnamese aspirations,
but at implanting American values on the Vietnamese and reassuring Americans. (This was true right through to 1967 when General Lansdale was back,
this time in a civilian capacity, and trying to run elections which, though
blocking out the Vietcong, would nonetheless, he hoped, be honest. He was,
however, receiving little support from the rest of the embassy on his idea, so
when Richard Nixon, an old friend of his, visited Saigon in mid-1967,
Lansdale seized on the idea of using Nixon to build support for the elections,
really honest elections this time. "Oh sure, honest, yes, honest, that's right,"
Nixon said, *"so long as you win!"* With that he winked, drove his elbow into
Lansdale's arm and slapped his own knee. Such were to be elections; like everything else they were to ratify American decisions and present American
policies in a favorable light.)

There were of course some official Americans who were not enthusiastic
about being manipulated by the executive branch. In late 1962 Senate Majority Leader Mike Mansfield came through Saigon at Kennedy's request.
Mansfield had visited Vietnam many times in the past and had been one of

the original liberal-Catholic sponsors of Diem (the hope of liberal-Catholic Americans of sponsoring a liberal-Catholic regime in Saigon). Since he knew a good deal of the background, he was appalled by the deterioration of Diem, the growing isolation of the man, the sense of unreality around the palace, and the dominance of Mr. and Mrs. Nhu. Mansfield had skipped some of the official briefings provided for him by Nolting and had instead spent a four-hour lunch with the American reporters, a lunch which confirmed his own doubts. The next day at the airport, as he prepared to leave, he was handed a statement drafted for him by the embassy (a small courtesy on the part of the ambassador in case the Senate Majority Leader did not know what to say). Mansfield, however, rejected it; and his own farewell speech, by its absence of enthusiasm, reflected his disenchantment. When he returned to Washington he gave Kennedy a report of mild caution for public consumption, but in addition he gave him a private account that was blunt and pessimistic about the future of it all. Kennedy had summoned Mansfield to his yacht, the *Honey Fitz*, where there was a party going on, and when the President read the report his face grew redder and redder as his anger mounted. Finally he turned to Mansfield, just about the closest friend he had in the Senate, and snapped, "Do you expect me to take this at face value?" Mansfield answered, "You asked me to go out there." Kennedy looked at him again, icily now, and said, "Well, I'll read it again." It was an important conversation, coming as it did about a year after the Taylor-Rostow mission and after a year of the policy of deliberate optimism. It showed that if this policy had not fooled anyone else, it had deceived the deceivers.

But the articles in the daily newspapers, combined with the reports from men like Mansfield, had slowly been having an effect on the President. Increasingly bothered by discrepancies in the reporting, he dispatched two of Harriman's people in late December to make their own check, Roger Hilsman of State and Michael Forrestal of the White House. He told Forrestal that in order to get at the truth he wanted a fresh look, but warned him not to become too involved with the journalists there and not to see events through their prism. Forrestal, he said, should find out what was really happening there and how the people of South Vietnam felt about the war.

Listening to the President, Forrestal, who had been devoting himself to Laotian problems and had not worked on Vietnam, sensed his own doubts beginning. Those doubts were confirmed when he arrived in Saigon and found that the only people who believed in the regime were Americans. He also discovered that their belief was in direct proportion to the importance of their position, and that the more independent their position, the less faith they had in the regime or the viability of the war effort. He reported to Kennedy in early February that "no one really knows how many of the 20,000 'Vietcong' killed last year were only innocent or at least persuadable villagers, whether the Strategic Hamlet program is providing enough governmental services to counteract the sacrifices it requires, or how the mute mass of villagers react to charges against Diem of dictatorship and nepotism." Forrestal foresaw a long and costly war and also reported that Vietcong recruitment within the South was so successful and effective that the war could be continued without infiltration from the North, a point which jarred Saigon and Pentagon and some civilian sensibilities, since much of the Washington thinking was postulated on the basis of invasion from the North.

BY EARLY 1963 THE PRESIDENT HAD BECOME UNHAPPY WITH HIS TEAM in Saigon; in particular he was dissatisfied with the reporting that was coming in, it was all too simplistic, too confident, and there was too little nuance, too little concern about the population reflected. But it was not so much a distaste for the Harkins and Nolting simplistic reporting as a distaste for the war itself and the problems of Vietnam, a belief that, as Forrestal had reported, it was not going to be easy, an intuition that it was somehow going to pull us in deeper and deeper. In private he began to voice concern over where we were going. He had a feeling that Harkins and Nolting did not share his misgivings, and that Nolting in particular, who was supposed to be the President's man there, had not been a particularly good choice. Maybe for some other President, but not for him. So increasingly it was his own White House staff which had to fight to limit the military instead of the President's ambassador to Vietnam. The more the reality of the commitment and what it was doing to the peasantry was unveiled, the more uneasy Kennedy became, but Nolting was not disturbed; he was committed to supporting the regime at all costs. What the President was learning, and learning to his displeasure (once again, the Bay of Pigs had been lesson one), was something that his successor Lyndon Johnson would also find out the hard way: that the capacity to control a policy involving the military is greatest before the policy is initiated, but once started, no matter how small the initial step, a policy has a life and a thrust of its own, it is an organic thing. More, its thrust and its drive may not be in any way akin to the desires of the President who initiated it. There is always the drive for more, more force, more tactics, wider latitudes for force.

Starting in mid-1962, this had begun to be true on Vietnam, and there was soon a split between the American military (and Saigon) and the Administration over four main issues: napalm, defoliants, free fire zones and the introduction of jet planes instead of outmoded prop fighter-bombers. The military quickly lost on jets, but both Diem and Nhu supported and in fact pushed the American military on all these points, an important insight into the way they regarded their own peasantry, the lack of rapport and root and sympathy for them. The position of Diem, and particularly Nhu, was that these weapons

were vital; they helped support the government, even though they inflicted
great pain and death on the peasants. In fact, Diem and Nhu both specifically
liked the use of excessive power. They still held to the mandarin psychology
of the population's responsibility to obey the government. An example of this
mandarin thinking was the theory that the population would so hate the killing and the awesome force of its government that it would automatically respect the government even more, and would turn on the Vietcong. It was an
attitude well out of date, for Indochina had been swept by twenty years of
revolutionary excitement and fervor unleashed by the Vietminh and
Vietcong, who had taught not Communism as the West knew it, but that a
host of new possibilities, among them dignity and justice, were open to the
peasants.

That attitude of Diem and Nhu was an important reflection of the
difference between the way they regarded Communism and the way the society did. The population was simply not that anti-Communist; it resented the
force unleashed on it more than it feared the enemy it was allegedly being
saved from. By the same token, a few years later the My Lai massacre would
become a major political embarrassment to the Thieu government because it
reflected the same attitude: in defense of the Saigon government's own existence and in defense of the American anti-Communism, far too much fire
power was inflicted on the reluctant Vietnamese people.

If the military lost on jets, it pushed very hard on the other issues. At the
beginning it was the only aspect of Vietnam that Kennedy really interested
himself in. Vietnam had been a low-priority item in early 1962, but these issues of killing were different, and the President specifically commissioned
both Hilsman and Forrestal to watch the military on them, to make sure that
nothing slipped by. He was convinced, and rightly so, that the military were
always trying to push things by him. And Hilsman and Forrestal found that
for the first time McGeorge Bundy was a genuine help on Vietnam, a sign of
the President's very real interest. Bundy made sure the door to the President
was always open, though often the points seemed small or even technical by
the standards of the period; they were not global. Napalm was the first one.
Harkins liked napalm, Diem and Nhu liked napalm; Harkins said it put the
fear of God in the Vietcong. It was just one more weapon in the arsenal, the
general said, and perhaps he was right; other weapons killed people just as
dead. Harkins pushed hard for the virtually unrestricted use of it, but there
was an element in it as an antipersonnel weapon that appalled Kennedy. It
was a weapon which somehow seemed to be particularly antihuman, and he
hated photographs of what it had done to people. He would talk with a certain fatalism to his staff about the pressure on him to use it. Now they want to
use it on villages, he would say. They tell me that it won't hurt anyone, but if
no one will be hurt by it, what do they want it for?

Then the military wanted defoliation, and once again the battle started. They wanted to start using it widely, for crop defoliation, but Kennedy held the line there; he did not want crops destroyed, no matter whose crops. Then they pushed for limited defoliation, just on lines of communication. They wanted to use it on the roads to make it harder for the enemy to ambush the troops. Our boys will be protected. Try it out, MACV said. Just a little bit, it will work and it will help win the war. Reluctantly, Kennedy considered giving partial permission, but he was advised by the State Department's legal section that any such use was a violation of the Geneva Conventions rules of war. So he said, well yes, but couldn't they try it out in some deserted country . . . Panama . . . or Thailand . . . or somewhere else; did they really have to experiment right there in Vietnam with all those people around? Finally he approved a limited use of it, just as he approved a limited use of napalm in battles where the population was not nearby.

Then Harkins argued for free fire zones, a place to drop unused bombs, because to carry those bombs back made it dangerous for the planes on landing. Kennedy asked his staff why they couldn't drop the extra bombs in the sea, since the United States had lots of bombs and the loss of a few into the South China Sea would not be a problem for this country and probably wouldn't hurt the ocean too much. But Harkins wanted the Iron Triangle, no people there; well, no friendly people, certainly, and eventually the military gained very limited free fire zones.

Gradually Kennedy began to hate it, and some of the men around him began to sense that they were losing control, they were having to fight too hard for moderate positions, they were running hard just to stand still. The military could just announce a policy on areas where there was a vacuum, and it was the civilians who would then have to fight back. Even worse, the military could gain the upper hand by asking for too much, and then, like a shrewd bargainer, settle for a little less. Ask for broad defoliation, and get access rights. Ask for unrestricted napalm, and get limited napalm, which would not be too much of a problem because those boys from the White House wouldn't be on every plane on every mission.

The White House was beginning to see that the people who were in charge of the mission in Saigon had begun to take on the coloration of the commitment, they were more militant than Washington, more committed to Diem than Washington. As for Harkins, he took the position that it was, after all, not his viewpoint which was reflected, but that of the host government. We were just out here to help these little people, and since they wanted these weapons and they knew more about their country than we did, we should find out what they needed and then deliver it. Nolting was not inclined to challenge the military; indeed, he invariably went along with Diem in his demands. Thus when Kennedy repeatedly urged Forrestal to push Nolting to lean on the military, Forrestal would find a certain resistance, a reluctance to take on Harkins because that would mean taking on Diem. It became obvious that Nolting was not really acting as the President's man in Saigon, but the problem was greater than that.

Kennedy had made the commitment without much enthusiasm and with a good deal of misgivings. He had made it not so much because he wanted to, but because he felt he could not do less, given the time and the circumstances. But he was never in any deep sense a believer, whereas in Saigon, Harkins and Nolting had become true believers. They believed their own statements about victory, and they were not cynical. But the struggle over the issues of force was important on another level as well: as the Vietnam problem grew in importance within the bureaucracy and separated those who felt it was primarily a military problem and a question of force, from those who felt it was essentially a political problem, these questions of napalm, defoliation, free fire zones and jet planes would serve as an early litmus test as to which side the various members of the government would choose.

The commitment was already operative, burning with a special fuel of its own—bureaucratic momentum and individual ambition—men let loose in Saigon and Washington who never questioned whether that something was right or wrong, or whether it worked or not. In government it is always easier to go forward with a program that does not work than to stop it altogether and admit failure. John Kennedy was fast learning that his personal and political interests were not necessarily the same as those of the thousands of men who worked in the government.

Chapter Twelve

IN SAIGON, THE MILITARY ASSISTANCE COMMAND NOW FUNCtioned as a powerful, organized, disciplined establishment which could control the loyalty of its people and churn out facts, statistics and programs to suit the whim of its sponsors at the Pentagon. It had defeated the protests of its own best people, it had determined that things were going well, that there was and would be optimism (at a Honolulu meeting in April 1963, Harkins was almost euphoric; he could not give any guarantees, but he thought it would all be over by Christmas. McNamara, listening to him, was elated—he reached over and reminded Hilsman that Hilsman had been there when it had all looked so black and that had been only eighteen months ago). So in early 1963 MACV had far more muscle than the comparatively frail civilian operation there; this had once bothered Ambassador Nolting but it no longer did, largely because he agreed with the conclusions of the military; he too saw the war through a military, not a political prism. In Washington, the dominant figure on Vietnam was not Dean Rusk, but Secretary of Defense Robert McNamara; it was he who dominated the action, the play, the terms by which success in Vietnam was determined. In the growing split between the civilians and the military over Vietnam, McNamara was allowed to be the referee. In contrast, the people from State who, like Harriman, were challenging the military's estimates, were placed in the position of being adversaries.

That McNamara's role was major, that he was by default usurping the role of the Secretary of State, did not faze him. He was intelligent, forceful, courageous, decent, everything, in fact, but wise. Wherever there was a problem for his President, he would press on, the better to protect his superior, the better to take the heat. One reason he rushed forward on Vietnam was because he was haunted by the fact that he had performed so poorly during the Bay of Pigs episode (years later, this still remained something of a joke among Kennedy insiders, and after Edward Kennedy drove off the bridge at Chappaquiddick, among the many who rushed to the Kennedy compound in Hyannisport was McNamara; there he was greeted by the insiders' good fellowship and jovial remarks about the arrival of the man who had handled both the Bay of Pigs and Vietnam).

He became the principal desk officer on Vietnam in 1962 because he felt that the President needed his help. He knew nothing about Asia, about poverty, about people, about American domestic politics, but he knew a great deal about production technology and about exercising bureaucratic power. He was classically a corporate man; had it been a contest between the United States and Hanoi as to which side could produce the most goods for the peasants of South Vietnam, clearly we would have won. If it had been just a matter of getting the right goods to the right villages, we would have won; unfortunately, what we were selling was not what they were buying. This man, whose only real experience had been in dealing with the second largest automotive empire in the world, producing huge Western vehicles, was the last man to understand and measure the problems of a people looking for their political freedom. Yet he was very much a man of the Kennedy Administration. He symbolized the idea that it could manage and control events, in an intelligent, rational way. Taking on a guerrilla war was like buying a sick foreign company; you brought your systems to it. He was so impressive and loyal that it was hard to believe, in the halcyon days of 1963 when his reputation was at its height, that anything he took command of could go wrong. He was a reassuring figure not just to both Presidents he served but to the liberal *good* community of Washington as well; if McNamara was in charge of something he would run it correctly; if it was a war, it would be a good war.

He could handle the military. That, of course, was the basis of his legend. Washington was filled with stories of McNamara browbeating the military, forcing them to reconsider, taking their pet projects away from them. Later, as his reputation dimmed and the defense budget grew (it was not just Vietnam, it was other projects as well), some of those who had been part of that Administration suspected that he had in no real way handled the military, but rather, that he had brought them kicking and screaming and protesting to the zenith of their power. At the very least, it turned out that he had controlled the military only as long as we were not in a real war and that the best way for civilians to harness generals was to stay out of wars. That wisdom would come later.

When McNamara entered the Administration in 1961, he had let his deputy, Roswell Gilpatric, handle Vietnam, a sure sign that it was not an important issue. As the importance and complexity of Vietnam began to be evident, he took it over himself, wanting to protect the President, sure of his capacity to handle it. He then began his series of flying trips to Saigon, the on-the-spot inspections in search of the truth, a brisk, confident McNamara on the move, being televised, seeing people (the dissenters carefully screened out), gobbling up the false statistics of the day. His confidence became Washington's confidence; the people in the capital knew that this able, driving man could handle the war, could handle the military machinery. The truth was that he had no different assumptions, that he wanted no different sources of information. For all his idealism, he was no better and perhaps in his hubris a little worse than the institution he headed. But to say this in 1963 would have been heresy, for at that point his reputation was impeccable.

HE WAS BOB, BOB McNAMARA, TAUT, CONTROLLED, DRIVING—climbing mountains, harnessing generals—the hair slicked down in a way that made him look like a Grant Wood subject. The look was part of the drive: a fat McNamara was as hard to imagine as an uncertain one. The glasses straight and rimless, imposing; you looked at the glasses and kept your distance. He was a man of force, moving, pushing, getting things done, *Bob got things done,* the can-do man in the can-do society, in the can-do era. No one would ever mistake Bob McNamara for a European; he was American through and through, with the American drive, the American certitude and conviction. He pushed everyone, particularly himself, to new limits, long hours, working breakfasts, early bedtimes, moderate drinking, no cocktail parties. He was always rational, always the puritan but not a prude. And certainly not a Babbitt—if he could give up an earlier preference for academe to go into business, then at least he would not be a Babbitt. He sat there behind that huge desk, austere, imposing. A Secretary of Defense of the United States of America, with a budget of $85 billion a year, not to mention a generous supply of nuclear warheads at his disposal, was likely to be imposing enough, anyway.

One was always aware of his time; speak quickly and be gone, make your point, in and out, keep the schedule, lunch from 1:50 to, say, expansively, 2 P.M., and above all, do not engage in any philosophical discussions, *Well, Bob, my view of history is* . . . No one was to abuse his time. Do not, he told his aides, let people brief me orally. If they are going to make a presentation, find out in advance and make them put it on paper. "Why?" an aide asked. A cold look. "Because I can read faster than they can talk." There were exceptions to this, and one of the most notable was his interest in 1966 in an electronic barrier for Vietnam as a means of stopping the infiltration (and thus the rationale for bombing); suddenly this took top priority and General Alfred Starbird, who was in charge of it, had access to him at any time and could always brief him orally. The boredom he showed when the JCS came over once a week was in sharp contrast to the interest he had when General Starbird was talking. Those who wasted his time—except of course those above him—would feel his cold stare, and this included almost everyone, even General Maxwell Taylor. The first time Taylor went over to see McNamara at the start of the Kennedy years, Taylor arrived a little early. He stood outside the Secretary's office while McNamara waited for the exact moment of their appointment. When it came, Taylor was held up on the phone for a few minutes because the White House had called him. So McNamara waited for Taylor and finally Taylor waited for McNamara a bit more, and then he went in and was given one of the icier treatments of his life.

Time was of the essence, to be rationed and saved; time was not just money, it was, even more important, action, decisions, cost effectiveness, power. It became part of private Pentagon legend that if you really wanted to make a point with McNamara, the best way was to catch him on one of those long flights to Saigon or Honolulu, hours and hours aboard planes where there was nowhere else to go, no appointments waiting. There are those who remember well a scene in October 1966 when Daniel Ellsberg, who had already turned against the war, cornered McNamara on a plane, and crowding over the Secretary, served him all the dovish papers that Ellsberg had written and saved up. There was a feeling of slight amusement on the part of one witness because of the almost obsessed manner of Ellsberg, a Dostoevskyan figure, and the fact that McNamara had no place to hide.

McNamara, who was under such pressure, always tried to conceal it, to be cool, to control his emotions, though not always successfully, and there was somehow a price to be paid. He would, for instance, while he was in Detroit, grind his teeth in his sleep, wearing down the enamel until Marg McNamara realized what was happening and sent him to a dentist, who had them recapped (a New York dentist just so there would be no gossip in Detroit, gossip which might diminish his legend and thus his power; his legend was his power).

Sometimes, to those around him, he seemed so idealistic as to be innocent. He never talked about power and he did not seem to covet it. Yet the truth was quite different. He loved power and he sought it intensely, and he could be a ferocious infighter where the question of power was concerned. Nothing could come between him and a President of the United States unless it was a potential President; thus his dilemma in 1967, when he was torn between loyalty to Johnson and Robert Kennedy. For all his apparent innocence, he had triumphed in the ferocious jungle of Detroit automotive politics, he was acutely aware of how to gain and hold power. It was not, however, a quality which surfaced regularly; if anything, part of his strength appeared to be his capacity to seem indifferent, to seem almost naïve about questions of power. One Defense Department aide who had visualized McNamara as the idealistic civil servant was stunned when he caught a glimpse of the other side of McNamara. The aide had been offered a job at the White House, and when he told McNamara about it, he was advised to refuse it because, McNamara said, though he was offered high visibility and glory, the job lacked real power. McNamara thereupon continued with a startling and brilliant analysis, department by department in the government listing, which jobs carried power in which department and why, and which jobs, seeming to have real power, in reality lacked it. He was, it seemed, a little less innocent and idealistic than the aide had thought.

That McNamara had such a good reputation in Washington was not entirely incidental—he knew about the importance of public relations, and played that game with surprising skill. Finding that his top public relations man at Defense, Arthur Sylvester, was a man of limited sophistication and ability, McNamara quickly learned how to use him to stand as a lightning rod and filter between the Secretary and the average working reporter, essentially to fend the press off and deflect the heat (leaving many reporters to wonder why a man as able as McNamara had a press aide as inept as Sylvester; the answer was that it was deliberate). At the same time he used Adam Yarmolinsky, a former Harvard Law School professor and a man with unusually good connections with the liberal establishment, to do the more serious job of protecting the Secretary's image with major writers and columnists, and it was Yarmolinsky who would write the letters to the editor tidying up McNamara's reputation after various critical articles.

IF THE BODY WAS TENSE AND DRIVEN, THE MIND WAS MATHEMATICAL, analytical, bringing order and reason out of chaos. Always reason. And reason supported by facts, by statistics—he could prove his rationality with facts, intimidate others. He was marvelous with charts and statistics. Once, sitting at CINCPAC for eight hours watching hundreds and hundreds of slides flashed across the screen showing what was in the pipe line to Vietnam and what was already there, he finally said, after seven hours, "Stop the projector. This slide, number 869, contradicts slide 11." Slide 11 was flashed back and he was right, they did contradict each other. Everyone was impressed, and many a little frightened. No wonder his reputation grew; others were in awe. For it was a mind that could continue to summon its own mathematical kind of sanity into bureaucratic battle, long after the others, the good liberal social scientists who had never gone beyond their original logarithms, had trailed off into the dust, though finally, when the mathematical version of sanity did not work out, when it turned out that the computer had not fed back the right answers and had underestimated those funny little far-off men in their raggedy pajamas, he would be stricken with a profound sense of failure, and he would be, at least briefly, a shattered man. But that would come later. At his height he always seemed in control; you could, said Lyndon Johnson, who once admired him and trotted him out on so many occasions, almost hear the computers clicking away. But when things went sour and Johnson felt McNamara's doubts, his tongue, always acid for those who failed him, did not spare his prize pupil. He would say to those around him, "I forgot he had only been president of Ford for one week." Yet even then, when his tenure as Secretary of Defense was coming to an end and he knew that his policy had failed, even then his faith in his kind of rationality did not really desert him. The war was a human waste, yes, but it was also no longer cost-effective; we were putting in more for our air power than we were getting back in damage, ten dollars of input for one dollar of damage, and the one dollar was being put up by the Soviet Union and not North Vietnam, anyway.

He was an emotional man as well, weeping at his last Pentagon ceremony, his friends at the very end worried about his health, both mental and physical, about what the war had done to his ethical framework. The Kennedy people in particular worried about him. He was a close friend of the Kennedys', gay and gregarious at dinner parties. Though not noted for his wit—no one had ever accused him of an overdeveloped sense of irony, which after all was to be found mostly in peoples and nations that history had defeated, and Bob was undefeated. He had a certain gaiety and ingratiating charm, an ability to talk about things other than shop. "Why is it," asked Bob Kennedy, "that they all call him 'the computer' and yet he's the one all my sisters want to sit next to at dinner?" That loyalty to the Kennedy family, which had begun in 1961, endured through tragedy after tragedy. "Bob," Ethel said to him after Chappaquiddick, "get up here, there's no one here but women."

It would not be surprising that in the latter part of the sixties, when a sense of disillusion with Camelot grew, that the Kennedy insiders in particular wanted to spare McNamara. They were by then quite willing to write off the war and the men who made it. Mac Bundy evoked no fondness, to say the least. He had given grants to Robert Kennedy's staff after the 1968 assassination, but there were still bitter feelings about his serving as a conduit for Johnson during the vice-presidential squabble of 1964. And Johnson was no favorite, the Kennedys had never been generous to him, nothing he did would ever please them. Max Taylor had been a favorite and there was some personal loyalty still there, but Taylor's strict adherence to the war, right through 1968, made it difficult to salvage him. With Bob McNamara it was different, he could still go out and play house games at Hickory Hill and they wanted to spare him from the responsibility; if McNamara had been in on the planning of the big escalation in 1965, and they doubted even that, then Lyndon had somehow pushed him into it. Bob, they thought, was always a little too eager to please (though at the time these events were taking place, George Ball would grow tired of having to repeat to his liberal friends that McNamara was fooling them; he might sound dovish around Washington liberals but he was rough as hell inside those meetings, and in 1965 he was always on the other side).

BOB McNAMARA WAS A REMARKABLE MAN IN A REMARKABLE ERA; IF at the beginning he seemed to embody many if not most of the era's virtues, at the end of it he seemed to embody its pathos, flaws and tragedy. No one could doubt his good intentions, his ability, his almost ferocious sense of public service, yet something about him bothered many of his colleagues. It was not just Vietnam, but his overall style. It was what made him so effective: the total belief in what he was doing, the willingness to knock down anything that stood in his way, the relentless quality, so that other men, sometimes wiser, more restrained, would be pushed aside. He would, for instance, lie, dissemble, not just to the public, they all did that in varying degrees, but inside, in high-level meetings, always for the good of the cause, always for the right reason, always to serve the Office of the President. Bob knew what was good for the cause, but sometimes at the expense of his colleagues. And indeed, experienced McNamara watchers, men who were fond of him, would swear they knew when Bob was lying; his voice would get higher, he would speak faster, he would become more insistent.

He embodied the virtues Americans have always respected, hard work, self-sacrifice, decency, loyalty. Loyalty, that was it, perhaps too much loyalty, the corporate-mentality loyalty to the office instead of to himself. He was, finally, the embodiment of the liberal contradictions of that era, the conflict between the good intentions and the desire to hold and use power (most of what was good in us and what was bad in us was there; the Jeffersonian democracy become a superpower). It was always there inside his body, Bob conniving and dissembling to do good and to hold power at the same time. Later, near the end of his tour, he went to Harvard, where in another and gentler time he might have been revered, but where now he was almost captured by the radical students, a narrow escape. That night, when he was speaking to a group of professors, someone asked him about the two McNamaras, the quantifier who had given us the body count in Vietnam, and the warm philosopher of the Montreal speech, a humanistic speech which seemed to cast doubt on the nation's—his own—defense policies. (When Johnson heard of the speech he flew into a rage, demanding to know who at the White House had cleared it, and when it turned out that it was Bill Moyers, this would speed Moyers' own departure.) He answered: "I gave the Montreal speech because I could not survive in office without giving it, could not survive with my own conscience, and it gave me another ten months, but the price I paid for it is so high in the Congress and the White House, people who have assumed I was a peacenik all along, that if I had to do it over again, I would not give that speech."

In 1968 he had gone to the World Bank—a job which was the very antithesis of his previous position as head of the greatest war machine in the history of the world, an act which seemed to some to have a touch of penance in it. He was willing to reminisce with old friends about the Defense years, with the exception of one subject which never came up, Vietnam. It still caused him pain and would not go away; there were reminders everywhere of what it had meant. Nor was the split in his own family a unique illustration of what the war had done to this country, in home after home: in the Robert McNamara family there was Bob McNamara, who was one of the great architects of the war, while in 1970 one of the leaders of the California peace movement, attending rallies everywhere, radical, committed, was his young son Craig.

HE WAS VERY MUCH IN PLACE AMONG THE KENNEDY PEOPLE, FOR THEY were rationalists all; they did not really dissent from the Eisenhower years, but as they entered office, had pledged to make the new Administration more effective. They would speed it up, make it work better, cut the flab off. For the cool, almost British young President, he was an ideal Secretary of Defense. He was not of the Establishment in the sense that Bundy was, nor had he served it the way Dean Rusk had, clerking all those years first in the State Department, then at the Rockefeller Foundation. Detroit was not part of the Establishment, but it was part of the functional structure, a place to be watched, its figures scanned by the Establishment to be sure that it could still outproduce Moscow and Berlin in heavy cars.

But if he was not of the Establishment, he had done his time and served well under Bob Lovett in the Air Force during World War II. McNamara was a man to take note of even then; one was sure he would be seen again, and his uncommon qualities, the skill and perseverance, brilliance and selflessness were not forgotten, and fifteen years later when Lovett, who had turned down Defense himself, was asked for names, he immediately mentioned McNamara, whose bright future had been realized. McNamara had kept straight ahead and had gone on to greater things at Ford; they had just made him president. Actually, he had first come to public attention in 1947 (though not by name), his achievements boasted about in a *Fortune* magazine article on Lovett. When Kaiser wanted to ferry all cargo by flying boats to overseas bases, Lovett had proved that it would require 10,022 planes and 120,765 air-crews to move 100,000 long tons from San Francisco to Australia, whereas the same task was already being handled by 44 surface vessels manned by 3,200 seamen. As casualties rose during the war, the article pointed out, Lovett had instituted Stat Control (Statistical Control Office), a world-wide reporting service anchored by a battery of IBM machines which produced life-expectancy estimates for every member of every aircrew. The idea was to prove to an airman that he had a 50-50 chance to come home while the war was still going on, and an 80 percent chance for survival. Eventually it became so efficient that it could predict how many planes would be available in every theater every day for every operation. It was, said *Fortune,* "super application of proven business methods to war, and so successful that a few months after hostilities ceased, the Ford Motor Company hired the two principal opera-tors." Thus McNamara entered on the scene, an imaginative and able cog in an enormously successful machine: business methods applied to war.

After the 1960 presidential election, the call went out from the talent scouts to the Ford Motor Company. Actually they had made contact even earlier, during the campaign. Neil Staebler, chairman of the Democratic party in Michigan, had suggested to Kennedy's brother-in-law Sargent Shriver that his friend Bob McNamara should head the businessmen's committee for Ken-nedy-Johnson, a job for which they were not exactly overwhelmed with appli-cants. Staebler pointed out that McNamara typified the new liberal business-man with the broader horizon, had considerable prestige among his colleagues throughout the country, had voted for Democrats in the past and came from the prestigious house of Ford. Shriver, a big-game hunter, liked at least part of the idea, Ford, but thought if we go for Ford, we'll go for the top, we'll get Henry himself, a decision which lacked only Henry's concurrence.

Somehow the McNamara idea was lost in the shuffle, but in December, Shriver, now in charge of the recruitment drive, called Staebler again: "How did your friend McNamara vote?"

"For Kennedy, I think."

"Could you find out?"

"Why?"

"Because we want him in the Administration."

Staebler warned Shriver that McNamara would not take the job. He was, said Staebler, the most conscientious of men, and now was just taking over a system built specifically around him. It was not just a question of replacing one man with another.

To Staebler, McNamara was different from the other auto executives. While the rest of the auto-making hierarchy was a solid Republican fortress, living in the same elegant suburbs, going to the same posh country clubs, McNamara was something of a maverick. He deliberately lived far from Detroit, in the groves of academe in Ann Arbor, his life style was different, and he had something of a sense of social responsibility. He supported Democrats from time to time, men like Senator Philip Hart and Congressman James O'Hara. He had not, rather vocally, supported Governor Soapy Williams, disliking Williams' close ties to organized labor, and indeed there were those in Detroit who felt there was a surprising intensity to McNamara's opposition to Williams, as though given a chance to vote Republican and be orthodox, he had seized it eagerly. He was liberal on most things, such as civil rights, but on labor, the great bugaboo in the auto industry, his views were surprisingly hard-line because labor kept interfering with his cost effectiveness and put constant pressure on the auto industry. McNamara and his Democratic friend Staebler used to argue regularly about labor's productivity, about the fact that American labor costs were too high, and that we were losing our competitive edge. Bob was, after all, the statistician; even in the Air Force, labor's role had been functional, not human, a factor rather than people.

Staebler did find out that McNamara had voted for Kennedy, and meanwhile the Kennedy people began checking with their people out in Detroit, getting political clearance. The chief of their people was Jack Conway, one of Walter Reuther's brightest aides, a United Automobile Workers political officer. To Conway, McNamara was by far the best of the breed. McNamara had never participated in the annual salary negotiations with labor (he was in a different department), but the two had worked closely in 1959 and 1960 during a major overhaul of the Michigan tax system when the Democratic party and labor were trying to bring in a state income tax. At the start, Ford and McNamara had both been strongly against the tax, but at the end of six months of committee work, McNamara changed his views and opposed the official Ford position, a switch which made him few friends in the auto hierarchy. He was, thought Conway, an impressive man to work with, the mind was first-rate, the intellectual discipline awesome, but more, you could engage him even when you disagreed, and you could even change his mind because his ego was not involved in his earlier stand. As for McNamara, he was finally impressed by the equity of the labor people's position. Conway had left with a strong and favorable impression of McNamara as a broad-gauged man, and he would help clear him later that year. McNamara was similarly impressed with Conway, and when he accepted the Defense job he asked Kennedy if he could offer Conway a job as Assistant Secretary of Defense for Manpower. But President of the AFL-CIO George Meany, no lover of Reuther, heard about it and blew up, blocking the job and creating a rift between himself and McNamara.

He was called to Washington and met Kennedy, who immediately liked him and offered him either Treasury or Defense. The Treasury job had little attraction; he asked one member of the Kennedy team what the Secretary of the Treasury does, and was told that he sets the interest rates. "Hell, I do more at Ford about setting the interests than the Secretary of the Treasury," he answered. He was bored with finances as an end in itself and felt more intrigued by Defense; one could serve more, contribute more, the challenge was greater. If one wanted a platform for national service, then Secretary of Defense under an activist President would be better than heading the Ford Motor Company. It was a better place to exercise power, to do more good, with greater visibility, particularly for someone who had always been somewhat uneasy in the automotive industry, his conscience never entirely at ease.

Their first meeting went very well; the puritan in McNamara made him ask Kennedy if he had really written *Profiles in Courage,* and Kennedy assured him that he had. McNamara expressed doubts about his training for the job; Kennedy answered that he knew of no school for Presidents, either. He demanded of Kennedy, and received permission, to pick his own men (much to the frustration of Franklin Roosevelt, Jr., who, having lent an honored name to the Kennedy cause by inveighing in West Virginia against Hubert Humphrey's courage and patriotism, hoped to be Secretary of the Navy. Roosevelt had tipped off reporters to where McNamara was staying in Washington, in hopes that as they questioned him they would find out about his own job. Thus the reporters trapped McNamara: "I hear you're going to name Frank Roosevelt Secretary of the Navy?" "The hell I am," McNamara answered. "But he's the President's friend," the reporter persisted. "I told the President I would pick my own men, and I'm not picking him." Perhaps not always his own men, since the job went to John Connally of Texas, a close friend of the Vice-President's).

Having accepted the job, McNamara went back to Detroit to get clearance from his boss, Henry Ford II, who, less than enthusiastic, let him go, for in giving the presidency to McNamara, a system and accounting man rather than a traditional auto man, he had based an entire production system around one highly specialized individual, and the functioning of that system was very much dependent on that one person. Now he was losing the man and keeping the system. In the meantime McNamara talked with past Defense Secretaries and other experts, and showed up a week later in Washington thoroughly prepared; in that short time he had mastered what the main issues before him were and singled out the major areas of work. He already seemed unique in his grasp of the situation, his control, discipline and energy. The Kennedy people, who were having the normal trouble trying to change from seeking office to assuming office, were impressed by the new Secretary, who seemed to be out and running while they were still in the standing start. He had developed that capacity at Ford, to prepare himself so thoroughly in the more intricate areas (his control of the most abstract figures was formidable) that other men, mere mortals, came away quickly impressed.

He managed to pick an uncommon group of bright, fast, analytical, self-assured men who in part helped lead us into the war in Vietnam, but who, unlike other layers of the Washington bureaucracy, would turn and help lead the fight to extricate the country from the war. It was said that in the Kennedy-Johnson years, the three places with the most talented people were the White House under Bundy, the Justice Department under Robert Kennedy, and the Defense Department under McNamara.

Even in the beginning he was completely sure of what he wanted to do, sure of the kind of people he wanted. While the talent scouts under Yarmolinsky were putting up different men, one of them had called Cyrus Vance at his New York law firm, because Vance was the kind of good, sound lawyer you put in a new Administration, and asked if he would like to be in the Defense Department. Vance said yes, as a matter of fact, he would. What kind of job, Cy? A service secretary job, I guess. What service? asked the talent scout. The Navy, I suppose. I was on a destroyer during the war—and so it was decided that Vance would be Secretary of the Navy. McNamara flipped through his dossier and said yes, this man has impressive credentials, but all my service secretaries have to have administrative ability of some kind, and this man doesn't. So Vance was given the job of general counsel to the Defense Department. Everyone else in the Administration was still learning, but McNamara already seemed to know, already the confidence was there. From the very start, he was an active, decisive Secretary of Defense, and this was not lost on John Kennedy.

Theirs was a relationship which was to continue with mutual admiration and ease, and McNamara was one of the few people working for Kennedy who crossed the great divide and became a part of his social world. Midway through the Kennedy Administration, in fact, a reporter working on a magazine article would ask McNamara who his friends were, and McNamara would answer, well, he had lots of friends. "But whom do you call when you want to relax and chew the fat or have a beer?" And McNamara answered, "The Kennedys—I like the Kennedys." He had left Detroit, though, at an enormous financial sacrifice, perhaps a loss of as much as $3 million (he had somewhat less than $1 million to his name when he went to Washington). At the time, one block of stock options was about to mature in just a few weeks and Henry Ford graciously suggested he delay two weeks in selling, but that would have interfered with his swearing-in ceremony and McNamara played by the rules. Besides, he was always far more interested in power than money. Power to do good, of course, not power for power's sake.

HIS GROWING UP HAD BEEN SIMPLE—AND ENVIABLE. GOOD PARENTS. Good values. Good education. Good marks. He was born in San Francisco in

1916, the son of Robert J. McNamara and Claranell Strange (thus the middle name, Robert Strange McNamara, upon which his critics would so joyously seize in later years). His father, who married late, was fifty when Bob was born; he was a sales manager for a San Francisco wholesale shoe firm. Father Catholic, mother Protestant, McNamara a Protestant. (Later, during the height of Lyndon Johnson's love affair with McNamara, the President thought of the Secretary of Defense as a vice-presidential possibility and called around to Democratic pols with the idea. "You could even see Lyndon thinking it out—the Protestants will assume he's a Protestant, and the Catholics will think he's a Catholic," one White House aide said.)

When he and his sister were small, the family moved across the Bay to an area of Oakland which featured a particularly good school system. They lived in Annerly, a nice middle-class section. More than forty years later his teachers would remember him with pleasure. Bob was always well behaved, never pushy, his work always ready in case you called on him; he prepared beautiful books on foreign countries—if only there had been more like him. On to Piedmont High, a school of high standing, where he received excellent marks. He was a doer, no jarred nerves, joining all the right clubs, honor societies, the yearbook, the glee club, president of a secret fraternity pledged to service. He was a very good student but not yet exceptional; an early IQ test put him above the norm, very bright but not exceptional.

From Piedmont he went to Berkeley at a time when Robert Gordon Sproul was turning it into a great university (McNamara greatly admired Sproul, and some friends felt that one of his secret ambitions was to leave Ford, if not for government service, then to head Berkeley). At Berkeley he was remembered as a student with a broadly based education and interests. His proficiency in math was beginning to show through, and his own grades came so easily that he had time to read and work in other courses. His professors assumed that he would become a teacher; he did not seem to have the kind of drive, the hustle, which one felt went with a business career; he seemed a little more scholarly. Those were good years, summers spent gold mining (unsuccessfully), climbing mountains, a sport which he quickly came to love, learning to ski, which he went at in typical McNamara style: find out your weaknesses and work on them, and then keep working on them. Man could conquer all by discipline, and will, and rationality.

From Berkeley he went to Harvard Business School, where he was an immediate standout. His unique ability in accounting control became evident, and he began to work at applying that talent to management techniques. He graduated, moved back to the Bay area to work for Price Waterhouse, and in 1939 started seeing an old friend named Margaret Craig. When he was asked back to Harvard Business to teach accounting, he married Marg (whom everyone would consider a good and humanizing influence on McNamara;

much of what was good in Bob, friends thought, came from Marg's generous instincts). At Harvard he was a particularly good teacher, well organized, with good control of his subject and enthusiasm for his work, but he was restless. World War II was approaching and he wanted to play his part; the Navy had turned him down because of weak eyes. He was trying to join the Army when Harvard Business School went to war.

ROBERT LOVETT, THE WORLD WAR I AVIATOR, HAD STAYED IN Europe after the Armistice. He had been plagued with a bad stomach, had lived far too much on baby foods, and thus had forsworn most of the social life that a well-connected young banker might be expected to enjoy. Instead he devoted himself to the political study of a decaying Europe and a military study of what the Hitler build-up would mean, particularly in the way of air power. He predicted accurately the fall of France, saw the rot in the fiber there, and sensed that it would be a war that no one could contain, in which air power, an embryonic factor in the first war, would become the decisive factor. He returned to America in 1940, and as a private citizen, while the rest of the country slept, he made his own private tour of all U.S. airplane factories and airfields to find out what America's air needs and resources were, and he was shocked by the inadequacy of what he saw. He foresaw vast possibilities for American airpower, given our industrial base; American industry could flex its muscle and build the greatest air force in the world, which would wreak massive saturation bombing against the enemy's industrial might. He had met James Forrestal through banking connections, and Forrestal, then Undersecretary of the Navy, sent him to see Robert Patterson, Assistant Secretary of War, where Lovett quickly became a special assistant, then Assistant Secretary for Air, and where his own private planning saved the United States vital time. When this country finally entered the war, some progress had been made in spite of ourselves. But it had not been easy; Lovett could not even find out how many airplanes there were in the country. Charles (Tex) Thornton, one of Lovett's aides, would remember that when they started in 1940, Lovett asked to see the Air Corps plan. There was much stalling, but Thornton insisted, *the* Air Corps plan, the overall plan for the defense of this country, and for its offense as well. The military kept delaying and delaying, and finally they brought down a plan for the aerial defense of New York City, with the dust still on it, apparently designed more to fight off the Red Baron than the new massive waves of air power being fielded in modern warfare.

Thornton was someone that Lovett immediately liked. He came from a small Texas town, was ambitious, bright and pleasantly extroverted; he quickly became one of Lovett's top deputies. Together they decided that in order to harness American industry for the great war effort, they needed first and foremost a giant statistical brain to tell them who they were, what was needed, and where. They asked Harvard Business School, the most logical place, to train the officers they needed for statistical control. This brain trust would send the right men and the right supplies to the right places, and would make sure that when crews arrived at a base there were enough instructors. It was a symbolic step in America's going from a relatively sleepy country toward becoming a superpower (a step which the acceleration in air power and air industry would finalize). We were already so big that our problem primarily concerned control as well as careful and accurate projection of just how powerful we were. (It was significant that twenty years later, when we were an acknowledged superpower, when Kennedy looked for a Secretary of Defense he turned to someone who was not really a production man, but the supreme accountant, determination of what we needed being more essential than the qualities of the old-style professional production man who ramrodded manufacturing schedules through, who went by instinct, and who knew nothing about systems control.)

The Business School accepted the proposition, and a group of the best young teachers was sought out. McNamara, who was already anxious to go into the service, agreed to become a teacher in the program. He was so effective, such an immediate standout, that Thornton soon pulled him from Harvard and attached him to the Army Air Forces. Finally, for the first time, McNamara had something upon which to fasten that energy, that drive, that curious cold passion. Those traits which would eventually be part of the legend began to emerge; until then he had been just another bright young man, intelligent and hard-working. Now he had a cause and a field to operate in. Thornton would recall that the young McNamara of those early days was strikingly similar to the mature McNamara: the same discipline, the concentration, the relentless work all day and night ("I'm sure that now that he's at the World Bank, only the Bank exists, and Defense is behind him, just as when he was at Defense, Ford was behind him, and when he was at Ford, there was really nothing else but his work," he would say).

Thornton sent him first to England to work out problems on the B-17 bomber program, finally got him a commission as a temporary captain in the Army Air Forces. But when the B-29 was being developed, he was pulled from other programs. This was to become the major project for the Air Force, the long-range bomber which was to prove so vital during the last year of the war, but first it needed to be organized and systematized. Other men would make their reputations on the development of the B-29, but Thornton later claimed that the genius of the operation was the young McNamara, putting all the infinitely complicated pieces together, doing program analysis, operation analysis, digesting the mass of facts which would have intimidated less disciplined minds, less committed minds, making sure that the planes and the crews were readied at roughly the same time. Since all this took place before the real age of computers, he had to work it out himself. He was the intelligence bank of the project, and he held the operation together, kept its timing right, kept it all on schedule. It was an awesome performance for a man not yet thirty.

McNamara had planned to go back to Harvard after the war. Challenges fascinated him, but not worldly goods or profit as ends in themselves. So why not return to Harvard, the teaching of those beloved statistics, it was amazing what statistics had done, it was awesome to imagine what they might do in the future. The life style of Cambridge appealed to him; he could enjoy the university atmosphere, he could talk with men who were in other fields and still involve himself in statistics. But Thornton, more outgoing, more entrepreneurial, a man with more imagination than the somewhat reserved McNamara, had other ideas. To Thornton the Air Force had not just been a part of a vast and impressive wartime enterprise but something more, a case study in instant corporate success. From a standing start, the Air Force quickly became cranked up into a supercompany, the most powerful and the most complicated industrial force in the world. It had gone from 295 pilots trained in the year before Pearl Harbor to 96,000 the year after, planes built, flight crews trained, all dovetailed. It had been a staggering task and an enormous success. And they had done it, not by the tired old men who had headed prewar companies, but by this group of talented young people that Thornton and Lovett had created, fresh young minds with modern skills, not tied to the myths, the superstitions and the business prejudices of the past.

Now, Thornton knew, there would be a reconversion from military to civilian production, and the business world would be filled with new opportunities. He took stock of his team: they were without doubt the most talented managerial team of the century, young men who had gained twenty-five years of experience in four years. Under normal business conditions they might not have attained comparable positions of power and influence until they were nearly fifty, by then having picked up all the old prejudices and undesirable traits of their predecessors. Thornton, the oldest and the most senior, was thirty at the time. None of the young men had any real ties to previous jobs; to go back to what they had been was like a general becoming a corporal.

Thornton began to think of the possibility of selling them as a group, all that expertise and managerial talent bound together. It was not just that they could bring a better price as a group, but more important to Thornton, if they were to accomplish something, really create something new and bold in the business world, then their chances were far greater as a group ("If you went in with one or two people you could get lost or chewed up; if you were going to convert a relatively large company quickly you needed a group," he would recall). When he talked it over with his team, they were enthusiastic. Only

McNamara had serious objections, he wanted to return to Harvard. The idea of business did not excite him. But there were financial problems: he had come down with a mild case of polio, and Marg with a more serious case, necessitating considerable doctor bills. ("I said, 'Bob, you've got those doctor bills and you can't go back there to Harvard on twenty-six hundred dollars a year,' and he thought and said, 'I guess you're right,' and he was on board," Thornton said.)

There were two immediate possibilities; one was Robert Young, the railroad man, and the other was the Ford Motor Company. Thornton went by to see Young, who offered him a job and said he could bring two or three men with him. And then there was the Ford Company, which seemed to offer the most challenge. It would have to be retooled and reconverted; they knew that financially it had not done well, though they did not know how badly it had done during the last twenty years, showing a profit only once since 1927, in the year 1932. The old man's long-time associate, Harry Bennett, had just been ousted and the reins taken over by Henry Ford II, their own age—he was twenty-eight—who now desperately needed to modernize the company that his grandfather had founded and then let slip. They sent Ford a cable which said in effect: Bright young management team, ran Air Force, ready to work. Thornton made an early contact; eight of them went out there and impressed Henry Ford and the deal was set. Ford told Thornton to set the salaries; they ranged from $10,000 to $16,000. Thornton gave McNamara the second highest salary. The group became the famous Whiz Kids: Thornton, McNamara, Arjay Miller, J. E. Lundy, Charles Bosworth, Jack Reith, Jim Wright, Ben Davis Mills, Wilbur Andreson and George Moore. It was an extraordinary decision for young Ford to make; however, at that bleak moment in his company's history he had nowhere to go but up. He was reaching beyond the normally closed auto business for a group of non-auto men, whose experience was not in the failure and stupidity of war, but rather in the technology of it, and indeed the technological success of war. Their chief lesson had been that you could control an organization by converting an abundance of facts and figures into meaningful data and then apply them to industrial production; these men were purveyors of what would be a new managerial art in American industry.

The Ford Company practices, both in production and in personnel, had an almost medieval quality to them. Under Henry senior and Harry Bennett the policies of the company were singularly primitive. The public was a problem, the unions were a problem, the bankers were a problem. If Ford built a car, it was the public's responsibility to like it. No modern managerial group was being trained. The company had no credit. Henry Ford's only son, Edsel, had tried to fight the policies, but Bennett destroyed him. After the family revolt which resulted in Bennett's expulsion, young Henry had inherited the shell of a company, the name and perhaps not that much more, at a time when General Motors seemed to employ the most up-to-date production and managerial techniques. Young Henry needed, above all else, instant executives; the company was losing $9 million a month. But he needed, as one friend would admit, two levels of management. One now, instantly, and one to come along. In hiring the Whiz Kids, he was taking care of the future, the near future, but the future nonetheless, so he shrewdly covered all bets and hired a senior level of management from General Motors, men in their late forties and early fifties who could go to work that day and help train his new intellectuals in the auto business. This was to be known in automotive circles as the Breech-Crusoe-Harder group, headed by Ernie Breech, then forty-nine, who had been at General Motors for most of his adult life, and was at the time president of GM's subsidiary, Bendix. He brought with him Lewis Crusoe, another high General Motors executive, now retired, and Delmar Harder, former chief of production of GM.

The arrival of the GM executive group, which the Whiz Kids had not known anything about, slowed down the latter's takeover of Ford (Thornton, restless, left after a year and a half for Hughes Aircraft, where he sensed greater possibilities, finally ending up at Litton Industries). But the system worked very well for Henry Ford. The young men were scattered throughout the company (with McNamara and Arjay Miller, who succeeded McNamara as president of Ford, working in finance). There they worked to convert the incredibly archaic, helter-skelter operation of old Henry to the new classic corporate style used at General Motors, with its highly accountable decentralized units, the different company operations turned into separate profit-and-loss centers where each executive would be held directly responsible, and where slippage and failure would be quickly spotted. The lead of General Motors in that postwar period was enormous: Ford had very little in the way of a factory, its machinery was badly outdated, not easily retooled. In contrast, GM had converted to war production, but it had been very careful to establish in its factory and production lines the kind of systems that could be easily converted to peacetime production. Chevy thus had a massive lead; it could bring out a car for much less than it actually did, but if it lowered its prices it would kill Chrysler and bring the wrath of the Congress down for antitrust. ("Don't ever hire anyone from the auto industry," Gene McCarthy, one of McNamara's severest critics later said of him. "The way they have it rigged it's impossible to fail out there.") So Chevy kept its prices higher and produced a much better car than Ford. The true difference between Ford and Chevy then was reflected in the used-car market: a two-year-old Chevy sold on the used-car market for about $200 more than a two-year-old Ford, a very considerable gap.

The prime aim of the two new management teams at Ford was to close the gap. Here Breech and McNamara combined their talents; they had to figure out how to produce a car that was at least partially competitive with Chevrolet, and at the same time make enough profit that could be plowed back into the company to build the desperately needed plants. They could not do it by borrowing from the banks, Ford's credit rating simply wasn't good enough, so they did it by skinning down the value of the car, mainly on the inside where it wouldn't be seen. Ford had always been known for styling and speed, so they kept that, and worked on having a modern design, with a zippy car, good for the youth market, though eventually, and sometimes not so eventually, the rest of the car would deteriorate (as was also reflected in the used-car price). The Ford buyers seemed to know it, but curiously enough, continued to buy Fords. By these means Breech got the money to buy and modernize the plants, while it was McNamara's particular genius to raise the quality without raising the cost, a supreme act of cost effectiveness. This was, of course, McNamara's specialty, and he had a bonus system to reward stylists and engineers who could improve the car without increasing the cost. The McNamara phrase—it came up again and again at meetings, driven home like a Biblical truth—was "add value rather than cost to the car." And slowly he and Breech closed the gap on the used-car differential while at the same time modernizing the company.

It was at Ford during this period that McNamara was being converted from a bright, hard-charging young statistician into a formidable figure, a legend, *McNamara* the entity, someone to respect, someone to fear, a man who rewarded those who met his standards handsomely, and coldly rejected those who did not.

If someone were to be driving with McNamara during work hours, he would see it: Bob was driving, but he was thinking of grilles that day, only grilles existed for him, cheap ones, expensive ones, flashy ones, simple ones, other cars rushing by on their way to lunch, on their way home, and Bob running it through his mind, oblivious to oncoming traffic, frightening his companions. Bob, watch the road, one would say, and if he were in a good mood, he might apologize for his mental absence. McNamara never stopped pushing; in those days he was watching Chevy—how was Chevy doing? The night each year when they got hold of the first Chevy, everyone gathered around in a special room and broke it down piece by piece into hundreds of items, each one stapled to a place already laid out for it, and they concentrated on it—no brain surgeon ever concentrated more—everyone muttering, wondering how Chevy had done this or that for a tenth of a cent less, cursing them slightly— so *that* was how they had done it!

When Thornton left, there was considerable curiosity as to who would emerge as the top Whiz Kid; it soon became clear that it was McNamara. He symbolized a new kind of executive in American business (later one friend would call him "dean of the first class of American corporate managers"), men who had not grown up in the business, who were not part of the family but who were modern, well educated, technicians who prided themselves that they were not tied to the past but brought the most progressive analytical devices to modern business, who used computers to understand the customers and statistics to break down costs and productions. At Ford what distinguished McNamara was the capacity to bring a detailed financial system to the almost total disorganization of the company. He was brilliant at systematizing, telling Ford where it was going before it got there. He set up a corporate accounting system which reduced the element of surprise in the business. His system of rewards for reducing costs provided incentive (though occasionally, in the view of his critics there, the system backfired, the rewards going to people and ideas whose efficiency would be only short-range).

He rose quickly because he was moving in something of a vacuum. Henry Ford was new and unsure of himself, particularly in the field of financial systems. To an uneasy, uncertain Ford, McNamara offered reassurance; when questions arose he always seemed to have the answers, not vague estimates but certitudes, facts, numbers, and lots of them. Though his critics might doubt that he knew what the public wanted or what it was doing, he could always forecast precisely the Ford part of the equation. He had little respect for much of the human material he found around him, the people who claimed, when he reeled off his overwhelming statistics, that they had always done it the other way in the auto business. Such people, when they challenged him, were often proved wrong. Slowly he surrounded himself with men who met his criteria, men who responded to the same challenges and beliefs, and he would respect their judgments. This was a formative experience in his life, because years later, when the doubters about Vietnam began to express themselves, they at first tended to be people who did not talk his language and who were very different from his kind of people. They did not think in terms of statistics, or rationalizing systems, and they did not support their judgments with facts as he knew them, but rather by saying that it did not smell right, or that it just did not feel right; he would trust his facts and statistics and instincts against theirs just as he had before at Ford when confronted by the businessmen who had doubted his facts and charts.

IN DETROIT HE WAS THE ODD MAN IN. THE AUTO WORLD IS A VERY special segment of America, with the normal American exaggerations blown even larger. Like a mini-Texas. It is a world closed in, auto men talk to other auto men, auto traditions passed on in generations of families. Ford people living among Ford people, General Motors among GM people. A Ford country club. A General Motors country club. Cocktail conversations about cars and the company. Dinner conversations about cars and the company. There is a self-belief that what they are doing is not only good for America, it is America. In this atmosphere McNamara was the last puritan. He came to it, met it on his terms, never really changing, conquered it by sheer mathematical and tactical ability, rose to the highest position, a penultimate corporate victory, forcing the head of the company to adjust an entire system to his style. McNamara was never *of* Detroit and never really *of* the auto industry. They were backslappers, good fellows, and he was never one for slapped backs, his or theirs. While they frolicked, he plowed through the unabridged Toynbee. Even his public relations man was different; other PR men specialized in expense-account lunches, plush trips, the usual lures to wine and dine and con journalists; McNamara by contrast paid a very handsome salary to a man named Holmes Brown because Brown was very good, knew a lot about the auto industry and was well informed. Brown's treatment of reporters was considered unusually Spartan by Detroit standards. McNamara preferred to live in Ann Arbor among the eggheads, many of them liberals and Democrats (at Ford executive meetings Henry Ford would occasionally mention contributions to the Republican party and then note with a certain distaste that "Bob here will probably give to the Democrats"), reading books, buying paintings. When the dealers and their wives showed up every year, the head of Ford would traditionally show them around while the wife would take care of the ladies for a day. Normally it meant fashion shows with mink coats. Under Marg McNamara they went for a tour of the University of Michigan cyclotron. Indeed it was said that the McNamaras deliberately managed to be elsewhere when Henry and Ann Ford gave great gala parties for their daughters.

But it was more than just a stylistic difference with Detroit, it was something far deeper. In business philosophy as well as personal life McNamara was a puritan, and the auto business is not the place for a puritan, nor is it necessarily the place for someone who has an abiding faith in man as a rational being committing rational acts. The buying of a car is not necessarily a rational act; it takes more than the transportation aspect to sell a car. Detroit is and always has been happiest when it can foist on a potential customer more than he needs, adding chrome, hard tops, soft tops, air conditioners, speakers, extra horsepower. McNamara was different; he thought the customer should be rational, and worse, in the eyes of some colleagues, he thought he *was* rational. The auto industry essentially believes the buying of a car is an impulse; McNamara insisted it was a rational decision. It pained him to approve a convertible, the idea that a customer would pay $200 more for a dangerous car that would deteriorate more rapidly offended him (after he left Ford and they made a convertible version out of his beloved Falcon he wrote a rare message to a friend at Ford: "You must be crazier than hell"). He believed deeply in the simple utilitarian car, that it was a raw, functional thing, that man seeks the highest form of efficiency without grace, and without psychological feelings at all. His opponents in the auto industry argued that this is not the way the world is, and in particular, it is not the way the auto industry is; man will opt for comfort and status every time, and has since men flaunted better-looking horses and carriages at one another.

But it was as if McNamara felt that there were certain things which were good for people and other things which were bad, and he would be the arbiter, he knew better than they. It was, said one friend, a quiet kind of arrogance. One of his colleagues thought he should have been the head of production at the Moskva works in the Soviet Union, the utilitarian man producing the utilitarian car for the utilitarian society, no worry about frills there. If he hadn't gone to work at Ford, thought another, he'd still be teaching at the Harvard Business School, probably happier, driving a VW to work and laughing like hell at all the fools around him with their big cars and automatic transmissions. He not only believed in rationality, thought a friend, he loved it. It was his only passion. "If you offended it at a meeting, you were not just wrong, you had violated something far greater, you had violated his sense of the rational order. Like offending a man's religion." If you did show a flash of irrationality or support the wrong position, he would change, speaking faster, the voice like a machine gun, cutting into you: chop chop chop. You miscalculated here. Chop. You left this out. Chop. You neglected this. Chop. Therefore you're wrong. Chop. Chop. Chop.

He was a powerhouse at those meetings, driving things through, always in great command, doing his own homework, never respecting those who did not (later when he was at the Pentagon a general would turn at a meeting and ask a colonel for the answer to a question, and it would be the general's last appearance around McNamara). His power was facts, no one had more, and no one used them better, firing them out, one after another, devastating his opponents (though sometimes friends would feel that there was a missing piece, that sometimes this brilliant reasoning was based, yes, on a false assumption). He was, if anything, too strong a personality; he so dominated meetings that other men felt submerged and suppressed. Sometimes his meetings seemed to less friendly eyes to have a sham quality. There would be a meeting, say, to plan a car, its style, content and prospective price. McNamara would arrive at the meeting with his own homework done, his own decisions made, so that he came with a fixed position. He would seemingly defer to the others, ask what they thought, yet there was an overpowering personality and ego there. He perhaps did not mean it to be that way, but despite the appearance of give-and-take, the whole thing would become something of a sham, the classic Harvard Business School approach with loaded dice.

Those who attended the meetings learned to play the game; the McNamara requests to speak freely were not to be taken too seriously. He would telegraph his own viewpoint, more often than not unconsciously, in the way he expressed the problem, and in particular he would summarize in an intimidating way, outlining point by point, using the letters of the alphabet, A through J, if necessary, and his position always seemed to win out in the summation. If you dissented or deviated, he listened, but you could almost hear the fingers wanting to drum on the table; if you agreed and gave pro evidence, he would respond warmly, his voice approving in tone. Gradually those who disagreed learned their lesson, and just as gradually he would reach out to men who were like him until he was surrounded by men in his own image. Those who knew him well could tell when he was angry, when he was going to explode. He would become tense, and if you looked under the table you could see him begin to hitch up his pants, a nervous habit, done because he knew he could not control his hands if they were on the table. The more restless he became, the more his antagonist assaulted his senses, the higher the pants would get, showing thick hairy legs. On bad days the pants might reach to the knees, and then suddenly he would talk, bang bang bang. You're wrong for these reasons. Flicking his fingers out. One. Two. Three . . . He always ran out of fingers.

Though he was often blamed for the Edsel (particularly by Barry Goldwater in 1964), he had remarkably little to do with it; the car was essentially antithetical to his position. The old GM people at Ford had long wanted to emulate the GM pattern, a different car in each of several different markets, different stalls in the market place (Ford-Mercury-Lincoln dealers were together, whereas the GM lines were sold separately). Finally they saw their chance: upgrade Mercury and slip the Edsel in between. The decision was made in 1955, a prime year, but the car came to fruition in 1958, which was a bad auto year, post-Sputnik, the worst year, for instance, Buick had. When the Edsel went bad, Lewis Crusoe had a heart attack, and McNamara was put in charge of all the car divisions. He consolidated some of the other divisions and put a stop to the Edsel.

Instead of playing games with consumer tastes, he spent those years fighting the battle to keep the prices down and the cars simple, fighting with the other people at Ford, fighting with the dealers. Always trading and swapping to hold the line. The dealers wanted more frills. The dealers wanted a crank on the front-window vents. And McNamara would say, all right, you can have that, but we'll have to take all the chrome off the car. Some of the men fought about the width of the car, wanting it wider so it could be a hardtop, which entailed a wider frame. McNamara would listen and tell them (words which would be remembered long after), "If you persist in demanding this, I'll have to take the car away from you." The men around him began to shade things in talking to him, not really lies, just a certain hedging of the truth to please him. For instance, McNamara wanted a two-speed automatic transmission, so he promoted a design which would perform as well as a three-speed but cost less. There were considerable doubts that the two-speed would work as well, but he was finally given assurances that it would; the engineers wanted it to work because *he* wanted it to work, because there would be bonuses and smiles of approval, but sadly it never did; it performed durably but sluggishly, just as his critics had predicted.

Yet he was good at Ford, no mistake about that. He brought his system to that declining empire at just the right time; they held the line, they did not decay and collapse as they might have, and they finally grew back, in part owing to his enormous drive and pressure, his utilitarian view, probably perfectly suited to what Ford needed and could afford at the time. His greatest triumph was the Falcon, the vindication of his years at Ford, the definitive utilitarian car, the direct descendant of the Model T, his ultimate contribution to cost effectiveness, a car low enough in price to compete with foreign imports but large enough to transport an American family around. He did not want a revolutionary car, just a classic, simple car. It was a great success, though not as great as McNamara had hoped; he envisioned a million in the first year, and it went instead to 600,000. Its success was to come just before he left Ford; it enabled him to gain the presidency, and he left on a note of triumph. But after he left, Lee Iacocca, who would eventually succeed him, said that Bob McNamara had damn near ruined Ford by pushing that Falcon, too simple a car, with too small a profit for the company. Iacocca symbolized exactly the opposite of McNamara in the auto world. For instance, he brought racing to Ford, and Henry liked that, Henry pictured with his pretty new wife in Europe after having virtually bought Le Mans, an invasion of American power and industry somewhat short of that flashed on D-Day. McNamara hated all that, hated racing, and now here was Henry and the Ford name advertising for it. Lee brought in the Mustang, a car designed for the American consumer in just the way McNamara's cars were not. They had looked at the design and thought, we have a doll of a car and people will buy it, and now let's figure out how to build it. Lee liked bigger, plusher, flashier cars, and to him the Falcon was a reminder that Ford might be growing customers for GM, bringing them into auto consumption, and then as they grew wealthier, turning them over to GM, which was stronger in the middle range of cars. So Lee was critical of McNamara, and so occasionally was Henry Ford, now more confident, now more his own man, and sometimes given to making statements which indicated a measure of disenchantment with McNamara, that perhaps the good old-style auto people were better than the new intellectuals.

IT IS NOT EASY BEING A PURITAN IN BABYLON, LIVING THE PRIVATE life of a puritan but competing with the other Babylonians in the daytime pursuit of profit and growth, and the Ford McNamara was an immensely complicated man. He would have been a simple man had he stayed on in a university, taught there, lived there, sent his students out in the world a little better for their experience with him, but essentially one man, no difference between the theory and practice of McNamara. But this was different. He who had little material drive of his own was committed to making it in the world of profit and excess and, indeed, greed (to hold power he had to be, above all, a successful businessman, and his power stemmed from his ability to do the job, to cut corners, to make profits).

So the ferocious businessman of Detroit was the humane citizen of Ann Arbor: he read the right books, went to local art openings in Ann Arbor, and supported the local cultural affairs, which always needed supporting. Marg belonged, of course, to the local UN group, and Bob and Marg were both members of a book club, which met once a month. Each person picked a book for a meeting, then all of them read and discussed it (with no more than two drinks at the meetings). Bob's book was Camus' *The Rebel*. His intellectualism was even then a little self-conscious; it wasn't so much that he was philosophical as he liked to be philosophical, he liked to improve himself (he was the final self-improvement man; he read an essay because it was an essay to be read), the man with the five-foot shelf of Great Books. Later, when he arrived in Washington, all that intelligence and force made some of the capital's more skeptical residents feel that there was a gee-whiz quality to his intellectual pursuits, McNamara a little self-conscious about intellectual pursuits, a part of the Great Book crowd . . . Bob and Marg to be improved . . . he had just talked to Barbara Ward and she said this and that. At the Robert Kennedy's Hickory Hill seminars, which were a symbolic feature of the vastly overrated New Frontier culture, more chic than substance, the women had to be either very pretty, or Mrs. Longworth, McNamara was a constant and deadly earnest student. He took the seminars more seriously than anyone else, always doing his homework, always asking a serious question.

As there was later in Washington, there was something of a split in the personality during the Detroit years, a switchover after 6:30 P.M. There was the driving, relentless, cost-effective executive of Ford during the day and the resident philosopher of Ann Arbor in the evening, one cold and efficient, the other warm, almost gregarious. It was as if he compartmentalized his mind; the deep philosophic thoughts were important, but they were not to be part of the broader outlook; if perhaps he were to stand for some of the good things in business he would do it *after* he took control of Ford. Subvert them first and then announce who you are. If later the immensity of the contradictions between his liberal instincts and the war in Vietnam would cause him grief, similarly the difference between his sense of social conscience and the enormous needs of great industry caused him problems earlier. It was as if the contradictions of our age were all within him. At Ford he could be an advocate of consumer rights, hating the way the parts system worked, with dealers forcing spare parts on customers (the dealers, of course, loved this because they could charge high labor rates for repairs). Although McNamara despised this system, he was also very much a part of it, because it was, yes, cost-effective, very lucrative, and the dealers in those years did not get the choice items from Detroit unless they sold the requisite number of parts to their customers. (Years later at the Pentagon he would be a symbol of an attempt to control the arms race and at the same time one of the world's great arms salesmen to other countries because it cut Pentagon costs, was good for the budget, looked good on the Hill, made the President smile.)

McNamara believed in car safety and thought it was important, yet he never really pushed it until 1956 when Ford was flat beaten by Chevy; Ford was in the last year of a three-year cycle and Chevy had a hot new car, a sharp new style, a V-8 engine, and Ford was dead and they all knew it. Since the Ford people realized that there was little in the way of options, they decided to sell safety; it was not often, one of them said, that you got to be on the side of both God and profits. It was McNamara's idea and decision. He had long been concerned about safety and wanted to bring it in; yet it was also a last-minute decision and a desperate one. They added some safety latches, a deep-dish steering wheel, crash padding in front, and called in J. Walter Thompson to do the campaign. The theme was that Ford was safe and safety was good for you, something that sounds mild to the uninitiated but which was revolutionary at the time. When the cars came out, Chevy was, predictably, a great success; the Ford was a bust and McNamara's job even seemed to be on the line.

Then he caught the flu and went to Florida for a rest. While he was gone some of the General Motors executives and some of their old friends at Ford tried a coup against McNamara. Apparently high GM officials called Henry and said—look, this is serious, you're ruining the auto industry, you're selling death, the image you're projecting is violent and ugly (cars, after all, were for pleasure and brought happiness. On the television commercials, handsome young men drove new cars and they met good-looking young women). With Henry's sanction a group of the old GM people took over some of McNamara's functions. It was, in effect, a takeover; he was, in fact, close to being out. But he rose from the ashes, saved not so much by the generosity of Henry Ford, or the Ford power structure, as by the 1957 Ford and by the much despised dealers, who knew they had a hot car (this was one of the two years while he was at Ford that Ford beat Chevrolet) and were willing to stay with the '56 in order to get the '57. So Ford decided to cut back on the '56 and minimize its losses. The new advertising was changed to style, performance, and yes—you could barely hear it—safety. It was not untypical of McNamara at Ford, and later at Defense, that he started with good intentions, touched with a certain expediency and a little dissembling, and ended up not with a success, but with something even worse, for it became part of the auto mythology that safety does not sell, safety is bad and hurts business. It would take another decade and an outsider named Ralph Nader who did not worry about hiding his intentions or making it in the business world, to put the full moral pressure on the auto industry to bring some safety and consumer reforms.

WHEN MCNAMARA WENT TO WASHINGTON, MOST OF HIS FRIENDS IN Ann Arbor felt that he left with a sigh of relief, that he had never really liked the auto industry, never found enough fulfillment (they thought also that Marg had always felt that selling cars was a little unbecoming, a little unsavory). It was as if, once he had found that he could make it at Ford and win, he was bored with the world, with the other men who could talk only about cars. It was as if, presented a challenge, he had mastered it in order to give himself credibility and respectability in the world of business (thus, if you were a success in the business world, met payrolls, made profits, you were a serious person, and your social and other opinions took on a more serious nature; you were not a simple do-gooder who has never lived in the real world). He made money for Henry not because he was interested in profits but because his power was based on his relationship with Henry, and Henry had charged him with this, thus it was his responsibility to make profits. (In 1955 he was asked to give the commencement address at the University of Alabama, and he wrote a speech which said finally that there had to be a higher calling for a businessman than simply making money. One of the Ford officials saw the advance text and insisted that the passage come out; McNamara was very bitter and thought of canceling the speech. "Damn it," he told friends. "I'm making more money for them than they've ever had made before. Why can't they leave me alone?" But friends told him that the Ford people had not said he couldn't say this, they had simply refused to permit it in the advance text. So he went down to the commencement and when he got to the controversial passage in his speech, he shouted it out so that it could be heard all the way back to Detroit.)

When he was offered the Defense job, his close friends felt they would not really be surprised if he accepted; he had, they thought, been looking for a larger and more satisfying stage. The only thing which would make him stay would be a sense of responsibility to Henry, certainly not to himself. There were people at Ford who were pleased, feeling as they did that the company under this coldly driving, efficient man had been too stifled. In Ann Arbor the pleasant liberals in his book club were pleased too, to see this humane man that they admired so much take on such an important new job as Defense. One of them, Robert Angell, the head of the sociology department and a member of McNamara's book club, who had admired the breadth of McNamara's mind, went to his classes that morning and instead of beginning with the regularly scheduled work, he talked movingly about McNamara, how lucky the country was to have this kind of man in such a difficult job, a man who was far more than a businessman, a real philosopher with a conscience and a human sensitivity. Later, when the Bay of Pigs happened, Angell and the others would receive something of a shock—how could Bob be involved in something like this? Angell, a very gentle man, decided, talking with some of Bob's other friends, that they had made Bob go along. And then McNamara went to Vietnam and came back, and Angell turned on his television set and there was Bob talking about putting people in fortified villages, and Angell wondered what had happened to Bob, he sounded so different. And his friends in Ann Arbor would watch him with his pointer as he crisply explained where the bombs were falling. In 1965 Angell would duly set off for the first teach-in against the war, held at Michigan, and he and the other friends would always wonder what had happened to Bob; they heard that Marg had been sick, that the war had torn Bob up, but they would not talk about it with him because Bob did not come back to visit them.

Chapter Thirteen

MᶜNAMARA HAD COME IN AT A DEAD RUN; BY THE TIME he was sworn in he had already identified the hundred problems of the Defense Department, had groups and committees studying them. He had his people plucked from the campuses or the shadow government of the Rand Corporation and other think tanks. They were cool and lucid, these men, men of mathematical precision who had grown up in the atmosphere of the Cold War, and who were students of nuclear power and parity and deployment, men whose very professions sometimes sounded uncivilized to the humanist. He took over the Defense Department for a Chief Executive who had run on the promise of getting America moving again (one pictured them always without overcoats and hats, moving and pushing quickly through crowds, always on the move; Kennedy had once gotten angry at Robert Bird, a reporter for the *Herald Tribune*, because Bird had written that the reason that this dynamic young man was able to campaign without an overcoat in the cold of New Hampshire and Wisconsin was that he wore thermal underwear), on the assumption that we were losing our power and manhood, *they* had more missiles. McNamara had assumed that his first job when he took over would be to hurry up production and close the missile gap, but he soon discovered that there was none. Shortly after the election McNamara told Pentagon reporters this, a statement which caused a considerable flap, particularly among Republicans, who had lost an election partly because of a nonexistent gap. How many God-fearing, Russian-fearing citizens had cast their votes to end the gap and live a more secure life, only to find that they had been safe all along. When Kennedy called McNamara the next day to find out what had happened, McNamara denied that he had ended the missile gap, a denial which made the Pentagon reporters, who had heard the statement with their own ears, very leary of his word in the future.

But it was true, there was no missile gap, so instead of increasing the might of the United States and catching up with the Russians, McNamara set out to harness the might, to control it and to bring some order and rationality to it, and soon, above all, to limit the use of nuclear weapons. To control the weapons, to limit them, to rationalize their procedures absorbed his time and his energy; and Vietnam, which was a tiny little storm cloud on the horizon, seemed distant, small, manageable, far from the real center of man's question of survival or self-destruction. It would be one of the smaller ironies of his years as Secretary of Defense that in making his arguments against nuclear weapons, forcefully, relentlessly, he had to make counterarguments *for* conventional forces, to build up those conventional forces. We had to have some kind of armed might, so he made good and effective arguments for conventional weapons (and if the Chiefs wanted to use them in Vietnam, to send American combat troops without nuclear weapons, he had to go along, since he had developed the thesis, the mystique of what conventional weapons could do with the new mobility). He gave them a rationale, for his overriding concern was quickly to limit the possibilities of nuclear war, to gain control of those weapons.

It was a very different time, the immediate post-Eisenhower years. The Chiefs, who were held over from the previous Administration (generals who believed in a more balanced posture, like Ridgway and Taylor, had been either winnowed out, or more or less ignored), were men who believed that nuclear war was a viable kind of military position; indeed, the entire American military posture was essentially based on a willingness to use nuclear weapons. That was an eerie-enough thought, and some people wanted to crawl away from it. Men such as Henry Kissinger, then of Harvard, had just made himself something of an intellectual reputation as a theoretician of tactical nuclear weapons (that is, finding something respectable between blowing up the world and being too soft), and there was thus something of a fad for tactical nuclear weapons. (Though one problem was that in the Pentagon's war games there always seemed to be a problem with the tactical nuclear weapons. No matter which side fired first, the other side would retaliate, and every time without fail it would somehow expand to strategic weapons; whoever was behind on the little stuff would let fly with the big stuff.)

Daniel Ellsberg discussed the subject of nuclear weapons with McNamara during a luncheon meeting; later he would remember the Secretary's passion on the subject. He was against using tactical weapons ("They're the same thing, there's no difference," he said, "once you use them, you use everything else. You can't keep them limited. You'll destroy Europe, everything"). Ellsberg had heard that McNamara was a man without convictions or emotions, but decided that this was a deliberately chosen pose, and an effective one, to cover real feelings. It was, he thought, an impressive performance, not just because of McNamara's almost emotional abhorrence of the weapons but because he understood the dangers of his situation: he had to keep his feelings hidden, for if the Chiefs or Congress found out how he felt he would be finished as Secretary of Defense. The whole might of America was concentrated on nuclear weapons, and we had sold the idea of nuclear retaliation to the Europeans; if the word got out of the Secretary's negative attitude, it would mean that the United States was virtually disarmed, so of course he would not be able to stay in office.

Shortly after lunch Ellsberg received a call from Adam Yarmolinsky, who had been present during the meeting. "You must not speak of this lunch to anyone. It is of the highest importance. Not to anyone. It must not get around." Ellsberg agreed, and then mentioned a rumor that the President himself felt the same way about the weapons. (There was a story going around hip Pentagon circles that Kennedy was unreliable, almost soft on nukes; he had been taken to visit a SAC base, and when he saw a 20-megaton bomb, he blanched visibly. "Why do we need one of these?" he asked. It caused a scandal in SAC circles because this, of course, was the standard bomb, they were all like this.) "There is no difference between them at all," Yarmolinsky answered.

McNAMARA WORKED HARD TO CHANGE WESTERN THINKING ABOUT nuclear policy. He set out to educate not just the Pentagon but his European colleagues as well, forming the Nuclear Planning Group for his European counterparts, men who were politicians first, not managers, and thus felt themselves particularly dependent on their generals. He forced them to build a table where only the defense ministers could sit. No prepared papers or set speeches were allowed, and they could not turn to their generals who then turned to their colonels. They came to the meetings, only one person from each country at the table, only four others allowed in the room, he hated crowds. At first it did not work too well because McNamara overwhelmed them, he was too strong a presence, but gradually he forced them to take political responsibility for defense positions, and equally important, build skilled professional staffs which could challenge the technical thinking of the military at the lower levels, point by point, so they would not be forced into blind choices at the highest level.

He worked hard to bring greater control to the entire nuclear system.

When he entered office he had found it surprisingly hair-trigger and chancy. The military had constructed a system in which the prime consideration was not control but getting the weapons into the air, no matter what; controls and safeguards were secondary. Even on the weapons themselves the safety features seemed marginal; there was, he decided, far too great a chance that one could go off in a crash, and he insisted on other safety features being added. He evolved PAL (Permissive Action Link), a system which was developed first as a technical device to lock up all nuclear weapons not under U.S. control; that is, the nukes in other countries. With that in mind he got development of it, his rationale being: I love nuclear weapons as much as the next man, but if we let these Greeks and Turks have them . . . Technically, none of the nuclear weapons here in the United States could be used without a specific order from the President; in practice, if the Chiefs felt that communications had failed, they could make a decision to use the weapons based on their best judgment. It was a very subtle thing; once he got started with the rationale of keeping them from the non-Anglo-Saxon peoples of NATO, he was able eventually to slip the controls on American weapons. Had the military been exactly sure of his intentions—they sensed them, of course—they might have blocked him from the start. At the end they fought and fought hard. After all, it downgraded the field commander, and to them, the threat that the reaction time was slowed down was greater than that a crackpot might take over the base.

HE FELT HIMSELF VERY MUCH ALONE, SURROUNDED BY HOSTILE forces in his quest. He had no following on the Hill and he felt that his detractors did, so his loyalty to the President, which was strong in any case, was doubly strong, the President was his only patron and protector, and his source of power. But if the President had doubts about him, then he lost power in this savage world in which he was operating. He was already a compromised figure. He was fighting for the highest needs of mankind, plotting against the bureaucracy, dissembling inside, but eventually the compromises that he made did not really work out satisfactorily, he had to give so much in order to appear respectable. To a degree the fault lay in the era. The nation was beginning to emerge from a period of enormous political and intellectual rigidity (it had virtually been embalmed) because of the Cold War, a period which nonetheless had seen a great jump in the technological might of the United States. The growth of the sophistication of weapons and the enormous increase in their price had given the Pentagon a quantum jump in power. Its relationship with the Congress, always strong, but based in the past largely on patriotism and relatively minor pork-barrel measures, was now strengthened by a new loyalty, based on immense defense contracts conveniently placed around the homes of the most powerful committee chairmen.

On how many fronts could he fight? If he had tried to turn the country around on chemical and biological warfare, for instance, Senator Russell surely would have opened hearings. Did you want a fight on everything? By holding them off on the B-70, a bomber which no one needed, he almost brought on a constitutional crisis, with the Congress passing the money that the executive branch did not want to spend. He was constantly fighting with the Chiefs, but also deciding how much each point was worth. On the test-ban treaty McNamara virtually locked them in a room for a week to fight it out with them. He made them promise that once he had broken an argument they could not go back to it, because he felt that arguing with the Chiefs was a lot like arguing with your mother-in-law; you win a point and go on to the next only to find that they are back at the first. So, for a week, hour after hour, he went through every objection they had, breaking them down point by point, until finally he won. He read his victory as a conversion. His aides felt differently, however; they felt he had shown how important the treaty was to him, and as one said later, it was virtually a case of going along with him or resigning. But how many issues were worth this much effort, particularly since many of these fights were not his by tradition? It should have been the Secretary of State, not of Defense, who was fighting for a nuclear-test ban.

Yet he took over at a time when the world was changing. The threats of the Soviet Union were not the same. There was no longer a Communist monolith. (The Chiefs, for instance, were far slower to accept the Sino-Soviet split than most people in Washington, believing it finally when the Russians massed troops on the Chinese border.) The bureaucracy around him often seemed more rigid than the needs of the world required. More missiles for NATO. More troops. Bigger bombers. It was as if at a crucial moment in history he sensed the problems and the end of certain myths and worked hard to correct them, yet as if finally it was all too much. His record clouded even on nuclear weapons. Had they tempered the arms race as they might have or had they helped push the Soviets into another round of mutual escalation of missile building?

HE COMPILED AN AWESOME RECORD IN WASHINGTON IN THOSE DAYS. He was a much-sought-after figure, a man of impressive qualities. In a flashy Administration which placed great emphasis on style, McNamara was at home. He had always liked style among people at Ford, judging them not only by what they said, but how they said it. He was popular at dinner parties and was considered unusual in that he did not bore women at dinner by talking about nuclear warheads. He was a friend of Jack and Jackie's, of Bobby and Ethel's, and yet he lived simply, driving his own car more often than not, a beat-up old Ford. He was gay when the occasion called for gaiety, sober when it called for sobriety. If he made enemies on the Hill, they were at least the right enemies—Vinson, Stennis, Rivers—men hardly revered by social-intellectual Washington. His congressional appearances were impressive, well prepared, grim and humorless. McNamara testifying on the Hill was not someone you wanted to cross. Yet he was unbending, he knew too many answers. The Hill didn't like that. He was perhaps a little too *smart*, and when Southerners say someone is smart they are not necessarily being complimentary. His deputy Roswell Gilpatric cautioned him, suggesting that it would be a good idea to go over and have a few drinks occasionally, get to know the boys, humanize yourself and your intentions. The oil in the wheels of government was bourbon. But McNamara would have none of it. He worked a fourteen-hour day already; if he did his job and presented his facts accurately and intelligently, then they would do their job by accepting his accuracy and there was no need to waste time in missionary work. He had his responsibilities and they theirs, and if they could not see the rightness of what he was doing, he did not think he could woo them by drinking. Probably he was right.

Yet even his enemies added to his reputation; they were the right enemies, the generals, the conservatives on the Hill. And if there were doubts about his sensitivity on some political issues, even his liberal critics found something admirable in him, his capacity to change, to follow the evidence and to keep his ego separated from his opinions. So as the Kennedy Administration progressed he seemed to have started toward a career as the classic Secretary of Defense, particularly working for a President of the United States who was wiser, whose political instincts were better and more sophisticated. The combination of Kennedy-McNamara seemed to work well. The President had a broader sense of history, a sense of skepticism, and it blended well with McNamara's sheer managerial ability, his capacity to take complicated problems of defense, which were almost mathematical in their complexity, and break them down. Kennedy understood the gaps in McNamara; even if he was brilliant, he was not wise. When Kennedy told him to bring back an answer on a question, McNamara would work diligently, come back, and present the answer to the question. If Kennedy noted that this was not the answer he wanted, McNamara would disappear and come back with the *right* answer this time. (In 1962 McNamara, always cost-conscious, came charging into the White House ready to save millions on the budget by closing certain naval bases. All the statistics were there. Close this base, save this many dollars. Close that one and save that much more. All obsolete. All fat. Each base figured to the fraction of the penny. Kennedy interrupted him and said, Bob, you're going to close the Brooklyn Navy Yard, with twenty-six thousand people, and they're going to be out of work and go across the street and draw un-employment, and you better figure that into the cost. That's going to cost us something and they're going to be awfully mad at me, and we better figure that in too. So Kennedy ended the closing down, but in 1964 under Johnson, McNamara came right back with the same proposals. Johnson, who loved economy, particularly little economies, light-switch economies, was more in-terested in the idea until Kenny O'Donnell, who had become one of McNa-mara's more constant critics within the government and who would later argue vociferously with Bobby Kennedy that most of the mistakes of the Ken-nedy era had stemmed from McNamara, pointed out that the shipyards al-ways tended to be in the districts of key congressmen, men like John McCor-mack and John Rooney, and though it saved a few million, it might cost them the Rules Committee.)

WHEN MCNAMARA BEGAN TO TAKE CHARGE OF VIETNAM THERE WAS A growing split between the civilians and the military over the assessment of Vi-etnam. Now McNamara, a civilian heading a military enterprise, was to be-come the principal figure, in effect the judge of the controversy, a man with civilian attitudes responsible to military pressures and military assessments (one of the problems with him on the war, a friend would later note, was that though he thought the military knew nothing about hardware and about weapons systems, he did think they knew something about running wars). But when he moved in on Vietnam he was not, as he was on so many other issues, aided by those bright young civilians from the Defense Department, the Whiz Kids, whom he usually let loose to become his own independent sources of information with which to break institutional information networks. Rather, he took over as if he were the desk officer, with John McNaughton later serving as his own aide. (In 1965 he finally sent the first of the Whiz Kids to Vietnam as a civilian member of the headquarters there. The young man's pessimism differed sharply from Saigon's optimism and had an important effect on McNamara's own doubts. The young man was Daniel Ellsberg.) McNamara, who had unleashed these young men elsewhere in the Pentagon, moved virtually alone in an area where he was least equipped to deal with the problems, where his training was all wrong, the quantifier trying to quantify the unquantifiable. What had worked for him so effectively in the past, the challenge of his own civilians loyal only to him and their craft, to the existing facts and preconceptions, was missing. He had no independent information with which to compete with the military's information; he had journalistic ac-counts, of course, but journalists were not serious people and even at the Pen-tagon they seemed like adversaries who existed for the sake of adversity.

Thus he went into Vietnam virtually alone. The reasons for keeping his civilians out are complicated. For one thing, it was a sensitive issue; the Chiefs were already somewhat neurotic about the use of systems analysis, sensing, not entirely inaccurately, that it was about to become a civilian JCS giving independent judgments. It was one thing to offer systems analysis in the technical areas, the mathematical and hardware areas, but quite another to compete with their judgment on a war, on the facts produced by a war. It would immediately have brought Stennis and Rivers down on him. The second thing was that though by and large he did not respect the military very much in *his* fields (which were in managerial decisions, rationalism, cost accounting), he did think they were professionals in one area, that whatever else, they knew how to fight at war; thus one did not mess with them in their area of specialty because it was very delicate in the first place, and in the second place because it went against their professionalism. And there was that confidence which bordered on arrogance, a belief that he could handle it. Perhaps, after all, the military weren't all that good; still, they could produce the raw data, and McNamara, who *knew data,* would go over it carefully and extricate truth from the morass. Thus the portrait of McNamara in those years at his desk, on planes, in Saigon, poring over page after page of data, each platoon, each squad, studying all those statistics. All lies. Talking with reporters and telling them that all the indices were good. He could not have been more wrong; he simply had all the wrong indices, looking for American production indices in an Asian political revolution.

There was something symbolic about him during those trips. He epitomized booming American technological success, he scurried around Vietnam, looking for what he wanted to see; and he never saw nor smelled nor felt what was really there, right in front of him. He was so much a prisoner of his own background, so unable, as indeed was the country which sponsored him, to adapt his values and his terms to Vietnamese realities. Since any real indices and truly factual estimates of the war would immediately have shown its bankruptcy, the McNamara trips became part of a vast unwitting and elaborate charade, the institutionalizing and legitimizing of a hopeless lie. Those trips seemed to symbolize the foolishness and hopelessness of it all, particularly if McNamara represented the best of the society. And memories of him still remain: McNamara in 1962 going to Operation Sunrise, the first of the repopulated villages, the villagers obviously filled with bitterness and hatred, ready, one could tell, to slit the throat of the first available Westerner, and McNamara not picking it up, innocently firing away his questions. How much of this? How much of that? Were they happy here? McNamara was always acting out his part in those carefully planned visits, General Harkins acting as his travel agent, and just to make sure the trip was a success, always at his side. (Years later, when McNamara had turned against the war, he talked with John Vann, the lieutenant colonel who had left the Army in protest of the Harkins policies, and the one who had shown statistically how badly the war was going. McNamara asked Vann why he had been misinformed, and Vann bluntly told him it was his own fault. He should have insisted on his own itinerary. He should have traveled without accompanying brass, and he should have taken some time to find out who the better-informed people were and learned how to talk to them.)

The Harkins briefings were of course planned long in advance; they were brainwashings really, but brainwashings made all the more effective and exciting by the trappings of danger. Occasional mortar rounds going off. A captured rifle to touch, a surly captured Vietcong to look at. What was created on those trips was not an insight about the country but an illusion of knowledge. McNamara was getting the same information which was available in Washington, but now it was presented so much more effectively that he thought he understood Vietnam. Afterward Arthur Sylvester, his PIO, told reporters how many miles he had flown, how many corps headquarters, province headquarters, district headquarters he had visited, how many officers of each rank. The reporters sat there writing it down, all of it mindless, all of it fitting McNamara's vision of what Vietnam should be. Vietnam confirmed McNamara's preconceptions and specifications.

One particular visit seemed to sum it up: McNamara looking for the war to fit his criteria, his definitions. He went to Danang in 1965 to check on the Marine progress there. A Marine colonel in I Corps had a sand table showing the terrain and patiently gave the briefing: friendly situation, enemy situation, main problem. McNamara watched it, not really taking it in, his hands folded, frowning a little, finally interrupting. "Now, let me see," McNamara said, "if I have it right, this is your situation," and then he spouted his own version, all in numbers and statistics. The colonel, who was very bright, read him immediately like a man breaking a code, and without changing stride, went on with the briefing, simply switching his terms, quantifying everything, giving everything in numbers and percentages, percentages up, percentages down, so blatant a performance that it was like a satire. Jack Raymond of the *New York Times* began to laugh and had to leave the tent. Later that day Raymond went up to McNamara and commented on how tough the situation was up in Danang, but McNamara wasn't interested in the Vietcong, he wanted to talk about that colonel, he liked him, that colonel had caught his eye. "That colonel is one of the finest officers I've ever met," he said.

And so he created the base of knowledge, first-hand, on which he would make his judgments and recommendations. It was all based on those terrible trips out there, the unwillingness to accept civilian assistance in challenging the military reporting, the unwillingness to adapt his own standards and criteria. In these crucial middle years he attached his name and reputation to the possibility and hopes for victory, caught himself more deeply in the tar baby of Vietnam, and limited himself greatly in his future actions. It is not a particularly happy chapter in his life; he did not serve himself nor the country well; he was, there is no kinder or gentler word for it, a fool.

IN THE SPRING OF 1963 THE WAR SEEMED TO COME TO A HALT. THE ARVN stopped initiating action. In Washington some of the civilians were becoming more and more dubious about the military reporting from Saigon, and Harriman, increasingly the dominant figure at State, was telling Roger Hilsman not to depend too much on MACV's reporting. It was all right for him to rely on CIA and journalistic dispatches as a basis for his own estimates and he could also use some of the military's facts, but without their conclusions.

On the political side, the government still seemed stagnant, unable and unwilling to reach an almost sullen population in the cities, and unable to counteract the sometimes subtle, sometimes ferocious Vietcong challenge in the rural areas. Yet there were few visible symptoms of the dissidence in the spring. But in early May 1963, Buddhists who were celebrating Buddha's birthday in Hué, the old imperial capital of Vietnam, were told by government troops to disburse. When they refused to break up, armored vehicles opened fire, killing nine people. The government, unable to reach out to its own population, unable to admit a mistake, blamed the entire incident on the Vietcong. This was the beginning of the prolonged Buddhist crisis which finally brought the Diem government to its knees. It became a full-scale political crisis as the militant, skilled young Buddhist leaders—sensitive to the new political forces and well aware of the changes in psychology and attitudes which twenty years of revolutionary war had brought about—offered the population, for the first time under the Diem government, an outlet for latent nationalist forces. For Diem and his government, sponsored by the Americans, represented, like the French before them, foreign coin, foreign language, foreign style, and the officers of Diem's army were tainted by the Western touch. Now, with the coming of the Buddhists, there was for the first time an outlet for a Vietnamese leadership which had no contact with the Americans, did not take their money and scholarships or visit with their ambassador. The leadership was brilliant, indigenous, nationalist in the true sense, and in no way beholden to the American embassy. The effect of this on the population was potent: the Buddhists became a spearhead for a vast variety of dissident groups, and with their ability made the rigid, unbending, ungenerous government look foolish. Under the press of the Buddhist protest, all the flaws, all the shortcomings, all the intolerance of the Diem regime came to the surface; so, too, did American impotence, the inability of the Americans to move the regime despite the deep involvement with it. To watch the regime stumble through the crisis over a period of five months was like watching it commit suicide; it proved its detractors prophets, its supporters fools.

In late May 1963 John Mecklin, head of the United States Information Agency in Saigon and a member of the Country Team, sat talking with two reporters. Mecklin had been an experienced reporter for *Time* magazine himself before taking this job, which he had accepted because he felt challenged by the Kennedy inaugural. He had arrived in Saigon full of enthusiasm, almost immediately sponsoring a contest to give the Vietcong another name which would indicate that instead of being legitimate guerrillas, they were just outlaws—a typical American gesture which died in infancy. With the Buddhist crisis developing into a full-scale foreign policy crisis, his own doubts were growing, and he would ultimately be a major dissenter. But now, as he sat with the reporters who were much younger, he was drawing on his reportorial expertise to forecast the events ahead.

The men to watch as the pressure of events grew, he said, were not Nolting and Harkins; they were already too committed, both by age, by generational outlook, by their public and private words on the regime. No, the interesting men were the two who were at the fulcrum, William Trueheart, the Deputy Chief of Mission, and Brigadier General Richard Stilwell, the new chief of staff to Harkins. They were, said Mecklin, in extremely difficult positions. They were both in their early forties and seemed to have brilliant careers ahead; yet the policy was clearly being challenged, indeed collapsing, and they might have to go against their superiors and perhaps their institutions as the pressures increased. Mecklin's point had a certain validity, and at first glance Stilwell seemed the more likely candidate to switch. Whatever else, no one would ever accuse Paul Harkins of being brilliant, but Stilwell was preceded by a reputation for brilliance; he was one of that special group of Army intellectuals, smooth, poised, sophisticated, a former CIA man, a staff officer for General James Van Fleet when he was director of military aid to Greece. Stilwell was well read, dropped the names of books he had just read, of writers and reporters and publishers he knew well and had just lunched with. He was a skilled and subtle briefer, and did not talk mindlessly of dead bodies, but he knew the lexicon of insurgency well, almost too well. He knew backgrounds, forces, and so the word was passed quickly in Saigon: See Stilwell, *Stilwell knows,* a hot general going places, a breath of fresh air after Harkins, and great things were expected of him. They materialized in a way; he got his second and third stars, and his career blossomed but he never challenged the Harkins line—perhaps the pressure the military staff system puts on a subordinate to go along is too great, perhaps it is unthinkable to challenge your superior. He became the hatchet man for Harkins, the man who personally quashed the reporting of the dissenting colonels, who challenged all dissenting views, who, though he was not in the intelligence operation, went through the intelligence reports, tidying them up.

Trueheart seemed, on the surface, a less likely candidate to break with the line than Stilwell. Not only had he faithfully followed the official line from the start but he was a Nolting man, brought to Saigon at the ambassador's personal request; the two were old friends and had stayed in very close touch. Nolting was the godfather of both of Trueheart's sons, and Trueheart seemed, if anything, more Nolting than Nolting, a little stiffer at first glance, a product of that same Virginia-gentleman school of the foreign service. An early memory of him in Saigon was his being asked to protest the expulsion of François Sully, a *Newsweek* correspondent. He had answered that it was not a great question; after all, Sully was a *pied-noir* (a term used to describe the French lower class in Algeria, like calling an American a redneck).

But in late June 1963 an exhausted and dispirited Nolting went on a prolonged vacation, despite the mounting Buddhist crisis. Nolting chose to sail in the Aegean Sea, where it was difficult to reach him (this became an important point because he felt Trueheart did not try hard enough to reach him and therefore was disloyal; others felt that there had been efforts to reach him but that he had made himself particularly inaccessible). With the crisis continuing to grow, Trueheart followed the straight Nolting line, but after a while, as Diem refused to negotiate and meet any of the Buddhist demands, as the protest mounted and reached deeper and deeper into the society, as unrest mounted in the military and as the government continued to mislead the Americans regarding its intentions, Trueheart opened up the embassy reporting. Together with Mel Manful, the political officer, Trueheart began to talk to dissidents, to Buddhists, and as embassy officials reached more of the society, the reporting changed. It went from blind support to being skeptical, cool and iconoclastic in its appraisal. Doubts were raised, questions asked. The embassy began to doubt that Diem could handle the Buddhist crisis, and it reported that the Buddhists had become the focal point for all sorts of dissidence and that the government was totally isolated. It also cast doubt upon Nhu's sanity, doubts which were accurate; Nhu was more and more on opium in his last years. The embassy saw Diem almost totally a prisoner of his family. The terrible thing, the embassy learned about the Diem regime in that crisis, was that all the clichés about it turned out to be true.

The change in Trueheart was crucial. His reporting was not so much anti-Diem (as opponents charged later) as it was analytical and detached, no longer blindly pro-Diem; it let loose a floodgate of doubts. For the first time, American reporting in Saigon resembled the American diplomatic reporting from China. Five months earlier only American journalists had been pessimistic about the war and the future; now the State Department people in Saigon were pessimistic, the CIA was pessimistic, the hamlet people were pessimistic, along with the journalists. Only the military held devotedly to the line of optimism. These doubts and divisions of Saigon were reflected in Washington, where Kennedy faced a divided bureaucracy. Earlier in the year he had seemed to be encouraging the Harriman group in its dissent; if not exactly siding with it, at least moving the play in their direction but doing it slowly, trying to prevent an open schism within his Administration, trying to keep from driving the military to the side of the right wing in Congress.

BY MID-1963 KENNEDY WAS A VERY DIFFERENT PRESIDENT WITH A very different sense of his own confidence and competence, more sure of himself, more dubious about the institutional wisdom of force in many areas of the world. He had been through the Cuban missile crisis, and that had restored all the credentials lost so early in the Bay of Pigs; he had handled himself coolly, had faced down the Russians, and though some, like Dean Acheson, did not think he had been forceful enough, the country had rallied to him. As he and his staff considered these his finest hours, so did most of the country, with the exception of the radical left, which thought too much had been risked for too little, and the radical right, which thought that too little had been risked for too much. Now newer, milder, more rational approaches were possible; the Cuban missile crisis had produced such a real vision of nuclear death, it had taken both the United States and the Soviet Union so close to so much of the reality of their propaganda and their threats that it also produced a possibility for a genuine thaw, and this he was now pursuing. Speeches and ideas that had not been possible in 1961 as he searched for his balance and confidence were now possible. On June 10 he gave perhaps the best speech of his Administration at the American University commencement. Here was an American President not just calling for a lessening of tensions, a greater attempt to control and limit the weapons of destruction, but also, and more important, calling upon Americans to redefine some of their attitudes toward the Soviet Union and toward Communism.

This was a landmark speech, coming after some seventeen years in which the American government had espoused the line that it was Soviet attitudes and only Soviet attitudes and actions which had brought on the Cold War, that the United States had been an innocent auxiliary to it all. It was, some thought, the beginning of the second part of the Kennedy Administration, the first part having ended after the Cuban missile crisis. It was as if he were liberated from the insecurities of his first two years with that one act, and now, more confident of himself, more confident of the nation's response to him; he was the President. The country now trusted him, the spurs were won; he could begin (slowly of course) to challenge some of the ideas and attitudes which had frozen so long in the government. The second part of his Administration, they felt, was marked by the search for a test-ban treaty with the Soviet Union, a milder and more tolerant tone in his speeches about the Cold

War, increasing doubts on Vietnam, and a general, growing awareness that one historic era was coming to a close, and by a desire to ride the changes without being destroyed, either by moving too fast on them, anticipating them too much, or by being too slow in recognizing the changes. For he had a feeling, which he passed on to some aides, that the country was ahead of Washington, Washington was living more in the Cold War than the nation. The country did not want war and did not want a constant nuclear tension with the Soviet Union. Kennedy was beginning to sense this and he would in his last major trip into the country find, not to his great surprise, that it was true. So by mid-1963 he was pushing for a test-ban treaty, and he was looking for a lessening of tensions. He was being plagued more and more by the question of the back-burner issue. Berlin, ironically, was on the back-burner now. The problem of Vietnam was proving very troublesome and now, as he had suspected, it refused to go away.

Faced with a divided bureaucracy, Kennedy gave the men around him an indication that he was uneasy with the use of force and dubious about reports of success. But he also felt uneasy about the question of change, of dumping Diem. He seemed to move with the doubters; the White House staff people, who had become increasingly pessimistic and were searching for alternate policies, found themselves encouraged by him. Encouraged, but not too encouraged. It was all still run carefully and cautiously; he wanted, they felt, to move the bureaucracy along, and the key man in this was apparently Robert McNamara. McNamara was still going on those trips to Vietnam, more and more often now, and coming back relentlessly optimistic. It was beginning to be known as McNamara's war, which at the time did not bother him. Some people in the government objected to his trips. When Roger Hilsman (who had been promoted to Assistant Secretary of State for Far Eastern Affairs, to replace Harriman, who was on his way up as Undersecretary) complained to the President about the fact that each time McNamara went out there, it resulted in a great amount of publicity which stirred the public interest in the war and brought out the fact that the United States was committed there (this was before the days when the major networks had resident correspondents, and thus the McNamara trips, bringing as they did major television teams, escalated the press coverage), Kennedy would answer yes, he knew it was a problem but he was having troubles there and the only way he could keep the Chiefs on board was to keep McNamara on board, and the only way he could keep McNamara on board was to let him make those trips.

One sign of the presidential distaste and disillusion with Vietnam was the change and the rise of Hilsman. He was, if anything, a talisman of the Kennedy years both in strengths and contradictions. He had started by being an enthusiast on counterinsurgency and thus the commitment to Vietnam. Yet at the same time, with Bowles gone, and Stevenson ineffectual, he was the government's leading advocate of a change in the nation's China policy. He still held to his enthusiasm for antiguerrilla warfare, but as the sour news came in from Saigon he began to wonder if the Diem regime was capable of waging any kind of political-military war, and he had grave doubts about both the policy and the use of greater force.

Hilsman had risen quickly in the bureaucracy; Kennedy liked him particularly because he was unafraid to challenge the military. One challenge was particularly memorable. At one of the first crisis meetings on Laos, General Lyman Lemnitzer, the Chairman of the Joint Chiefs, had shown up at the White House in order to brief the President, and suffered a mild humiliation at the White House gate. Since the police there were not prepared for him and his staff, his aides were not allowed to enter, so Lem had to struggle through carrying his charts and cases all by himself. A greater humiliation lay ahead. Lemnitzer began his briefing, charts ready, pointer poised. First the big picture: This is the Mekong Valley. Pointer tip hit the map. Hilsman, watching, noticed something, the point tip was not on the Mekong Valley, it was on the Yangtze Valley. Hilsman rose, went to the board, took the pointer. "General," he said, "you're mistaken, the Mekong Valley is right here." A switch of the pointer. But Lem's humiliation was not over. Hilsman did not sit down but continued the briefing, pointing out the key features of the Valley until finally the President said, "Mr. Hilsman, would you mind letting us hear the military briefing from the Chairman of the Joint Chiefs of Staff . . ." Later, when Hilsman was teased about this by friends, he protested, "But he was pointing at the wrong river . . ."

It was this very audaciousness which delighted Kennedy, the willingness to take on the military; in fact, when Hilsman had been moved up to Director of Intelligence and Research at State, he was told by Rusk that he was specifically not to challenge the military view. When he got back to his office, he received a White House phone call. A very high official congratulated him on his promotion and noted that by now he had probably been told by the Secretary not to push the military, but he was to disregard that last bit of advice; he had been promoted precisely because he did take on the military and he was to continue to challenge them. So he did, first at INR and then as Assistant Secretary for Far Eastern Affairs, his rise and Harriman's rise seeming to coincide with Kennedy's doubts. Kennedy used to call Hilsman in the morning to complain about the military's repeated attempts to give their own optimistic assessments of the war (the Kennedy public relations program was backfiring) until finally Hilsman, on Kennedy's orders, drafted a national security paper forbidding any general officer to go to Vietnam without the written approval of the Assistant Secretary of State for Far Eastern Affairs.

The struggle in the bureaucracy during the summer of 1963 centered mainly around intelligence and interpretation of the war. There was no essential challenge to goals, although there were increasing interior doubts in the minds of some civilians about them. The basic controversy was on a more primitive level; after all, why challenge your goals if you are attaining them? If the military were right, if the war was being won, then the problems being reported by the civilians were exaggerated, minor squabbles among Vietnamese intellectuals blown up out of proportion by jittery civilians. So in the summer Hilsman, still at INR, began to challenge the military's estimates with great regularity, an assault as much as anything on McNamara, who still held to the military's figures. It was convenient for McNamara to stick to these statistics, since they were not only the thing he knew best, but more important, by holding to them he did not get into a fight with his generals over the failure of the existing policy, and thus perhaps have to confront the pressure for a new, expanded policy. He simply froze his attitude: it was all going well, the statistics were there to prove it, and he was not interested in trying to find out why there were two different sets of information, and what lay behind the difference. Civilians traveling around with him to Saigon in those days found him surprisingly rigid; they tried to discuss their doubts with him but he would not really listen. When they said the Diem government was losing popularity with the peasants because of the Buddhist crisis, McNamara asked, well, what percentage was dropping off, what percentage did the government have and what percentage was it losing? He asked for facts, some statistics, something he could run through the data bank, not just this poetry they were spouting. And as far as charges that his data bank was corrupt and unbalanced, reflecting only the vested-interest optimism of the government and of MACV—why, their data bank was just as corrupt. They now factored in only people who had doubts, they did not listen to anyone who was optimistic.

This was a very revealing insight into McNamara. Both at Ford and at the Pentagon he had always loved statistics and facts, particularly those which confirmed what he wanted to prove, and now he was making the same accusation against bureaucratic opponents that others had made against him. He did not seriously investigate the negative claims because he did not choose to go that path; however, years later, once he had switched sides, he could be very good at finding dissenting statistics. Then he consciously used the CIA instead of his own Defense Intelligence Agency (which he had invented) to respond to his dovish questions, and when a particular CIA agent showed signs of pessimism himself, McNamara would turn out to have lots of time to listen. But in 1963 he systematically fought off any challenge to the military estimates, and he and Hilsman in particular had some fierce confrontations: as the Buddhist crisis continued, Hilsman seized on it as one more means of showing that the government was ineffective, that the crisis was bound to affect the war effort, since, though the ARVN officers were Catholics, the

NCOs and privates were Buddhists. When Hilsman made these claims, McNamara would flash back: Where are your figures? Where is your research?

So Hilsman commissioned Lewis Sarris, one of his deputies in INR, to do a major study on exactly this question. Sarris was to be an important figure in Vietnam, not so much for the role he played as for the role he did not play. His instincts were totally political and very true. He knew exactly what the limitations of the American presence were, how poorly the war was going; later he predicted accurately that the bombing would not work. Yet his views did not count; he was a pure intelligence man, not operational. He never got on the team, he never advanced his career as Vietnam expanded as a place to make a reputation. In a world of achievers he was a non-achiever. In 1963 Sarris was, however, briefly important because Hilsman, his superior, fought for him and for his opinions. So, encouraged by Hilsman, Sarris carefully pieced together a major report. He used some of State's material, some journalistic accounts and a good deal of the military's own reporting to compile an estimate which showed that the war effort was slipping away, that the Buddhist crisis was undoubtedly hurting it (he tied the Buddhist crisis to the war effort, and on this he may well have been wrong; the Buddhist crisis and the decline in the war effort coincided, but the military decline may have been based on more deeply rooted problems). Sarris knew exactly what figures to take from the military's accounts (in effect most things, but never the bottom line), and the result was a devastating report on the course of the war.

The military were furious and when Hilsman pressed the report at several high meetings, McNamara and General Krulak fought back bitterly. The Joint Chiefs were very angry: it was one thing for the State Department people to challenge Diem's popularity, to talk about the political problems (though of course the military frequently trespassed upon the political area by arguing that Diem was effective, his commanders were what they were supposed to be, the system worked), but it was quite another thing for State to challenge military estimates. Sarris' findings were absolutely wrong, they claimed, but even more important, they questioned the right of State even to produce such a report. State must not trespass onto the military's area.

After one particularly bitter assault by the military, when McNamara carried the ball and Hilsman received little support from his superiors, and when the report clearly was an embarrassment to Rusk, McNamara scribbled a note to Rusk saying: "Dean: If you promise me that the Department of State will not issue any more military appraisals without getting the approval of the Joint Chiefs, we will let this matter die. Bob." (The note, so revealing of the period is now framed and hangs in the living room of one of the dissenters from that period.) Rusk was of course uneasy with this kind of estimate, anyway, not so much because it was pessimistic, since he had grave doubts himself, but because he was a strict chain-of-command man himself and did not like State's getting into the Defense area; in a question involving the military he had an instinct to give primacy to Defense, and not to cause problems.

McNamara's role was a reflection of his shrewdness as a bureaucratic player, since it meant that from then on State would be handcuffed in its analyses of the situation. It could only report on the politics of the country, and the political situation was not good, it was bad and getting worse. But if the war effort remained untouched, if the war effort was going well, as the military repeatedly claimed, then there were no serious problems. It was a shrewd move on McNamara's part, designed to a certain extent to take the important decisions away from people he could not control. Thus, working between the President and the Chiefs, he would become the central civilian, he would determine what the President wanted and needed, and what the Chiefs would permit on a given issue, and he would be the negotiator. In addition, it was aimed at silencing critics, which it did temporarily, though in the growing collapse of the entire Saigon military and political structure there would be similar papers and estimates which Harriman, his bureaucratic opponent, continued to promote, making sure they were seen by the rest of the government. There were papers from Hilsman, cables from Trueheart: Has McCone seen this one? Has McNamara seen it? What about Gilpatric, did he see this one?

That particular meeting would not help Sarris' career; he would be known thereafter by the military as the "coup-plotter," and he would never rise in the Department. In 1969 one of the bright young State Department officers on Vietnam whose own career had been helped by Vietnam would find that a reporter was going to interview Sarris about the 1963 period. "Sarris?" he said. "*Lew Sarris?* Why him? He seems to me to be a pathetic figure; why, he sits in the very same office and does the very same thing that he did in 1962." Which was true; he still sat there years later, still making the estimates, which were still rejected and disputed; others came and were usually wrong and had their careers advanced; Sarris was right and remained there. As for Hilsman, he was bouncy, full of himself then, but someone sitting there and watching the faces of McNamara and the military would think that this was a bright and bumptious young man, and hope for his own sake that his protectors stayed around to protect him. As for McNamara, he held to his statistics, though much later, in 1967, he would change and convert to dovishness. When he did, he went through a personal crisis. He would confide to friends that if they had only known more about the enemy, more about the society, if there had only been more information, more intelligence about the other side, perhaps it would never have happened; though of course one reason there was so little knowledge about the enemy and the other side was that no one was as forceful as he was in blocking its entrance into the debates.

BY EARLY JULY 1963, WASHINGTON KNEW THAT IT HAD A MAJOR crisis on its hands. Though under great American pressure Diem had finally negotiated a partial settlement with the Buddhist insurgents in mid-June, it became clear shortly afterward that the government had no intention of implementing the concessions. A couple of weeks later, the intelligence community predicted that Diem would fail to carry out the provisions of the agreement and that it was very likely there would be either a coup against him, or an assassination. Saigon itself became filled with rumors of coups, and by early July at least three major plots had begun to form, reflecting different generational and regional preferences. In Saigon, Trueheart became more and more discouraged with the government; if Diem promised something to him, Trueheart found that it was repudiated the next day in the English-language *Times of Vietnam*, a newspaper controlled by the Nhus; worse, the darker forecasts of the *Times of Vietnam* over a long period of time more accurately reflected the government policy than the official promises of Diem. Thus while Diem was promising one thing to the Americans, in private sessions with his family he reverted to the harder line pushed by his brother and sister-in-law. If Diem promised to be conciliatory about the Buddhists in action and tone, the *Times of Vietnam* would soon charge that the first Buddhist priest who burned himself to death had been drugged. (Was this true? Kennedy asked Hilsman. No, answered Hilsman, religious fervor and passion was all that was needed.) In Washington, Kennedy was again discussing with his advisers the possibility of separating the Nhus from Diem, an idea which had long tantalized Americans, and received a pessimistic response. It was really too late. At the same time Trueheart passed on a variety of good liberal American suggestions to Diem: Diem should meet with the Buddhist leaders, should appoint Buddhist chaplains for a predominantly Buddhist army (which had only Catholic chaplains) and make a warm conciliatory speech about religious freedom. Trueheart received, in response, an excessively polite smile and thanks from Diem, that and nothing else; Trueheart was beginning to learn the lessons of Durbrow.

When Nolting went on vacation in early July, the President decided that a new ambassador was needed; though Kennedy was unhappy with Nolting (who also wanted out because of pressing family responsibilities) and did not trust Nolting's version of events, he also realized that part of Nolting's problems was the policy itself, the decision to commit the United States directly to Diem, which had originated in Washington; thus he himself was more than partly responsible. It just hadn't worked and it was time to look around for a replacement, for an ambassador who would become less emotionally involved with Diem, and who was, as far as the Vietnamese were concerned, less a symbol of direct American commitment to Diem. Some people in the White House and at State pushed for Edmund Gullion, who had been a friend of Kennedy's for years. They had first met in Indochina ten years before when Gullion was the leading dissenter from the French optimism; Gullion had since become Kennedy's perhaps most successful ambassador during the difficult crisis in the Congo, where he had shown a considerable ability in cloaking American policy in terms which were reasonable to indigenous nationalist sentiment. But Gullion was not anxious for a return to Saigon, and Rusk was less than anxious to have Gullion there, so on Rusk's insistence Kennedy chose Henry Cabot Lodge. The appointment of this patrician, symbol of the Establishment, defeated candidate for the U.S. Senate by Kennedy himself in 1952, defeated candidate for the Vice-Presidency by the Kennedy-Johnson ticket, made the liberals in the Administration uneasy (though Rusk and the military were pleased). The reason for Kennedy's choice was obvious. If Vietnam turned into a disaster, what could be better than to have a major Republican name associated with it (which for the same reason made some high Republicans unhappy about the appointment).

Since it would take Lodge a certain amount of time to be prepared (he had to enroll in the counterinsurgency course), Nolting returned in mid-July for one last chance as ambassador. Those were very unhappy days. Nolting found Diem uncommunicative and unresponsive; Nolting, who had acquiesced to Diem on so many things in order to have money in the bank for just such an occasion as this, now found that he had little influence after all. If he was alienated from Diem, so he was separated from his own embassy. Trueheart he accused of disloyalty, but not just Trueheart, also Rufus Phillips in the strategic hamlet program, Mecklin at USIA, the AID (Agency for International Development) people, and many of the CIA people. His only allies now were the military people. The others in the embassy were sympathetic: they liked him personally, they knew how hard he had worked and the odds that had been against him, the personal sacrifice he had made, but it no longer worked, if indeed it had ever worked. Now that it had failed, everyone but Nolting accepted it, and there was a certain pain for him in watching his unwillingness to let go.

His last days there were particularly painful; the Nhus, exploiting his loyalty, involved him in a bogus ceremony designed to identify them with the Americans. It was an Orwellian scene: all the strategic hamlets in the country had allegedly competed for the honor of being named after Nolting; they had written essays, describing what the ambassador had done for their country. The winning hamlet had been chosen. Nolting would now visit it. He tried to get out of it; then, trapped, agreed and became furious when reporters said his acceptance was reluctant. He presided at a fake ceremony in front of stone-faced, stoic Vietnamese. The Vietcong soon knocked over the hamlet.

With everything collapsing around him, he turned in his fury on his old friend Trueheart and accused him of having destroyed the trust which Nolting had so carefully built up. Trueheart's protestations that he had worked loyally for the policy, but that the months since May had seen the disintegration of that fragile hope, fell on deaf ears. The more Nolting realized that Trueheart's reporting was accurate, the more he blamed Trueheart for not holding it together. If Nolting was impotent, then it was Trueheart's fault, not the fault of history or of the policy. So when he went home he would write his final efficiency report about his once trusted deputy, entering into Trueheart's personnel file the most damaging of all assessments, a charge of rank disloyalty, saying that he had brought this man Trueheart to Saigon, had placed his trust in him, and Trueheart had betrayed that trust, had undermined everything Nolting had worked for. It was powerful stuff and it almost destroyed Trueheart's career. Hilsman, Harriman and others wrote answering letters, that Trueheart had worked loyally for one policy, but as that policy foundered he had reported its failure accurately and had continued to represent the best interests of the United States. Still, it would take Trueheart an extra six years to get his ambassadorial post (in Nigeria), and by that time Johnson was no longer President and neither Rusk nor McNamara was Secretary. At the ceremony Jonathan Moore, who had worked as a deputy to William Bundy all those years and who knew what Trueheart had gone through, would tell Trueheart's son Charles that it was overdue, long overdue, it should have been done a long time ago.

But now events were out of control, no one could do anything. If people, Nolting said, would only keep their eye on the ball, if they would only stop being distracted by all this political activity. All of this was a side issue. The job was to win the war. Yet he was shaken. A television team that came to do an interview in his office saw him take down a portrait of Jefferson and replace it with one of Washington, explaining that Washington was less controversial. Finally it was all over, and on August 15 Nolting, a rather lonely figure at the airport, talked about the mutual traditions of the two countries "of humility and tolerance, respect for others and a deep sense of social justice." The next day another monk burned himself to death, and within a week Diem and Nhu had crushed the Buddhists with a bloody midnight raid on their pagodas, disguising their private security army in uniforms of regular soldiers in order to put the onus on the army (and thus have the society put the blame on the army and turn more against it, in what was of course a political war).

The embassy had been caught unaware by the strike on the pagodas, including John Richardson, the CIA station chief, who was in a state of shock,

with many Vietnamese thinking that since it was Nhu who had engineered
the crackdown and since Richardson was deeply involved with Nhu, the raid
had CIA approval. But the cover story soon faded. It fooled the embassy and
Washington for about forty-eight hours, but American journalists had called it
right from the moment it happened. It ended an era and a policy, and later,
describing those events, John Mecklin wrote: "Thus the Diem regime's final
gesture to Fritz Nolting, flagrant abrogation of its solemn last word to this fine
man who had staked his career on the regime's defense."

IN WASHINGTON THE HARRIMAN PEOPLE HAD BEEN PUSHING FOR
months for a policy which would separate the Americans from the Ngo family; they still thought victory in a political war against the Vietcong possible,
but felt it would not work with a government which unified all the population
against its very dictates. Week after week in July and August, events had
proved them right and the pro-Diem faction wrong: the regime had been unbending, had been unwilling to broaden its base, and above all, unable to deal
with its own population. This last was crucial—the question was not so much
whether the Buddhists were totally legitimate, but whether the government
had the ability to deal with them ("We will throw them the banana peels for
them to slip on," said one young Buddhist priest, accurately describing Buddhist plans and government reactions). Now any chance for a settlement had
been destroyed with the crackdown which had also shattered the illusion of
people like Nolting that the United States had influence with Diem. In contrast to Nolting's optimism, the Harriman group had predicted that the Ngo
family would crush the monks. Thus within the bureaucracy its estimates and
prophecies had been largely accurate, while the predictions of Taylor and
Nolting had been increasingly inaccurate.

In America, the Buddhist crisis had been a growing embarrassment for the
young Catholic President. The photographs of soldiers bringing their billy
clubs down on Buddhist monks had been montaged on front pages with stories of the loss of life of young American officers. If in the past Kennedy had
worried about right-wing opposition to the loss of part of the free world, now
he was worrying about liberal reaction to American blood being spent for a
petty family dictatorship. So when Lodge arrived in Vietnam (his mind already made up about the Ngo family before the attack on the pagodas, and
inwardly enraged by this gesture aimed as much against him as anyone, presenting him with a *fait accompli*) he was already determined to broaden
American policy, to move it, at the very least, away from the Nhus, and failing that, away from Diem himself.

With the Vietnamese military pressuring the Americans to absolve the army from responsibility for the crackdown, the Voice of America soon began broadcasting honest assessments, placing the blame on the Nhus. In addition, Lodge received a cable from Washington saying that the Nhus must go, that alternative leadership possibilities be investigated, that the Vietnamese military be told that the United States would no longer support a government which included the Nhus. It was, in effect, the go-ahead signal for a coup (no one in Washington or Saigon thought Diem would ever drop the Nhus; if it had been unlikely before the crackdown, it was even more improbable now).

The cable had been drafted by Harriman, Forrestal, Hilsman and George Ball on Saturday, August 24, at the President's suggestion. Though Rusk was out of town, he was consulted regularly, and he was helpful. He even strengthened the cable, inserting provisions for supplying the generals with matériel should they be cut off during a breakdown (it was, significantly, a military suggestion on the part of Rusk; the old CBI planner still lived). McNamara and John McCone, Director of CIA, were on vacation, and Taylor was out of reach, having dinner at a restaurant. With McNamara out of town, Gilpatric was in charge at Defense, and he said the cable sounded fine, acceptable, he had no objections. At CIA, Richard Helms, whose doubts on Vietnam had always been considerable (reflecting the pure intelligence estimates rather than the operational end), told them that it was about time they moved this way, what had taken them so long in the first place? Forrestal dealt with Krulak, whose job it was to get clearance from General Taylor, which he did, though technically after the cable had gone out (Taylor did not know that the cable had already left, but he disagreed with nothing in it).

Later, when the principals gathered in Washington, there were second thoughts among some of them, particularly as each learned that some of the others had misgivings (it was a stunning example of how the domino theory worked if not with nations in Southeast Asia, then certainly with high government officials who wanted to sense which way the wind was blowing and did not want to be caught alone going against it). Taylor in particular was unhappy about the way it had been maneuvered. He thought everyone else had agreed, but of course they had not, since they had been out of town. There began to be murmurings to friendly journalists that Hilsman had pulled something slick. He had become the Washington target for the more conservative members of the government and for conservative journalists. Harriman was certainly no target; and one did not take on the President lightly; Forrestal was a quiet figure bearing a great Cold War name; but Hilsman, Hilsman was talkative, ebullient, almost outrageous, a lovely lightning rod. The President was furious with the cable mix-up; he was already fed up with the division within his government and the resulting newspaper coverage from Washington and Saigon which emphasized the split in his government. It was particularly strong from Saigon, where the entire mission had come apart ("This shit must stop," he told an aide after one particular journalistic reflection of governmental dissension).

Now when some of his closest officials began reneging on a cable he thought they had agreed on, Kennedy blew up. He was furious at some of them for waffling, and furious at Hilsman and Forrestal for having been so sloppy as to leave an emergency exit for dissent, knowing that moving a bureaucracy toward a given objective was a difficult process, and when done, it should be done. Kennedy lashed out at Hilsman and Forrestal for incompetence, a rare and very real burst of presidential anger ("The lesson," said the cool McGeorge Bundy, a bystander to all of the debate, "is never do business on the weekend"). But if Kennedy was annoyed at Hilsman and Forrestal, he was even more annoyed at the men who were now backtracking (showing their doubts not so much to him as elsewhere). So the next time they were gathered he looked at them and said, the voice very cold, very distant, that there had been some doubt about the cable, that it might have been precipitous. Fortunately it was not too late to change. Do you, Mr. Rusk, wish to change? No. Do you, Mr. McNamara, wish to change the cable? No. Do you, General Taylor, wish to change the cable? No. Do you, Mr. McCone, wish to change . . .

THE UNITED STATES WAS MAKING IT VERY CLEAR TO THE SAIGON military that it was ready for a coup. On August 29 Lodge cabled Rusk:

> We are launched on a course from which there is no respectable turning back: the overthrow of the Diem government. There is no turning back in part because U.S. prestige is already publicly committed to this end in large measure and will become more so as the facts leak out. In a more fundamental sense there is no turning back because there is no possibility, in my view, that the war can be won under a Diem administration . . .

There was a flood of cables back and forth between Saigon and Washington, arrangements made about the possibility of a coup, which Vietnamese general to talk to, how to go about it, the extent to which the United States could be involved. Even the CIA station chief, John Richardson, who until recently had been so close to Nhu, was a surprising advocate of a coup, and a prophet that the coup would come and come quickly ("If the Ngo family wins now, they and Vietnam will stagger on to final defeat at the hands of their own people and the Vietcong . . . If this attempt by the generals does not take place or if it fails, we believe it no exaggeration to say that Vietnam runs serious risk of being lost over the course of time").

But the generals, who met covertly with the Americans, did not move. The

Nhus had caught them off balance with their strike against the pagodas, and tightened control on forces around Saigon; the Americans, who had long told the generals that only Diem would receive support, had now switched, but so quickly that they caught the generals unprepared. They wondered if the Americans really meant it. When General Harkins contacted the Vietnamese generals to imply that a coup was all right, wasn't he still an agent of Diem? When the CIA people talked about logistics, didn't it mean that Richardson was feeding all this back to Nhu (Nhu was telling people that it did)? Saigon, always filled with rumors, seethed with intrigue. And the generals did not move. Why hadn't they? State cabled Lodge. "Perhaps they are like the rest of us, and are afraid to die," Lodge told a friend.

But if there was not a coup, it marked the end of our total belief that Diem and Diem alone could be the instrument of American policy, a blind commitment to one irrational family. In the struggle within the American government it seemed that for the moment the civilian forces were dominant, though there were varying degrees of doubt among the civilians about whether a coup could be staged at all. Some, like Forrestal and to an increasing degree Robert Kennedy, were more and more dubious about the whole thing, while Rusk and Lodge, for instance, viewed an overthrow of the Diem regime as advantageous, as a way of winning the war.

Chapter Fourteen

THE FAILURE OF THE VIETNAMESE GENERALS TO ACT HAD
not by any means ended the debate within the Administration; what it did
essentially was move it back to the point where it had existed before the
crackdown on the pagodas, which had accelerated doubts and shifted positions. It had changed Rusk, McNamara and Taylor slightly and temporarily.
Now that the generals had failed to move, all three wanted to get back to a
position of business as usual, get on with the war. Thus, just a week after they
had all agreed on the necessity for a change, they signed off again. At a high-
level meeting on August 31, McNamara emphasized that the most important
thing was to reopen channels of communication with the Diem government;
Rusk talked again of the need to regird the anti-Communist forces, to get rid
of the Nhus, and to prevent Diem from striking against his top military
officers. At the meeting the burden of the case against the regime was borne
by Paul Kattenburg, the young State Department officer who had worked in
Vietnam for many years in the fifties. He was at this point chairman of the Interdepartmental Working Group on Vietnam and more than anyone in Washington knowledgeable about the country. The Vietnamese people loomed
large in his assessments, and he had a real feeling for the fabric of the society
there. He had once believed there was a right way to make our policy work;
now he felt Diem was hopeless and had begun to doubt that it could be done
at all. When Rusk suggested that there was no chance of the coup now,
Kattenburg was not so sure, he thought it was almost too soon after one very

inflexible policy, and that more time and more gestures were needed. He quoted Lodge as saying that if the Americans tried to live with the Diem regime, with what Lodge termed its sense of false promises, its bayonets on the streetcorners, then the United States would be forced out in six months. Then Kattenburg summed up; he had known Diem for ten years and the story had always been the same, one disappointment after another, always Diem had failed to live up to promises, he had relentlessly turned inward and away from reality. Diem, he affirmed, would not change; rather, this hope had been one of the oldest American illusions. Nor would he part with Nhu; instead the support for him would continue to dwindle, as it had in the past. In this case, Kattenburg said, the wise thing would be to get out of the country honorably. It was an important moment—the first time at a high-level meeting anyone had really said the unthinkable, coming significantly from the man who knew the most about the fabric of the society and the limits of it.

Kattenburg was quickly challenged by Max Taylor. What did Kattenburg mean by "forced out of Vietnam in six months"? He answered that in six months, as it became more and more obvious that the Western side was losing the war, more and more Vietnamese would go over to the Vietcong (by the rules of the game set by McNamara, he was not allowed to say what he really thought, which was that the war was probably lost already, that the military's optimistic estimates were illusory, that it was far later than anyone thought; State could not challenge Defense estimates).

Nolting took issue with Kattenburg. Although he allowed as how Kattenburg knew the cities, and yes, this political protest was taking place in the cities, and Diem was slipping in the cities among the intelligentsia, but out in the countryside, where the war was being fought, it had little effect, out there the people faced reality, and out there we were winning the war. At which point Rusk added that what Kattenburg had said was speculative, and anyway, one thing was clear, we would not leave Vietnam until the war was over and won, and the United States would not support a coup. To this McNamara agreed.

It was again a key moment; here was Rusk, whose job essentially was to forecast political events and weigh political subtleties and political limits, saying that come hell or high water the job would be done, putting down his own subordinate (years later, after publication of the Pentagon Papers, he told interviewers that he had erred in underestimating the strength of the enemy). So there was in the meeting a sense of business as usual. The time for a coup had come and gone; the policy in the past had always been to stand in Washington and paper things over in Saigon, and that was the trend now. Whatever the problems, we could live with them, get on with it; the problem now, as they would soon learn, was that there was precious little left to paper over.

Though Nolting had participated in the debate, he was almost finished as a player; he was no longer ambassador and he had little post-tour credibility as a witness. What credibility he did have was systematically destroyed by Harriman, who was brutally trying to remove the last remnants of Nolting's legitimacy. When Nolting criticized Kattenburg, Harriman had moved in with a ferocity which startled the others in the room. "We do not," he said angrily, unable to contain himself, "particularly value what you say since you were on vacation and unavailable for two months, and it is because of *your* reports, the weakness of them, that we have this very problem of information." The attack was so fierce that Kennedy had to restrain Harriman, to make him stop, saying that he, the President of the United States, wanted Nolting to finish. But Nolting had left that meeting white-faced and shaken, and his last months in government were bitter ones. He was an outsider, using a small office at CIA, watching the policy disintegrate, finally leaving the government to become an international representative of the Morgan Bank (and to write various newspapers a commemorative letter on the annual occasion of Diem's death, a date which in the country Nolting professed to love had become a national holiday). Yet if Nolting was finished as a player, there was still a great debate left on what to do, and that debate would focus on intelligence estimates, whether the war was being won or not.

IT WAS AT THIS POINT IN A BITTERLY DIVIDED BUREAUCRACY THAT Maxwell Taylor was in the central position, and his behavior in the divisive months of the summer of 1963 would shed a good deal of light on how he would react in future struggles over Vietnam. As before, the pressures on him reflected two very powerful and conflicting loyalties, one to the President and one to his uniform. He was a divided man, and this would become more and more apparent as Vietnam continued to disintegrate. As the limited commitment he had helped author was becoming increasingly untenable, so was his own position.

He had held strongly to certain basic military policies—based on the need to fight brush-fire wars—during the Eisenhower Administration, and he had been out of step with the Administration then. If he had not resigned, then he had at least resisted the temptation to sign on (succumbing, thought some friends, would have brought him the chairmanship of the Joint Chiefs, but would have cost him dearly in terms of loyalty to the Army). So he had walked the tightrope, satisfying neither the Eisenhower Administration, which viewed him as being on the edge of disloyalty (unannounced dissent), nor satisfying the young colonels on his staff who wanted larger and more modern roles for the Army (they did not realize that Max Taylor did not like to fight when other people owned the battlefield). During his four years as

Chief of Staff of the Army he had been undercutting as subtly as he could the Eisenhower policies of massive retaliation, with testimony on the Hill, with subtle leaks to the right journalists. Since he had always been against what he considered a futile policy, he had never become Chairman.

It was with this image of being both a restrained and moderate general that he had arrived back in Washington, his book just published, *The Uncertain Trumpet* ("We have the ability to wage total war. We can trigger near total destruction. But can we defend Berlin—South Korea—Vietnam—Iran—Thailand—America?" said the dust jacket). He had been a convenient figure for Kennedy, as Kennedy was a convenient figure for him, each serving the other's purpose. Kennedy, too, wanted to get away from the doctrine of massive retaliation. Kennedy wanted to rebuild the Joint Chiefs with younger men who were, if not directly loyal to him, at least cut more in his mold; Taylor was willing to do the same thing. (Taylor and McNamara were pushing for younger officers, switching the criterion for promotion, leaving busted careers in their wake. Men who one day had been too young for their next assignment would wake up and find themselves too old for it.) But now that he had made it back, Taylor faced the delicate job of balancing his loyalties to both the Administration and the uniform, a task for a man with a good political sense, which Taylor had. He was the kind of general that civilians liked, felt at ease with, felt they could trust. Civilians, looking at other generals, felt all they understood was their own problems; Taylor saw a wider periphery of interests, he understood what civilians wanted and why, and his career would be furthered by them. He was not blindly attached to his uniform; he was reasonable and above all *civilized* about things. Civilians, looking for allies, always liked him.

Now he faced two interests which were by no means compatible: the Kennedy people, young, ambitious, aggressive, talked boldly about their anti-Communism. But that anti-Communism was not imbedded in them as a lifeblood, it was not their mission. They were willing to ride it out from time to time, but they were men essentially committed to a rational order. The military, in contrast, particularly the senior military, were very different. The Cold War was their mission, defense against the aggressor enemy; since they had to be prepared to die for their mission, they also had to believe in it. Since the Communists were the aggressor enemy, anti-Communism was the textbook of their life, and their political center was far to the right of the Kennedy political center. Success in the Kennedy Administration meant reading subtle changes in the world and the Administration's reaction to them; bureaucratic success in the military meant getting along with your superiors and understanding their whims, and their whims were deep in the lifeblood of the Cold War. (Occasionally, however, a general like David Shoup would bemoan the extent to which anti-Communism had become part of American military doctrine—too much hating—and the attempt to create a countering ideology. Shoup did not like that, he did not believe in demonology. The job of the Marines, he said, was not to be anti-Communist, it was to wait until the President said "Saddle up and go," and then to saddle up and go.) And then, of course, Taylor had to contend with an instinct (particularly among the Air Force and Navy people) to use force in any situation, and failing in the first dose of force, to use more force, then more force.

At times these different pressures posed no problem. On the Bay of Pigs, Taylor had been a good critic of that particular disaster, and on the Kennedy attempts to limit nuclear testing and harness the arms race he was completely loyal to the Administration. He believed nuclear war was an irrational solution, and the sooner the nuclear race was turned around the better. But that had always been the Army's position. Now, with the problems of failure on Vietnam closing in, the urgency of what to do next, he would be in a different spot. Vietnam was a reflection of his military strategy (however incomplete) at this point; it was an experiment in a new kind of limited war. But if the Taylor-Rostow strategy failed, then what? Other generals would take over who were not so civilized, not so committed to the Administration, not so appalled by the specter of nuclear weapons. The Air Force, for instance, believed its weapons, its bombs, its nukes could do it all, and it was always ready to go. Thus the Air Force by itself, and with its friends on the Hill (since, of the three services, the Air Force required the most hardware, the biggest contracts, the closest links with industry, it had the most connections on the Hill), moved the center of the debate over a few notches to the right, which led generals like Taylor to believe that when they gave in a little on the use of force, the important thing was not so much that they were acquiescing, but that they were holding the line against something worse, protecting us from the Air Force with its nukes and missiles.

So if Vietnam collapsed, it would pose this particular problem of what to do next. If limited force had failed, would there be more pressure for greater force? Taylor had been able to try out his own concept of the limited commitment to stop the brush-fire war by putting Paul Harkins there, not because Harkins was the ablest general around, but because, far more important, he was Taylor's man and Taylor could control him. Now, in the middle of the crisis, with the State people despairing about Diem and about the conduct of the war, Taylor wanted to hold the line, to keep up the appearances, to keep from failing at what they were trying. As the struggle continued he kept Krulak in line, he kept Harkins in line, and he slowed McNamara's own tendency to swing over.

Taylor would in the ensuing weeks prove a formidable bureaucratic player, as some, like John Vann, had already learned. As the debate over information mounted he was determined to keep as much control as possible over military assessments. In September, with the bureaucracy as divided as ever, Kennedy decided to try and get information from both Lodge and Harkins on a long list of specific questions. The request was very much the President's and he asked that Hilsman compose it. The cable itself reflected a vast amount of doubt about the progress of the war. Eventually the answers from both men came in: the Lodge report was thoroughly pessimistic, while the Harkins report was markedly upbeat, filled with assurance, but also bewildering because it seemed to be based on the debate in Washington rather than the situation in Saigon. In it, the puzzled White House aides found a reference by Harkins to an outgoing cable of Taylor's. They checked out the number of the Taylor cable, but could find no record of it in the White House. Sensing that something was wrong, one of the White House aides called over to the Pentagon for a copy of the Taylor cable, giving the number, though being careful to call a low-ranking clerk, not someone in the Chairman's office who might have understood the play. The young corporal was very co-operative and came up with the answer the aides wanted, a remarkably revealing cable from Taylor to Harkins explaining just how divided the bureaucracy was, what the struggle was about, saying that the Hilsman cable did not reflect what Kennedy wanted, that it was more Hilsmanish than Kennedyish, and then outlining which questions to answer and precisely how to answer them.

The cable had been unearthed just before a key National Security Council meeting. The White House staff was very angry and felt that Taylor had been completely disloyal, although Kennedy himself was more fatalistic than upset, being perhaps more aware of the conflicting pulls on Taylor's loyalty. At the end of the meeting, however, Kennedy asked Taylor to come in to a private office, like, thought some of the others, a little boy summoned to the principal's office. (If Kennedy's respect for Taylor slipped a little, it went up for Harriman, who, not knowing of the secret Taylor cable, had nonetheless not liked the Harkins response and had told Kennedy before the meeting that there was something funny about it, somebody was playing games on him. "Harriman really is a shrewd old SOB," Kennedy said later.) In the intensity of the debate the incident quickly passed, although it did convince some of the White House staff members of what they had suspected all along, that Harkins' response and attitudes were being almost completely controlled by Taylor, with Krulak acting as something of a messenger between them, and with McNamara's own position thus limited by his necessity of going along with what were deemed to be military facts. Later the civilians asked to have a set of cable machines in the White House so this sort of thing could be monitored, and the military readily agreed. The next day some fourteen machines were moved into the White House basement, grinding out millions of routine words per day, and the civilians knew that they were beaten by the sheer volume, that it was impossible to monitor it all. They surrendered and the machines were moved out, almost as quickly as they had been moved in. As for Taylor, there were those in the White House who thought him disloyal to the President, though it was clear that he felt he was acting for the President's own good, protecting Kennedy from himself and the people around him. He, Taylor, was civilized, there were far worse people waiting in the wings if it didn't work out, and so all of this was being done for Kennedy's own sake.

NOW SUDDENLY, UNDER CRISIS CONDITIONS, THE KENNEDY ADMINistration was finding itself confronted with the questions it should have faced and resolved almost two years earlier, when it slipped into the larger commitment. The political problems of Vietnam now seemed very real because they had acquired greater American potential, and they did not go away. For the first time the State Department people were making something of a case for the basically political nature of the war. The things that so many, like Durbrow and Ken Young, had said in the past about the Nhus seemed only too true, and now in the glare of international publicity the Administration had to come up with answers. The Administration's hopes that there might be an easy coup had dimmed. There was that old illusion, the separation of the Nhus from the government. On September 2 the President himself went on television with Walter Cronkite and tried to disassociate the United States from the harshness of the regime and talk about the limits of the American role in a guerilla war—it was, he said, "in the final analysis . . . their war. They are the ones who have to win it or lose it." Then he talked about possible changes in policy and personnel which might help the war effort. In Saigon at the exact same time, Lodge was with Nhu, trying to get him out of the government, and perhaps out of the country. There seemed to be some progress—there would perhaps be an announcement saying that the progress against the Vietcong was so great that Nhu could now retire. However, four days later Nhu went into a tirade and said that he would not leave the country, though he might leave the government. Experienced Americans in Saigon and Washington realized that this too was a fraud, that there was no such thing as Nhu out of the government as long as he stayed in the country. With this in mind, the National Security Council met again on September 6, and heard the same two factions, ending in the same negated view of policy. The civilians said it was hopeless with Diem, and the military said that it was equally hopeless without him. McNamara, pressing the military side, said this was a good time for Lodge to start talking with Diem again and restore relations to normal. Sitting in on the meeting and listening to both sides cancel each other's arguments was Robert Kennedy, and he asked the questions that should have been asked two years earlier.

Perhaps no one person reflected the embryonic change in Administration and in American attitudes toward the Cold War as did Robert Kennedy, the change from tough and aggressive anti-Communism toward a more modest view of the American role, and a sense of the limits and dangers of American power. He was, in mid-1963, in the middle of his personal journey, his own attitudes very much in flux. He had entered the Administration as perhaps the most hard-line member of the entire inner group, and in fact, the job he had really wanted was not at Justice but at Defense, where he wanted to be the number-two man, specifically in charge of ending what he and others in the Kennedy group believed was a missile gap. If he were at Defense, he told friends, he could serve as the ramrod, pushing through newer, tougher programs, and be a watchdog for his brother. At the same time he would be gaining valuable experience in foreign affairs, which he wanted, and similarly, escape going to Justice, where he feared his reputation as the cop of the family would become more permanent.

He was already being haunted by this idea, that no matter what he did or how he served his brother and his country, the public would think of him as the ruthless cop. So he had pleaded with his brother, and Jack Kennedy did take the matter up with McNamara, suggesting that if he needed a deputy at Defense there happened to be a very good one in the Kennedy family. McNamara smiled and the President-elect quickly protested that Robert Kennedy was very able indeed. McNamara nodded and said that he had never doubted that, but if the President would think for a minute—suppose he were a senator and wanted something done at Defense, would he call the Secretary of Defense or would he call the President's brother? The President understood. The next day Robert Kennedy was talking with a friend and the subject of the job at Defense came up. "Well," he said, "that's out. If you were Bob McNamara, would you want the President's little brother always there spying over your shoulder?"

So he had entered the Administration, against his will, at Justice, but he had played a major role in foreign affairs. It was Robert Kennedy who had been primarily responsible for the counterinsurgency enthusiasm. Toughness fascinated him; he was not at ease with an America which had flabby waistlines. The enemy both at home and abroad was determined; we had to match that determination. If he worked until midnight, and on driving home saw the lights on in the offices of Jimmy Hoffa's Teamsters Union, then he turned around and drove back to his office. The standard by which he judged men was how *tough* they were. Early in the Administration, when he was overwhelmed with speaking requests and was turning almost all of them down, he had received one from a Polish group. He immediately seized on it: "Let's do this one. I like the Poles, they're tough." He had been a major force in promoting the career of Maxwell Taylor and diminishing that of Chester Bowles; his relationship with Taylor was different from his relationship with other men in the Administration. With almost everyone else his questioning was hard and relentless; he did not really respect age or title. But with Taylor he was markedly uncritical; whatever Taylor said went through almost unchallenged. He was genuinely in awe of Taylor's war record, the fact that he had dropped by parachute into Normandy and that he had run a special mission for Eisenhower behind the Italian lines. For Bobby Kennedy those were real credentials.

There were several qualities which set him apart from others in office. The first was total confidence in his relationship with the President. The second was an almost absolute insistence on being well and honestly briefed. The third was a capacity, indeed an instinct, to see world events not so much in terms of a great global chess game, but in human terms. As such he retained his common sense, it was at least as strong as his ideology (when others were talking about a surgical air strike against Cuba during the missile crisis, he said very simply that he did not want his brother to be the Tojo of the 1960s). Out of all of this came the final characteristic, the capacity to grow and change and to admit error.

In 1962 he had stopped at the Saigon airport long enough to say that we would stay in Vietnam until we won, but he had also learned a very important lesson: that most of the official reporting was mythological. He was supposed to be briefed at the airport terminal by the top members of the mission, all of whom, in one another's presence, assured him that everything was just fine, everything was on target. "Do you have any problems?" he asked. No, said everyone in unison, there were no problems. He looked at them somewhat shocked by the response. "No problems," he said, "you've really got no problems? Does anyone here want to speak to me in private about his problems?" And then one by one they talked to him at length and it all came pouring out, a brief and instructive lesson in what people would say for the record and what they would say in private.

By 1963, as his perceptions had developed, he was no longer just the President's little ramrod brother with a simplistic, hard-line view of the world, but now he had a new reputation, as the best man in government to bring an unconventional idea to. Some of the people working under Harriman, like Forrestal and Hilsman, felt themselves encouraged in their doubts by Robert Kennedy and felt that he more than anyone else in the upper level of government regarded the war as a *war* and in particular a war where civilians might be paying a particularly high price. His questions at meetings always centered around the people of Vietnam: What is all of this doing to the people? As his skepticism grew about how well the war was going he would ask, "Do you think those people really want us there? Maybe we're trying to do the wrong thing?" His common sense, among other sensibilities, was offended by it.

Now in the early fall of 1963, sitting in these meetings, listening to one side say that it could not be done with Diem, and the other side say that there was no one but Diem, he was appalled. Perhaps, he said, this was the time to consider withdrawing. It was a brief moment, but he was focusing on the central question, which everyone else, for a variety of reasons, had avoided. Up to now the debate had always been on the peripheral questions, in large part because it was safer that way. By concentrating on Diem, the liberals could attack the policy without being necessarily accused of softness on Communism. Diem had proved himself illiberal, and that was why the policy was failing; going further than that was a tenuous thing and might arouse considerable opposition. A bureaucratic doubter could keep his *bona fides* only by saying that he was for the war and for South Vietnam; it was only Diem he was against. Perhaps it was symbolic that the first senior official who questioned the overall policy was Robert Kennedy, totally secure in his place in the Administration, and also secure in his credentials as an anti-Communist. The question he raised was not discussed; it was still too sensitive a point. Perhaps that was how he intended it, as a beginning, an airing of a new idea, and giving it just a little respectability.

Thus with both sides still negating each other, with everyone in Washington still committed, they decided at the September 6 meeting of the National Security Council to try one more special report from Saigon. Each side pushed for representatives from Saigon to report back in Washington, and for its Washington people to visit Saigon and report back. McNamara wanted Krulak, and Harriman, equally tough in the infighting, made sure that a foreign service officer of comparable rank went along. Joseph A. Mendenhall, a senior officer who had had experience in Vietnam and who was fed up with Diem, was chosen. In addition Harriman, notified that two key members of the American mission in Saigon had changed their views, lobbied for them to come back with Krulak and Mendenhall to brief the White House. They were Rufus Phillips, who ran the crucial strategic hamlet program, which was part political and part military, and John Mecklin, head of the USIA in Saigon. Phillips was an ace in the hole for Harriman and his group. Whenever there had been pessimistic civilian appraisals in the past, the top figures in the mission had always used the strategic hamlet program as their counterargument: how could anyone say the political situation was bad when the hamlet program, which was the key to the rural success of the commitment, was going so well, was way ahead of schedule? But if Phillips was willing to discuss the failuresofthehamletprogram—whichwouldreflecton*military* failures as well —then this would be significant, far more important than anything Mendenhall could say. Harriman had come upon some of Phillips' quite pessimistic reporting in recent weeks, and he had taken great delight in having it shown around Washington. He had told Forrestal to make sure McNamara saw it, and on September 1 the report was sent to McNamara. There was no immediaate response from the Secretary, but Harriman was ready to play for bigger game.

To the military, Krulak was the most important figure. He was the military's most skilled bureaucratic player in Washington at the time, a figure of immense import in the constant struggle over Vietnam. He was the special assistant to the JCS for counterinsurgency, though of course he had no background on guerrilla warfare. What he really did was serve as a messenger between Saigon and the Pentagon, and represent the military at intergovernmental meetings, where his special assignment was to destroy any civilian pessimism about the war and to challenge the civilian right to even discuss military progress, or lack thereof.

He was the shortest Marine in the Corps' history, which had earned him the nickname Brute, and his toughness, reputation and nickname appealed to the Kennedy sense of vigor and drive. He was a very good briefer, not falling back on clichés but expressing his points in powerful, cogent terms. This fascinated and delighted McNamara, who hated briefings by most of the generals, and he remained a McNamara favorite long after it became clear that Krulak had participated in serious misrepresentations to the President. He was charming and sophisticated, and he did his staff work well; if anyone needed a paper on Vietnam, Krulak's office could cough it up much faster than those bumblers at State. He did not neglect the social end of it; he drove by Justice and picked up Bobby Kennedy on the way to meetings, courting him assiduously; he played golf with John McCone at Chevy Chase. He was strong and aggressive, and yet for all of that, quite subtle. Doubters on the policy like Michael Forrestal were always impressed how subtle Krulak could be in private, sharing their doubts—yes, he, Krulak, wasn't blind, he knew these problems existed—though of course speaking differently in meetings. He was, for all the intelligence and charm, a proponent of the straight MACV-Harkins line, as the official minutes of the special counterinsurgency group reveal for that crucial period ("February 7, 1963 Krulak says real progress is being made in the struggle. Vietcong morale is deteriorating . . . March 14, 1963 Krulak says Vietcong activity is at a level 50 percent below last year . . . May 9, 1963 Krulak, back from a Honolulu meeting with Harkins, says that all trends are favorable . . . May 23 Colonel Francis Serong, Australian guerrilla fighting expert, expresses doubt on the Strategic Hamlet Program saying it is overextended, and that it has left vast areas from which the Vietcong can operate freely. Krulak immediately and violently challenges him . . .").

Now Krulak would travel with Mendenhall, for what was to be a special report for the President. He was to use his eyes and ears to represent the President of the United States. He did nothing of the sort. He and Mendenhall spent some time together in Saigon; then they went different ways. Mendenhall had his doubts confirmed and Krulak went out into the field. Before he did, however, he picked up a voluminous report specifically prepared for him by Harkins and Stilwell, filled with all the good indices. The report would now become not a Harkins report, but a Krulak report. When they were at the airport, ready to leave for Washington after their four-day whirlwind tour, David Shepard, Saigon deputy head of the USIA, asked Mendenhall what he thought. "What you people have been reporting, only worse, and I'm going to tell the President that," Mendenhall answered, "but I think I'm going to have trouble bringing Krulak along."

It was an understatement; the reports they gave at the next National Security Council meeting could not have been more different. For Krulak the important thing, the shooting war, was fine, it was going according to schedule, particularly out there in the countryside. If there was any dissent about the regime, it was aimed at the Nhus, not at Diem. Diem was good. Our man. Respectable. All we had to do was stay with the program. Since Mendenhall was not allowed to challenge the military reporting, he described the collapse of the civilian morale, the atmosphere of fear and hatred in every city, and he said that yes, the government had finally succeeded in unifying the population—though against itself. The war in the countryside, he said, was now secondary to the opposition to the regime.

When Mendenhall had finished, the President looked at both and said, "You two did visit the same country, didn't you?" Well, said Krulak, it was easy to explain; he had been out in the countryside among the troops where the war was taking place, while Mendenhall had been among the students and the intellectuals. Whereupon Nolting challenged Mendenhall: everyone knew that Mendenhall was against Diem, and had been for several years. As for the paralysis in government now, we had had paralysis in government before, in 1961, and we had overcome that. We could overcome the problems if we put our minds to it, Nolting said, if we didn't get caught in the side issues.

Well, said McGeorge Bundy (who had become increasingly disenchanted with the entire situation, the messiness and self-defeating quality of the regime, an American-supported government turning American weapons on its own population), in 1961 the fear and paralysis had been caused by the Vietcong and we had overcome it by strengthening the war against them; now it was the government itself which was causing the fear and the paralysis, and it was a little difficult to strengthen a war against a government.

John Mecklin spoke next. As a correspondent in Indochina during the French war he had lived through it all; he had started out trying to sell Diem both to the Americans and to the Vietnamese, and now he could no longer even sell the regime to himself. It was all finished as it stood, he said. It was time for the United States to put pressure on the regime to change. Since this might bring on a civil war, he recommended the possibility of sending in U.S. combat troops to fight the Vietcong. If Kattenburg's earlier suggestion about

getting out had been voicing the unthinkable, so was the idea of combat
troops—after all, this whole mess was a result of what had been arranged precisely in order to prevent the need of combat troops.

Now it was Rufus Phillips' turn, and his briefing was doubly important because it was the first informed frontal attack upon the military reporting, and
also because it was given by a man who had a particularly good reputation in
Vietnam, Lansdale's own chosen legatee. If Lansdale had been the main
figure of the Good Guy American philosophy in the fifties, Phillips was very
much in his image. Recruited off the Yale campus by the CIA, he had been a
part of the early Lansdale group, and had been in charge of having Vietnamese astrologers predict dark days for the Vietminh and happy days for Diem.
In early 1963, as his people in the Delta reported the breakdown there of the
strategic hamlet program, Phillips had responded to their warnings, had visited the areas himself, and was horrified. Now, coming before the President,
he was admitting the failures of his own program, in itself a remarkable moment in the American bureaucracy, a moment of intellectual honesty. He had
known Diem and Nhu for ten years, he said, and they had gradually lost touch
with the population and with reality. The Vietnamese now felt that their government had to change, and he agreed. As for General Krulak's earlier statement that the political problems had not yet touched the Vietnamese officers,
it was simply not true; but American officers were under direct orders not to
talk to their Vietnamese counterparts about politics, and the Vietnamese
knew this. So the testimony of American officers in the field about Vietnamese
politics was bound to be limited. At this point Krulak interrupted him: the
Americans in the field might not know about politics, but they knew whether
or not the war was being won, and they said it was going well.

Now Phillips made his direct attack on the military reporting. Yes, the war
was going reasonably well in the areas north of Saigon, where there was little
action. But in the Delta, where most of the fighting was taking place, it was
going very badly. The Vietcong were taking over the Delta without a struggle; in the last few weeks, fifty hamlets had been overrun. What made this
even worse, he said, was that the Buddhist crisis had not even reached the
Delta yet. And, said Phillips, this was not the view just of his people, many
Army officers felt the same way. In fact, Phillips had brought with him a report from the provincial adviser in Long An province, one of the most popu-
lated areas in the country. Phillips had stumbled on the report by accident:
Earl Young, a civilian who was Phillips' man there, had been reporting for
some time that the Vietcong controlled 80 percent of this populous province.
Young had told Phillips he was not alone in his pessimism; the provincial adviser (in this case an American major detailed to advising the province chief)
agreed with him completely, and had in fact been reporting precisely this to
MACV but had gotten no response from his superiors. The major had there-

fore turned over his reports to Earl Young, who turned them over to Rufus Phillips, who had supplemented his own impressions with a small but impressive example of field reporting by the military.

So the battle raged. Krulak immediately jumped Phillips. Phillips was putting his judgment ahead of General Harkins', a senior military official, a man of seasoned judgment who had more people working for him, more information at his disposal, and who knew how to evaluate military reports. He, Krulak, would take General Harkins over Phillips any time (the implication in his voice was that Phillips was very young, thirty-three years old, at best a captain, and captains should not challenge generals). With Krulak going after Phillips, Harriman went after Krulak: Harriman said he was not surprised that Krulak was taking Harkins' side—indeed he would be upset if he did not. Harriman said that he had known Krulak for several years and had always known him to be wrong, and was sorry to say it, but he considered Krulak a damn fool. When this storm had passed, Phillips finished: he wanted to say that despite what Krulak felt, the war was not being won militarily, and it was going badly. And anyway, he emphasized, you could not talk about it being won militarily, it was above all a political war.

With that, with the government as badly split as before, the meeting broke up, but the military estimates had been seriously punctured. In addition, in the turning around of Phillips, a bench mark had been passed. It was a symbol of Lansdale turning as well; the people who had invented Diem were now leading the assault against him. Too, it was a sign that the Good Guys, the Americans who thought there was a right way, a middle way of dealing with Vietnam if we had the right programs and did the right things, and who believed that the Vietnamese wanted us there, were beginning to despair. If they failed, and they were failing fast, desperate now to find, eight years later, some last-minute substitute for Diem, then there was a chance that American policy in Vietnam would be directed by people who felt we ought to be there whether the Vietnamese wanted us or not, whether we helped them more than we hurt them, that the answer lay not in the right people handling the right programs, but simply in superior force.

If the military had had their estimates punctured by Phillips at the National Security Council meeting, then the MACV officials made sure that those who did the puncturing would live to regret it. None other than General Richard Stilwell would lead a subsequent investigation, which was designed not to find out whether or not the Phillips charges were true, but instead to find out how Phillips and Young had got hold of the Long An report. For a time there was serious talk at the highest levels of MACV of charging Phillips and Young with security violations; however, that idea was dropped after Ambassador Lodge defended them. But the major who had written the report was reprimanded, given a bad efficiency report and immediately transferred out of

Long An to the least attractive post available, which happened to be a National Guard slot. The stakes were getting higher and the game was getting rougher.

In addition, the Army was beginning to function more and more like a separate organism, responding to its institutional needs, priorities, vanities and careerism. Challenged by outsiders, by civilians, it responded by protecting its own senior officers.

In August this reporter did a major survey of the deteriorating military situation in the Mekong Delta. I had been called by two friends who were senior advisers to Vietnamese divisions and who were appalled by the collapse of the ARVN and the appearance of formidable new Vietcong battalions sweeping almost without opposition throughout the Mekong Delta. My story was published and told of big new beefed-up battalions of 600 and 1,000 men, very well armed with captured American weapons. The article suggested that the war was being lost and that the high-level optimism about the Delta was comparable to the French optimism that preceded their debacle at Dienbienphu. The story staggered the President, who was an avid newspaper reader, and who took journalists seriously. He asked the military to comment on it, and word was sent through channels from Taylor to General Krulak to General Harkins that this was particularly important, that it was bad enough to be taking heat because of the Buddhist crisis, but if the President thought the war was going poorly as well, the whole game might be over. (The story in the *New York Times* was so similar to the briefing then being given at the Pentagon by Lieutenant Colonel John Vann that though Vann had been out of Vietnam for several months and had not talked to me, serious thought was given to court-martialing him.) The assignment was given not to MACV's intelligence section, but to its most gifted general, Dick Stilwell, who thereupon, without consulting his top advisers in the Delta, prepared a massive file, filled with charts, graphs and statistics, which took the newspaper account apart word by word; each word received at least a paragraph. The Stilwell account found the journalistic account inaccurate, indeed "the picture is precisely the opposite," he reported. The only problem, as the Pentagon Papers would later note, was that the newspaper account was right and the Stilwell-Krulak account was wrong. Sound misreporting did not impede the careers of either Stilwell or Krulak (additional stars would come their way, and Krulak would just miss out on being Commandant of the Marine Corps), but it did offer a fascinating insight into the way the military worked. Loyalty was not to the President of the United States, to truth or integrity, or even to subordinate officers risking their lives; loyalty was to uniform, and more specifically, to immediate superior and career. It was an insight into why the military in Saigon, despite all the contrary evidence in the field, despite the arrival of as bright an officer as Dick Stilwell, managed to retain their optimism. The

Americans in Vietnam, long frustrated by the ineptitude of their ARVN counterparts, and by the fact that ineptitude guaranteed career advancement, had come up with a slogan to describe the ARVN promotion system: "Fuck up and move up." They did not realize that by now the slogan applied to their own Army as well.

Chapter Fifteen

THE KRULAK-MENDENHALL TRIP HAD NOT REALLY SETTLED anything; it had simply proved to the President that his government was still seriously divided. The return of Phillips had convinced him, however, that the war was not going well, and that the military reporting was not to be trusted. Kennedy was by this time very frustrated: he told aides that he could not believe a word that the military was telling him, that he had to read the newspapers to find out what was going on; at the same time, the more he read the more he was reminded of the depth of the division in his Administration and the failure of his policy in Vietnam, and he would, in turn, rant against the reporters in Vietnam. By mid-September he had decided that the problem was not so much the question of information, whether or not the war was being won, as a question of slowly shifting policy and still trying to hold his government together.

On September 17 McNamara asked to go to Vietnam on another trip, but Lodge and some of the other State Department people were strongly opposed to it. In the past McNamara's trips had not been glowing successes; they had tended to emphasize the dominance of the military over the civilians and to equate statistical results with reality. In addition, the civilians, who normally liked McNamara, had found him surprisingly inflexible on Vietnam. But Kennedy insisted that he be allowed to go; indeed, there were those in the White House who suspected that the idea for the trip had originated with Kennedy. After some protests against the trip by Lodge (resulting in an announcement that McNamara was going to Saigon at Lodge's request), McNamara and General Taylor left on September 23 for Saigon. One of the things they were to investigate was the possibility of cutting down some of the U.S. aid projects as a symbol of disenchantment with the Ngo family. Inadvertently some of these programs had already been cut off, by a bureaucratic fluke. Though some of the civilians, including Lodge, had argued for it, Kennedy had held the line; he had not been prepared to take this first step until he was more sure that the Vietnamese military was at least one step ahead of him and was ready to replace Diem. But in early September at one high-level meeting the principals had been talking about whether or not to cut off commodity aid, when David Bell, who was head of AID and who was not regularly a high-level player, said rather casually that there was no point in talking about cutting off commodity aid, he had already cut it off.

"You've done what?" said a startled President of the United States.

"Cut off commodity aid," Bell answered.

"Who the hell told you to do that?" asked the President, since this was no small action; it could easily bring down a government.

"No one," said Bell. "It's an automatic policy. We do it whenever we have differences with a client government."

And so the President sat there shaking his head, looking at Bell and saying, "My God, do you know what you've done?" (There were those in the government who suspected, however, that Bell would not have moved without approval or encouragement from some superior at State.)

ALMOST LITERALLY FROM THE MOMENT HE ARRIVED, McNAMARA found a new Saigon command; instead of the old unified Harkins-Nolting view of the war, he found Lodge and Harkins barely speaking to each other. In fact, as McNamara was descending from his plane Lodge assigned two staff members to block the general so that Lodge could greet him first, leaving an angry Harkins pushing at the human barrier, shouting, "Please, gentlemen, please let me through to the Secretary."

It was a fascinating trip; the military controlled the itinerary, but Lodge had McNamara as his house guest. It was there that Lodge worked to change McNamara's view of the war, at breakfast time rushing in people from the provinces who were armed with pessimistic statistics. Then Lodge's time would be up, and McNamara would go off on the prescribed Harkins-Taylor tour, all the young officers geared up long in advance, charts and optimism at the ready: Yes, sir, all programs are go, sir; we're getting with the program, sir. The young officers briefed Taylor and McNamara, Harkins standing a few feet behind them, the smile on his face, all the curves were up.

It went on like this for several days and finally they reached a province in the Delta where Rufus Phillips' people had reported enormous Vietcong progress. A copy of the Phillips report had been made available to McNamara in the morning when the military briefing began. Taylor was standing there impressive, asking helpful leading questions: Major, we know what a good job you're doing and that this situation is under control, and we wonder if you could tell us about it? . . . McNamara had tried to penetrate these briefings in the past without much success but this time he was prepared, he had read a pessimistic paper on this same province. So finally the entire civilian-military split seemed to have come down to one place, one war, two views of it. Had the major, McNamara asked, read the report of his civilian colleague in the Hamlet program? Yes, sir. Did the major agree with the civilian appraisal? Pause. Finally the officer said yes, he did. Why, then, asked McNamara, hadn't he reported it himself? Because his civilian colleague reported it and because he himself had reported only the military situation as set by guidelines from MACV.

At this point General Taylor looked at the officer very coldly and said that it appeared he had been falsifying reports. No, sir, said the young officer, my report was accurate as far as it went. With that they moved on to the next stop, but McNamara's attitude had changed for the first time; his own doubts had grown, he had penetrated the military reporting.

On the way back the two men, so different in their perceptions and loyalties, worked out their divergent views of Vietnam. Like much of what had come out in the past, and even more of what was to come in the future, two separate attitudes were contained in one report, badly bastardized. It reflected a trade between McNamara and Taylor on a number of things: McNamara accepted Lodge's estimates that we could not succeed with Diem, and got major new doubts about the regime and major new pressures against it into the report ("It is very fortunate for the country to have a man of the breadth and scope of Bob McNamara as Secretary of Defense," said Lodge the day after McNamara left, a big grin on his face, having just swallowed *that* canary). Taylor held the line on the military estimates and optimism, so that the opening line of the report stated that the military program "has made great progress and continues to progress." The programs were going very well, the shooting war was fine, 1,000 Americans would be out by Christmas, and the whole American commitment would be finished by the end of 1965. The report also, given the ever-increasing noises about withdrawal from Vietnam, reiterated the intention of the Defense Department to stay there:

The security of South Vietnam remains vital to United States security. For this reason, we adhere to the overriding objective of denying this country to Communism and of suppressing the Vietcong insurgency as promptly as possible. (By suppressing the insurgency we mean reducing it to proportions manageable by the national security forces of the GVN [Government of (South) Vietnam], unassisted by the presence of U.S. military forces.) . . .

Taylor and McNamara went on to say that they had found the government increasingly unpopular, although the Vietnamese military were "more hostile to the Vietcong than to the government." The report said in a rather revealing reference to American policy: "Our policy is to seek to bring about the abandonment of Diem's repression because of its effect on the popular will to resist." (Repression for repression's sake was permissible, but repression which hurt the war effort was regrettable.) It recommended keeping the commodity aid shut off, besides holding back on a number of other aid projects, including CIA money for Diem and Nhu's private palace guard unless it was used to fight the Vietcong. "Correct" relations between the United States and Diem should be maintained, along with the search for contacts for what was termed "alternative leadership," something Lodge badly wanted and was already gearing up to do. The request was typical of the policy and the frustrations and divisions and dishonesty of it all; it said in effect that the United States should look elsewhere for leadership and away from Diem even though the war was being won, and that the war was the only important thing. It was an assessment that the civilians would live to regret, since it would later appear that they had switched governments and helped topple a government which was still winning the war. They knew that this judgment was false, but they had never challenged it, because of their own previous wishful thinking, because of their inability to control their own bureaucracy, and because, above all, of a belief that telling the truth to the American people was unimportant. They—both Kennedys, Rusk, Lodge, Harriman, Hilsman, Trueheart, Forrestal—knew the war was being lost, but they never got it down on paper or into their own statements, or into their briefings with congressional leaders. A lie had become a truth, and the policy makers were trapped in it; their policy was a failure, and they could not admit it.

Back in Washington, McNamara and Taylor went to the White House to read the report. Some of the civilians were uneasy with the optimism still contained in it (Bill Sullivan, Harriman's man, had argued against it on the plane ride back), particularly against pulling out of troops. Mac Bundy, at the urging of some of his staff, questioned it. "Is this wise?" he asked. "Aren't we setting a trap for ourselves?" But they would find no flexibility. Someone questioning Bill Bundy, still at the Defense Department, about the wording and the dangers inherent in it, got a shrug. "I'm under orders," he said. Taylor, he told others, wanted the reference to the troop withdrawals left in as a means of pushing the Vietnamese. Hilsman, asking McNamara about the wording, found him brusque, almost rude, and later, Hilsman said, when McNamara read the statement publicly, it was as if he were reading an ultimatum. The

President himself was unhappy about it, but was fatalistic; he could have leaned on them and pushed for more, but he had a sense of the delicacy of the whole thing, that he had moved one key player, McNamara, considerably with this one mission, and McNamara had in a limited sense moved Taylor (though without truly changing him or opening him up; it was as if McNamara had dragged a reluctant Taylor a few gradations on the calibration of attitude). So Kennedy knew that if he were having troubles with his bureaucracy in moving them a notch or two at a time, they in turn were having troubles with their bureaucracy.

As everything about Vietnam was compromised, so too was this report by McNamara and Taylor, but Kennedy was not that worried. He knew Vietnam was bad and getting worse, that he was on his way to a first-class foreign policy problem, but he had a sense of being able to handle it, of having time, that time was somehow on his side. He could afford to move his people slowly; too forceful a shove would bring a counter shove. It was late 1963, and since 1964 was an election year, any delay on major decisions was healthy; if the Vietnamese could hold out a little longer, so could he. Besides, other things were beginning to come together. He had signed a limited nuclear test-ban treaty with the Soviets, the civil rights march on Washington had come and passed, and had not hurt his Administration; rather, by its dignity and grandeur and passion, it had reflected the aspirations of have-not Americans with a sense of majesty that probably had helped his Administration. Kennedy felt that the country's doubts about him and his Presidency were ebbing, that his real popularity, not the visual popularity, but a deeper thing, was beginning to form, that the idea of him as President was beginning to crystallize. So he did not want to rush too quickly, to split his Administration unnecessarily. There was always time. The date of the McNamara-Taylor report was October 2, 1963.

AT ALMOST THE SAME TIME GENERAL DUONG VAN MINH, THE MOST respected military figure in the South, a man close to the Lansdale group since the early days when he had helped fight the banditlike Binh Xuyen sect, contacted Lou Conein, an old friend of his, and asked if they could talk. Conein had been in Vietnam for eighteen years, mostly with the CIA; he had been one of the first Americans parachuted in at the end of World War II. He knew the non-Communist Vietnamese military well, since they had been his recruits, as he liked to say. Shrewd, irreverent, colorful, he seemed an American version of the audacious French paratrooper, someone sprung to life from a pulp adventure thriller. He knew the country, and the people, and he flirted with danger, it was danger that made life more exciting. Two fingers were missing from one hand, and stories were told all over Saigon as to how those fingers had disappeared, in what noble or ignoble cause; reporters who knew

Conein well and liked him and whose phones were always tapped referred to him in their own code as "Three-Finger Brown" after a baseball pitcher named Mordecai Brown. The American command in Saigon despised him; he had, they suspected, been there too long, gone too native; he was erratic, untrustworthy, playing the game of adventurer—the most dangerous kind. He was also one of the very few Americans who had any credibility with the Vietnamese military, who despised Harkins and regarded Harkins as an extension of Nhu (later, as dealings with the Vietnamese generals became more involved, the White House cabled Lodge suggesting that it would be nice if someone more respectable than Conein could be found, and Lodge answered yes, he agreed, but there was no suitable substitute, and General Tran Van Don had "expressed extreme reluctance to deal with anyone else").

With Lodge's approval, Conein met General Minh on October 5 and they talked for more than an hour. General Minh said that the war was being lost, that the senior Vietnamese officers (himself, Tran Van Don and Tran Van Kim, all respected and none of them commanding troops because they had followings of their own, and were thus considered dangerous by Nhu) felt that a change had to be made. He wanted to know what the American attitude toward this was; he did not want American assistance, but neither did he want the Americans to thwart them. They had to move and move quickly, he said, because regimental and battalion commanders were now too restless and were pushing for a coup (which confirmed a Hilsman-Sarris estimate made a month earlier that the generals would not move immediately unless pushed from below by junior officers). Conein said that he could not answer them until he had talked to his superiors; Minh said he understood. He mentioned three possible ways of removing the regime: assassination of both Diem and Nhu, a military encirclement of Saigon, or open fighting between loyal and disloyal units. Conein said that the United States would not advise on which plan was best. Minh also wanted to know whether U.S. aid would continue if the generals were running the government. Ambassador Lodge immediately answered that the United States would not thwart a coup, would review Vietnamese plans, other than assassination plans, and would assure the generals that U.S. aid would be continued to another anti-Communist government.

With this the end was in sight for the Diem regime. Lodge, the dominant player in Saigon, shrewd, forceful and tough, did not believe anything the government said, nor much of what the U.S. military said. He cut Harkins out of much of the cable traffic, believing the general was a problem both in Washington and in Saigon, where he might leak information to the Ngo family. Ironically, Harkins was an old family friend from Boston, which made Lodge wary of being openly critical of the general's reporting, so he tried simply to by-pass him ("The Ambassador and I are certainly in touch with each other but whether the communications between us are effective is something else. I will say Cabot's methods of operations are entirely different from Amb. Nolting's . . ." Harkins said in an angry cable to Taylor on October 30.) Before he went to Saigon, Lodge had prepared himself fully in Washington, including long talks with Madame Nhu's parents, who were highly critical of their daughter's politics (her father, Tran Van Chuong, was ambassador to the United States and had resigned, along with the embassy staff, after the crackdown on the pagodas). Lodge felt that all the charges against the Ngo family were true, that Nhu could not be separated from Diem, that the war was being lost, that since there was going to be a coup anyway, the U.S. position should be to neither encourage it (except perhaps slightly; that is, by not discouraging it) nor thwart it. He predicted, accurately, to Washington, that Diem would make a request for U.S. help, and that the U.S. attitude should be that its capacities were far less than Diem's.

By mid-October Lodge had convinced the White House, which was in a receptive mood, that a coup was going to take place, led by the generals, unless the Americans openly betrayed them. He thought that it was all for the better, that the chances of a new government being far more effective than the old were at least even. In that he was right; in Saigon at least three major plots were still brewing, plus a counterplot by Ngo Dinh Nhu; it was no longer a question of a coup, but of which coup. By October 6 Kennedy had wired Lodge telling him that although the United States did not wish to stimulate a coup, it did not wish to thwart one either, that Lodge should keep in touch with the generals and find out what their plans were. However, the U.S. role should be covert and deniable; indeed, Lodge should pass on Kennedy's instructions verbally to the acting CIA chief (John Richardson had been sent home at Lodge's request because he was too much of a symbol of the direct U.S. relationship with Nhu), so that no one else would know of the contents.

The weeks of October passed with coup fever building in Saigon. Diem and Nhu had won the first round with the pagoda strike, but it soon became evident that it was a temporary move, that while it had left the opposition disorganized at first, in the long run it was galvanizing the opposition, making it virtually total. A form of madness seemed to take over in Saigon. Having crushed the Buddhists, the government had moved against college students, and having crushed them, moved against high school students, and after they were crushed, and finding rebellion in elementary schools, it cracked down on them, closing those schools too. In hundreds of homes of government officers, brothers and sisters had been arrested. In Saigon, a journalist for Catholic magazines and until then a vehemently loyal supporter of the family, took American journalists aside to tell them of past Ngo injustices against the Catholic Church, a means of separating the Church from the accelerating insanity of the family.

Lodge, biding his time, letting the family guess his intentions, began to deal with Diem and found him as unresponsive as ever. Diem asked about rein-statement of American aid, and Lodge parried by demanding the release of hundreds of arrested Buddhists and students. Diem, Lodge later reported, offered a vast number of excuses. Finally Lodge said, "Mr. President, every single specific suggestion which I have made, you have rejected. Isn't there some one thing you may think of that is within your capabilities to do and that would favorably impress U.S. opinion?" According to Lodge, Diem gave him a blank look and changed the subject. It was in fact a tactic which had worked in the past: give the Americans at best a vague promise, count on them to be so committed to you that they would never turn aside; also that whoever dealt with you would be afraid to face domestic reverberations if he failed with you.

With the coup imminent, Harkins discovered in late October that he had been cut out of major decisions and cable traffic; in addition, he was irate over Lodge's pessimistic assessments of the military status. Now, on October 30, he reported back to Taylor that he doubted a coup was coming. General Tran Van Don had told Conein that it would take place before November 2, but when Harkins asked Don he denied any knowledge of a coup. In addition, Harkins reported that he had sat with Generals Don and Minh for two hours the previous weekend and neither had mentioned a coup (which was of course true; both generals regarded Harkins as the last Diem loyalist in the country).

The Harkins cable unsettled an already jittery Washington, and later that day there was a nervous Bundy cable to Lodge saying that despite what Lodge had said, the U.S. role on a coup could be crucial; he demanded more military information on what the generals were going to do, which units they had and which they lacked. Lodge answered that it was essentially a Viet-namese affair, though of course it was possible to give to Diem the informa-tion that Conein had received from the generals, which would place the United States in the position of being traitors. If at this point, he warned, we pulled back on the generals, it would guarantee that Diem and Nhu would never change, nor could they ever be moved. The United States, he con-tinued, was trying "to bring this medieval country into the 20th Century and . . . we have made considerable progress in military and economic ways but to gain victory we must also bring them into the 20th Century politi-cally . . ."

Bundy was still not satisfied with the Lodge answer. He cabled once more suggesting that the United States could control Vietnamese events, that he was not suggesting the betrayal of the plotters but perhaps a delay until there were better chances of success. But it was too late, the final plans were in mo-tion. On November 1 the Saigon embassy and CIA predicted in their early reports to Washington that a coup would come that day; MACV, which was supposed to be the best-informed on what the Vietnamese military were doing, dissented and said it would not come (when the coup did take place, MACV called up the embassy and asked to have the cable killed).

Shortly after one o'clock in the afternoon, troops committed to the generals began taking over key points in Saigon. Ngo Dinh Nhu had been tipped off earlier by one officer that a coup was coming, and true to form, instead of trying to break it then, he had devised an enormously elaborate countercoup which was designed to lure the plotters into the open, destroy them, destroy the Buddhists and all American sympathizers and raise such havoc that the Americans would be glad to have the Nhus back in power. As the first incidents took place, Nhu was confident it was his own countercoup set in motion. By the time he realized that he was mistaken and that he had lost control, he and Diem were practically surrounded, only the palace guard remained loyal. Since their situation was almost hopeless, Diem and Nhu asked the generals to call a halt and negotiate demands, but the same thing had happened before, in 1960, when Diem used it as a means of smashing a coup and gaining time for loyal units to enter the city. Now the brothers tried it again, but there were no loyal units. At four-thirty in the afternoon Diem finally called Lodge, and the embassy preserved this record of the conversation:

DIEM: Some units have made a rebellion and I want to know what is the attitude of the U.S.?

LODGE: I do not feel well enough informed to be able to tell you. I have heard the shooting, but am not acquainted with all the facts. Also it is 4:30 A.M. in Washington and the U.S. Government cannot possibly have a view.

DIEM: But you must have some general ideas. After all, I am a Chief of State. I have tried to do my duty. I want to do now what duty and good sense require. I believe in duty above all.

LODGE: You certainly have done your duty. As I told you only this morning, I admire your courage and your great contributions to your country. No one can take away from you the credit for all you have done. Now I am worried about your physical safety. I have a report that those in charge of the current activity offer you and your brother safe conduct out of the country if you will resign. Had you heard this?

DIEM: No. (And then after a pause) You have my telephone number.

LODGE: Yes. If I can do anything for your physical safety, please call me.

DIEM: I am trying to re-establish order.

The fighting continued through the night and into the early morning. By the time the rebels took the palace, Diem and Nhu were gone, having slipped out through a secret tunnel. They fled to the Chinese suburb of Cholon, where they remained in touch with the generals. Reportedly they finally accepted safe-conduct out of the country, but were picked up by the insurgents, and on orders of the new junta, killed while in the back of an armored personnel carrier. The body of Ngo Dinh Nhu was repeatedly stabbed after his death.

It was all over. One day photographs and statues had been everywhere, but not just of Diem, of his sister-in-law as well, a personality cult. The next day it was all gone, the statues smashed, the posters ripped through, his likeness left only on the one-piastre coin. In the streets the population mobbed the generals and garlanded the troops with flowers (one combat officer from the Delta later recalled that it was the first time he liked being a soldier, the first time he felt popular with the people). When Lodge himself walked through the streets, he was cheered like a presidential candidate. For the Americans it was a high moment, yet it would soon be followed by darkness; the reality of how badly the war was going would now come home as the death of Diem opened the floodgates of reporting and allowed officers to tell the truth. In addition, the one factor which had briefly in the nine years of the country's existence given even the vaguest element of unity to a non-Communist South Vietnam was gone—opposition to the Ngo family. For Diem the responsibility had been too much; he was a feudal leader, a man of the past trying to rule by outmoded means and dependent upon outside Caucasian support. There were many epitaphs written for him in the next few weeks, but curiously and prophetically the best one had been written some eight years earlier by Graham Greene:

Diem is separated from the people by cardinals and police cars with wailing sirens and foreign advisers when he should be walking in the rice fields unprotected, learning the hard way how to be loved and obeyed—the two cannot be separated. One pictured him sitting there in the Norodom Palace, sitting with his blank, brown gaze, incorruptible, obstinate, ill-advised, going to his weekly confession, bolstered up by his belief that God is always on the Catholic side, waiting for a miracle. The name I would write under his portrait is the Patriot Ruined by the West.

In Washington almost everyone concerned had seen the coup against Diem as somewhat inevitable. Taylor, reflecting the position he and Harkins had created, had been the most reluctant. But there was one other figure strongly opposed to it, who had rumbled about it, disliked it and would have fought it, had he exercised the power. He did not exercise the power, and neither his opinion nor his opposition was taken very seriously; perhaps had the issue involved legislation on the Hill or a conflict in Texas politics the others might have paid serious attention to his dissent, but not in the field of foreign affairs, where he was considered particularly inept. His name was Lyndon B. Johnson. He had hated the coup against Diem from the very beginning. All this talk about coups. Cops-and-robbers stuff, he said, coups and assassinations. Why, he and Ralph Yarborough had their differences down in Texas but they didn't go around plotting against each other, murdering each other. "Otto Passman and I, we have our differences, God knows he can slow up a lot of God's good work for mankind," he said, "but I don't plan his overthrow." In the summer, as others challenged the regime, Johnson had occasionally attended meetings and had defended it. The important thing, he had said, was to get on with winning the war. He felt genuine admiration for Diem as a man. Oh, he had his problems, but "in Texas we say that it's better to deal with the devil you know than the devil you don't know." When Johnson went to Vietnam in 1961, he had personally symbolized an American commitment to Diem, and part of his allegiance stemmed from this, that he had been the conduit of a promise, so arguing against Diem was arguing against Johnson; but some of it was broader, a somewhat more simplistic view of the world, and of who was a friend and who was an enemy. Friends were real friends, they signed on with you. Ayub Khan of Pakistan, for instance, was a friend. He spoke our kind of language, committed himself to our side, was willing to fight; Johnson would complain to those he suspected of having pro-Indian sympathies "of what *your* Indians are doing now." Arguments that Ayub was an American friend because he was using American aid against India rather than against Communists, and that India had five times as many people as Pakistan and thus deserved a certain amount more consideration, did not move him. Ayub was a friend, but these Indians, they never committed themselves. A contract was a contract, a deal was a deal, you held out your hand and they held out theirs and that was the way it was done. Even Tshombe— Johnson was a not-so-secret admirer of Tshombe, who, after all, alone among all those Africans, was willing to say he liked us and disliked the Communists.

The talk about the overthrow of Diem hit a very negative chord; he didn't like these young amateurs running around causing problems (often the people who were most against Diem seemed also to be the people who were against *him*, those people in the White House, not the seasoned professionals like Rusk, and this did not help his attitude). So he came to dislike and distrust the men who he thought were engineering the pressure against Diem, the young White House types, the brash know-it-all Hilsman, the young reporters out there who were, he said, traitors to their country—all these young people who had not even been through World War II, challenging senior people. Though he usually exempted John Kennedy from all criticism, on this subject he did not; he felt that Kennedy had played too great a role in the whole affair, and a few months later, after Kennedy had been assassinated, Johnson would turn to a friend and say, in an almost mystical way, that the assassination of Kennedy was retribution for the assassination of Diem. So in the months of 1963 when Kennedy was so carefully moving the bureaucracy over, the President, who was usually very careful about Johnson, had not worked on his Vice-President; he had been preoccupied with other matters, with moving more central players, and he had simply neglected to work on Johnson. No other word. Neglect. It did not, however, seem important at the time.

THE MONTHS OF SEPTEMBER AND OCTOBER WERE VERY GOOD ONES for John Kennedy, rich in themselves, full of promise for the future. Above all the beginning, perhaps just the beginning of an end to a particularly rigid era of the Cold War. Not the end of the Cold War, the problems were too great and too deep on both sides. Some of the competition was very real and would always remain so; but perhaps turning back the paralyzing effects of it, the almost neurotic quality which had provoked a country to reach beyond its own real interests because of domestic fears which had been set up at home. The opportunity had come first in the post-Cuban missile thaw, and Kennedy had explored it, cautiously, again not too quickly.

There had been the speech at the American University about a reappraisal of attitudes toward the Communists, and he had encouraged and dispatched Averell Harriman to work out a limited test-ban treaty, which was the first break in the almost glacial quality of the Cold War. It had not come easily; the bureaucracy itself was not really prepared for a change and there was considerable resistance within the government. The Chiefs were opponents (though they finally went along with a limited test-ban treaty in order to kill off pressure for a comprehensive one). Taylor was helpful here, in part because he thought nuclear war impossible for a democracy. McNamara was dubious at first and then a genuine ally (in large part because of the pressure and reasoning from his aide John McNaughton, one of the two or three most important men in the government in the fight to limit the arms race; but McNamara by the very act of appointing McNaughton had in effect created a disarmament lobby in Defense, something which Rusk had not done at State). Mac Bundy was neither a help nor an opponent. He did not push it, and he did not use his position to expedite it, but he made sure that the advocates had all the access to the President they needed.

Rusk was the least enthusiastic. In fact, one White House aide had first sensed that Rusk might be innately more conservative than the other Kennedy people, even before the inauguration, when Rusk had taken him aside and asked, "What's all this talk about disarmament, they aren't really serious about it, are they?" It was not so much that Rusk was against test-ban treaties as that he was a status quo man. The world was a static place, it changed very little, and then, very slowly. These differences, these divisions existed for very real and valid reasons and they would always exist and one did not push; pushing meant risks, on the Hill, with NATO allies, with the traditionalists in the foreign service; one moved slowly and was grateful for very small changes. Things like disarmament were for the Stevenson people and should be debated at the UN, and were for American domestic consideration by the liberals, but were not serious things (though later, when Johnson made it clear that he wanted a nonproliferation treaty, and when an issue like this was no longer groundbreaking, no one worked harder or more effectively for it than Rusk).

So with these Administration differences, based upon institutional and personal viewpoints, the outlook on the test-ban treaty was surprisingly similar to attitudes on Vietnam, with the President particularly interested in securing a test-ban treaty, and with Harriman far ahead of Rusk in willingness to take what was deemed political risk in accomplishing it. Harriman had wrestled it out with the Russians; he, more than anyone else in the government, believed that the time was ripe and that it could be pulled off, although there were a few, like Wiesner, who felt that in the previous negotiations with the Russians a treaty had been possible, but the U.S. negotiators had been too conservative. This did not mean that the bureaucracy and the Hill were ready by a long shot for change on the arms race. The Hill seemed to be dubious, particularly the Armed Services Committee, and the bureaucracy itself was filled with potential opponents. In the spring of 1963, for example, when there was no real idea that a test-ban treaty was coming, the word slipped out that Senator John Stennis was going to hold hearings on the state of the nation's preparedness. The preceding negotiations with the Russians had come surprisingly close to a treaty, and there was a feeling that things might be moving in that direction. But the threat of Stennis' hearings was a serious one. In the hearings the conservatives would summon the generals, who always call for more preparedness and lament America's present weakness, they create a more antagonistic climate, they worry the Senate and they worry the President; in all, they create a record which opponents of the treaty can work off. Some White House representatives went to see McNamara and warned him what was coming. McNamara was rather casual about it at first. He did not think that they were that close to a treaty. Anyway, if he made his case too soon, it would be easy for the opposition to counter it. Let Stennis have his hearings, he said, and we'll wait. The White House people bowed to his superior judgment.

A few weeks later they heard that John McCone had lent CIA specialists on nuclear weapons to Stennis, to help him make the case against the treaty— McCone had always opposed the treaty—and the White House people sensed that things might be more serious than they had imagined, and that this was in effect a confirmation that Stennis and McCone thought the treaty might be close. So Mac Bundy's deputy, Carl Kaysen, got together with Abe Chayes, the State Department's legal adviser, and with McNaughton, who was an expert on arms control, and decided that their instincts about being worried were good ones. They went back to McNamara and spelled out their doubts;

he listened for a few moments and then said—I agree, you're right and I was wrong; it is more serious, and you're now the committee to oversee the executive branch's argument. McNaughton is the chief, and you're to put together our case, check out who the witnesses are, and balance the record.

Thus were the Stennis hearings negated. As summer ended and it became a question of going before the Senate with the treaty, the Administration was far from confident about congressional support (later the 80–19 vote would imply that it had been a piece of cake all along; the truth was that the balance had seemed quite fragile at the start, and a vote near the two thirds needed for ratification was really no victory; it was almost an incitement to enemies as much as a change in the Cold War). With a Senate vote looming ahead, the Administration decided to test the waters in its own party. It sent an emissary to Dean Acheson to find out how Acheson felt on the treaty. It was a delicate mission, for Acheson, though a Democrat, was a good deal more hard-line than most of the young men running the government, and his opposition at this point might be critical, might just divide the Democrats in the Senate and encourage opposition to the treaty. They found, however, that Acheson was surprisingly sympathetic, but he did say there was something he objected to, and that was the way Averell Harriman was using the treaty negotations to promote himself to Secretary of State. Couldn't they do something about Averell, make him act his age? And so the message was brought back to the White House, and slowly they put together their forces on the Hill. It had not always been a sure thing, but the vote was very good, better than they expected, and the President was pleased. It was a highly personal victory; it had not been some force loose in the country which had pushed him forward, with the Administration harnessing it at the last minute (as civil rights would be), but rather something that his Administration had committed itself to and pushed through. He told friends that he had made the test ban the keystone of his foreign policy; if he lost in 1964 because of it he would be willing to pay that price.

In the fall the President had been scheduled to go on a tour of Western states that Mike Mansfield had promoted, a conservation tour in essence, where he would praise wide open spaces and high mountains and clean rivers. It was not a subject which particularly interested him (conservation was not yet ecology), but Kennedy was glad to be leaving Washington. The trip did not start well. He made two poor appearances, and then in Billings, Montana, he was scheduled to give another boring speech, boring himself and his audience, and in the middle of it he mentioned the test-ban treaty, and as he did, the crowd responded with force and immediacy. It was a real rapport, not the carefully calculated applause lines which often mark a political speech, hackneyed calls to party or national fidelity written into a speech, the audience responding faithfully if listlessly on cue. Kennedy, who was above all a good politician, whose ear was fine and always tuned, and who sensed his audience well, adjusted immediately and continued on the peace theme, accelerating the tempo and the intensity, and the crowd responded. He talked of the nuclear confrontations of the last two years, first Berlin and then Cuba, and he said: "What we hope to do is lessen the chance of a military collision between these two great nuclear powers which together have the power to kill three hundred million people in the short space of a day. That is what we are seeking to avoid. That is why we support the test-ban treaty. Not because things are going to be easier in our lives, but because we have a chance to avoid being burned."

From then on through the Far West, the trip was the same; he strayed more and more from conservation and into the test-ban treaty, and everywhere the crowds were very good, and very responsive. The last night he went to Salt Lake City, where the crowds along the route were the best yet, and when he entered the Mormon Tabernacle, allegedly the enemy camp, he received a five-minute standing ovation as he walked in. Here again, in what was alleged to be Birch country, Goldwater territory, he challenged the theses of the far right and talked of the problems of living in a complicated world. He had long suspected that the right in America was overrated as a political force, that there was an element of blackmail to its power, and now he was convinced that the country was going past old and rigid fears of the Communists, that it was probably ahead of Washington in its comprehension of the world and its willingness to accept it (and if not ahead of Washington, at least far ahead of where Washington thought it was). He sensed that there was a deep longing for a sane peace and sane world. He knew that Goldwater would be his opponent in 1964 and now he felt that he could beat Goldwater badly and end some of the fears which had haunted American politics since the hardening of the Cold War. That and his own popularity, the fact that he was no longer considered too young. The 100,000 margin was a thing of the past.

The following evening both Tom Wicker and Sander Vanocur, the *New York Times* and the NBC White House correspondents, respectively, sought out Press Secretary Pierre Salinger and suggested that the Western trip had uncovered a new and powerful issue. "Yes," said Salinger, "you're right. We've found that peace is an issue." So it had come that in the last months of his life his Presidency had turned, and not by chance, it had coincided with the first major step away from the barren path of the Cold War. It was perhaps not surprising that the first step away from the glacial quality of the Cold War would take place with the Soviet Union on something like a test-ban treaty. It was an area of less political risk; there were checks, on-site inspections against violation, and these were part of the treaty. The burden of proof in a domestic political confrontation would be on the opposition to a treaty:

Why do you oppose it, what proof have you against it? But on the question of whether or not a country would go Communist, the risk was higher, the burden of proof would be on the Administration rather than on the right-wing opposition. The question would be, Why did you lose that particular country? rather than, Was the loss of that country worth a nuclear confrontation? Was it worth a major American land war? So the first break had taken place here, and though it was historically a small break, it was a beginning, and it belonged to both Kennedy and Khrushchev. By that special irony the problems which had haunted him in his meeting with Khrushchev in Vienna in 1961 were past him now, he had come to terms with them, with his own sense of himself, with Khrushchev's estimate of him, and above all, with his country's estimate of him. But Vietnam, which he had conceived of as part of the price of making American power and determination credible to the Communists, was coming apart even as the U.S.-Soviet balance seemed to be stabilizing.

FOR A BRIEF MOMENT AFTER DIEM'S DEATH, VIETNAMESE OFFICERS were able to report honestly about what had happened in the war, what the situation was. The embassy was staggered under the impact of what was coming in from the field; the situation was far worse than it had expected, even in some of the more pessimistic quarters. There was, it turned out, no strategic hamlet program in the Delta to speak of; in many areas where the embassy had been reasonably confident, it turned out there had been few incidents precisely because the Vietcong totally controlled an area and did not need to launch any attacks. (As the reports came in, the Harkins-MACV line would immediately change to accept negative aspects of the reporting and claim that it had been going very well until the coup, but since then, the government had completely fallen apart and the war had started to go badly.) One brief example will suffice; about two weeks after the coup I went to the 7th Division area just below Saigon in the Mekong Delta; there a new general, Pham Van Dong, was conducting an operation. General Dong was talking about the misreporting and pointed to a district chief, said that the district chief had been an old aide of his and would tell the truth. "How many villages are there in your district?" the general asked him.

"Twenty-four," answered the official.

"And how many do you control?" asked Dong.

"Eight," answered the official.

"And how many," said Dong with a grin, "did you tell Saigon you controlled?"

"Twenty-four," said the official, looking somewhat sheepish.

ON NOVEMBER 21 HENRY CABOT LODGE FLEW TO HONOLULU ON
the first leg of a trip to Washington, where he planned to tell the President
that the situation was much worse than they thought; even Lodge, who had
been pushing the idea that the war was going badly, was shocked at just how
discouraging it really was, and he planned to tell Kennedy that there was
serious doubt as to whether any government could make it any more. He
never delivered the report; in San Francisco he heard the news of the assassination in Dallas, and that Lyndon Johnson was sworn in. Lodge asked the new
President if he should simply return to Saigon; no, said Johnson, they ought
to talk anyway. And so they met, and the message, that it was all bad in
Vietnam, that hard decisions were ahead and not very far ahead, was delivered to a brand-new President, unsure of himself, unsure of the men around
him, unsure of his relationship to the country, and the country's acceptance
of him. He was above all unsure of himself in foreign affairs, more suspicious
of the world around him and of enemies than his predecessors. (A few weeks
later a group of reporters gathered to have dinner with Johnson at the home
of Phil Potter of the Baltimore *Sun,* an old Johnson friend. The reporters
asked various questions. Russell Baker, one of them, asked what the first thing
was that had gone through Johnson's mind as the shots were fired and Rufus
Youngblood threw himself on Johnson. "That the Communists had done it,"
Johnson said, and Baker would remember being shocked by the reply, it had
seemed so primitive.)

If Vietnam was to be saved, Lodge said, it was Johnson who would have to
make the tough decisions. "I am not going to lose Vietnam," the new President
answered. "I am not going to be the President who saw Southeast Asia go the
way China went." Lodge then asked him what kind of political support he had.
"I don't think Congress wants us to let the Communists take over Vietnam,"
Johnson answered. It was the first sign. There would not be many more for a
while, but it was an instant response and an important one. But hard decisions
on Vietnam were the last thing he wanted right away; he wanted first to help
the nation (and himself) absorb the psychic shock it had just gone through
(which he did by a whirlwind of activity), to establish as much continuity as
possible, to hold on to the Kennedy men, not just the big Kennedy men at first,
but all of them. ("I need you more than he did," he would say, pressing them,
pushing them, imploring them to stay. He invited the White House people, not
just Bundy but many of them, to lunch, a friendly swim first, then everyone was
marched over to the swimming pool, stripped down naked in a tiny dressing
room, with the result that Robert Komer was so nervous that he dove in with his
glasses on, and the rest of the swim was devoted to diving for Komer's glasses.)
He intended to secure the Kennedy legacy, prove his own worthiness to accept
the torch by pushing the Kennedy legislation through Congress, then he would
run for President against Goldwater in 1964, and finally, elected President in

his own right, have a Johnsonian Presidency, a big one, an Administration all his own. All that would take time, and for a start he wanted to hold the world at bay; he did not need any additional and extraneous problems from the world, and particularly not from Vietnam.

So the men around him set out almost immediately to hold the line, to protect the President, to delay decisions on Vietnam as long as possible, to keep it, if at all possible, off the front pages, to make as few decisions for as long as possible. Vietnam, however, was his, and a few days later he walked over to the State Department, assembled the gentlemen of that vast house of employment, and reminded them that he was the only President they had (just to make sure that they got the message, he had taken Speaker of the House John McCormack with him, that trembling, frail old man who was next in line in succession, a graphic illustration of the truth of Johnson's words). He gave them a pep talk, emphasizing the importance of what they did, the difficulty under which they did it, the lack of recognition, saying he understood all this (which was not true. Of the many departments of the government, they constituted the one he was least sympathetic to; his view was not unlike that of Joe Kennedy. He believed them sissies, snobs, lightweights who sacrificed too little and thought themselves better than their country). He closed with one statement which sent cold chills into a few of the doubters who had been working on Vietnam under Harriman: "And before you go to bed at night I want you to do one thing for me: ask yourself this one question . . ." Pause. Then slowly, for emphasis, each word a sentence: *"What have I done for Vietnam today?"* Then he left. Almost three years earlier, Douglas MacArthur had told John Kennedy, in a discussion about the coming problems of Asia, that the chickens were coming home to roost for Kennedy. But instead they would come home for Lyndon Johnson.

JOHN KENNEDY WAS DEAD. HIS LEGACY WAS A MIXED ONE. HE HAD come in at the latter part of the Cold War; at the beginning he had not challenged it, though he had, in the last part of his Administration, begun to temper it. On Vietnam his record was more than cloudy. More than any other member of his Administration, he knew the dangers of a deep U.S. involvement, the limits of what Caucasian troops could achieve on Vietnamese soil, and yet he had significantly deepened that involvement. He had escalated the number of Americans there to 16,900 at the time of his death, with more than 70 dead (each dead American became one more rationale for more dead Americans); more important, he had markedly escalated the rhetoric and the rationale for being there. Although he seriously questioned the wisdom of a combat commitment, and at the end had grave doubts about the viability of the counterinsurgency program, whether we should be there at all, he had never shown those doubts in public, from the rostrum of the bully pulpit. The only thing he had expressed doubts about was the Diem regime, that and little more. His successor had to deal not so much with Kennedy's inner doubts so carefully and cautiously expressed, but with his public statements, all supportive of the importance and significance of Vietnam. In addition, his speeches and programs had raised the importance of Vietnam in American minds; his commitment had, by the publicity his Administration gave it, become that much more vital, and had led to that many more speeches, that many more newspaper stories, that many more television stories on the Huntley-Brinkley show.

Kennedy had of course in the last couple of months privately expressed a nagging doubt: Could it be done? Was it worth doing? He had always feared the combat-troop idea; the French, he said repeatedly, had not been able to deal with the Vietnamese with 300,000 men, how could we? This was a political war; one could not produce military answers. He was increasingly dubious about the whole thing, about just how effective any Western presence which required force could be in Asia. It seemed to do more harm than good in order to survive. Just before he died he took Michael Forrestal aside and told him that he wanted Forrestal to make a special trip to Cambodia to see Prince Sihanouk. Forrestal's specific mission would be to convey Kennedy's personal and political warmth, Kennedy's belief in the kind of neutralism Sihanouk followed, that we felt we understood him better now, and that we wished him great success. That in itself marked a change from the more hostile attitude of the past, when Washington had been forced to accept the essentially anti-Cambodian anti-Sihanouk attitude of South Vietnam. In the last few weeks of his life he had talked with some aides, such as Kenny O'Donnell, about trying to paper it over through 1964, keeping the commitment away from Goldwater as a target, and then trying to negotiate his way out. He had spoken similar words to Mike Mansfield, though omitting the reference to the 1964 election, simply talking about de-escalating, letting out his misgivings about our involvement. The men who were close to him in the White House felt that these doubts were growing all the time. And certainly he had been burned in the past. He knew the limits of force, and he knew the limits of what the generals recommended, and the limits of institutional wisdom. What was it he had said to Harriman at the time of Laos: It's political, if they don't want me to go to war in Cuba ninety miles from home, how can I go to war 12,000 miles away? And yet, and yet . . . More skeptical, more subtle than his public pronouncements, he had nonetheless failed to deal with Vietnam as a political problem. His response, if not combat troops, had been highly operational and functional and programmatic. He had worked to conceal the truth about Vietnam from the public and had markedly increased the American commitment, and he had severely limited the hand of a fresh, unsure successor. And he had passed on to that successor the brilliant, activist can-do Kennedy team, a team somewhat tempered in the past by Kennedy's own skepticism, but which now found itself harnessed to the classic can-do President. He had deepened the commitment there, and he had, in a way, always known better. He had preached, both in his book and in his speeches, about the importance of political courage, but his Administration had been reasonably free from acts of courage, such as turning around the irrationality of the China policy. In this most crucial area the record was largely one of timidity.

Chapter Sixteen

LYNDON JOHNSON SEEMED IN THOSE FIRST FEW MONTHS TO BE always in motion, running, doing, persuading; if later much of the nation, bitter over its seemingly unscheduled and unchartered journey into Southeast Asia, turned on him and remembered his years with distaste, it was grateful for him then, and with good reason. His mandate seemed to be to hold the country together, to continue to exhort from those around him their best, to heal wounds and divisions. Kennedy had been the man who experimented, who ventured into new areas, civil rights, and in so doing caused division and pain. He had jarred our nerves in taking us places we had not intended to go; now Johnson would heal not just the pain caused by the assassination but the tensions caused in the venturesome days of some of the Kennedy policies. The healer. If later one of the Johnson qualities which caused doubts among the nation's critics was his force, the very *abundance* of it—the great capacity to plead, to bully, to beg, to implore, the capacity to manipulate them to what he considered his interest and the nation's interest—in those early days he was much hailed for it. He was not berated for being a manipulator then, that term would come later. His ability to drive men to a program and policy beyond what they themselves considered wise was considered a national asset, since the men he was manipulating were largely old tired conservative Southern congressmen who headed committees and thus blocked progress. A powerful Presidency was still considered very desirable in those days; the problem was seen as too much power in the Congress and too little in the executive branch, which was exactly the way that man of the Congress recently transferred to the executive office, Lyndon B. Johnson, felt.

THE DECISION IN THOSE EARLY MONTHS WAS TO HOLD THE LINE ON Vietnam, to hold it down and delay decisions. Too many other things took primacy over it; since Vietnam had always, as far as American policy there was concerned, reflected American developments rather than Vietnamese events (the Buddhist crisis was one of the rare occasions which were primarily *Vietnamese* and contrary to what the Americans wanted), it was, despite the collapse of successive governments, imperative to keep Vietnam quiet. Though the men around Johnson were crisis-mentality men, men who delighted in the great international crisis because it centered the action right there in the White House—the meetings, the decisions, the tensions, the power, *they* were movers and activists, and this was what they had come to Washington for, to meet these challenges and handle them—in 1964 they deliberately avoided a sense of crisis on Vietnam, with the exception of the Tonkin Gulf incident, which became an incident in large part because they needed a congressional resolution. Thus events which might have been played up were played down. Provocations by the other side, the very same kind of alleged provocations which in 1965, when we were ready and geared up (that is, the presidential race run, the President elected, the inaugural given) would stir us to action, retaliation, escalation, first of words and then deeds, these acts were disregarded in 1964.

In Saigon there were attempts to stop the coups, to stop these malignant acts which kept getting in the American newspapers and which made it harder and harder to convince the American public that the struggle there was necessary. So 1964 became a year when Vietnam could no longer be kept on the back burner; events there would thrust the country, the frailty of it all, in front of the American people, but it was a year in which the highest level of American policy makers refused to accept the necessity for making important decisions, tried to delay them, to buy the President a little more time. Besides, Lyndon Johnson liked choices and options. So it was a lost year; opportunities were lost for possible political negotiation, of re-evaluation of American attitudes, of perhaps convincing the American public that it wasn't worth it, that the Vietnamese themselves did not care that much about the war. Instead of that, they held the line. They did not think time was working against them and decided not to deal with Vietnam in 1964, but to keep their options open. They would not be entrapped, they would make their decisions carefully and in their own time (they were above all functional, operational, *tactical* men, not really intellectuals, and tactical men think in terms of options, while intellectuals less so; intellectuals might think in terms of the sweep of history and might believe that twelve months would make little difference in Vietnam, that if the sweep of history was bad in 1964, it would probably, if anything, be a good deal worse in 1965). They could, they thought, control events, but it was all an illusion. Time had been closing off options relentlessly since 1945 and 1946, when it would have been easy to have a political settlement, a favorable one, with the United States dealing from strength, but ever since those days, the possibility had steadily diminished as the other side, the Vietnamese Communist forces, had become progressively stronger and the United States had become increasingly committed to the idea (then hardly part of its global outlook) that Vietnam was vital.

Thus past years had shown that time diminished options, and this would be true in 1964 as well. A year later the Communists would be that much stronger, the government in Saigon that much weaker, and the United States, having used force in Tonkin, that much more committed. Events, George Ball would write in 1965, a year later, in beginning his final and most important paper in trying to keep us out, and drawing on a quote from Emerson, are in the saddle and tend to ride mankind. When they came to make the final fateful decisions, there would be options, but the real ones would be long since lost; the options they would deal with in 1965 were artificial ones. Given their outlook and their conception of the country and of their own political futures, they would be driven to certain inevitable, highly predictable decisions, but they still had the illusion that they could control events. They were rational men, that above all; they were not ideologues. Ideologues are predictable and they were not, so the idea that those intelligent, rational, cultured, civilized men had been caught in a terrible trap by early 1964 and that they spent an entire year letting the trap grow tighter was unacceptable; they would have been the first to deny it. If someone in those days had called them aside and suggested that they, all good rational men, were tied to a policy of deep irrationality, layer and layer of clear rationality based upon several great false assumptions and buttressed by a deeply dishonest reporting system which created a totally false data bank, they would have lashed out sharply that they did indeed know where they were going.

Yet the old dilemma of Indochina was now finally coming to its illogical conclusions. Being good and decent men, they could not use nuclear weapons, not on first strike at least, perhaps in retaliation, though. They were the policy makers of the greatest nuclear power in the world, except that they could not use those weapons—indeed, their private defense policies were based on the unwillingness to use nuclear weapons—particularly against a small nation in a guerrilla war. Yet because of the Cold War legacy, the loss of China, they could not lose more territory (contested territory; uncontested territory was another thing) to the Communists. And yet we could not fight a long limited war. Korea had been deeply unpopular, and now finally the illusion of a viable South Vietnamese government able and anxious to fight for its own sovereignty was dying. We could not let go, and yet we did not want to get in.

THE LEADERSHIP OF COURSE WAS VERY GOOD. THE LOSS OF KENNEDY was mourned, and yet Johnson, this new President . . . he was a powerhouse, a mover. He went after the same programs that Kennedy had wanted, but with more force. McGeorge Bundy, sensing grave doubts about Johnson in his White House shop, where the relationship to Kennedy had been so personal, where the men had been something of a reflection both of Kennedy and Bundy, lectured some of them, telling them not to be such Eastern snobs about Johnson, to cast that arrogance aside. Perhaps he did not have the elegance of his predecessor, but he got things done, and perhaps, being somewhat weak in foreign affairs, he would need them more; there would perhaps be a greater role to play. So it would, some thought, be an Olympian union, the Kennedy staff and style in foreign affairs, and the Johnsonian force in domestic events. And if they were impressed by Johnson, not just the force, but the fact that there was, for all the braggadocio, far more subtlety to the man than anyone had realized, as if some of the roughness of style and of language was a deliberate attempt to hide his sensitivity—he was impressed by them. He had never had men like these working for him. McNamara, the head of Ford Motor Company. "The ablest man I've ever met," he called him. Bundy, flashingly brilliant, the dean of Harvard College, working for this old boy from San Marcos State Teachers College. He did not really like Bundy, sensing at times a patronizing attitude, though occasionally so delighting in him, in Mac's style—Mac briefing, tidying up a complicated question, so professional, so clean—that a small amused smile would come to his face, like a hitting coach watching a fine hitter or a connoisseur watching a great ballet dancer. Mac was dancing, and dancing for *him*. It was an art form. And Rusk . . . Rusk had been the head of the Rockefeller Foundation, a Rhodes scholar, and Rusk was intelligent and cautious, a wise person.

He was in awe of men like these and he judged them by their labels. Other men who had worked for him were just as able, but he knew them all, knew their faults and their weaknesses, and he had put his stamp on them. But these men were different. They were not Johnson men, he had not put his stamp on them, finally broken them, made them his, seen that they too, like everyone else, had their faults. That would be later, and only Rusk would be spared; McNamara would be someone who had "headed Ford for only one week." Bundy was "just a smart kid. Period." But now this remarkable team that Jack Kennedy had assembled was working for him, Lyndon Johnson, whom in the old days they would never have even voted for, let alone worked for. Lyndon Johnson, who knew all the faults of some of the great men on the Hill, was markedly uncritical, and accepted judgments from them which he might have questioned from his own men. Years later George Ball, who, having fought with Johnson on the war and lost, retained a considerable affection for him, would say of that period and Johnson's relationship with the Kennedy luminaries that Johnson did not suffer from a poor education, he suffered from a belief that he had had a poor education.

IN 1964 THE LEADERSHIP, CONFIDENT OF ITSELF AND ITS PRO-fessionalism, held back on making decisions on Vietnam and allowed the bureaucracy to plan for war. There were signs of this in early 1964; indeed, if you put the signs together in retrospect, they were largely negative. However, that all seemed more obvious later; they were well concealed at the time. At the time, the political men around the President were busy planning for his election campaign, and for the Great Society to come, and they were sure that Vietnam was somehow a stumbling block over which they would not stumble, that Johnson, in the words of the speeches being written, wanted no wider war, that he would, as he himself thought, reason with the other side. Yet gradually, even in early 1964, the play was being held closer and closer, and there were fewer and fewer players and decision makers; others, doubters, were slowly being cut out of the play. Those who were running it were running it on a straight nuts-and-bolts basis, and the various forecasts of the intelligence agencies were being brushed aside. These estimates were still very dark, but the attitudes were still very programmatic.

McNamara was learning the hard way about Vietnam; when he went there in December 1963 he had begun to know what to look for in the field. He still did not know how truly resilient the other side was or how weak the fabric of the South was (in discovering that the other side was stronger, he did not realize that the balance was virtually irreversible; he believed that more effort, the right programs, more matériel might turn the tide). He had also learned how to penetrate Harkins' briefings and he had become angry over what Harkins had told him in the past, and it showed this time. There was one session when he was questioning a junior officer and he sensed that the junior officer was about to be candid, except that Harkins and General Stilwell kept interrupting, trying to intercede and stop the young officer from answering. Suddenly McNamara turned to them, the anger open and visible, his face red —"I asked that Major the question and I want an answer." It was a very tense and bitter scene. On his return to Washington he got together with McCone, who was also bothered by the reporting from Saigon, feeling that too much had been filtered out in the previous years, and they decided to do a joint CIA-Defense intelligence survey of the situation, which they felt was very bad; at least they ought to serve the President with as honest an evaluation as possible. But the Joint Chiefs of Staff blocked it, they wanted to control their flow of information; reporting and re-evaluation of reporting was a very sensitive subject. The proposed survey might reflect unfavorably on some very important generals, and it might, by its forecasts for the future, take some of the play away from the military (instead of just reporting how bad the situation was, it might predict the likelihood of the other side to reinforce). And it might—which it did—give a far more pessimistic appraisal of the status of the war than MACV was providing.

So the JCS held off, but the CIA decided to go ahead with the study anyway, and sent a team of about twelve men, all experts, all with about five years' experience in the country. They were billed officially as "joint team," though the JCS sent back channel messages to MACV saying not to believe it. Once again the military was able to hold on to its version of reality, this time against the best efforts of the Secretary of Defense; the report of the special team was very pessimistic, but it had no effect on the overall evaluation.

Above all, there was no real investigation of what kind of a deal might be worked out with Hanoi and the Vietcong, what neutralization might mean. So a year for political exploration was lost, and the reason for this was to be found in the character and outlook of the Secretary of State of the United States, a man who believed in force, who believed in the commitment, who believed that the proper role for the State Department would come after the military had turned the war around and State was charged with negotiating a sound peace, and who believed that the Secretary should defer to the President, should not be a strong figure in his own right. Where a Harriman or a Ball might have seized the initiative, might have begun his own explorations for peace, might have decided that politically Vietnam was hopeless, and therefore militarily as well, Rusk was content to wait, to let events come to him. He was convinced that the military estimates were accurate, that the generals could achieve what they said they could. He was a forceful, determined, hard-working, intelligent man who was in charge of the political aspects of American policy, and he would have made a very great Secretary of Defense, it was his natural constituency. He did not push negotiations in that period because he did not believe in them, and he feared that the very idea of negotiations would make the weak fabric of Saigon even weaker.

DEAN RUSK HATED TO CHALLENGE THE MILITARY ON ITS NEEDS AND its requests because he feared a State-Defense split such as had existed between Dean Acheson and Secretary of Defense Louis Johnson, and he would do almost anything to avoid it. In particular, he did not like to be out front on a policy, and he was content to let McNamara surge into the vacuum of leadership, poach on his terrain. All of this was the bane of his subordinates at State, who again and again, when they heard of some projected Defense policy for Vietnam, would go to Rusk and protest it, trying to get him to intervene, to limit it all. Very rarely would they succeed even to the extent of getting Rusk to call McNamara and bring the matter up, and when he did even this, he was usually brushed aside by an assertive and confident McNamara. Thus in 1965 when State heard that the military was about to use massive B-52 bombing raids on Vietnam, subordinates went to Rusk and pleaded with him to block the bombing; its effect in Vietnam was dubious and its effect throughout the rest of the world was likely to be disastrous. They had argued forcefully with him and finally Rusk had picked up the phone and called McNamara.

They listened as Rusk relayed their doubts: "Bob, some of the boys here are uneasy about it." Was it really necessary, he asked, he hated to bother McNamara on a question like this . . . Then Rusk was silent and they could almost visualize McNamara at the other end crisply reassuring Rusk. And then McNamara was finished and Rusk was talking again: "Okay, Bob, in for a dime, in for a dollar." And he hung up.

DEAN RUSK WAS A MAN WITHOUT A SHADOW. HE LEFT NO PAPERS behind, few memories, few impressions. Everyone spoke well of him and no one knew him, he was the hidden man; he concealed, above all, himself and his feelings. All sorts of people thought they were good friends of his. They had known him for a long time—Rhodes scholars, old and intimate friends, called by someone wanting to find out about Rusk, said they would be glad, eager to talk, yes, Dean was a very old friend, and then it would always end the same way, the preliminary insights into Dean, that he was a good fellow, responsible, hard-working, intelligent, serious—that and little more. Perhaps a sense finally that he had never been young. And then the faltering admission that on reflection they knew very little about him.

He loved being Secretary of State, the title and the trappings and what it meant. He was aware, to the day, of how long he had held office, and he would say things like "I am now the second oldest foreign minister in the world" . . . "Today I am the second most senior member of NATO." One record that he wanted and never achieved was that of Cordell Hull for American longevity; Rusk held the office for the second longest period in history. Not bad. A small corner of the history books. Many of his critics, the ones in the Kennedy Administration, talked about his imminent departure and denigrated him, but they left after their two years, sometimes voluntarily and sometimes not so voluntarily, to write their books, while Rusk remained. Always the professional. It was an important part of him, that foreign affairs was a profession and he was a professional, a serious man doing serious things. He had studied at it all those years, apprenticed at it under the great men, Marshall, Acheson, Lovett, worked his way up in State, where his rise was nothing less than meteoric (his detractors forgot that at a time right after World War II when the competition at State was ferocious, Rusk rose more quickly than anyone else in the Department). Then he was briefly out of government, went into the shadow-cabinet world of the foundations, and then back to Washington, back to the beloved profession, a chance to hold the torch passed not so much by Roosevelt, Truman and Kennedy as by Marshall, Acheson and Lovett, hold it and pass it on to someone else, eight years later, with the world in the same condition, probably not any better, but hopefully no worse, that was all he asked, he would say. No better, no worse.

He was a modest man in an Administration not known for its modesty, self-effacing in an Administration not known for self-effacement. He hated the amateurs, the meddlers, the intellectuals around him, playing with power, testing their theories on the world. Quick, glib men dancing around Georgetown cocktail parties, Schlesingers, Galbraiths, Goodwins, Kaysens, people of that ilk. Making their direct phone calls to the President, breaking regular channels with their phone calls and shortcuts.

He worried about the liberals, he was one himself, although not too much of one: did they really understand the Communists, weren't they too likely to come to Washington just long enough to meddle in foreign affairs and fall victim to their own good intentions? Foreign affairs was something special, it was filled with pitfalls for well-meaning idealists. A brief scene: 1962. The Soviets had apparently resumed testing. Kennedy was trying to decide whether to test again. Adlai Stevenson asked what would happen if the United States did not test. Jerome Wiesner answered that American weapons were better, so that if there was a delay in the resumption of testing, what he called a benefit of the doubt delay, it would not make much difference. Then Stevenson (would-be Secretary of State, the man for whom in 1960 Rusk had served as the Scarsdale chairman of "Citizens for Stevenson," Rusk's highest political office) said that perhaps the United States ought to take a small risk in the strategic balance on a question like this, that it ought to try for moral leadership. Rusk interjected at this point: "I wouldn't make the smallest concession for moral leadership. It's much overrated." A young White House aide remembered the conversation, which shocked him, and from then on always thought of Rusk in that context; he thought that when Rusk died that should be inscribed on his tombstone, his epitaph.

A PROUD MAN. A POOR MAN. PROUD OF HIS POVERTY IN A WAY, sensitive about it, but that sensitivity showed in his pride (who else in that chic egalitarian Kennedy period, when they were pushing so hard to improve public education and get an education bill passed, sent his children to public schools?). He was almost defiantly proud of his lack of wealth, mentioning it often to aides in the Department, that this job had cost him money. When he was first offered State in 1960, he told Harriman that he did not think he could accept it because the job meant a considerable financial sacrifice. Harriman told him not to worry, there would be plenty of job opportunities, lucrative offers after he finished, but Harriman was wrong. Neither could have foreseen Vietnam and what it would do to Rusk, making him virtually unemployable, making him, because of his decision to ride it through, the prime target for its critics, or the second prime target after Johnson. He would be vilified, but he was proud and refused to answer the attacks, the criticism, he was above it. Friends pleaded with him to answer some of the criticism, to fight back, but he deemed it improper, not so much for himself personally, but for the office.

A controlled man. Always patient. An extremely good diplomat in at least the limited sense of the word, that is, being diplomatic with other human beings. He would go up to the United Nations every year to meet the vast hordes of foreign ministers come to the opening session, meeting with each one, handling them well, believing that his aides, who thought that this particularly thankless task should go to an underling, were wrong (just as he thought they were wrong in 1962 when he refused to forgo presiding at one of the two huge diplomatic dinners given by the Secretary of State each year to go to Nassau, where Kennedy was meeting with Harold Macmillan to discuss U.S. and European nuclear defense systems. He sent George Ball in his place, instead of going to Nassau himself and letting Ball handle the dinner, which gave McNamara a chance to play too large—and clumsy—a role at Nassau. Those who knew the role of the Secretary believed, first, that it was all too typical of his deference to Defense, and second, that Rusk, more cautious, more thoughtful and more reflective than McNamara, might have stopped the decisions of Nassau, decisions which encouraged De Gaulle to go it alone in Europe and keep England out of the Common Market). When he met all the foreign ministers, he gave each equal time, showing the physical stamina of an old workhorse, great endurance, and always that control. Never, if possible, public or private nakedness of man or spirit or ideas, even at what many thought his greatest triumph, an appearance before a House committee considering civil rights legislation when he startled everyone by giving very strong testimony ("If I were a Negro I think I might rise up")—one of his finest moments, the committee applauding, the press applauding, his aides proud, delighted. When he left the committee room he turned to a friend and said, "You don't think I went too far, do you?" Control was important, it was part of your discipline, of your attitude; it went with the position. If you lacked it, how could the men below you have it? If an aide walked in on Rusk while he was reading a piece of paper, the Secretary would continue to read it, even as the aide was on top of him. It was a highly disconcerting habit, and Rusk would explain simply that years before, he had vowed that when he picked up a piece of paper to read, he would finish it. Nothing swayed him. Sometimes that conscious quality of his control struck some of the men around him as in part at least a protection against insecurity; by holding strictly to the form he was protecting himself, not letting himself go.

He was a modest man: a symbol, in personal style, with the control and the sense of the adversity of life, the discipline needed to meet that adversity, of a passing era. You played by the rules of the game and the rules were very strict, you did not indulge the whim of your own personality, you served at the whim and will of those above you. Dean Rusk did not, so to speak, do his thing. He was the product of an era, and a particularly poor area and harsh culture where exactly the opposite behavior was respected and cherished: the compromising and sacrificing of your own will and desire and prejudices for the good of others, the good of a larger force. Sacrifice was important, and the very act of sacrifice was its own reward. All this was a part of him; he was, the men around him thought, a true Calvinist. Indeed, years later when Senator Eugene McCarthy wondered if Rusk's views on China were real, a friend assured him that they were, that Rusk was very much in the tradition of Dulles, a Calvin come to set policy, but McCarthy, who loved to mix theology and politics, shook his head and said no, not Calvin; Calvin had only written down his philosophy, he had not inflicted it on others. Rusk, McCarthy said, was Cromwell to Dulles' Calvin. He was Rusk, the poor Georgia boy to whom the Good Lord had given a good mind and a strong body and a great capacity for work, and it was his obligation to use those qualities. This was something that Lyndon Johnson, who had that same sense and came from similar origins, understood completely. Rusk was, in his way, something of a hired hand to these great institutions. His upbringing had taught him to serve, not to question (which immediately set him apart from many of the Kennedy people who had been propelled by their propensity to question everything around them). Once, in an interview in Georgia, Rusk talked of the traits instilled in him by a Calvinist father. He defined it as a "sense of the importance of right and wrong which was something that was before us all the time. I think there was a sense of propriety, a sense of constitutional order, a sense of each playing his part in the general scheme of things, with a good deal of faith and confidence, with a passionate interest in education . . ." He did not question these institutions; they had become what they were not by happenstance but because wise men who had thought a long time had deliberately fashioned them that way; nor did he severely question their current attitudes, which again had not arisen by happenstance; indeed he found American and Western institutions admirable in contrast to the disorder which existed in the rest of the world.

He was part of that generation which felt gratitude for what was offered him. It was in that sense generational; his attitudes were close to those of a previous generation, while in the Dean Rusk family the values would change, would be less conservative: a son would work for the Urban League and would be part of the anti-Whitney Young movement because Young was too moderate; a daughter would marry a Negro. In this family, as in many others, children were more confident, more willing to challenge the existing order. "Rusk," said someone at the White House who knew him well and liked and respected him, "was different from the rest of us. He was poor and we had not been, but he really was more of my father's generation. You don't show feelings, you don't complain, you work very hard and you get ahead, and there was a sense that his mind was not his own property, that he was not allowed to let it take him where it wanted to go; there were instead limits to what you could think. Strict confines."

THE LAND WAS HARD AND UNFERTILE AND TAUGHT ITS OWN LESSONS, stern lessons. The virtues were the old ones and the sins were the old ones, and the Bible still lived. No one ever expected life to be easy, and forgiveness was not the dominating trait. It was not a land which produced indulgence of any sort, and people who grew up there did not talk about life styles. They talked about God, about serving, about doing what He wanted. It was much admired to make use of what God had given you and to obey authority. If you didn't, dark prophecies were offered and you were considered, at the least, wayward. One kept emotions inside. Rusk himself on the subject: "We were rather a quiet family about expressing our emotions under any circumstances. I think this was part of the reticence. Perhaps it goes with the Calvinism. Perhaps it comes from the Scotch-Irish. Perhaps it comes from the tough battle with the soil in the family that has to wrest a living out of not too productive soil in Cherokee County." Rusk remembered going to the funeral of his grandmother as a little boy. Funerals for some families in those days were noisy affairs, the deceased mourned loudly, the love and loss measured by the amount of weeping and moaning. The Rusk family was different; it asked the mourners not to cry, and the neighbors, puzzled, asked why and a member of the Rusk family answered, "We feel it inside." We feel it inside. Some fifty years later Dean Rusk would, perhaps not surprisingly, cable his ambassadors to stop using the word *feel* in their cables; he was not interested in what they felt. When he was assaulted by the Kennedy people, by the liberals, by the intelligentsia, pilloried, he always turned the other cheek. We feel it inside. Endure pain, endure insult, it is right to do so: if you have been faithful to your beliefs and your heritage, then all will right itself. Rusk and Dulles, both moralists; Dulles spouting his moralism publicly, almost flagrantly, preaching it from his international rostrum; Rusk feeling it perhaps even more deeply, keeping it inside.

His father was a preacher in a culture which produced and respected preachers, as New York City would later produce and respect psychiatrists. Stern upbringing, hard work and reverence. Other children coming to the Rusk house on Sunday mornings were allowed to look at the funny papers, but not the Rusk children, they were denied this touch of levity. The Lord's will. Later the parents softened a bit and allowed the children to read them once in a while. Though Robert Hugh Rusk was a poor white, he was not trash; though they were of modest means, there was a sense of tradition in their house and a belief in what education could do, a passion, Dean would call it. Farther west, in Texas, in almost similar circumstances a young Lyndon Johnson would grow up with the same almost mystical belief in education and what it could do.

One of twelve children, Robert Rusk had put himself through Davidson, one of the South's best schools; from there he went on to Louisville Seminary, where he became an ordained minister. Eventually he had to leave the ministry because of a throat ailment; thus perhaps the house became even more Calvinist than a preacher's house, as a kind of atonement for the failure of the vocal cords. His wife, Frances Elizabeth Clotfelter, was "the best-looking girl in Rockdale County, I believe," Rusk would say of her, the serious ambitious young preacher getting the prettiest girl. "She was a very hard-working woman, as any wife of a family in poor circumstances in those days, or modest circumstances, would be. She made most of our clothes. We did our own washing of course. I have on my front porch now the black wash pot under which I had to build hundreds of fires to fire up the family wash. She herself had gone to normal school and had done some teaching and strongly reinforced my father's interest in books and learning. And also a devout worshiper at the Presbyterian church." All three sons would do well. One rose high in government, very high indeed; Roger became a professor of physics at the University of Tennessee; and the oldest, Parks, who had less schooling because he had to do more physical work, became a successful journalist. In 1912, when Dean was three years old, heavy floods cost the Rusks their crops, and they moved to Atlanta, where the children were raised. "The land didn't want us," said Roger.

Young Dean was very church-oriented. A sister would remember him walking around the house reading the Bible aloud. The family committed the Bible to memory, and one of the best ways to learn was to read it aloud. He was active in Christian Endeavour, a sort of after-hours group of young people who put extra time and effort into the study of the Christian life. He attended church twice a week regularly, and at least until he was midway through high school he intended to become a minister, but about that time broader horizons began to open up.

It was a good boyhood, so simple and basic that Rusk believed (inaccurately) for much of his life that he was delivered by a veterinarian. There were always difficulties and hardships, but they were the kind that could be dealt with, so that there would develop in the grown man a belief that any obstacle could be overcome, that hard work made no challenge insurmountable. He got his first schooling in a simple Atlanta schoolhouse, half of which was uncovered, with canvas screens pulled over part of the building when it rained. So he went to school in the open air, carrying woolen sacks in the winter, bringing hot bricks to school in the morning and putting them in the bottom of the sack to keep it warm. In the sixth grade young Dean was told by his teacher on the first day of school that he must wear shoes the next day, they were trying to stop hookworm. Dean went home with the message to his mother. Since shoes were scarce in the Rusk family, Mrs. Rusk wrote a note saying that the teacher ought to look after her end of the job, which was educating, and Mrs. Rusk would look after her end, which was feeding and dressing the children; Dean returned the next day barefoot, and proud of it.

He would regard his own rise as a personification of the American possibilities, and he would see in the American-Rusk story a moral for other people. Cherokee County, he would later point out, was an underdeveloped area, with typhoid and other problems, but it had all changed and become modernized. "I've been able to see in my lifetime how that boyhood environment has been revolutionized with education, with technology, with county agents, and with electricity—all that helping to take the load off the backs of the people who live there. Now I can see that this can happen in one lifetime, I disregard those who say that underdeveloped countries still need two or three hundred years to develop because I know it isn't true. Because I've seen it with my own eyes."

Dean was very good in school, though once he lost in a spelling bee because when he came to the word "girl," he spelled it "gal." Could there have been a Secretary of State with origins, with traditions more perfectly attuned to Lyndon B. Johnson? It was not surprising that their relationship was different from almost any other in that period of 1964. They felt so comfortable in each other's company that if they were on a plane, they would fall into conversation that was almost giddy, like two schoolboys back together after a summer vacation. And was it not true, thought the men around Rusk, that his accent, which under Kennedy had been somewhat Scarsdale, became more Georgia again? Once Lyndon and Dean were walking around the Ranch, followed by a group of high Washington aides, Johnson taking great pride in showing all the artifacts. One in particular delighted him, an antique piece which he pointed out to the somewhat bewildered Easterners. "You and I know what this is, don't we, Dean?" There was a smile of acknowledgment from Dean of a memory which took him back many years. It was an old indoor potty.

As a young boy he had dreams that took him beyond Cherokee County; even then he was fascinated by the military. During World War I Dean, not yet ten years old, and Roger would cut out pictures of soldiers from newspapers and paste them on cardboard. Thousands of them, Roger would recall. Roger and Dean would dig thirty-foot trenches and follow all the battle plans. "There wasn't a rich kid in town who had as many soldiers as we did," said Roger Rusk, adding, "What people don't understand about Dean is how deep are his military inclinations. It's part of our Anglo-Saxon heritage. The South always had a military disposition." That tradition is very real. The South is filled with minor and major military academies, and produces an abnormally high percentage of career officers and Medal of Honor winners. This was also part of Rusk's life (both his grandfathers had fought in the Civil War, though on the Confederate side, and later when he had to fill in his security forms and was asked to list any relatives who had tried to overthrow the government of the United States, he would put down both their names).

He was a rare person in that era, a young man who went through high school and yet graduated from college with *eight* years of ROTC training, for besides his religious instruction he had come across something else which fascinated him, military training. He spent four years at Atlanta Boys High in ROTC, rising to command all ROTC units in Atlanta, student colonel. "Well, of course, in the South, most of us as we were growing up just took for granted that if there was to be trouble, if the nation was at war, that we would be in it. The tradition of the Civil War was still with us very strongly . . . We assumed there was a military duty to perform . . . We took that as a perfectly natural part of being an American." The blending of the religion and the sense of military duty, a belief in it as the most natural kind of thing, was not by any means a contradiction. The values of the region were still very close to the frontier, a hard land, with many enemies, a code which taught that if evil stalked, you did not turn the other cheek; if you were soft or tolerant of evil, it would devour you.

Rusk had been encouraged to seek a Rhodes scholarship by a high school teacher who had been to Oxford. Here was this promising young man of truly uncommon industry and discipline, the brightest boy in the school, who spoke well on his feet—why shouldn't he do well before the Rhodes interviewing board? And it was typical of Rusk, serious and single-minded, that in high school he had already set out a goal like this. He worked for two years as a clerk in a law office to earn the money to go to Davidson, where he once again excelled in his studies, his ROTC and his YMCA work, and where he compiled a sufficiently good record to become a likely candidate for a

Rhodes. He was Phi Beta Kappa and captain of the ROTC, and he played on the basketball and tennis teams, which was all very good for the Rhodes, Cecil Rhodes having preferred to advance sound minds in sound Caucasian bodies. The Rhodes committees are local blue-chip Establishment groups with a strong scent for the future good citizen. Rhodes scholars as a group tend to be intelligent but more respectable than restless, more builders than critics, and the personal interview is highly important. Those who show indications of doing good are lauded, and such qualities are respected and encouraged, but there is doubt about someone very young who is deeply alienated.

Rusk acquitted himself predictably well. He was questioned about what seemed like a contradiction in his record, his interest in international affairs and the eight years of ROTC, and answered (visions of the Fulbright committee to come) that the American eagle on the Great Seal has arrows in one claw and the olive branch in the other, and the two have to go together. He won the scholarship, and it would be the crucial link, the propellant for him. In a nation so large and so diverse there are few ways of quantifying intelligence or success or ability, so those few that exist are immediately magnified, titles become particularly important; all Rhodes scholars become brilliant, as all ex-Marines are tough. To make it in America, to rise, there has to be some sort of propellant; sheer talent helps, but except in very rare instances, talent is not enough. Money helps, family ties and connections help; for someone without these the way to the power elite can seem too far, too hopeless to challenge. The connection is often a Rhodes scholarship. It is a booster shot that young men are not unaware of, that will make the rest of their lives a good deal easier. Doors will open more readily, invitations will arrive, the phone will ring (thus one young applicant brought before the Rhodes committee was asked at the end of his interview what he would choose for the epitaph on his tombstone. He quickly answered, "Rhodes scholar," and got his grant).

From then on Rusk would be someone of note; in any application the title would jump out, *Rhodes scholar*. As a staff officer during the war, what he said would have meaning, he was a Rhodes, therefore an intellectual, a soldier-intellectual. Later, to a President of the United States under criticism from the intellectual community for his policies in Vietnam, it would seem very comforting: My Secretary of State is a Rhodes scholar. His accomplishment would make that very genuine modesty and tolerance of others even more becoming: Dean is a Rhodes scholar but he puts on no airs. So the Rhodes, coupled with Rusk's intelligence, his enormous industry and energy and ambition, would carry him far and open up the great Eastern centers of power for him. Dean Rusk, Rhodes scholar.

THESE YEARS COINCIDED WITH THE DEPRESSION BUT THAT SEEMED TO have little effect on Rusk. Other men coming out of the rural South of that period may have been affected by the poverty they saw around them, but Rusk was always interested in international affairs, not domestic ones. In his two years at Oxford, he was even by the standards of those days considered extremely hard-working and diligent; he won coveted awards in England and gained a respect, as many Americans did, for those special qualities of the British, understated humor (in rare moments when he is relaxed and feels himself among real friends, Rusk can be very funny indeed, but it is not a side of himself that he likes to show in public, as though somehow levity detracts from the office. It was only when he was among those who he knew already respected the office that he would let himself go). He also spent a semester in Germany and watched Hitler coming to power. The most lasting memory of those Oxford years was a belief that the best-educated and most elite young men of England with their Oxford Union had given Germany the wrong impression, signaling that England would not fight; it was, he would tell friends later, the worst possible indication, and England might have been better served if the signal had reflected something closer to the heart and determination of the average workingman. The lesson was that the upper class was a little spoiled and faddish, that intellectuals and elites were not entirely to be trusted, that there was often greater shrewdness and wisdom in the mainstream.

He came back to America in 1934 and took a job at Mills College in California teaching political science, wrote a little, and rose quickly, becoming dean at the age of thirty. In 1937 he married one of his students, Virginia Foisie. In 1940, with his ROTC commitments still alive, he was called to active duty as an Army captain in command of an infantry company. Shortly afterward, just before Pearl Harbor, he was put in charge of military intelligence for British Southeast Asia. Captain Rusk, Major Rusk, finally Colonel Rusk. These were good years. Playing on a great team, doing something that mattered and was of value, using all that training, effecting things; above all, being a part of something important. No one who ever knew Dean Rusk doubted that they were satisfying and exciting years. Some men had too much war, a bad war, had left too much of themselves behind and could only hope to shed the uniform the day it was over, if not sooner, but for Rusk it was a fulfilling time, with tasks he was well prepared for and found he did well. He was far from Cherokee County, and it was in a sense liberating; unlike so much of life, what you did had meaning. Studies by Lloyd Warner, the sociologist, showed that Americans had never had such a sense of purpose, usefulness, of being needed, as in the war, and Rusk was a good example.

He served first in Washington and then in the China-Burma-India theater, in the New Delhi section, where he became deputy chief of staff. He was an operations man as well, and his intelligence and extreme diligence put him a notch or two above the men around him. Two qualities emerged for the first time which were to propel him further upward. The first was that he was a very good diplomat, which was particularly important in the tense and often explosive atmosphere of Delhi, where the final days of an empire were flashing by, the final prejudices, the last kicking of the wog. True, the British were our allies and we needed them, but the Americans were idealistic, anti-imperialist, and despised British colonialism. They believed in the new order which they were helping to create, and hated the way the British treated the Indians. If most of the Americans there reacted to it, General Joe Stilwell, the classic American anti-imperialist, the man who was on the side of the little fellow, with his instinctive commitment to the poor and wretched, rebelled the most. He was, in the words of Harold Isaacs, "an impatient and puritanical soul, hating liars and grafters and men in pinstripe suits." He naturally hated British colonialism, and he broke a lot of crockery and wounded some sensitive feelings at headquarters, he was not a headquarters man. But Rusk was. In the short-tempered world of New Delhi, where we both needed and hated the British, Rusk was the good guy, the man who handled the touchy tempers; he was smooth where Stilwell was abrasive. You talked with Rusk and you knew he was for the same things you were for. He hated the racism of the British, the arrogance of the colonialist, but in a divided atmosphere, he was someone everyone could talk to. He was the good soldier who was also a good diplomat, and these were not qualities which were lost upon that supreme soldier-diplomat George Catlett Marshall, public servant personified.

No one grasped like Marshall the vast complexities of the war, and the political problems as well; he was also aware of the coming of the United States as a superpower and of the future decline of the British, aware of the need to harness the British potential and yet to understand their limits without offending them. It was not by chance that he had reached down and chosen Dwight D. Eisenhower, that general who was the most subtle politician, as his Supreme Commander in Europe, a man brilliant at synthesizing the work of others, extracting their best qualities, and controlling his own anger (so good, in fact, at controlling his own rages when need be that years later, when Joe McCarthy slandered George Marshall and called him a traitor, Ike, fine diplomat, good pol, for the good of the party and the Republican crusade, swallowed his pride and loyalty and excised criticism of McCarthy and defense of Marshall from his speech). It was these same qualities which had caught Marshall's eye about Rusk—intelligent without being egomaniacal, well educated, a good man.

There was one other quality which had begun to surface, Rusk's writing ability. Is there such a word as "expositor" for a man who writes almost classic expository prose? If so, Rusk was a brilliant expositor; he had a genius for putting down brief, cogent and forceful prose on paper—a rare and much needed quality in government. There was no descriptive, flowery writing, but brief, incisive action cables for men who, already overburdened by words, had too little time. He had been virtually discovered as a writer through the cables he sent back from that theater, and after a while, in the nerve ends of the Pentagon, people began to talk about this young officer out there. General George (Abe) Lincoln, a West Point man who was also a Rhodes scholar and a key man in that special underground world of military intellectuals teaching at the Point, spotting talent, making sure that it was promoted into key slots, had been impressed by the Rusk cables and he asked a friend who this Rusk was, he seemed like a hell of a man. "You don't know Rusk?" the other officer answered. "I thought you were at Oxford together. Why, Rusk is a Rhodes scholar." Then Lincoln, who was a talent scout for Marshall, began to pay closer attention and Rusk became singled out. Lincoln soon decided that Rusk's reports were the best there were, which was quite an accolade, since the competition was very stiff; Bedell Smith, after all, was writing for Ike from Europe.

Toward the end of the war Lincoln decided that they would need Rusk on some of the upcoming political problems, so he persuaded the Delhi headquarters to let Rusk come back to join a very special political-military group which was going to determine the political divisions of the postwar world working directly under Secretary of War Henry Stimson, with Lincoln as the connecting officer. Since the State Department had become moribund during the war, with all the talent having been siphoned off to the military, this was the creation of a new instant State Department, comprising talented young men who were having to make quick decisions on what the postwar map would be, which country should accept surrender, where various countries would be divided. It also had to prepare the Japanese peace terms (which meant getting the right terms, getting Chiang, MacArthur and the British aboard, and doing it quickly, because hundreds of thousands of lives might be lost). It was highly pressurized work, with lives in the balance, but also a sense that a mistake, the wrong line drawn, the wrong island given away, could come back to haunt you years later. The group was in effect the forerunner of the National Security Council, and the problems it faced were very tough: whether or not to let some Dutch marines back into Indonesia; where to divide Korea as the Russians came pouring through—it was Rusk who, checking with old maps, picked the 38th parallel. And deciding, as the war came to a close, to go along with the pressure from the British and French and let the British accept the Japanese surrender in Indochina, a particularly fateful decision as far as Vietnam was concerned.

John McCloy was the head of the group, which also included General Charles Bonesteel, a Rhodes scholar and one of the Pentagon's intellectuals (who would, like Lincoln, become one of Rusk's lasting friends—his old friends tended to be from the military); James Pierpont Morgan Hamilton; Andy Goodpaster, a bright up-and-coming officer who was also a Rhodes scholar (later the influence of Lincoln in all this would become so profound that his men would be known as the Lincoln Brigade).

In this high-powered group, Colonel Rusk dealt on an equal level with four-star generals and the great figures of World War II. It was in this period particularly that he caught Marshall's eye. Rusk intended to stay in the Army; these had been happy years with the military. He liked the atmosphere in which he worked and he thought that there would be a need for men like him in the new Army. His future seemed secure, the first star was on its way, and with Rusk's special credentials, the intellectual qualities which would now show, the second and third would not be far behind. Not being a West Point man, perhaps he would never be Chief of Staff, but he would certainly be a top staffman and it would be a good and useful career.

It was at this point that Marshall asked him to go to State. Marshall, who had been so brilliant at promoting the bright young men in the Army and speeding their careers in the military, now wanted to redress the balance and move talent back to State. He prevailed upon Rusk, and Rusk somewhat reluctantly agreed; he had worked with the State Department people doing some of the planning for the United Nations and now, with the war over, he went to work for State in the UN bureau, eventually becoming director of Special Political Affairs.

If Marshall wanted him to do something, Rusk did it. Marshall was his hero, the embodiment of all that was desirable, all that a man should be. Twenty years later Rusk would repeatedly quote Marshall—Marshall had said this, Marshall had done that. He would quote Marshall on the military approvingly (always give them half of what they're asking and double their missions), and he followed Marshall's mode of operation. Marshall the ex-general was staff-oriented; Rusk would be staff-oriented. Marshall the ex-general was always correct and went through proper channels; Rusk would go through channels and be appalled by anyone who did not. Marshall did not deign to answer criticism; Rusk, proud, would also not deign to answer criticism. As Marshall had admired the sense of service and the intellectual capacity of the best of the military, so would Rusk, and he would quote Marshall approvingly about the modern American army, and particularly those men who had come to the fore because of World War II, a generation which had come to manhood between two great wars, superior men, learned, wise. Having a lot of time on their hands during the war, they went to special schools, read a great deal, traveled a great deal, used that leisure time well, went beyond the parochial bounds of their jobs and their careers. They were superior men, superior to comparable men whom you found in peacetime jobs, who had less sense of service. Thus he shared Marshall's admiration for the military, without wondering perhaps if it was equally applicable to another time.

He admired Marshall's virtues, the urbanity, civility; the Virginia gentleman, and yet distant, never intimate; never write your memoirs, confide in no one but the President. Always put duty and country above self. Marshall had given up the chance to head the invasion of Europe because Roosevelt needed him in the less dramatic job in Washington; after the war he had taken on the China mission for Truman, trying to negotiate an agreement between Mao and Chiang while protecting the President, by the very use of his great prestige, from the immediacy of political fallout on that supercharged question, mediating between Chiang and Mao. Rusk took a demotion from Deputy Undersecretary to become Assistant Secretary for the Far East because it had become a hornet's nest; Rusk was willing to take all the brutal criticism of the war in Vietnam because the more he took, the more it might shield the President. Rusk was upset after his term not because the criticism of Vietnam had been so personal, but far more important, because he feared it was sweeping America away from courses of foreign policy in which he deeply believed. He thought the new drift very dangerous, to this country and to the world, which had been held together by that foreign policy (was it surprising that of the policy of containment, the greatest edifice had been given the name of his mentor, the Marshall Plan?).

Marshall was austere, impressive, selective with his praise; years later Rusk took aside aides who would work through the night and into the morning, passing on those Olympian words: "I will never forget what George Marshall said one day when he was Secretary of State. I had worked fourteen hours long into the morning and as I was leaving his office, he said, 'Mr. Rusk, you've earned your pay today.' So I took that lesson from the greatest man I've ever known. If you have very good people it isn't necessary to compliment them. They know how good they are." Marshall was genteel, always the gentleman, above the fray, never entering into petty fights; when Rusk left the government in 1952, he eschewed the rough-and-tumble of the business world or politics, where it was very hard to be both successful and a gentleman, and found comfort in the less savage world of the foundations, where you could hold on to the old values and still rise. As Secretary, he brought this sense, this lack of jugular instinct back into the government, a lack of willingness to fight with the sharp young Kennedy people, or Harriman, or Defense, or any other force. A bright aide would remember the situation early in the Administration when the question of the publicly owned satellite arose. The top State people gathered and decided that State was *for* the publicly owned satellite, and there was a sense of excitement among some of the new people, why, they had just seen policy set. But State, having taken a position, did not get behind it, used no force or pressure, left the issue to low-ranking assistants, who were cut up very badly, since State turned out to be the only organ in the government which was for it. On something like a satellite, if you want it, you get behind it, very hard, otherwise you let it alone completely.

Marshall, too, had been above the crowd, confiding in the President and in few others, and Rusk would be the same. It was not proper for him to get into fights with twenty-nine-year-old headhunters and bright desk officers who seemed to want to challenge all their superiors, so the Secretary of State reserved his counsel for the President of the United States, driving people at State mad and indeed irritating the President. But in Rusk's emulating Marshall in every way, there was a difference, and it was a crucial one: Marshall had become Secretary after a full and distinguished career. He did not need to raise his voice, he was *George Marshall.* He might be wearing his civies, but those stars were still there, in his mind and everyone else's; his austerity made his achievements seem greater still. By contrast, Rusk was a man of far less achievement. He had moved upward so quietly, left so little impression behind of posture or belief that no one had seen him or heard his footsteps except for a few insiders. He did not leave a record. More brilliant men had left a record, and though it may have been a good one, they were betrayed by it and by the times, and they had disappeared. Thus Rusk emulating Marshall. Rusk as Marshall. Marshall without Marshall.

It would become fashionable later among Kennedy people to portray Rusk as a man of some mediocrity and it was a widely shared belief of many Kennedy insiders that Rusk's greatest problem in those years was simply brain power, he just wasn't as smart as that bright Bundy group. There was an air of patronizing, a sort of winking to each other about Rusk, about the need to check with the good people at State, which did not mean Rusk. Yet in the late forties and early fifties he was considered the most professional officer at State by many who knew the Department well. He rose faster than anyone else, in harder times under more difficult circumstances; in five years he went from an Assistant on loan from the War Department to office director for the United Nations to director of Special Political Affairs to Deputy Undersecretary of State for Political Affairs, the highest career job. The most striking thing was that he was not associated with any particular policy or viewpoint. He was intelligent and able, and yet it was symbolic of Rusk, the shadow man, that he could have this career and yet not be identified with any policy, so that later he could be a man of NATO, a man of the United Nations, a man of the Rockefeller Foundation, a man of Marshall, a man of Dulles and a man of Stevenson, all without apparent contradiction. It was a time when the post-World War II policies of stabilizing the world and fending off a totalitarian enemy were clearly set, policies which Rusk could wholeheartedly believe in; and under the direction and the assumptions of other men he could make a total commitment of all his energies. He was doggedly hard-working and yet his meteoric rise did not seem to offend the men around him; other men with family connections or aristocratic backgrounds rising so fast might have been prima donnas, might have been abrasive to contemporaries, but not Rusk. He was invisible to them (indeed, when the North Koreans crossed the 38th parallel, Rusk, with his special background in the United Nations, was sent to New York to negotiate the United Nations troop force, which he did secretively and personally, telling none of the Americans in the UN what he was doing, appearing one day at the U.S. mission, nodding, and then leaving later without having said anything or left a single trace, not a tip of his hand, not a piece of paper behind, leaving them the impression that he was Chinese).

He never inflicted his problems on superiors, nor questioned their judgment. Lovett would in fact remember Rusk, an Assistant Secretary, showing up one day exhausted, his face almost green. Shocked, Lovett asked what was wrong. It turned out that one of the Rusk children had scarlet fever; the family was quarantined and Rusk had been up most of the night washing sheets, never complaining, never asking for help. Lovett was appalled—my God, Dean, we have lots of people around the department just for things like that.

He was Marshall's and Lovett's and finally Acheson's boy in those days, cool, competent, unflappable, dogged in carrying out policies which they set, years in which the very bases of the great policies of the Cold War were set down. The world seemed to those men who were the architects of the policy parallel to the one which had existed before the war; a totalitarian force was at work threatening Western Europe, the lines had to be drawn, only force would work. The lessons of Munich were very real and still lived; through mutual security with the force and guidance and leadership coming from the United States, the West would provide the answers which had been applicable in 1939 but which had been neglected then. This time we had learned the lessons of history, and the mistakes would not be repeated. The United States would take the place of Britain; it would balance, stabilize and protect the world. And so the lessons were clear for young Dean Rusk: whatever the United States set out to do it could accomplish. There was a great centrist political strength in the United States; further, when confronted by the strength and, most important, the determination of a just and honorable democracy, the totalitarian forces of the world would have to respect that power.

IT WAS EXTRAORDINARY THAT IN THIS PERIOD RUSK AVOIDED THE one dangerous issue of the time, on which he seemed to be an expert. The issue was China, the one major place in the world where Communism would become entwined with nationalism and cause major domestic problems for the United States. The fall of China would send American policy—first domestic and then inevitably foreign—into a crisis and convulsions that would last for more than two decades and give the policy in Asia a hard-rock interior of irrationality. Good men of genuine honor and intelligence would have their careers destroyed. Rusk's own saints would be smeared. Marshall pilloried by McCarthy, that one career in America which seemed beyond reproach was reproached. Acheson, the man who as Secretary of State had been the great architect of containment, became badly tarnished because of China, guilty of harboring traitors and homosexuals. The Dean Acheson College for Cowardly Containment of Communism, in the words of Richard Nixon, who even then had a feel for a good phrase. Other towering men in the State Department were wounded, set back in their careers. George Kennan, Bohlen, an impeccable old-school boy like Chip Bohlen having trouble being approved as ambassador to the Soviet Union in 1953.

The handful of genuine experts in the China field saw their careers totally destroyed, driven out of the Department, a scarlet letter branded into them. But not Dean Rusk. Rusk was clean, and the Kennedy people were reassured —be grateful for small favors—though the very fact that Rusk had not been involved in the China problem, that he was not burned, should have been some kind of warning. Yet he had been Assistant Secretary of State for the Far East in that period, but not only that, he had volunteered for the job, taken a demotion from the job as Deputy Undersecretary and asked for FE, which seemed the suicide seat; the Department was already under terrible pressure from the right and from the Hill. He told Acheson someone had to take the job and he was qualified. "I fit it," he said. "You get the Purple Heart and the Congressional Medal of Honor all at once for this," Acheson answered. And thus into the pit. Except in a curious way, by the time he took the job, though it was an exhausting, demanding place, it was no longer the pit.

Those who had been hurt, the real experts, were the young men who had been in China during the storm, who witnessed the collapse of the old order, the death of feudal China in the late forties; as they had watched the rise of the new China they saw the inevitability of its victory and they said so, and they were later victimized by their own prophecies. O. Edmund Clubb, a foreign service officer in China for twenty years, had been interested in Chinese Communism as early as 1931 and was attacked even then because of the attention he paid to it—if he was so interested in it, didn't that mean that he liked it? (His security file would contain a particularly mindless list of suspicions of people from an earlier day who disliked his energy in analyzing the early roots of Chinese Communism.) Davies and Service had been saying that the Communists were going to win, suggesting that the United States get ready to deal with the new China. Like it or not, the future is theirs, Davies wrote, and we had better recognize it. Of course they were right, and predictably, China fell. Chiang had spread himself too thin rather than conserving his troops and resources and concentrating them in more limited areas, thus forcing the Communists to deal with him (as Davies, among others, was suggesting). But there was little disposition to accept the inevitability of Chiang's decline (particularly on the part of Republican congressmen who were pushing intensively for a more rapid demobilization to bring the boys home at a time when the only American action which might have affected the balance in China would have been the commitment of hundreds of thousands of American troops to China to save Chiang). Instead, scapegoats had to be found and they became the State Department officers in question, both in Washington and in China.

But Rusk went to FE *after* China had fallen; it was a *fait accompli,* and he was in no way involved. Deeply anti-Communist himself, a containment man, he was in fact a man who seemed to give to those around him a sense that there were moral overtones to the Communist conquest of the mainland, that it was wrong, that a real enemy was installed there, an immoral government. This viewpoint did not get him into trouble on the Hill; if anything, at a time when State had particularly bad relations, Rusk had good relations (the shadow-cabinet Secretary of State, John Foster Dulles, ever sensitive to the nuances of the Hill, spotted him as a comer, would want to befriend him, and Rusk of course was wise enough always to stay in with the outs, which meant that he and Dulles would have a very nice quiet friendship). Thus Rusk entered the job clean; he was not associated with the past, he was on neither side of the great issue (had he been on the pro-Chiang side he would eventually have become unacceptable to the Democratic party). Then, less than two months after he took the job, the Korean War broke out, and it made him even less likely to be controversial, made him safer. There was a real enemy now, everyone rallied round the flag and the policy. A real war, a real enemy, they both cleared the air, everyone came on board. State's job was to co-operate with the military, to make sure that things got done. The job became more functional than anything else; since the Allied forces fought under the UN flag, Rusk was particularly valuable because of his knowledge of the UN and he had a good deal to do with compiling the UN manpower lists. The complicated and destructive problem in State of where you stood on China evaporated; there was a team now and everyone was aboard; and here was Rusk, playing his role, effective, hard-working, he was State's man working for the military.

The Korean War was to prove a difficult and often painful experience for Rusk; in some ways the frustrations of a limited land war in Asia were as painful for him as they were for the American military. He was part of the civilian decision-making process which had set the particular limits of the war, which had in effect created sanctuaries for the enemy—for good reasons, certainly, but making American boys fight under terrible hardships which seemed very difficult to explain. This meant that Rusk the civilian was limiting Rusk the soldier. Some of those who knew him well in that period felt that the Korean War was perhaps the most painful experience of his career before Vietnam. There were two reasons for this: first, the sense of being at least in part responsible for the limits under which American troops fought, and second, a sense of responsibility because he had not forecast the Chinese entry into the war. He would talk about this a great deal with close friends (finally those who worked with him during the Vietnam war and wanted to push him toward dovishness, wanted to turn him on a specific issue against the military, would know that the only way they could do it was by mentioning China— well, suppose China came in if we escalated beyond a certain point in a certain way—and they played on it very skillfully, using China as a decoy for broader dovishness, since their other reasons were disregarded; later there may have been lingering regrets of Rusk about the escalation, not that we got into it, but perhaps that we did it too slowly, we had felt too many inhibitions. Rusk's reservations about the use of power in 1965 and 1966 were not those of other civilians who felt we had used too much power; they were almost exactly the same as the senior military, that we had used too little). But Rusk had not warned us about Chinese intervention in Korea, and he felt the burden of the latter stages of that conflict in a particularly personal way.

If Rusk sometimes seemed to say *mea culpa* about China, there was good reason. For if Vietnam is a major Greek tragedy, it is compiled of many minor scenes which come together in one great epic. In 1950 one of those scenes was unveiled in the Far Eastern bureau of the Department of State. There Assistant Secretary Rusk prided himself on his knowledge of China (though later when he was Secretary of State an assistant who knew him well described him as a "real Grandma Moses on China," each year asking the China desk a list of detailed and somewhat archaic questions on China, including, for instance, the chances for secession of various areas, the possibility of the return of war lordism). The head of his China desk was Edmund Clubb, intelligent, dogged, a little heavy-handed in his writing, but he was that rarest of men, a genuine expert—not only on the new China but on the Soviet Union and the Manchurian border area as well. He was, in the view of some of his contemporaries, less graceful as a writer than Service, less sophisticated than Davies. He had made many enemies as a young foreign service officer among the older, more traditional and wealthier American community in China, the upper-class America of those small foreign enclaves. And when he started to study the Chinese Communists in the early thirties, this in itself aroused suspicion—wasn't he making too much of these people? They were, after all, only bandits. Wasn't he too sympathetic? When the dark clouds gathered and the China experts were pilloried, Clubb was included. One of the ten charges against him was that he had associated with Communists in Hankow in 1931–34.

But now he was back in Washington as China desk officer when the Korean War started. Actually, he had been on vacation in late June, but in view of developments in Korea he had cut short his leave. Knowing the Chinese and the intensity of what they considered grave matters of national security, Clubb, between mid-July and early October, submitted three separate official memoranda warning of the danger of Chinese intervention. But though it was his special area of expertise, he was not included among those who attended the critical meetings between Truman and MacArthur at Wake Island, and his warnings went unheeded. Years later he would think that his superiors in the bureaucracy already knew that he was scheduled to undergo a major security investigation by the Department's Loyalty-Security Board. So instead of concentrating on using his particular knowledge at a time when it was most desperately needed, Clubb was to spend the year 1951 fighting the bitter and painful battles of his security process. Then, early in 1952, he was cleared of the charges against him—but was simultaneously assigned to the Division of Historical Research. Knowing that his career had been effectively savaged, he retired from the foreign service; his very special expertise was lost to the U.S. government, and Dean Rusk proceeded upward at the same time with his career.

RUSK WOULD TURN OUT TO BE A HARD-LINER ON THE NEW CHINA, AND once the Korean War started he would be at ease; the war and the competition with the Communists was almost a moral thing. The United States obeyed the law; the Communists broke it. We wore white hats and they wore black; our GIs did not rape, they gave away chewing gum. In fact, a speech of his in that period is particularly revealing because the words are real, they are believed:

Our foreign policy has been reflected in our willingness to submit atomic weapons to international law, in feeding and clothing those stricken by war, in supporting free elections and government by consent, in building factories and dams, power plants, and railways, schools and hospitals, in improving seed and stock and fertilizer, in stimulating markets and improving the skills and techniques of others in a hundred different ways. Let these things stand in contrast to a foreign policy directed towards the extension of tyranny and using the big lie, sabotage, suspicion, riot and assassination as its tools. The great strength of the United States is devoted to the peaceful pursuits of our people and to the decent opinions of mankind. But it is not healthy for any regime or group of regimes to incur, by their lawless and aggressive conduct, the implacable opposition of the American people. The lawbreaker, unfortunately in the nature of things, always has the initiative, but the peacemaking peoples of the world can and will make themselves strong enough to insist upon peace . . .

It was vintage Rusk, and he believed it. What Rusk said was an expression of his real views. (In 1965 Rusk would meet with a group of high school seniors and discuss the reasons why we were escalating in Vietnam; a member of his staff who was there thought it was a forceful but simplistic presentation of a hands-out-of-the-cookie-jar view. The next day, however, he was stunned when he saw an "Eyes Only" memo on the same subject from Rusk to the President, the highest level of security possible for documents, and it was word for word the exact same presentation.)

Rusk's speech gave vital insight into his thinking; here was a man who believed in his origins and experiences—the democracies were ipso facto good and the totalitarians were ipso facto bad, and this helped explain the force of his positions. But it also explained some of the danger of his tenets because they were held by a man so wedded to certain concepts and truths that he did not reckon with the whimsical quality of history, that the forces of history can just as easily make the democracies aggressive, that to some small states, large democracies look tyrannical, that justice and decency have various definitions in different parts of the world. These were the words of a man who advocated his own concepts, whether the world was ready for them or not. The world would have to adapt to him. Yet the steadfastness of his beliefs was also his greatest asset; he believed, he was not ambivalent. He believed in both the might and the decency of America (having never dealt in the domestic processes, he was uncritical of them; he was willing to accept the high school civics class theory of their reality). If America was both honorable and strong, and turned that strength in the right directions—which had been charted in the postwar years as containment of the totalitarians—then our side would triumph. Perhaps not easily, perhaps the struggle would be long, but eventually quality and class would tell. In 1965 and 1966, as the Vietnam war began to look more and more difficult and George Ball and others would tell him of their doubts, that it was a lost cause, Rusk would say, again and again, that when a great nation like the United States of America puts its shoulder to the wheel, something has to give: Yes, I know that the French were there and the political situation is bad, and it may be worse than you say, but I can't believe that when a great nation like the United States puts its shoulder to the wheel . . . More than a belief, it was a matter of faith, really.

He had, he repeated to Vietnam critics, been through the same kind of struggle, heard the same kind of doubts before. It was in December 1950, after the Chinese had entered the Korean War, catching MacArthur unprepared, cutting up an entire division, and then pushing down quickly against disorganized American units. MacArthur panicked and was sending back what Lovett would call "posterity papers" which covered him against all eventualities, saying that he was meeting the entire Chinese nation in battle. His cables were having a shattering effect at the United Nations and on the

Joint Chiefs, and there was talk of pulling out of Korea and even of pulling out of Japan. The JCS cabled back to MacArthur that the first order of business was preservation of his troops, if necessary to consolidate them into beachheads, as he had recommended. It was at this point that Rusk steadied everyone. He was very forceful: it just was not that bad, he said; there were limits to what the Chinese could do, and American might was not totally impotent. Perhaps we had been overextended when they came in, but the same thing could happen to them. It was time for everyone to calm down, to pay less attention to the tone of MacArthur's cables and to try and sense what our possibilities were and their possibilities were. Since General Matthew Ridgway was saying somewhat the same thing, the two were able to steady the Washington hands, and Dean Acheson would later say that this was Rusk's finest hour.

Acheson was also impressed with Rusk's toughness during a great subsequent bureaucratic struggle over the question of releasing prisoners of war in Korea. Thousands of the Chinese and North Korean prisoners did not want to be repatriated; the Pentagon, anxious to get American prisoners back, was willing to accept a simple man-for-man exchange. With the military pushing for this formula, and desperate to get its own men back, the bureaucracy seemed ready to go ahead. But Rusk forcefully and with great passion made them hold the line. To force prisoners back to a country against their will, he argued, was a violation of almost everything this country stood for. It would be inhumane, and immoral. Despite great pressure he stuck to his position and eventually won; voluntary repatriation became the policy.

YET THOSE YEARS WOULD ALSO SEE A CHANGE IN AMERICAN AND State Department attitudes on China and Asia; it was part of a national phenomenon. China, a beloved and somewhat mysterious ally, had gone Communist, and worse, that new regime had engaged us in a brutal land war (smiling, dutiful, loyal Chinese had almost overnight become yellow hordes, mindless functional Communist ants, a shocking new reincarnation). This brought a domestic crisis of sorts, accelerated the coming and the importance of Joseph McCarthy and led to the hardening of political and bureaucratic attitudes on Asia; in particular State and its Asian bureau became militantly anti-Communist. Years later the Democrats would take particular pleasure in blaming Dulles for those policies and for that rigidity; Dulles did make an attractive target, with his righteousness and his tendency to pontificate in public, and with his opening of the doors of State to security people. Although Dulles helped change the personnel by permitting the destruction of the existing men, the policies had nonetheless changed during the latter years of the Acheson Administration, when Rusk was his Assistant Secretary at FE. The young State Department officials trying to make American policy in Indochina less dependent upon the French Foreign Ministry, and more committed to an indigenous nationalism, would find no friend in Rusk (in fact, the day after the United States decided to intervene in Korea, Rusk had made a list of recommendations for new policies in the area, including a vast increase in military aid to the French). Instead they would find less interest than ever in the subtlety of the political problems, less disposition to look for differences in the kind of war taking place in Korea and Indochina. It would be the business-as-usual attitude, which gave the dominant hand to the European desk. In those years, American support for the French would increase considerably, and the French rhetoric about fighting in Vietnam for the free world, which we had always mocked in the past, would become our rhetoric and find its way into the speeches of high officers in the State Department, notably the Assistant Secretary for FE, Dean Rusk, as for instance in a speech on Asia in November 1951; a time when the French were paying only the slightest lip service to the demands of Vietnamese nationalists:

The real issue in Indochina is whether the peoples of that land will be permitted to work out their future as they see fit or whether they will be subjected to a Communist reign of terror and be absorbed by force into the new colonialism of a Soviet Communist empire. In this situation, it is generally agreed in the United States that we should support and assist the armies of France and of the Associated States in meeting the armed threat in Indochina. . . . We are trying to build, the enemy is trying to tear down. It is hard to organize a constitutional society of free men; it is easy to impose a reign of terror . . .

For the truth was that despite the Democratic desire to blame Dulles for the commitment to Southeast Asia, the creation of South Vietnam, and the invention of Diem, the roots of the change in American policy actually predated Eisenhower's coming to power. The really crucial decisions were made at the tail end of the Truman years, with Acheson as Secretary of State and Rusk as his principal deputy for Asia. This was the period when the United States went from a position of neutrality toward both sides in the Indochina war to a position of massive military and economic aid to the French. The real architect of the American commitment to Vietnam, of bringing containment to that area and using Western European perceptions in the underdeveloped world, was not John Foster Dulles, it was Dean Acheson.

Acheson. A handsome man, the right kind of handsomeness, not matinée-idol handsome, but respectable-handsome. He looked like a Secretary of State; in fact, it was hard to think of him as anything else. Had he been a banker he would have looked too respectable to be simply a financier; he looked more worldly and urbane than a man who simply dealt with money. He became a Democratic icon of the fifties both because he had been viciously attacked by McCarthy and had stood the attack without flinching (personally, if not professionally), and because he would not turn his back on Alger Hiss (who was of course a member of the Establishment in very good standing; a remarkable amount of what Acheson was committed to was at its heart class). His reputation in the fifties because of those McCarthy years, a quirk of history really, was somehow that he was a soft-liner, and that Dulles was the hard-liner. If anything, the reverse was true. It was not so much that Dulles was softer, but for all the bombast of his speeches, the verbal right-eousness in public, there was an element of private flexibility (the great cor-poration lawyer who can make a resounding appeal in the courtroom and then a more subtle private deal in the judge's chambers), whereas Acheson was the hard-liner who felt that Dulles' policies were extremely dangerous and that the defense budget was too small. Acheson was always the true inter-ventionist who deeply believed that the totalitarians might exploit the democ-racies. He was not soft, Acheson, he never was. He was Wilsonian, but new-generation Wilsonian, Wilson flexing old ideals with new industrial and tech-nological might, Wilson with a longer reach.

He was the son of a British Army officer who went to Canada, fought against a half-breed insurrection in Manitoba, and later became an Anglican minister and eventually bishop of Connecticut. Dean Acheson's upbringing was stern (in fact, he once wanted to be Solicitor General of the United States, a job for which he had been recommended by the Roosevelt Adminis-tration, only to find that he was blocked by Attorney General Homer Cum-mings, who was from Connecticut, the reason being that the senior Acheson had found Cummings too frequently divorced and had withheld a marital blessing). His background was clerical-military and quite traditional; like other proper young men he went off to Groton (writing of Franklin Roosevelt years later, he would say: "Ten years older than I, he had left our school be-fore I got there, but he regarded my having gone to it as a recommendation"). From there he went to Yale, where he received a gentleman C, and then to Harvard Law, where for the first time the excellence of his mind began to flash. He became a favorite of Supreme Court Justice Felix Frankfurter, who got him a clerkship under Louis Brandeis; with that, his career was under way.

The young Acheson was an offbeat Democrat, and a somewhat unlikely one. He was excited by Teddy Roosevelt and bored by Taft, and was finally brought into the Democratic party by Woodrow Wilson, a figure of austere, almost harsh moralism, with the same bent toward both the Atlantic countries and internationalism. Acheson was a conservative and proper young man, ca-pable at his tenth Yale reunion in 1925 of giving a speech which dealt with re-gaining control over a burgeoning government and criticized the government for interfering too much in human affairs. He was almost classically a man of the Establishment—the right backgrounds, the right schools, the right clubs, the right connections. Indeed, in 1933 he entered the Roosevelt Administration in the best Establishment tradition of the old-boy network ("In May 1933 two old friends, Arthur Ballantine, the Republican holdover Under Secretary of the Treasury, and James Douglas, Assistant Secretary, also awaiting relief, asked me to lunch with them. The new Secretary, Will Woodin, was, they said, a man after our own hearts who would need congenial friends. Would I come to meet him at lunch. The lunch was gay and uninhibited . . . I was hardly back in my office before the operator announced Secretary Woodin calling. Would I become Under Secretary of the Treasury?").

The first tour with Roosevelt did not work out well: Acheson was more conservative than the Administration on fiscal policies, and ill at ease with Roosevelt's loose, disorganized personal style, which he considered "patronizing and humiliating. To accord the President the greatest deference and respect should be a gratification to any citizen. It is not gratifying to receive the easy greeting which milord might give a promising stable boy and pull one's forelock in return." He eventually resigned and only returned before the beginning of the war because his own fierce interventionism coincided with Roosevelt's needs; in 1941 he was made an Assistant Secretary of State.

While he never felt comfortable with Roosevelt, personally or politically, he was later very much at ease with Truman, a feeling which most members of the Establishment came to share. Roosevelt was too political a figure and thus too capricious, and Truman had more reverence for the wisdom of the Establishment (one of the differences was that Roosevelt, having come from that particular class, was a good deal less in awe of it, be it in foreign affairs or anything else. He knew too much about them; he was broader than they. Acheson, and men like him, would come to be admirers of Truman, in part because he gave them a very free hand and took them at face value, but there was a certain condescension at first toward him: John Carter Vincent would recall Acheson saying at the beginning, "John Carter, that little fellow across the street has more to him than you think.") Joseph Alsop, a journalistic extension of Acheson, would tell a reporter, "Stewart [his brother] and I were still patronizing toward Truman then because we thought the big successes of his Administration were owing to the big men in the Cabinet—Marshall, Forrestal, and the others. But it is a rule that a President must always be given final credit for *all* his Administration's successes and the final blame for *all* its failures . . . We admitted in our column several times that we had underestimated Truman, and several years ago we wrote him a letter of apology. Dean said it would make the old man happy and I believe it did . . ."

The big man. Acheson was of course the big man of the Truman years. Marshall was beginning to age; the China mission after the war had taken a good deal out of him and had not gone well, and when he eventually served as

Secretary of Defense he never seemed to catch hold, as if something had gone out of him. The Defense Department, preoccupied with its own problems and reorganizations, was not as influential as State in the late forties. In the late forties and early fifties, Acheson was a rising figure there, both as Undersecretary, from 1945 to 1947, and then as Secretary from 1949 to 1953. Not by chance would he call his memoirs *Present at the Creation.*

In 1947, when congressional support for aid to Greece and Turkey was wavering, when the British, clearly bled white by two world wars, could no longer function as the dominant Western power, the torch was passed to the United States, and it was Acheson who assisted in relaying the torch of Anglo-Saxon sanity and order. The British said they could not bail out the Greek economic situation, which was near collapse, nor could they underwrite the modernization of the Turkish army. Reading the cables at the time, Loy Henderson, then director of the office of Near Eastern and African Affairs, thought "that Great Britain had within the hour handed the job of world leadership with all its burdens and all its glory to the United States."

With congressional leadership dubious, it was Acheson who rallied everyone; he painted a picture of a world slowly being infected by Communism, country by country, one rotten apple contaminating the barrel. Only the United States stood between freedom and this latest totalitarian threat of all Western civilization. The dark ages were the alternative: the Russians would get control of the Mediterranean, then Africa, then Asia. In Europe our friends would feel the impact. He said it forcefully and with passion; these were not sham views. Fine, said Senator Arthur Vandenberg, but "if Truman wants it he will have to go and scare hell out of the country."

This became the origin of the Truman Doctrine. Truman, charged with scaring hell out of the country, did exactly that, to such a degree that when the message for the Doctrine went before Congress it surprised Secretary Marshall, then flying to Moscow. Uneasy with the extent to which the anti-Communist element was stressed, Marshall sent a cable to Truman questioning the wisdom of this presentation, saying he thought Truman was overstating the case. Truman replied that after talking with Senate leaders, he felt sure that this was the only way to get the message through. So it was that Acheson, even more than Marshall, was the architect of containment, the architect of an attitude of universality toward Communism (one could not struggle with them in Europe and acquiesce to a different form of them in Asia. It was not a time for subtleties. Subtleties blew up in your face).

But he was not a man concerned or interested in Asia; he was a man of Europe, which was the serious world, with values that were Western, Christian, democratic-elitist. It was not really Europe as a whole that shared his values, but specifically Anglo-Saxon Europe; as one went farther south and the people became darker and more Mediterranean, they tended to be less worthy and dependable (with the exception of Portugal's Salazar). But Europe was the world: the Russians to be stopped there, the British held together and given a rest period, the French encouraged to be more worthy of us and their own past, the Germans to be re-created in our image. The French were perhaps the most troublesome, surprisingly unstable for a major European power, insisting always on being French. The underdeveloped world was not a serious place. Though Acheson presided as head of State at a time of great restlessness and changes in the colonial world, with its deep longing for a new order, there is little evidence of it in his memoirs other than a certain irritation with Nehru for his lack of appreciation for Acheson's grace and wit as a host. Instead, his is an Anglo-Saxon book, dealing mainly with the passing of the torch.

IT WAS THIS BASIC DISINTEREST IN THE UNDERDEVELOPED WORLD, A belief that it was not only less important but somehow less worthy, and above all the unwillingness to rock any European boat, which came back to haunt, if not him, then his country and his party on Indochina. In October 1949 Acheson, now Secretary of State, talked about Indochina with Nehru, who was extremely pessimistic about the French experiment there ("the Bao Dai alternative," as it was known). He outlined the failings of the prince and said that the French would never give Bao Dai the freedom necessary to hold the hopes and passions of his people. Acheson told Nehru he was inclined to agree, but that he saw no real alternative. This was an odd answer, since he was in effect saying that we were committed to a dead policy. Nehru, who like other newly independent Asian leaders refused to recognize Bao Dai, told Acheson that Ho Chi Minh was a nationalist, albeit a Communist. Nehru argued that European judgments on the failures of popular fronts were specious in an Asian context, and Acheson replied by talking about France and Italy. But at that early date, Acheson knew the French cause was both wrong and hopeless.

Even that attitude would shift in the waning days of 1949 and the first days of 1950. It was not that events in Indochina were different, but that domestic perceptions in the United States, pushed by developments in China, were changing. No longer would the Americans be so even-handed, if that is the word, in their policy toward Indochina. Up until that point Walton Butterworth, still Assistant Secretary of State for the Far East, was fighting valiantly against all the French attempts to involve us in the war with aid and arms, but things were fast moving out of his control. Among other things, the fall of China to the Communists had released a vast amount of money which had been ticketed for Chiang Kai-shek, and there was now talk of giving some of it to the French in Indochina. Philip Jessup, the ambassador-at-large for the Administration, was to go on a special mission in which part of his assignment was to bestow official recognition upon the Bao Dai government (which we had previously thought worthless). After the recognition, the Bao Dai government might receive some leftover China aid. Jessup was to be accompanied by Ray Fosdick and Everett Case. Of course the American options were steadily narrowing; the most hopeful possibility by this time was Bao Dai, since the Ho Chi Minh alternative was now long gone. If we could not support him up to 1949, when there was no domestic pressure, it was impossible now. Bao Dai represented a frail, non-Communist, nationalist alternative, even if the French were co-operative, which they were not likely to be.

Jessup carried with him a letter from Acheson to Bao Dai saying that the Americans were delighted that he had been chosen to lead Vietnam. Jessup, an authority on international law, considered this a letter of recognition. After the visit he went to Singapore, where he held a press conference praising his own visit and saying that the United States was extremely pleased that the French had granted the Vietnamese independence. There was an immediate uproar in Paris, and Jessup was ordered by Washington to give a second press conference, in which he very carefully stated that he had referred to Vietnamese independence within the French union. Once more we had caved in to the French; even within the already limited and probably futile framework of working with Bao Dai, the United States was accepting further limitations. Rather than being the high-water mark of the U.S. commitment to Vietnamese nationalism, it was a reflection of one more concession to the European ally. All in all, it was not a happy trip; on his way back to the United States, Jessup learned that he would have to answer McCarthy's charges that he had an "affinity for Communism."

Thus even the recognition of Bao Dai was neutralized, but the American aid to the French cause would come and come quickly. A follow-up mission was appointed by Acheson, headed by a California publisher named Robert Allen Griffin. Its purpose was to determine whether or not to send arms and other military equipment to the French. In Washington, Butterworth, who had consistently fought this kind of thinking, sensed that this was Acheson's way of signaling an end to an unwanted policy. It was, he thought, an old Department way of switching policies while the same men were still there—send an independent commission, with the advance knowledge that the result would be a new line. A separate survey. A new position. Butterworth was finishing up his tour, anyway. He who had come in so clean and fresh because John Carter Vincent had taken too much heat had now taken too much heat himself. Just as there had been trouble getting Vincent an ambassadorial post which required Senate confirmation, Butterworth would have the same problem: when the Department wanted to send him to Sweden as ambassador, it had to cancel this for a lesser position because of Senate pressures.

Not surprisingly, the Griffin mission found that the Communist threat to In-

dochina was so acute that it advised the State Department to concentrate on
short-range assistance in order to help the French achieve immediate political
and military stability. It was not surprising because the reasoning was different: the given was not whether it was wise to aid the French, whether this
was the right side or not, but whether the French needed the aid. Of course
the French said they needed the aid. Thus began a major new policy of aid to
the French in this colonial war, a policy by which the United States would
eventually almost completely underwrite the costs, $2 billion worth, and
would by 1954 be more eager to have the French continue fighting than Paris
was.

There was, however, still one small detail to be taken care of, the question
of whether the military equipment and economic aid would be channeled
through the French or through the Bao Dai government. The French had
been suspicious of American intentions from the start, believing that the
Americans were eager to replace them in Saigon. Paris was filled with rumors
to this effect. Would the Griffin mission mean that? In March 1950, while the
Griffin mission was on its way home, Lieutenant General Marcel Le Carpentier, the French commander in Indochina, said in a statement filled with the
feeling of the time (and with a good deal of insight into why the French lost):
"I will never agree to equipment being given directly to the Vietnamese. If
this is done I would resign within twenty-four hours. The Vietnamese have no
generals, no colonels, no military organization that could effectively utilize
the equipment. It would all be wasted, and in China the United States has
had enough of that." (The French of course needed the aid because they were
being beaten by Vietnamese.)

Le Carpentier would have no problem; as it always did in conflicts between
its anticolonialism and its anti-Communism, the United States backed down
completely. The equipment arrived, through the auspices of the French; the
Vietnamese were on the sidelines, a simple people, not capable of producing
colonels and generals. So Griffin recommended that we give military aid; the
only question now was, With what kind of leverage? Acheson had already
talked with the Philippine statesman Carlos Romulo, one of the few Asians
who was considered respectable both in Washington and in Asia, and Romulo
warned him that the trouble with giving the French aid was that the moment
it was done, you lost all leverage and influence.

In May 1950 Acheson made his decision; again it was not based upon what
was good for the Vietnamese or what the needs were on the scene. It was a
dual decision; it reflected, first, the general intensifying of the Cold War, and
the consequent greater inability to make a distinction between any two parts
of the Communist world; second, and perhaps more important in the case of
Acheson, it was, like the original Potsdam agreement, a reflection of Indochina as a peripheral area, unimportant in terms of the real world and rela-

tionships with European allies. At this time the Americans, who wanted to stabilize Europe with a new and powerful pro-Western and anti-Communist anchor on the Continent, were pushing to revive the West German economy. The British were uneasy about American intentions, and the French were openly recalcitrant, fearing, as they had good reason to, the specter of German economic might and muscle, followed inevitably by German political might and muscle, and fearing this at least as much as they did the specter of international Communism. Then Robert Schuman, one of the great Europeanists of the French government, came up with a plan which would regulate European production of coal and steel under an ultranational regulatory body, and which would let the Germans have far greater coal and steel production. Thus the French had come around to the American demands for European protection and a rebuilding of the West German economy. But there was to be a sweetener. The French economy was troubled, the defense bill for the prolonged and distant war was mounting all the time; they could no longer afford it, and they needed American help for Indochina. On May 7, 1950, the day when Acheson learned of the Schuman Plan, he also agreed to give military aid for the war. It was a quid pro quo decision, though it was not announced as such (later Acheson admitted privately to friends that it was). The desire to strengthen Western Europe against the Communists would see us strengthening a Western nation in a colonial war.

The next day it was announced that the United States would give aid; it was a turning point in the postwar history of American policy; we would begin to finance a colonial war. But if the war was to be financed, then it could no longer be known as a colonial war, but as a war of freedom against Communists. Freedom of speech for the Vietnamese suddenly became an issue. In the past the State Department's statements on Indochina had carefully abstained from defining the war as the French defined it; now, that too would change. On May 8, after making his deal with Schuman, Acheson announced: "The United States Government, convinced that neither national independence nor democratic evolution exists in any area dominated by Soviet imperialism, considers the situation to be such as to warrant its according economic aid and military equipment to the Associated States of Indochina and France in order to assist them in restoring stability and permitting these states to pursue their peaceful and democratic development."

Stability, that was the key word, to bring stability to that land, though stability as we defined it was colonialism as the Vietnamese defined it. Freedom to them was instability and revolution. Just as the policy had gotten turned around, so too had the words; as our policy had become an aberration, so too, and this was to continue for the next twenty years, our language. Yet the Acheson decision did not stand out as something terrible, an obvious turning point; rather, it was clearly part of the times and part of an era, the fifties were not a time for subtleties and distinctions. The day after the decision was announced, the *New York Times* commented editorially: "We cannot ask France to sacrifice for Indochina, merely then to give it up. Neither can we dictate terms to France, because we are not prepared to step in. Indochina is critical—if it falls, all of Southeast Asia will be in mortal peril." All of this, of course, was before Korea.

WHATEVER DESIRE TO DISCERN DISTINCTIONS IN THE COMMUNIST world existed in June 1950 (and they had been fast diminishing) ended on June 25, when the North Koreans crossed the border to the South. Two days later Truman announced the American response, and the Korean War was on. Eventually China (because of American miscalculation) entered the war, and all of this made Vietnam totally and definitively part of the great global struggle. Immediately after the start of the Korean War, Assistant Secretary of State Dean Rusk made a brief list of steps to be taken in Asia; one of the priorities was a sharp increase in military aid to the French. In Washington, American statements reflected French statements; Acheson, who had once seen Ho as something of a nationalist, now was a hard-liner on the war. After Senators Homer Ferguson and Theodore Green made a trip through Asia they returned deeply concerned about what was happening there. They found that wherever they went, most people thought the Americans were supporting a colonial war, which was very damaging to the American reputation for being on the right side and against colonialism. Acheson moved to reassure the senators: they had it all wrong, they had completely misunderstood. It was not nationalism which was being fought there, he told them, it was Communism. The two were incompatible; you cannot be both a Communist and a nationalist. It was all very simple, he said.

It was a marvelous and definitive answer, reflecting the American capacity, and particularly the Achesonian capacity, to see things through our eyes rather than through anyone else's. Since the situation was clear to Acheson, it should also be clear to the Vietnamese. That self-assurance which blinded him here always served him well against his critics; he did not lack for confidence. But there was a touch of genuine naïveté about the world. In 1951 Acheson met with Jean de Lattre de Tassigny, the famed French commander of the Indochina forces, a French MacArthur. De Lattre explained some of the problems of fighting an elusive enemy in a war without fronts. Then he told Acheson that his greatest need was to train Vietnamese officers, since the Vietnamese would not fight under French officers. Acheson in turn grandly suggested that American officers do the training, explaining that the United States had demonstrated in Korea that it knew how to train Asian officers and the French didn't. The wars, he thought, and the problems, were the same.

ONE IMPORTANT MINORITY VOICE WAS RAISED IN THE STATE DE-
partment at the time—George Kennan's. There was an element of irony in his
dissent, because it was his cables from Moscow toward the end of the war
which had fascinated James Forrestal and which had led to a marked escalation in his career and reputation. But Kennan had resented the way his ideas
had been used; as American foreign policy hardened after the war, he had a
feeling that his ideas were being exploited by his superiors, one element of a
broad outline of thinking plucked out by them for their purposes, which were
not necessarily his; he was outlining a very complicated thing, and they were
not interested in the complications. Kennan had little illusion about Soviet
postwar intentions. He knew they would make certain moves which they considered in their national interest, and that we should be prepared for these
moves. But he had not foreseen and did not want the spiraling tensions and
arms race as the Cold War mounted, and by 1948 he had become the highest-
ranking dissenter on what he termed the increasing militarization of American foreign policy. He had dissented on NATO, since, as far as he was concerned, the Marshall Plan was sufficient; Soviet penetration of Western
countries, he felt, if it came at all, would come from within, it would not
come in the form of Soviet tanks rolling across France. When the Korean War
broke out he argued with Acheson that this was not a Soviet attack, but that
almost surely the Soviets regarded this as a Korean civil conflict.

By 1950 Kennan had become very unhappy with the growth of the military
influence in American foreign policy, and the instinct to have a simplistic approach toward the Communists as one great monolith; and he was uneasy
with the embryonic attempts to do in Asia what we had done in Europe. As
American involvement in Indochina deepened, he had written a long memo
to Acheson saying that the French could not win in Indochina nor could the
Americans replace them and win, and that we were now, whether we realized it or not, on our way toward taking their place. He wrote that if the Vietminh won, it would look like a Communist takeover at first, but eventually
the local forces would find their own level, and the indigenous people would
run things in their own way. Nationalism would inevitably express itself in
hundreds of ways, and the people would not be dominated by Moscow or Peking. What he was really saying was that this was nature taking its course, a
step in the national evolution of the people.

It was not a position which Kennan had come to easily, but he had been
talked into it by a member of his staff at the Policy Planning Council, none
other than John Paton Davies, already being hounded for his China prophecies. Kennan, basically a Europeanist like the others, had been against the
idea of coming to terms with the Vietminh, but Davies had turned him
around. Davies insisted that American policy makers had to get out of the
habit of looking at Communism as a moral issue. Rather, he said, when a local

indigenous force for a variety of reasons has a chance to form an insurgency, the metropolitan government would not be able to defeat it. Davies was extremely skeptical of the American capacity to put trained people into the field to deal with the complexity of these problems, having seen Americans failing at the same thing in China. Davies convinced Kennan that there was no real future for the West in areas like this, and yet the dangers were not so real as they seemed. The local forces, for example, would have to sell the same raw material to the West that they had in the past. It was, of course, similar to Davies' thinking on China, which was that the Chiang government was never much of a friend, it was too Chinese; as such it inevitably had built-in conflicts with us, and thus, similarly, the Mao government could never be much of a friend to Moscow. The best thing we could do in situations like this was to deal with the realities and hope for the best; many of these forces were simply outside our control, and by trying to control them we could not affect them but might, in fact, turn them against us.

Kennan's brilliantly presented arguments, based on the ideas and evidence of Davies, did not change American thinking on Vietnam. The new Assistant Secretary at FE, Dean Rusk, was too much of a traditionalist, a believer that we had to rally a government and not show faint-heartedness. The Kennan-Davies view remained a minority one, all but ignored in the rising domestic tensions and anti-Communism; Kennan's ideas would surface again, some sixteen years later, when the Senate Foreign Relations Committee belatedly held hearings trying to trace the course which had brought us that far.

SINCE THE COURSE WAS ALREADY SET, THE MEMO HAD NO EFFECT AT the time. We picked up the French war and the French assumptions. We financed the war for the next four years, and considered it part of our great global strategy. The architects of the major change had been the Democrats and Acheson, albeit under pressure from the right. In 1952 the Democratic Administration was defeated and the new Republican Secretary of State would lend his own loftiness and grandeur to that particular French cause. Indeed, as the war progressed and the realities of the paddies came home to Paris, the two countries, America and France, seemed to switch sides. The French, who had been eager for the war and for American support, became increasingly dubious, and the Americans seemed more eager for the war than France. And developments showed what strange paths our own smaller compromises would lead us to. Dean Acheson, who had always thought the French cause a false one and who had once seen Ho as a nationalist, and who had made the decision to give arms more as an afterthought, found himself sucked along by the pull of that which had been let loose. In 1953 and 1954, out of office, he met regularly in Princeton with his former State Department associates, and at the time of Dienbienphu he and his aides (with the exception of Kennan) agreed that the United States was making a great and perhaps fatal mistake if it did not go to the rescue of the French and join in on the war. Soft old Dean Acheson. Soft old Democrats.

ALTHOUGH RUSK HAD NOT CHANGED THESE POLICIES HIMSELF, SINCE it was Acheson who was in command, he certainly acquiesced and had no qualms about it. He became a formidable articulator of the policy. The people who wanted a hard-line China policy, on the Hill and at *Time* magazine, found in him a more than acceptable advocate, and he was a very able man to have around during a change in policy (though when he first took over the job at FE, he held to the existing line that the fall of Nationalist China was the Kuomintang's own fault, and in June 1950, just before the Korean War, he had called the rebellion there comparable to "the American revolt against the British"). In fact, it was a speech of Rusk's on China to the China Institute in May 1951 which seemed to mark the new, harder policy. Chiang, not the Communists, were the legitimate rulers of China; the Mao government represented foreign masters. "Forthright speech," said *Time* approvingly; it was a speech which made headlines throughout the country and was reprinted in major news magazines, occasioned a protest from the British, a denial from the State Department that it represented a new policy, and finally a cat-and-mouse press conference by Acheson himself in which he said that it represented nothing new—but it was stronger than the old, wasn't it?

. . . We and the Chinese, for example, have had a vital interest in the peace of the Pacific. Each of us wants security on our Pacific flank and wants to be able to look across those vast waters to find strength, independence and good will in its great neighbor on the other side. It was inevitable that the driving force of Japanese militarism would sooner or later bring China and America together to oppose it, just as we had moved 40 years earlier to support China's independence and integrity against threats from Europe. The same issues are now posed again—and are made more difficult to deal with because foreign encroachment is now being arranged by Chinese who seem to love China less than they do their foreign masters.

∞

The independence of China is gravely threatened. In the Communist world there is room for only one master—a jealous and implacable master, whose price of friendship is complete submission. How many Chinese, in one community after another, are now being destroyed because they love China more than the Soviet Union? How many Chinese will remember in time the fates of Rajk, Kostov, Petkov, Clementis and all those in other satellites who discovered that being Communist is not enough for the conspirators of the Kremlin?

The freedoms of the Chinese people are disappearing. Trial by mob, mass slaughter, banishment as forced labor to Manchuria, Siberia or Sinkiang, the arbitrary seizure of

property, the destruction of loyalties within the family, the suppression of free speech
—these are the facts behind the parades and celebrations and the empty promises.

The territorial integrity of China is now an ironic phrase. The movement of Soviet
forces into Sinkiang, the realities of "joint exploitation" of that great province by Moscow and Peiping, the separation of Inner Mongolia from the body politic of China, and
the continued inroads of Soviet power into Manchuria under the cloak of the Korean
aggression mean in fact that China is losing its great Northern areas to the European
empire which has stretched out its greedy hands for them for at least a century.

∽

Hundreds of thousands of Chinese youth are being sacrificed in a fiery furnace, pit-
ting their waves of human flesh against the fire power of modern weapons—and without heavy equipment, adequate supply or the most elementary medical attention.
Apart from Korea, the Chinese are being pressed to aggressive action in other areas—
all calculated to divert the attention and energies of China away from the encroach-
ments of Soviet imperialism upon China itself.

∽

Events in China must surely challenge the concern of Chinese everywhere—in For-
mosa, on the mainland and in overseas communities. There is a job to be done for
China which only the Chinese can do—a job which will require sustained energy, continued sacrifice and an abundance of the high courage with which so many Chinese
have fought for so long during the struggles of the past decades. The rest of us cannot
tell them exactly what is to be done or how. We cannot provide a formula to engage
the unity of effort among all Chinese who love their country. But one thing we can
say—as the Chinese people move to assert their freedom and to work out their destiny
in accordance with their own historical purposes, they can count upon tremendous
support from free peoples in other parts of the world. . . .

It was strong stuff. There was another speech that night, by John Foster
Dulles, and it was mild by comparison; but it would not hurt the career of
Dean Rusk to have been a little more anti-Mao than Dulles that night. Rusk
would not remain Assistant Secretary very long, however; the Republicans
were on their way back, and they would use the charge of State Department
softness on Communism as the major weapon in their return to power. Many
of the people in State would be badly hurt during this period, but not Rusk, in
part because his own views were indeed hard-line, but more than that, because of an almost unique capacity to stay out of trouble. (After MacArthur
was fired and returned to give his "Old soldiers never die" speech, State knew
there was going to be a congressional inquiry on MacArthur. Yet Rusk did not
go with Acheson to the Hill at that time, though he seemed the logical candidate, being the man for Asia; instead it was Adrian Fisher, the Department's legal counsel, a man who normally would not receive that assignment.)
The Republicans, with Dulles leading the way, attacked the policies of the
past, the immoral compromises, the weakness of the Democratic no-win containment, policies in which Rusk had been one of the lesser architects. But no

matter, Rusk and Dulles got on fine; they had worked well together on the Japanese peace treaty and had kept in touch, and Rusk's views on China were obviously acceptable.

After the Republicans were elected in 1952, which meant that Dulles, chairman of the board of the Rockefeller Foundation, had a new job, Secretary of State, he started to look for a staff for State, but he also needed someone he liked and trusted for the important job of President of the Rockefeller Foundation, and he recommended his young friend Dean Rusk. So Dean Rusk was once again promoted (the best people, who had correctly predicted the fall of China, would see their careers destroyed, but Dean Rusk, who had failed to predict the Chinese entry into the Korean War, would see his career accelerate. There had to be a moral for him here: if you are wrong on the hawkish side of an event you are all right; if you are accurate on the dovish side you are in trouble). He would maintain, this man whose surface identity was as a Democrat, a very close friendship with Dulles. Years later, when Dulles' secretary met Rusk, she said she felt she knew him well. Mr. Dulles had liked him so much, had spoken about him and had told her that any time Mr. Rusk called from New York, she was to put the call through directly because Mr. Rusk was very special, and Mr. Dulles certainly did not do that with many people. Robert Bowie, the head of Policy Planning under Dulles, would confirm this, whenever Rusk was in town Dulles would call him and say—Rusk's here, I want you to spend the day with Rusk, tell him everything we're doing.

So color Rusk neutral, or color him amenable, or hard-line. Who was he, which side was he on? He left State for the next best thing, the head of a great foundation at an unusually early age, only forty-three, and there were to be great things ahead. He had survived the most delicate and politically dangerous period in recent State history, and he had come out stronger than when he went in (with both sides). He was deft enough to retain his friendships with Lovett, Acheson and their friends, to secure new friendships with Dulles and Henry Luce, and yet to send occasional smoke signals to the Democratic liberals that he was on their side. At the same time he was handing out the tax-exempt money of the very wealthy, holding on to a safe and secure base, where risks were minimized. He had a little more interest than in the past in the underdeveloped world, earmarked a little more money for Africa and Asia. So he spent those years of the fifties meeting the wealthy and powerful in New York, making no enemies, waiting for the next phone call from the next President. Making no enemies.

But the Kennedy years were not particularly easy ones; Rusk found himself surrounded by men he considered amateurs, people playing with the processes, interfering with serious men. Rusk was a man who believed in the processes; in fact, in that 1960 *Foreign Affairs* essay he had written advertising himself to the next President, he had said that processes were more important than people, but this was an Administration which believed in the importance of people and their attitudes. (In that sense he and Harriman could not have been more opposite. Harriman believed that you changed policies by changing people, that you fought the bureaucracy; Rusk thought the bureaucracy was something you came to terms with, that its attitudes existed for very real reasons.) The Kennedy style upset Rusk, the young men from the White House trying to get their hands into foreign policy, playing at it, looking over at State and finding bright young friends of theirs, bringing them to NSC meetings so that the Secretary, yes, the Secretary of State would be giving advice and have it challenged by some hot young desk officer. This was a recurrent situation, which he found virtually a violation of his office, and it made his natural tendency to speak only to the President even more marked. Faced with a situation like this he became even more tight-lipped, and he would doodle. Those who knew him well could detect from his scribbling the amount of tension and distaste he felt, and they would decide that the younger and more outspoken the desk officer, the greater the doodle index.

Rusk himself must have sensed the disdain for him around the White House. (He had once scheduled a briefing on nuclear weapons for the high-level officials, believing that they needed to know more about what the weapons would or would not do—and it was a chilling experience. Glenn Seaborg did the briefing on American missile capacity, and afterward, as they were all going back to the White House, Rusk turned to the two high-level White House people with him and said, "It's all very complicated, isn't it? You never know when those things will really work when it comes right down to it, do you?" And one of the very senior White House men answered, "Well, if they don't, you'll never know, Dean.")

He was a man of the past, not entirely at ease with either the direction or style of the new Administration (this included the President himself, who liked to cut through channels and deal with foreign visitors as informally as possible, just the two of them, with no one else around if possible. Rusk hated this; he always wanted someone there, at least an Undersecretary. He was wary of the dangers of a too-personalized diplomacy; it was the same kind of irritation with violation of processes that Acheson had felt about Roosevelt). Yet for all the stylistic problems, the relationship with the President was not bad. True, the President never called him by his first name, and there were hurts absorbed along the way (before Kennedy met with De Gaulle and Khrushchev, he wanted to take a day off and spend it at Villa Serbelloni, the Rockefeller Foundation study center on Lake Como, which Rusk arranged; then Kennedy failed to invite Rusk for the day, and Rusk was particularly wounded). But in addition to his capacity to get things done, and to get things down on paper with great precision of language (once there was a major conflict between Fred Dutton, who was an Assistant Secretary for Congressional Relations, and Bob Manning, Assistant Secretary for Public Affairs, and their interests were clearly antagonistic. Rusk listened to each of them state his case; then he called in a stenographer and dictated a perfect memo which satisfied both of them, a remarkable accomplishment), he was very good going up on the Hill for Kennedy, which was what Kennedy wanted most, a lightning rod there; the more Kennedy departed from the past and tried the new, the more valuable Rusk was on the Hill.

Above all, the Secretary of State deferred to the President (years later, during the Johnson Administration, when Nicholas Katzenbach tried to push Rusk a little on Vietnam, Rusk held back, he was not going to pressure the President on foreign policy, whereupon he gave Katzenbach a long dissertation on the constitutional prerogatives of the President. Katzenbach finally interrupted and said he knew about the Constitution, but a man could be a damn fool and be constitutional). Rusk had a great sense of the function of the office; he believed in people playing their parts, that and no more. He believed that if the Secretary and the President did not agree, it was virtually a constitutional crisis. When Rusk set forth his views forcefully at a National Security Council meeting it was a sure sign that he had already conferred with the President, found that they agreed and thus had been encouraged to speak out within the bureaucracy. But in all of this there was one curious anomaly; Rusk, who had risen to what was the second most powerful position in the nation, did not really covet power. He liked being Secretary of State, liked the title and the job and the trappings and the opportunity to serve; but at the point where you dominate, force yourself and your ideas forward, he shrank back. He did not like to be out front, to take a position of genuine leadership. He really was a modest man in a job which does not entail modesty but demands that the incumbent fight and dominate an entire area of policy making.

Those who worked with him in those days thought he was very good and subtle on the parts of the world where the real issues were already settled; it was only when the idea of change, of softening some of the tensions of the Cold War were involved that his conservatism showed, his uneasiness with new direction, his belief that the other side might exploit our overtures. He was no help at all to the young men, who under Harriman were trying to change the China policy in the Kennedy years; indeed when there was finally some pressure at the Policy Planning Council for a re-evaluation of our China policy, it was Rusk's response that instead of the Department taking the lead, it pass the idea back to the Council on Foreign Relations. Perhaps, he suggested, the Council could undertake a study of Communist China, some books to look at the subject anew (the Council did study the subject, producing a book some four years later). When some people at State wanted to push for recognition of Outer Mongolia as an opening wedge in coming to terms with China, Rusk was no help, indeed he acquiesced to pressure from the Hill and from Nationalist China to shelve the issue. He had been no help in the Kennedy years, but in the Johnson years he became even more of an adversary on a potential new China policy. In fact, in late 1965 McGeorge Bundy, who was relatively open on the issue of coming to terms with China, made an unusually revealing comment about both Rusk and Johnson. Some of Bundy's White House staff people had just pushed through a policy which would open up the possibilities of limited travel in China. They were congratulating themselves on what they had accomplished, but Bundy added a cautionary note on the lessons learned during the struggle for something as small as this. "This President," he said, "will never take the steps on China policy that you and I might want him to take unless he is urged to do so by his Secretary of State. And this Secretary of State will never urge him to do so."

No wonder then that their relationship was so easy, and no wonder that of all the Kennedy people Rusk was the most at ease under Johnson. For Rusk believed in protecting the President from difficult decisions if he wanted to be protected, he believed in containment, he believed in our morality, as opposed to the immorality of the Communist world, and he believed in the use of the force, the primacy of the military, and deep down that the war was a crucial test in Vietnam, and that it was essentially a military problem. He believed, finally, that whatever doubts he had were secondary to what the President wanted to do (so that years later a man who was close to him would say that though Rusk's instincts were divided, albeit probably more for the use of force than against, he could, had Johnson or Kennedy wanted to pull out, easily imagine Rusk having no problem at all assuming the role of main articulator of a policy of withdrawal, going before the Senate Foreign Relations Committee, patiently withstanding the assaults of the Senate hawks).

It was all these factors which allowed State to play such a dormant role in the year 1964, when the political situation in Vietnam continued to collapse and the strength of the Vietcong became ever more evident. When, under normal procedures, it should have been pushing harder than any other organ in the government to come up with political alternatives, when it should have been sending out warning signal after warning signal to the White House about the darkness immediately ahead in the tunnel, saying that the tunnel was getting longer and darker, State simply did not pose deep and probing questions. Instead it geared itself up on straight operational questions: how much fertilizer for this province, how much barbed wire for that. Nineteen sixty-four was a lost year, and much of the loss was attributable to the attitudes and disposition of Dean Rusk.

Chapter Seventeen

IN THE FIRST COUPLE OF MONTHS THE MOST FORCEFUL FIGURE OF the Johnson Administration on Vietnam was Robert McNamara, and it was he who set the tone. Rusk would develop a good relationship with Johnson and there was a natural affinity between the two men, but he did not start off as the strong man on Vietnam (later he would become a pillar of support for the policy as criticism mounted, but this was quite different from being an architect). In those days Rusk's subordinates despaired of him, of his unwillingness to use his platform to play more of a role on Vietnam, his attitude that it was primarily a military problem. He hadn't even visited the country, and there were those in State who thought he should.

At this time Bundy did not have an easy relationship with the new President. Johnson had felt Bundy's disdain in the past, had heard that Bundy mocked him around town, and there was almost an assumption on Johnson's part that Bundy's Eastern elegance and grace had somehow been aimed at Johnson. Bundy's position would later improve, both because McNamara deliberately worked to sell Bundy to Johnson and also because Bundy took a vacation in the Caribbean, and when he did, the White House machinery seemed to fall apart. No one else knew how to push the buttons and move the papers the way Mac did, and Johnson operating without a Bundy found he needed one. However, the relationship was never an easy one, not then, not ever. But McNamara was another thing: from the start Johnson was in awe of him. McNamara, he told friends, was the ablest man he'd ever met in government, so bright, so forceful, so intelligent. He knew so much, and yet unlike intellectuals who knew things, which Johnson did not necessarily admire, McNamara was a doer, he moved things, he worked, a man after Johnson's heart. He had made it by himself in the rough world of business, which impressed Johnson, and then he had given it up, all that money, millions of dollars, and all that stock, to serve the nation.

But it was McNamara in those days who was strong and assertive; if Johnson was a new and untested President, McNamara was a sure and tested Defense Secretary, at the height of his reputation. Because Johnson depended on him, McNamara seemed to surge forward, to become even more assertive and aggressive. Some White House aides felt they could almost mark the change from January 1964 during the brief Panama crisis when there was some uncontrolled sniping and the question arose whether American forces should go into Panama after the snipers. Sitting in the White House with a small group, Johnson had begun a monologue on the sanctity of contracts, a discourse with a high degree of Teddy Roosevelt in it. What a terrible thing this was. By God, in Texas a contract was the most sacred thing there was. And then suddenly, without a word spoken, McNamara jumped up and went to the outer room and called the commander of the troops in the Canal Zone and told him to send them out to patrol in Panama. Some of the White House old-timers watched him uneasily; they thought it was not the way he would have behaved under Kennedy.

If he abhorred a vacuum elsewhere in particular he disliked one on Vietnam, and to an extraordinary degree he took charge of Vietnam. He would complain privately, when political problems on Vietnam were brought to him by civilians, that why didn't they ever go to Rusk with these things, but at the same time he managed to cut out more and more turf for himself. He had been visiting Vietnam often in the past, he had dealt with it, had virtually been the desk officer. He knew it, and knew the President, and he was determined to protect him on Vietnam. If there was to be criticism of the Administration in 1964, let it be of McNamara rather than his Chief. In very late 1963 and early 1964 he, more than any other governmental figure, set the tone and direction, representing Washington in Saigon, and Saigon in Washington, making himself the key figure, and thus ensuring, among other things, that the Administration's attitudes on Vietnam would be primarily military, for McNamara, good civilized businessman and liberal, was nonetheless Secretary of Defense, the man of hardware, and he had to react to the Joint Chiefs of Staff and keep them in line. It was not just a matter of what he wanted, it was a matter of what he could negotiate between the Chiefs and the Administration. He had to come to terms with his constituency, so his attitudes, his love of statistics, his determination to quantify everything, his almost total absence of sense of nuance and feel, were also dominant. (In 1964 Desmond FitzGerald, the number-three man in the CIA, was briefing him every week on Vietnam, and FitzGerald, an old Asia hand, was made uneasy by McNamara's insistence on quantifying everything, of seeing it in terms of statistics, infinite statistics. One day after McNamara had asked him at great length for more and more numbers, more information for the data bank, FitzGerald told him bluntly that he thought most of the statistics were meaningless, that it just didn't smell right, that they were all in for a much more difficult time than they thought. McNamara just nodded curtly, and it was the last time he asked FitzGerald to brief him.)

In December 1963 when McNamara had gone back to Vietnam, he had come away quite depressed. He had found out the degree to which the military had misled him in the past. In addition, the new government was not taking hold, the Vietcong still seemed to be growing in strength. Now he was really beginning to see how bleak the entire picture was. On this trip he had also spent a good deal of time checking the infiltration and discussing means of dealing with it. This would be important because as frustrations with the new government and the conduct of the war mounted, as the United States found itself face to face with failure in the South, it would concentrate more and more on areas that it felt could affect its power. The North. Hanoi. Thus increasing evidence of the failure of the antiguerrilla measures and techniques would push Washington to more and more emphasis on the role of Hanoi in the insurgency, the belief that if we could use our power against Hanoi, we could affect the origins. Thus in 1964, from frustration, Hanoi would grow as the villain; we would believe, first, that Hanoi was the source, and second, that we could, by threat of bombing, determine Hanoi's willingness to underwrite the war. Both of these attitudes would continue to harden, and the players would come to accept them in 1964 in direct proportion to the failures in the South, despite the fact that the intelligence community was warning, first, that the problems were political and in the South, that even if you could shut the country off, the war would continue at virtually the same rate; and second, that there was considerable doubt about how much the threat of bombing would determine any actions of the North Vietnamese. But the thrust of the government was clear; if Saigon turned out to be incompetent, if all those plans and ideas and assistance failed in the South, then there had to be a new rationale. During his December 1963 trip, McNamara had talked at length with the military about covert operations against the North, going over the plans for them. In reporting to the President, he called the plans excellent and he had put General Krulak in charge of working out a program for Johnson on covert operations against the North. It would be known as 34A.

AT ALMOST THE SAME TIME, IN JANUARY 1964, THE JOINT CHIEFS OF Staff moved to expand the war. In a memorandum for the President they decried the limits placed on them in the past ("The United States must be prepared to put aside many of the self-imposed restrictions which now limit our efforts, and to undertake bolder actions which may embody greater risks"). It was clearly the Chiefs' testing of a new President to see how much pressure he could take and what results it would bring. In the past they had identified the source of opposition not so much at the normal center, the State Department, but at the White House; now they were experimenting to see whether with a new President and new failures of the old programs there might be more give, a relaxing of the restrictions; they were also doing what came natural to them, which was to ask for more force, to keep the ante above what the civilians wanted. They characterized the problem in the South not as a political problem, but one of being on the defensive:

Currently we and the South Vietnamese are fighting the war on the enemy's terms. He has determined the locale, the timing and the tactics of the battle while our actions are essentially reactive. One reason for this is the fact that we have obliged ourselves to labor under self-imposed restrictions with respect to impeding external aid to the Vietcong. These restrictions include keeping the war within the boundaries of South Vietnam, avoiding the direct use of U. S. combat forces, and limiting U. S. direction of the campaign to rendering advice to the Government of Vietnam. . . .

The Chiefs recommended a wide range of escalatory measures, principally designed at widening the war, and striking at the North. Thus the scenario was being written in which Hanoi would become increasingly the villain, a villain who had been allowed too free a hand. Once the Chiefs took the position, then McNamara would have to turn to it—particularly if there were additional failures in the South, something which was inevitable—and if McNamara had to react to it, so would the rest of the Administration. If nothing was going to be decided in 1964, then the Chiefs were at least staking out their position (restlessness with the existing situation, which was defensive and wasteful). No comparable political positions were being staked out. The Navy and the Air Force were particularly enthusiastic on this theme; their role in the war had been much too small so far, and an expanded war, a war directed against the North, would allow them to use air power and, in the case of the Navy, carrier-based air power. If the Army had doubts about the efficacy of an expanded war, and it did wonder what air power could effectively do, it was also restless with the existing rules of the war; part of its own ideology was to forge ahead, not to permit sanctuaries, not to use less than maximum force. If an enemy was an enemy, then you lashed out at him. Aware of some of the dangers of an expanded war, and aware of the limits of air power on interdiction, the Army nevertheless was swept along. There would be, in an expanded war, enough room for everyone.

IN WASHINGTON THE HOPE THAT THE NEW GOVERNMENT OF GENERAL Minh, General Don and General Kim could be used to hold the line and begin to prosecute the war had soon vanished. There was little action and little intensification of the war, since these pleasant, emasculated men, having lived under both the French and the Diem governments for so long, made their own accommodations. They were charged with a desperate situation, and faced an enemy who was above all a revolutionary force; the last thing these men were was revolutionaries. They were nice upper-class men with no desire to repress the population, and no sense at all of the harsh demands on them. They could not cope. In addition, they had moved against Diem partly to head off pressure from younger officers who were themselves conspiring against Diem. Taking power had not necessarily removed that pressure and unified the society, but had, after all these years of harsh authoritarian rule, increased the desire for diversity in the South. The almost feudal factionalism of the South still remained a basic political problem among non-Communists, after the one factor which had briefly unified the society—the distaste and hatred for a sick regime—had disappeared. Even the military did not automatically rally around a military leadership, as the Americans learned; young officer was divided from old officer, northerner from southerner, air force from ground officer. In early 1964 there were rumblings of new coups, and of divisions. Nguyen Khanh, commander of the forces in the II Corps area in the Central Highlands, the last general to join the coup against Diem and a favorite of Americans, told his American advisers that he planned to pull a coup against the generals. The report was duly passed to MACV headquarters (and word of it unofficially went to the embassy, which took the position that it did not want to know anything). In February, Khanh deposed the generals, which pleased Harkins, who despised them and had always considered Khanh his special favorite of the Vietnamese officers (because, for one thing, Khanh spoke the best English and was considered the most pro-American).

But the coup would accelerate rather than slow down the surface political instability of the country (the real political instability was basic to the country, old and dying institutions being supported by an outside power against newer, more modern internal drives), for the immediacy of the American acceptance of Khanh, plus the fact that in contrast to how difficult the coup against Diem had been, how easily Khanh pulled his, would underscore the frailty of political control in Saigon. It would encourage rather than discourage other plotters.

Washington may not have realized how little all of this affected the average Vietnamese, but it wanted, above all, surface stability; it had never worried about subsurface instability because that was not visible to the American electorate. It could not, particularly in an American election year, sell the idea of aiding a beleaguered little ally if the ally was more beleaguered by his own officers and battalions than the enemy's. So when Khanh pulled his coup Johnson was, if not angry, irritated and nervous; he was being assured that this was good, that the old generals were sloppy and pro-French while Khanh was our kind of officer, pro-American, he liked us, he would get with the program, that he was a doer, the kind of young nationalist we wanted to encourage and develop, young nationalist and *pro-American*. So Johnson had acquiesced, since there was nothing else to do—there was his ambassador in Saigon holding up the triumphant hand of Khanh like a winning boxer. But Johnson told his staff he wanted "no more of this coup shit." If they had to plot, he said, let them plot against the Vietcong. It would, he said, kill him with the Congress and the newspapers. He couldn't sell this war if they were going to play musical chairs. And he wanted this message brought to them: he wanted them to shape up and cool it. He chose his special messenger, the Secretary of Defense, who would also look over the situation, since the Chiefs were pushing for more force.

McNamara arrived with presidential orders that there were to be no more coups, and the embassy was ordered to get McNamara and Khanh on the front pages everywhere, to make it clear that Khanh was our man. The order to get front-page exposure came through the USIA office, where Barry Zorthian, the officer in charge, decided to have McNamara and Khanh barnstorm together. McNamara would campaign, even babble a few slogans in Vietnamese, thus setting an example for Vietnamese politicians of how to reach out to their own people; when McNamara was gone, Khanh would continue to campaign, and win the people. Zorthian, the most subtle member of the embassy, a man whose own skepticism about the mission was considerable but who was brilliantly effective in quashing doubts in others, asked a staff member what McNamara might say which would be good in Vietnamese. So they went off together, McNamara and Khanh, the United States presence in Asia symbolized by the face of the Secretary of Defense, cameras clicking, McNamara saying, *"Vietnam moun nam, Vietnam moun nam"*—Vietnam a thousand years, Vietnam a thousand years. They made the news shows, the Huntley-Brinkley show. Poor stiff, graceless Robert McNamara, hardly gifted at public relations in his own country, looking particularly foolish as a campaigner (later when Johnson, still in love with McNamara, thought of him as a possible vice-presidential candidate, the ablest man he had ever met, one of the reasons the idea was blocked was memories of that pathetic little barnstorming trip in Saigon). It was an appalling trip, but it worked in that it got McNamara on the front pages, though of course it did not work in stopping coups; it showed the Vietnamese not that the Americans were committed to Khanh, but that the Americans would go with whoever held the reins; for if Khanh was the new American model Vietnamese as far as Washington was concerned, the Vietnamese read him more accurately: just another former French corporal playing the game of intrigue.

As the decay in Saigon became more evident, McNamara was also charged with looking into the possibilities of bombing as a means of bringing more pressure to bear on Hanoi. Would it have to be done, and if so, should it be done immediately? Or could we wait? These were questions which the government was pushing at the President; if Vietnam was falling apart, perhaps the bombing could hold it together. It would rally Saigon and at the same time it might make Hanoi ease off on the pressure. Thus it was a card to be played perhaps without committing the President, to be played and then pulled back. It could even help protect the President. So even as McNamara was striding through the streets of Hué, the bureaucracy in Washington began to intensify its study of the bombing possibilities, and also started working on pinpointing targets. McNamara himself returned from Vietnam in mid-March with a pessimistic appraisal of the situation in Vietnam, reporting that the situation in the countryside had deteriorated, the Vietcong had up to 90 percent control in key provinces in the Delta, and neutralist sentiment was rising. Not surprisingly, he focused most of his attention on what could be done to affect the war by pressuring Hanoi. He did not recommend bombing; he had checked first with the President, and the President was not ready for it. But he did not want to be in conflict with the Chiefs; so he recommended that they go ahead with the planning of what they wanted, concentrating on two particular types of bombing. The first would be a quick strike, to be launched within seventy-two hours, primarily in retaliation for specific guerrilla incidents. The second part was the real bombing program. This, unlike the other, would not be tit for tat; it would be ready to go on thirty days' notice, and it would be a major strike against the North's military and industrial centers. These would be sustained raids, in effect what Rostow had been talking about for more than three years. A real bombing program, the use of the threat of bombing to coerce Ho Chi Minh to de-escalate the war rather than lose his precious industrial base.

McNamara made these recommendations officially on March 16, after checking how far the President wanted to go on the subject (which was that he wanted the study in the works, that and nothing more; he wanted his options open). On March 17 the National Security Council met, and Johnson and McNamara played out their charade, using the National Security Council as a forum to inform the rest of the Administration of their intentions. The President told the NSC that he wanted the planning on the bombing to go ahead energetically, which gave the military what they wanted. The generals had not really expected a bombing program this early; as this was an election year, they knew that the President, as Bundy told the principals and McNamara relayed to them, had "his problems." It was not something they talked about, but there was an awareness of his difficulties. The main thing was that they were permitted to go ahead with the planning.

In addition, the McNamara report (written by John McNaughton), was by itself a particularly significant document. In its preamble it set out the aims of American policy, and the rationale for the objectives. It was significant because these aims had not been so clearly stated before, nor would they be subsequently. In fact, another version of them would become the critical inner governmental paper on American objectives; years later, in looking back over the papers which had determined the goals of the war, the staff which compiled the Pentagon Papers came up with Nassam 288 (National Security paper 288). It was based on the McNamara paper and was almost word for word identical. Nassam 288 said:

> We seek an independent non-Communist South Vietnam. We do not require that it serve as a Western base or as a member of a Western Alliance. South Vietnam must be free, however, to accept outside assistance as required to maintain its security. This assistance should be able to take the form not only of economic and social measures but also police and military help to root out and control insurgent elements.
>
> Unless we can achieve this objective in South Vietnam, almost all of Southeast Asia will probably fall under Communist dominance (all of Vietnam, Laos, and Cambodia), accommodate to Communism so as to remove effective U.S. and anti-Communist influence (Burma), or fall under the domination of forces not now explicitly Communist, but likely then to become so (Indonesia taking over Malaysia). Thailand might hold for a period with our help, but would be under grave pressure. Even the Philippines would become shaky, and the threat to India to the west, Australia and New Zealand to the south, and Taiwan, Korea, and Japan to the north and east would be greatly increased.
>
> All these consequences would probably have been true even if the U.S. had not since 1954, and especially since 1961, become so heavily engaged in South Vietnam. However, that fact accentuates the impact of a Communist South Vietnam not only in Asia, but in the rest of the world, where the South Vietnam conflict is regarded as a test case of U.S. capacity to help a nation meet a Communist "war of liberation."

It was, in fact, the Secretary of Defense playing the role of Secretary of State, and going ahead with the straight domino theory, though the CIA and the other intelligence agencies were reporting, quite the opposite, that the dominoes were not all the same size, shape and color, that the loss of South Vietnam might have less impact outside the immediate Indochinese peninsula, that the other countries reacted to very different political pressures, and that Vietnamese nationalism, left over from the colonial war, which was the principal force aiding the Vietcong in Vietnam, might have no effect in a country which had not undergone a colonial experience. But the McNamara position did not take into account the aftereffects of the French war which might make Vietnamese Communism different; instead, Communism was some great force which was sweeping right across a wide area.

It was an important moment, even though immediate action was postponed. The given, which was that there was a country called South Vietnam, that it wanted to be free and had to be denied to the Communists, hardened within the bureaucracy, as did the ostensible reason for holding it, the domino theory. (Johnson himself did not take the domino theory seriously; he was far more worried about the loss of a country to the Communists and what this would do to him in terms of domestic politics, though this could not be expressed so bluntly in an official paper.) These assumptions became realities, became the given. Since McNamara had noticed the increase of neutralist sentiment in Vietnam, the kind of sentiment which might lead to a neutralist coup, a coalition government which would ask the Americans to leave, he warned the President there was a real danger of this, that U.S. policy must be aimed against this threat. Three days later Johnson cabled Lodge that he was intent on "knocking down the neutralization wherever it rears its ugly head, and on this point I think nothing is more important than to stop neutralist talk wherever we can by whatever means we can." At the very time that they were talking about keeping their options open, they were closing them off. They were not questioning the given or the assumption of Vietnam; they were determining that the country would stand, like it or not, able to stand or not. They were not distinguishing between Communism in Vietnam and why it was successful and the exterior Communist threat to other countries in the region. And they were not analyzing to what degree the people of South Vietnam did or did not sustain the Vietcong. McNamara made his assessments in a vacuum, and the kind of challenge to them that might have taken place was absent. State made no rejoinder, there was no debate over the assumptions of the facts, no discussion of possibilities of negotiation. The man who was in charge of the counterassessments at State, William Bundy, had just come from McNamara's shop and he was entirely agreeable to the goals. Thus, without seeming to make a decision, while on the contrary seeming to avoid a decision, the bureaucracy both at Defense and at State had been given the go-ahead, and told in effect to start planning for war. It was not so much that Defense was strong; it was that State was both weak and amenable.

WHILE McNAMARA WAS IN VIETNAM, THE STATE DEPARTMENT HAD been preparing a major study on the bombing at the Policy Planning Council under Robert Johnson. The study had been ordered at the beginning of the year but little had been done about it then; suddenly McNamara went to Vietnam and the timetable was speeded up, the answers were to coincide with his return. There was enormous pressure for an answer to the question:

Would the bombing work? Perhaps there was going to be a decision to bomb, after all.

Robert Johnson himself had not been eager to take on the job of preparing the study. As Rostow's deputy, he knew how strongly his boss felt on the subject of bombing, that it was above all *the* answer, the vital card, and though he liked Rostow personally, he disagreed strongly. His own impression was that Vietnam was coming apart and would continue to do so, and he thought it would be difficult to do an honest paper with Rostow in charge. Nonetheless, he finally accepted the job. He put together a staff of about six people, all intergovernmental men, all pure intelligence people. The study dealt solely with the bombing and they had to identify the main questions. First: Would it work? Would Hanoi drop its support of the Vietcong if we pressured by bombing? Then: What were the upper levels of the U.S. commitment? What would bombing do in the way of bringing about meaningful negotiation? What would be the problems of exiting, in case of failure? What would be the problems of justifying the U.S. action in legal and moral terms? What was the problem of defining American objectives and Communist possible reactions? And finally: What would the effects be on the Sino-Soviet split?

It was, in the classic sense, a pure study. It reflected the genuine expertise of the government from deep within its bowels, not its operational functions, not its ambitions, not its success drives. None of the staffers represented vested interests, and none really saw his future being affected by either a positive or negative study. They considered all kinds of bombing, quick tit-for-tat retaliations and massive, prolonged saturation bombing. They worked under intense pressure for about two weeks, eight hours a day, six days a week. When they finished they had a stack of papers about a foot high and the essential answer, which was no, bombing the North would not work.

Basically the study showed that the bombing would fail because the North was motivated by factors which were not affected by physical change and physical damage. The North Vietnamese were not hooked on the idea of economic growth determination (which was one of the great hang-ups of Rostow), but were determined to extend their regime's control to the entire country rather than maintain their industrialization. That was what motivated them, and that was what they considered their unfinished business. They had invested a great deal in it and they would continue to invest in it; no North Vietnamese government could afford to do less. Hanoi, the study said, enjoyed the nationalist component of unity and the Communist component of control, which made for an organized, unified modern state. Given their standard of living, their determination, bombing would not affect them, other than produce a tendency perhaps to strengthen the regime's control. There was also a consensus on one key point: if you threatened the North with escalation you would soon know whether or not it would work because they would have to respond before you started (that is, they would never fold their hand under duress and go to the bargaining table, because once there, all the United States would have to do was threaten once more to start bombing and they would have to concede more).

Nor was anyone particularly optimistic the bombing would improve South Vietnamese morale. The study implied that escalation would not bring negotiation, that it would place at least as much pressure on the United States as on Hanoi, and that the subsequent problems of de-escalation would be even more difficult to deal with. Bombing would have raised the stakes, South Vietnam would have become much more important as an issue, a South Vietnamese regime would have become even more dependent upon the United States (which had just bombed the North, partly to improve Southern morale). So the position, in terms of extrication, would be even more complicated.

In addition, the study showed that there would be a considerable international outcry if the United States bombed the North, that this would seem a disproportionate response to what the North was doing in the South (which reflected a feeling that few Americans had, about how repugnant bombing was to the rest of the world, since much of it had been bombed, while America had done some of the bombing but had never been bombed itself), and that while this would not pose a serious problem if quick success was achieved, it would become sticky if the war became drawn out, as it was likely to be.

It was an important study because it not only predicted that the bombing would not work, and predicted Hanoi's reaction to the pressure, which was to apply counterpressure, but it forecast that the bombing would affect (and imprison) the American government. That was particularly prophetic because America did eventually bomb with a view to bringing the North to the conference table. It would find that it was, instead of changing the North, sticking itself to a tar baby, and that nothing could take place in the way of talks or negotiations, no word of peace exchanged as long as the bombing continued, thus forcing an American President to change and undo his own fragile political balance and give up hopes of a second term in order to get back a card for the purposes of negotiation, a card which had been played in the first place to bring negotiations.

The Johnson study had very little impact, for a variety of reasons. The first was that Policy Planning is not an operative area, it is not a place for doers, and over a prolonged period of time in the State Department its influence had steadily decreased. As the Cold War had advanced and hardened, there was less and less need for it; what the United States wanted to do, the internal and domestic implications of a policy, became more important. So Policy Planning was off the beaten path. Rostow, the current head of it, had been sent there by Kennedy in a moment of Kennedy's disenchantment. For all its talented people, it did not enter into policy making, it was a not serious place. The elephant was great and powerful and preferred being blind. That was one problem. The second problem was timing; though the study had been rushed through with the idea of coinciding with the McNamara report on bombing, the President had let McNamara know that he did not want to make any major decisions for the present, and so the bombing was put on hold, and the decision delayed. Similarly, the massive and significant study was pushed aside because it had come out at the wrong time. A study has to be published at the right moment, when people are debating an issue and about to make a decision; then and only then will they read a major paper, otherwise they are too pressed for time. Therefore, when the long-delayed decisions on the bombing were made a year later, the principals did not go back to the old Bob Johnson paper, because new things had happened, one did not go back to an old paper.

Finally and perhaps most important, there was no one to fight for it, to force it into the play, to make the other principals come to terms with it. Rostow himself could not have disagreed more with the paper; it challenged every one of his main theses, his almost singular and simplistic belief in bombing and what it would accomplish. He did not censor the study, but he worked to suppress it and as a result its distribution was quite limited; neither Rusk nor Bill Bundy was enthused by it (in other days Harriman might have forced it upon everyone), and it was very closely held. Later in the year, however, parts of the report were bootlegged through the government, and one part of it played a major role in confirming the doubts of George Ball and provided much of the raw material for his dissenting papers. So the government was able to weed out its own caution, and keep it out of the mainstream; if it is kept out of the mainstream, it does not exist. And so it did not exist.

EVEN SO, THE SLATE HAD TO BE WIPED CLEAN. NOT ONLY WAS THERE A need to negate and remove the Policy Planning study, but there was a need to have a piece of paper which would be intellectually reassuring. In April a special intelligence study was ordered, which meant that though many of the same experts would participate, the results would be radically different, because the military intelligence people were brought in. A Special Intelligence Estimate is a very formal procedure, with very definite patterns. CIA, for instance, chairs it, which means that the Agency's role shifts dramatically. Instead of giving pure intelligence, the Agency people become bureaucratic. They are told to come up with a piece of paper and they want to provide that piece of paper; thus they seek a consensus. In addition, they are working against a deadline, which means the softening of their own estimates in order to get the military to come along. Thus the State Department experts, the Intelligence and Research people, lose an ally (CIA), which has become bureaucratic, and gain an enemy, the military.

And the military, in a case like this, can be very tricky in its intelligence estimates; it is the job of the military intelligence people to get along with their superiors. Rusk and Bill Bundy, for example, did not directly try to influence their own intelligence people (they often ignored them, but they did not meddle with them; rather the real problem in 1964 for the INR people was trying to get the attention of their superiors, trying to get someone to fight for them). But the JCS and their intelligence people are quite different; the light colonels and bird colonels, bright men on their way up, are soldiers; they are in uniform, they know what the JCS wants, they are servants, and they have bright careers ahead. An Air Force intelligence officer will not, for instance, say that the bombing will not work. So in an intelligence estimate like this, the INR experts are not going against comparable intelligence officers; instead, they are going against wholly committed men (very intelligent men, and men whose private estimates may be quite close to what the INR people are saying).

State would see grays, the military blacks and whites; State would see doubts, the military certitudes. And State would always end up being conciliatory; its terms were not as firm and hard and sure as the military's. INR could never be sure of what it was saying, and somehow the military always seemed sure; they had facts and they had military expertise. If State tried to challenge them, it was blocked off. State could not make judgments on military possibilities, things which involved military expertise. Yet at the same time the military were constantly poaching on State's territory ("We will bomb X and Y, and you can't tell us that they won't feel it, that they won't quit then"). There was, for example, a major argument over whether or not explosives could close the Mu Ghia Pass. The State people argued that rather than closing it, explosives would widen it (which is exactly what happened). The military were sure explosives could close it. They were experts on explosives, this was their trade, so how could State know—what did State know about bombing?

To a degree, the Army was sympathetic to what the INR people were saying. The Army people had always had their doubts about the effect of interdiction by air, but the services would bind together under the gentlemen's agreements which protect their autonomy and mythology (the Army did not challenge the Air Force on its capacity to bomb, and the Air Force, though reflecting considerable doubts, did not challenge the Army on its capacity to fight a politically oriented land war in Asia, though later each branch's intelligence estimates of the other's failings were quite accurate; the Army was good on the failures of the bombing, the Air Force was good on the limits of the land war). But in the overall intelligence estimate, the arrival of the military shifted the weight of the study. CIA was neutral and compromised in order to have a finished piece of paper and the political people were brought down to a minority viewpoint, largely footnoting their dissent. The crucial factor was that the President would ask, What is the vote? and the vote would be yes, the bombing would do it. Thus did the government protect its capacity to go against its own wisdom and expertise.

Chapter Eighteen

VERY SUBTLY IN THE LATE WINTER AND INTO THE EARLY spring of 1964 a change began to take place within the government and the bureaucracy. It was something which was not announced, but Vietnam gradually became a more sensitive, more delicate, and more dangerous subject. As such it became something spoken about less and less, the decisions became more and more closely held, and the principals became even more guarded with whom they spoke on the subject. They did not want to be seen with known, identified doves; they did not want to be considered soft. If they had to meet with, say, a reporter known as a dove, they would let friends know that it had to happen, as Bill Bundy did, but with an inflection in his voice of what-else-can-I-do, and a pleasure in telling aides that he was keeping the dove journalist waiting, which was what a dove deserved. Or at the White House, where the subject became more and more sensitive, Chester Cooper, a former CIA analyst who was extremely knowledgeable about Indochina, found that it was more and more difficult to reach McGeorge Bundy on the subject as the questions became graver and the failures more apparent. Cooper began to write memos to his boss expressing his grave doubts about the situation in Vietnam, but he soon found that the subject was so delicate that it was better to write them by hand so that Bundy, reading them, would know that not even a secretary had seen these words and these thoughts; such doubts did not exist except in the most private sense between two men.

Actually, changes and nuances like these were indications of which way they were going, although they were not signals that the outside public, or for that matter, the men involved themselves, could read. Part of this was the growing sense of failure over Vietnam and part of it was the new style that Lyndon Johnson had brought to the White House and the government at large, a sharp contrast to the Kennedy style, which was post-Bay of Pigs to ventilate an issue as much as possible within the government. Above all, Johnson believed in secrecy. He liked to control all discussions; the more delicate the subject, the more he liked to control it. Thus by his very style Johnson limited the amount of innergovernmental debate, partly because debate went against his great desire for consensus, whether a good policy or not, a wise one or not. The important thing was to get everyone aboard; if there was consensus there was no dissent and this was a comforting feeling, it eased Johnson's insecurities.

So the reins of debate began to tighten and be limited, and the bureaucracy began to gear up for war. Individual doubters began to be overwhelmed by the force of the bureaucracy, the increasing thrust of it, mounting day by day, like the current of a river as it nears the ocean. And no one symbolized the force of the bureaucracy against the stand of the individual, the incapacity to be oneself because the price of being oneself meant losing one's governmental position and respectability as a player, more than a young Harvard Law School professor named John McNaughton.

He was the least known of the major players; his life and that of his wife and a young son ended tragically in July 1967 in a freak plane accident, a light private plane smashing into the jetliner carrying the McNaughton family. Yet when the Pentagon Papers were published the impression was that he had been the leading hawk of the era. His name seemed to be on almost every other paper, and the documents were appallingly functional and mechanistic, drained of any human juices (the public reaction to the McNaughton papers was not much different from that of his staff, which after his death had had to go through his papers and came across a private file of memos from McNaughton to McNamara, so closely held that only the two had seen them, in which they had debated and measured the troop and bombing commitments, and it was, said one of his staff members who had loved McNaughton, "like finding a secret John McNaughton"). In the Pentagon Papers he seemed to symbolize the inhumane and insensitive quality of that era, undoubting, unreflective, putting the quantifying of deaths and killing and destruction into neat, cold, antiseptic statistics, devoid of blood and heart.

Yet in many ways quite the opposite was true. No one at a high level of government had served his country better on the question of disarmament than John McNaughton. He had a genuine, cold passion for arms control, and he had helped bring McNamara and the Defense Department around to the limited test-ban treaty. Equally important, no one in the high levels of government in 1964 had greater and more profound doubts about the wisdom of the policy the nation was following in Vietnam, and no one argued more forcefully with his immediate superior against the particular course. And having lost that argument, when someone else—perhaps from State, perhaps from CIA—made the same points which McNaughton had just made to McNamara, no one tore those arguments apart more ferociously than John McNaughton. Once he left Tom Hughes, the brilliant State Department official who headed INR after Hilsman, feeling that the wind had been knocked out of him. Hughes had made an extremely pessimistic appraisal of the chances for success in Vietnam and a rather positive estimate on the vitality of the enemy. McNaughton looked at him and said with disdain, "Spoken like a true member of the Red Team," the designation for the Vietcong-Hanoi side in the war games.

McNaughton was the classic rationalist, and he prided himself on this. When he taught evidence at Harvard Law School, he specialized in defining the difference between reality and illusion. He would walk into a law class, pull out a toy pistol, shoot a student and then take sixteen different versions of what had happened. Then he would point out to his class the difference between what they thought they had seen and what they actually saw, carefully extracting the hearsay. Facts, always facts. Define what people are saying. He could come back from meetings at Harvard, or later in the Defense Department, and replay the meeting, to the delight of subordinates, not just what each person had said, but what he meant when he said it and why he was saying it. He would bring out the prejudices, and tear at the whole petty, self-protective fraud of a meeting. Thus he was a brilliant bureaucratic gossip. He was completely detached, being able to look at a situation with all his own prejudices removed. Logic and facts alone counted; if he had any prejudice at all, it was a bias in favor of logic.

Though he had been a Harvard Law School professor, he was markedly different from the rest of the Cambridge crowd. His roots were not in that Eastern establishment; instead he was the scion of Pekin, Illinois, the son of the owner of the local newspaper there. He was a man who almost flaunted his Midwestern quality, who could put on the twang at a moment's notice and mimic his origins. Not only that, and more important, he could mimic the styles of his Eastern colleagues, playing the role of the country hick, letting the smooth Easterners know that John McNaughton was a little different, that he might in a sense be a good liberal like the rest of them, but that he had his own identity and it was a little more skeptical of their attitudes. He had once run the family paper in Pekin and also gone back once to run for Congress; it was a very good race, but he lost and returned to the East.

Tall and cool, almost brusque (was the brusqueness a cover for shyness because he was a gangling skinny six foot four?); not a particularly good teacher and not liking to teach that much (he did not intend to go back to Harvard Law after his tour in government), disliking the military and making it obvious (though he was perhaps Mcnamara's most trusted deputy at the end of his life, he could never have succeeded him as Secretary of Defense; there was too much antagonism built up there, even among the younger brighter military officers who felt what they considered Mcnaughton's contempt not just for the old-fashioned bombs-away generals, but for themselves as well, the men who felt they were working for the same thing as McNaughton and were hurt by his brusqueness and rudeness). Since he was not of that Eastern elite, he was not wedded to their ideas in national security, to containment in Europe, to the arms race, and to the domino theory. From the moment he joined the Defense Department he had begun to question the wisdom of some of America's commitments, what were considered then the realities of foreign policy and now are considered the myths. The young men around him, who were schooled in the language and litany of the Cold War, regarded him with certain misgiving. Wasn't this a kind of Midwestern isolationism showing? Wasn't it too bad that McNaughton hadn't taken the right graduate courses with Kissinger and the others so he would *know* about these things, as they knew?

Instead he brought an intuitive doubt to many of the issues; he did not, as many of them did, accept all the assumptions of the Cold War. He was perhaps the most iconoclastic member of the government, questioning privately and sometimes publicly the most sacred assumptions, and he could sit with Senate aides, this man who held such power at the Defense Department, its budget always rising, and say, "How much do we really need for the *defense* of the United States of America? Only the defense, to defend its shores? . . . Well I suppose the maximum for the defense of our shores is one billion dollars. So all the rest of our defense budget relates to what we regard as our responsibilities as a world power?" Probably the best definition yet of a country emerging as the new Rome, by one of the head Romans himself.

He was also totally driven and very ambitious; he projected his working hour to the minute. Roger Fisher, a Harvard Law School friend, calling him for lunch, would find that McNaughton was busy—was it that important? And Fisher said yes, and then McNaughton said, "All right, make it twelve thirty-five and we'll have a sandwich," and at 12:35 the door would open and Fisher went in, and a sandwich it would be, for ten minutes. The first thing that Fisher, who was worried about the direction of American policy in Vietnam, said was that McNaughton was too tied to the daily routine, that he was overworked and needed time to think, not to rush more and more papers through, but to stop and to reflect and look ahead, and in particular to think about an idea which was a favorite theme of Fisher's, what the political objective of American policy was, what we wanted Hanoi to do.

"Look at my schedule," McNaughton said, and Fisher protested that the schedule had to be pushed aside. He didn't care how many meetings there were, how much pressure there was, how many five-minute increments marked on that carefully kept schedule; this was the most important thing for McNamara's chief political officer. "No," repeated McNaughton, "look at my schedule." Finally Fisher did and there, after all those tiny meetings and tiny increments, five minutes each, he had blocked out five hours, from 1:15 to 6:15, and noted: *"What are we trying to get Hanoi to do?"*

He was a man after McNamara's heart in this, the quantifying of everything, the capacity to break things down, to do it numerically and statistically. Even when he spoke against the arms race, to limit it if not halt it, his terms often seemed curiously mechanistic, as if human beings never entered the calculations. In 1966 McNaughton was asked to meet with a group of sociologists and economists headed by Kenneth Boulding, to explain what McNamara was trying to do at the Pentagon. McNaughton agreed because some old friends were organizing the meeting, and he gave a particularly brilliant performance on the McNamara revolution, on cost effectiveness, a presentation of both force and brilliance, and yet curiously unsatisfying, so that finally one of the young sociologists got up and said, "Mr. McNaughton, I've had enough. All your facts, all your statistics, all your slide rules, all your decisions—you speak it all so well, and yet where is *man* in all this, Mr. McNaughton? Where are his needs, and where are his problems? Does all of this do him any good? Or does it do him more harm?" McNaughton rose again and said, in effect, *touché:* "At last someone's made the point. All day long I've been talking with you and you've been giving me the standard left-wing stuff, and you've been debating whether we count better than you do, and now finally we have something, and the trip is worthwhile for me."

In 1964 McNaughton was very unsure of his relationship with McNamara, he was never in his position than McNamara was in his. He was almost mesmerized by McNamara; he had never seen anything like him and admired the Secretary without reservation, being almost slavish in his subservience. That and being extremely ambitious, and wanting, now that he was operating in the big and fast world of Washington, to remain there. So he became at once the man in the government where two powerful currents crossed: great and forceful doubts about the wisdom of American policy in Vietnam, and an equally powerful desire to stay in government, to be a player, to influence policies for the good of the country, for the right ideas, and for the good of John McNaughton. Though he was a Harvard law professor, there was no more skillful player of the bureaucratic game than John McNaughton, for he understood the bureaucracy very quickly and how to play at it, and he learned this, that his power existed only as long as he had Robert McNamara's complete confidence, and as long as everyone in government believed that when he spoke, he spoke not for John McNaughton but for Bob McNamara. That, with its blind loyalty and totality of self-abnegation, meant bureaucratic power, and John McNaughton wanted power. Any doubts he had were reserved for McNamara, virtually alone, and perhaps one or two other people that he knew and trusted, who would not betray him with gossip, so that the word would not go around Washington that McNaughton was a secret dove. Nor was he at all unaware of the enormous political sensitivity of even thinking like a dove, and of doing dovish papers. In late 1964 he assigned Daniel Ellsberg to the job of looking for ways of rationalizing the American way out of Vietnam—if everything collapsed. It was in effect to be a covering White Paper along the lines of the China White Paper. The secrecy involved in Ellsberg's assignment was paramount: Ellsberg, McNaughton made clear, was to talk to no one else about his assignment, not even his colleagues in the McNaughton shop. He was not to use a secretary on his reports but was to type them himself. In addition McNaughton wanted to make clear that this very assignment might damage Ellsberg's career, that a repeat of the McCarthy period was possible. "You should be clear," he repeatedly warned Ellsberg, "that you could be signing the death warrant to your career by having anything to do with calculations and decisions like these. A lot of people were ruined for less."

Yet the doubts expressed in the Ellsberg papers clearly reflected McNaughton's own doubts. In 1964, rather early, John McNaughton had begun thinking the darkest thoughts, touching very quickly on the central problems of Vietnam, not whether it was a question of personnel, getting better people there, or better programs or more equipment, but whether we should be there at all, whether, to use an almost isolationist term, those people wanted us there. Was it worth it, shouldn't we perhaps just get out quickly at a lower price? He had few illusions about the ability of our Vietnamese allies, and the more he studied the war, the more respect he had for the Vietcong. He was capable, in 1964, of listening to aides brief him on the quality of Vietcong leadership and motivation, and saying almost offhandedly, in a rare off-guard moment, "If what you say in that briefing is true, we're fighting on the wrong side." Knowing that McNamara did not yet share these doubts, he was very careful about getting some corroboration before he went head-on to his boss with them. And in this increasingly tense atmosphere, as he looked for someone to share his doubts with, someone who knew something about Vietnam and would not talk out of turn and just might be dovish, he finally decided that he might find a co-conspirator, not at State, State was too gossipy, but at the White House, there was less bureaucratic entanglement there. The White House was safer; it was somehow a more private place. Michael Forrestal was an old friend of McNaughton's, they had worked together on the Marshall Plan, and very early in the game McNaughton had sensed Forrestal's own growing doubts about Vietnam. Since Forrestal was a key link in the Harriman group and had spent a good deal of time in Vietnam, he was the ideal man to talk to and would be able to confirm or refute McNaughton's suspicions.

There was something very clandestine about their meetings, beginning in the spring of 1964. McNaughton would call Forrestal to find out if he was free for a chat, nothing formal. Then he would arrive at the White House at five-thirty, which was not easily done, the traffic was very heavy going against him but it could not be done the other way, Forrestal could not visit McNaughton at the Pentagon without causing great suspicion. People would ask, What's Forrestal doing at the Pentagon? Isn't he just a little bit soft? This was the cool, bureaucratic McNaughton, conspiring for the good of mankind, not about to get himself tagged as unrealistic nor for that matter his boss either, because any doubts about him would also reflect on McNamara; above all, he and McNamara would be realistic.

Yet in these private meetings all his doubts would pour out. He had done his homework and the more he did, the more it bothered him. The lawyer's mind asked the cutting questions: If the government in Saigon was weak and probably not viable, was it worthwhile to try and bolster it? This seemed questionable because if it was weak it would probably stay that way and you simply would become more involved without having any effect on it. Do you really want to commit yourself more to something that sick? Would it make a lasting difference if we bombed or sent troops, or would that be a gimmick with a brief positive effect, which would very quickly lose its impact upon such a fatigued and divided society? Was there really anything there to build on, was it a government, or was it something we called a government because we wanted an illusion through which to enact our policy? Were we committing ourselves to something that did not exist, and if so, wasn't it extremely dangerous? Bombing bothered him. Everyone now was planning the bombing. But could you really bring people around, change them, by punishing them? Did we know enough about their standard of living to know whether it would really affect their daily existence? It was a vintage McNaughton performance totally without passion, performed not so much by conviction or morality as by rationality. He simply hated the proportions of it, the sense that we were totally losing perspective, and that if events took their course we would be fools in the eyes of the world, victims of our ego.

McNaughton found in Forrestal a sympathetic listener and a man who largely confirmed his own doubts, and by the same token, the more McNaughton evoked from him, the more Forrestal found his own doubts crystallizing. But he was not yet as pessimistic as McNaughton; he did not think the dark picture he painted of the world of Saigon would necessarily entrap the United States. He was sure that it could be avoided somehow, that there were options, that good intelligent men in Washington could control decisions and avoid the great entanglement.

McNaughton was not so sure. "The trouble with you, Forrestal," he once said, "is that you always think we can turn this thing off, and that we can get off of it whenever we want. But I wonder. I think if it was easy to get off of it, we would already have gotten off. I think it gets harder every day, each day we lose a little control, each decision that we make wrong, or don't make at all, makes the next decision a little harder because if we haven't stopped it today, then the reasons for not stopping it will still exist tomorrow, and we'll be in even deeper." Even as he spoke, Forrestal felt chilled, for McNaughton was not just challenging what was going on in Vietnam, there were lots of people in Washington who were doing that, what he was challenging was even more basic: the illusion of control, the illusion of options, the belief that whenever Washington really wanted to, it could pull itself together and handle Vietnam. He was challenging, then, not just the shabbiness and messiness of Vietnam, but the most sacred illusion of all, the capacity of Washington to control and manage foreign events.

Having finished with Forrestal, McNaughton would go back and pour out his doubts to one man, Robert S. McNamara, a man he was still in awe of. McNamara would override them, he would dampen them, it would be business as usual, and McNaughton, the secret dove, would emerge from the Secretary's office and hide his doubts, because he still wanted to be a player, and he knew there was no power at the Pentagon if he differed from McNamara at all. So John McNaughton would attend meetings where some of George Ball's people might express their doubts, the same skepticism he felt, but he would tear them apart, into little pieces, almost rudely. Later, after the war had been escalated and he had become more confident of his relationship with McNamara and more sure that the war was wrong, some of his close aides began to wonder what would happen if the President ever asked him what he, John McNaughton, thought about an escalatory move, not what the Defense Department thought, not what McNamara thought. In 1966, when the question of bombing the oil depots at Haiphong came up, and the President was going around the room trying to get a consensus, one after another they all signed on, McNamara said yes, it was time to take them out. The Chiefs and then Rostow signed on. Ball dissented. And finally Johnson turned to McNaughton, who had been arguing violently in private against this, and McNaughton said simply, "I have nothing to add, sir."

He fought it within himself, and fought it with his chief, but already the thrust of his own institution was so strong that he could not resist it. He would become a doubter and a pessimist who also picked bombing targets and did much of the planning and supplied much of the rationale, working very closely with McNamara. There were those who knew them both who thought that McNamara must have found it very reassuring to have this eminently civilized and rational man, the flower of Pekin, Illinois, working with him as he planned the war.

IF THE THRUST OF THE BUREAUCRACY WAS BECOMING MORE OBVIOUS at Defense, then what was happening at State was more subtle. The group there which had been fighting the policies of the past on Asia, which had challenged the official estimates from Vietnam and the ability to win with Diem, always maintaining that the war was primarily a political problem, was being systematically dismantled. Although it was one of the most important developments in 1964, it went almost unnoticed; there was, for instance, no reporting about it in the country's great national newspapers or magazines (as there had been almost no reporting on its formation). The group had jelled late in the Kennedy Administration, breaking through some of the policies of the past. Perhaps not even deliberately these men were now slowly being filtered out of the policy-making decisions, in part consciously because they had questioned the policies but to an even larger degree unconsciously, not so much because they were skeptical, but because they seemed too negative. Another reason was that both in their attacks on Diem and in their disdain for Rusk and Vice-President Johnson, they had made enemies, not powerful then but powerful now. Dean Rusk, no longer liaison man to the Hill, was increasingly becoming Secretary of State. Thus Harriman, Hilsman, Trueheart, Forrestal and Kattenburg very quickly became nonplayers. First Paul Kattenburg. He was the lowest-ranking of the players but he had perhaps been the most important because he knew the most about the country. He had been in Vietnam all through the fifties, fighting both from Saigon and from Washington for the group which wanted more emphasis on nationalism as opposed to the group which simply wanted to go along with the French and seek a military solution, a group which in 1950 and 1951 was headed by Dean Rusk. Kattenburg's early doubts about the French had not helped him; he was separated from the issue in the fifties, moved to Latin America and then the Philippines, and it was only in 1962 that he was rehabilitated by Hilsman, who had known him as a fellow Yale Ph.D. candidate. Rehabilitated on Vietnam, Kattenburg in Washington had provided much of the expertise which Harriman and Hilsman had forced into the upper-level struggles, and as they gained some bureaucratic control of the issue, Kattenburg himself began to emerge as a player, coming to meetings, bright, nervous, not very subtle. When asked to speak, he spoke his mind freely, thus offending some of the powerful men in the room. In August 1963 he had reported that the Diem-Nhu regime was very bad, and he had gone further, he had expressed doubts about the cause even beyond Diem and Nhu and said that perhaps we ought to think about getting out, statements which in a different era, eight years later, when the Pentagon Papers were published, made him look like a prophet, but which at the time made him seem particularly dangerous and untrustworthy, and the military then marked him for later disposal.

In late November, Kattenburg had gone back for a second trip to Vietnam and he was shocked by the evidence of decay. The ARVN seemed to him a defeated army, the political situation was as fragile and divided as ever and in no way coming to terms with the reality of the problems of the society. As far as he was concerned, it was all over, the Vietcong had all the muscle and dynamism, the government side seemed weak and hopeless; time, if anything, was on the side of the Vietcong. For someone who had worked through the Indochina war, as Kattenburg had, and who knew the force of the enemy, the traditional and historic weakness of the anti-Communist side, it was all too clear; the only thing ahead other than steady deterioration was for the United States to enter with combat troops and thus replace the French.

When he returned from his trip in January 1964, he cornered Hilsman and said that the whole thing was nothing less than poison, that it would poison anybody and anything it touched, that everyone who went near it was going to be stained by future events. The war was lost, he said, had been lost for some time, in fact had always been lost. He told Hilsman that he wanted out, that there was nothing ahead but disaster. Hilsman, who felt that Kattenburg had become something of a liability, someone that the military were out to get, was ready to oblige. So Kattenburg, who was head of the Interdepartmental Working Group on Vietnam, was made a regional planning adviser, a less important job which did not entail political planning for the war itself. Before he left he said in his last report that the war was lost, that if the United States went in, it would take about 500,000 troops, five to ten years, and about 5,000 casualties a year, which was not a bad estimate, although the last figure was quite conservative. The estimate was not, however, considered conservative at the time, and at one of his last meetings he got into a furious argument with Bill Bundy, who was then Assistant Secretary of Defense for International Security Affairs, the job that John McNaughton would soon hold. Bundy, who was McNamara's chief political adviser, had denounced Kattenburg and said, it was the kind of word he used, that Kattenburg was performing a *disservice* by his pessimism. The pessimism was unwarranted, *it was not that bad,* an injustice to the people working there and serving there, that they felt yes, the signs were bad, but it could be turned around. It was just as well to forget these doubts and this negative talk, Bundy said, because we were going to stand there, we were not going to let it go down the drain. Bundy had shaken Kattenburg and convinced him that the Washington direction was not good, that Defense was getting tougher and tougher, but that at least Bundy spoke for Defense, that perhaps there was some hope at State, where he was working.

In his new job Kattenburg began to concentrate on possibilities for negotiation, what it would take, what we might ask for, and in particular a scenario using Charles de Gaulle as an aid in trying to get out. It was a job he felt at ease in, particularly since his old office, the Vietnam Working Group, rather than asking long-range questions about the policy, was instead simply supplying nuts and bolts as needed by Saigon. He was working there, somewhat contentedly, if not terribly optimistic, in early 1964 when a new Assistant Secretary of State for Far Eastern Affairs was appointed; it was William Bundy. Shortly afterward Kattenburg was transferred from even his new job and put at the Policy Planning Council, where he stayed for two years, eventually allowed back to State proper as long as he did not touch Vietnam, and where he would finish his career. He never became an ambassador, but was eventually moved over to the Foreign Service Institute, where he taught young foreign service officers about the pleasures of their career until, in 1972, at the age of fifty he had to retire.

THE NEXT TO GO WAS BILL TRUEHEART. HE HAD PLAYED A MAJOR part in making the estimates from Saigon more realistic, and in so doing, had angered the Saigon military command and Taylor to a point beyond recall. So had Ambassador Lodge, but Lodge was something else, a person of such prestige and independence, and with an ability to go to the press—and the opposition party—that had there been a showdown conflict between Lodge and Harkins over which of them would remain, then Harkins would have been homeward bound on the next boat, and the military realizing this, settled for Trueheart's head. In late October 1963, Trueheart's career had looked very good; he had taken risks, but he had powerful protectors. Hilsman was a protector who had important people working above, and he had just told Trueheart that there were good things ahead, that they would eventually like him to come back and head the Southeast Asia desk, including Vietnam, with the title of Deputy Assistant Secretary of State for Far Eastern Affairs. It would have meant a major career promotion. Trueheart took the offer from Hilsman to Lodge and asked the ambassador what he thought. They both agreed it was a good thing for Trueheart and that he should accept it; however, since Lodge was new, Trueheart should remain in Saigon through the spring and then return to his new job at State. But it did not work out that way; in December 1963 Trueheart was told that he was wanted back in Washington immediately. It would shortly become very clear that he was wanted not so much in Washington as out of Vietnam. He had caused trouble, made enemies, angered the military, and the military wanted him out. It was McNamara who had gone to Rusk asking that he be switched; McNamara was responding to pressure from the generals because he did not like people who made trouble and cast doubt upon the assumptions.

What happened upon Trueheart's return was even more interesting. He had been the top political officer coming back from a country where political estimates were of the essence, and by natural events he would have moved either to an ambassadorship, or a major desk job involved with Vietnam. Instead, he was now under a shadow: he would not become a Deputy Assistant Secretary, nor an ambassador, and he would not be involved with Vietnam. He was made the desk officer for all of Southeast Asia, a marvelous job if it had not been for the fact that it specifically *excluded* Vietnam. One more doubter had been removed. As such he was finished as a major player, and although he was outside of the main action he continued to try to be a player, working with George Ball to some degree, and more important, trying to keep the war from spreading into other countries as the military in 1965 and 1966 pushed for raids into Cambodian sanctuaries, raids which he felt would broaden the war.

What happened to his successor was even more revealing. By early 1964 the players were still at a point where they hoped to get something for nothing, that they could stave off messy decisions by sending the right Americans to influence the right Vietnamese to get with the right programs. Since personnel was the easiest thing to deal with, the principals went at the choice of a new Deputy Chief of Mission as if it were one of the crucial moves on Vietnam, perhaps a decision to turn the tide. Everyone was involved, the search was intense, and the names of the five best young officers in the foreign service were turned up, including the name of an officer named David Nes. Since Lodge was considered somewhat difficult to get along with, his approval was necessary, and the names of all five were sent to him. Lodge remembered Nes, who had several years earlier been Deputy Chief of Mission in Libya. When Lodge arrived in Tripoli late at night on a tour, Nes had won points by meeting Lodge at the airport, and instead of taxing his by then travel-fatigued mind by throwing him in with the right Libyan people or briefing him on the possibilities of Libya going Communist, Nes recommended that Lodge drive out to Sabratha if he wanted to see the most beautiful sunset in the world. Lodge did just that, finding it a rare sunset indeed, and marking Nes down as a young man of style and sensitivity. So of the five people suggested to replace Trueheart, Lodge chose Nes, he of the Libyan sunsets, and Washington, paying due attention to Lodge's choice, took a serious look at Nes. Everyone got to look at Nes. First Roger Hilsman, Assistant Secretary for the Far East; then George Ball, the Under Secretary of State. Well and good. Then Dean Rusk himself, a bit unexpected, but then, Vietnam was no ordinary assignment; the Secretary probably wanted to give a few words of warning on the complexities of working with Lodge. Then word came that McGeorge Bundy at the White House wanted to see him, which was a little unusual, but of course, Bundy liked to keep a finger in things. He asked Nes a lot of questions, and when Nes was about to leave, Bundy said, "Now I think the President would like to see you," which made Nes a little nervous and wondering what was up, a potential DCM being appraised by the President of the United States. He was ushered in for a surrealistic session with Lyndon B. Johnson, who asked many questions, none about sunsets. He talked about Vietnam, and then he turned from Nes to talk to Bundy, though the conversation was obviously orchestrated for Nes's benefit: Well, it was tough out there and there were a lot of people who were ready to run and ready to give up, but they better forget that, because Lyndon Johnson did not intend to lose Vietnam. Truman may have lost China, and that had been a mistake, but Lyndon was not going to go down as a President who lost Vietnam. The words were very strong and they seemed to punctuate the meeting; the President then rose and Nes rose, ready to save Vietnam and Lyndon Johnson. The President came over to Nes, and suddenly the treatment was very physical, giant arms and hands bearing down on Nes's slim arms and shoulders, flesh squeezed, physical and psychic messages imparted. What messages? Nes thought. Then the President turned to Bundy and said, "I hope Nes here is the kind of guy who goes for the jugular because that's what we need out there."

Thus branded with the Pedernales approval, Nes sped to Vietnam in search of jugulars, though the only jugular that would finally be cut was his own, for having soon found that the war was going poorly, that the military optimism was a fraud, he clashed openly, and unsuccessfully, with General Harkins. Deputy Chiefs of Mission who clash with four-star generals almost always lose, no matter how good their case. A few months after his arrival Nes was headed back to Washington, where he found very little interest in debriefing him. Hilsman was gone by then, and Bill Bundy, who seemed distinctly uncomfortable when they met, gave Nes the feeling that he was locked in, there was no give, no flexibility, no desire to learn. Rusk did not see him, nor anyone at the White House. Of the people in the government, only George Ball seemed genuinely interested in talking with him and trying to find things out. But Nes had a strong feeling that no one wanted to touch anyone who had angered the military, that if the military had turned on you, you were dead. He found that the real outlet for his dissent and disenchantment was not within the bureaucracy but on the Hill with Senator Fulbright. In the fall of 1964 he wrote a long and prophetic memo saying that trying a little harder, feeding more American officers, more programs, would have no effect, would only "hasten the day of total Vietnamese military and administrative collapse. We will then be in virtually the same position as the French in 1954—except that they had several hundred thousand veteran troops on the ground at their disposal."

ROGER HILSMAN HAD BEEN A MARKED MAN FROM THE DAY OF THE Kennedy assassination. He had probably made more enemies than anyone else in the upper levels of government, partly because of the viewpoints he represented, partly because of the brashness with which he presented them, partly because of his constant inclination to challenge the military. He had angered Johnson because of his role in the pressures against Diem, and he had angered Rusk for two reasons: first, he had repeatedly gone out of channels, by-passing the Secretary. Hilsman's ebullience had not bothered the Secretary when Hilsman was at INR because then it was his job to have a lot of ideas, but it had bothered him ever since Hilsman became operative at FE. Second, he was an irritant with the military and Rusk hated people who caused any friction with the military. McNamara and the Chiefs had been after Hilsman because for more than a year he had been one of the main thorns in their side. He consistently challenged their estimates and their honesty, which they were not about to forget, and now he was operating with the same enemies, minus some powerful friends, in particular John Kennedy, who had both encouraged his dissent and feistiness, and protected him and his protectors.

The loss of Hilsman would be a crucial one because as the fulcrum of the pessimistic group, he had linked the younger and less important players and political estimators with the top-level players such as Harriman. When Kattenburg was being pushed aside, Hilsman had tried to protect him. He had known that the knives were out for Trueheart, so he organized a group to write letters for Trueheart's personnel file, countermanding the charge of betrayal entered by Nolting. Though in early 1964 Johnson was making an all-out effort to keep Kennedy people of all sizes, shapes and persuasions, Hilsman himself was an exception. Johnson did not like him, did not like his bumptiousness, the policies he had followed and the enemies he had made, among them of course Lyndon Johnson. He simply had to go. Later, after he resigned, he would say that he had resigned in protest of the policies, and some friends of his were furious with him; he was opposed to the bombing and to combat troops, but at the time he was eased out these were not yet the central issues and Hilsman, who gloried in bureaucratic infighting, would have been quite willing to weigh in. When he knew he was leaving the government, he did talk with his friend Averell Harriman about it, and he forecast a dark view of the future on Vietnam, telling Harriman that his group was being disassembled and that it was all going to be very tough. At first Harriman argued with him and then did something which was very rare for him, admit to pessimism about policies and about the future. He said yes, it was very bad, and if he were Hilsman's age he would get out too, and they both knew what *that* meant, that Harriman felt if he was not operative in government he would soon die. This view was confirmed to Hilsman a few weeks later by Marie Harriman, who, still bitter about Johnson's treatment of her husband, said that he would endure some of the humiliations because if he left the government now, it would all be over.

So Hilsman left, though Johnson—not wanting him to resign, no one quit Lyndon Johnson—knowing every man's price, knowing that Hilsman's father had once been Commandant of Cadets at the Philippine Military Academy, and that Hilsman had grown up there and had an enormous attachment to the Islands, offered him the ambassadorship to the Philippines, a job Hilsman regretfully turned down.

AFTER HILSMAN, IT WAS HARRIMAN'S TURN. HE HAD BEEN AN INcreasingly open, almost defiant critic of Rusk in the last couple of months of the Kennedy Administration, scarcely able to conceal his scorn for a man who did not seize power, did not use it and exploit it thoroughly, who seemed to withdraw from it at the last minute. Harriman was not a man to hide his scorn or his feelings, and what with his other qualities, his forcefulness and ruthlessness, no one could ever accuse him of subtlety. He had created deep-seated hostilities in Rusk, hostilities which now surfaced; and it turned out that enemies of Rusk's were also enemies of Johnson's, so Harriman, no matter how hard he tried, could not make it with Johnson. He had gotten along with all these other Presidents, the supreme courtier to them, and he was a great Democratic party loyalist, but here was a Democratic President who would not bite.

First Bill Sullivan, whom Harriman had promoted and used as his man in the apparatus, was removed. Sullivan had traveled with Taylor and McNamara to Vietnam, as Harriman's eyes and ears. He had reported back to Harriman the nuances of the trips, who was moving which way, and he had cut Harriman in on cable traffic that he might have missed. Now he was put in charge of the Vietnam Working Group directly under Rusk and McNamara. Then eventually Harriman himself was moved aside. He did not lose his title at first, simply his influence; but by 1965 he was a roving ambassador again. In 1964, however, he was moved off Vietnam and given Africa, put in charge of running rescue operations there in the Congo, stopping the left-wing Congolese troops, the Simbas.

If he had once again fallen from grace, it was not for lack of trying to maintain position, this old expert on the care and feeding of Presidents. He had gladly humbled himself in the immediate pursuit of gaining the affection of Lyndon Johnson. Through small, deferential, sometimes blatant acts he had shown Lyndon that he was his man, handwritten notes fragrant with flattery of Johnson, but it had not worked (he would, in late 1965, finding that some of his liberal Administration friends were becoming critical of the policy, accuse them of biting the hand that fed them). Johnson was unbending. Why they did not connect is difficult to determine—were there too many scars inflicted in the past in Democratic party struggles? Not likely, really, because they had never been that far apart. Was it too strong a connection to the Kennedys at the end without, to the general public, Harriman's having the Kennedy-style stamp the way McNamara and Taylor bore it, thus bearing the onus of Kennedyism without the benefits of it? Was it that Marie Harriman, sharp-tongued and outspoken, had made too many tart remarks about Johnson during his depression days as Vice-President? Or was it Harriman himself, too single-minded, too ruthlessly seeking power, too much the outsider wanting to enter the Administration in the early days to bother with the second tier of government, concentrating his affection on the top-level people only, the President, his brother, Mac Bundy, McNamara, and showing his rude and brusque side to the others, such as Johnson, forgetting that most basic rule of politics: always stay in with the outs. Probably more the last than anything else, but a combination of the forces.

However, when the war was escalated in 1965, Harriman quickly moved to make himself the unofficial minister in charge of peace, knowing that though they were not yet ready for it, when the policies failed, they would need to negotiate, and they would need the help of the Russians, and then they would have to turn to him. Which they did. And he would be the best of all possible things, an important player again.

AND THEN MICHAEL FORRESTAL. HE HAD BEEN A VITAL PART OF the Harriman group, the link between Washington and Saigon, traveling back and forth frequently, his own doubts increasing at almost the same time that President Kennedy's doubts were growing. His position in the Administration had been more personal and social than professional. In addition to his longstanding friendship with Harriman, he was linked to the President by a newer friendship (though of course Joe Kennedy and Jim Forrestal had been friends). He was part of Kennedy's professional as well as social life. For Jackie liked Mike Forrestal, and later, after the assassination, he was one of the people who would be an escort for her.

He was not by nature a driving, ambitious figure or particularly interested in becoming a professional bureaucrat. Although he had been weaned on the Cold War (and bore the name of the first Secretary of Defense, the classic Cold Warrior), he had a sense that something was coming to an end in Saigon; what and how he did not yet perceive. At thirty-six, he was young enough to see that the commitment was not working and would not work but old enough to be tied to the past, to believe in it, in the necessity of stopping Communism, the belief that we were better than the Communists *everywhere* in the world, and in addition, that it would be a terrible thing if a large part of Asia were closed off to us. Now, in 1964, with John Kennedy dead and the problems in Vietnam mounting, he felt himself less and less able to operate. Robert Kennedy seemed dazed and lost; Harriman, upon whom Forrestal depended for toughness, was functioning less and less; Mac Bundy no longer seemed to encourage his access to the President, nor to be terribly interested in sharing doubts. By mid-1964 the whole thing was getting tighter, with Johnson being aware that Vietnam was something that would not be swept under the rug, and wanting only his closest and most senior people to work on it, not junior people linked to Bob Kennedy. It became harder and harder for a known doubter like Forrestal to find senior players interested in talking about the long-range problems of Vietnam. Perhaps they did not want to hear his doubts because they had doubts enough of their own.

In July 1964 Johnson switched Forrestal's job, moving him out of the White House to a line job at State on Vietnam where he could work on nuts and bolts, integrating the military and the civilians in the pacification program—perhaps the gravitational thrust of Vietnam would carry him along and end his doubts and he would become a team player, the way a comparable switch had changed Bill Sullivan. He spent much of the rest of 1964 working on daily minutiae on Vietnam, losing his taste for the whole thing, and losing his sense of being able to function. He worked in the late fall with Sullivan, on a plan which became known as the Sullivan-Forrestal Plan, which was a doomed attempt to buy off the military on bombing. It would give them a few things but not everything, the tempo was slower, the targets fewer, and hopefully, far from population centers. It was to be covert, and it would, hopefully, bring negotiations. It was, he realized somewhat in retrospect, aimed more at the American military than at the North Vietnamese, and not surprisingly, it did not fool the Pentagon for a minute. In late November, as part of the Bill Bundy Working Group, he wrote a paper on how we could negotiate our way out. No one seemed terribly interested. In January 1965, depressed personally and professionally, he quietly left the government.

THUS, WITHOUT ATTRACTING MUCH ATTENTION, WITHOUT ANYONE commenting on it, the men who had been the greatest doubters on Vietnam, who were more politically oriented in their view of the war than militarily, were moved out, and the bureaucracy was moved back to a position where it had been in 1961, more the old Dulles policies on Asia than anyone realized. Those men had surfaced too quickly on Vietnam and fought on what turned out to be a peripheral issue, namely, whether or not to go with Diem, not whether to stay in Vietnam or get out. They had spent all of their force on it, and they won the battle but in a real sense lost the war, for in the struggle almost all of the doubters had become marked men; they would not be major players again on Vietnam because they had antagonized Lyndon Johnson with their opposition. It was as if an orange crop had bloomed too quickly during an unseasonal hot spell in Florida, only to be quickly killed off by a devastating frost that soon followed. Significantly, the only important doubter who stayed in the inner circle was George Ball, the Undersecretary of State. One of the reasons why he remained a player in 1964 and 1965 was that he had not interested himself in Vietnam very much in 1963 and had *not* been an important player during the Diem struggle of that year. He had been preoccupied with Europe and had allowed Harriman and his group to carry the Vietnam fight. Thus, unscarred by earlier skirmishes, he was still around to fight in 1964. Similarly, the systematic removal of the players from 1963 meant that though there was dissent and debate, some of it serious and forceful, in late 1964 and 1965 over whether to bomb, and whether to send combat troops to Vietnam, it never reached the ferocity of the preliminary struggle of 1963, when the real divisions within the Kennedy Administration emerged and when men fought on Vietnam with absolutely everything they had, not as gentlemen, but as players who intended to win and to destroy their opposition in the process. By 1964 the political side had been disassembled, the players changed, so that the balance was uneven, the odds were hopelessly on the side of force, and there was, despite Ball's eloquence, a sense of doom about what he was doing. Though the most important question of Vietnam was whether to go all the way in or all the way out, it did not in any way provoke the greatest bureaucratic struggles of the period; rather, the first of these had taken place in 1963 over the issue of Diem. In the aftermath State's doubters were so depleted that State easily acquiesced in the 1965 escalation; and the second great bureaucratic struggle took place in 1968, when Defense, not State, had changed, and when new and antibureaucratic civilians at the Pentagon were finally able to force another debate over the limits of escalation. Thus by late 1964 the possibilities of great debates were ebbing, and they had diminished the selection of the various players. Nowhere would the difference show more markedly than in the choice of the new Assistant Secretary of State for Far Eastern Affairs.

IN FEBRUARY 1964 ONE OF THE MOST IMPORTANT CHANGES OF players took place with Hilsman's resignation. His successor was William Putnam Bundy, who came over from a similar position at Defense, bringing his attitudes with him, above all both a man of force and a man of the bureaucracy. He had served in three quite different capacities under three very different Presidents, and he had risen under all three. The job of Assistant Secretary of State for Far Eastern Affairs is a crucial one, perhaps on the subject of Vietnam the most crucial one. If there were doubts on Vietnam, they should have been voiced first of all by State. And in the case of Vietnam the position of the Assistant Secretary for FE was particularly vital, for the skepticism, the expertise, an empathy for the origins of the insurgency, all that knowledge which dated back to the French Indochina war and which came from the various lower-level experts in the Department, would have to filter through the Assistant Secretary and Undersecretary. He was the pivot, the man who had contact with the Secretary and Undersecretary, while at the same time the lower-level men, the experts, had 90 percent of their contact with him. So if it was the Assistant Secretary's job to implement the policies of his superiors, it was also his job to fight for the judgments of his subordinates. Thus, if the doubts and pessimism of the lower-level State people did not filter through to the principals in Vietnam (and they did not), it was primarily the fault of the Assistant Secretary. If anyone should have made the principals uncomfortable in their determination to go ahead and use force, it was a strong and uncompromising Assistant Secretary. For it was not American arms and American bravery or even American determination that failed in Vietnam, it was American political estimates, both of this country and of the enemy, and that was the job of State, and in particular of the Assistant Secretary. If, perhaps, there had been no McCarthy period, no ravaging of the precious-little expertise, the Assistant Secretary might have been someone very different.

Under normal conditions it might have been John Paton Davies, Jr.; he and John Stewart Service had seemed equal in overall ability, but those who knew them both well thought Davies was more likely to succeed in the operational aspect of government, to move up into the part of the Department where an expert begins to exercise power, while Jack Service was more cerebral, ticketed perhaps for a post as an ambassador, or for a major role at the Policy Planning Council. Had it worked out that way, with John Davies as Assistant Secretary, it might all have been different, because this would have meant that one of the principals was a genuine area expert. He would have been able to explain to his peers and his superiors the danger signals, the toughness of the fabric of the enemy, and the weakness of the friendly society. He would have been able to fight for the views of the intelligence people, in large part because those would have been his own views. But John Paton Davies was not in the State Department at the time, he was not in Washington at the time, he was, in fact, not in the country at the time. He was sitting in Peru manufacturing furniture, calling himself "an unfrocked diplomat." He was watching American policy in Asia, and he was appalled by it.

He was not an optimist about the incumbent Administration; he regarded the excitement and the promises of the New Frontier with a considerable amount of skepticism. He had become, involuntarily, a good deal more of an expert on political and bureaucratic timidity than he had ever intended. He watched from his distant vantage point as Kennedy and Nixon ran against each other, and their banalities on Quemoy and Matsu did not bring him any great confidence that they were ready to come to terms with the irrationality of America's China policy; the Democratic party, if anything, still seemed to be very much on the defensive, and this did not bode well either for the China policy or for John Davies. His wife had listened to shortwave accounts of the Kennedy election victory and was genuinely excited. Nixon was a reincarnation of Dulles, but these were their people, their friends coming back into office. Rose Kennedy herself was a good friend of Lucretia Grady, the mother of Patricia Grady Davies; they were both of the same generation, both of that special Catholic aristocracy in America. Lucretia Grady was a real political trooper who had worked hard for the Kennedys in the campaign, giving parties and raising money. There would be some influence there, and there was talk between the women that something would be done for John Davies, his name cleared, his security clearance reinstated, his ability to make a living restored.

A few weeks after the election Patricia Davies felt even better when she learned that the new Secretary of State would be Dean Rusk. Dean was a friend, a good friend of John's; they had served together in the CBI theater, and what could be better than have an old friend heading the very institution that had wronged her husband? Then day by day as the other names of the Administration were announced she was even more enthusiastic: Kennan and Harriman, two old friends who knew John Davies' real worth and had stood by him during his long and terrible ordeal. This was going to be so much better than the atmosphere of the old administration of John Foster Dulles, who had fired her husband. John Davies, however, was more cautious; he did not think the new Administration was in any great hurry to change past policies, and if they were not willing to take any political heat to change a policy of irrationality toward 700,000,000 Chinese, then it might be too much to expect them to take a great deal of heat, or even a little heat, for one fallen and easily forgotten comrade. John Davies had always viewed human nature with an abiding skepticism, and he had rarely been wrong.

They were living in their own self-imposed exile in Peru, and while he ran the furniture factory, she helped him and did some interior decorating on the side. They had recast their lives after he was fired in 1954; at that point, when McCarthy's charges finally caught up with him, he was serving in Peru (he had been transferred from a more important job in Berlin because he was under investigation); they had remained in Peru, starting their own factory.

They were not particularly good at the furniture business, at least in the financial sense (some of his designs, however, won international prizes), and they had made as many mistakes as one could possibly make, they had union problems in their tiny shop; nothing had gone easily. But they had managed to make a living since that date in 1954 when John Davies was forced out of government, and from that date on he never looked back. His past had died, the career as a foreign service officer had died, and the China he knew had died. He would not look back nor mourn the past. He spent the day after he was fired from his profession with Theodore White, but though they were old friends from China, they did not discuss the past. John Davies had walked in, carefully checked White's apartment for microphones—he was already showing that much effect from his persecution—and then he had talked of the future. Only the future. He had unfurled a map of Peru. He was going to go to the inner slope of the Andes and carve out a new living. He would not let his life dwindle into a special kind of idleness and frustration, sitting by a phone hoping for someone else to determine his fate and his future. John Davies would not pass on his failed hopes to his children. He would instead determine his life himself. He was a man of ferocious pride; though he was practically without means, he would not, even when separated from the Department, sign a release which would have brought him several thousand badly needed dollars, because resigning would deprive him of his own professional papers and perhaps a future chance to challenge what had happened to him and to write honestly of it. He was not anxious to remain in America, it was his country and he would not criticize it, but again, he did not want his children to grow up in an atmosphere of condescension, political insecurity or fake sympathy. So Peru it would be.

There he created his new life. He moved his family away from the luxurious American ghetto of Lima into a native quarter, partly because the American section was a good deal more expensive and also because he wanted to be out of that particular all-American atmosphere, more suburban than the most antiseptic of suburbs at home. If he was going to live overseas he wanted his children to grow up in a truly cosmopolitan climate. After all, he had grown up in that kind of special atmosphere of being a poor expatriate forced to live both in and off a foreign culture, and he did not think it had hurt his childhood at all. In Peru his family became exclusively his world. He was the patriarch of a large family growing larger; though he and his wife were not young, they started a second tier of their family, three more children were born, making a total of seven. It was, thought friends of theirs, done as an act of the human spirit as much as anything else. Life centered, not as it might have under normal conditions for most successful Americans in the achieving society, on job and career, but rather on home and family. It was a special kind of childhood for the young Davieses: with a father who was very demanding of them, setting high moral, intellectual and human standards, and yet who was always there and always, for all his sternness, very gentle with them.

By contemporary American upper-middle-class standards they were reasonably poor. They wore hand-me-down clothes, yet they made the most of what was around them. They went exploring, setting off every weekend and every vacation for trips into the interior, always in the same tired old 1953 station wagon, which the children were somewhat ashamed of, always hoping that it would not break down. Slowly the children of John Davies came to realize that of them, their father was the greatest adventurer; he always wanted to try something and learn something new. By 1961 there was a touch of irony to this: John Davies living outside the fancy swish of the New Frontier, which by ability, style, charm, connections and professionalism he seemed to be bred to, but instilling in his children some of the stoicism which was part of the frontier values and virtues he had learned on another frontier as a missionary's child in China. His children grew up uncorrupted by the plush, air-conditioned alienation of American middle-class life (when the family returned to America in 1964 Mrs. Davies believed her children were better for the hardness of their life. The family seemed to have traditional values and a strong sense of loyalty at a time when the children of most of their friends were on some kind of drugs).

While John Davies sent his children to Peruvian schools, he made sure that their education was complete. He was their unofficial tutor in the classics and in contemporary events; he made them read the *New York Times* and asked them questions about it, seeking not just the right answers, but answers which showed that they could think. He made them listen to classical music and quizzed them. They talked of many things, but one thing they did not discuss was his past and specifically the McCarthy investigations; there seemed to be a tacit agreement that it was not to be discussed. He did not want anybody's sympathy, and he particularly did not want his children to feel sorry either for him or for themselves. Later, as they grew older and went off to college, they became more aware of his past and began to ask questions. They did not feel sorry for him, but became quite proud of him, particularly of the fact that he was so steadfast, that he had made the State Department people fire him rather than docilely resign and take their money and save *them* from embarrassment. A resignation would of course have been beneficial to him as well, giving him a decent and desperately needed pension, but he turned them down. He had done nothing wrong, and that ferocious and stern pride, product of that missionary background, did not let him compromise with his honor. He was, they thought, a linear and secular descendant of the Christian martyrs.

They became aware of the strain on him, the sacrifice, the lack of money, the loss of his beloved profession, and sometimes they wondered if he would ever show the strain. But he always seemed so gentle and so comforting, and the flashes of emotion and tensions, the break in the control, were so rare that they would stand out. When Sacha Davies was fifteen, she wanted to be a singer, and she remembers waltzing in one evening and saying that when she grew up she would be a famous singer and make a million dollars and give it all to her father, and John Davies, suddenly raging, anger flashing through him, his voice very tense and harsh: "I don't need your money! Don't ever mention that to me again! I don't want anyone's money!" And then the storm passed.

There were few reminders of China, because China, too, was part of the past. Occasionally when an old friend from those days, like Eric Sevareid, showed up, they would reminisce. Once Jack Service came down and stayed with them for a week and they were joined by C. J. Pao, the Chinese ambassador to Peru, a boyhood friend, and there were barbecues, with the three of them going off into the night singing old Chinese songs, a touch of sadness in the air, China, the real China, in the past for all of them.

HE WAS NOT, OF COURSE, VERY WRONG ABOUT THE KENNEDY ADministration. Having a good many friends there meant little. He knew that Harriman and Kennan had pressed his case, and Arthur Schlesinger was working on his behalf, as was McGeorge Bundy. But his old friend Rusk seemed preoccupied; there was little word from him. Soon after Kennedy took office Harriman let his old friend know that nothing could be done in the first term; his clearance was one of the wondrous things which would take place in the second term. Davies was not surprised, but he remained even more dubious and suspicious about the integrity and brilliance of the Administration. In 1962, hearing that Sargent Shriver of the Peace Corps and the Kennedy family was in Peru, Davies looked up from his desk to see Shriver, surrounded by a phalanx of young Peace Corpsmen heading for his office. Davies simply fled out the back door, thinking it was some cheap political trick (which perhaps it was, though during the fifties Shriver, who was quite good on civil liberties, had been regarded as something of the family Communist by a more conservative Joe Kennedy and his son Robert). Shriver came and left without seeing Davies, and when his wife, Patricia, heard about it, it was one of the few times that she was genuinely angry with him.

Thus their life in exile. The rest of the nation was caught up in a mood of high style and excitement about its power and its role in the world, yet those who knew most about the price the country had paid—or had not paid—were far from the centers of power, far from the hubris of the American age. After they finally returned to America in 1964, they ran into an old friend. He asked

Patricia Davies how it had been, and he would remember both the answer and the way she said it—"We've had a terrible time"—but she said it gaily.

DAVIES WAS THE SECULAR PURITAN. THAT SPARTAN, UNCOMPLAINING quality had its roots in his childhood, and in later years as his children grew up and learned with fascination of their father, they believed that the missionary background was more a part of him than he knew; that if he had rejected the overt Christianity for atheism he nonetheless retained the values and outlook of his boyhood, the stoic sense of accepting what life gave you.

John Paton Davies senior, who was one of nine children of a Welsh immigrant, went as a Baptist missionary to China, the most exotic and marvelous place to do God's work (indeed his son would write of it some sixty years later: "Churchgoing Americans—and that was most Americans—had grown up believing that of all the Lord's vineyards, China was perhaps the most beloved"). The boyhood in China during the time of World War I was a true frontier experience, hard and unsparing, oil lamps, milking cows to get your own milk, growing up with Chinese kids. "It puts iron in your blood," his ninety-one-year-old father remarked in 1969. John Davies could recall living in the village of Chen Tu as a boy when two opposing war lords put it under siege. His mother wrote letters to both sides demanding a cease-fire, which was finally granted. Then Mrs. Davies marched out with her two sons, protected by the soldiers of one war lord, finally tipping the soldiers with what was known in China as rice-wine money, but in the families of missionaries as tea money.

In the twenties China was alive with great forces coming into conflict, one order was collapsing, a new one was rising, it was really a China afire. Death and suffering were all around him; he became inured to them. As a boy and as a young man, Davies was a knowledgeable witness to revolution; the son of Michael Borodin, there to organize China for the Comintern, was a classmate at school, as were many of the boys who would become leaders in the divided China of the thirties and forties. He grew up with China in his blood, with a kind of skeptical love for it, not a naïve love for it. He learned to love China the hard way, for like Service and other sons of missionaries, there was a certain disillusion in realizing the futility of their parents' work. They knew that whatever else happened, China was not going to be saved and modernized by coming to Jesus Christ; China was China, and Christ was alien, Western, white. But if this was true, then their parents, selfless, decent people, were wasting their lives in at least one sense, and friends thought this accounted for much of the skepticism and irony which marked John Davies' outlook for the rest of his life. Growing up as a young American in China had already made him something of an outsider; now as a young man, jarred loose from the perceptions of his parents, he was even more intellectually and culturally independent at a surprisingly young age. From this would come John Davies the outsider, cool, involved intellectually but uninvolved emotionally, the perfect reporter. If anything, he was brought up with a sense of the vastness of China, resistant to outside influence, be it Western Christian or Western capitalist or Western Communist, China determined somehow to come up with its own definition of itself formed on its own terms. It was a brilliant and far-reaching vision, but it did not necessarily serve him well.

His unique intellect was honed even more by a college education which was part American, part Chinese; even the American years were unique. In the late twenties he was one of eighty students admitted to the experimental college started at the University of Wisconsin by Alexander Meiklejohn, an innovative educator who had just been fired from Amherst. Protected by the liberalism of the La Follettes, this was to be the special college, the attempt to mold the classical mind with the classical education. There were no classes as such, the emphasis was to be on *education*, on opening the mind. The first year was spent studying nothing but Greek civilization, the second nothing but nineteenth-century American civilization and comparing the values of the two civilizations. In a way it was a spawning ground for revolutionaries, young men who went back to their hometowns, making too many ripples; after only four years the school was closed, largely upon the protests of parents who objected to their children coming back and asking too many disturbing questions. For Davies it was a marvelous time, the best of a university flashed before him. He was a good student, intelligent, a little reserved, as though somewhat bemused by all those college hijinks around him. But the education further developed an already identifiable quality in him; it taught the students to think in terms of civilizations, not just in terms of governments. After all, governments come and go, but civilizations linger on. There were certain values, beliefs, qualities which would prevail, no matter what the outward form of the government. These were lessons which Davies later applied to the contemporary world, and it would explain why his reporting was so profound; it was always touched with a sense of history. He saw something in a country and the society far deeper than the events of the moment. His reporting intuitively reflected the past as well as the present, and it marked him as no ordinary reporter or observer.

After two years at Wisconsin he went back to China, where he spent one year at Yenching University, studying alongside those who the Chinese hoped would be their modern leadership. That year was a particularly adventurous one; he was old enough now to explore the country on his own and at one point he set off for Inner Mongolia, an area at that time ravaged by typhus and famine. His real problem there, he would write, was not revolution or war but lice, so he filled a talcum can with sulphur and sprinkled it on his food, in the hope that the sulphur fumes would exude through his pores and drive off the lice. Instead he simply became violently ill for a couple of days.

When the year was up he returned to the United States (the first leg of the trip was by the Trans-Siberian Railroad, a marvelous long journey for a young man). He graduated from Columbia and took the foreign service exam; by 1933 he was an officer in China, and for the next twelve years, with the exception of two years back in Washington, he was to watch and report from the country he knew best. But first, upon arrival, he was to become even more professional. He spent his first two years as a language attaché, honing his already unusual knowledge of the country and language to an even finer degree. For two years he was at Peking University, his own tutor working with him long hours on Chinese language, history and culture. It was, he would recall, a very serious thing, and yet an enormously stimulating time; John K. Fairbank was there doing his postgraduate work, and there were journalists like Edgar Snow and Harold Isaacs around as companions. It was the making of a genuine scholar-diplomat.

HE WAS FULL-BLOWN, SURPRISINGLY SOPHISTICATED, GAY AND erudite, but there was always the quality of the outsider about him, as though he were, no matter what the situation, always a little removed from it, bemused, listening, not unsympathetic. The journalists there, like Sevareid and White, loved him and thought that with his mind and background, he would have been a magnificent journalist. They liked being around him for his ability and also for the pleasure of his company. Once Sevareid and Davies were flying over the Hump when they had to parachute. A small group made the jump, and it was Davies who led them back through difficult and dangerous terrain, negotiated with not necessarily friendly Naga tribesmen (later during the McCarthy period after Davies had been fired, Sevareid would broadcast for CBS a brief piece entitled "Defects of Character, But Whose?" in which, describing that incident, he said: "For I thought then, as I think now, that if ever again I were in deep trouble, the man I would want to be with would be this particular man. I have known a great number of men around the world under all manner of circumstances. I have known none who seemed more the whole man, none more finished a civilized product in all a man should be—in modesty and thoughtfulness, in resourcefulness and steady strength of character"). Davies could be quite witty as well (friends would remember a ditty he wrote about Gandhi: "Nonviolence is my creed/Noncooperation in word and deed/Red hot Mahatma Gandhi is my name/I wear my dhoti up around my crotch/Drink goat's milk instead of Scotch/Red hot Mahatma Gandhi is my name . . .").

To his contemporaries he symbolized what the foreign service should be, expert, analytical and brave, and above all, perfectly prepared for what he was doing. He knew China, the people, the language, and he watched the revolution sweeping the country. It was, he would say then and later, an implosion, not an explosion, that is, the collapsing inward of a civilization, a nation shutting itself off from the world, determining within itself its destiny. He was with General Joe Stilwell in 1938 as the Japanese marched south, ravaging whatever was in their way. He was puzzled as to why a civilized people like the Japanese would commit such atrocities, and pondered it for some time. Part of the answer, he decided, was that the troops were simply motivated by duty to their emperor; the second reason, more interesting in the light of events thirty years later in Vietnam, was "the idealistic belief that the mission is also a crusade to liberate the Chinese people from the oppression of their own rulers." When the Chinese peasants showed signs of resenting this liberation "it is a shocking rejection of his idealism," and the Japanese soldier raged against "the people who he believes have denied him his chivalry."

He would eventually become the top American political officer in China, Stilwell's most trusted adviser. It was an extraordinary time: history flashed before them like a constantly ongoing newsreel, and they were part of it. Very early in the game, in the thirties, Davies had sensed that Chiang would never make it. He was not China, he was only a part of it, and that part was diminishing all the time. The transition from feudal China to modern was a fragile one at best, but under the pressure of the Japanese invasion it became virtually impossible; the Japanese invasion simply magnified all the weaknesses and insecurities in Chiang and made him more vulnerable. He was not big enough to use the Japanese as a means of rallying his people; thus the more the pressure against him built up, the more isolated he became. It was Chiang who bore the brunt of the Japanese attack and he was not equal to it. Years later Davies' friend Teddy White would remember Davies' mind, the precision of it; if he disliked Chiang it was not emotional, it was because Chiang couldn't cut it and was therefore useless.

Davies was by this time very much in the Kennan, and what would later be the George Ball, school: the man who sees the forces of history, is dubious of using morality as a test and thinks that intelligent realpolitik is the best policy. He was as dubious of the morality of intense anti-Communism as he was of the morality of Communism. He had few illusions about the Communists and what they represented. Even in 1938 when they were nothing but guerrillas, he was capable of telling Agnes Smedley, a Mao sympathizer who wrote for the Manchester *Guardian*, not to commit herself as totally as she wanted to, to bear in mind that it was all very exciting and romantic *now*, with the revolution being on the upswing; it was idealistic, full of promise, high resolve and a warm comradeship because of mutual dangers shared against common and powerful adversaries. But if it succeeded, he warned her, the Communists would become powerful and corrupt and she would feel disillusioned and betrayed, used and cast aside. Why didn't she just report, like the other correspondents? "I can't," she answered him, "there is no other way for me." (Later, when he went through his ordeal of the McCarthy years, his attitude included no small amount of scorn for his oppressors, partly because they were accusing him of views he had always thought preposterous.)

The war years did nothing to change his mind. Events happened step by step as he had predicted. Chiang became more rigid and isolated from reality, while the Communists picked up more and more momentum, touching something deep and powerful in the country. The future of China was theirs, he would cable his superiors, and we had better come to terms with it whether we liked it or not. But he never had any particular illusions about China, about how good and pro-American the Nationalists were or how evil the Communists were; he saw them both as being primarily Chinese, seeking China's special destiny; more Chinese than foreigners knew, more Chinese, perhaps, than they knew themselves. The United States, he believed, should let events take their own course (if only because there was no alternative; in China you could not control events, and if you tried, you were sucked into something monumentally futile). If anything, America should try and encourage independence for Communist China from Moscow, and above all, not push Mao into Stalin's hands.

Davies was, it is an understatement to say it, ahead of his time. In October 1944 he went to the Yenan base of the Communists, along with a small group of Americans including Teddy White, to get a feel of their leaders. One day he and White were having lunch with Ch'en Chia-k'ang, who was something of a liaison officer with the Americans and in effect a foreign ministry desk chief for the United States. The lunch would soon become embarrassing for White, because of Davies' treatment of Ch'en, which was nothing short of brutal. Davies kept picking away at his host on the subject of a solid Sino-Russian alliance, like a bullfighter going after a bull. Asking question after question, Davies forced his host to compare the Russian proletariat with the peasantry. There was such skepticism in his voice as to be almost mocking: What did they really have in common? Wasn't there an old historical enmity that lurked beneath the surface of the new friendship? Weren't there differences in culture, differences in race, differences over borders? Wouldn't the Chinese have to remain subservient to Moscow as long as they were in the Soviet orbit? How could that be squared with a desire to assert China's real destiny as a great power?

The more Davies ruthlessly pressured his poor host to admit that there were long-range differences, the calmer Ch'en Chia-k'ang remained. To him, he assured Davies, it was unthinkable that Russia and China would ever be enemies; since they were both Socialist states, there could be no problems or disagreement. Years later Teddy White would remember that luncheon with an eerie feeling; perhaps Davies had seen the future more clearly than the Chinese Communists themselves had.

If Davies saw events ahead of the Chinese Communists, he saw them ahead of his own country as well. That he, so skeptical, so tough-minded, would be blamed for ideological weakness and soft-minded reporting was ridiculous, yet it would happen; a surprise even for a man schooled to expect very little from human nature. But Patrick Hurley, whose mission to China to unite Mao and Chiang during the war had ended in failure, the same Hurley who thought that the Chinese Communists were like Oklahoma Republicans except that they were armed, needed a scapegoat after Chiang's debacle. Old and senile, he turned against Davies and the other Chinese officers, accusing them of having deliberately betrayed Chiang (and Hurley). It was a foolish charge of a foolish man, but the nation was ripe for a little demonology and scapegoating. That there would be right-wing attacks after China fell was not surprising; what was surprising was how little the people who knew better, the Establishment, fought back.

Thus began the long ordeal of John Paton Davies and other China experts. Starting in 1948 and continuing through 1954, he underwent nine security investigations. Again and again he was cleared, but the experience itself was debilitating and destructive, poisonous, always leaving doubts. Besides newspaper charges, guilt by association, the failure of friends to stand by, even the very questioning seemed to imply his guilt. (Typically, *U. S. News and World Report*, December 1953: "The Strange Case of John Paton Davies. Investigated since 1945, He's Still a Diplomat.") His case was made more difficult by an additional tactic of the right wing. After China fell, Davies had suggested a complicated covert CIA program which would use China experts somewhat sympathetic (or at least not antagonistic) to the regime as an outlet to the new China, perhaps as a way of keeping the country open and as a means of getting American information in and Chinese information out. Instead, right-wing members of the CIA blew just enough of the program to make it look as if Davies were trying to have the CIA hire a bunch of Communist agents; it was a kind of mindlessness that was special to the period, and it was a particularly difficult charge to defend against because the program was classified, and an honorable explanation would have violated security. At first when the charges began he had not been particularly upset; it had seemed like the final rantings of a senile old man, Hurley, and though he knew things might be a little uneasy back in the States, he assumed that right would triumph. Besides, his immediate superior, Harriman, backed him 100 percent. But as it became clear that the Republican party was determined to use the China issue as a means of getting back in power, his spirits dropped and he had a feeling that it would end badly. By 1952, he remembered, it was like a rabbit being shot at in an open field.

The temper of the times was very special, notable for a kind of national timidity and dishonor. Some friends stood behind him, others did not (Rusk did). Davies, ever proud, found it hard to ask others to testify in his behalf; when someone like Teddy White volunteered to, which was rare, he was touched. But those who offered to appear paid the price themselves; two weeks after White testified in Davies' behalf, his own passport was lifted. Davies became a particular target of McCarthy's, linked in McCarthy's charges somehow to Alger Hiss and Harry Dexter White. In 1954, because of McCarthy's pressures, he was investigated for the ninth and last time. This time he was accused not so much of disloyalty as of nonconformity. He was finally found guilty of "lack of judgment, discretion and reliability." Dulles, who wanted as little conflict with Congress as possible, upheld the decision. He did not talk with Davies, but through subordinates passed the word that it would be a healthy thing if Davies resigned instead of forcing Dulles to fire him. This, it was said, would be good for Davies and save him embarrassment (it would also save Dulles embarrassment). Davies, ever unflinching, refused to resign, and sought a confrontation with the Secretary. Dulles summoned him to announce that the board had found against him. "Do you agree?" Davies asked. "Yes," answered Dulles. "I am sorry," Davies said. Davies' manner at the meeting, thought one Dulles aide, was almost flippant, his jacket thrown over his shoulder like a cape; it was conduct unbecoming to a foreign service officer, though of course the aide had not been investigated nine times. Later Dulles, ever the moralist, quietly let Davies know that if ever he needed a letter of recommendation, why, Foster would be pleased to write one. It was an offer which was not taken up. By then Davies was on his way to his new life; the best of a generation of Asian experts had left his profession.

It was the end of one life and the beginning of another; more important for his country, it was the end of one kind of reporting and expertise in Asia. The best had been destroyed and the new experts were different, lesser men who had learned their lessons, and who were first and foremost good anti-Communists. If there had been a prophetic quality to Davies' China reporting, there was no less a measure in the letter he had submitted to the final review board:

When a foreign service officer concludes that a policy is likely to betray national interests he can reason to himself that, as ultimate responsibility for policy rests with the top officials of the Department, he need feel no responsibility for the course upon which we are embarked; furthermore his opinions might be in error or misunderstood, or misrepresented—and so the safest thing for a bureaucrat to do in such a situation is to remain silent. Or, a foreign service officer can speak out about his misgivings and suggest alternative policies, knowing that he runs serious personal risks in so doing. I spoke out.

His only crime, John Finney of the *New York Times* would write fifteen years later, was that he had been both too honest and too far-sighted in his reporting from his area; if that had been a crime, there would be few, reporting from Asia in the next fifteen years, who would repeat it. Instead, officials became good solid anti-Communists; they told their missions, as Ambassador Nolting did, not to look at the opposition, not to meet with it, not to think of alternatives, but rather to get the job done, that was what Washington wanted. The Americans who followed John Davies would be very different, they were determined to impose American versions and definitions of events upon Asian peoples. It became easier to be operational rather than reflective. Reflection brought too many problems.

From Peru, Davies watched America struggle through or try to glide through the post-McCarthy period, and he observed the deepening involvement in Vietnam with a sense of foreboding. There was, he thought, a certain inevitability to it, and for him at least, there was a terrible logic to events. If with his family he seemed gentle and thoughtful, he was nonetheless not without his scars. What had seemed skeptical now sometimes seemed cynical; he seemed to bear the special pain of a man determined not to show pain. He finally decided to return to the United States, partly because he felt his children should live in their home country for a while, partly because he wanted to clear his name, not for his own sake but for that of his wife and children. Periodically old friends tried to introduce him to some of the new young men working in the Administration on Asia, some of what were known as good guys on China. The meetings went badly because Davies did not respond well to the swift young Kennedy and Johnson people, he was not linked to them and he was determined that he not show hurt. They, in turn, found it hard to choose the right words in the presence of a man who was legend and hero to them.

In 1964 he began the long process of clearing himself. He found an excellent lawyer named Walter Surrey, who was willing to fight for him. But even then, Surrey and Davies would find the State Department an ungracious and ungenerous place, less than anxious to right an old wrong. It would in fact take five years of fighting the Department to get clearance. Surrey asked for a review of Davies' case; the State Department reviewer, Wilson Flake, a former ambassador to Ghana, looked at the record and saw no reason to reopen it. Surrey, however, persisted year after year, with little co-operation from Secretary of State Rusk. In 1966 Bill Bundy, then Assistant Secretary for Far Eastern Affairs, tried to put Davies on an advisory panel of Asian experts; Rusk rejected him. He would go as far as accepting John Fairbank, the controversial Harvard scholar, but Davies, he said, was politically unacceptable.

In 1967 Surrey wrote directly to Rusk asking for a review of Davies' case; Rusk, preoccupied with Vietnam, never responded. Out of this would come a quiet, lingering bitterness toward Rusk, a feeling that he, more than others, had been less than he should have been. The matter might have died there, but Surrey persisted, and others in the Department, slowly, cautiously, came to Davies' support. Months passed, years passed, and eventually Undersecretary Nicholas Katzenbach helped nudge the case along, despite ferocious efforts on the part of the Department's security people to obstruct progress. Finally, in mid-1968, fourteen years after he had been fired, John Davies was cleared. He was cleared in the last months of the Johnson Administration, when it was too late and all the damage both to a man and to a policy had been done. But even then the State Department did not have the courage to admit that it had corrected an old injustice. Instead of issuing an honest and candid statement, it leaked the news of the reinstatement to a reporter for the *New York Times*; the timidity still lived.

Davies himself began to work again as a consultant and as a writer, and when the Nixon Administration recognized China a year and a half later and it reappeared on the face of the map, Davies found himself something of a celebrity. Important journalists began to talk about him as a candidate to be the first American ambassador to Peking. In the summer of 1971 his young son was getting married and the Davieses sent out invitations for a reception; in the past they had usually gotten only a 50 percent acceptance to their parties, but this time everyone showed up, including, as the children put it, "the real chickens."

John Davies remained shy about going on radio and television and had a feeling he might be exploited now that he had been rehabilitated. In late 1971, sensing that they were being used by the people around them, and tired of having their young daughters mugged on the way home from public schools, John Davies and his wife decided it was time to pull up stakes again, that adventure lay elsewhere, and moved to Spain.

So John Paton Davies or Jack Service could not serve—men, extremely knowledgeable about the area, whose primary viewpoint was political. And yet the post was crucial, doubly so, because the Secretary of State himself was a man who believed in force, whose first love had been the Pentagon, and who did not like to challenge the views of the generals. So the selection for the man to fill the slot below him, to replace Hilsman, was of genuine importance. But instead of it going to a man of the area, it went to a man classically of the bureaucracy, a believer in force, and a man whose last job had been at the Pentagon under McNamara, who was in awe of McNamara, and who brought a photograph of McNamara to hang on his wall at State. As well he might, for the idea of his new job had come from McNamara; McNamara, good bureaucrat, always liked to have his people spread around the government, and it would not hurt to have Bill Bundy, his own man, at a crucial slot at State. The suggestion had gone in from McNamara and finally came back to Harriman for his response, and Harriman, who still had some control over this area, did not fight the appointment. He thought Bill Bundy was a very good bureaucrat and bright, and that he might give State some badly needed muscle. Besides, he was sure he could handle him. So he acquiesced. Consequently, by the middle of 1964 State did not have its men at Defense; Defense had its men at State. There was Bill Bundy, a classic insider's man. His name would probably be on more pieces of paper dealing with Vietnam over a seven-year period than anyone else's, yet he was the man about whom the least was known, the fewest articles written. There were no cover stories in the news magazines, no long profiles. A shadowy figure on the outside center of power, lowest man on a very high totem pole. In photographs of the group, the other faces were recognizable: Bob, Dean, Mac, Lyndon, and then that tall thin fellow on the side. A patrician, you could tell that, perhaps a slight resemblance to Mac. Mac's younger brother? No, he would get tired of telling people, he was not Mac's younger brother, he was Mac's older brother. What was it Lyndon called him? (Lyndon always professed to have trouble with people's names when he wanted to put them down a little. Kissinger would become Schlesinger, Dick Goodwin became Good*man*, George Hamilton the actor-suitor would become Charley.) Johnson respected Bill Bundy but did not like him, spotting in him that supercilious quality which, so long in developing, was not easy to shed, even for the White House. Hating all superciliousness, but particularly Groton-senior-prefect superciliousness, Johnson would call him "that other Bundy." That other Bundy.

William Putnam Bundy, two years older than McGeorge Bundy, had left remarkable records wherever he went, Groton, Yale, Harvard Law School (which inclined him to tell others who sometimes doubted him and his positions that their problem was that they lacked a lawyer's training and eye). More of an ambitious mother's hopes were invested in him, and yet always pursued by that younger meteor, always living in the shadow of Mac's extraordinary achievements and accomplishments, which somehow dimmed the luster of his own quite remarkable career. He was not as quick as Mac, and not as open. Mac had competed in the somewhat more open environment of Harvard, where sheer brains counted, whether they were immigrant brains, blue-collar brains or WASP brains, and he had triumphed there, his connections not hurting a bit. But the process had ventilated him (Mac knew the value of a Kaysen or Wiesner), and he liked brains for brains' sake, whereas Bill had made his way up through the more closed profession of the inner bureaucracy, particularly the CIA, where connections and birthrights were far more important. He had done very well at the CIA, at a time when it was decidedly the profession of the upper-class elite, the right people looking out for one another's sons and friends. It was a profession and a craft which demanded considerable ability, which he had, but which also responded even less to new forces and egalitarian pressures of America. There was a tendency in Bill Bundy, when challenged, to rely, or at least to seem to rely, even more on his background, to seem more the snob and more arrogant, a belief that Bundys are just a little different and better than mere mortals.

He himself was not without his own political scars from an earlier period. He had always done well in the government, and had been a particular protégé of Allen Dulles', an affection which he reciprocated. Dulles had been more than a boss, he had been a friend and also a protector. When William Bundy had one rather frightening run-in with Joseph McCarthy in the fifties, he had the good fortune to work for the right Dulles, who had chosen to protect his staff. The incident took place in July 1953. McCarthy went after Bundy partly as a general means of attacking Acheson, and partly because it was fresh governmental meat, the CIA this time. There were two points McCarthy used against Bundy, the first being a brief period of time in 1940 when Bundy was an employee of the Library of Congress and for four months belonged to a group called the United Public Workers of America. The second was more dramatic, McCarthy's desire to question Bundy on $400 that Bundy had contributed to the defense fund of Alger Hiss. (He had not, Bundy explained later, known Hiss, but he had worked as a young lawyer in the same firm with Alger's brother Donald Hiss. He sensed that the Hiss case was going to be very important and he wanted Hiss to have a very good attorney "the first time around. We had some knowledge of the Sacco-Vanzetti case in my family and I thought it important that he had a good lawyer the first time around," the latter being a reference to his great-uncle A. Lawrence Lowell, who had upheld the Sacco-Vanzetti decision, and whose reputation was thereupon tarnished.) Bundy had told all this to Allen Dulles, who said not to worry. Then, in the summer of 1953, when McCarthy went after him, Bundy was about to leave for Europe, and there was a question as to whether McCarthy would subpoena Bundy. Allen Dulles worked out a deal with the White House by which there would be no subpoena; Bundy would be allowed to go on his European vacation, and Dulles would develop a special procedure to check all loyalty at the Agency. McCarthy tried to fight the European trip, but Dulles absolutely refused to cave in, no one on his staff was going to be exploited by McCarthy; Bundy went off, and came back to continue working at the CIA. Allen Dulles, he thought, was a very different man from Foster (on the day that Foster had let George Kennan, perhaps the State Department's foremost intellectual of a generation, leave the service "because I don't seem to have a niche for you," Allen had driven into town to see

Kennan and to offer him almost any job he wanted at the CIA). But it was not a pleasant experience, just as the tormenting of his father-in-law, Dean Acheson, had not been a pleasant experience; it had a profound effect on the young and ambitious career servant and made him very careful about leaving himself open for any future attacks on his softness.

He was extremely well connected in the inner traditions of American government, the Stimson-Bundy connections and the fact that he was Dean Acheson's son-in-law, but there were also many who felt that he was Allen Dulles' long-term choice to be the eventual head of the Agency. Though he was the nominal Democrat in the Bundy family, he had not done particularly well at the beginning of the Kennedy Administration, partly because he had mouthed the Acheson anti-Kennedy line during the 1960 period, and his father-in-law felt that he should have had the job which went to Mac. Instead he went from CIA to Defense in 1961 as Deputy Assistant Secretary of Defense for International Security Affairs under the Assistant Secretary, Paul Nitze, who was Acheson's special favorite (he had been head of Policy Planning under Acheson). When Nitze was appointed Secretary of the Navy, Bundy was moved up to his job. Those who worked under Bill Bundy in those days remember an almost electric sense of power: he worked for McNamara, he had a brother at the White House, there were links everywhere to the very top, decisions were made and Bill and his shop were in on it. He liked the McNamara job, and friends there felt that when he was made Assistant Secretary of State for Far Eastern Affairs he left reluctantly, that there had been a virtual father-son relationship, despite the similarities in age. He was totally happy there.

While Rusk and McNaughton, both very good bureaucrats, had worked in the outside world, Bill Bundy had spent most of his adult years working within the government. After CIA and Defense, an even more successful career was beckoning. Becoming Secretary of State, Secretary of Defense or head of the CIA was a very real possibility for him in 1964 at the comparatively young age of forty-six. He was extremely adept at playing the bureaucracy, savvy, able to finesse it, there was no better interdepartmental and crossgovernmental man than Bill Bundy, cutting across lines if necessary, and then, if someone was a person to be wary of, going back later and healing a wound. He could cut through it and he could go outside it if need be. Very good at paper, just like his younger brother and like the Secretary of State, letting both sides speak their piece, and then Bill Bundy grabbing the middle position and dictating the paper, getting both sides in, and moving the paper to his view. During those years at State he was very careful to follow all the paper traffic. He was a good dictator, and knew who at State was good at taking dictation and who was not, insisting on the best clerks, a good clerk was someone who could take dictation and handle paper. He read quickly, and if anything, too quickly; there were those around him who believe that in 1967 he misread Hanoi's answer to the San Antonio formula because he read it too quickly and was preconditioned to think that they were never going to respond.

Yet he was a puzzling man too. He had such good manners and came from such a fine tradition, yet he was the classic mandarin, abusive and rough on those who worked for him, obsequious to those above him, with almost no such thing as an equal relationship. The one eventual exception was John McNaughton, who held Bundy's old job at Defense and was thus equal in rank and ability and toughness, although Bundy tested him out at the beginning, trying to let him know that Bill Bundy was just a little more senior, a little more superior. On the phone, with just a trifle of condescension, trying to help McNaughton really: I'm sure, John, that if you check with Bob you'll find that it's all okay . . . No, Bob wasn't there . . . but Cy was there, and it's really all cleared, John . . . I'm sure you'll see . . . But McNaughton was just as shrewd a bureaucratic player and he soon let Bundy know that he spoke for McNamara, and thus gained a rare parity. Subordinates had to suffer what bordered on temper tantrums, as if all the contradictions of Vietnam were too much and produced resulting seething tensions: Get off that goddamn phone. . . . Where the hell is that paper? . . . This damn paper isn't fit for an eighth-grader. Yet to his superiors it was yes, Mr. Secretary . . . no, Mr. Secretary . . . yes, Mr. President—which reminded those around him of nothing so much as the best senior boy at the old school working between the headmaster on one side and the boys on the other, or the beloved senior clerk in a great firm who anticipates every whim of his superiors and terrorizes the clerks beneath him. He was the classic civil servant really, who believes he has succeeded if he meets the demands on him from the top of the matrix, and does not represent the bottom to the top (in contrast with his eventual successor at Defense, Paul Warnke), which is all right if the top of the matrix knows what it is doing. So he was this great Brahmin, William Bundy, really a very great clerk.

He did not bring his subordinates into the play at all, and would brook no faintheartedness; in fact, it was believed by the fall of 1964 that real doubters on Vietnam could not serve in his section. Nor, and this was equally important, did he bring subordinates into any kind of discussion on Vietnam but quite the opposite; he worked to head off any serious questioning. When doubts arose among some of the younger men, he would stop them, they would not go further. "The President had already decided on that," was a favorite line, or "We won't chase that hare," or "We won't open that can of worms," but the message was the same: don't argue with us, we know where we are going. Since his subordinates were almost completely excluded from discussions on Vietnam with Bundy, except for minor technical matters, they found that if they wanted to pick up a trend of the direction of policy, the best way was simply to be in his office when he was talking to trusted outsiders on the phone, where he would ruminate, talk more openly, give a sense of the play. Only certain people could be trusted and they had to have certain credentials, and those credentials would turn out increasingly to be breeding and a fondness for the use of force.

Bill Bundy was extremely well read, a deeply educated man who brought a real intellectual background to his work, a bureaucrat, thought his friends, who had a secret craving to be a historian. In addition, unlike the other top players, he knew something about Southeast Asia. He had dealt with the problem in the past working with the Office of National (Intelligence) Estimates at the CIA from 1951 to 1959, where Chester Cooper, the staffman who was writing pessimistic notes to McGeorge Bundy, was charged with Far East evaluation and Bundy was doing overall general evaluation. During the French war he had read all the traffic, and had thus, unlike the others, gained a sense of the history which they were contending with. Later, in 1964, when a squadron of outmoded B-57 bombers were routed back to the Bien Hoa air base from the Philippines, some of the younger men at State and the White House argued vigorously against leaving them there, saying that they were useless and could only serve as a temptation to the Vietcong, who would be almost obligated to attack them and blow them up; besides, security was undoubtedly terrible. So the real risk was that if the Vietcong moved, we would have to make a countermove. In a rare exception to his general rule, Bundy agreed, and he even went to see Rusk and posed the problem (the B-57s would not really change the direction of the war, but they would present unnecessary risks). Rusk listened and more or less agreed, and then called McNamara, who said that the military needed the planes, and Rusk called back to his subordinates and said that the military said they needed them, and State had not given a good-enough reason not to put them there. So, foolishly, they stayed there, until in November the Vietcong did blow them up, prompting the JCS and Taylor to recommend immediate retaliation, which surely would have taken place then, except that it was Election Eve. But what the incident showed was that Bill Bundy knew something about Vietnam, and had more sophistication about the war and the enemy than most of the players. Brains were not his problem; it was a question of assumptions, and ambition.

His move to State was an important step. At Defense he had shown no doubts about the policy. He had never been for any of the pressures against Diem, his recent attitudes on Vietnam had been oriented toward the military, and he held his new job in part because he had in no way angered or irritated the hawks of the government; in fact, he had worked well with them and had their confidence. He had come to State to make sure that State co-operated with Defense, and he was perfect for the job, since he had lived through the Cold War years and believed in all the attitudes of them; he was not Acheson's son-in-law for nothing, and was perhaps even more than his brother a man of force. He believed in covert operations from his CIA days and believed that we were justified in what we did because the Communists inevitably were worse. He was a man who, in the words of his new boss, Lyndon Johnson, would "run it in through to the hilt." But curiously enough, though his new job at State was seemingly a promotion, his father-in-law, Acheson, always zealous of Bill's career, was not particularly enthusiastic, and there were two reasons why. Part of it was Acheson's doubts about Rusk; to Acheson, Rusk was a failed figure on his way out (Acheson, hearing people say that they did not know what Rusk was thinking during crucial meetings, would respond, "Did it ever occur to you that he wasn't thinking?"), and he thought Bill would be better served by staying with McNamara, *there* was the real powerhouse of the Administration—perhaps McNamara would be going over to State and Bill could make the transfer then. But the second reason for Acheson's doubts was Vietnam itself; he sensed that FE was going to be a graveyard, and that anyone working there would be charged with either liquidating the war or escalating it, and he did not want Bill Bundy caught in this particular trap. He made these reservations known to the President, but they had no effect; Bill Bundy got FE.

IT WAS AN ODD YEAR, 1964, THE CALM BEFORE THE STORM; THE bureaucracy was, in a phrase which the Vietnam war would help create, doing its own thing, planning away, storing up options. The military were beginning to check out bombing sites, and deep in the bowels of the Pentagon, trained professional staff men who knew something about contingency plans were working on what might be needed if we decided to go to war, and if we needed ground troops, and if so, which units would go and which reserve units might be called up. All ifs, of course, but the Pentagon was ready. At the top level, through much of 1964, there was still lip service to optimism. But the advisory commitment was a passing stage; in the back-channel world of the Army, where the *word* was far more important than the public statement (the public statement of a military man allowed no dissent, it was built totally upon loyalty to policy, to chief, and thus was without subtlety, so that the *word* was the truth, the word was that it was all coming apart, and we might have to go in there with the first team). Much of the Army brass had never really believed in the advisory commitment; they had accepted that role because it was the only role authorized, but it was not a satisfactory role. It excluded more elements of the military than it permitted in, it handcuffed more than it liberated, and so American generals were quite capable of saying what a great thing the advisory role was, how well we were doing, what great fellows the little ARVNs were, Little Tigers, and believing it, and yet at the same time never believing it. They thought it was all a lie, but it was the only lie available, and you did what you were told, though with your own way of winking: Don't knock the war in Vietnam, it may not be much but it's the only war we have. Or on the definition of the adviser: an adviser is a bastardized man-made animal which is bound to fail. Until 1964 the war in Vietnam had not really even been a war, but now they were getting ready, just in case this country wanted to go to war.

In the country and in the government, however, there was no clear sense of going to war. Each person working around the President saw Johnson through his own special prism, and had his own impressions of Vietnam confirmed. Thus the domestic political people assumed that Johnson was committed to the programs that they were preparing, and thus what was peaceful in his rhetoric was the real thing. The national security people did not talk to the domestic people; no one walked both sides of the street. The national security people were above politics (except for their desire to protect their President and keep him in office, which would also keep them in office as national security people), and if they thought about the dark consequences of the road ahead, they were somehow sure that a confrontation could be avoided. They were, in particular, believers in the idea that the threat of force would make the use of force unnecessary. So if they played their roles properly—and they were all crisis veterans now; they wore the battle ribbons of the Cuban missile crisis and knew how to negotiate through danger, to show the willingness to use force, to convince the other side of the seriousness of their intent, to pass their messages as civilized gentlemen—they could prevent both war and aggression. As 1964 progressed and ended, it became apparent that the Cuban missile crisis had been the test run for Vietnam, that the Vietnam planning was derivative from the missile-crisis planning: enough force but not too much force, plenty of options, careful communication to the other side to let him know what you were doing, allowing him to back down. They were very confident of themselves and their capacity to wield power. The dry runs were behind them. They could handle events. They had confidence in themselves and in each other.

Perhaps if the people who knew a good deal about Vietnam (the fact that the weakness in the South would continue and grow worse, that the other side would react to force with the patient, dogged determination which had marked the French war, that there was no way to bluff Asian Communist peasants) had gotten together with the domestic political people who knew something about Lyndon Johnson, which way he would react to certain pressures, then they probably could have plotted the course of the future. But the national security people did not know Johnson, which would be part of the problem. They were all new to him, and they had little sense of his real instincts and subtleties. To foretell what would happen in Vietnam, what Johnson's reaction would be and what the enemy's reaction would be to Johnson's moves required a combination of expertise which no one had. Therefore, in 1964 each man saw his own estimates as the deciding ones, pulling from the contradictions of Administration rhetoric what he wanted to believe. If a person was dovish, then he was dovish for forceful reasons, and he assumed that the principals were probably dovish too; and if he was hawkish, he assumed that he could control events. It was a time when the play became more and more closely held by the principals, and that as doubts about the future grew, the willingness to discuss them and share them diminished; as they grew more serious, the doubts became more private than public, as in the case of John McNaughton.

Chapter Nineteen

IN THE WHITE HOUSE, LYNDON JOHNSON WAS IN THE FIRST stage of becoming a President; he wanted to keep not just Vietnam at arm's length but all foreign problems. In the first months of 1964 he wanted to play from strength, not from weakness; domestic policy was strength, foreign policy was weakness. If one had to deal with foreign policy, then it was best to deal at the very top, to personalize it (as he did during the Panama Canal Zone crisis, picking up the phone and calling the President of Panama). He was not at ease with the general class of people who made diplomacy their profession, particularly ambassadors. They were, after all, the worst of two worlds, being both State Department people and foreigners. As a result, he almost refused to see the members of the diplomatic corps. "Who are these people?" he would say. "Why do I have to see them? Have Rusk see them. They're his clients, not mine."

The list of ambassadors waiting to see the President grew and grew. Some could not assume their responsibilities and make the official Washington diplomatic circuit until they had first paid a call on the President. In desperation, groups of envoys were run through, one group including the British ambassador. On another occasion it was decided to run the French and the Vietnamese ambassadors through together, the idea being that since they both spoke French, it would make things easier. At the last minute this idea was vetoed.

Those visitors who were granted what were supposed to be important private audiences often found that Johnson had invited some member of the press or friend visiting the White House to come along for the meeting. When Prince Bernhard of the Netherlands showed up for a private meeting he found himself being photographed with a dozen or so White House tourists who had been selected by Johnson with the invitation "Come on, have your picture taken with a *real* prince." Eventually, under pressure from his staff and from Rusk, it got a little better. More than most men, Johnson could put himself in the other politician's position and see his problem (he once told Harold Wilson, facing a difficult re-election, not to come and do his campaigning on the White House steps). But he did not like problems in the abstract; he was a politician and he preferred dealing with other politicians at the moment of crisis—that was reality and he felt more at ease in that kind of pressurized atmosphere.

A strategy for 1964 slowly began to evolve: fend off the outside world, particularly Vietnam. Keep Vietnam quiet, do not explore its problems, and do not reflect upon them, but keep them papered over. Make it a functional, factual issue, send more aid, more weapons, a few more men to Saigon. The doubters were to be cleared out. The man in charge of keeping the commitment running as smoothly as possible was McNamara. Above all, it was not to surface as an issue in 1964; it was to be controlled, and managed, and kept away from the reaches of Barry Goldwater; it was not to be an issue for the right. Goldwater would be the candidate against Johnson, and he appeared to be a particularly easy mark; he would drive Americans back to political divisions answered years earlier. If anything, Goldwater would serve a convenient purpose, he might propel Lyndon Johnson into his own Presidency with a momentum which Johnson would be hard put to create himself. Anything that diminished the possibility not just of a victorious election but of a real landslide, which would allow him to take the Congress by storm in 1965, was to be avoided. Vietnam was the most identifiable trouble spot.

Thus if he could keep his people together, the liberals and the Democrats, then he was confident the issue would be Goldwater, and by early 1964 it was clear to him that his real problems—in that they could create serious factional rifts—were, first, his relationship with Robert Kennedy, which was particularly touchy, and second, the broader aspect of handling the Congress, using it in effect as an umbrella, on the question of Vietnam. The matter of the Congress was made all the more difficult because while Johnson wanted it as a weapon to fend off a potential challenge from the right, his problem at the moment was not with the right wing in the Senate, but with the left wing, where Senate liberals were beginning to mount increasing numbers of attacks on the American presence in Vietnam. Thus he faced the problem of going to the Congress to stop the right and becoming involved in a Pyrrhic battle with people from his own party.

The problem of Robert Kennedy was a special one. The relationship between him and Johnson had always been marked by coldness, suspicion and barely concealed dislike. Now both men were jockeying for the right to be John Kennedy's legatee. Robert Kennedy had the right to it by blood and by emotion, but not by law; Lyndon Johnson had no emotional base at all, but he had it by constitutional right. The last thing he needed or wanted was a split between himself and the Kennedy people; he could understand a passive opposition from Kennedy loyalists, but an open one would have dire consequences. It would divide his party, severely limit his capacity to govern and sustain the image of Johnson as the usurper. What he wanted, and what he eventually achieved, was to take hold of the Kennedy legacy in 1964, carry out Kennedy programs with Kennedy men, at the same time diminishing the role of Robert Kennedy; then run for President and win on his own, and thus shed the Kennedy mantle. But in order to get rid of the Kennedy mantle he first had to gain control of it. All of this required deft handling. Johnson was partially aided in the business of neutralizing Robert Kennedy by the fact that all the key men of the previous Administration now worked for him, so the Attorney General could not make an outright challenge against his late brother's closest advisers. Yet at the same time Robert Kennedy had ambitions of his own, and by the spring of 1964 he was openly campaigning for the Vice-Presidency, precisely the position Lyndon Johnson did not have in mind for him (a landslide victory against Goldwater would become less of a personal triumph if there was a Kennedy on the ticket. The press, which was Eastern and pro-Kennedy, would give Robert Kennedy considerable credit for the victory). So Robert Kennedy was a serious potential problem in 1964, unlike Barry Goldwater, who was regarded as something of an asset.

The Congress was a more complicated problem: if an issue as fragile and volatile as Vietnam became a major part of the upcoming political campaign, then Johnson wanted some kind of congressional support, for protection. He was very much a creature of Congress: to him the Congress was the country and he wanted the Congress on board, partly as a way of keeping the country on board. As early as May 1964 Dean Acheson stopped a White House friend at a cocktail party and said that he thought Vietnam was going to turn out much worse than they expected, that it was all much weaker than the reports coming in—Acheson assumed that if the official reporting was beginning to be a little pessimistic, then it was surely far worse—and that it might be very tricky in the middle of the campaign. He thought the President ought to know this and ought to try and protect himself. Acheson's warnings paralleled the President's own suspicions, and he asked the people around him to start thinking in terms of a congressional resolution. This would protect him from the pressures on the right, and would force Goldwater to support whatever the President was doing on Vietnam, or isolate him even further. Bill Bundy drafted the first copy of the resolution, a document of purposely vague intent and proportions, signifying that all good Americans were behind their President against the invidious enemy.

For a time it was debated within the inner councils whether or not to send the Bundy resolution to the Congress, but Johnson was lying low for the moment. Ernest Gruening of Alaska and Wayne Morse of Oregon were already making waves in the Senate, and Morse in particular was prickly, with that compelling sense of international law and an almost faultless sense of where the weak spot in an issue resided. Morse, Johnson told friends, was a tough one, the kind of man who could hurt you and expose your weaknesses even when he was standing alone. A formidable opponent. "My lawyer," Lyndon Johnson sometimes called him, hoping that a little flattery would rub him the right way. An able and abrasive man. And Johnson knew too that if Gruening and Morse had surfaced, then there were others hiding in the cloakrooms who might spring at him, more covert in their doubts, but ready to jump if they smelled blood. Even Fulbright, who was an old friend, was showing signs of independence. And Johnson knew that his own case for a vote of confidence was a thin one, that the more prolonged scrutiny Vietnam received, the more difficult it would be for him. The whole point of the resolution was to paper over tensions, not to increase them. Johnson always believed that his problems in the Congress lay in committee rooms, not on the floor, that once a bill or a motion came out of a committee, the President could get it through the Congress. (If the committee was the problem, then the Senate Foreign Relations Committee was potentially a center of opposition.) So in June his own intuitive sense of the Congress told him that the time was not right, that he could not just spring the resolution on the Congress, but rather he must mold it to events, and if possible tie it to an issue of patriotism. Something would have to come along.

So he would bide his time on the Congress. In the meantime it was McNamara's job to keep Vietnam in hand to tidy it up. Within the government the discussion of it became more and more limited; it became more closely held. Only the very top people were involved on the decisions and the drift of it; the others, the second- and third-echelon people who had been playing some part, were moved out. Letting McNamara be the front man for Vietnam was handy in a number of ways. He generated confidence not only to the President himself but to much of the Washington community; he was at the height of his reputation with liberals, and he was a Kennedy figure in a way that Rusk was not; thus he neutralized potential opposition. Liberal Democrats, by now co-opted by the Kennedys, could not effectively protest the drift of the Vietnam policy without criticizing at least by implication their own people. McNamara was the star of the Administration; he was able to continue his close personal relationship with the Kennedys, his regular visits with Jackie Kennedy, and at the same time receive praise such as Lyndon Johnson had never accorded mortals in the past. He was the ablest man that Lyndon Johnson had ever dealt with, the President told people; there was no one like him for service to his country. "He wields that computer and those figures like King Arthur wielded Excalibur," Jack Valenti told the President.

"Like what?" the President asked.

"Like King Arthur wielded Excalibur," Valenti repeated.

"More like Sam Rayburn with a gavel, I think," the President said.

"Same thing, Mr. President," Valenti answered.

IF McNAMARA WAS REGARDED WITH AWE IN WASHINGTON, THERE were those in Saigon who had watched his trips to Vietnam with mounting disbelief. They thought that his glib press conferences, the statistics rolling off, were hopefully put-ons, that at least McNamara himself did not believe in what he was doing. Nothing fazed him, he showed no uncertainty, he plunged straight ahead. If he was learning, he was learning too little too late. Indeed, even as he became somewhat more knowledgeable in 1964 and 1965, it was not entirely a blessing. The very process of learning was achieved at the expense of his becoming more deeply involved, more attached to and identified with the problem, and thus more committed to finding a solution. Having helped bring us that far, he felt himself under extra pressure to see it through.

He had learned in late December 1963 and early 1964 that Harkins had seriously misled him and he was furious, and Harkins was in effect finished; the only reason he would be allowed to stay on a few months longer in Saigon was to save face. Not Harkins' face, but the face of the people in Washington who had put him there, not the least of them Robert McNamara. If he were pulled back under the mounting evidence that the war had been going poorly all along, it would be an admission that the Administration had been either taken in by faulty reporting, or worse, had itself been lying. If its past estimates were not to be believed, then how could one fend off critics of present estimates? In addition, when Harkins was finally brought home, the attitude in Washington was again simplistic: a bad general was going to be replaced by a good general; it was not the whole system, the bad war, which had produced such fraud, it was simply the wrong general. Thus one replaced him with the best general around. Individuals *could* make a difference.

In June 1964 General William C. Westmoreland became the commander of American forces. On June 22 Lyndon Johnson held a ceremony for Harkins at the White House, where he presented him with an oak-leaf cluster for his Distinguished Service Medal. As was the President's wont, particularly in cases where he did not believe what he was saying, he resorted to considerable flattery in his description of Harkins, noting that though the general would soon retire, "I have asked Secretary McNamara, who has such great and unlimited confidence in this great soldier, to have the general remain in the Washington area so that we may benefit from his broad knowledge of and his experience in the various theaters of the world, and particularly Southeast Asia." (McNamara had of course lost confidence in Harkins, in fact was very bitter about him, telling interviewers such as Professor Henry Graff of Columbia that Harkins had failed in Vietnam.)

At this point Harkins uttered one of the most revealing statements ever made by an American commander. He was an optimist, he said. "I guess I was born one, and I continue to be an optimist about Vietnam." As such, he was very encouraged by recent reports. The way would be difficult, it would require time and patience. "I am reminded of our own Revolution," the general continued. "It took eight years to get through our Revolution, and then we ran into some of the toughest guerrillas that we ever want to run into any place—the American Indians. We started what we call in Vietnam today an oil spot moving across the country. The last Indian war was 1892, over a hundred years after we started our Revolution. There is a social revolution going on now in Vietnam. They are not at the stage to say 'We the people,' but when they do get to that stage, then things will be fine . . ." The general's view of revolution was nothing short of remarkable; if an SDS member had formulated it for him, it could not have been more perfect for the radical left.

IN MAY AND JUNE THINGS BEGAN TO LOOK BETTER AND BETTER FOR the President. In the past, Johnson had not particularly liked polls, partly because he did not like what they told about himself, but now some of his staff began to do some testing for the President among the citizenry. The first results were very good: though George Wallace had run well in the Indiana primary, the impression was that the white backlash against Negro progress was not yet a real issue (in addition, some of the President's staff told him that Goldwater, an economic conservative as well as a racial one, would have trouble moving in on the blue-collar people, who felt an immediate empathy with Wallace). The polls showed Johnson running well among people who had never liked him before, and cutting in on large segments of Republican voters (one poll taken by Oliver Quayle in the spring of 1964 showed that half of the people who had voted for Nixon in 1960 were now for Johnson). The message confirmed his own intuition; it was going very well, and he did not need Robert Kennedy on the ticket; if anything, given the restlessness in the South over civil rights, Robert Kennedy, who as Attorney General had been the Cabinet officer most deeply involved, might even hurt him. Now he moved to end the Kennedy threat.

Jack Kennedy had never taken Lyndon Johnson's attacks upon his youth and his family seriously, but Robert Kennedy had; Jack Kennedy had always treated Vice-President Johnson courteously and with great sensitivity; Robert Kennedy had not. The antagonism between the two men was very real. Friends thought the origins went back to the 1960 convention, when Johnson had attacked Jack Kennedy in a personal way, and even more important, had attacked Joseph Kennedy personally at a press conference, saying, "My father never carried an umbrella for Chamberlain." John Seigenthaler, Bobby's closest aide, who was at the press conference, had reported back to Kennedy that he was sure now that Johnson knew he was going to lose, that he was desperate. Robert Kennedy remembered the incident, as had Johnson, and a year later at a dinner party Johnson, the Vice-President and outsider, took Bobby, the Attorney General and insider, aside and said, "I know why you don't like me. The reason you don't like me is because I made those remarks about your father at the press conference and they were taken out of context and I was misquoted." Kennedy denied that he knew what Johnson was talking about. "Yes, you do," Johnson said, "you know what I'm talking about and that's why you don't like me." The next day Kennedy called Seigenthaler and repeated the conversation to him, and Seigenthaler dredged up copies of the quotes from four different newspapers; it had, after all, stayed in both of their minds a long time. None of the tensions had eased after Johnson became President, and Robert Kennedy and the people closest to him felt that Johnson was somehow a usurper. Johnson, sensitive to Robert Kennedy's feelings, had worked hard to ease the pain, but he had met little success.

Now in the early summer of 1964 he knew that Robert Kennedy was promoting himself for the Vice-Presidency. He tried to head it off, using McGeorge Bundy, among others, as an emissary (the fact that Bundy, nominally a Republican, was willing to run this kind of errand for Johnson particularly infuriated Robert Kennedy, and Bundy's connections with the inner Kennedy group were badly shattered). All of this failed. In late July the President called Robert Kennedy in and told him he would not be on the ticket, that he had a bright future in politics but this was not his year. Johnson would be pleased to have him run the campaign. Their talk seemed to have gone very well, but later Johnson called in three White House correspondents for a leisurely lunch. He described the meeting with Kennedy and could not restrain his talents as a mimic; he demonstrated how Bobby had gulped when the news was broken. Within a few hours the story was all over Washington, complete with Johnsonian embellishments; Robert Kennedy was furious. Johnson soon went on television to say that he had decided against naming any members of his Cabinet to the Vice-Presidency. Thus Johnson took care of Robert Kennedy, and the way was clearer to his own Presidency, but he had paid a price; the tension between the Kennedy people and the Johnson Presidency was more real than ever.

But he still had to deal with the question of the Congress as far as Vietnam was concerned. He wanted that extra protection before he went into the campaign. At the end of July he got his way; an incident in the Gulf of Tonkin provided the factor of patriotism that he had sought for his congressional resolution. It was to be called the Tonkin Gulf incident, and in reality it had begun back in January, when the President and his top advisers gave permission to General Krulak and the restless JCS to go ahead and plan a series of covert activities against the North under the general code name of 34A. These would be run from Saigon under the command of General Harkins (though of course the Vietnamese would be nominally in command), and the purpose would be to make Hanoi pay a little for its pressure on the South, to hit back at the enemy, to raise morale in the South, to show Hanoi we were just as tough as they were, that we understood the game of dirty tricks and could play it just as well as they did. (Which, of course, we could not.)

In that sense the origins of the Tonkin Gulf went back even farther, to the height of the Cold War tension in the late forties, which had seen the growth and acceptance of a certain part of the Cold War mentality: the idea that force justified force. The other side did it and so we would do it; reality called for meeting dirty tricks with dirty tricks. Since covert operations were part of the game, over a period of time there was in the high levels of the bureaucracy, particularly as the CIA became more powerful, a gradual acceptance of covert operations and dirty tricks as part of normal diplomatic-political maneuvering; higher and higher government officials became co-opted (as the President's personal assistant, McGeorge Bundy would oversee the covert operations for both Kennedy and Johnson, thus bringing, in a sense, presidential approval). It was a reflection of the frustration which the national security people, private men all, felt in matching the foreign policy of a totalitarian society, which gave so much more freedom to its officials and seemingly provided so few checks on its own leaders. To be on the inside and oppose or question covert operations was considered a sign of weakness. (In 1964 a well-bred young CIA official, wondering whether we had the right to try some of the black activities on the North, was told by Desmond FitzGerald, the number-three man in the Agency, "Don't be so wet"—the classic old-school put-down of someone who knows the real rules of the game to someone softer, questioning the rectitude of the rules.) It was this acceptance of covert operations by the Kennedy Administration which had brought Adlai Stevenson to the lowest moment of his career during the Bay of Pigs, a special shame as he had stood and lied at the UN about things that he did not know, but which, of course, the Cubans knew. Covert operations often got ahead of the Administration itself and pulled the Administration along with them, as the Bay of Pigs had shown—since the planning and training were all done, we couldn't tell those freedom-loving Cubans that it was all off, could we, argued Allen Dulles. He had pulled public men like the President with him into that particular disaster. At the time, Fulbright had argued against it, had not only argued that it would fail, which was easy enough to say, but he had gone beyond this, and being a public man, entered the rarest of arguments, an argument against it on moral grounds, that it was precisely our reluctance to do things like this which differentiated us from the Soviet Union and made us special, made it worth being a democracy. "One further point must be made about even covert support of a Castro overthrow; it is in violation of the spirit and probably the letter as well, of treaties to which the United States is a party and of U.S. domestic legislation. . . . To give this activity even covert support is of a piece with the hypocrisy and cynicism for which the United States is constantly denouncing the Soviet Union in the United Nations and elsewhere. This point will not be lost on the rest of the world—nor on our own consciences for that matter," he wrote Kennedy.

But arguments like this found little acceptance in those days; instead the Kennedy Administration had been particularly aggressive in wanting to match the Communists at new modern guerrilla and covert activities, and the lines between what a democracy could and could not do were more blurred in those years than others. These men, largely private, were functioning on a level different from the public policy of the United States, and years later when *New York Times* reporter Neil Sheehan read through the entire documentary history of the war, that history known as the Pentagon Papers, he would come away with one impression above all, which was that the government of the United States was not what he had thought it was; it was as if there were an inner U.S. government, what he called "a centralized state, far more powerful than anything else, for whom the enemy is not simply the Communists but everything else, its own press, its own judiciary, its own Congress, foreign and friendly governments—all these are potentially antagonistic. It had survived and perpetuated itself," Sheehan continued, "often using the issue of anti-Communism as a weapon against the other branches of government and the press, and finally, it does not function necessarily for the benefit of the Republic but rather for its own ends, its own perpetuation; it has its own codes which are quite different from public codes. Secrecy was a way of protecting itself, not so much from threats by foreign governments, but from detection from its own population on charges of its own competence and wisdom." Each succeeding Administration, Sheehan noted, was careful, once in office, not to expose the weaknesses of its predecessor. After all, essentially the same people were running the governments, they had continuity to each other, and each succeeding Administration found itself faced with virtually the same enemies. Thus the national security apparatus kept its continuity, and every outgoing President tended to rally to the side of each incumbent President.

Out of this of course came a willingness to use covert operations; it was a necessity of the times, to match the Communists, and what your own population and your own Congress did not know was not particularly important; it was almost better if they did not know—it made it easier for them to accept the privileges and superiority of being a democracy; thus it was better for Stevenson to go before the United Nations and lie, he was more convincing that way; thus it was better for the citizens, the editorial writers, the high school graduation speakers to believe that we were different as a country. And a few chosen citizens working discreetly in Washington would do the dirty work for them. A public service.

So the people of the United States did not know about 34A, nor did the Congress, but that was of no importance. Of course Hanoi knew, it was not fooled, and by and large, slowly, the rest of the world would know, but the Congress of the United States would not know what the United States was up to. Thus in terms of the central state's attempt to lead and manipulate a potentially resistant society, the covert operations were doubly handy; if no one knew about them, then it bothered no one; if they did become public, if there was a Communist challenge to them, the public and the Congress would be forced between choosing their own side or the Communist side. A question of patriotism, then.

The idea of subversion, of dropping in teams to blow up bridges, create harassment, be they frogmen or men parachuted in, was doomed from the beginning. The North Vietnamese government was both forceful and popular, and it was particularly invulnerable to exterior subversion (at one time there had been a base for subversion, the large Catholic minority which might have been a problem for Ho in its dissidence, and might have been a major source of espionage for Western powers. The United States had, however, helped remove this possibility in 1954 by encouraging the Catholics to go South—using loudspeakers which claimed, in Vietnamese, that the Virgin Mary had gone South and it was time to join her. This had created a somewhat more anti-Communist society in the South, perpetuating an illusion of anti-Communism there, essentially a transplanted anti-Communism, but it had also removed from the North any real possibility of internal subversion). So in 1964, when frogmen swam ashore or Vietnamese commandos were parachuted in, almost invariably they were picked up immediately by the North Vietnamese security teams.

In the early summer of 1964 the operations under 34A were intensified. The war in the South was not going well, and this was a way of slapping back at the North and also warning Hanoi surreptitiously that its attacks were not going unnoticed, that there was a payment inherent in its war. The subversion attempts proved predictably futile; at the same time, more annoying to the North Vietnamese, though hardly damaging, was the use of unannounced bombing raids along the Laotian border, and the use of South Vietnamese PT boats in hit-and-run commando raids against North Vietnamese naval installations on the coast. Although the latter did not cause much harm, the pressure in the North for some retaliation was building up. The PT raids, though involving Vietnamese crews, had been planned and initiated by the command of MACV, under General Harkins and Mac Bundy. McNamara and Rusk had full knowledge and control of them. In the real sense, these were American operations.

ON JULY 30, SOUTH VIETNAMESE PATROL BOATS BASED IN DANANG had taken off for a raid on two North Vietnamese bases; the attack took place on July 31. At almost the same time an American destroyer named the *Maddox* was on its way toward the same coast, its mission to play games with the North Vietnamese radar, to provoke the radar system. Using highly expensive and sophisticated equipment, the *Maddox* could simulate an attack on the North, thus forcing the Chinese Communists and the North Vietnamese to turn on their radar. At this time the Americans could pinpoint more accurately where the other side's radar installations were located, just in case there was ever a need to have them charted. As the *Maddox* headed toward its mission on July 31, it passed the returning South Vietnamese PT boats; unaware of the other mission, it thought at first they were Soviet boats. On August 1 the *Maddox* began her mission, which was, in North Vietnamese eyes, a provocative act and seemed to be part of the overall assault which had begun on July 31. On August 2 the *Maddox* sighted three North Vietnamese PT boats, was attacked by them, and destroyed one. Aboard the *Maddox*, radio intercepts of North Vietnamese traffic made clear that it considered the *Maddox* patrol part of the overall 34A operation, and this information was cabled back to the Pentagon (McNamara would soon testify before the Senate Foreign Relations Committee that it "was clear" that the North Vietnamese knew these were separate missions; similarly, on August 6, McNamara would claim that the *Maddox* was attacked when she was thirty miles from the North Vietnamese coast. In truth the attack began when the *Maddox* was thirteen miles from a North Vietnamese island, and earlier in the day the ship had been much closer to the mainland). Out of this, and a subsequent incident on the following days, was to come the Tonkin Gulf incident, the first bombing of the North, and almost immediately the Tonkin Resolution. But in particular, out of all of this would come the sense that *we* had been attacked, and *we* were the victims.

Johnson's first reaction was that whatever else, we had been fired on in an area where we had a right to be; thus our ships, the *Maddox* and a companion ship, the *C. Turner Joy,* should continue their activities, otherwise we would be pushed farther and farther back. Meeting with Rusk, McNamara and

Bundy, Johnson discussed retaliatory measures. For the moment the President was unwilling to bomb the North; he wanted to know more about what was happening, and he didn't think this episode in itself was worth it. We didn't, he told them, lose anybody in this fight, we had sunk one of their boats. Now we would just show them that we weren't going to move, they couldn't run us out of those waters, and we would kick the hell out of anyone who tried. At the same time Johnson used the hot line to reassure the Soviet Union that we intended to continue naval operations in that area, but that we did not intend to widen the war. Meanwhile Rusk told his subordinates to go ahead with the drafting of a congressional resolution backing the President in eventualities like this.

Captain John Herrick, who was the commander of the Tonkin Gulf patrol, was cabling back that he thought continuance of the patrol "an unacceptable risk" because of the North Vietnamese sensitivity to the *Maddox* foray; since Herrick was privy to the radio intercepts, he knew what the North Vietnamese were thinking, which was that this and the 34A activity were all one raid. His warning cable had little effect; Washington was in no need to pull back or be cautious. If anything, quite the reverse was true; the Chiefs and some civilians in the Pentagon had been pushing for acts against the North which were at the very least provocative, such as sending low-flying jets over Hanoi in order to create sonic booms, which would push the North to some kind of reaction. Johnson had held the line on that, but he had given permission to go ahead with the radar harassment patrols as well as the 34A missions, and now that had in fact created just the provocation that some of the Joint Chiefs wanted.

The next day, August 3, both the *C. Turner Joy* and the *Maddox* were ordered back into the same dangerous waters as a sign that the United States would not back down. Almost immediately the North Vietnamese appeared to challenge them, in what would become the second Tonkin incident. Whether there had been an attack was somewhat unclear (in fact, much of the Tonkin Gulf controversy centered around whether or not an attack really took place, or whether the two destroyers were firing at each other, or whether in fact the military deliberately faked an incident in order to create the retaliation). The evidence on Tonkin is still clouded, in part because McNamara's story was so filled with old-fashioned lies, but the evidence, clear or not, is peripheral to the real question of what had taken place in the days immediately prior to the incident, and what kind of U.S. and South Vietnamese provocation had taken place. Because of the secrecy and the covert nature of the operation, because of Administration lies, both the Congress and the public were seriously misled. That was the central issue, not whether or not there was a second Tonkin episode.

On August 4 Captain Herrick radioed back that the intercepts showed the North Vietnamese still thought this was part of a 34A mission. By 8 A.M. Washington time (8 P.M. of the same day in the Gulf) it became clear that some sort of incident was taking place; at 9:52 Washington time both destroyers signaled that they were under constant attack. Throughout the morning there were unclear and fragmentary reports of combat. By noon Johnson was lunching with Bundy, Rusk and McNamara (at the same time James Thomson, the specialist on Asian affairs on the Bundy staff, was asking White House staff member Robert Komer what they should do in moments like this. "What we do," said Komer, "is go to lunch. In situations like this the big boys take over"). There would be retaliation this time, Johnson made clear. Bombing most likely. At lunch they continued to discuss the alternatives and gradually firmed it up. American planes would be used, and they would hit bases which harbored the patrol boats. The JCS had provided a list of six sites, but Rusk, who was always worried about the Chinese, suggested eliminating the two northernmost bases because they were too near the China border. Reconnaissance photos showed berths for forty-seven PT boats, with only thirteen of them in the two northern bases. We ought to hit the remaining thirty-four with everything we had, Rusk said, and let the other thirteen be. They would still be there in case we needed to go back, and that would give us an option for the future. Thus was the list drawn up.

Johnson was still demanding more information on what exactly had happened out there. More and more pressure to confirm that an attack had taken place came down through military channels to the commanders on the spot. At best the reports back indicated that an ambush had taken place, although details were very vague and confusing. By 5 P.M. Johnson was summoning congressional leaders to the White House; even as the leaders were on their way there, the planning for the retaliation was going ahead. When Johnson met with the congressional leaders at 6:15 he outlined the day's events (without, of course, mentioning the 34A activities) and told them what he intended to do. He emphasized that it would be a limited retaliation, and said he wanted a congressional resolution; he was assured of their support, for both the actions and the resolution. I'm not going in, he told them, unless the Congress goes with me. At 10 P.M., with the Pentagon still sending out urgent messages demanding details of the incident ("Who are witnesses? What is witness reliability? Most important that positive evidence substantiating type and number of attacking forces be gathered and disseminated"), the first planes were leaving the aircraft carriers *Ticonderoga* and *Constellation*. The war planes hit the four PT-boat bases and the oil depot at Vinh. The next day McNamara reported that twenty-five of the thirty boats in the bases had been either damaged or destroyed, and that 90 percent of the Vinh depot had been wiped out; indeed, at Vinh "the smoke was observed rising to 14,000 feet." So in a way it had begun. We had shown ourselves in an act of war. We had perhaps committed ourselves more than we knew.

The next day the President was in a relaxed mood. He was talking with a few chosen reporters, telling them how the decision had been made—everyone had been for it, no one had been soft—and then he leaned over to a reporter and smiled. "I didn't just screw Ho Chi Minh," he said. "I cut his pecker off."

About eight months later, when Johnson complained to civilians about the military handling of the war (he was also good at complaining to the military about the pressures put on him by civilians; he was always trying to show to each side that he was really with them but that there were others blocking him, so they had to trust him), he brought up the Tonkin incident, how hard it had been to get exact information on what was taking place. It was a terrible example of what he had to put up with. "For all I know, our Navy was shooting at whales out there," he said with a grin.

THE DAY AFTER ALL THE MEETINGS, WHILE THE IMPACT WAS STILL just settling, McGeorge Bundy gathered the White House staff together and said that the President had decided to go for a congressional resolution calling for a general posture in Southeast Asia. Thus if anything more serious happened during the forthcoming election, he would have the resolution in his hip pocket, and he would be able to deal with both Hanoi and the Congress, one a sure adversary, the other a potential one. After Bundy finished, Douglass Cater, a White House adviser on domestic issues, was one of the first to speak up. "Isn't this a little precipitous?" he asked. "Do we have all the information . . . ?"

Bundy looked quickly at him and said, "The President has decided and that's what we're doing."

Cater, new in the White House, persisted: "Gee, Mac, I haven't really thought it through."

Bundy, with a very small smile: "Don't."

WALT ROSTOW, STILL AT POLICY PLANNING, THOUGH MORE AN enthusiast now of the policies as they became more and more hard-line, was very pleased; a few days later friends who lunched with him at State found him almost expansive. Things, he told them, could not have gone better had they planned them exactly this way.

Which seemed to be true at the moment for Lyndon Johnson. As long as he moved ahead toward escalation he had kept the right fairly quiet, and the left had been bothersome but not dangerous. Now a confrontation had taken place where our boys had been fired on, where national patriotism was at stake, and he could lock up both sides. Particularly the right. It would kill Goldwater. And in the Senate he could move under cover of the flag. People like Morse might try and oppose him, but after an incident like this, it would be much harder. In addition it would not be some slow, ponderous hearing where they could bog him down; there would be an element of immediacy to it, and the hearings would take place in the heat of battle. All the better for him. So he immediately decided to go for the congressional resolution; it was too good an opportunity to miss. He did not miss it, and the first person he co-opted was his old friend Bill Fulbright.

Fulbright was an odd combination of public man and private man, Arkansas and the Senate's link to the Establishment. He was a public official, publicly elected, and yet he seemed to be an ally of the elitists, sharing their view of the private nature of national security. He had good ties to Georgetown and the Metropolitan Club, he was a disciple of Acheson's and he agreed with most of the centrist foreign policy objectives of those years, occasionally fighting with Dulles, but generally being a key partner to the containment and postcontainment policies of the fifties. It was not just that he agreed with the objectives, but in addition, he was agreeing to a somewhat acquiescent and secondary role for the Senate, not challenging the executive branch's assumptions or information and not building up the kind of machinery on his Foreign Relations Committee which might result in different information and thus different conclusions (the Congress, noted one assistant to a senator, was the only understaffed bureaucracy in Washington, particularly on foreign affairs; Vietnam, however, would change all of that). Fulbright preferred not to create an opposition center; indeed, even after he and his committee had emerged as the main opposition to the President's policy on the war, Fulbright was distinctly uncomfortable with his new role. Rather, he liked to hold the committee somewhat in the background and to wield influence on a personal basis. A public man giving private consultations. He would be consulted, his advice weighed; as such he had always been a good friend of the court. Being an adversary was not a role he had sought under any conditions; it was out of character, but it was particularly out of character with a fellow Democrat and friend in the White House. He liked having his committee; he also liked playing the game.

If he had believed in the major assumptions of the previous era, he had in 1961 begun to change, as it seemed that the world was changing. He had opposed the Bay of Pigs and privately he was increasingly unhappy with the direction of the policy in Vietnam—the United States as the anti-Communist policeman of the world. Vietnam and the Dominican Republic intervention would turn him into a major foreign policy critic, but that still lay ahead in

August 1964; he was a particular favorite of the President's, Johnson having engineered the coup against old Theodore Green which gave Fulbright his prized committee, and there had been reciprocal favors. Fulbright gave the Johnson operation a little class; Johnson allowed the more reserved Fulbright to rise and hold power without getting his hands dirty. Those had been good days; Johnson the Senate Majority Leader, always putting his personal imprimatur on things, had referred to Fulbright as "my Secretary of State," and there was little doubt that Fulbright was the Johnson candidate for Secretary of State in late 1960, the Vice-President-elect lobbying hard and persuasively. Johnson was in fact somewhat annoyed that Fulbright did not work harder for the appointment, and did not push harder himself. But it had been a long and mutually beneficial friendship, Johnson, the powerhouse of the Senate, opening things up for the more cerebral Fulbright, Fulbright with soft-spoken elegance, his reputation as the resident intellectual of the Senate, giving a certain tony quality to Johnson's operations.

Now, facing Goldwater in the forthcoming election, and faced with the tricky issue of Vietnam, Johnson called in a due bill from Fulbright, and asked him to manage the resolution through the Senate. It was a crucial request and Fulbright accepted, not just because of the threat of Goldwater, though that was the reason he would later give, but largely because, for all his misgivings, and he had plenty of them (he knew that Johnson was not entirely to be trusted, but he also thought that Johnson might manipulate others, but not his old and dear friend Bill Fulbright), he was still part of the old partnership, a very junior partner, because he did not like an adversary role. All things being equal, he preferred to work in tandem, making his opposition in private. He always thought that if it were more serious, if Vietnam became darker, if they really did head toward war, somehow Bill Fulbright would be consulted. By that time he and the President would be in almost total opposition; besides, Johnson had others now to tone up his own reputation, the brilliant and flashing men of the Kennedy Administration, McNamara, Bundy and Rusk. He no longer needed the intellectual benefits that went with being a friend of Bill Fulbright's, he had all his own new advisers. Later, with friends, Fulbright would be somewhat bitter about this particular point, all those flashy Harvard people had excited Johnson, he thought they were all so smart, and Fulbright, why, Fulbright was simply an Arkansas hillbilly from the Senate, and Johnson had mastered that world, he knew all *their* mistakes and weaknesses. He was in awe of his new advisers, but not his old one. It was a particularly bitter point for Fulbright, who had based so much of his hopes not on his constitutional relationship to the Presidency, but on his personal one.

So Fulbright, in a move he would spend the rest of his life bitterly regretting, accepted the job of shepherding the Tonkin Gulf Resolution through the Senate. The decision reflected all the ambivalence both of Fulbright's views

on foreign affairs and on his view of his own position. He had grave doubts
about the war, and he knew the dangers of the wording of the resolution he
was pushing through, but he was also willing to take the risk. Having done
things and played the game with Johnson in the past, he was willing to try it
once more, though Fulbright was unusually independent and courageous. The
stigma of going against the President on an issue of patriotism was not one
that any senator sought—which of course was exactly why Johnson was sending his resolution hurtling toward the Hill. The key moment was when he
pushed it through the Foreign Relations Committee. Morse, irascible,
forceful, an expert both on international law and Lyndon Johnson, warned
Fulbright that this was not a limited resolution, that if you knew Johnson and
the way he operated, this was clearly intended as an all-purpose measure, the
first and more than likely the last he would send to the Congress. Morse, who
had fought lonely and successful battles against Dulles on resolutions over
Quemoy and Matsu, had a particularly good reputation as a man willing to go
it alone on an issue of conscience; his sources within the bureaucracy were far
better than those of the average senator.

On the night of August 4, while the second Tonkin incident was beginning
to wind down and American planes were already on their mission, Morse received an anonymous phone call from someone at the Pentagon who was reasonably high up and who obviously knew a good deal about destroyers. The
caller told Morse that he understood that the Oregon senator was going to oppose the forthcoming resolution. In that case he should ask the Secretary of
Defense two questions. He should ask to see the *Maddox*'s log (which would
place the ship closer to shore than the alleged site of the incident reflected),
and he should ask what the real mission of the ship was. Morse, who had already smelled a rat, was now convinced that the Administration's case was
even flimsier than he had suspected, that this was perhaps a provocative incident on our part, and he even suspected that it had been deliberately initiated
in order to get the resolution through Congress.

The next day Morse begged Fulbright to hold real hearings on the resolution and warned him that the wording was far too general and far too open-
ended for any President, particularly Lyndon Johnson. Fulbright answered
that they didn't have time, that it was an amergency. What emergency?
Morse asked. I don't know of any emergency. Instead Morse insisted that this
was the proper time to hold real hearings on Vietnam, to ventilate the issue
and to summon genuine expertise. He had in mind calling the dovish generals,
Ridgway, Gavin, Shoup, Collins, and then some international-law people, and
then perhaps witnesses who knew something about the political situation in
the South. The sum of the hearing, he was sure, would have been to cast such
doubt about any venture in Vietnam as to make any resolution a good deal
more limited, if not bottling it up altogether. Morse was absolutely convinced

that the instincts of his colleagues were more dovish than was apparent, and that expert testimony by former generals would give them heart. Fulbright turned him down and decided to ram the resolution through in a crisis atmosphere with patriotism a key factor; at a joint meeting of the Foreign Relations and the Armed Services committees, where both McNamara and Rusk testified for forty minutes, Fulbright was a friend of the White House. Morse alone asked unfriendly questions and cast the only dissenting vote.

That day and the next, Fulbright continued to serve as the floor manager for the resolution. The ambivalence of Fulbright about the whole issue was reflected in seemingly contradictory answers he gave to doubting senators, John Sherman Cooper of Kentucky and Gaylord Nelson of Wisconsin. Looking at the resolution, Cooper felt it was surprisingly open-ended, and raising a number of questions, finally asked Fulbright, "Then, looking ahead, if the President decided that it was necessary to use such force as could lead into war, we will give that authority by this resolution?"

"That is the way I would interpret it," Fulbright answered. "If a situation later developed in which we thought the approval should be withdrawn, it could be withdrawn by concurrent resolution. That is the reason for the third section."

But his answers to Senator Nelson were very, very different. Nelson, warned and primed by a very bright young member of his staff, Gar Alperovitz, who would later become a major revisionist historian of the Cold War, was extremely uneasy. Perhaps more than anyone else, he asked the right questions about long-range problems and difficulties. He thought the resolution gave the executive branch far too much power, in fact gave the President the power to change the American mission in Vietnam. Fulbright tried to dissuade him; this resolution was consistent with the past and rather limited mission. But Nelson persisted; this might mean a land war in Asia. Again Fulbright tried to reassure him on the basis of information from the White House. "Everyone I have heard has said that the last thing we want to do is become involved in a land war in Asia; that our power is sea and air, and that this is what we hope will deter the Chinese Communists and the North Vietnamese from spreading the war," he said. Nelson was still not reassured; he let Fulbright know that he intended to enter an amendment which would specifically continue to limit the American role there to advisory, training and support missions. It was an amendment against a land war. Fulbright conferred with the President, and found that the White House did not want the amendment. Johnson said that one amendment would bring countless others, the whole thing would come unraveled; it would spoil the language of the resolution, which had been very carefully chosen, and above all it would give the wrong impression, it would imply to Hanoi that the Congress was not behind its President. Besides, the President told Fulbright, the resolution was *limited,* no one wanted to get into a land war in Asia, that was the last thing they wanted; it was aimed not so much at Hanoi, he implied, as at Goldwater.

So Fulbright went back and reassured Nelson that his amendment was unnecessary, though he noted that the Nelson amendment "is an accurate reflection of what I believe is the President's policy." (A few months later, as the war escalated, Nelson sharply attacked Fulbright on the floor of the Senate, and Fulbright in turn publicly and profusely apologized to his Wisconsin colleague.) But Nelson withdrew his amendment and the debate came to its somewhat sterile end. (Recounting the congressional enthusiasm for the Tonkin message, Johnson in his autobiography would cite with some glee the Fulbright-Cooper exchange, making no mention of the Fulbright-Nelson one.) On August 7 Morse, with Gruening the only two senators to vote against the resolution, said: "I believe that history will record that we have made a great mistake in subverting and circumventing the Constitution of the United States . . . by means of this resolution. As I argued earlier today at great length, we are in effect giving the President . . . warmaking powers in the absence of a declaration of war. I believe that to be a historic mistake." He was right, of course. Johnson had it both ways; the Congress signed on without really declaring war. It was a great day for the private exercise of power; the most public of bodies, the Senate of the United States, had seen fit to acquiesce without any serious challenge to the manipulations of the executive branch. It was perhaps the last great political hurdle for Johnson as he faced the pressures that were mounting.

What was important was that the step had been taken at a very considerable price. The Secretary of Defense would mislead the Congress on a number of specific points, and the most important point of all, the role of the covert operations in initiating the entire prolonged Tonkin episode, was omitted from discussion (in his autobiography Johnson would later pass over this very lightly, claiming that on August 3 McNamara had fully briefed the Senate leaders on the 34A operations. It was simply not true). Thus the crisis atmosphere and the issue of the flag seemed to dominate the proceedings; the Communists had provoked us, as Communists were wont to do; obviously we had to respond, to show firmness. But the full story, that we and our American-owned proxies had been provoking them at the time they retaliated, was left out. It was a crucial omission, for it colored the entire subsequent debate, and allowed the Administration to use the most potent of all weapons in the proceedings, the issue of the flag. Had the real story been known, there would surely have been full Senate hearings, and the more they dragged on, the more they would have cast doubt on the President's position. In private testimony before the Senate committees at the time, McNamara had gone out of his way to dissociate the *Maddox* patrol from the 34A missions; similarly he was disingenuous to the point of open dishonesty about what the mission of the 34A boats was, what the extent of U.S. control of their missions was, and what his own knowledge of 34A day-to-day operations was (he was fully informed, as was Rusk).

It was not surprising that years later a reporter interviewing Wayne Morse, by then an ex-senator, would find him more intense in his retrospective anger toward Fulbright than toward Johnson; Fulbright, Morse thought, had played the game when he should have known, and in fact did know, better. But as part of an overall consensus, the hold on the Congress was very thin, as thin as the wording in the resolution was vague. Fulbright would feel that he had been lied to and misled, and finally, with great misgivings—going against the advice of his more conservative Senate staff, and with the urging of his committee staff, he began a series of speeches that would lead to a major break with the Administration. The relationship, once so warm ("To J. William Fulbright, than whom there is no better," Johnson had recently autographed a photo), would become bitter and hostile. Knowing that Fulbright liked to be on the inside, Johnson deliberately tried to isolate him, to mock him in private, calling him "the stud duck of the opposition"; and he would talk to friends of Fulbright's laziness, his vanity. Fulbright in turn dissented first in speeches, and then, by early 1966, with major hearings on the war, calling a series of forceful and eloquent witnesses, Kennan, Gavin, and others.

If at that time the Republican party with its triple tongue of Rockefeller-Nixon-Goldwater was not furnishing the country with intelligent, informed, thoughtful analysis of the war, and it was not, then no matter, because the Senate Foreign Relations Committee, reluctantly or no, had become the center of opposition. The opposition to the war, kindled there, would help turn the country and particularly the crucial liberal-egghead wing of the Democratic party against the war, and would lead, to a very considerable degree, to Lyndon Johnson's withdrawal from the 1968 race. And if the Senate and Fulbright had been noted for their lack of assertiveness in the serious questioning of American foreign policy, then that era ended with the Tonkin Resolution. A new age would dawn, in which all the major assumptions of American foreign policy would be challenged, and Bill Fulbright, the least likely adversary for Johnson, feeling personally betrayed, would become the leader of a hostile and bitter opposition which no longer believed anything emanating from the White House. The resurgence of a real and independent U.S. Senate on the foreign policy of the United States would date from Tonkin. The old order, the assumption that the executive branch knew better because it was privy to better inside information, would end, as would the corollary, that the President of the United States could be trusted. For Lyndon Johnson, the Tonkin Gulf Resolution was a victory, but like so many things he was to do in the coming year, it produced short-range gains with far more serious long-range problems. (However, ironically, the lack of legal authority for the war continued to bother not just the critics of the war but the President as well, and in 1965, as the escalation mounted, he turned to Nicholas Katzenbach, the Attorney General, and asked, "Don't I need more authority for what I'm doing?" Katzenbach assured him that he did not, that on a legal basis he had all the authority he needed with the Tonkin Resolution. But Johnson was still bothered by the idea, and he raised the same point with his congressional liaison people and his friends on the Hill, and they told him not to go for more legal justification, that he would get hit from two sides: by the people who opposed him on the war, and by those who supported him but thought they had given him enough authority already.)

JOHNSON HAD NOT MOVED PRECIPITOUSLY ON THE CONGRESSIONAL resolution, as some on his staff had wanted, rather he bided his time; and when the right moment came, he taught the North Vietnamese a lesson ("touched them up" was the phrase which he would use from time to time). So they knew they were dealing with Lyndon B. Johnson, a man to be reckoned with, a man who was not afraid of force and who would lay it on the table. At the same time he had got the Congress over to his side, silenced the dissenters, locked up the press, and even locked up poor Barry Goldwater, who after some phone calls endorsed the Johnson approach to Tonkin. Johnson was hailed as a man of wisdom, balance and *restraint;* the contrast with Goldwater, who seemed anxious to turn all problems over to the Joint Chiefs, was marked. Here was a man of restraint, a man of judicious force, neither of the left nor of the right. But if Tonkin made things easier it was because it was a fraud; it left the President with the illusion that he could use force, and use it effectively, simply by turning it on and off, that he could get in and get out without any fuss, that he could teach the North Vietnamese a lesson and they had no response (which was not true, they would immediately respond to the Tonkin incident, showing anyone who cared that when kicked, they would kick back—indeed Tonkin itself had been precipitated by an instance in which they had retaliated at a destroyer because of actions against them. Tonkin was not just an escalation on our part, it was an escalation on *their* part as well, showing that they would meet force with force). That was one illusion; the second was that consensus warmaking worked, that the President could get all but the extremes to agree to a judicious way of going to war, and that it would hold as long as he took the center, and that he could rally and strengthen his position by force; and finally, that as he had been in control during Tonkin, controlling the response to the North Vietnamese attack and gaining just what he wanted domestically with it, the President could continue to stay in control, to use events to his advantage.

Although Johnson's success was an illusion, the short-range results were remarkable. The polls were better than ever, the press comment was better than ever (even Walter Lippmann seemed pleased, because Lippmann, a believer in an American policy of blue water and clear skies for the Pacific, that is, staying out of land wars, thought Johnson was signaling the limits of the United States in a Pacific war rather than just the beginning). "In a single stroke Mr. Johnson has, at least temporarily, turned his greatest political vulnerability in foreign policy into one of his strongest assets," wrote Lou Harris, the pollster, on August 10. No less than 85 percent of the nation approved the raids. In July, Harris noted, 58 percent of the nation had criticized Johnson's handling of the war, while after Tonkin public opinion virtually reversed itself, and 72 percent approved. More and more people, Harris found, wanted us to take the war to the North (though of course there was very little polling about what that meant, whether we should take the war to the North if it meant a prolonged and bloody ground war in the bargain).

But Tonkin protected Johnson from the one issue which he had feared and where events might slip away from his control. While it had improved his standing in the polls, it had, ironically, sharpened the differences between him and Goldwater (and it had both in his mind and the minds of the men around him convinced them of their right and their capacity as well to manipulate the American people and the Congress). Having handled, he thought, the Congress, the people and the enemy, the way was clear now to his own Presidency. In late summer he moved away from the shadow of Jack Kennedy, his own legislative program and his foreign problems, to run for the Presidency as his own man, for the Johnson years, and he did it joyously and with zest. It was no wonder that he loved running in 1964, a chance to bask in the kind of national admiration he had never received before, though the admiration was at least as much anti-Goldwater as it was pro-Johnson; Goldwater had done for Johnson what Johnson could never do for himself. He had magnified those Texas virtues and minimized those Texas warts; the warts disappeared not so much because they were no longer there, but because the press and the public in the summer and fall of 1964 chose not to see them. Rather, the virtues became evident; Johnson was frequently described as a healing man, indeed he would refer to one of his main speeches as the one in which he was "healing the wounds." He was the man who could bring the different regions together, who could overcome his own regional prejudices if the nation would overcome its prejudices against him. Roy Wilkins would say of him, yes, the President seemed to be a great man destined for great things, but that Texas accent did make him, Wilkins, a little uneasy; and no less a figure than Martin Luther King, Jr., saw more hope for him, more commitment from him for Negro rights than from John Kennedy, King seeing in Johnson a desire to cleanse a soul.

His energies became almost mythological; they were our energies, his dreams were our dreams. Business leaders came over to him, made uneasy not by Goldwater's preference for free enterprise, but by their fear that in blowing up the Kremlin men's room, he might blow up their factories as well. The young did not protest him. He sat at a mass rally in Detroit with Walter Reuther on one side of him and Henry Ford on the other. Was it possible? Was this the land where our fathers had struggled? "I never had it so good," he said that day in Detroit. To visitors at the White House he loved to show slides of people reaching out to him at campaign rallies. "Look at them," he would say. "Just look at them." Negroes, in their last year of being content to be known as Negroes, rallied to his side. More than rally—"Those Negroes cling to my hands like I was Jesus Christ walking in their midst," he told friends. He was for one magic moment what he had always wanted to be, the centrist consensus candidate, loved by all his people. He savored it, becoming expansive in the riches that the campaign brought to him; he had the issues locked up. There were only three national concerns, anyway, he told reporters traveling with him on the plane. "Everybody worries about war and peace. The men worry about heart attacks and the women worry about cancer of the tit."

It was all his; Jack Kennedy had started it and Lyndon Johnson had finally put it together and held it together and now he was reaping its dividends. To James Cannon, a reporter from *Newsweek*, which was jointly owned by the Washington *Post*, he would mockingly complain about the *Post*'s treatment of him and then open the paper, where there were eight stories on the front page, three editorials about him, all favorable, and three columnists praising his wisdom. As Johnson went through the paper, checking off the stories, his grin began to grow, and he finally said, "See? Nothing but a house organ." And to Charles Mohr, the White House correspondent for the *New York Times*, who, when granted an interview and finding nothing of great import to ask about, all great issues settled momentarily, asked about some internal White House procedural question, Johnson laughed and said, "Here you have a chance to interview the President of the United States and the leader of the entire free world. And you ask a chickenshit question like that."

As the campaign progressed, even the greatest sophisticates in the country, the New York jet set, rallied to his cause, opened a discothèque called the LBJ, where chic young people danced beneath giant photos of that somewhat mournful face. Everywhere he campaigned the crowds were good and they responded to him, to the good life he was bringing them. He cast aside the security advice of the Secret Service people, and surged into the throng, and they loved him and he gave back his warmth and his energy. The times were good now and there were better ones, golden years, ahead. His record would make people forget Kennedyism—oh, a few snobs, the Georgetown Ivy Leaguers, might remember how they had danced in those brief years, but the rest of the nation would be reading about the Great Society and Lyndon Johnson and what he had done for *all* of the people. It was no wonder he tried to keep Vietnam out of his mind, as far from a place of debate as possible. When someone asked him later why he had not involved the public more in the question of Vietnam, he was told: "If you have a mother-in-law with only one eye and she has it in the center of her forehead, you don't keep her in the living room."

Oh, to run against Barry Goldwater, he of the quick tongue and the quick atomic trigger. It was not that he actually advocated nuclear war, it was just that he talked about nuclear war so much that he *seemed* to be advocating it (reporters covering Goldwater noted that in one thirty-minute speech alone, Goldwater mentioned nuclear weapons, war and devastation twenty-six times). In the past, Lyndon Johnson knew, there had been doubts in the public mind about him, not doubts about the Johnsonian ability to get things done, but about his ethical sense, doubts about his restraint, doubts stemming from his *Texanisms*. But Goldwater, the man of the real right, cleansed him of his sins; the more Goldwater campaigned, the better it was for Lyndon Johnson, a rare case where exposure of your opponent was a blessing. In case there was any question about what Goldwater might do with the issue of the war, the Administration was careful to send a young naval officer in civilian clothes to Goldwater's headquarters each day to pick up his advance speeches; thus the Administration was prepared to answer any charge on the war almost before Goldwater made it. If Tonkin had tied up the nation, it had also tied up Goldwater, good old-fashioned patriot that he was. So Barry Goldwater made it possible for Johnson to run as he had always wanted and as he felt most comfortable, not as a man of ideology or region, but as someone who simply wanted to do good for all the folks. It was a lovely thing to watch, Lyndon out there, healing the wounds, as he put it.

The signs were good everywhere, in the polls, in the people who came to the White House. He was ebullient; he loved calling people into the White House, showing them the polls, and telling them what it would mean in the next session of Congress. He was going to win and win big, and he was going to get a real Congress, and there was nothing in his way. "We'll have nine, eh, maybe even eighteen months before the Hill turns around on us," he would say. "We have that much time to get it all through." And then he talked of his plans, his dreams, what he would do, the education legislation, the housing program, the domestic vision, and he pushed his domestic staff to work harder and harder on domestic legislation, driving them relentlessly, always aware of the limits of time. "When you win big," he would say, recalling Franklin Roosevelt's experience, "you can have anything you want for a time. You come home with that big landslide and there isn't a one of them who'll stand in your way. No, they'll be glad to be aboard and to have their photograph taken with you and be part of all that victory. They'll come along and they'll give you almost everything you want for a while and then they'll turn on you. They always do. They'll lay in waiting, waiting for you to make a slip and you will. They'll give you almost everything and then they'll make you pay for it. They'll get tired of all those columnists writing how smart you are and how weak they are and then the pendulum will swing back."

So you had that time and you had to use it, and he wanted everyone ready; when they came out of the election he wanted it all lined up. Then sometimes, when the others were gone, he would turn to the men around him and continue to talk about the Congress, and he would do something rare for him in those days, he would mention Vietnam. You had to control the Congress and keep it in line, keep it from thinking it could run over you. From smelling blood on you. That meant controlling Vietnam, keeping it down. If you didn't handle Vietnam, the Congress would know and would strike at you, and would lose its respect for you. If he seemed weak as a President in dealing with Vietnam, he was sure it would undermine him politically. Hell, Truman and Acheson had lost China, and maybe it wasn't their fault, but they were blamed for it, and when it happened the Republicans in Congress were waiting and jumped on it, and Truman lost the Congress and then the country—it hadn't happened over domestic issues, remember that, he said, and Truman and Acheson were as strong anti-Communists as anyone he knew. Well, he did not want the blame for losing Vietnam, it might mean the loss of other things he wanted. So Vietnam became more than just a piece of terrain, it was something linked to the rest of his program, to his whole Presidency. Something you had to watch. It might not do you a lot of good, but it sure as hell, he said, could do you a lot of harm.

At the convention, *his* convention, there had been barely any challenge to his supremacy. Some kids and some Negroes from Mississippi tried to get in, tried to stir up trouble, trouble that would only help Goldwater, so he calmed them down, in his usual way, telling the liberals it was their job to take care of that Mississippi business, or else their man, Hubert Humphrey, would suffer. That was the price. And so they had quieted down the Mississippi people, and Humphrey had been on the ticket ("My link to the bomb throwers," he had called Humphrey in the old days when he used him as an opening to the Senate left, though Humphrey was far from a bomb thrower any more), and it was one more victory for centrist pluralist politics over the extreme fringe.

American politics—the kind of coalition politics he knew best still worked —still delivered. The people might not always like it, but they had no alternative to it. Or did it work? Was it still effective? Or had there been a major change in the attitudes of the people, and in particular among his party's special constituents, the liberal intellectuals, changes which were momentarily obscured by the one issue of 1964, Goldwater? If the benefit of Goldwater

was that he dominated the campaign, the price was that he obscured other issues and warning signals, subtle changes in the society, for events and attitudes in America were very much in flux, and if anything, 1964 was a landmark year in American life. The people in power seemed to be very much in
control of events; the Cold War still existed and high-level American political
attitudes were still shaped by it; the old liberal Democratic coalition still held
together, though some of the participants in it were increasingly uneasy with
one another. On the surface, things seemed as they had in the past, only perhaps a little bit better. But it was a time when icons were about to be shattered, and when the order was about to change.

There was a growing citizen restlessness which was not reflected in the political order; the politicians and a good many in the population had very different definitions of who the enemies were and what the problems were. For
the existing political structure still believed that America was threatened
from without, while an increasing number of educated, articulate Americans
felt the dangers were from within. The politicians in Washington were responding to issues which no longer affected large numbers of the people, and
as a corollary, increasing numbers of people were bothered about elements of
their life which were not defined as political issues. The gap between the politicians and the public, particularly an articulate educated minority, was growing, and nothing would widen it like the war in Vietnam. The government itself was still geared up to hold the lines in the Cold War, but a particularly
influential part of the citizenry believed that it was a thing of the past, that
the arms race was futile and destructive, that the enemy was really bigness,
technology and the government itself. Liberals had always grown up thinking
big and powerful government was good; now for a variety of reasons they
were moving back from that position. So there were stirrings in the land; they
had not surfaced as political forces and it would have taken a uniquely sensitive political figure to both perceive them and incorporate them into his policies. Lyndon Johnson certainly did not sense them; he saw power residing
where it always had in the past and he had little sense of where it might go in
the future. Perhaps some of these stirrings might have surfaced earlier, but
the sheer charm and style of Kennedy had helped co-opt some of the dissidence and defuse some of the restlessness. Kennedy was intellectual, stylish,
liberal and young, and thus seemed like them and of them; Norman Mailer
had seen Kennedy as the existential President whose very presence would
somehow make American intellectual and political life better.

Now in 1964 the cracks in the concrete were beginning to show in a variety
of places, and the coming of the war would heighten the very restlessness
which was just beginning to emerge. Hollywood of course had always supported the Cold War; at best a movie like *High Noon* was an oblique criticism
of the McCarthy period. But generally certain things were sacred, and Holly-

wood seemed to be particularly good at grinding out films on the Strategic Air Command. In early 1964 nothing seemed to symbolize better the conflicting forces and changes of attitude, the new and the old, than the appearance of Stanley Kubrick's movie *Dr. Strangelove*, and the review of it by Bosley Crowther in the *New York Times*. The Kubrick film was an important bench mark; it attacked not so much the other side as the total mindlessness of nuclear war, portraying how the irrational had become the rational. It was wild black humor at its best, and it touched some very sensitive nerve ends. But Crowther, who knew where the line should be drawn, was appalled and called it a sick joke: "I am troubled by the feeling which runs all through the film, of discredit and even contempt for our whole defense establishment, up to and even including the hypothetical commander in chief. It is all right to show the general who starts this wild foray as a Communist-hating madman convinced that a Red conspiracy is fluoridating our water in order to pollute our precious body fluids . . . But when virtually everybody turns up stupid or insane—or what is worse, psychopathic—I want to know what this picture proves . . ." (Significantly, as the change of values intensified in the middle and late sixties, there would be almost a complete turnover in the critics for all the major publications, such as the *Times*, the Washington *Post*, *Newsweek* and *Time*. The older reviewers would be moved aside and younger, more radical critics quickly promoted in film, books and the theater. Traditional outlooks still marked those publications' political attitudes and reporting, but publishers, realizing that times were changing, had accommodated in their cultural sections; the result was that sometimes a paper like the *Times* seemed to have a split personality; its political reporters hailing what its critics shunned.)

In 1964 Lenny Bruce, who a few years later would become a major cultural hero, was being prosecuted by the District Attorney's office. Bruce would lose the case, but what he stood for—the essential change in attitude—would win. Bruce was saying that individual foul epithets were not obscene; it was the tolerance of all kinds of inhumanity by people in power which was genuinely obscene. His definition of obscenity was rapidly gaining acceptance. He was by no means simply a popular nightclub comedian; he was linked to the same broad assault on the society's attitudes that Kubrick was part of.

There were other political reflections. Young whites went to Mississippi that summer to attack segregation, but they made it clear that they were attacking the entire structure of American life and that Mississippi was merely the most visible part. Their activity led to the formation of the Mississippi Freedom Democratic party, which caused the one sour note as far as Johnson was concerned at the convention. There they were quickly put down, but what the Freedom Democrats symbolized politically, deep and abiding dissent from the processes and an unwillingness to compromise on terms dictated by the existing power structure, would live and grow. By 1968 many of the people who had helped put them down at the 1964 convention were with them, and the Democratic party itself seemed threatened.

At the same time the civil rights movement itself was winding down; there was a new and growing Negro discontent. There was a new anger in the air, particularly in Northern cities. A sense of bitterness and hate seemed to pervade, and traditional civil rights leaders were pushed aside. Riots started in the ghettos of Harlem, Rochester, Jersey City and Philadelphia, and other cities would soon follow; as the ghettos burned, the civil rights movement was coming to an end. More alienated and more scarred leaders such as Malcolm X rose. They were protesting not just legal segregation, but the very structure of American life. The problem was not a Negro problem, they said, it was a white problem. They did not want In, they wanted Out. They did not want programs; indeed, in the changing mood of the black communities, leaders who were seen co-operating with the white structure soon lost part of their credibility.

In California, at Berkeley, the university that was once a special monument to pluralistic free education, there was a growing student restlessness and a growing dissatisfaction with student and American life. When the protests were put down clumsily by local authorities, the students banded together and formed the Berkeley Free Speech Association; it was the first step in which a new educated youth of America flashed its power and its desire to have a say in political events. They were protesting many things, including the sheer size and insensitivity of the giant university, known as the multiversity. Their enemy was the president, Clark Kerr, a good liberal technocrat, a decent man trying to manage an enormous complex. He was, William O'Neill would write, "anything but a despot. He was, in fact, the Robert McNamara of higher education, a skillful manager of complex systems." Berkeley was the beginning of a growing student protest which sometimes seemed unable to define its exact enemies, but which came together on the issue of the war as Johnson escalated in Vietnam. But to them, bigness, technology and bureaucracy was as much of an enemy. Even as Berkeley was breaking out, a young lawyer named Ralph Nader was finishing his book on auto safety, and he would come to symbolize the citizen protest against the government and against the corporation, a belief that government co-opted good ideas and served the large and powerful forces, and that a citizen, to be effective, had to work outside the government.

Yet for all this change and embryonic change, there was little of it reflected in the political processes. The attitudes of the existing parties were much as before. If anything, the government seemed determined to take fears and attitudes which had grown about the Soviet Union in the Cold War and now imperially export them to the underdeveloped world, Cuba, the Dominican Republic, Vietnam. This would in turn heighten the alienation among many who thought the enemy was now the government, the bureaucracy, the military. What had happened was that reality and public attitudes had outstripped Washington political attitudes, and the country needed serious reform and changes. Perhaps it was a problem between a society where the cultural and intellectual attitudes were shaped by new modern media, whereas political attitudes, and particularly American congressional attitudes—of which Lyndon Johnson was a prime student—were still locked in the feelings of small-town America of twenty and thirty years earlier. To Lyndon Johnson, the Mississippi Freedom Democratic party was like a gnat to be squashed on his way to the convention, a tiny irritant in a time of great joy, but it would be a symbol of other forces which would have dire consequences. Even later, as Johnson made his decision to have both the Great Society and the war, the war for the conservatives, the Great Society for the liberals, he would be giving the latter something that much of the American liberal intellectual community was no longer interested in; indeed, as Gene McCarthy noted in 1968 after he made his challenge against Johnson, "he keeps going to them with the list of bills he's passed—the laundry list, and he doesn't know that they aren't interested any more."

Chapter Twenty

H<small>E WAS THE ELEMENTAL MAN, A MAN OF ENDLESS, REST-</small>less ambition. Nothing was ever completed, each accomplishment was a challenge to reach for more. He was a politician the like of which we shall not see again in this country, a man who bridged very different Americas, his early days and attitudes forged by earthy, frontier attitudes, and whose final acts as President took us to the very edge of the moon. He was a man of stunning force, drive and intelligence, and of equally stunning insecurity. The enormity of his accomplishments never dimmed the hidden fears which had propelled him in the first place; he was, in that sense, the most human of politicians. There was about Lyndon Johnson something compelling; the more he tried to hide his warts, the more he revealed them. His force and power were such that when he entered the White House, the intellectual architects of his own party believed firmly that the greatest political benefits in America were produced by a strong, activist President; it was a negative testimony to him that when he left many of these same people talked of limiting the role of the Chief Executive, of strengthening the powers of the legislature and of local governments. Perhaps there was something of the inherent contradiction of democratic pluralistic America in the contradiction of Lyndon Johnson as President; the country had become so large, so powerful, yet so diffuse and disharmonious that only a man of his raging, towering strengths and energies could harness the nation's potential. That energy, when properly harnessed by him was marvelous, but given his powers, his drives, his instinct to go forward, it was disastrous if he was harnessed to the wrong policies. America then seemed faced with the dilemma of being overgoverned or undergoverned, and no one would ever accuse Lyndon Johnson as President of being content to undergovern. He would never let the history books say of him that he had been content to sit on the sidelines, to be a gentle, leisurely President, letting events take their course. He would control and dominate events, and the history books would tell of the good that he had done. Everything was on a larger scale for him, the highs were higher, the lows lower. He did not dream small dreams. Nor did he pursue small challenges. He pursued History itself, a place, perhaps, on Mount Rushmore, though there were were those who knew him who felt that Rushmore was too small, that it was Westminster Abbey, the history of the West. His speech writers were enjoined to read everything about Churchill, to help give Johnson a Churchillian twist.

Greatness beckoned him. Even as Vice-President he got to meet some elder statesmen when Kennedy dispatched him to Europe. He liked Adenauer, who was warm and pleasant, but he did not like De Gaulle, who was aloof and arrogant. However, he was impressed by De Gaulle, with his sense of grandeur and sense of history, De Gaulle who had greeted him with these words: "What have you come to learn?" That was greatness and that was history.

Later, when he had become President, he never took his eye off history. When an expert on documents warned him against using the auto pen (an automatic pen which reproduces the signature of the busy executive) and said that Jack Kennedy had used it too frequently and promiscuously, and that there were too many Kennedy letters which were not true Kennedy letters in the exact historical sense (including, the historian knew but did not have the heart to say, one from President John F. Kennedy to Vice-President Lyndon B. Johnson), Johnson took the admonition seriously. He signed all letters himself; history was history, one did not cheat it, a Johnson letter was a piece of history. Everything was a piece of history, and it was to be treated with proper respect; on board the presidential jet, he often doodled as he spoke with reporters, and if he left to talk with someone else and noted a reporter moving to pick up a scrap of presidential doodle, he did not find it beneath himself to walk back and snatch it away. Thus no unauthorized bits of Johnsonian history. He kept everything—letters, photographs, furniture—and it was not surprising that when he left office he speeded his own monument along. The Lyndon Johnson Library rose quickly and massively (while the Kennedy Library was still housed in a warehouse in Boston), and the real curator of the Lyndon Johnson Library would be Lyndon Johnson.

His appetite for achievement was never tempered. Not a contemplative man himself, he was not surrounded by many contemplative men.

He preferred men who said yes, it could be done, and they would do it: cut the budget, dam a river, pass the bill, write the speech. He was a doer himself, and one of the most striking parts of the Johnson memorabilia of those vice-presidential years are his letters from Jackie Kennedy asking Lyndon to please do this, and please take care of that; whenever Jackie wanted something done, accomplished, a job found for a friend, she had turned to Lyndon. And he liked doers around him: McNamara was a man after his own heart; he did not want ideology, he wanted action and energy. Looking at McNamara's fabled excellence at Defense, Johnson decided that one reason for it was the brilliance and drive of one of McNamara's deputies, Joseph Califano, and he set out to bring him to the White House. Eventually Califano joined the White House staff, where he began to submit endless numbers of memos. Sometimes, it was even alleged, he put his name over the work of subordinates, and there was some grumbling about this. When Johnson picked it up, when he heard another trusted staff man imply that Califano was not perfect, he reacted almost fiercely: *Don't you criticize Califano. There's never been a man around me who wrote so many memos.*

He was a man with an extraordinary attention to detail, which was very important to him; larger conceptions might not mean that much, but if he knew the details he could control the action, he could control subordinates. So he always knew details about everyone, more about them than they knew of him. Early in 1969, after the election, after it was all over, his attention to detail still lived. An aide wanted to go to New York to look for a job, but Johnson was unhappy about the trip. He did not want any job hunting until after the inauguration; it was, after all, one more reminder that he was leaving office. So having given his reluctant approval, he remembered later that day to call the White House booking office to make sure that the aide had paid for his own ticket. Always the search for a weakness in another man, always the hunt for something that might be used against him later.

Always that attention to detail, details not just of big things, but little things as well. Nothing was too small for Lyndon Johnson to master and manipulate. Even as Senate Leader, when he was about to go back to Texas for the weekend and time was of the essence, a fellow Texas congressman had some constituents in tow who had a problem on soil irrigation. Did Johnson have time for them? Of course he did, come right in the office, this soil irrigation is a serious problem. In the middle of the conversation, as he listened to them, nodding his head, exchanging views, without changing stride he switched from irrigation to the subject of his aide George Reedy's shirts. "You know, that boy Reedy never packs enough white shirts." He picked up the phone and dialed a number. "Hello, Mrs. Reedy, this is Lyndon Johnson. What size shirt does George wear? . . . No, no, no, he's a bigger man than that. George takes a bigger size." Briefly he argued Mrs. Reedy down, got her to accept *his size* Reedy. He put down the phone, continued talking about water irrigation, picked up the phone again, called a large department store, demanding the manager. "This is Lyndon Johnson and I need four white shirts sent over to my office right away . . . No, no, I need them right away . . . Yes, you can do it, I know you can, you're a can-do fellow. I know you and I won't forget it." He hung up the phone and went right back to irrigation again, without a break in his trend of thought, having done George Reedy's work for him, having assured Mrs. Reedy that she did not know what size shirt her husband wore, and having convinced the manager of a major department store that he was a real can-do man.

He was a relentless man who pushed himself and all others with the same severity, and demanded, above all other qualities, total loyalty, not loyalty in the traditional sense, not positive loyalty as John Foster Dulles had demanded, but total loyalty, not just to office or party or concept, but loyalty first and foremost to Lyndon Johnson. Then Lyndon Johnson would become the arbiter of any larger loyalty. Those who passed the loyalty test could have what they wanted. And he always knew who violated that loyalty, who said one thing to him and another thing to a possible enemy. No one could run as good an intelligence network inside Washington as Lyndon Johnson; as President he always knew who had dined with Robert Kennedy. He knew when the loyalty of his followers was waning before they did. No one was more loyal than Lady Bird. Of Marvin Watson, his last political operator, a man of great rigidity and little political sensitivity, Johnson, fiercely protective, could say that there was only one person more loyal than Marvin Watson and that was Lady Bird. High praise indeed. One reason for the long and intimate friendship between Johnson and Abe Fortas was the fact that despite the Johnson inner circle's doubts about the political acumen of Fortas, he was one of the few major Democratic doyens of Washington who was loyal to no other major Washington figure. He was Lyndon's man. Lyndon of course liked to personalize things: his people, his staff, his boys, his bombers. To a young Air Force corporal trying to show him the presidential helicopter—"This is your helicopter, sir"—he answered, of course, "They're all my helicopters, son."

He was ill at ease with abstract loyalty, loyalty to issue, to concept, to cause, which might lead one to occasional dissent, a broader view, and might mean that a man was caught between loyalty to civil rights and loyalty to Lyndon Johnson. One reason that he was never at ease with the American military was his knowledge that their loyalty was very special, that it was first to uniform and to branch of service, and only then to civilians in the most secondary way. Loyalty was crucial: Washington, after all, was a city with enemies everywhere, with sharks swimming out there waiting for any sign of weakness. Thus the inner circle had to be secure, truly secure; particularly a man with as profound a sense of his own weaknesses and vulnerabilities as Lyndon Johnson wanted men around he could trust.

"How loyal is that man?" he asked a White House staffer about a potential hand.

"Well, he seems quite loyal, Mr. President," said the staffer.

"I don't want loyalty. I want *loyalty*. I want him to kiss my ass in Macy's window at high noon and tell me it smells like roses. I want his pecker in my pocket." When Neil Sheehan interviewed Johnson about McNamara in early 1967, before the break on the war, he was surprised to hear Johnson talk about McNamara in terms not of ability, but of loyalty. "If you asked those boys in the Cabinet to run through a buzz saw for their President, Bob McNamara would be the first to go through it. And I don't have to worry about Rusk either. Rusk's all right. I never have to worry about those two fellows quitting on me." And even two years later, after he had parted from McNamara, after the pressure of the war had become too much for the Secretary of Defense, Johnson could talk with more compassion about McNamara than he could about McGeorge Bundy. In his opinion McNamara had folded, had come apart not just because the war was too much of a problem for his ethical composition but because he had been torn between two great, perhaps even subconscious loyalties: one to the Kennedy family, which had meant a commitment to Robert Kennedy, along with his ambitions and dovishness, and a second to Lyndon Johnson and his Presidency, and that was too much. The other loyalty, Johnson would say, was a prior one. But of Bundy he felt there was no real loyalty to the Kennedys (a judgment in which Robert Kennedy had concurred), nor to Johnson, but only toward self and sense of class. The Kennedys, of course, wanted comparable loyalty, but they were always more subtle about it, and more secure in themselves, and thus less paranoiac; they had a far better sense of touching people by seeming to appeal to higher instincts. The Kennedys were for civil rights, therefore people who were for civil rights should be for the Kennedys. The Kennedys demanded loyalty out of confidence, Johnson demanded it out of insecurity. The Kennedys were for the same things you were for, that was their message; they offered you the best chance of achieving it, and by turning to you, they demonstrated your own excellence. They never presented people of considerable self-esteem with such blatant either-or choice of loyalty as Johnson did, and they somehow managed to put it on a higher plane. They were plagued by fewer doubts about themselves and they had fewer fears that intimates might reveal their shortcomings to a threatening and hostile world at large.

His almost desperate need for loyalty was the other half of the coin of insecurity of this great towering figure who had accomplished so

much, was so much a man of Washington, and yet in so many important sections of the city felt himself an alien, the Texas ruffian among the perfumed
darlings of the East. It was a profound part of him; his sense of being alien, of
the prejudice against him, was never assuaged (in October 1964 when George
Ball handed in his first memo against the war, Johnson turned to an aide and
said, "You've got to be careful of these Eastern lawyers. If you're not careful
they'll take you and turn you inside out"). He was haunted by regional prejudice, and even the attainment of the Presidency did not temper his feelings.
Later, after he had left office, he became convinced that it was his Southern
origins, not the war, which had driven him out, that *they* had lain in wait for
an issue, any issue, and had used the war, which was their war in the first
place, to drive him from office. In July 1969 he sat in Texas, an ex-President of
the United States, and listened to the news of the tragedy of Edward Kennedy and Mary Jo Kopechne at Chappaquiddick, and became convinced by
the second day that Teddy Kennedy would get off scot-free. He became almost bitter about the injustice of it all; Kennedy would get off because he was
a Kennedy, there was a double standard, "But if I had been with a girl and
she had been stung by a bumblebee, then they would put me in Sing Sing," he
said. Even as President he had been haunted by these feelings: "If something
works out, Joe Alsop will write that it was Bundy the brilliant Harvard dean
who did it, and if it falls flat he'll say it was the fault of that dumb ignorant
crude baboon of a President," Johnson would complain, and he would remind
people again and again that in the chamber where these great decisions were
made, there sat the head of the Ford Motor Company, a Rhodes scholar, the
dean of Harvard University, and one graduate of San Marcos State Teachers
College. He had triumphed over one area of Washington, the doers, the movers, men of the South and West, shrewd insiders, but he had always failed in
another area, the taste makers, so much more Eastern, more effete, judging
him on qualities to which he could never aspire, all the insecurities confirmed.
Hearing in the late fifties that Walter Lippmann was important in the taste
making of Washington, that he set and determined everyone else's taste, and
knowing that Fulbright knew him well, Johnson had insisted that Fulbright
bring him together with Lippmann, which Fulbright with great misgivings
had done. It turned out to be a predictably horrendous evening, Johnson giving Lippmann the treatment, an evening of exaggeration and braggadocio,
Johnson showing his worst side to the genteel and gentle, self-contained
Lippmann, confirming all the worst doubts about the lack of subtlety in this
gargantuan figure. Johnson, aware of this, terribly aware of enemies everywhere, of Georgetown's distaste and the Metropolitan Club's distaste, sometimes even as President seemed to want to aggravate the sore, trying to emphasize what the Easterners would consider his own boorishness, trying to
inflict some crudity on them, demanding that they accompany him into

the bathroom for conversations during the most personal of body demands, virtually driving Douglas Dillon out of the Cabinet by this maneuver alone.

This very earthiness was very much a part of him, and he reveled in it; he was the earthiest man in the White House in a century; his speech was often obscene, shrewd, brilliant. Of one Kennedy aide he could say, "He doesn't have sense enough to pour piss out of a boot with the instructions written on the heel." Trying to get rid of J. Edgar Hoover and then finding it was simply too difficult, he admitted, "Well, it's probably better to have him inside the tent pissing out, than outside pissing in." Asked by reporters why, when he was Senate Majority Leader, he had not taken a particular speech of Vice-President Nixon's seriously, he said, "Boys, I may not know much but I know the difference between chicken shit and chicken salad." And once, driving around the Ranch showing its sights to a CBS television team, he stopped in the midst of particularly rough undergrowth to urinate. "Aren't you afraid a rattlesnake might bite it?" a CBS cameraman asked him.

"Hell," said Johnson, "it *is* part rattlesnake."

He was a man of primal force. Not a man, in the words of James Reston, that you would hand your hat to without thinking twice. His genes were seemingly larger and more demanding than those of other men; he dominated other men, leaning on them, sensing that every man had his price or his breaking point. (Once a young and very ambitious staff member was challenging him on an important point and was being unusually persistent in his opposition. Johnson took it for a while and then said very softly, "You know, Joe, you'd make a great Attorney General." The staff member folded like an accordion.) He knew the uses of force, of flattery and threat, honing in on the weakness like a heat-seeking missile, cataloguing each man's weakness in that incredible memory, to be summoned forth when necessary. Always wanting to know a little more about a potential friend or potential adversary. And everyone was a potential adversary. As President he enjoyed reading FBI files, they gave him lots of tidbits about some of the people he had to deal with. He had, there is no other word, a genius for reading a man instantly, for knowing how far he could go, how much he could push, what he could summon from the man, when to hold on and when to let go. He often took too much, leaving men who had worked for him depleted, exhausted and feeling that they had been misused.

The people who worked for him lived in mortal fear of him. He humiliated them in front of their peers, then sometimes rewarded them, dressing down one staff member while others watched, then later in the day awarding the staffman a Cadillac, winking and explaining to someone else that it helped bind a man to strike with munificence when he was down. He would call in all the press officers from the different departments and chew them out like a drill sergeant, saying they had been doing a terrible job, he hadn't been on the front page in weeks except for lighting a goddamn Christmas tree. Lighting a goddamn Christmas tree! Now he was going down on the Ranch and he wanted them to get him on page one every day; they better dream up something and get it on the first page. On he went, leaving the men in the room, some of them quite distinguished men in their own professions, feeling that they had been crushed and degraded. Or Johnson telling Cabinet members that they wouldn't dare walk out of his Administration, no one was going to walk out on Lyndon Johnson because they knew that if they did, two men were going to follow their ass to the end of the earth, Mr. J. Edgar Hoover and the head of the Internal Revenue Service.

In front of visiting dignitaries he was wont to put up his feet on Jack Valenti's lap and use it as a stool. Similarly, when he was visiting Nehru in 1961 as Vice-President and the meeting was breaking up, Johnson turned to an aide and asked if a press conference had been arranged. When the aide said he knew nothing of a press conference, Johnson berated him in the most forceful terms, finally telling the aide, "The only way to deal with you is to handcuff you to my belt, so you'll be there when I need you." His close aide Walter Jenkins in particular lived in terror of Johnson, who had borne down on him so often and so hard that there was little left. Once when an exhausted Jenkins was about to take a brief nap, he told Bill Moyers to guard the office for thirty minutes. Moyers, who like his boss was an excellent mimic, got in the doorway a few minutes later and did a magnificent imitation of Johnson catching Jenkins napping. Jenkins turned first from total panic to total anger: "Don't you ever do that again . . . Don't you ever do that again . . . Don't you ever . . ."

There was in all of this more than a small element of the bully in Johnson and an occasional misreading of people. Even then he learned quickly. When General Wallace Greene, the Commandant of the Marine Corps, attended his first high-level meeting with the President, he was appalled by the way the President treated the people around him, abusing them, almost humiliating them, and Greene decided immediately that he would not take this. So the first time Greene spoke up, it was on the subject of Vietnam. Johnson did not like what he was saying; Greene was very hawkish and said he thought too little force was being used, and Johnson began interrupting him: "Speak up! Speak up! I can't hear what you're saying. Speak up!" Greene waited deliberately; then he looked up at Johnson and said in his carefully controlled voice, "You can hear what I'm saying and so can everyone else in this room," and calmly continued to speak. Greene noticed that from then on, whenever he appeared at the White House, Johnson seemed to solicit his advice and opinion, and marked him down for a bully, though of course not many men would enter the National Security Council with the same sense of confidence in himself as the Commandant of the Marine Corps. (General Greene was not the only person who sensed this; Gene McCarthy in 1967 told friends that he thought Johnson was a bully, and that if the early primaries were not good, he would come apart rather than fight back.)

But generally Johnson had that brilliant sense of how far to push and this made him particularly effective in the U.S. Senate, where he could employ his knowledge at close-range maneuvering, where his shrewdness, remarkable intelligence and sheer energy would overwhelm lesser men; totally uncorrupted and never distracted by other pursuits, he considered the Senate, and his maneuvering there, his life. Manipulation of another human being was deemed normal and indeed necessary to the job. But it was a different thing when Johnson was in the White House, where he could extract from people what he needed and wanted, and then when he was finished, when the Johnson stamp was indelibly, and sometimes too indelibly, on them, Johnson would let them go (which often left a bad taste, a feeling after the fact on the part of people that they had been exploited, which was true, they had been, though for the greater good). Once, even before it all went sour on Vietnam, when Johnson was at the height of his accomplishments, he had complained to Dean Acheson about the fact that for all the good things he was doing, he was not beloved in the hearts of his countrymen, and why was that? Acheson looked at him and said simply, "You are not a very likable man." Indeed, those who knew him best (men like Clifford and Fortas, who enjoyed that rarest of things, his respect) were uneasy about working for him. In 1967 Johnson sent an emissary to talk with Clark Clifford about the possibility of his becoming Attorney General, a suggestion Clifford dismissed because he was afraid the job would undermine that fragile balance between being something of an equal and then overnight a total servant having to bear those tongue-lashings.

Johnson would forever quote a maxim of his father's: if a man couldn't walk into a room and tell who was for him and who was against him, then he wasn't much of a politician. Of course Lyndon Johnson could do it like no other man, ipso facto he was a great politician. Thus a key to Johnson was the capacity to move men to his objective and away from their own charted course. That was the way to achieve things: deal with men at close combat, man to man. He believed this deeply, almost too much so. Since he was not a contemplative man, a man who read books, and since he had little belief in the rhythms and thrusts of history, he was convinced that you could accomplish things by reasoning with leaders, by moving them to your goal, manipulating them a little, and that finally, all men had a price. In part this helped bring him into trouble in Vietnam, with his instinct to personalize. He and Ho Chi Minh, out there alone, in a shoot-out. He would find Ho's price, Ho's weakness, whether it was through bombing the North or through threatening to use troops and then offering Ho a lollipop, massive economic aid and regional development, a Mekong River Delta development project. This time he would find himself dealing with a man who was a true revolutionary, incorruptible, a man who had no price, or at least no price that Lyndon Johnson with his Western bombs and Western dollars could meet. But it would take him quite a while to find out that he had met his match. For a long time he thought that he could handle Ho the way he handled senators and bureaucrats, and opponents. Put a little squeeze on him, touch him up a little, then Ho would see the light, know whom he was dealing with and accept the lollipop.

NOTHING EXISTED FOR HIM BUT POLITICS. THE IDEA OF HIS GOING TO A symphony or reading a book was preposterous, and before he took office he would boast of how little he read. When a young Senate staff member named Bill Brammer wrote a brilliant novel about Johnson entitled *The Gay Place*, Johnson did not read the book but was annoyed, not so much about the portrait Brammer had drawn of him, but about the fact that Brammer had written the book at night while working for Johnson, when he clearly should have stayed up late answering Johnson's mail. (If he was not a great reader, in his earlier incarnation, he became sensitive about this failing once he assumed the Presidency, particularly when his lack of reading was contrasted with Kennedy's voracious reading.)

Hugh Sidey of *Life*, who had written of Kennedy's reading habits, decided to do a similar article on Johnson's. He started with George Reedy, who told him that yes, Johnson was an avid reader. What books? Sidey asked. All Reedy could think of was Barbara Ward's *The Rich Nations and the Poor Nations*, a book on how the rich should help the poor which Johnson had liked because it was similar to his own ideas. From there Sidey went to see Moyers. Yes, said Moyers, he was an avid reader. What books? Well, there was Barbara Ward's book *The Rich Nations and the Poor Nations*. And from there to Valenti, who said Johnson read more books than almost anyone he knew. What books? Valenti hesitated and thought for a moment, then his face lit up. Barbara Ward's *The Rich Nations and the Poor Nations* . . . Even the book he read was of course a can-do book, a book which was about how to make things work; he had little time for light activities. Both his successor and predecessor were sports fans, but Johnson had little interest in football or baseball. Once Lana Turner was promoting a movie in Washington; aides had arranged for her photo to be taken with a group of senators, including Johnson. The schedule for the day was duly shown him, including the appointment with Miss Turner. He looked at it for a moment and then asked, "Who the hell is Lana Turner?"

He was the totally political man, living and breathing for the political act.

Yet he was curiously a man of Washington more than of the nation, a man who for most of his career harbored national ambitions, and yet who knew amazingly little about national politics as opposed to Senate politics, perhaps because he was afraid that if he ventured forth, people would treat him as a Texas ruffian. So the Senate had remained his theater, and he had mastered it and orchestrated it, the big things and the little things. Unsure of himself outside, he had remained where he was safe and secure. Because of this he had tended to see the country and its politics through the particular prism of the Senate. He believed in 1960 that since Senator Tom Dodd of Connecticut was for him, this meant that he was doing well in New England, and he did not realize what had happened to him until he reached Los Angeles. The problem there was of course not just that he read the country through the Senate, but he had so terrified his own people that they did not dare tell him bad news. Larry King, now a magazine writer and in those days a legislative assistant to a West Texas congressman, was one of Johnson's area representatives in 1960, assigned the Rocky Mountain area. He went out to work his section, found it very weak and was eventually summoned back to Washington for a meeting of area representatives, all the rest of whom were Texas congressmen. Johnson presided at the meeting, and one after another they made their reports. It was all marvelous: New England was very strong for Johnson, despite the seeming Kennedy strength. New York looked good. The great industrial states were hard and fast. Finally it was King's turn. "Well, I guess I'm working the one part of the country where we've got problems, but things don't look very good at all," he began. "Now, in Wyoming you say Gale McGee is for you, but I'm not so sure. He's staying out of it and telling his people to be neutral but I think they're leaning to Kennedy. And in Colorado . . ." Johnson gave him a very hard look and cut him off. "Next report," he said.

At Los Angeles he found out what the Kennedys, with their surer sense of national politics, had done to him. Washington and the Senate were his mirrors; he was big in the Senate and Kennedy was small there, usually absent. If he knew this, then others would know it too and know who the real man was. If conservatives and hawks were more powerful in the Senate (which they were, more often than not controlling the key committees, Russell, Stennis, etc.), it was a sign that the conservatives were more powerful in the country. If the liberals were prone to make speeches and never got things done in the Senate (the more they talked, the more of a guarantee it would be that they would be outside the real corridors of power), then it was a sign that they were regarded the same way in the country.

He looked at the East and its politics long after he came to terms with the big-money people of the Southwest with an enduring rural Texas sense of alienation. He did not, for instance, like the big-city bosses as politicians, not liking the culture of the cities they represented, the trailing Catholic priests, the lurking labor leaders who probably didn't like Southern accents; but he was impressed by them as men, with their capacity to control their environment, their sense of presence, their ability to tell him how many votes a given district would produce. In contrast, Kennedy was not impressed by them as men, he knew them all too well; he was spawned by that tradition and wanted not so much to move up in their world as to move out of it, but he was impressed by them as politicians, liking not them but their methods.

Johnson viewed an area of the country not so much in ethnic and social terms but as an area which had sent certain men to Congress. He was best and most effective not as an open politician who seeks the Presidency (Kennedy had absolutely destroyed him there) but as an insider's man, working privately in the great closed corridors, always cloaked in secrecy until the good deed was done. There was a reason for this. He could be an excellent campaigner, and knew his own regions well, but what he had dedicated his career and his working hours to was the accumulation of power as a parliamentarian. Once he had established himself in what was virtually a rotten borough or safe seat (and come to terms with the upper tier of the new Texas power establishment) he proceeded to build up his connections and his possibilities as a Senate parliamentarian, trading his chance of appealing to wide national blocs of voters for the opportunity to work quietly on the inside to influence other legislators in private. He sought due bills on the inside, not due bills to the various great national lobbying groups, except as his and their interests occasionally coincided. He dealt similarly with the press; he held, charmed and commanded reporters who were intrigued by the inner workings of the institution of the Senate itself (notably his close friend Bill White who had written a biography of Robert Taft and a book on the Senate entitled *The Citadel*, and finally a book on Johnson himself, entitled, not surprisingly, *The Professional*) rather than reporters who were committed more to issues and to ideology, and who, like elements of the public at large, regarded him, because of his great parliamentarian sleight of hand, as something of a wheeler-dealer. Nor did he help himself with reporters by telling them that if they played the game the way he wanted, wrote the stories the way he told them to, he would make them all big men. His view of the press, they soon found, was that in his eyes they were either for him or against him. There was no middle ground. They were either good boys, in which case he felt he owned them, or they were enemies.

Given that safe seat back in Texas, he could concentrate the full force of his attention on his role within the Senate; given regional prejudices against Southerners, he could probably not aspire to a serious race for the Presidency; given the split between the South and the North within the Democratic party, the chance for an ambitious Texan to serve as something of a bridge between the conflicting forces also encouraged him as a man of the inside. The men from the North, for instance, rarely held such safe seats—their constituencies were often too narrowly divided—and had to devote more of their time to coming to terms with their own regions. If they mastered these regions they thought in terms of national ambitions and continued to channel their efforts outside the Senate. He was thus a man of the Senate because it fit his abilities and his possibilities.

In addition, it fit his personality. He did not particularly want to be out in front alone on a policy; he was not by any instinct a loner, and in the Senate, if he did his work well, the responsibility (and potential blame) could be broadly shared. He liked as many other fingerprints on the door as possible (in fact, when Johnson wrote his book on his presidential years, he spent a great deal of time and effort not discussing the wisdom of his policy, but emphasizing the consensus quality of it, how many others had been on board and wished him well).

HE LIKED TO THINK OF HIMSELF AS SOMETHING OF AN ABE LINCOLN, the country boy learning by oil lamps, and later, as President, loved to feed his own legend and richly embellished it, taking visitors around the old homestead, describing how simple it had been, a tiny little shack, until finally his mother interrupted him in front of several visitors, and said, "Why, Lyndon, you know that's not true, you know you were born and brought up in a perfectly nice house much closer to town." (In the same way he claimed that an uncle of his stood at the Alamo, which under most conditions would be all right, except that the whole point of the Alamo was how few men stood there, which made it tough on them against the Mexicans but somewhat easy for later historians to check whether a Johnson forebear had been there, and to find that one had not.) He was, in reality, despite the poverty that was around him in those Depression days, a member of a part of the American aristocracy, albeit Texas Hill Country aristocracy. An ancestor was president of Baylor University, and his family gave Johnson City its name. His father had served as a member of the Texas Legislature at a time when membership was limited to those who could afford to live in Austin during the biennial session, and Sam Johnson's seat had been held previously by his father-in-law, Joseph Baines. Thus there was a sense of tradition in the family, and if from time to time during the Depression there was not a lot of money, the Johnsons had land, influence and connections. They were landed aristocrats, though the land was often harsh.

He was a young boy that teachers would pay extra attention to. There was no doubt ever in his family that he would go to college, and when he did, messages about his arrival preceded him and connected him with a job in the office of the president of the school, and almost as soon as he graduated, there was a job in the local congressman's office. Lyndon was a man with some in-fluence and connections, and most of all, respectability. Most of that respecta-bility and much of the drive within him came from his mother, Rebekah Baines Johnson. (In 1968 when Harold Lasswell, pioneering expert on psy-chology and the political personality, gave an interview on Johnson's person-ality, he said, "One thing of outstanding interest is the extent to which John-son had to struggle to achieve independence from his mother. She was an ambitious, domineering woman who thought she had married beneath her. She was determined that this lad would be a great success and she pushed him very hard . . . It puts the son in a conflict. On the one side there is a tendency to accept domination and on the other hand a rebellious tendency to reassert one's independence and masculinity and sense of adequacy . . . It is a reasonable inference that Johnson was very much concerned about re-maining independent of outside influence. His subsequent political career—with his demand to make his own decisions, and his demand to *control* a situa-tion [italics Lasswell's]—has these very deep roots." This evaluation might have been debatable, except for the fact that when the interview reached the White House, it was immediately Xeroxed and gleefully passed around among some of the President's closest and oldest friends and was much admired for its insights.) For Rebekah Johnson was a person of great force, a great sense of herself, and of her son's destiny; in his own mind she would become a mytho-logical figure. (In "A Family Album," a brief volume on the Johnson and Baines families which she had written and which was published after her death, with a foreword by the then President, in 1965, there are some signs of her special hold on Lyndon. She told of Lyndon in elementary school reading, as befitted a class leader, a poem of his own choosing, entitled, curiously enough, "I'd Rather Be Mamma's Boy." She also reprinted an essay Lyndon published when he was twenty-two in the college newspaper, entitled "To Our Mothers." ". . . There is no love on earth comparable to that of a mother. Our best description of it is that of all types of earthly love, it most nearly approaches the divine . . .") Later when he was grown he would talk of his mother to friends: she was the finest, the most intelligent woman he had ever met, and therefore anyone who reminded him of her would have a brighter career ahead of her. Rebekah Johnson had, of course, always be-lieved in Lyndon; all her hopes, which had not been realized in her own life, would be attained through him. When he was elected to Congress, she wrote him:

My darling boy:
  Beyond "Congratulations Congressman" what can I say to my dear son in this hour of triumphant success? In this as in all the many letters I have written you there is the same theme: I love you; I believe in you; I expect great things of you. Your election compensates for the heartache and disappointment I experienced as a child when my

dear father lost the race you have just won. How happy it would have made my precious noble father to know that the first born of his first born would achieve the position he desired.

The Johnsons were part of the power structure of the Hill Country, the men who had power and who got together with the other men who had power, the Hill Country establishment, so to speak, and they conspired to bring about what was needed. A bridge. A highway. A hospital. Get rid of a bad teacher at the school. Decide who ought to be the candidate for which office. You had your own network of people, your own people arranged and you didn't go public with it until the time was right. (Years later McGeorge Bundy would tell friends that there was one thing you could not do with Lyndon Johnson and that was to go public with it, and by going public, Johnson meant talking to anyone else.) You never talked, not in the open. To do good, to get things done, to help the folks, to be powerful, you stayed private; you didn't go to the people, you helped the people. There was a considerable distinction here; if you were a serious man and wanted to get things done, you had to do them *for* people. Manipulate, but manipulate for their own good. He grew up in that environment and it never left him. In that particular art form there was no one quite like him, the art of doing good for people in spite of themselves. Even when he went to Washington, he mastered the inner corridors of power, getting things done. (Russell Baker, then a young reporter for the *New York Times*, was sent to cover the Senate in the early Johnson years and would recall one of his first meetings with Johnson. "How are you liking the Senate?" Johnson asked. "Well, I like it, but it's not what I thought," Baker answered. "I thought there would be more speeches, more debates, more arguments on the floor." Johnson leaned over, grabbed Baker, looked him in the eye: "You want a speech, you go see Lehman and Pat McNamara. They'll make you a speech. They're good at making speeches." An edge of contempt passes. Johnson now closer to Baker. "You want to find out how things are *done*, and you want to see things *done?* You come to me. I'll tell you all that.")

In Washington his first great mentor was Sam Rayburn, Mr. Sam, who as Majority Leader held great power, who exercised it wisely, meting it out judiciously, but who was never a public figure, never gave long speeches, never tried to get his name in print. Mr. Sam was the first teacher, and the second was Senator Richard Russell from Georgia, who taught him more about Washington, how to maneuver, how to get people indebted to him. In later years Johnson would tell friends how Dick Russell had operated, Russell the bachelor, always with plenty of time for young bright congressmen when they first arrived, taking them around at night, carefully guiding their careers and their social lives, making profound impressions on them with his generosity and intelligence, moving them ever so slightly into his orbit of influence. However, Johnson did not talk about the other half of his particular relationship with Russell, which was similar to that which he had enjoyed with Rayburn and others back in Texas, which was of the bright eager young man who brilliantly cultivates a lonely, forceful, older man of great power (Russell was a bachelor, and Rayburn, briefly married, might as well have been). That was a Johnson specialty, and helped lift him above the average young congressmen of his time. Johnson seemed to be the perfect pupil for both Rayburn and Russell; they were like fathers, he was almost sycophantic, thought some around them, but later, having gone beyond both of them, he could at times be harsh and contemptuous in talking about them. Yet the lessons were clear, these were men who got things done, who did not hang around the fancy men and indulge in the fancy talk of Georgetown dinner parties. These were men.

Like Rayburn, Johnson became an immensely successful parliamentarian, a man of the center able to move slightly to the left or the right depending on his needs and his party's needs, able to accommodate to the Eisenhower years with few problems (leaving Democrats the feeling that the Eisenhower election over Stevenson had upset neither him nor Rayburn; indeed the congressional leadership was so acquiescent to the Republican White House that the liberals created a Democratic Policy Study group as a means of charting a more independent course). Johnson could move slightly to the left on civil rights as national ambitions began to touch him, but he could also serve as a brake within his party if it moved too far to the left. Similarly, one of the reasons why the Democratic party did so little on major tax reform in the decade of the fifties was the relationship Johnson had with the big money in Texas and their proxies in the Senate (he could say of Senator Paul Douglas of Illinois, a constant critic of the oil-depletion allowance, that Douglas would understand it just a bit better if there were a few oil wells in Cook County).

There were two reasons why he was so successful: his own hold on the Senate, and the fact that, teamed with Rayburn, he controlled both branches of the legislature and could control, through Rayburn, the appropriations aspect of legislation. He could thus, for example, keep the military on a long-enough leash to allow them to plan their new weapons systems, and on a short-enough leash to have them keep coming back for more. His congressional position gave him considerable influence within the party of the fifties, a party caught in the conflict between its Southern-dominated Congress and a Northern-dominated mass. If Richard Russell tried to assert the party leadership through the Congress it would split the party, and someone like Hubert Humphrey, representing the liberal-labor elements of the coalition, did not have the horsepower to stand for the party in the Congress. So Johnson was the go-between; each adversary armed him against the other, their divisions fed his strength, he was the compromise figure. He was acceptable to the Southerners, but not really of them, but the more the Northern wing of the party rebelled, the luckier they felt they were to have Johnson. But if he was regionally acceptable to the South, he was for the same reason probably regionally unacceptable to the rest of the party. But he could, holding power in the Senate, make Humphrey glad to deal *with him*, giving the liberals just enough to keep them from going into open rebellion and asserting independent, though futile, leadership.

He loved the Congress and studied it; he could catalogue the strengths and weaknesses of every man there. The strength of a man put him off, but his weaknesses attracted him; it meant a man could be used. Whereas Kennedy had been uneasy in the face of another man's weakness, it embarrassed him and he tended to back off when a man showed frailty, to Johnson there was a smell of blood, more could come of this. But he understood men only through that one prism, how they performed and handled the Congress (even on the subject of the loss of China, it was the fact that in losing China, Truman had first lost the *Congress* which haunted him. The reaction to the loss had not necessarily come from the population, it had come from the Congress). This attitude was a weakness in itself, for not everyone shared his thirst for congressional work or his opinion that it was the only forum. One reason he misjudged John Kennedy as an opponent was that he did not take Kennedy seriously in the Senate. Kennedy clearly did not care, did not really bother with his congressional work and was therefore not, in Johnson's eyes, an entirely serious person.

As Lyndon Johnson admired men who got things done, men to be measured by their achievements, surely so too would the nation; it would choose a doer, a *man*, not a handsome young talker, a *boy*. As congressman and senator he created his own network of power, men who worked through him to move things, and he extracted his particular price and added more layers of power to his original base. But it was always done privately; he went partially public only after it was all done, and even then, when he dealt with the press, he was the private man, calling in a small claque of reporters whom he knew and trusted. He would sit down and explain his great victory, though within certain limits; he would not compromise future victories for the sake of immodesty now. And the reporters would play the game, they knew the ground rules: how much credit would go to Lyndon—never too little, mind you—and how much to the others, perhaps a little extra credit to a particular senator to ensure even greater co-operation the next time around. Out of this came his almost neurotic view of the press, two very conflicting views: first, that you owned the press, you summoned them and they wrote good stories, and second, that the press was an enemy, it was disloyal, that if it did not belong to you, then someone else had bought and thus you had to be wary. Rich publishers. Or the Kennedys. Or the big interests. Thus you had to get in there quickly and make your pitch. When Bill White left after covering Johnson in the Senate for the *New York Times* he was replaced by Russell Baker, and Baker heard about the change about six o'clock one evening. A few minutes later there was a telephone call and a booming voice over the phone, and it was, it said, Senator Johnson, what great news that Baker would be covering him, they would get along very well, even better than Johnson had with Bill White. Baker's reputation as a fearless reporter was going to be made; anything Baker wanted to know, his friend Lyndon Johnson would tell him. Anything. Johnson loved the *Times*, admired Baker's work. "For *you*, I'll leak like a sieve," he said.

He was concerned about the reputations of the reporters who covered him and worried about their professional prestige, since it was a reflection of his prestige, particularly during the vice-presidential years. When *Time* magazine decided to switch the assignment of John Steele, who had long been *Time's* envoy to Johnson, and replace him with a younger man named Loye Miller, the Vice-President was particularly upset. Was this another humiliation? Another taste of vice-presidential ashes? Steele and others in the *Time* empire rushed to reassure him: it was just the opposite, it was a re-evaluation in *Time's* eyes of the importance of the Vice-Presidency, and Loye Miller was the best they had, their brightest young star, scion of a great newspaper family, his father was a famous editor in Knoxville. There were brilliant things ahead for Loye Miller, and in recognition of the very big things ahead, perhaps the biggest ones, he was being given this choice assignment, this plum, an intimate relationship with Lyndon Johnson. And Johnson smiled and welcomed Miller. It is one of the sad aspects about great flatterers like Lyndon Johnson that among the few things they are vulnerable to is flattery. Shortly afterward Johnson was in New York and of course paid a state visit to the head of the Luce empire, Henry Luce himself. Johnson began with a long tribute to Luce, what a great man he was, how much the communications world of America owed to him, and yet even the greatest men eventually had to step aside and Johnson was delighted by the knowledge that he, Johnson, could vouch for the remarkable young man who would succeed Henry Luce, this fine, handsome, talented, brilliant young man, a scion of a great newspaper family. Some of the *Time* executives noticed a look of surprise and shock on Luce's face as Johnson was carrying on. After the Vice-President left, Luce grabbed a high-ranking aide and asked, "Who the hell is Loye Miller?"

The stories of his flattery soon became legendary. He had learned as a congressman that those out of power are surprisingly susceptible to the flattery of those in power, that flattery by someone in power becomes a special form of recognition. As he rose to higher and higher positions he resorted to greater and greater flattery, finding that few resisted it or were offended by it and that, indeed, most people accepted it as God's truth. The Johnsonian view of their abilities was similar to their own. Soon Washington was filled with stories of Johnsonian flattery and exaggeration, of Johnson telling Adlai Stevenson that he should be sitting in the President's chair, of Johnson telling Arthur Goldberg to leave the Court and go to the UN and make peace because the next man who sits in *this* chair is going to be the man who brought peace in Vietnam. But there were some occasions of mistaken identity and problems caused by the flattery. In July 1967, for instance, after John McNaughton was killed in an airplane crash, Johnson decided, at McNamara's urging, to appoint an able but little-known Washington lawyer named Paul Warnke, who had been working with McNamara as counsel to the Defense Department. Johnson was determined to pass on the news himself, to flatter Warnke and to impress upon him the importance of being Assistant Secretary of Defense for International Security Affairs, and most of all, the importance and goodness of Lyndon Johnson. So he told his secretary to have the switchboard get Warnke. Shortly thereafter the switchboard located John Carl *Warnecke*, an architect and social friend of the Kennedys' who was better known in Washington and a frequent visitor to the White House.

Jack Warnecke got on the phone to hear the President of the United States say, "Mr. Warnke, this is Lyndon Johnson, and Bob McNamara has been telling me of all the great things that you have been doing for your country, how much and how generously you have given of your time, and how helpful you have been, and I am calling to say thank you."

Warnecke, who had been doing a little work with McNamara on the Kennedy grave site, quickly answered that that was very kind of the President, but he had really done very little work.

"No, Mr. Warnke, this is not time to be modest. We know all about you. There is no man I hold in higher esteem than Bob McNamara and Bob is saying a lot of fine things, very fine things about you. Mr. Warnke, Bob McNamara is a great American and a great Secretary of Defense."

Warnecke acknowledged that he too admired Bob McNamara and considered him a great American.

"Mr. Warnke, it is refreshing to talk to someone like yourself, a man who could make a great deal of money in private life and yet is willing to give of himself to his country."

Warnecke answered quickly and truthfully that the sacrifice was very small.

"Mr. Warnke, I know better. *I know that you have truly done a fine job for your country* and we are not unaware of it—we know of your dedication, and, Mr. Warnke, Bob McNamara needs you and I need you, and I am calling you today because I am naming you as Assistant Secretary of Defense today and it will be in tomorrow's paper. We are proud of you."

At which point Warnecke understood and felt himself stumbling over the phone: Yes, a great honor, very touched by it, great regard for President Johnson, great regard for Bob McNamara, worked with him on grave sites, but perhaps a mistake had been made, he could not accept. He was an . . . architect, an architect could not run things at Defense. Paul Warnke, a lawyer . . . perhaps they wanted Paul Warnke . . .

He could hear a slight halt at the other end of the phone, and then Lyndon Johnson, as effusive as ever, saying, "Mr. Warnke, *you too have truly done a fine job for your country,* but it does appear that perhaps a mistake has been made." And so Jack Warnecke did not become an Assistant Secretary of Defense, and the next day when Paul Warnke received a call from the President naming him to the job, he was puzzled that the President was so brief, almost curt.

Stories like that, about his flattery and about his exaggeration had started out as something of a private joke among the reporters who covered him. It seemed amusing early in the game, when things were going well; they saw it as part of his attempt to control everything in his environment, to make things turn out the way he wanted, his desire to dominate everything, even the official record. At first it had been small things which amused them: his insistence that he drank bourbon, when in fact he drank Scotch; his stories about an uncle who had stood at the Alamo, when no such uncle had existed. His gradual expansion of his own rather thin war record (which brought him one of the least deserved but most often displayed Silver Stars in American military history) to the point where he could tell a somewhat surprised historian named Henry Graff, invited to the White House to report on Vietnam decision making, that he had earned the Silver Star for helping to shoot down twenty Zeros. Later it expanded to versions of whom he would appoint and whom he would not. In 1964 Dick Goodwin, a former Kennedy speech writer, came back to work for Johnson, and not being a blushing violet, immediately let Hugh Sidey of *Life* know he was back, and in fact showed him a draft of a speech. Sidey, looking for a subject for his weekly column, decided to write about the return of Goodwin as Johnson's principal speech writer, only to find that despite the fact that Johnson had been using Goodwin's drafts, the President insisted, in a face-to-face confrontation, that Goodwin had not written for him. Oh, perhaps a little research here and there, but no speeches. Wasn't that right, George? Reedy gurgled slightly, a sound of both yes and no. Finally Johnson took Sidey aside and drew a diagram of White House responsibilities. Nowhere did Goodwin appear. At the last moment Johnson wrote in a category, "Miscellaneous," and penciled in the name

"Goodman." At first these anecdotes enlivened the White House press corps and made for fine after-dinner stories; later, as the pressure of Vietnam mounted and the President's credibility problems centered on greater issues, they would not seem so amusing.

HE WAS NOT A MAN TO BE UNDERESTIMATED; HE SOUGHT POWER AND found it, and relished exercising it; he did not like being out alone on a position and he was brilliant at working others to a position which he intended to take so that they would stand together, there would be plenty of protective coloration. As a man of great force and intelligence, he had mastered a certain kind of power as no one had in Washington in years; he performed in the Senate with such subtlety and skill that there were newspapermen in Washington who would leave their offices to go down to the Hill to watch him when there was a particular scenario coming up, knowing that it would above all be a performance, orchestrated, skilled and almost joyful.

With all that ability, however, there were limits imposed by the regionalism. What he had exploited also held him back. Even at the 1960 convention, when he was chosen for the Vice-Presidency, it was not a recognition of the breakdown of the regional prejudice, but rather a confirmation of it; he could help bind a badly divided party, he could work with the South and try and hold it to what would be a traditionally liberal campaign in the North. It was not that inviting an office; it is a somewhat futile office under the best of conditions, but these were even worse conditions for a man as restless as Johnson, who had been a powerful figure as Majority Leader and who would serve a strong-willed President younger than he. It had more than the usual elements of being the end of the road, and only Sam Rayburn's deep animosity toward Richard Nixon, toward the Nixon who had called the Democratic party the party of treason, the attack upon the loyalty of an institution that Mr. Sam revered, made him advise Lyndon to take it. That he might help beat Richard Nixon.

Even then his old enemies rebelled and there was talk of a floor fight against him; the liberals and labor leaders from the great industrial states were less than grateful for his leadership in those congressional years. Yet Johnson had been a liberal, perhaps even, it was said, a Texas populist, who had been one of Franklin Roosevelt's most loyal New Dealers, a young man who had been anointed in Washington upon his arrival by none other than FDR himself. FDR, he liked to say, had been like a daddy to him. Was Johnson liberal, or was he conservative? His bitterest enemies were the committed Texas liberals, the Yarborough people, the Texas *Observer* people. They knew him back home. Who was he, anyway? Liberal, conservative, or just very ambitious? He was the kind of man who seemed to be at ease with the power structure of Texas, the richest and most conservative of the rich and conservative, and yet in the spring of 1960 he could tell friends and reporters flying back from a campaign meeting in Binghamton, New York, while complaining about the fat cats he had met that night, "No member of our generation who wasn't a Communist or a dropout in the thirties is worth a damn."

Johnson's first major job in the Depression had been as an assistant to Richard Kleberg, a conservative congressman and owner of the vast King Ranch. This job had brought no great ideological hardship; rather, Johnson seemed more irritated by Kleberg's laziness than his politics. He went back to Texas in 1935 to head the state's National Youth Administration. There, helping to find work for young people, he was also building a political base, and when there was a sudden vacancy in 1937 caused by the death of the incumbent congressman, Johnson immediately declared himself a candidate.

It was at the time of the first low point in Franklin Roosevelt's presidential history. Awed and intoxicated by his own 1936 landslide (46 out of 48 states), Roosevelt had moved to change the one institution in the nation which still blocked his program, by attempting to expand the Supreme Court. He immediately overstepped his popularity; the reaction was quick and intense. All sorts of opposition to Roosevelt which was then dormant suddenly surfaced, and this was particularly true of Texas: the President's enemies were clearly using the Court packing as a means of rallying support against him. (Almost twenty years later Johnson was still acutely aware of this, and after his own landslide victory against Goldwater he was ferocious in pushing legislation through as quickly as he could, always as though time were running out, saying that once the Congress feels it has given too much, it is bound to react and reassert its own independence.) Of the seven candidates running for the Texas seat in the special election, only Johnson wholly committed himself to the New Deal, so when he won, it was a symbol which Roosevelt grasped at.

The President interrupted a vacation to greet the new young congressman in Galveston the day after the election, and thus did Johnson start his career twice blessed. Sam Rayburn, his father's old friend from their days in the Texas Legislature, had just become House Majority Leader, a powerful ally for a freshman congressman; now the President himself was committed to him, telling the bright and powerful men of the New Deal to watch out for this young congressman from Texas, he was a hot one. And out of that first year came friendships specifically forged at Roosevelt's direction, which would last Johnson's entire career, ties to men like Abe Fortas, Ed Weisl, William O. Douglas. He was also given a seat on the Naval Appropriations Committee, a choice assignment on a committee which was the forerunner of the House Armed Services Committee. In those days he was Roosevelt's man, straight and simple; even in showdown conflicts with Rayburn he chose Roosevelt; it was the height of a new powerful Presidency, and the White House could do more for a young congressman than anyone else.

But Roosevelt's popularity would soon ebb in certain sectors of the country and Texas was one of the first to feel a new conservatism. A young ambitious politician in Texas would not want to look like a prisoner of the New Deal; in 1941 when Johnson made his first race for the Senate he found that Texas was changing, that the New Deal was less popular there and that he was beaten largely because he bore the onus of the New Deal. Too liberal, too much of a spender. He would not make that mistake again. Slowly he began to change his image, and he began to assert a certain independence from the Administration and to concentrate on armed preparedness as an issue, a decision which offended neither Roosevelt nor Texans. He stayed with the New Deal as long as he could, though he declared his independence from it soon after Roosevelt's death.

As the coloration of Texas politics changed, so did Johnson. The new oil money was beginning to dominate the old rural agricultural economy, and an ambitious young congressman who coveted a Senate seat had to come to terms with it. The oil money had gone after Sam Rayburn in 1944 and if it had not cost Rayburn his congressional seat, as the oil people intended, it forced him to stay home and campaign during the 1944 convention, thus depriving him of any chance to get on the ticket with Roosevelt. Lyndon Johnson, who did not intend to stay in the House and who planned a statewide race, had to come to terms with the new money in the mid-forties. He did it by developing close ties to George and Herman Brown, old contracting friends who had moved into oil by getting into natural-gas transmission, buying the Little Big Inch pipe line in 1947. The Browns buffered Johnson with the oil people and eased the transition for what Robert Novak and Rowland Evans in their excellent book on Johnson would call "a lateral movement into the center of the new oil power." He had paid his price. Thus he had become respectable; he had done it to survive, but it was typical of the price the Democratic party in general was paying to stay in power.

At the end of the war and in the immediate postwar years Johnson made himself even more respectable with the Texas business community by becoming an activist for defense spending. He could be vigilant on the subject of defense spending against the Communist expansion, and simultaneously forge growing links to a massive new industry beginning to flex its muscle in American society. He was typical in that era of many in the Democratic party who were more than glad to change the political subject in the postwar years from the domestic reform of the New Deal to defense and foreign policy. In the House and later in the Senate, Johnson became both an advocate of greater defense spending, and at the same time, with that special duality of his (the kind of duality which allowed him to turn the lights off at the White House while sending the Pentagon budget skyrocketing), became known as a tough critic of potential waste in military spending. He became an advocate of greater air power, breaking with the Truman Administration on this issue, accusing the Administration in effect of not making our air wing adequate (in the postwar years the poor Army could never match the Air Force for congressional support. There was always much more political and business interest in a contract for a multibillion-dollar airplane than there was for an Army contract for new webbing on boots).

His dissent with the Truman Administration never hurt his relationship with the President, who knew exactly the game Johnson was playing; he had played it himself. Yet Johnson's belief in military preparedness and defense spending was a very real part of his outlook, an extension of the way he had felt in 1941 when he helped Roosevelt prepare this country for a war which seemed so distant to many Americans. To be for defense spending in those days seemed to be against isolationism, so in those years he was identified as a great friend of the military. Technically, he was; he helped them get the money they needed, though actually he did not like them or admire many of them. Johnson, who was always so well prepared himself, always better informed than his subordinates, thought they were sloppy in their work, that they left too much to subordinates, and he was uneasy with their parochial view and prejudices, and with their definition of loyalty, which was too limited by his standards. It was to service, not necessarily even to country, and certainly not to Lyndon Johnson. They had to be watched; it was all right when they were temporarily on your side, but they could not really be counted on.

Added to his belief in defense spending and a need for preparedness came a very real belief in the Communist threat. (When he was President and as criticism on the war mounted, he convinced himself that there was a real Communist conspiracy at work in Washington; his feelings about it hardened and became stronger as sentiment against the war—and against him—also mounted during the sixties.) In Texas, as he made this transition, it allowed him to get along with the big boys and show them that that can-do ability didn't just work for the poor and the underprivileged. But this also meant that as a senator committed to greater defense spending, to larger defense contracts, he was not disposed to challenge the prevalent anti-Communism of the day, nor the theories which required such great defense spending. To challenge them, to study them too intensely, might have meant to find them wanting and thus necessitate a cutback in defense spending. So the instinct for force, for greater military might, had been nurtured in and by Johnson; it was at once both very real and very convenient, which was a powerful combination for any politician, and he was a symbolic part of a particular phenomenon of the fifties and sixties which found the military budget dominating American life and the great advocates for even greater spending, the Democrats, ostensible members of the party which was soft on Communism.

VERY SUBTLY, IN THE LATE FORTIES, HE HAD MADE THE TRANSITION from New Deal congressman to sound and respectable senator who did not frighten the big interests of Texas. A change of emphasis really. In the early fifties he made his way up the Senate ladder, not through connections to the national Administration, but rather through connections to Richard Russell and Senator Robert Kerr of Oklahoma, personification of the Southern big-interest wing, and in the late fifties he would undergo another transition. He had never been totally content to be just a senator. Now, as national ambitions stirred him, he became a man who spanned regions. He was not of the South but of the *West,* he could pilot civil rights legislation through the Congress, he could heal, he could understand the heartache of both sides, and also he had genuine ability. In discussing his own presidential race, Jack Kennedy had said that he had a right to run for it; no one else had more ability except Lyndon, and Lyndon could never make it because he was a Southerner. The prejudice against him never disappeared, and the sense of prejudice, the hurt always remained in Johnson, made him more interesting and, curiously, more sensitive. Even when he was placed on the ticket in 1960 he was put there to help Easterners, first Jack, who would hold office for eight years, and then perhaps Bobby. And he felt the pain of those three years of the Vice-Presidency; President Kennedy had been particularly aware of his sensibilities, but not everyone else was so sensitive (except for Rusk, who shared the same origins, humiliations and enemies). Johnson, who had always known about one thing, power, who held it and who did not, knew that as Vice-President he was a living lie, that his title was bigger than his role, that he did not have power, that younger, faster men with no titles held and exercised more power. And then suddenly, shockingly, he was President, the awkward easy-to-caricature Southerner replacing the beloved handsome slain Eastern President, shot down in Dallas, a hated city in Johnson's own Texas. That did not ease his own sense of the prejudice against him as he acceded.

So the perfectly prepared and trained and tuned parliamentary leader moved into the most public office in the world, an entirely different office for which all his previous training was in some ways meaningless, indeed the wrong training; he had learned many of the wrong things. The Presidency is a very different power center; it is not a particularly good place from which to perform private manipulation and to do good things for the folks in spite of themselves. It is at its best when a President identifies what he is and what he seeks as openly as possible, and then slowly bends public opinion toward it. If the President is found manipulating or pressuring a lower figure, putting too much pressure on a congressman, it can easily, and rather damagingly, backfire. Harry Truman was a success in the White House partly because he was openly, joyously and unabashedly Harry Truman; he was what he was, he gloried in attacks on his inadequacies, they being in general the inadequacies of most normal mortal men, and he made his limitations his assets; the American people had a sense of identification with him and what he was trying to do. Franklin Roosevelt was a fine back-room manipulator, but he always had a sense of the public part of his office, of it as a pulpit, and he used the rhythms of radio expertly in seeming to bring the public into his confidence. Lyndon Johnson never could. His office was above all public, but he could never communicate with the people, never be himself.

Journalist after journalist, politician after politician, businessman after businessman exposed to the private Johnson treatment, the full force of the man, the persuasiveness, the earthiness, the intelligence, came away impressed. Many of Washington's most sophisticated writers regarded Johnson as their favorite politician because of his earthiness, because he was so real that despite all his attempts to be clever and crafty and hide his style and his vanities and faults, he never could; and it was this earthiness, this particular quality to him, to his insecurities, which made him so interesting, so human. It was the lack of ability to control what he was and shield what he was which made him more likable than many politicians who were ideologically more sympathetic. But despite the great capacity to communicate from that office and despite his own enormous capacity to communicate, Johnson was curiously ineffective as a public communicator in the White House. He would not let the real Lyndon Johnson surface, the forceful, dynamic and very earthy one; not trusting himself, he did not trust the public. He did not feel he could be himself without hurting his Administration. The real Johnson was saved for the private rooms, and the public Johnson was a new Johnson, modest, pious, almost unctuous, and it did not come over very well. The public, which, despite the fact that it did not know Johnson and had never met him, knew instinctively that whatever else, this was not the real man.

This was part of it. The other part was related, the attempt to use the office, to manipulate, but to do so for the good of mankind, which is all right under ideal conditions (in that people do not particularly like being manipulated, even for their betterment, and if it doesn't work out, then they become particularly ungrateful about it, as the Senate did after the Tonkin Gulf Resolution. To a certain degree the Senate knew it was being manipulated, that the wording of the resolution was deliberately vague, that it was not a good idea to take your eyes off Lyndon Johnson; it knew it was not asking hard questions and playing the role it should have, but it was also willing at that point to acquiesce and be manipulated rather than ask the hard questions.

But if the war did not work out, and it did not, then there would be a sense of bitterness and even betrayal over the manipulation). Even when Lyndon Johnson passed vast amounts of legislation through the Congress in 1964, there was some uneasiness about him. He was, in the public mind, too much a "politician," he was a wheeler-dealer, you had to watch his hands. Even at his most successful moment there was not that much the public could identify with and say that it had participated in; it was his private act for them; nor could they identify with his personal qualities. So it was in no way inconsistent with his training that in 1964 the public Johnson seemed to campaign in one way while the private Johnson was being pulled in the direction of escalation. (In his memoirs he would clear up the discrepancy between his eventual acts and his campaign rhetoric against having American boys do what Asian boys should be doing. He had, he wrote, simply been implying that he did not intend to get into a ground war with *China*, which had nothing to do with Vietnam because we were already involved there.) If escalation finally was what the people needed and what was good for them, then Lyndon Johnson would make sure they would get it, but it would be better not to frighten them or confront them too openly with it. In 1964, as Lyndon Johnson learned to be President, and for a brief period enjoyed being President, the public man and the private man were doing very different things and going in very different directions.

HE MIGHT, THOUGHT HIS PRESS SECRETARY AND ADMIRER, GEORGE Reedy, have been a gigantic figure as prime minister, a man to stand along with Pitt and Disraeli and Churchill, if the parliamentary system had existed here. He was, thought Reedy, particularly well suited for its kind of leadership, a view strikingly similar to that of the man who had been for him in 1960 at Los Angeles and who in 1968 had helped drive him out of office, Eugene McCarthy. McCarthy, questioned in 1968 about his earlier support for Johnson, said he had been for him for prime minister, not for President, because given a particular course, he could get more out of it than almost any other man. But was he a man to chart a course himself? Under the British parliamentary system he would have faced the challenge of his peers, tough, sharp, examining, who feared neither him nor his office. But there was no comparable challenge at the White House, where no one really stands up to the President, where there is no equality, where no one tells the President he is wrong. For the Presidency is an awesome office, even with a mild inhabitant. It tends by its nature to inhibit dissent and opposition, and with a man like Johnson it was simply too much, too powerful an office occupied by too forceful a man (Johnson's own style in the Senate of trying to take the mark of another man from the start to break him quickly was a quality which had served him, if not the others, well. But it did not work so well in the White House. Other men were already too inhibited, they did not need the extra force of the incumbent to put more fear, respect and awe into them). Now he was too powerful a man with no one to slow him down. He was in an office isolated from reality, with concentric circles of advisers who often isolated rather than informed, who tended to soften bad judgments and harsh analyses, knowing that the President was already bearing too many burdens, that he could not accept more weight, that it would upset him, and also knowing that if they became too identified with negative views, ideas and information, they too would suffer, their own access would diminish (a classic example of the former of the two problems would be Bob McNamara telling Arthur Goldberg midway through the escalation, when Goldberg raised a negative point to him, that it was certainly a good point but would he please not raise it with the President, it would only upset him).

Now there was a giant of a man in the White House who made the imposing office even more imposing and who personalized the office. Doubts about a policy might seem like doubts about him: were you doubting him, were you disloyal? And Johnson, who in domestic matters reveled in his own expertise (calling in the staff working on a bill and questioning them, matching his own, often superior knowledge of it against theirs, ventilating the problems), was very different in foreign affairs. He was much more reserved in his participation and was prone to limit the discussion, as if somehow the discussion might show up his weaknesses. He had inherited the Kennedy people, who had always impressed him, but though they were the same men, they were used in a strikingly different way. Kennedy had been aware of the danger of isolation and the inhibitions the office placed on men, and he had deliberately confronted his senior people with young bright nonbureaucratic men from other parts of the bureaucracy, trying to challenge the existing assumptions; Kennedy did not view dissent as a personal challenge. Once Kennedy had played the diverse viewpoints against one another, once there had been an inner debate, he would use some of his own people to filter it down, to analyze it, and then finally make his decision. Even as a presidential candidate he had sat among his aides as they discussed issues, decisions, positions, all of them equals; as President they were no longer equals but he had encouraged the same diversity, realizing that it was healthy. As President he had been more of a judge than a participant, but he had held it together and set the tone. And it was Kennedy who knew the other players and their weaknesses, that McNamara was a man of great loyalty and force, and of a certain kind of intelligence, but of perhaps limited wisdom, brave in the bureaucratic sense, but that the imposing strength masked equally imposing weaknesses. He liked Bundy too. Bundy seemed so much like him, kept him out of trouble, sometimes he would know better what Kennedy wanted than Kennedy himself did. Only Rusk bothered him, with his reluctance to take strong and forceful positions. He respected Rusk's proficiency, his loyalty, his control, the subtlety of his political instincts and his performance on the Hill, but he was bothered by his overdependence on the system. He never felt at ease with Rusk, and in the last part of the Kennedy Administration both John and Robert Kennedy were talking with intimates about the possibility of a new Secretary of State.

The Johnson style was very different and it made different men of the chief presidential advisers. They would bear his stamp, and that made his Presidency different. From the start there was a different atmosphere, a more constrained one, less free, a little more fearful; whether this was deliberate or not, it was the result. (It showed in all sorts of ways, and made the isolated White House even more isolated. Kennedy, for instance, had liked newspapermen and had talked freely to them himself, so freely in fact that Richard Helms of the CIA once called *Newsweek* executives to suggest that perhaps Kennedy's relationship with Ben Bradlee, their Washington bureau chief, was constituting a major security leak. But if Kennedy liked newspapermen and the press, and kept up with what different reporters were writing, then his staff had to do the same, and this in many ways opened up the executive branch. Reporters as such were not necessarily enemies. But Johnson viewed the press, with its different definition of loyalty, darkly; it was in essence a hotbed of enemies. If Johnson did not like reporters and did not see them, then his aides did not either, and they could explain away any critical reporting by the fact that the reporter was personally unfriendly to the Johnson Administration.)

So there was a difference in the way the men were used. Johnson did not like the free flow, and did not reach down to younger men in the various offices. He believed that youth in itself was a sign of inexperience. (In 1968, during the great post-Tet events, the Wise Men had arrived to be briefed. What they heard jarred them, and it was reflected in their attitudes. Johnson wanted to know who had briefed them. He was given their names, young men in the various departments, and asked, Who the hell are they, who are these people? When he was told he said, How the hell can they know anything? They weren't even around during World War II.) So the lower-level men did not appear and did not ask the questions which Johnson himself was unable to ask. His was a far more structured government; decisions were made at the very top, in part because of his almost neurotic desire for secrecy. The more men who participate, the more gossip there is going to be, the more rumor that maybe Lyndon Johnson himself didn't make those decisions, that he needed people to make them for him, or worse, that there was disagreement at the top level of government, thus perhaps an inkling, an impression, that the decision was not perfect. So the way to control secrecy was to control the decision making, to keep it in as few hands as possible and make sure those hands were loyal, more committed to working with the President than to anything else. Besides, these were big men who had been given their jobs by Jack Kennedy.

Thus the decisions on Vietnam would be made by very few men, and the players would be different from those under Kennedy. To Johnson, McNamara was not just a forceful statistician and bureaucrat, his judgment and wisdom were invoked; Rusk, who had been something of a liaison man with the Hill before, became a genuine Secretary of State, a wise, thoughtful man, a man not too quick on his horse. So rather than the previous Administration's decision making, where a variety of opinions were sought and filtered down, this was a very structured one, a place where Rusk could feel much more at home, and headed by a man who liked to hold his decisions as close to him as possible and who had an obsession with consensus. That in itself was an illusion as far as foreign policy was concerned. Consensus was primarily the mark of the domestic politician and particularly of someone who was working in the Congress, trying to sign on as many people as possible to a policy (perhaps not the best policy, but a policy which the broadest range found acceptable and bearable; thus it could more readily be pushed through Congress, and more important men could not attack it later on if they had been part of it), but consensus in foreign affairs was likely to be different. Although such a consensus might make the various signatories feel safer and more comfortable, it would not necessarily make the policy any wiser. But to Johnson, a man of some timidity and considerable caution despite the bluster, a consensus was safer, the footprints were covered. He was not a man with a sense of history, a man who had a particular belief in the lone man dissenting, in the man going against the ostensible grain. He was trying to get everyone on board in an office where the best decisions are often the loneliest ones.

Chapter Twenty-one

EVEN AS THE BUREAUCRACY WAS GEARING UP ITS PLANS FOR bombing, the upper level of the bureaucracy and many of the principals were meeting in the Pentagon to program war games for Vietnam. It was an elaborate procedure, with the lower-ranking staff people spending two weeks before the arrival of their superiors in planning and setting up the games. The actual scenario reflected the real situation in Vietnam as accurately as possible. The situation in the South was bad, the play was now up to the United States, would it bomb, and if it did, what would be the North Vietnamese response? Though there was nothing unusual about the idea of having war games—they are constantly being programmed in the game room of the Pentagon—these games were different, and all the players knew it; it was as if this was a dry run for the real thing. The players were not the usual semi-anonymous figures from the lower floors of the government, but some of the great names of the government, men like Curtis LeMay, and General Earle Wheeler, and John McNaughton; and to let everyone know that it was not some light exercise, representing the President of the United States was none less than McGeorge Bundy, a sign somehow that although this was a war game, it was as close to reality as it could be.

The only problem with the war games was that they did not go well. The real question was to test out what would happen if we bombed the North. It quickly became apparent that very little would happen. The Red (or Hanoi) Team had some very good players, a smart general like Buzz Wheeler, and

Marshall Green of the State Department; the Blue Team had men like Bill Bundy, General LeMay and McNaughton. Hanoi had all the advantages; the bombing of the infiltration routes did not seem to bother it. The more the United States moved, the more men it could send down the trails. For every American move, there seemed to be a ready countermove for Hanoi; the blockade of Haiphong saw the North Vietnamese simply put more pressure on the U.S. military bases in the South and slip more men down the trail. We bombed and they nudged a few battalions into the South. We bombed some more of the greater military targets, and because we were bombing them we had brought in a surface-to-air (SAM) antiaircraft missile site to protect the South's cities against North Vietnamese or Chinese bombing. So they put the SAM site under siege, and in order to protect the site, which was staffed by Americans, we had to bring in Marines, at which point they nudged a few more men down the trail. The moment the Marines landed we had more difficult logistic problems, and the Vietcong simply applied more pressure to all supply routes, blowing up railroad tracks, ambushing convoys, making the small bases held by Americans increasingly isolated, dependent upon air supply (because there was little patrolling), and moving their machine guns in closer and closer to the bases, and beginning to shoot down the resupply planes. The enemy was turning out to be very savvy, very clever, and to have just as many options at his disposal as we did at ours. Maybe even more. What was particularly disturbing, the civilians on the Blue Team were discovering, was that he could meet the U.S. escalations at surprisingly little cost of his own.

North Vietnam had, noted a civilian player, always seemed like such a small country, until you got involved in a war game; then, programmed from their side, their army seemed very large, about 250,000 men, and it was so easy just to send a few divisions down the trails and those divisions somehow did not disturb the mass of troops left behind in the North. The bombing, they soon found out, seemed to have little effect on their military establishment; Hanoi could disassemble it, move it to rural areas, use camouflage, and run on very little logistic support in the American sense. Indeed, the more the Blue Team players pushed, the less vulnerable the North seemed to the kind of limited bombing envisioned (limited in the sense of using either the military system or the industrial system as bombing targets, and excluding cities and irrigation dikes). There was a growing sense of the elephant struggling with the gnat, and Marshall Green, who had the most experience in Asia, at one point noted that if his (the Red Team's) airfields were bombed, he would move all his women and children to the airport and make an announcement to the world that they were there, and then dare the Americans to keep bombing.

It was all very frustrating for the Blue Team and particularly for General LeMay, who was the classic Air Force man and who hated the restraints imposed by civilians. He sensed that a new kind of war was coming and that once again the military would be frustrated, that sanctuaries would be given, that air power would be misused. At one of the intermissions he began a running dialogue with Mac Bundy which reflected his own frustration and his belief (and later the military's belief) that bombing should be used all-out against the North, that if we bombed we should bomb to level them, and Bundy's view (the civilians' belief, which would surface in 1964 and again in 1967) that there was a limited amount that bombing could do. We were, LeMay said, swatting at the flies, when we should really be going after the source, the manure piles. Bundy deflected that one, and LeMay continued: they had targets, oil depots, ports, dikes, and if they existed and we were their enemy and we were enemy enough to fight them and to die, we should tear it all down. "We should bomb them into the Stone Age."

"Maybe," answered Bundy, "they're already there."

But LeMay was still not satisfied, and he seemed restless and irritated. "I don't understand it," he said. "Here we are at the height of our power. The most powerful nation in the world. And yet we're afraid to use that power, we lack the will. In the last thirty years we've lost Estonia. Latvia. Lithuania. Poland. Czechoslovakia. Hungary. Bulgaria. China . . ."

"Some people," said Bundy, "don't think we ever had them."

LeMay, with a wave of the cigar, a quick flick of the ash: "Some people think we did."

The second set of war games went a little better. General Wheeler had switched sides, and though there were certain continuing problems of Asian responses (a massive air attack cut all rail links between North Vietnam and China, but a Chinese general simply released 50,000 men to replace 50,000 North Vietnamese troops who would then move into the South), there was a subtle difference now. That was a greater U.S. willingness to commit more and more of its resources to the war, and corollary change among the North Vietnamese, a downplaying of their willingness to meet the larger American commitment. Despite the more favorable outcome of this game, however, few of those who played in both of them left sanguine; the real lesson of the games, and it was not a lesson they wanted to talk about, was not how vulnerable the North was to U.S. bombing, but rather how invulnerable it was, how much of an American input it would require to dent the North Vietnamese will, and how even that dent was not assured, and finally, for some of the more neutral observers, the fact that the basic strategy of limited bombing already split the civilians and much of the military.

THE COLLAPSE IN THE SOUTH, THE ONE FORCE WHICH THE AMERICAN leaders could not control, continued unabated. The Americans had always had the illusion that something might turn it around; a new leader in South Vietnam who would understand how to get with the program; a realization on the part of the South Vietnamese that their necks were on the line, that the feared enemy (the Americans' feared enemy, though perhaps not the feared enemy of the Vietnamese), the Communists, were about to walk into Saigon. Or magically, the right battalion commander would turn up to lead ARVN battalions into battle against the Vietcong, or the right program would emerge, blending arms and pig-fatteners together to make the peasants want to choose our side. But nothing changed, the other side continued to get stronger, the ARVN side weaker. One reason the principals were always surprised by this, and irritated by the failure of their programs, was that the truth of the war never entered the upper-level American calculations; that this was a revolutionary war, and that the other side held title to the revolution because of the colonial war which had just ended. This most simple fact, which was so important to the understanding of the political calculations (it explained why their soldiers would fight and die, and ours would not; why their leaders were skillful and brave, and ours were inept and corrupt), entered into the estimates of the American intelligence community and made them quite accurate. But it never entered into the calculations of the principals, for a variety of reasons; among other things to see the other side in terms of nationalism or as revolutionaries might mean a re-evaluation of whether the United States was even fighting on the right side. In contrast, the question of Communism and anti-Communism as opposed to revolution and antirevolution was far more convenient for American policy makers.

For members of the intelligence community, the war was directly linked to the recent past; they saw deep-rooted reasons for Vietcong successes and Saigon government failures. As far as the intelligence community was concerned, history was alive and gaining its revenge in Indochina; as far as the principals were concerned (and it was a very American attitude that Vietnamese events and history began only after the Americans arrived and took charge), nothing had existed before because it had not been done, tended to, examined by Americans. The Americans were tempting history by ignoring it; after all, in the past they had been able to dominate events by the sheer force of their industrial capacity, which had exempted them from much of the reality of the world. Nowhere was this so openly reflected as in a report by Maxwell Taylor which he brought back to the country at Thanksgiving time in 1964. He was recommending greater escalation, and he talked at great length about the political weakness of the South:

. . . there seems to be a national attribute which makes for factionalism and limits the development of a truly national spirit. Whether this tendency is innate or a development growing out of the conditions of political suppression under which successive generations have lived is hard to determine. But it is an inescapable fact that there is no national tendency toward team play or mutual loyalty to be found among many of the leaders and political groups within South Viet-Nam. Given time, many of these [words illegible] undoubtedly change for the better, but we are unfortunately pressed for time and unhappily perceive no short term solution for the establishment of stable and sound government.

Then, added Taylor, still perplexed about it all:

The ability of the Viet-Cong continuously to rebuild their units and to make good their losses is one of the mysteries of this guerrilla war. . . . Not only do Viet-Cong units have the recuperative powers of the phoenix, but they have an amazing ability to maintain morale. Only in rare cases have we found evidence of bad morale among Viet-Cong prisoners or recorded in captured Viet-Cong documents. . . .

Thus did the Americans ignore the most basic factor of the war, and when they did stumble across it, it continued to puzzle them. McNamara's statistics and calculations were of no value at all, because they never contained the fact that if the ratio was ten to one in favor of the government, it still meant nothing, because the one man was willing to fight and die and the ten were not.

So the Americans ignored the real key to Vietnam, only to have successive collapses of the South Vietnamese continue to confront, astound and disturb the American planners. The inability of the South Vietnamese to behave like Americans was particularly puzzling, and chief among those puzzled was the man who had become the U.S. ambassador to Vietnam in July 1964, Maxwell Taylor, a man who was supposed to be a soldier-intellectual and to understand both the war and the enemy, but who in fact understood neither.

In June, Henry Cabot Lodge had gone home, the call of the Eastern establishment too great upon his ears as Goldwater neared the Republican nomination, a challenge and affront far greater to Lodge than it was to Johnson; it was a challenge to the traditional Republican leadership. He had gone back ostensibly to help the belated campaign of William Scranton as the moderate Eastern challenger to Goldwater, but he was not above hoping that lightning might strike for himself, a hope that would turn a little bitter when he found out later in the year that his old friend Dwight Eisenhower had wanted *Lodge* to run when Lodge had interpreted it as simply the general wanting *someone* from the East to run against Goldwater.

When Lodge announced his decision to come back, there had been no dearth of candidates to take his place, including Robert Kennedy, who was still trying to find mission and duty and purpose in the postassassination days (Johnson wrote him a compassionate note saying he could not risk the dangers to Kennedy's life inherent in the Saigon job), and the Good Soldier Rusk, ready to resign and take the job of ambassador. When Taylor, who had been serving as Chairman of the Joint Chiefs for the past two years and had accomplished all that could be achieved in that career, also volunteered, willing to peel off his four stars, Johnson gladly chose him. It was a time when he wanted to move things in Vietnam without really touching them, affect events while doing nothing; thus one moves names, celebrities, and what better name than Max Taylor, citizen-soldier, a liberal, an intellectual, a quoter of Greek, a man who knew something about war and politics, and above all a friend of the Kennedys' (thus tying up Robert Kennedy even more; indeed some three years later, when Robert Kennedy began to dissent on the war, the Administration used Taylor to bring him back a step and a half). Better still, if one wanted to keep his options open, if there was going to be a decision to cut and run, then what better name under which to cloak it than Maxwell Taylor. A cool man in a cool era, Max Taylor.

Which was not the way he saw it. As far as American officials in Saigon were concerned, Taylor gave them their marching orders on July 9, almost immediately upon his arrival. He had summoned the mission council together, that group of a dozen Americans who ran the country, or tried to run it, and he briefed them on what he considered to be American objectives. There were, he said, four alternatives. The first was to throw in our hand and withdraw. The second was accommodation through negotiation, which he said was a sign of political weakness. The third was to take military action against the North, which could be done by the South Vietnamese air force, with or without U.S. participation, either in retaliation for specific acts of violence or as part of a general deterrent. These reprisals, he said, would threaten all that Ho Chi Minh had accomplished in his homeland in the last decade and could provide him with a strong incentive to change his mind. The fourth and final option was to improve and expand the in-country pacification program (i.e., within the South Vietnamese borders) with special emphasis on the so-called eight critical provinces. The U.S. government was, he said, following option four while preparing for alternative three. "No consideration is being given to alternatives one and two, because they are tantamount to accepting defeat," Taylor said. "Failure in Southeast Asia would destroy and severely damage our standing elsewhere in the world." With that he was finished; he had in effect told the men who would be running the operations in Saigon that we were not going to lose Vietnam, that negotiation was out of the question. We would stand. Among the men listening to him, there to get guidance, was his old protégé, the new commander of the U.S. military mission in Saigon. General William C. Westmoreland, a man who was neither brilliant nor, for that matter, presumptuous, would come away from the meeting with the belief that he had been told to hold Vietnam. Which in fact he had.

So for the third time Max Taylor would become a major player on Vietnam, which had begun in 1961 as a test case for the Administration's new strategies of war, and Taylor more than anyone else had been the author. He had, at the start, been looking more for a limited war than a guerrilla war, but you took what you could get, and he was never too sharp on the distinction and the political significance of the latter. It was his military recommendations which Kennedy had partially followed in authorizing the advisory and support mission. Taylor had hand-picked Harkins, so that he himself could control the reporting from Saigon, a reporting system which he had not only orchestrated, but what was worse and more dangerous, come to believe. Taylor had been coolly critical about the Bay of Pigs because it was the work of other men and other agencies with other beliefs, but he would not, in turn, be so detached about Vietnam, which was his work, and where his reputation rode. He was almost the last person in the government to accept the failure—there is no other word—of the Kennedy limited commitment because in large part it was his failure and because he stood for the middle way, the limited war. The entire experiment in Vietnam had been based on the idea that a great power could get by with a small war in Asia. It was deep in the public mind and the minds of his military contemporaries that Taylor was, like Ridgway, a member of the Never Again Club: U.S. Army officers who, embittered by the frustrations of Korea, vowed that never again would they fight a land war on the Asian mainland without nuclear weapons. Thus if a small war failed, the failure would be one of doctrine; more, it would play to the advantage of the more militant men in the Pentagon who believed you had to use greater quantities of force, total force if necessary.

Thus in 1964 his pessimism was not so great as might have been expected; if things were perhaps not going well, he did not see them as going that badly. In the first few months after his arrival in Vietnam he was not as pessimistic as Westmoreland, because he was tied to past optimism, which Westmoreland was not, and because he feared the consequences of the failure of the advisory and support mission, which Westmoreland, ready and just a little eager to be a commander, did not. Taylor did not in mid-1964 particularly believe in the bombing, thinking that it would lack military effectiveness—certainly in interdiction—nor was he particularly enthusiastic about the idea of combat troops. So even before he left for Saigon, Taylor wanted to maintain the kind of commitment which already existed. He talked openly with a handful of Pentagon reporters about the bombing, telling them he was against it (some of the other Chiefs were already pushing it). It was likely to be ineffective, and as far as interdiction went, it was more difficult to interdict than the Air Force thought, he said. He was more of an authority on that particular subject than he wanted to be, having served as an Army general in Korea and having been hit by Chinese divisions which the Air Force had failed to interdict. Though he would later become an advocate of the bombing, during much of 1964 he was a critic, particularly of its use in a *military* sense. He was uneasy about it politically, since it might involve us more deeply, and simultaneously take too much of the burden and psychological responsibility for the war from the South Vietnamese, a factor which always bothered him.

He changed his views on the bombing in the latter half of 1964, and after that to a limited degree on sending combat troops. It was a crucial change in the cast of characters. For as a member of the Never Again Club, the linear descendant of Matt Ridgway, whose proudest boast was that he had helped keep us out of the French Indochina war, Taylor was, when he became ambassador, the most prestigious American then in uniform. Max Taylor before a Senate committee would have been a powerful advocate for the decision not to escalate, but when he turned, the President lost a compelling reason for staying out. At the very end, in the final rounds of decision making, Taylor voiced doubts about the use of combat troops, but by then it would all be beyond him. He would be replaced by other, more powerful players, and at the moment when his word carried weight, he had approved the escalation. His role was vital: Washington is a gossipy town both in and outside the government, and the coming of the Xerox machine has made it more so; so when Taylor's cables came in during the last part of 1964 calling for bombing, they had a profound effect upon the bureaucracy.

The reasons why he changed were varied; an awareness of the failure in the South, an irresistible pressure to justify what you are doing, to compensate for the latest miscalculation, which carries you on further and further past cutoff points without knowing they have been passed. Too much had already been committed, too many men, too much honor, too much prestige, too many white crosses to turn back. And he changed, too, because he had changed constituencies. He had gone from Washington and become a spokesman for the American community in Saigon, living in that intense, almost irrational atmosphere of men who talked only to themselves and others like them, and who came to believe that whatever else, Vietnam should not be lost, and for whom the domestic problems of the United States were quite secondary. From Saigon the United States seemed distant and small, Vietnam was the important thing, the center of the universe; the careers and the decisions centered there. In Washington, if the particular men making the decisions did not have many ties to the poor and there were few representatives of the underclass at the meetings, there was at least a broader view of the United States and its needs, a certain sanity. Later, however, as the war progressed, the particularly hothouse, isolated quality of the Saigon military headquarters in Saigon and the American embassy would begin to find its counterpart in the White House and other centers of power in Washington (as the President rose and fell with events in Vietnam). So in the last months of 1964 Max Taylor changed; he had not intended to go this far but there was nowhere else to go, no more forks in the road, even for a supremely detached man like Maxwell Taylor.

MAXWELL DAVENPORT TAYLOR, THE KENNEDY GENERAL, IMPRESSIVE even in civilian clothes. The words to describe Max Taylor came easily to all journalists: Distinguished career. Soldier-statesman-intellectual. The *New York Times*'s "Man in the News" profile of Taylor when he went before the Fulbright committee, a profile so flattering that it was used in his lecture brochure, was titled "Soldier and Statesman," and naturally, under the photograph, there was, God save the mark, this caption: "Somewhere between Virgil and Clausewitz." It began, not untypically for him:

It was characteristic of General Maxwell Davenport Taylor, star witness today at the Fulbright committee that he quoted Polybius, a Greek historian of the pre-Christian era. "It is not the purpose of war to annihilate those who provoke it, but to cause them to mend their ways," General Taylor quoted. . . . General Taylor's reference was characteristic because he has long been known as a soldier-scholar, equally familiar with Polybius and Virgil as with Caesar and Clausewitz. When he was superintendent at West Point in the late 1940s he advised cadets to study the dissenting opinions of Supreme Court Justice Oliver Wendell Holmes . . .

A striking-looking man. Always in fine shape, tennis racket in hand, always ready to play tennis, to stay lean and trim. Very good at getting junior officers to play tennis with him. Very correct, almost curt. "Major, tennis tomorrow at three?" "Yes, sir." And then tennis for an hour, the major exercising Taylor, just like a masseur giving a work-out. The hour over, still very correct and curt. No friendship. "Thank you, Major. Tomorrow at three?"

Not a favorite of other generals, who thought him aloof and self-centered and did not entirely like him, never one of the boys; the other generals uneasy during the Kennedy years about whether Taylor represented Kennedy or them, whether their views were getting through. Not a man to relax, not even in those moments when there might have been time, flying across the ocean in old propeller airplanes. While the other officers would gossip and talk shop, who had which command, who was on the way up, there Max Taylor would be, reading a German magazine. Even when he finished reading, would he come over and talk, be with the boys? No sir, he would sit back and take out a pack of small cards, look at a card, and look out the window, and then look back at the card again. Max was memorizing Japanese. Will power. Discipline, always discipline. Different from the other generals. The others were not surprised. They had gone to school with him at the Point and even then, as a young boy from Keytesville, Missouri, he was different. All business, all ambition, cold as ice, determined; he was going to be someone.

He had had a flawless career. He was fourth in his graduating class at West Point, and was voted "most learned" in his senior year. But he was not just one of those bright boys who are at the top of their class but who fade as they get into the other, more demanding world of military command; rather, this was a fine mind in an officer who had the capacity to command and to lead, a man who would come on quickly in the middle stages of his career, taking off when he became a colonel. Taylor graduated in 1922, shortly after one war and nineteen years before the next one. It was a time when George Marshall had changed the Army and was determined to open the doors of learning to his officer corps, doors which might ordinarily have been closed. Marshall, who was dissatisfied with the leadership of World War I, believed in expanding the mind and the man in preparation for command in an ever more complicated modern world and army.

Taylor's mind was first-rate; not, in the view of some of his contemporaries, a particularly restless or doubting one, or one tuned to the disorder of the world, wondering why that disorder existed, but rather one tuned to the order, to control the disorder, a mind to master facts rather than challenge them, an attitude which was entirely within the traditions of his service. It was as if it were all a matter of will power, learning a remote language and learning it quickly, but perhaps little knowledge or curiosity about the mores of the people who spoke the language, what moved them and why. The result was that despite his travels he was a surprisingly unchanged and rigid man, and when he came to Vietnam in 1961 he saw it more in terms of his World War II and Korean experiences than in terms of the French experience. His recommendations were based largely on how to exploit the new technology, how to make the Vietnamese army more mobile. He was a man without much sense of feel or nuance, but that was not readily apparent; instead, he seemed by comparison with other generals to be a vastly superior man. He was very good at languages, it added enormously to the legend that Max Taylor was an intellectual and a linguist, fluent in several languages, French, Chinese, Japanese, Spanish, German and Italian. He had linguistic control without any feeling for the people: people were to be molded.

He had a fine peacetime record between the wars, this serious, disciplined young man, who seemed apart from much of the peacetime Army, and the slots were good and the superiors impressed. When the Japanese invaded China, and Colonel Joseph Stilwell needed a Japanese-speaking aide, Captain Maxwell Taylor was sent out in 1937. They got along well. Taylor found himself, besides other responsibilities, charged with being something of a diplomatic buffer between the irascible Stilwell and the turbulent world around him. Taylor handled the Stilwell assignment well; clearly he was an unusual man of unusual abilities. George Marshall, who was then keeping a little black book where he entered the names of particularly able young officers whom he planned to push ahead to command if war came (so that many of the best of the World War II generals were catapulted to command ahead of nominally more senior men), made a note about Taylor. When World War II came, Taylor was ready, an airborne commander, the best of the best, part of that elite group which would dominate the Army command during the postwar years (Ridgway, Gavin, Taylor, Westmoreland). At the time of the Italian campaign, when an airdrop of the 82nd Airborne into Rome was a possibility, Eisenhower chose Major General Taylor for a special mission behind the German lines because he spoke the language and was a cool officer who would not lose his head. Taylor performed the mission, moved past German positions by PT boat, slipped into Rome, and returned back to Eisenhower's headquarters, having recommended against the drop. It was a mission which caught the particular fancy of Robert Kennedy many years later. Taylor was later given command of the elite 101st Airborne (Westmoreland would later command it), while Gavin, his chief rival in ability and dash, had the 82nd, both of them dropping in Normandy on D-Day. (Years later, when Taylor was at the White House, the question arose of whether to keep the Davy Crockett—a two-man nuclear weapon, a nuclear bazooka really—in the military inventory. The White House staff, led by Carl Kaysen, wanted to get rid of the Crockett, and Taylor wanted to know why Kaysen was unhappy. "Because it makes a very big bang for such a small outfit," Kaysen said. "What do you mean?" Taylor asked. "Well, suppose a corporal and a sergeant get cut off from their regular unit and become surrounded—do we really know enough about them, about what's going on in their heads, to give them a nuclear weapon?" Taylor answered, "I've been a troop commander and I've never been out of touch with any unit in my command," which left Kaysen amazed, wondering about all those little units scattered across the French farmland on D-Day. But Taylor was, Kaysen noted, different from other generals even on this; he had asked, Who doesn't like it and why? not What do *you* know about it?)

Taylor had been at home when the 101st was cut off during the Battle of the Bulge and was rushed back just as the division was rejoined. He came out of the war with his career on the way up (at the end of the war he had moved to deactivate the 82nd and have the 101st make the victory parade through New York, but Gavin had managed to switch those roles, so it was the 82nd, not the 101st, which marched before cheering millions). Ahead of him were the choice assignments which go only to an up-and-coming officer. Superintendent of West Point, a post which only the truly anointed get, then first U.S. commander in Berlin, another plum assignment, and a highly political one (where he became a close friend of William Draper's, a former Assistant Secretary of War, who was working with General Clay and who was extremely influential in the redevelopment of Europe. Draper took a special interest in Taylor's career, helping him to get a job at Mexican Power and Light Company in 1959, and then eventually the job at Lincoln Center, which was in part designed to bring him into the New York area and to meet influential people). During the Korean War he was given command of the Eighth Army at the time hostilities were drawing to a close. He sensed accurately the political balance of the war, took his troops to the 38th parallel and a little beyond, and then waited for the political disposition of the war. He went on from there to Tokyo to command all ground forces in Japan, Korea and Okinawa, and finally, in 1955, with Ridgway in open conflict with the other Chiefs and the Eisenhower Administration, Taylor was brought home to become Chief of Staff of the Army, the most coveted position within his profession.

TAYLOR IS DIFFERENT FROM MOST GENERALS. A LONER. A MAN WITH A broader view of the military role, with a sense of the balance between the military and civilian, and the subordination of the military to American politics; a belief that the military must adjust to the civilian side and must not try and fight the greater organism (though the war which he helped to plan would in many of its ironies do more to isolate the military from the larger organism and make it a separate entity with separate values and requirements than anything in recent history; it would almost single-handedly undo much of the work that men like Marshall and Taylor himself had done in trying to liberalize and broaden the Army as an institution, and encourage a broader range of officers). If he was not particularly well liked by some of his contemporaries, there was nonetheless an almost universal respect for him; more important, he was liked and respected by high-level civilians. He was in fact, and this was one of the keys to his success, a general that civilians liked and felt at ease with, and trusted; he was thus a political general in the classic sense, the way Marshall and Dwight Eisenhower were, able to go to the limits of one constituency and work as a bridge to another, to understand the needs, limits and tastes of civilians and give them what they need. MacArthur had tried to be a political general too, but it had never worked. He had been too brazen; he had believed his own speeches. He had tried to adapt the greater organism to the values, styles and beliefs of the smaller one, believing that this was possible, that the harder, more rigid, more openly patriotic mores of the military would triumph in civilian life, that the civilians were ready and waiting for this kind of leadership and would rally to it given a chance. MacArthur had terrified vast numbers of people; and was a complete political failure. It was never possible to think of MacArthur without his uniform, whereas it was always possible to think of Marshall and Eisenhower and Taylor in civies. A high-level civilian dealing with MacArthur would always know that there was no give, that any accommodation would have to come from the civilian, whereas with men like Taylor there would be accommodation, flexibility. Some of these men had, after all, had plenty of chances to work in Washington as young officers, to study in the politically charged atmosphere there, lobbying, writing speeches, meeting congressmen and senators. Ike, for instance, friendly, easy grin, good mind, good writer, had been a fine lobbyist and a very good speech writer ("Remember those great speeches MacArthur made from the Philippines?" he once told a friend, a rare moment when the greater inner ego flashed outside. "I wrote all those").

Marshall had dominated one era, and now Taylor seemed on paper to be part of that tradition. Since he was too proud to wear a hearing aid, he was denied a political career of his own. Besides, he had never returned from a triumphal war like Eisenhower; the wars where he played a major role, Korea and Vietnam, were reflections of a modern age, frustrating, messy, unsatisfactory, unheroic except to the men who had fought there. Yet he had managed to reach the summit of a career, to be the leading military officer of an era. Eisenhower made him Chief of Staff of the Army, Kennedy brought him back to Washington and then made him Chairman of the JCS, Johnson sent him to Saigon as ambassador. And in 1968, after that war cost Johnson his Presidency and Richard Nixon had been elected, there he was in Washington, with his own office in the Executive Office Building (his title was Chairman of the President's Foreign Intelligence Advisory Board), advising Nixon on Vietnam. Pictured going in and out of National Security Council meetings. A great survivor.

He was always a great survivor; he had a capacity to meet a crisis head-on and survive. Nothing had shown this better than the major power struggle within the military which took place in the fifties; it was an unusual test of him and his beliefs. At the time, Eisenhower had been President for more than two years, and despite the fact that a West Point graduate was in the White House, the morale of the Army was very low. It was the golden age of the Air Force; Ike was cutting the budget, promising a bigger bang for a buck, and there was an emphasis on massive retaliation. The military seemed prepared to fight the biggest war of all, either that or no war, a political policy made somewhat simpler by the fact that the Republicans under Eisenhower could foster a policy like this and not be charged with being soft, for spending inadequately on the nation's defenses. The Republicans were never on the defensive on the issue of patriotism. The coming of the military-industrial complex, the big new contracts awarded the Air Force, had given it far more muscle on the Hill than the other branches of the service, and the Army's roles and budget were being sharply reduced. There was a feeling among many of the Army's top officers that it was now dangerously close to not being able to fulfill its functions, that it could not fight intermediate, brush-fire wars. This had caused much unhappiness in Chief of Staff Matthew Ridgway, who retired in 1955 after one frustrating tour; his farewell statement, a harsh critique of the inflexibility of the Eisenhower policies, was held back by Secretary of Defense Charles E. Wilson, who made it a classified document, but a young officer smuggled it out to the press. It was a tense time.

With Ridgway retiring in June, Taylor was called back from Tokyo by Wilson for a long talk, which reflected how well Wilson understood the coming political problems for an Army Chief of Staff. ("He then began to cross-examine me on my readiness to carry out civilian orders even when contrary to my own views. After thirty-seven years of service without evidence of insubordination I had no difficulty of conscience in reassuring him, but I must say I was surprised to be put through such a loyalty test," Taylor would later write in *The Uncertain Trumpet*.) Shortly thereafter he was made Chief of Staff.

Taylor's moves were going to be watched by the Army command, but by now none more closely than a group of talented young colonels which had been assembled by the Army as a special secretariat for the Chief of Staff, as if to be his political-intellectual planning staff, to decide what the Army's needs were, what its budget should be, and to evaluate the proposals of the Air Force and the Navy. This was known as the Coordinating group, a new office prompted by the fact that the military world had become infinitely more complicated, the range and sophistication of missions and problems had gone beyond the range of a few overworked generals; it was in effect the coming of new managerial planning techniques to the once happenstance and more leisurely planning of the U.S. Army.

The young officers, all colonels on the way up, had been carefully selected for this secretariat; they were the pick of the Army, all of them certain to make general; all but one were West Pointers, all in the top 10 percent of their promotion class, with good combat records and staff service, and intellectual capacity. Many were working on their master's degrees. They saw the Army withering away beneath them; they believed, as Taylor did, that massive retaliation did not fit a complex world, that the world would be unstable and that the future for the Army was its capacity to fight brush-fire wars in places like Algeria and Indochina. The sense of rebellion against the drift of the Army had started informally with two or three of them discussing it, and finding their own doubts and concerns shared by others. They were not prompted by any parochial conviction, by Army chauvinism or search for career advancement; indeed it might and finally did end some promising careers. They were concerned about what they felt was the most serious question an officer could face: whether or not the Army was able to perform its mission.

After a while the colonels began to meet more regularly and more formally, keeping notes, and by the summer of 1955 they were putting together papers on the Army's problems; they discovered that they had a consensus not only among themselves but among their contemporaries throughout the Army. They found little response among most of the senior officers. Yes, agreement that things didn't look good at all, but a warning that they were treading on dangerous ground by challenging the policies of the Administration. The generals, the colonels decided, had their stars and wanted more, and were no longer sufficiently restless. Only one general gave them encouragement, James Gavin, then Deputy Chief of Staff for Plans, a man who believed above all in mobility and who was bothered by the same frustrations as the colonels. He listened to them, encouraged them, and served in an unofficial way as their adviser, using them as his own sounding board.

It was at this point that Taylor came home; the colonels were curious as to what this would mean. The Army grapevine word was that Taylor was good, and might, being an old airborne man, be extremely sympathetic. So when Taylor returned in the summer and brought with him the draft of a paper called "A National Military Policy," the colonels became excited: here was the man they had been looking for; here was a new Chief of Staff saying exactly what they had been saying, bothered by the same things, coming up with the same answers. And here was a man who would fight for his beliefs; he would not be doing all this unless he intended to fight (the program as outlined in his paper was in essence what he would call for in *The Uncertain Trumpet*). What impressed the colonels the most was that this was not staff work, a vague paper whipped up by an ambitious staff for an indifferent or reluctant general officer; this was by the man himself. They knew this because the paper was so poorly typed that they had asked a staff officer if he knew who was responsible for all the typos, and he told them that Taylor had written and typed it himself on the way back from Japan.

Taylor had turned his paper over to the colonels for critique. They tore it apart, added, cut, sharpened it, and wondered whether it was too anti–Air Force in tone. When they finally finished working on it and handed it back to Taylor, they asked him what he planned to do with it. He said he thought he could issue it to the Army for consideration. The colonels dissented sharply (in retrospect, said one of them years later, "I shudder to think how outspoken we were, a bunch of colonels standing up to the Chief of Staff, telling him what he had to do. But it was a reflection of how serious we thought the matter was"); they told him it was not enough, that Taylor was in this too deeply, that the Army wanted and needed more than a paper stating what it already knew. They suggested that he turn the paper over to the other Chiefs for comment. Taylor agreed, and in early 1956 this was done. They, not surprisingly, did not respond at all. "Noted," they would scribble on it upon receipt, which disappointed Taylor, who felt he had been fair and objective.

For a time the issue seemed to stall, and then the most intense and driven of the colonels, a young officer named Donovan Yeuell who had just come back from four years in Germany and picked up a master's degree at Georgetown, started to push the problem again. Yeuell watched for a chance to be alone with Taylor, and found out that the Chief was going to the New Orleans area for three days to be with the Corps of Engineers; Yeuell and another colonel got themselves assigned to the trip. They bided their time, and then one day, which Taylor spent sightseeing on an old paddle wheeler, they cornered him. He was alone and there was no place to hide. They asked him if he believed enough in the paper, which he had written and they had refined, to fight for it. He said he did. At this point they told him they needed a controlled and deliberate campaign to inform the press and the public. It would not have to be traced to Taylor, they claimed. They had outlined about twenty steps of the campaign, including congressional and journalistic connections. The Army, they said, had more friends on the Hill than it realized; people like Senator Henry Jackson were sympathetic and wanted to help, but they needed some help from the Army, two- and three-star generals, and these generals would have to come into the public eye. They told Taylor there would be some heat, that he could not go up against Eisenhower, Radford, Twining and Charlie Wilson without taking heat, but the case to be made was very strong. Though Taylor was noncommittal, they found him very sympathetic during the three-hour session, helping to construct the scenario, saying he knew this particular senator or that columnist, vetoing their idea of ghost-written anti–Air Force articles ("How the Air Force Failed in Interdiction in Korea") as too risky.

At the end of the paddle-boat tour, Taylor looked at them and said, "Okay, I understand what you've said. Now put it in a memo." Yeuell did, and shortly afterward there was a paper on the new military program, and on the public campaign for it. After Taylor signed it, he called in Yeuell and said, "Yeuell, you're really asking me to stick my neck out." Yeuell answered that if he fought for the program he would have an Army, otherwise he could spend his years simply sitting in the office ("I was a real believer, full of myself and my beliefs—willing to put my career and my life on the line for them," he would recall fifteen years later). Taylor read the memo, agreed that it was an accurate account of what he had committed himself to do and signed a paper to that effect, thus committing himself to a program of exposure for the Army viewpoint.

Meanwhile the colonels were getting set up to go ahead with their program. The head of the secretariat was a brigadier named Lyal Metheny who worked regularly with the Secretary of the General Staff, another brigadier named William C. Westmoreland (Westy was in effect Taylor's secretary, determining who did and who did not see the Chief). The colonels themselves were now full of enthusiasm; they were all aboard with the exception of one young officer named William Depuy who was uneasy about the whole thing and who felt that his contemporaries were pushing too hard and were going to get their superiors in hot water (Depuy would go on to a particularly noteworthy career, serving as Westmoreland's chief of operations in Vietnam, and being in effect Westmoreland's egghead, helping to design the search-and-destroy strategy).

The colonels began to collect papers backing up their points, and began to write articles hinting at the new strategy and outlining the Army's role. Similarly, Taylor had begun to send them around the country in groups of two to tell other officers at the posts, and particularly the service schools—which are vital to the Army's intellectual life, the centers of thought, where the hand-picked meet with the hand-picked—what was happening. There they explained the new military program, and more important, that they were going to fight for it. The question everywhere was a simple one: Is *he* going to fight? Is the Chief with us? They assured everyone that he was. The question then became how best to go about the public campaign. Since 1956 was an election year, they wanted it to be a campaign issue and decided to gear up as quickly as possible for a national campaign. Yeuell started talking to his brother-in-law Wallace Carroll, then news editor of the *New York Times* Washington bureau. Carroll said that the *Times* would not move unless the Army high command was behind it; the *Times* would not report just for restless colonels. Slowly, the *Times* people were introduced to the generals, assuring the *Times* that the Army was behind the program. When the *Times* was finally confident of the depth of the commitment, Carroll asked for some of the staff papers, which the colonels turned over and which became the basis for articles by Anthony Leviero in May 1956 ("Inter-Service Rivalry Flashed").

The story hit the Pentagon like an explosion. Wilson was in a rage, and the Army brass quickly folded. The Coordinating group was immediately broken up. The colonels were ordered not to come to their offices. Yeuell's files were cleaned out and burned. Wilson told reporters, "There's a bunch of eager beavers down in the Army staff, and if they stick their heads out again I'll chop them off." Within the Army command the colonels were told that Westmoreland, who was halfway in and halfway out of the cabal, had assured Taylor that he would take care of the colonels for him and clean it all out. Yeuell, who was investigated three times in one year, went to the War College a year ahead of schedule, but eventually lost faith in the Army and drifted out of it. Metheny, one of the other leaders, was immediately transferred to a meaningless post in Florida; the others were quickly and quietly switched in their assignments.

Later that week in May, Wilson called a press conference and assembled the Chiefs to prove that they were all on the team; Taylor, asked if there had been a revolt, answered that there was none (which was technically true, since it had been an authorized rebellion) and also quite carefully failed to repudiate the colonels; he walked a very tight rope indeed. But he did not fight for the colonels, and the campaign was dropped then and there. Later that year Taylor went to see Eisenhower to ask him to reappraise their defense policies, with Ike reportedly asking what was wrong with them. But Taylor stayed on, served two consecutive two-year tours as Chief of Staff, and then in 1959, after he had left, wrote *The Uncertain Trumpet,* thus strengthening his reputation. To many younger officers, however, he had turned out a major disappointment, a man who was the ablest person to sit in that office for many years but who had not fought for what he believed and who finally played the game, which he did rather skillfully, becoming closer and closer to the Democrats as Eisenhower's second term wore on, and as the Democrats picked up the issue of preparedness. This helped link him with the Kennedys, and it would become an article of faith among the Kennedy people (for instance, in the Schlesinger book) that Taylor had resigned when he had in fact *retired.*

But there was less feeling for him in the Army and even among some of the other Kennedy-style generals, especially Jim Gavin, who had also been a critic of the defense policies in the 1950s. In fact, Gavin testified before the Johnson Senate Preparedness Subcommittee hearings; when Senator James Duff of Pennsylvania asked him about casualties in a nuclear war, Gavin answered that there would be 425 million casualties. The hearings were supposed to be private and censored, but someone had conspired to make the Gavin testimony public, and the Japanese were horrified because of all the fall-out which would blow across their land. When the testimony surfaced, Gavin became the scapegoat for the Army's position and was in effect forced to leave the Army. He did so with a certain bitterness, feeling that Taylor had sacrificed him (and there was a feeling among some other general officers that Westmoreland, who was half a Taylor protégé and half a Gavin protégé, had rushed the resignation through a little precipitously). The result was a certain division within the airborne clique in the Army, and a lingering distaste in Gavin for Taylor.

TAYLOR HAD BEEN VERY HELPFUL TO PRESIDENT KENNEDY IN THE early days, Robert Kennedy would say in 1968 (when he was running against the war and reporters haunted him with questions about Taylor and the origins of the war). Which he had. He had come in as military adviser to the President, a filter to the Joint Chiefs, but he had not remained there long. After the Bay of Pigs, Kennedy had relied on him as his chief investigating officer; Taylor had been very thorough in analyzing the failure of the breakdown in planning, though in retrospect his report seemed to deal too little with the political realities of such a venture, instead being concentrated on the technical failings (not enough ammunition; the fact that like most green troops the brigade had fired too quickly and used up too much ammunition).

But he had been of value to the Kennedys and McNamara in trying to reshape the grand design of strategy, away from nuclear dependence, and he had given the change in policies a certain respectability; he was an imposing figure to have on your side. In trying to gain some kind of control over the military, Taylor had been a considerable help, and part of the counterinsurgency fad, which Bobby Kennedy promoted in 1961, was an attempt to work outside the existing bureaucracy to Kennedyize the military programs, as if to take some of the planning and decision making away from the Chiefs, who were not Kennedy people.

It quickly became clear to Kennedy that this was not adequate and that he needed more control of the military. Since Taylor as a civilian assistant lacked real leverage, he soon returned to uniform as Chairman of the Joint Chiefs. His was not an easy role, caught as he was between the conflicting pressures of two very different constituencies: the Chiefs with their totality of commitment to the early lessons of the Cold War, the Communists were enemies, the only thing that mattered was force, and maximum application of it, and the Kennedy Administration, nervously and gingerly and slowly beginning to move away from some of the rules of the Cold War. Taylor was particularly valuable to the Administration on nuclear control, and among the White House confidants of the President there was a feeling that if Taylor was not exactly the intellectual he was supposed to be ("He is a very handsome man, and a very impressive one," said Averell Harriman in 1967, "and he is always wrong"), there was genuine warmth toward him based more than anything on the test-ban treaty. He had been very helpful then, and in June 1963, when Kennedy decided to give the American University speech in which he would announce that the United States would not be the first to test in the atmosphere, a White House staff member had the job of clearing it with McNamara, Gilpatric and Taylor. He called the general and explained what they were planning to say and what they were doing and suggested that Taylor might want to check with the Chiefs; Taylor answered no, he did not think he needed to check with them, since it was basically a political matter for the President to decide, not a military issue. It was a very special act, a mark of his deference to the President on something the President cared deeply about; Taylor knew that if he asked the Chiefs they would object strenuously, so he decided not to ask them at all. As far as the White House was concerned it was Taylor at his best, and there was a mutuality of gratitude.

This had been a happy time for him, back in uniform, working with a President he liked, on particularly good terms with the President and even better ones with the Attorney General (Jack Kennedy had once said that he would stick with his old friends once in the White House, that the White House, the center of everyone's desire for influence, was not a good place to develop new friends, but McNamara and Taylor were the prime exceptions to that. They were the professional associates who had bridged the gap, a gap which held a certain element of good old-fashioned snobbery to it, and became personal friends. In Robert Kennedy's case his friendship with Taylor was even more remarkable, since Taylor was not known for having close friendships of any kind, particularly not with men more than twenty years his junior. Friendship with younger men was not normally something he encouraged, but then, there are exceptions to every rule). After the assassination, Taylor and McNamara would visit Jackie regularly, working very hard to keep her spirits up, visits that she particularly prized. And later, when Taylor became ambassador to Vietnam, the friendship with Bob Kennedy continued, and a friend of Taylor's would remember one moment with the general that was in stark contrast to the everyday Taylor, usually so aloof: the scene was the airport when Taylor was returning to Saigon after a visit to Washington. Bobby and Ethel and innumerable children were there to see him off, arriving a few minutes before Taylor, rushing aboard the plane and leaving notes for him pinned everywhere, hidden here, folded under this seat, and on the ceiling, notes of fondness and trivial jokes. When Taylor, normally so cold and distant, found them, he was absolutely transformed, laughing and affectionate. If there were holes in his discipline, it should not be for anyone below the rank of Attorney General.

But it was no wonder that Robert Kennedy liked him, that Jack and Jackie had liked him; that Lyndon Johnson felt comfortable with him, that he was one more reassuring figure in that era. He was so reasonable and so professional. The very best of the breed. The right officer for the American century. He seemed to embody the American officer of the era; he gave off vibrations of control and excellence and competence, and indeed he seemed to represent something that went even beyond him, the belief of the United States military that they were the best in the business. Wars on the plains of Europe and the jungles of the South Pacific were behind them, the struggles against the Chinese hordes in Korea loomed, in retrospect, increasingly as a victory. Now we were at the apex, the new technology added to the old valor, the average officer now the graduate of an endless series of service schools, bearing graduate degrees from America's great universities. So Taylor had seemed to be speaking almost for the American era in June 1963 when he gave the commencement address at West Point; he had chosen as his topic "The American Soldier," as Ralph Waldo Emerson in 1837 had spoken on "The American Scholar." As Emerson had declared American scholarship free from dependence upon Europe, so now Taylor said he was doing the same for the American soldier:

I have often felt that a West Point graduation should sometime have been the occasion for a similar address dedicated to the American Soldier—and I use that term broadly this morning to mean the American man-at-arms be he soldier, sailor, airman or marine. Like other forms of American scholarship, American military thought was also once in European bondage, but likewise has become emancipated. Our Civil War marked the turning point in this trend. Drawing confidence from the experience acquired in that war, American military leadership became more and more independent of the European tradition which once controlled its thinking and limited the soar of its initiative . . .

Yet as I said at the outset, no orator has thus far seen fit to memorialize the deeds of the American Soldier and of American arms. Even if an Emerson were here today with this purpose—and all too clearly one is not—any oration in praise of the independence of the American soldier would be largely postlude to the present fact of the ascendant role of America in military affairs.

Abroad this ascendancy of American arms and American military concepts is accepted as a matter of course—it is imperfectly or reluctantly recognized at home. Abroad the successes of our armed forces in World War II and Korea and the visible deterrent power of our arms today as shown in the Cuban crisis have enforced this appreciation of American primacy—for in the military field as in other fields of endeavor it is success that brings conviction.

Abroad, the success of the American military effort has led to an inquiry into its causes, into the form of its concepts, and the nature of its tactics and techniques. Hence allied and neutral representatives send their representatives to our military schools in vast numbers—last year approximately 17,000 students came to the United States to learn the American way of waging war and of keeping the peace. These same countries draw heavily on our military literature to guide their own studies. A few decades ago we in the United States learned from foreign military text books. In the Superintendent's quarters here at West Point some of you have no doubt seen the desk of Sylvanus Thayer, the great superintendent whom we know as the Father of the Military Academy. There you have noted some of the military texts to which he turned for counsel in administering West Point at about the same time that Emerson was delivering his oration in Cambridge. Most of these books are in French, a few in the English of the mother country. Today, the library of any foreign military academy is apt to be filled with books written in the English of the military centers of the United States. Last month I stood on a hilltop in Iran and with the military representatives of the CENTO alliance watched with the Shah a military demonstration presented by the Iranian Army and Air Force. The explanation to the assembled international audience was made in English by Iranian officers in uniforms similar to the U.S. field uniform and the briefing bore the unmistakable mark of Fort Benning or Fort Sill. One sensed the influence of the American Soldier in his role as teacher of the armies of freedom.

Yet, said Taylor, though Americans boast of all accomplishments and are not an immodest people, there were few who boasted of the accomplishments of the American soldier, great though they were,

the lands, seas and air spaces which they have conquered and the prisoners which they have taken dwarf the deeds of the great conquerors which provided the familiar faces in the history books of our childhood. But still no orations are devoted at home to the ascendancy of the American Soldier. Why is this so?

Our incomplete answer would be that we Americans are made uneasy by the responsibilities of military leadership. As a nation we are still the prey of clichés about men on horseback and of the dangers of the military to democracy. We still have trouble distinguishing between what is military and what is militaristic; between what is peaceful and what is pacifistic. We must perhaps progress further toward maturity before there will be wholehearted acceptance at home of the continuing need for a large and respected military profession in the United States in the same way as there is a need for a class of businessmen, professional men, scientists, clergymen, and scholars. Uncle Sam has become a world renowned soldier in spite of himself . . .

If the Kennedy Administration had come to power to be the rationalizers of the great new liberal Democratic empire, then they had found the perfect general; their social and academic hubris was matched by his military self-confidence. His were not the attitudes of a man about to be deterred from his path by a little peasant revolutionary Army. Not in the American century.

Chapter Twenty-two

BUT THE SAIGON YEARS WOULD NOT BE HAPPY ONES. AFTER all those years learning control, discipline, making those the touchstones of his life, Max Taylor was now confronted by the wild irrationality, the deviousness, the maliciousness and venality of the South Vietnamese. It was somehow unfair; people who are about to be saved from the Communists should feel some element of gratitude, and at the very least that gratitude should surface in the form of knowing they were being saved, and more important, wanting to be saved. There he was in Saigon, in mid-1964, proconsul of a great empire which had a firmer sense of its mission than its ally; the Americans more committed, more willing to die than the South Vietnamese. It was all very puzzling. No common cause. No consensus. Could there be anarchy when the Communists were at the gates of the city? Remind them, Dean Rusk, Taylor's new chief at State, would cable him, of Ben Franklin's statement that they would either hang together or hang separately. All those years in the military, where there were certain standards and rules; where young men treated their superiors with respect; where you gave an order and it was obeyed; where a uniform meant you were all on the same side. Now here in Saigon, all of that meant nothing, medals won on the plains of Europe against the world's second mightiest army meant nothing; he was dealing with these boys, most had never heard a shot fired in anger. Everything went so badly; Nguyen Khanh, who had appeared so dramatically on the scene in February as the new prime minister, and whom the Americans had seized upon, the first American-style leader, had turned out to be not American style, but Vietnamese style, with Diem's weaknesses without Diem's strengths—neurotic, paranoiac, disliked by both older officers and younger officers, and like his predecessors, totally overwhelmed by the political problems he faced. Khanh and Taylor argued regularly, ever more bitterly, until by the end of his tour Taylor, representative of the mightiest nation in the world, was virtually *persona non grata* in the weakest nation in the world.

It was always like that; Max was so organized, disciplined, trying to transfer that rationality and logic to this Alice-in-Wonderland world. When he complained to one of his civilian aides about a propaganda program they were using which the Vietnamese did not like and wanted to drop, the aide suggested it be dropped. Was it logical that it should be kept? asked Taylor. Yes, said the civilian. Was it a sound program? asked Taylor. Yes, answered the civilian again. "Well, if it's logical and sound, we'll keep it," Taylor said. And later, during a period of revolving-doors governments, when Air Marshal Nguyen Cao Ky had come to power, Taylor would take two *New York Times* reporters aside and tell them that if Ky got the premiership he would give up the air force, the vital power balance in any coup, since government troops, unlike the Vietcong, were not used to being strafed. Jack Langguth, one of the reporters, was somewhat startled by the suggestion and asked, "Do you really think he'll give up the air force, which is the only power base he has?" Taylor said he did. "Why?" asked Langguth. "Because he promised me," answered Taylor.

The worst thing for him was of course that nothing worked. It was a roller coaster—more advisers, more gear, more threats to the South Vietnamese, more threats to the North. He was at the confluence of it now, the architect of limited war, and particularly this limited war, caught between the failure of it and the threat of a greater war, between his vanities and his beliefs that the United States would not be defeated here, that the loss of prestige for a great power in the face of a small guerrilla army would be a major catastrophe. It had all come home to him, Max Taylor, who had always been able to control things. Now control was getting away from all of them. What they had held on to, the counterinsurgency, was slipping away, and in early August 1964 he began to grasp almost desperately at solutions. Since the Vietcong could not be defeated in the South, the answers would have to be found elsewhere, and for the first time he began to change on the bombing. It now became a possibility; significantly, he did not recommend bombing for military reasons (he was, as Westmoreland also was, dubious about the military effectiveness of bombing, knowing as he did the reluctance of his kind of civilian superiors to use the kind of bombing that the real hawks, the LeMays and the Wally Greenes and the McConnells wanted. They wanted total bombing, they were ready to annihilate the opposition. Taylor was too civilized a general for that, and he served too civilized a set of superiors to believe that they would permit something like that; the whole point of the new strategy had been to get away from total force, be it nuclear or nonnuclear force).

Taylor wanted it for political reasons. In the past he had opposed bombing because he was unwilling to commit the United States to the use of greater power against the North, which meant greater involvement; otherwise, he felt, the United States would find itself at war with the North with a very weak government in the South. Now he was changing. In his August 18 message to the President he said: "Something must be added in the coming months." That something would be bombing; the right time for starting a campaign of reprisal, he suggested, would be January 1, 1965, a time conveniently after the election. Ideally, we should tell Khanh that we would begin to bomb for him and the South Vietnamese if he could show the United States that he was ready for it and brought a new era of stability to Saigon. Thus the bombing was a political lever, a reward; if they were good and cleaned up their house, we would bomb, and show our greater willingness to commit ourselves. Of course the one lesson the Vietnamese leaders had learned over a decade was that the United States was more desperately anti-Communist than they were, and that the more the Vietnamese failed, the more the United States was willing to put in. As if to confirm this, the same Taylor message also told Washington that perhaps January 1 would be too late, in which case the United States would go ahead anyway and simply hope that Khanh would come around.

Eventually Taylor and George Ball would be on opposite sides of the same great question, whether to bomb or not, while presenting identical evidence, the almost total weakness and instability of Saigon. There was another reason, which would move the others, the idea that bombing was a card, you played it, it was not necessarily a final act. Everyone else seemed to think that Hanoi valued its industrial base so much that it would do almost anything to protect it, including calling off the war in the South. Why not try it and find out? At the very least it would punish Hanoi, which was something; there was a feeling that Hanoi deserved it, it had been punishing them and Saigon without paying any price. The change in Taylor was that of a key man in the key slot —a strong ambassador in a divided or uncertain bureaucracy has enormous power—something that symbolized the gradual transformation of the other players: it was not so much that Taylor was stupid or inept, though he was far from brilliant; he was, and this was symbolic of all of them, a desperate man in a desperate situation, unable to turn back, having come this far.

Events in the fall would turn him completely toward the bombing. Just as the pre-Tonkin covert operations had led to the Tonkin incident and the sense in this country and among many of the principals that the other side had provoked us, the principals triggered the situation at Bien Hoa which, when it exploded, filled them with righteousness against the enemy. On November 1 the squadron of obsolete B-57 bombers which had been moved from the Philippines to the air base at Bien Hoa (over State's objections) was hit by the Vietcong; five Americans were killed, seventy-six wounded and six of the bombers destroyed. Thus the Vietcong had matched their symbols against our symbols; anyone wanting to know what their attitude toward the bombing would be in the future had his answer right there. They would meet our air power with increased pressure against targets in the South.

What was most important about the Bien Hoa attack, however, was not the fact that the United States had left the planes there, or that the VC had hit them, or that the ARVN security was predictably inept. What was remarkable was the reaction of Max Taylor. The attack infuriated him, and his cables back to Washington, which had always in the past been restrained and almost conservative in tone, were now strikingly different, angry, reflecting almost outrage that they could do this to the symbols of the United States of America, of which he himself, as ambassador, was the great symbol. A sign of arrogance on the part of the other side, tinkering with the giant. He wanted to retaliate and retaliate immediately, and he was surprised and a little angry when Johnson, facing an election in two days, did not respond, and he complained openly to friends in the mission and to journalists. But this, as much as anything else, pushed him over on the bombing. From then on he was committed. He was angry at Hanoi and eager to punish, and he wanted not just tit for tat but the major bombing program as well, using as his argument that it would improve morale and give us more influence in the South, since the South would now have to prepare for greater pressure from the North. So with Taylor, as with some of the others who advocated bombing, the attitude was not particularly one of belief but rather one of why-not. This would after all buy time for Saigon; we would not take over the war.

But as he switched in the late fall of 1964, it was a decision which had a powerful effect on the principals within the bureaucracy; if Max was getting on board, then there was little else holding them back and it was more evidence than ever that this was the way they would have to go. Besides Taylor's protégé William C. Westmoreland there was, however, one key member of the top mission staff who had grave doubts about the bombing: the CIA station chief, Pier de Silva, a West Point graduate himself, and a man who, friends thought, had an almost pathological distrust of the military. He accurately forecast that the bombing would have virtually no effect other than provoke Hanoi into sending more troops down the trails; it would not invade in the classic military sense. This was somewhat unusual, since the military assumption in 1964 was still that if the North came down, it would come down in traditional division formation, making a good target for American power. When Robert Kleiman of the *New York Times* interviewed generals in February 1965 about what Hanoi would do, he was told by a member of the Joint Chiefs that if they came down, it would take "eight U.S. divisions, just like in Korea" to stop them and we did not need to worry about getting the U.S. troops in advance because we could fly them there faster than the North Vietnamese could march. A civilian with military experience in Saigon estimated that it would take four divisions; another high-ranking member of the Saigon command said two divisions; and one of Saigon's top planners said one U.S. division, then added prophetically, "I don't think they're going to do it that way. As a matter of fact, we just picked up a broadcast report on how they took a division, broke it down into smaller component parts, and then practiced infiltrating it and reassembling it in the South. I don't think they're coming down Korean style, the country's just not right, the narrow coastal plain, no good routes—they just couldn't conduct a conventional advance in force."

Even as Taylor was recommending bombing, he knew that this in itself was not enough, that if you bombed you would need troops. But he was bothered about sending combat troops, and he did not want to cross that bridge if necessary, partly because of the problems of Americans fighting in a political war and turning the population toward the Vietcong, but even more because he felt there was a crossover point at which, as the Americans put in men, the South Vietnamese would let down even more on the job, and the process of Americanizing the war would be accelerated. It was a question which bothered him a great deal in the fall of 1964. What was the Plimsoll line, as he called it, was it 75,000 or 100,000, or was it 150,000? At which point did they quit and turn it over to us, requiring more Americans? But if it bothered him, he was still convinced that whatever happened, he could influence American decisions, that he could apply the brake if necessary, that he was at the crucial spot, the ambassador, with Westmoreland somewhat under his wing and thus under his control. This illusion tempted him, as it would eventually tempt other principals, to believe that they could control events and decisions, determine and check the flow. Which would not turn out to be entirely true: as ambassador he was the senior American only as long as there were no American troops; the moment the troops arrived the play would go to Westmoreland.

But if the question of troop levels bothered Taylor, he was sure of his ability to keep it down. So it was in late November 1964, right before Thanksgiving, before his crucial trip back to Washington, where they would, now that the President was elected in his own right, make some critical decisions, that Taylor gathered his senior staff together in Saigon. It was, thought one witness, a momentous occasion, Max aware of it, somehow more aloof than other men. Standing there, handsome, reserved—somehow those four stars seemed visible even when he was in civies—he had turned to them, this man who had been a charter member of the Never Again Club, and said, "I am going to see the President and I am going to advise him that the way things are going we will need American troops here. I intend to tell him this anyway, but I think it will help, it will make my position stronger, if I could tell the President that all of you here agree as well. I think I should warn you, however, that we may ultimately need as many as one hundred thousand."

THE ELECTION ON NOVEMBER 3, 1964, HAD GONE JUST THE WAY Johnson wanted, perhaps more so. He had received 43 million votes and Goldwater 27 million; he had 61 percent of the vote, the greatest percentage any American President had ever received. He had the Congress, a gain of thirty-seven seats in the House and with an enormous Democratic majority of sixty-eight Senators in the upper chamber. He had carefully camouflaged the question of Vietnam, removing it from debate, from the public eye and from the journalistic eye (Theodore White's coverage of the 1964 campaign, *The Making of the President*, a series known for its thoroughness in backgrounding major issues as well as men, is quite revealing: there are eighteen references to Bill Moyers and fourteen to Kenny O'Donnell, both of whom worked in Johnson's political process during that period, and no references to Bill Bundy or John McNaughton, who were carrying the burden of the preparations for war. Max Taylor, who as U.S. ambassador was the central figure in Saigon, was mentioned only twice, a reflection not on White's journalistic ability, but on Johnson's ability to separate the issue of the war from the political process and to hide the decision making). Yet Vietnam had not gone away; even while the President was in the final, hectic, joyous weeks on the campaign, receiving a kind of adulation rarely accorded a political figure, the bureaucracy was grinding away methodically, coming to its positions. The principals had been ready to bomb at the time of the Bien Hoa attack; the pressure to do something, almost anything, was growing. Almost immediately after the election they moved toward the decision on bombing, and on November 8 Dean Rusk sent a crucial cable to Max Taylor in Saigon saying that the working group was intensively preparing alternatives to the present policy:

Our present tendency is to adopt a tougher program both privately and publicly against them. We propose to decide very soon that if there is no change in Hanoi's position we would start in January a slowly graduating military action on Hanoi, in conjunction with negotiating moves. Such course of action would be less drastic than a course of full attacks. The working group is going to get everything in order.

Rusk asked Taylor to comment on the Saigon side, the idea being that it would be in order when the bombing took place, and he had also urged that Taylor impress the South Vietnamese with the importance of holding together. On November 10 Taylor answered Rusk, beginning with a rhetorical question:

What is the minimal level of government stability before we go in? I would describe it as maintaining law and order in the cities, securing vital areas from Vietcong attacks, and working effectively with the U.S. We don't expect such a government for three or four months. It is highly desirable to have this kind of minimum government before accepting the risk inherent in any escalation programs.

But, Taylor pointed out, if the government faltered we would still consider attacking the North "to give Pulmotor treatment for a government in extremis." As for the instability, Taylor reported:

I know of no words of eloquence or persuasion that have not been tried in the past. At the moment the problem is not with the government, but with major outside groups such as Buddhists, Catholics and politicians . . .

FOR THE JOINT CHIEFS OF STAFF IT WAS AN UNSETTLING TIME, JUST AS it was at the other extreme, for the intelligence community. If the intelligence community had a sense that events were getting out of control and that the restraints were being lifted, the Chiefs had something of a similar feeling from an entirely different viewpoint. They thought it was all moving toward their business, their profession, and yet, even as events progressed, as the inevitability of combat neared, they had too little sense of play, too little sense of control. They had assumed that they would move into a larger role, their advice, their professionalism summoned; the civilians around the President moved aside, the Chiefs moved to center stage.

But it did not happen that way; instead they found the President, if anything, more nervous than ever about being with them, as if somehow afraid of giving the impression that he was getting into a shooting war, and thus listening to the military, and influenced by the military (they would learn about Lyndon Johnson that he was far more willing to be seen with them and photographed with them later when he was *de-escalating* the war and when he needed their coloration to protect him from the right; whereas in 1964 and 1965 the last thing he wanted was the impression that he was under their spell and influence). They found themselves moving closer and closer to a real war, and yet more and more separated from the President, and among some of them grew a sense that this would again be another frustrating bitter war, a civilians' war, and that they would be isolated once more. They did not feel at ease with the President, largely because they were sure he felt uncomfortable with them; they sensed his distrust, the fact that he wanted to keep them at arm's length, and his desire to use both McNamara and Taylor to filter them out.

They neither liked nor trusted McNamara (nor McNaughton, McNamara's chief aide in working with them, who made even less effort to conceal his contempt for them) and they felt that the Secretary was constantly manipulating them, that he did not really represent their position to the President, although he claimed he did. They were sure that he denigrated them, that somehow when he talked with the President they were the enemy, people to be fended off, and that he tried to keep them from seeing the President. ("It's your constitutional right," he would tell them, "but if I were you I wouldn't do it. He doesn't like you to come over and I can do it better for you.") So they saw the President only twice in the months right before the President made the decision to escalate. Many of them would come to despise McNamara; as the war progressed and the problems mounted he would symbolize their frustrations, the embodiment of all evil. (In August 1966, at Lynda Johnson and Chuck Robb's wedding, McNamara approached General Wally Greene, Commandant of the Marine Corps, a man who loathed him, and said that he was puzzled, he was losing his influence with the President and he wondered why. Did General Greene know why? Greene thought to himself, You're losing your influence because you've lied to him and misled him all these years. Greene would feel somewhat the same way about Lyndon Johnson by the end of his tour. Asked by a historian to consent to an interview for the Lyndon Johnson Library, he said yes, if they had asbestos tape in the recorder.) The only general that McNamara had trusted as late as mid-1964 was Max Taylor, a man the other Chiefs did not necessarily trust, feeling that Taylor was not one of them and that he represented Taylor, not them, to the politicians. Earle Wheeler, who had replaced Taylor as Chairman of the JCS, they liked better; he was, they felt, more honest, but they also thought Wheeler was overwhelmed by the problems of the civilians who were always playing politics.

So there was a strong feeling, even as events were moving ahead toward escalation, that they were on the outside looking in. They were General Curtis LeMay of the Air Force, Admiral David McDonald of the Navy, and Wally Greene of the Marine Corps (not a statutory member of the JCS, but an important figure within the group because of his forceful views and because of the fact that the Marines would be the first troops to go), and they were all very hawkish. The Air Force believed in air power and bombing, old-fashioned, unrelieved bombing; the Navy, anxious to show that the carrier still worked and to get its share of roles and missions in what had been largely an army show up to now, was hawkish; and Greene was hawkish. They were simple men, products of their training, environment and era, and they believed in the old maxims of war. If you had to go to war you used force, and if you used force, you used maximum force. If we were going to bomb, then it had to be saturation bombing of every conceivable target, and they would pick the targets. Obliteration of the enemy.

The closer they got to a decision, however, the more they sensed that it was going to be nervous, inadequate, half-hearted bombing, starting slowly and working their way up. It was exactly the reverse of everything they believed, it signaled the enemy that more was coming, it allowed him to move his resources around and protect himself from bombing, to decrease his losses and increase American ones. All the Chiefs were signed on to a heavy bombing campaign, but LeMay and Greene were the most aggressive; they wanted to hit the irrigation dikes as well. Hit everything there. If it wasn't worth hitting it wasn't worth going to war. If you sent troops in, you sent in enough to do the job, 600,000, 700,000 perhaps, and not spaced out over a couple of years, allowing him time to build up his own logistical base, you did it immediately; and you went on a wartime footing, you called up the reserves and you let the nation know it was into something. War, they felt, was a serious thing, and not just the Marines and a few Air Force pilots should have to pay for it. They were in that sense old-fashioned men. Not every one of the Chiefs was quite so hawkish; General Harold K. Johnson, the Army Chief of Staff, was dubious about the whole thing, including the bombing, and to all intents and purposes he had voted against the bombing, raising such doubts for so long that it was in effect a negative vote. Wheeler himself was more modest in what he felt could be done; his own views were probably closer to those of the more hawkish generals, but he also considered himself a representative of the President and committed by the Constitution to understand the President's problems, even if deep in the recesses of his own heart he did not really sympathize with them.

So at the end of 1964 the Chiefs felt they were left out, that the civilians were making the decisions (the military moved the civilians over in the play; because of the military the civilians were more hawkish. But they were still civilians, and they held the levers of power, and deep down they were contemptuous of the Chiefs. It was years later, when the decision making on this *war* was analyzed, that the names and faces of the civilians came easily to mind, but the names and faces of the Chiefs remained a mystery. Was it Earle Wheeler or Harold Johnson at Army? Curtis LeMay or John McConnell at the Air Force? David McDonald or Thomas Moorer at Navy? When General Harold Johnson, Chief of Staff of the Army, was having lunch in February 1965 with two *New York Times* reporters, he said that he had no great desire to go to war in Vietnam. He knew too well what it would be, Korea all over again, only worse, an enemy using sanctuaries, the United States unable and unwilling to use its full power, all the old frustrations again. He was not anxious for it. Not at all.

If General Johnson was not hawkish, and was worried about another ground war in Asia, his colleague Wally Greene was far more hawkish. In late 1964 Greene was going around to the various service schools, Army and Marine Corps, and talked to the officers, giving a very militant lecture, saying that we should go in there and get the job done, use everything we had. This was the job to do and we ought to do it. It was all very upbeat and at the end he would turn to his audience and ask who was with him, and there would be a roar. A show of hands, he would say, let's have a show of hands of those who want to go. Lots of hands up. And those who don't want to go? Always fewer hands. And always, it turned out, the hands of men who had served there recently as advisers.

WHAT WAS MOST STRIKING ABOUT THIS PERIOD AS EVENTS CLOSED IN on the principals was how little exploration there was of the consequences of their route, what might happen if the more pessimistic appraisals were accurate (which were the appraisals of the intelligence community) and what it might do to the country. And in the same sense, there was a refusal to consider what the alternatives to escalation really were. A question that was almost never raised was whether the Vietnamese might or might not be better off under Ho, and to what degree the success of the Vietcong was a reflection of this. The kind of men who might have the doubts, who might at the top level of players have the insight and knowledge of some of the men in the intelligence community had long since been winnowed out. The men who had been politically inclined in their view of the war had also been filtered out. Only one man was left at the top level who had open doubts on Vietnam, and that was George Ball. He had not been a participant in the earlier bureaucratic struggles; he was something of an outsider as far as the Kennedy circle was concerned; he was a man of Europe and he had not considered Vietnam that important. Now, starting in 1964 and through the crucial months of 1965, he argued compellingly, forcefully and prophetically against the escalation, so prophetically that someone reading his papers five years later would have a chilling feeling that they had been written after the fact, not before. Later it would be said of Ball that he was a devil's advocate, the house dove, a safe dove trotted out by a shrewd President for the record, so that later when the historians came to dissect the record they would find that Johnson had been careful, thoughtful and had listened to all sides. (The devil's advocate story originated with Jack Valenti in 1964 when word started getting out that Ball was fighting against the policy. It was a deliberate attempt to show that there was no opposition, that it was all one big happy consensus within the government, when in fact Ball was making a strong dissent.)

In arguing against the escalation, Ball was saying that it was doomed. He was alone among the foreign policy people saying this, which did not bother him; he felt he needed only one of Johnson's domestic people to argue for the domestic side, to say that the American people didn't want war, that anti-Communism was ebbing as an issue. If only one more voice . . . If. If. He had spent the year working it out on paper, writing long memos, twenty pages or more, giving them to Johnson, feeling this was the best way to approach him rather than seem to debate him in small meetings, and each time he did, Johnson would study the memo all night and then question him very carefully. Johnson would show up the next morning without the memo, but able to cite page and paragraph without looking at it: "George, you say on page fourteen . . ." and "George, here on page eighteen . . ." George Ball had the strong opinion that in late 1964 and early 1965, Lyndon Johnson was a very troubled man.

GEORGE BALL SEEMED AN UNLIKELY MAN TO MAKE A CASE FOR THE doves and against the Establishment. He was first and foremost a Europeanist; perhaps more than any man in that government, even more than McGeorge Bundy, he was a man of Europe. His career had always been involved in Europe and in economic matters; he was an American disciple of Jean Monnet. He possessed a singular lack of concern, some of his colleagues in State thought in the early days of the Kennedy Administration, for the problems of Africans and Asians. Those in State who in 1961 and 1962 wanted to move American policy away from the old Europe-oriented colonial-power view of the underdeveloped world felt that Ball was the main antagonist in the Department, the man most likely, for instance, to take the French–Belgian–British–Union Minière view of sustaining the Katanga secession rather than the new-forces people's view of ending it, thus gaining love and affection elsewhere on the African continent. It was one more irony of the war that George Ball would make his first national reputation—something he had always wanted and had been somewhat denied—as a man who had been prophetic on Asia, since he had been concerned about Vietnam in the first place because he feared (as did many Europeans) that it was going to divert America from its prime concern in the world, which was the European alliance.

Ball was a more iconoclastic man than the Eastern group that Jack Kennedy had gathered around him; he was a Stevenson loyalist, a Democratic party worker, a good New Deal lawyer from Chicago who during the height of the McCarthy period was willing to represent Henry Wallace, a former Vice-President of the United States, when no one in Washington would. Ball had come to Washington with a cold and skeptical eye and a willingness to challenge assumptions. He did not, for instance, consider it a particularly bad thing for most of Africa to go Communist, thinking in fact that it might serve the Communists right to wrestle with the enormous problems of new countries; it might bog them down a little, and perhaps not win them many new friends. The exception, of course, would be an underdeveloped country particularly rich in minerals like the Congo, in which case the attitude of the

European patron country might change (and as it changed, so would Ball's). He had a certain unorthodox view of the world and a lack of preconception, except of course for an almost automatic instinct toward anything which promoted traditional European unity (he was the foremost advocate of the implausible MLF, a cartoonist's delight and a politician's nightmare). It was not easy to pin him down in the old split between the Acheson hard-liners and the Stevenson-Bowles faction in the Democratic party; there was a certain allegiance to Stevensonian liberalism, perhaps with a line a little harder and a little less idealistic in foreign policy. ("George," noted a friend, "has a certain moral framework to his ideas, but he would be absolutely appalled if someone ever said that he did. George is very careful to camouflage his moral concerns—so he can be a better and more realistic player.")

Ball was a devotee of traditional nineteenth-century power politics; he felt that power is real, something that is almost tangible and has to be dealt with: thus, stay out of Vietnam; do not dissipate power in a situation where it is not applicable; nothing destroys power more than the misuse of it. He liked to look ahead and think of the United States in ten years: his dream was of an alliance of the great industrial powers of the world. There were only a few of them that were truly important, he felt, that had genuine power: a United Europe, one great power with primacy over Africa; the Soviet Union with primacy over Eastern Europe; Japan with primacy over Asia, including China; the United States with primacy over Latin America. If he was more hard-line than Stevenson and more power-oriented, he was less anti-Communist than Acheson, sensing that economic and industrial power rather than Communism and anti-Communism would divide the world. He was more like George Kennan than Acheson (though with his sense of Europe and his strong commitment to stronger links there, he was by 1963 the Acheson candidate for Secretary of State, Acheson being disenchanted with Rusk for not being stronger and more forceful, and sensing that Ball would be a driving force, seizing the initiative and pushing McNamara somewhat into the background).

His pre-election relationship with Kennedy had been marginal, and he had not been in line for a particularly good job. Ball, himself uneasy about entering a somewhat anti-Stevenson Administration, never became a part of the inner Kennedy group; rather, he existed in something of a no man's land for those first years. He was a man of immense pride, and he regarded much of the Kennedy style and dash with considerable skepticism; those snappy young men running around in the White House did not necessarily strike him as brilliant. He was a man of considerable zest, enthusiasm and egocentrism, and he did not defer to those around him in Washington. He was probably the most traveled man of that group in Washington, the best read, and certainly the most elegant in speech. He was also a good deal more worldly than the others. He wrote well and took a special pride in the language. Where others in high places were fascinated by having subordinates who were doers, activists, finely tuned young men, Ball was quite different. The young men he brought to him were decidedly intellectual; he judged them, it seemed, not so much on their ability to move paper and make phone calls, as on their wit and literary style. He was not in awe of McGeorge Bundy, thinking Bundy too much the pragmatist (Bundy in turn would call Ball "the theologian" because of too much belief, and occasionally irritated by Ball's independence and individualism, once said to him, "The trouble with you, George, is that you always want to be the piano player"). Part of the tension between them, of course, was that each saw the other as a possible successor to Rusk. He was less than admiring of McNamara, sensing quite early the weaknesses in him, doubts which had been intensified by the Skybolt affair.

A man of genuine intelligence and force, Ball rose at State on his ability, and because he was acceptable to all factions. Independence and ability, rather than being the good corporate man, he felt, should bring success in government, and besides, he simply was not constituted to be a good, obedient corporate figure. He got on particularly well with Rusk during the Kennedy years. The friendship survived remarkably well, despite the vast disagreements over Vietnam. (Years later, when Rusk's reputation was at its lowest, a reporter, interviewing Ball about the war, would mention Rusk and would be stunned by Ball's almost vehement answer, *"I love Dean Rusk."*) Ball had a sense for Rusk as a human being that few others had in that era. Perhaps since both were outsiders in the Kennedy years, Rusk opened up more to Ball than to others. That, plus a certain gratitude to Rusk for permitting him as Undersecretary to dissent so strongly on Vietnam ("I cannot," says one member of that Administration, "imagine McNamara letting Ball dissent like that. Nor, for that matter, can I imagine George letting Rusk dissent if Ball had been Secretary and Rusk Undersecretary"). The men could not have been more different. Rusk had a certain skillful knowledge about a vast number of problems, but was relatively thin and not too deep in any of them; Ball was interested in few things, but when he became involved in a subject—Vietnam, the Kennedy Round tariff negotiations, Cyprus—he would tear into it, break it down into component parts, master it, overwhelm it. Rusk served as Secretary of State with an overpowering sense of being a civil servant, a superclerk, an attitude which placed strong limits on his individual rights, whereas Ball, with a fierce sense of his own ability and prerogatives, felt that he was there to say what he believed. Rusk seemed ill at ease with *power;* Ball sought it avidly.

He was a strong and forceful figure in all those years; in an Administration where too many of the figures were corporate men or gilded clerks, Ball was something surprisingly unique and old-fashioned, an independent man. He had enjoyed a good relationship with Jack Kennedy, and without demeaning himself at all, he enjoyed perhaps an even better one with Lyndon Johnson. He had come away impressed with the force and sense of vision of Johnson, the desire to commit human energy to human good, the almost naïve belief in the powers of education. As Johnson slipped into his war Presidency, Ball was sometimes reminded of a story about Woodrow Wilson arriving for his inaugural, getting off at Union Station on a rainy day, talking to a friend about the forthcoming years, Wilson saying that he started his Presidency that day; all his life he had prepared himself for it, for the real problems of domestic reform. Then pausing and adding, "Wouldn't it be a great irony if I had to spend my time dealing with war." He liked Johnson and sensed the forces at work in the man, and he liked his job, and even when he made his dissent on Vietnam it was done not as an adversary of the court, but as a friend; there was no threat of resignation. George Ball had worked too long and too hard to get where he was to stomp out in anger. Ball believed he was doing the wise thing, and he did not think that in the long run it would necessarily hurt his chances of becoming Secretary of State. He was at ease on the inside; the harsh criticism which later fell upon the architects of the war was completely alien to him. In 1971 when the Pentagon Papers were published and Ball's dissents were made public he was very low-key about it, he played down his wisdom, if anything he seemed the major defender of his old antagonists.

Ball had been a member of the Strategic Survey team which studied the effects of the Allied bombing on Germany during World War II, a study which revealed how surprisingly ineffective the bombing had been, that it had rallied German morale and spurred industrial production. Since bombing had not worked against a major industrialized state like Germany, which abounded in tangible targets, Ball had immediate doubts about Vietnam (doubts which were not assuaged by conversations with his friend Thomas Finletter, Secretary of the Air Force during the Korean War, and an early Vietnam dove who had pointed out the limits of bombing during the Korean War); Vietnam was after all a peasant nation with very limited industrialization. In addition to his doubts about bombing, Ball had doubts about the war in general. He had served as France's American legal counsel during the fifties, years which had given him a deep and continuing feeling of uneasiness about entering the Indochinese swamps as well as a sense of distrust for any Western military estimates from Saigon and somehow a belief that there were always more of *them* (the enemy) than any Westerner ever figured. He had watched the French military over eight years, always asking for a little more matériel, a little more time, and always running into more Vietminh. To him, the war was unwinnable, or at least it was for a civilized government, and it might have profound domestic consequences; the French democracy had almost collapsed under its weight. Ball did not foresee the full extent of the negative fallout of the war, that it would drive out the President and virtually

destroy the Democratic party as an operative institution, sharpen generational and racial conflict in the country (alienating the best of a generation
from the institutions they were by tradition supposed to enter and serve), but
in a more vague sense he knew that if something like this was tried and failed,
the consequences would be very serious. In addition, Ball, more than anyone
else in official Washington, sensed that once started, the course had a certain
inevitability to it: each day it would be more difficult to bail out; the idea of
options was all an illusion. Years later he would tell friends that two things
had done incalculable damage during the 1964 and 1965 period; the first was
the ease with which a democratic government moved into covert operations
and let its highest men become stained by participation in such operations;
the second worst thing was the idea that there were options which could be
kept open. Quite the reverse was true, he would say. Events were always
changing, inaction closed off alternatives; when events were going badly, time
worked against you, and when events were going well you did not need options. Thus the time when there had been the most choices was in 1946; the
time when there were the fewest, in 1965. He was an insider with something
of an outsider's viewpoint in 1965, and one of the reasons he had not been in
awe of the Kennedy people was that for all their flash and reputation he considered himself, by his own estimates, wiser and more a man of the world
than they. And he was right.

Bothered by the direction of the war, and by the attitudes he found around
him in the post-Tonkin fall of 1964, and knowing that terrible decisions were
coming up, Ball began turning his attention to the subject of Vietnam. He
knew where the dissenters were at State, and he began to put together his
own network, people with expertise on Indochina and Asia who had been
part of the apparatus Harriman had built, men like Allen Whiting, a China
watcher at INR; these were men whose own work was either being rejected
or simply ignored by their superiors. Above all, Ball was trusting his own instincts on Indochina. The fact that the others were all headed the other way
did not bother him; he was not that much in awe of them, anyway. He would,
knowing there was a meeting the next day, stay up all night working on a
paper, questioning the men around him, going through books on Indochina,
and then he would write and rewrite his papers, and have his staff play the
part of the opposition as he went through the dry run. And he would go off to
battle, taking genuine delight in it, and his aides could sense the excitement,
the adrenalin was really pumping. He would often return, not depressed, but
almost exhilarated, *Johnson was listening*. He was getting to him. We're getting through, he would say, and then he would start talking about the next
paper. To him, Johnson was the most sympathetic man in the room, a real listener, and he had the feeling that Johnson was not so much ill prepared for
foreign affairs as he *felt* that he was ill prepared, made insecure by all these

intellectuals around him. Even Ball himself. "George, you're an intellectual too," Johnson would say. "I know it, and you know it."

Since Ball had not been in on any of the earlier decision making, he was in no way committed to any false hopes and self-justification; in addition, since he had not really taken part in the turnaround against Diem, he was in no way tainted in Johnson's eyes. While some of the others, implicated in the origins of the commitment, were either psychologically involved (in the case of Taylor) in trying to make their estimates come true, or (in the case of McNamara) having miscalculated earlier and thus feeling they must protect the President and share the responsibility (a belief which sucked many good men farther into the quagmire, and would help account in part for the peculiar behavior of Robert McNamara), Ball was freed from the mistakes of the past. He had, at the time of the original Kennedy commitment, warned that 15,000 men would become 300,000; that was his own prediction, and it was not a bad one.

And so now he began, first by writing a memo to Rusk, McNarama and Bundy expressing his doubts, and expecting that Bundy would pass the memo on to the President. But to Ball's surprise the memo did not reach Johnson, so the next time Ball passed his memo to Bill Moyers, the bright young assistant of Johnson's who showed his own doubts on Vietnam largely by encouraging other doubters to speak and by trying to put doubters in touch with one another. Moyers passed the memo to the President, who encouraged it, and so, beginning in the early fall of 1964, Ball emerged as the voice of dissent. Ball argued that the ground troops would not work, that the United States would repeat the French experience, soon costing us what few friends we had in the South, that the situation "would in the world's eyes approach that of France in the 1950s." But he also argued vigorously against the bombing, saying that if the United States used air power, Hanoi would feel the need to respond, and failing to have air power, they would respond with increased ground forces. He cited U.S. intelligence estimates that if Hanoi chose to, it could infiltrate two divisions through Laos and the demilitarized zone in two months. What he was in fact doing was systematically compiling all the evidence that the intelligence community, the real experts on Southeast Asia, had compiled, all the stuff which normally had been filtered out, and was using it at the level of the principals.

A copy of the Policy Planning study which Robert Johnson had put together was smuggled to him. He was in effect choosing to see that which everyone had decided not to see. He argued that the bombing would not, as its advocates were claiming, have very much effect on South Vietnamese morale. Rather, he said, it might affect the upper level of the government, and even that rather briefly and impermanently; it would never take root in the country. While the others kept talking about South Vietnam as if the government and the people were somehow linked, for Ball, South Vietnam was not even a country. As for the effectiveness of the bombing on morale, he was suspicious; he cited a post-Tonkin CIA study made by Vietnamese-speaking Americans which showed that of about two dozen Vietnamese questioned, all but one disapproved (the one being an American-trained airborne sergeant). He denied all the peripheral arguments, that we had to stand in Vietnam because if we did not, our allies in Europe would be nervous and unsure of us (an argument which McGeorge Bundy was to become fond of). He submitted, quite accurately, that this was the official view, that our allies formally said things like this, but the reality was quite different, even among the Germans: they did not consider the South Vietnamese to be the equal of themselves in legitimacy, and the real fear in Europe was that the United States was going to be diverted from its primary concern in Europe by less important adventures in Asia. And to Ball, the arguments of Mac Bundy and Taylor that we must bomb to shore up the morale of the South Vietnamese because the government was so frail that it would otherwise collapse was foolishness of a high order. It was all the more reason *not* to commit the power and reputation of the United States to something that weak. The South Vietnamese were, he noted, allegedly a people about to be overrun by their sworn enemies, and if they really cared about the freedoms we were so anxious to protect, why did we have to make a gesture like this to convince them to save themselves?

He looked farther down the road, warning that we were essentially dealing from a position of weakness despite what we thought, and perhaps almost most important of all, he challenged that greatest of American assumptions, that somehow, whatever we did, the other side would lie down and accept it. He pointed out *that we did not necessarily control the rate, the intensity and the scale of the war.* The enemy, he noted, was not entirely without the means of response. In October 1964 he had written in answer to McNamara and Mac Bundy: "It is the nature of escalation that each move passes the option to the other side, while at the same time the party which seems to be losing will be tempted to keep raising the ante. To the extent that the response to a move can be controlled, that move is probably ineffective. If the move is effective it may not be possible to control or accurately anticipate the response. Once on the tiger's back we cannot be sure of picking the place to dismount." Here he was prophetic again, as Johnson, once committed, would find himself in a terrible squeeze, the military pushing relentlessly for more force, for escalations which they claimed would end it quickly; yet each of these moves would seem to bring in the Chinese. Thus nothing that could be truly effective against the North Vietnamese could be tried without the fear of a much larger war which Johnson wished to avoid. The things which could be done against Hanoi without bringing in the Chinese were always, accordingly, ineffective.

So Ball made his dissent, and he made it powerfully, and if he was not changing the men around him he was certainly affecting the President, touching those doubts which already existed in the President's mind. Ball was making the President very unhappy, and thus he was slowing down the process. Was the President waffling? Might he turn back? Sometime in the fall of 1964 Joe Alsop feared that he was, and set out to help clarify the way for the President. Hearing that George Ball was making a major dissent on Vietnam, Alsop wrote on November 23 that Ball's "knowledge of Asia could be comfortably contained in a fairly small thimble." What Ball was not telling the President, even though he was European-minded, was, Alsop wrote:

The Ball memoranda further assert that the trouble in Vietnam is damaging the United States in Europe without bothering to note that a gigantic United States failure in Vietnam will virtually give the European game to General Charles de Gaulle. . . . A majority of President Johnson's chief advisers are certainly on the do-something side and the more able and courageous appear to favor doing something pretty drastic.

Alsop, still uneasy about the lack of decision and possible portents, wrote on December 23:

There are plenty of discouraged Americans in Saigon who think the President is consciously prepared to accept defeat here. They believe that he cannot bring himself to take the measures needed to avert defeat, and they therefore suspect that he is simply planning to wait until the end comes and then to disclaim responsibility. But since the President has the means to avert defeat he cannot disclaim responsibility. It will be his defeat as well as a defeat for the American people and for millions of unhappy Vietnamese. It does not seem credible that Lyndon B. Johnson intends to accept and preside over such a defeat. But the alternatives open to him are narrowing very fast.

It was another example of something that Alsop did brilliantly; he was an odd man, sophisticated, talented, arrogant; his real talent and perhaps his real love lay not in writing about politics but about archaeology. If his political writing did not last long and did not read well years after, it was not a fault of intellect, it was something else: it was that Alsop was a man of Washington and its power, and he wrote to the power play of the day, he wrote not to enlighten but to *effect*, to move the principal players on decisions like this. And in that sense there was a brilliance, for he had an unerring sense for the raw nerve of each player, for knowing how to couch his arguments in terms which would make them most effective, not on the general readership but on the individual himself. He knew intuitively that the thing Johnson feared most was that history would write that he had been weak when he should have been strong, that Lyndon Johnson had not stood up when it was time to be counted, that his manhood might be inadequate; and in late 1964 and early 1965 he played on that theme masterfully; the Alsop columns on Johnson were part of a marvelous continuing psychodrama. For instance, on December 30, again noting that Johnson might be too weak to take the necessary steps, Alsop wrote:

The unpleasantness of making the required effort does not need underlining. But it must certainly be underlined that the catastrophe now being invited will also be remarkably unpleasant. For Lyndon Johnson, Vietnam is what the second Cuban crisis was for John F. Kennedy. If Mr. Johnson ducks the challenge we shall learn by experience about what it would have been like if Kennedy had ducked the challenge in October, 1962 . . .

And so there it was, posed again: Did Johnson have as much manhood as Jack Kennedy? In Washington, Walter Lippmann would read those columns with a sick feeling and tell friends that if Johnson went to war in Vietnam, at least 50 percent of the responsibility would be Alsop's; at the White House, Johnson, who never liked or trusted Alsop (later, when the latter was virtually the only columnist in town still supporting the war, he would read the columns and rage against Alsop for closing off his options, for trapping him in, and he was deeply suspicious that the Bundys, who were old Alsop friends, were the sources of the leaks). He was very angry about the columns, but he was not unaffected by them. They posed the question as he knew it might be posed out in the hinterland, as he, Lyndon Johnson, might pose it himself against a political adversary.

WHILE THE BUREAUCRACY IN WASHINGTON WAS WORKING ON ESCA-lation, Taylor was negotiating the Saigon mission to virtually the same position: it would be bombing, but limited bombing.

The Bill Bundy working group, the people immediately under the principals, had formulated the policy in the late fall, and their proposals were discussed at the late-November meetings. The group had been instructed to come up with various options, but those concerning negotiation had been moved aside, and the options were all ones of force (there had been one proposal of the civilians, which was a fraudulent use of force, and was based on the instability in Saigon and the fear of McCarthyism here at home. It was to launch a short, intense bombing campaign, show that it had no effect on the South, then to blame the South for its own instabilities and to get out. It was in effect a flash of power and a retreat. The Chiefs immediately vetoed it).

The Bundy group had presented the President with three options. Option A was light bombing, more reprisals and more use of covert operations, essentially more of the same with light bombing thrown in. Option B was the Chiefs' suggestion, minus the dikes—very heavy massive bombing right from the start, including the Phuc Yen airfield at Hanoi and cutting the rail links with China. And Option C, the moderate solution (it was typical of the bureaucracy to present its predetermined position by putting one option to the left of it and one to the right of it, thus it was recommending the just and moderate position), the slow squeeze, which allowed the United States to put increasing pressure on Hanoi while "keeping the hostage alive" while still permitting it to pull back if it wished to. This was the McNamara position, the moderate one, designed to give the Chiefs something of what they wanted, yet give the civilians the opportunity to control it, to turn it down, turn it up, turn it off; it was the solution which allowed the civilians presumably the most control. One reason why the Chiefs, who did not like it and believed it was a false use of force, did not fight it more vigorously was their assumption that if it failed, which it probably would, the civilians would have to turn to more and more force. The civilians always thought they were smarter than the military and understood them better than the military understood the civilians; the reverse was true, in fact; the military always read the civilians better. The minimal force necessary to keep the Chiefs on board had been worked out between McNamara and the Chiefs, and the architect of it was that most curious combination of human being and bureaucrat, the divided man, John McNaughton, who was quite capable of doing the most precise kind of planning and paper work for the bombing and then coming back, and almost with pleasure, telling a few chosen aides that it had not yet jelled, the President had not yet bought it, Johnson was still referring to it as "this bombing bullshit."

It also was a more political kind of pressure; it allowed more possibilities for negotiation, and this was an argument McNamara liked. The JCS position did not allow flexibility, and with its greater use of force might bring too great and too premature an international pressure for negotiation, whereas the moderate solution, McNamara believed, deflected pressure. It was more civilized, it would be easier to fend off both friends and enemies at the UN, and besides, it was more political in its aim, which was to get the North Vietnamese to the table. So even as the government seemed to be turning unanimously toward bombing, it was in fact very far from unanimous. The civilians wanted the bombing almost as a feint, a card to play; the military essentially wanted it as an instrument of war, a lever of force, an end in itself. Thus the seeming unanimity on bombing was a very thin conditional agreement of very different men who would momentarily come together for sometimes very conflicting reasons.

What was significant about the proposals the Bundy group presented to the President was that all three of them included bombing; there was really no political option at all. What was also significant was that the Assistant Secretary of State for Far Eastern Affairs was recommending and pressing options that went markedly against the beliefs and instincts of the men below him and of the intelligence community. Thus the man in charge of political estimates for an area was going ahead even though the political expertise was largely against him, particularly since the intelligence estimates within his working group were, if anything, seemingly more oriented toward force and the success of force than they were in reality, the actual view being somewhat clouded and compromised by the presence of the DIA (Defense Intelligence Agency) people, who were not about to say blandly that bombing would not work. In the final recommendation to the working group, the experts forcefully challenged the Rostow thesis that Hanoi would succumb to the bombing in order to protect its new and hard-won industrial bases. It said:

> We have many indications that the Hanoi leadership is acutely and nervously aware of the extent to which North Vietnam's transportation system and industrial plant is vulnerable to attack. On the other hand North Vietnam's economy is overwhelmingly agricultural and, to a large extent, decentralized in a myriad of more or less economically self-sufficient villages. Interdiction of imports and extensive destruction of transportation facilities and industrial plants would cripple D.R.V. [Democratic Republic of (North) Vietnam] industry. These actions would also seriously restrict D.R.V. military capabilities and would degrade, though to a lesser extent, Hanoi's capabilities to support guerrilla warfare in South Vietnam and Laos. We do not believe that such actions would have a crucial effect on the daily lives of the overwhelming majority of the North Vietnam population. We do not believe that attacks on industrial targets would so greatly exacerbate current economic difficulties as to create unmanageable control problems. It is reasonable to infer that the D.R.V. leaders have a psychological investment in the work of reconstruction they have accomplished over a decade. Nevertheless they would probably be willing to suffer some damage to the country in the course of a test of wills with the U.S. over the course of events in South Vietnam.

Thus, even with the sweeteners thrown in for DIA—the idea that the military pressure would hurt them more than the CIA and INR people believed— it was a clear warning against bombing. Nonetheless, it had no effect, other than feeding Ball's dissent.

If the Washington bureaucracy had decided on a course and veiled serious discord in an aura of consensus, the matching part, Taylor representing the mini-organism of American Saigon, was surprisingly similar. He again represented what seemed like a consensus for modified bombing (starting with low-level flights in Washington's Option A and then switching after thirty days to Option C, a relatively similar conclusion), but it was a false consensus, and he was, like his counterparts in Washington, playing down the estimated North Vietnamese reaction that his own intelligence community was giving him. He was discussing possible U.S. actions, and more by silence than anything else, implying that the North Vietnamese response might be somewhat different from what he was being warned (he would soon go further and deliberately downplay pessimistic estimates of his intelligence people rather than frighten Washington off a course he wanted). But his consensus was thin; his top CIA man, Pier de Silva, thought the bombing futile; his top military aide, William C. Westmoreland, did not think the bombing would be militarily effective. He thought the real problem was in the South, and thought it would take ground troops. Yet Westmoreland was willing to go along for the political reasons specified by Taylor, who was the chief political officer. Westmoreland was also willing to go along because he wanted troops and he sensed that this was simply one last bench mark on the way to the inevitable decision to send troops, indeed the troops that would be needed to provide security for the air bases would be the beginning of an American combat commitment. So though Taylor seemed to bring unanimity, much of it was a sense of signing on despite great doubts or signing on for quite different and unexpressed reasons.

THE TWO SIDES WERE SUPPOSED TO MESH IN THE LATE-NOVEMBER meetings. They did not. Lyndon Johnson was still not satisfied that bombing was the answer. Rusk did not doubt the necessity of holding South Vietnam and denying it to the Chinese and Hanoi (which was his view of the origins of the pressure), but he was not sure bombing was the answer, nor did he think it would be easy to turn it on and off as the proponents argued. Johnson was on the fence, and Rusk, uneasy in his own right about the bombing, was waiting to see which way the President wanted to go. Johnson's own fairly strong political instincts had been stirred by Ball's dissent, and he was discovering that despite the seeming unanimity of his principals, their belief and confidence in what they were proposing were not exactly convincing. Under questioning it developed that they were proposing it more because they did not have anything else to offer. So it was not entirely reassuring. Of the principals, McNamara and Taylor seemed the most confident, and McNamara, who had a remarkable ability to present answers in terms a superior wanted, was arguing that bombing was not final, it was political, and finally, at a relatively low cost; at the very least it would buy time. There, that was reassuring: it was not final, not irreversible and it bought time (for a President who clearly did not want to make decisions and who wanted to buy time). The President, who had earlier seemed ready to go on Vietnam once the election was over, was now becoming skittish again; he told associates that the war was in the South. Ball was making him nervous, and the turmoil in Saigon was making him uneasy. How could he bomb the North when some colonel or corporal in a tank might take Saigon the next day? he asked. Couldn't Taylor make it clear to those people that the President wanted to help them, the United States was prepared to play its role, but not unless they got together? Why couldn't they get together? he asked.

So the Taylor mission to Washington, which was supposed to sew everything up, did not; the decisions were still open. Events were closing them down, but the President was unhappy about the trap he found himself in. He was still looking for a way out; if Ball was not changing the direction of the play he was slowing it down. And there would be moments, when after a particular dissent by Ball, the President would turn to him and say, "All right, George, if you can pull me a rabbit out of a hat, go ahead," meaning trying to settle it without losing.

As it got darker, the play became more tightly held in Washington, with the bottom-ranking players being Bill Bundy and McNaughton. There were little signs that it was getting tougher: Bill Bundy went to the Council on Foreign Relations and gave a talk on Vietnam; he seemed to say that there would not be a wider war, and then, when the Council sent the notes on his speech back down to Washington to be cleared, they had to be rather heavily edited. The line was hardening, the winds were blowing in a different way, it was clearer and clearer that they were going to go North. Little signs. A high State Department official who was working on one policy paper and trying to get a drift of the play was by chance invited to the White House in December. He found the President surprisingly relaxed; stories of his boyhood came flashing out, stories of the Senate, slipping it by them, all punctuated by colorful language, and then suddenly, knowing why the State Department man was there, slipping in the phrase very quickly, as though it were almost unimportant, "Well, I guess we have to touch up those North Vietnamese a little," and then he was back again regaling his audience, all in the vernacular.

ALLIES WERE BEING SUMMONED TO SYMPATHIZE WITH, IF NOT JOIN, the American commitment to Vietnam. The least sympathetic of all was Charles de Gaulle, who was opposed to American policy for a vast variety of reasons, the first being that it would not work, and the second, that he saw a chance, as America moved back from Saigon, for a greater role for France in linking up with underdeveloped countries, an alternative for the underdeveloped world between the American, the Soviet and the Chinese possibilities. De Gaulle, who had been through the whole bitter thing before, had seen what it had done to France; and if he was not the fondest American friend in the world, he was nevertheless wary of seeing a Western power once more mired down in a guerrilla war. As early as 1963 he had begun to advocate neutralism for South Vietnam, and he had also discussed an American withdrawal. It was a suggestion which Washington regarded as being distinctly unfriendly and representing, rather than French good will toward the United States, French designs to re-establish primacy in this area. Rusk had been particularly uneasy about the specter of neutralism, and with the support of the mission in Saigon, believed that it would tend to weaken the resolve of the Vietnamese government. So in December 1964, Johnson dispatched George Ball to talk with De Gaulle, to try and win him over on our side, and failing that, to make him at least a little more sympathetic to the U.S. mission in Saigon, and to give him a sense of which way the play was going.

In sending Ball, the President had of course chosen the foremost dissenter within his government, thus following a familiar formula of using a dissenter to speak for the policy. It would tie Ball more to the policy, even if his dissent failed, and it would lessen the unlikely possibility for Johnson that Ball might stomp out of the government in anger over the policy. So as far as Johnson was concerned, he was the ideal man to make the representations to De Gaulle, which he did, reflecting the Rusk and to a lesser degree the Johnson view of the reasons for going ahead.

Ball told De Gaulle that in the past both the United States and France had wanted a viable South Vietnam, but since it was becoming increasingly difficult to sustain the government in the South "within a reasonable time," the United States might have to take action against the North, even though this might entail the risk of involving the Chinese in the war. The United States did not want to do that, Ball said, but Hanoi would have to learn that we were serious. Though some people talked about a diplomatic solution, the United States had grave reservations. Perhaps some other time, but not now; it was all too fragile in the South, and even talk of negotiation might undermine the South Vietnamese government and lead to its collapse and a quick Vietcong victory. As for negotiating with the North Vietnamese and the Chinese, there were limits there, and they were not known for keeping their word. The United States believed in talking with the Communists, but only when it had some balance of force there, enough to make them want to talk. Right now the U.S. position was too weak. Thus the United States would have to make a stand, it had to teach the Chinese Communists to stop pushing their neighbors around; the United States considered China to be similar to the Soviet Union in 1917, primitive, and aggressive toward its neighbors. With this Ball finished; he had given the pure Rusk line, a view that he could not in his own heart disagree with more.

De Gaulle, in turn, told Ball he did not agree with anything he had said. China was in no way comparable to the Soviet Union as a power, even the Soviet Union of 1917. It was a nation without real power; it lacked the real base for it, the military, industrial and intellectual resources which even 1917 Russia had. It would have to consolidate its own power and would not be aggressive for a long time. As for Vietnam, he said he understood the problem; France had once held the same illusion and it had been very painful. It would be nice if the U.S. position was correct, but he felt that he knew something about Vietnam; it was a hopeless place. He was obliged to say that he did not believe the United States could win, that the more it put in militarily, the more the population would turn against it. The United States could not force its position by power; rather, it must negotiate. Ball said that this would not be understood in South Vietnam, that if the United States approved a cease-fire, Ho Chi Minh would exploit it. But De Gaulle interrupted him: it was hopeless, and France would not be part of any escalation; the United States would fight alone. Vietnam was a filthy place to fight, France knew only too well. But, he added, as the meeting broke up, France would be glad to serve as a friend any time the United States was looking for negotiations. (In a blunter sequel to this, in June 1966, the Administration sent Arthur Goldberg, once again the dissenter within the government, to France, giving Goldberg strict instructions to tell De Gaulle the American position, but he was under no circumstances to ask De Gaulle's opinion, instructions which fazed neither Goldberg nor, of course, De Gaulle. So Goldberg gave once more the complicated and fragile rationale for American policy, and when he was through, De Gaulle smiled and said, "Are you finished?" "Yes," answered Goldberg. "No one has asked me my opinion, but there are some things I would like to say. First of all, you must pull out," the French leader said. "But won't it go Communist?" Goldberg asked, playing his part. "Yes, it will go Communist," answered De Gaulle. "But isn't that against us?" said Goldberg. "Yes," answered De Gaulle. "But it will be a messy kind of Communism." A hint of racism, Goldberg thought. "Not a Russian or even a Chinese kind of Communism. An Asian kind. It will be more of a problem for them than for us.")

DECEMBER 1964 WAS NOT A HAPPY MONTH FOR THE MAN WHO HAD dispatched George Ball, Lyndon Johnson. There were of course moments of euphoria, when he loved being President as he had enjoyed the landslide. When he was at his most expansive he was as sure as the men around him that the situation in Vietnam could be dealt with, that the men around him were every bit as wise as their biographies claimed, that in fact they knew more about Vietnam than he did, that their confidence was real. He had unleashed the bureaucracy during the entire year; now it had crystallized its positions and he was having trouble keeping up with it. The men around him were responding to what they thought he wanted (plus their own instinct to use force), and he was responding to what they wanted. But he was never at ease, he sensed that it was never going to be as simple as they said, and there were darker moments when the doubts did not go away. He told them to stop the provocative naval acts around the North because, as he said, "I have every right in the world to let Lady Bird and Lynda Bird walk in that park out there"—and he pointed at Jefferson Park—"without fear of being mugged. But that doesn't mean I have to send them out there unescorted at four in the morning." And he could complain to those who came to see him, liberals mostly, that all the Chiefs did was, come in every morning and tell him, "Bomb, bomb, bomb," and then come back in the afternoon and tell him again, "Bomb, bomb, bomb."

He was beginning to wrestle with himself, aware of what escalation might do to his domestic programs, wary of the military's promises, knowing that it might be easier to start than to finish, that it was his record and his Presidency which were at stake, and aware also of the charge that might be made against him if things went sour—that he was soft, and that he had lost a country. His enemies, he knew, were lying in wait out there to turn on him if he went wrong on Vietnam, to destroy him for other reasons. What good would it do, he told friends, not to spend American resources on the war if you lost the war, and in losing the war, lost the Congress? Yet knowing also that if he went ahead he might lose the Congress, too, and might lose the Great Society. He would say to friends, talking about his dilemma, "If we get into this war I know what's going to happen. Those damn conservatives are going to sit in Congress and they're going to use this war as a way of opposing my Great Society legislation. People like Stennis and Gross. They hate this stuff, they don't want to help the poor and the Negroes but they're afraid to be against it at a time like this when there's been all this prosperity. But the war, oh, they'll like the war. They'll take the war as their weapon. They'll be against my programs because of the war. I know what they'll say, they'll say they're not against it, not against the poor, but we have this job to do, beating the Communists. We beat the Communists first, then we can look around and maybe give something to the poor." It was, said a man who was with him that night, eerie listening to him speak, like being with a man who has a premonition of his own death.

So in January it still hung in the balance; the President had decided but was unwilling to put his decision into practice. But there seemed to be consensus: If the South could get itself together they would probably bomb the North; it would be a smaller, almost covert bombing at first and then it would move into the Bundy-McNaughton slow squeeze; the paper work should go ahead, Bill Bundy should start notifying the various interested allies, and Max Taylor should get the South Vietnamese in line, letting them know that if they could shape up we would bomb the North to help them. And so the bombing decision seemed to have been made, made but not committed, and it was one of the marks of the breakdown in the entire decision-making process that because the bombing was going to be an instrument to prevent the use of combat troops, to win the war cheaply, to flash American technology and will without really using them, the decision was a piecemeal one. Lyndon Johnson liked slicing the salami thin, he could slice a decision as thin as any man around, so he and his decision makers sliced this one very thin: they made the decision on the bombing, and only on the bombing, in a vacuum. The subject of the troops, of the inevitability of them if the bombing failed, was rarely discussed. Even the subject of troops for perimeter defense was barely mentioned. It did not come up for a variety of reasons; for one thing it was not a subject that Lyndon Johnson wanted to hear. It made him very uneasy and unhappy and so he did not encourage it, nor did the people around him, like Mac Bundy (who did not necessarily fully understand the inevitability of it). As for the men who should have known better—that one step might well lead to the other, that there was a Rubicon and that with bombing they had to assume that they were crossing it—men like Taylor and the Chiefs, they were in no hurry to bring it up and make the President live with it. They sensed that if the full magnitude of each decision hit him, that the bombing decision might well be a bombing-troop decision, then they might be somewhat less likely to get the first go-ahead (in Taylor's case, talking about troops meant not getting the bombing, which he wanted, instead of the troops, which he did not want; in the case of the other Chiefs, it meant not getting more bombing and more troops). The entire bombing decision was complete and full as far as bombing went, and almost totally unrealistic as far as the true implications went, the implications of getting into a real war. There was an unofficial decision on the part of the principals not to look at the real darkness, to protect the President from what might be considered unpleasant realities, not to ask the hard questions. (If anything there was almost a deliberate attempt to avoid thinking and looking at the larger consequences, and above all of the likelihood of the North Vietnamese reaction, which was quite predictable. In Saigon in early 1965 the CIA completed two massive intelligence estimates on the situation in Vietnam and the possibilities for the future. The man in charge of them for the Agency was an experienced analyst who had spent more than ten years working on the country and who had been consistently prophetic about events. Now in his estimates he predicted that the Vietcong, and in particular the North Vietnamese, had an enormous capacity to escalate if the United States bombed. Not only that, but on the basis of everything known about them in the past, their responses to Western pressure, it was likely that they would use that capability. These estimates were sent back to Washington as part of an overall U.S. mission report, but by the time they left the office of Ambassador Maxwell Taylor, the paragraphs which told of the North Vietnamese response were missing. Thus in effect the mission was in the position of asking for bombing, while concealing comparable estimates that this would expand the war. It was said that an unexpurgated version went back to the CIA.)

So instead of returning to Saigon with a completed bombing package, Taylor had returned with instructions in which Johnson complained about the lack of progress in pacification and instability in the government. The President said that he wanted a "stable and effective" government in Saigon before he moved against the North; this was necessary in the South, he wrote, even if Hanoi cut off its aid to the Vietcong. "Since action against North Vietnam is contributory, not central," he continued, providing a revealing insight into how the government really regarded the problem, "we should not incur the risks that are inherent in such an expansion of hostilities until there is a government which is capable of handling the serious problems involved in such an expansion and of exploiting the favorable effects which may be anticipated from an end of support aid directed by North Vietnam." The President then said the United States would be willing to use minor bombing raids in the Laotian area and sea patrols against the North while the Vietnamese pulled themselves together and stabilized their government. Then, once the government was stable ("firmly in control") and in command, the United States would be willing to start steadily mounting air attacks on the North, and "the U.S. mission is authorized to initiate such planning now with the GVN [Government of (South) Vietnam] with the understanding that the U.S. Government does not commit itself now to any form of execution of such plans."

This explained Taylor's fury two weeks later when Nguyen Khanh and the young Turks, including Air Marshal Ky, dissolved the High National Council, a group of civilian elders, and made a large number of political arrests during the night. The timing could not have been more inauspicious: Washington was finally getting itself revved up; the exact plans for the bombing were being determined; Bill Bundy had flown to New Zealand and Australia to alert them to the fact that the United States intended to bomb (the New Zealand government answered that it did not think it would break Hanoi's will and thought that it would in fact heighten infiltration); Harold Wilson had been briefed (and received the news with less than enthusiasm). Everything finally was falling into place.

All it took was for Max Taylor to hold the line in Saigon to keep the Vietnamese military in line, to get the surface stability which Washington required. And once again the Vietnamese had blown it; they aided their enemies in Washington who said they were not worth American lives, and who said they were not a government, and not a nation and not worth fighting for. Taylor was in a rage; they had, he felt, gone against him personally; he had given his word to President Johnson that he could handle them, provide the stability, thus it was a personal insult. He summoned the young generals and lined them up against the wall in his office. When they tried to sit down, he did not permit it, and they were dressed down like West Point cadets. They were lieutenants at best, these young kids, running around playing at governing a country. All the veneer, the idea that they were really sovereign, had disappeared and he treated them as he really felt, that they were junior officers in a kids' army, and he read them out. "Do all of you understand English? I told you all clearly at General Westmoreland's dinner we Americans were tired of coups. Apparently I wasted my words. Maybe this is because something is wrong with my French because you evidently didn't understand. I made it clear that all the military plans which I know you would like to carry out are dependent on governmental stability. Now you have made a real mess. We cannot carry you forever if you do things like this. Who speaks for this group? Do you have a spokesman? . . ." (The idea of Taylor thinking he could speak like this to the Hanoi leadership is inconceivable and shows the difference between the American view of the South and the North. Air Marshal Ky was furious, later telling friends, "He must have thought we were cadets. I've never been talked to in my life like that. I wouldn't let my father talk to me like that.")

Although they were warned that America would stand for no more, that they could not toy with a great power like this, that American support was becoming more difficult, they did not believe it. They had already learned that the worse things got and the more the Americans threatened them with disengagement, the more the Americans coughed up; that they had sunk the hook deeper into the Americans than the Americans had sunk it into them. As if to convince them that for all the fury, it would be business as usual, Taylor said as they were leaving, "You people have broken a lot of dishes and now we have to see how we can straighten out this mess."

In spite of Taylor's invectives, it had not been completely one-sided; they had talked back to him as well. Later that day a high CIA official came across one of the young officers, General Nguyen Chanh Thi, who seemed to be in a jovial mood, an enormous grin on his face. Why the big grin? the CIA man asked Thi. "Because this is one of the happiest days of my life. Today I told the American ambassador that he could not dictate to us." It was a small sad footnote to the South; the only way genuine anti-Communist nationalism could surface was in talking back to the American ambassador.

THE BRINKS HOTEL WAS ANOTHER AMERICAN SYMBOL IN SAIGON. IT was a bachelor officers' quarters, an American world that Vietnamese need not enter unless of course it was to clean the rooms or to cook, or to provide some other form of service. It stood high over Saigon and its poverty and its hovels, a world of Americans eating American food, watching American movies, and just to make sure that there was a sense of home, on the roof terrace there was always a great charcoal grill on which to barbecue thick American steaks flown in especially to that end. This lovely American symbol was named not for the Dulles policy of toying with war, but for General Francis

Brink, chief of MAAG (the Military Assistance Advisory Group) during the fifties, a man not known for his insight into the new Asia. In the early fifties, while the French war was still going on, there had been an American mission meeting and someone had said that there were increasing reports that the Chinese Communists were giving aid to the Vietminh. And they had all turned to General Brink to see if he had any confirmation, but he didn't seem worried. "I've been in the Far East for much of my life and I worked for Stilwell and there's one thing I know and understand and that's the Chinaman and I've never known the Chinaman to give anything to anybody."

The Brinks being a symbol of the American presence, it was perhaps not surprising that on Christmas eve 1964 the Vietcong planted a bomb there, blowing it up, killing two Americans and wounding fifty-eight others. The incident seemed to those already committed to bombing one more tweaking of the giant's nose; Taylor in particular wanted to retaliate, and so did the Chiefs. But Johnson was still hesitant, particularly about bombing during the Christmas season. He cabled Taylor that he did not want to move against the North unless he was sure that American security was faultless ("I have real doubts about ordering reprisals in cases where our own security seems at first glance to be very weak"). Then he pointed out that he wanted the American mission in greater "fighting trim." He wanted dependents out. And Johnson, the man who felt he could reason with anyone, was unhappy about the political situation in Saigon. Why couldn't we line them up better, and get them on the team? Why did we have this "lack of progress in communicating sensitively and persuasively. I don't believe we are making the all-out effort for political persuasion which is called for. I don't know if we are making full use of the kind of Americans who have the knack for this kind of communication" (which of course infuriated Taylor, who was already fed up with trying to deal with Vietnamese politicians). Then with pressure for bombing and possibly even combat troops constantly upon him, he added:

In regard to recommendations for large-scale bombing: I have never felt that this war will be won from the air and it seems to me that what is much more needed and would be more effective is a larger and stronger use of rangers and Special Forces and Marines or other appropriate military strength on the ground. I am ready to look with favor on that kind of increased American effort directed at guerrillas and aimed at stiffening the South Vietnamese. Any recommendations that you and General Westmoreland make in this sense will have immediate attention from me although it may involve an acceptance of larger American sacrifices. We have been building our strength to fight this kind of war since 1961 and I am ready to substantially increase the number of Americans in Vietnam if it is necessary to provide this kind of fighting force against the Vietcong.

It was an interesting insight into Johnson: the pressure was building on him all the time to bomb, the bureaucracy had reached a consensus, and yet he had not yet joined it; he was a good listener to what George Ball was saying because he believed what Ball was saying, that the bombing would not provide any great answer. So even this late he was dubious about the bombing and he was not recommending combat troops; what he was suggesting was in fact more of the same, more irregular American units trying to stop guerrillas. It was, in effect, a suggestion that they do more of the same, but do it better.

They had turned to the bombing out of their own desperation, because what they were doing no longer worked and because bombing was the easiest thing. It was the kind of power which America wielded most easily, the greatest technological superpower poised against this preposterously small and weak country. ("Raggedy-ass little fourth-rate country," Lyndon Johnson called it during the great debates, complaining to John McCone of the CIA about the lack of information coming out of Hanoi. Wasn't there someone working in the interior of their government who would slip out with a stolen paper saying what they were going to do? "I thought you guys had people everywhere, that you knew everything, and now you don't even know anything about a raggedy-ass little fourth-rate country. All you have to do is get some Chinese coolies from a San Francisco laundry shop and drop them over there and use them. Get them to drop their answers in a bottle and put the bottle in the Pacific . . ." McCone, who was not noted for his sense of humor, sulked for several days.) Since, after Korea, this country was sensitive about ground wars, bombing would not seem like going to war, but combat troops would. Besides, the decision makers were men from the successful areas of American life, they believed in the capacity of American production and technology to satisfy human needs; therefore the deprivation by bombing would have effect. It was particularly hard for them as a group to understand how very little effect something like bombing would have on revolutionary Asian Communist-nationalists, other than to make them more determined. They were all private men, and thus the idea that the 1964 election mandate might be quite different from going to war had very little effect, except on George Ball, and to some degree on Lyndon Johnson.

Chapter Twenty-three

AND SO IT WAS THAT 1964 PASSED, BRINGING LYNDON Johnson to the Presidency on his own as a peace candidate, and now on the brink of going to war. But the bombing allowed them a rationale for thinking that it was not war, it was just bombing, a way increasingly in their own minds, of *not* going to war. Something that would be over shortly and quickly; the use of power to prevent using power. So it was that a subtle thing had taken place over the last year and a half; in their desperation, in their grasping at almost any rationale, anything to do, the principals had turned to the Rostow thesis for bombing, with its built-in reassurances—Rostow, whom they had snickered about earlier, whom they had not really taken seriously. Walt was not exactly a joke, but he was not entirely a serious figure, either, too involved in his own world, always talking about bombing, a zealot in an Administration uneasy with zealotry. Now, with the bureaucracy grasping at straws, Walt was no longer the semicomic, peripheral figure. He was a zealot with an answer, and as such he was about to become, for lack of anyone or anything better, a very influential intellectual—the wrong man at the wrong place with the wrong idea. But it was reassuring that he seemed to have answers, and right then, answers were what they desperately needed.

There was another man who seemed to have answers, and that was Robert McNamara; if we were turning to a technological war, a war which could be fought antiseptically, war without death, then he, the master of this new modernized war machine, was the right man to have there. In January, McNamara once more became the forceful advocate of escalation, of going ahead with the bombing plan, of using force, but not too much force. With Lyndon Johnson still dragging his feet, McNamara set out to convince him that bombing was at least the first answer, McNamara being pushed by the Chiefs, his constituency. He was, after all, not one to turn away from a challenge. The mark of him in government, his imprimatur, was his capacity to say that something could be done, understood, mastered, accomplished. To say that something could not or would not work or that it was beyond the reach of this most powerful nation in the world was to admit not just human frailty, but to fail in a very special and almost terrible way. McNamara hated failure; he had conquered it all his life, risen above it, despised it in others. Besides, and this was later easy to forget, he was very much a part of that era; he had been particularly close to Mac Bundy, the intellectual, and influenced by him. McNamara wanted to win, to move Castro out, to deny Vietnam to the Communists; his speeches warning of the Chinese Communist peril preceded those of Rusk as Administration documents. In discussing Vietnam, he was capable of telling aides that there was something worse than physical enslavement, that there was enslavement of the mind the way the Communists practiced it. He would later shed much of that viewpoint, or at least seem to shed much of it (he carefully fended off questions on what he really thought by pointing out that as head of the World Bank, he had no viewpoints, no politics). Besides, he was already so much of a part of Vietnam's history that it was becoming a large part of him.

So he pushed ahead. Aides remember him in those days busy making the case for escalation, building up the evidence. Even as the bombing decision hung in the balance he assigned two staff men to check on Vietcong torture against Americans. The Vietcong had recently captured two Americans, a captain and a sergeant, and had committed appalling atrocities against them, which was unusual because in the past, atrocities had been used regularly against the South Vietnamese but not against Americans. So in February the two staff men were on the phone to Saigon because McNamara wanted something to present to the President as a means of convincing him to go along with the bombing campaign. The idea was that if there were many incidents like this, the mutilation of Americans, the President would have to react and the American public simply would not stand for it; thus the first soldier becomes the rationale for the second soldier. The word was that this was very important to McNamara and that he wanted every detail, all of it, spare nothing. So the aides spent what was to be the night of the Vietcong attack on Qui Nhon on the phone to Saigon getting all the atrocity information they could, which was very gory. (A few days later, after the Qui Nhon attack, when the President finally made up his mind, the word came down from McNamara that it had been very effective with the President.)

The idea of cutting losses, as George Ball suggested, was unacceptable—so much was already invested, it concerned prestige and honor. Indeed John McNaughton, his chief deputy on Vietnam in 1964 and like his boss a great quantifier, outlined the reasons for going into Vietnam and escalating, and assigned 70 percent not to save dominoes, but to avoid a humiliating American defeat; the second, and in McNamara's eyes—though not Rusk's—less important reason was to keep Vietnam and other adjacent territory from the Chinese, and to that McNaughton assigned 20 percent; and finally the official reason, the one for the high school history books, to aid the South Vietnamese so that they could have a better life was given 10 percent. Westerners, it seemed, were much like the Asians they always talked about; when it came right down to it, they wanted to save face. They could not cut now, the President had been brought this far, and the damage to him and the Administration, though not necessarily the country, if they pulled out and suffered a humiliating loss would be too great.

Bob McNamara was not blindly optimistic (later, after it had all failed, he would tell this reporter that he had always doubted the bombing, that anyone who knew anything about bombing in World War II would be dubious about what it would accomplish, a startling admission from a man who had urged the bombing to the President as forcefully as he did), but it was more likely to work than not. It was worth trying, and if it didn't work out, it could always be stopped. Thus the later frustration of McNamara, who would always favor whatever bombing halt was being proposed, wanting at once to negotiate but unable to give Hanoi terms under which it would negotiate, offering instead terms which for Hanoi meant surrender. But if McNamara had doubts, he was also, much more than Rusk, action-oriented. His instinct was always to do something, to move something, above all to *try* something. Besides, the case study of the Cuban missile crisis was still vivid in his mind and in the minds of the others (he was experienced in crisis management, whereas Johnson was not; a veteran Secretary of Defense, a rookie President); this was the precedent for what they were planning now. They would, as they thought, use power in the same slow, judicious manner as they had during the missile crisis. Not too much, not too little. Signaling clearly and cautiously their intentions (that is, that they did not want to go to war). Rejecting the radicals on both sides ("the wild men waiting in the wings," McGeorge Bundy called them at the time, linking in equal insanity and irrationality those who wanted to get out with those who wanted to obliterate North Vietnam). Being in control of the communications all the way through. Riding herd on the military and keeping them away from all but technical decisions. Which was fine, except that they made one fatal mistake; they forgot that in the Cuban missile crisis it was the *Russians*, not the Cubans, who had backed down. The threat of American power had had an impact on the Soviets, who were a comparable society with comparable targets, and little effect on a new agrarian society still involved in its own revolution. Thus, though they were following the same pattern as they had in the missile crisis, they lacked a sense of history, and what had seemed so judicious before became injudicious in Vietnam. The bluff of power would not work and we would be impaled in a futile bombing of a small, underdeveloped country, an idea which repelled most of the world and increasing numbers of Americans.

When it came right down to it, McNamara had doubts about the bombing in his mind, but those doubts were not reflected in the meetings. He was forceful, intense, tearing apart the doubts of the others, almost ruthless in making his case; those around him were sure that he was being encouraged by the President to do this; he was too much the corporate man to go as far as he did without somehow sensing that this was to be his role. He was, Ball found, quite different in private sessions than in the major meetings where Johnson presided. When Ball prepared paper after paper for Johnson, he would first send them to the other principals, and occasionally McNamara would suggest that he come by and talk the paper over before they went to see the President. Ball would find McNamara surprisingly sympathetic, indeed there seemed to be a considerable area of agreement. Sometimes John McNaughton was present and McNamara would note that McNaughton was in general agreement with Ball, that he had great doubts about the course they were following. So Ball often left feeling that he had made some impression, that he had stirred some doubts in McNamara, that there was the beginning of an area of agreement. But then, in the real meetings, with Johnson present, it would be quite different: McNamara, the ripper now, his own doubts having disappeared, could not afford to lose an argument, or even express partial doubt; partial sympathy for Ball might hurt his own case. So he plunged forward, leaving Ball somewhat surprised and dominated by his force, his control and his statistics. McNamara may have realized that there was an enormous element of chance to what he was proposing, that he was only for it 60–40, but it seemed at the meetings that he was for it 100 percent. There was never anyone better at a meeting; it was a performance, really—programmed, brilliantly prepared, the right points fed in, in just the right way. It was done without emotion, that was a key point, it always seemed so objective and clear; and yet it carried conviction. Conviction and certitude without emotion. When he finished everyone knew what to do. The modern man.

He was extremely tough in those late 1964 and early 1965 meetings. Perhaps bombing wouldn't work, but what was the alternative? Defeat? Humiliation? Withdrawal? "George here," he said, "is exaggerating the dangers. It is not a final act," it could be turned off, pushed up, and it would have effect. It seemed the lowest risk. We had to do something, he said, we couldn't just stand there. We had to act. His statistics on force ratios showed that the South was collapsing (the JCS had told Westmoreland in the fall of 1964 that the material he was sending on the decline in the force ratio—that is, stepped-up enemy infiltration, the massing of Vietcong units, the inability of the ARVN to mobilize—was having a strong effect on McNamara. Please send more, they cabled Westmoreland, they could use it well with him, it was something he understood). So he was carrying the brunt for escalation in January 1965, with Rusk still on the fence, not wanting to get out, but uneasy about going ahead. And Mac Bundy seemed to be siding with McNamara. Although he had been in agreement on the bombing in the past, he was in no sense committed on the issue of Vietnam. He was biding his time, committed on tit-for-tat reprisals but still uncommitted on a real bombing campaign, and in no sense supporting Ball; if anything, quite the reverse.

Up until now McGeorge Bundy had never played a major role on Vietnam, either in the early days, in the Diem period, or during the early debates on bombing. He was not particularly interested in Asia (indeed he would finally give as a major reason for his conversion the need to keep our reputation to back an ally credible with our European friends), and the messiness of Saigon did not appeal to his orderly mind. As the debate on bombing and escalation raged, he had been more of an adjudicator, trying to keep himself out of it to a large degree, trying to present to the President as honestly and coldly as he could the various alternatives and possibilities, and above all, trying to keep the flow going, trying to let the President know when he had to make a decision, when the buffer zone of time was running out, being very operational and functional and not really looking down the long road.

His relationship with Johnson had been improving steadily for about a year. When Johnson first came in, their mix had not been very good at all. Johnson had regarded the White House staff as something of a hostile area, not without cause, since the Bundy group *had* felt a certain contempt, the attitude being: How do you keep him at bay, how do you placate him without telling him anything and without violating the Constitution? The tension from those days had existed after Johnson took over, though in the eyes of the Kennedy people Bundy tried quite hard, in fact a little too hard, to make the transition to Johnson, a transition which demanded extraordinary tests of loyalty, which Johnson took no small pleasure in submitting Bundy to. It was not easy, but Bundy and Johnson had worked out their relationship, Johnson occasionally taking great pleasure in having Bundy work for *him*, delighting in Mac's sheer style. "My intellectual," he called him. And they had both, each needing the other, put aside their distaste for the other's style, Bundy for the rages of Johnson toward subordinates, including occasionally even him, for his making Bundy deliver papers while in an open-door bathroom ("Mac, I can't hear you

. . . Mac, get closer . . . Mac, get in here"), and Johnson for his part put aside, although he never forgot, that Bundy epitomized a breed and tradition which had long felt itself superior to the Lyndon Johnsons of the world.

Now in late January decisions were coming up on Vietnam and time was running out. McNamara and Bundy talked it over and decided it was time to move the President off the dime, and they came up with the idea of a trip to Vietnam by Bundy as the eyes and ears of Johnson. Though the memo suggesting the trip was a Bundy memo, the two of them had worked it out together, both so committed to activism. The memo, which went to Johnson on January 27, 1965 (significantly, right after the inauguration), said that decisions could not be delayed any longer, that the present course could only bring "disastrous defeat." We had to move all-out to negotiations or use more force, and they recommended the latter:

Both of us recognize that the ultimate responsibility is not ours. Both of us have fully supported your unwillingness, in earlier months, to move out of the middle course. We both agree that every effort should still be made to improve our operations on the ground and to prop up the authorities in South Vietnam as best we can. But we are both convinced that none of this is enough and that the time has come for harder choices.

The memo also noted that Rusk did not agree:

What he does say is that the consequences of both escalation and withdrawal are so bad that we simply must find a way of making our present policy work. This would be good if it was possible. Bob and I do not think it is.

So there it was, the activism, the can-do, the instinct to go forward, and the alliance of Mac Bundy and McNamara, operating in tandem to increase their bureaucratic power; two were better than one, they were not alone, and it put the pressure on *Rusk,* who did not like being alone, to accommodate. Their position was thus noticeably strengthened. (Later, as the war progressed, aides to the three men would be appalled by the way the three stayed in touch with each other by phone every afternoon to be sure that each was in the same position, that no one had changed, that they were all still lined up; and in fact, later, after Bundy left and Rostow took his place, Rostow used this as a form of brilliant gamesmanship to keep McNamara on board, to keep him off balance, dangling little bits of new Vietnam information in front of him, the latest body counts, so that McNamara and Rusk both became overwhelmed with Vietnam trivia.) Now he, Bundy, should go out there and take a look. Vietnam doubters who knew Bundy and his instinct to be operational, to use force, and his closeness to McNamara, were not optimistic about the outcome of the trip. Yet it was an important moment within the bureaucracy, for Mac was not considered to have signed on, and it was known that the President was wavering, that Ball was making his stand; perhaps there might be a chance of changing it, what with Mac going there, a man of force but a man of a great intellectual tradition, the dean of Harvard College. He was then still ambitious, and though he would later point out that it had been obvious from the very start that no one could separate Rusk from Johnson, the consensus of those around him was that he believed that he had a chance to be Secretary of State and that it was one of the prime motives in his actions in those days.

At the State Department there was some rancor about the trip, based on the view that if the President wanted his own look he had the entire State Department there to look for him, and on the belief that no one going to Vietnam cold could make any kind of assessment in that hothouse atmosphere, everyone in Saigon lined up to give as intensely as possible the case for escalation. ("Brainwashing," George Romney would call it in 1968, and be immediately jumped on by all sorts of people, like Robert Kennedy, who had been brainwashed themselves and never known it or admitted it.) In addition, the Intelligence and Research people at State were opposed to the trip for reasons of their own; Hanoi, they pointed out in a memo, knew that a bombing campaign was being considered by the Americans and that the Bundy trip was related to it. Thus Hanoi would view the Bundy trip as a real fact-finding trip and would try to influence Bundy's decision by showing that it did not fear bombing, and the way it would do this was by provoking some kind of incident while Bundy was in Vietnam. The same memo noted that of the three places which housed planes, Tan Son Nhut, Bien Hoa and Pleiku, Tan Son Nhut was the most likely to be attacked because it was the most open, and, being in Saigon, would be connected with the Bundy trip. In addition, the memo said, the fact that Soviet Premier Aleksei Kosygin would be in Hanoi at the time was enormously important, since the Russians, in the immediate post-Cuban missile crisis atmosphere, were almost sure to tell Hanoi not to push forward, that it was all too dangerous and they might do well to cool it a little. So an incident would show that Hanoi was not dependent upon Soviet aid, that the Soviets could not dictate to them, particularly since, if the Americans went ahead the way Hanoi sensed they would, and bombed, the Russians would be forced to support Hanoi, anyway.

Events began to move quickly. On February 2 Lyndon Johnson announced that McGeorge Bundy was going to Vietnam for a special review; as a small signal to men within the bureaucracy, John McNaughton, McNamara's trusted aide, would go with him. On the same day, in a news event which seemed unrelated then but would seem somehow linked, years later, Martin Luther King and 770 other civil rights protesters were arrested in Selma, Alabama; 500 more were arrested the next day. On February 4 Lyndon Johnson said he was hopeful of an exchange of state visits with the Russians in the following year. "I believe such visits would reassure an anxious world that our two nations are striving towards the goal of peace." On that day Kosygin left for Hanoi: Bundy was already en route. In Saigon, Bill Depuy, General Westmoreland's closest adviser, briefed the press saying that eight government victories in recent battles with enemy troops in battalion strength should have discouraged the Vietcong from attempting to stand up to government forces in conventional battles. Even then, optimism still lived for the public.

On February 7 the Vietcong struck the American barracks at Pleiku in the Central Highlands; it was a quick, efficient attack, the kind of thing that they specialized in, a mortar attack, nothing unusual really. Considerable planning in advance to be sure the distances were right; no peasants in the area sympathetic enough either to the government or the Americans to warn them. Standard for the war, except that this time it was aimed at Americans. This time they changed it; INR had been right, no one was going to push them around or threaten them. Eight Americans were killed and more than sixty were wounded. (A small footnote to it, and a tip-off to the difficulty of fighting there, would come a month later when Tom Wicker of the *New York Times* asked General Harold Johnson, the Army Chief of Staff, how many men it would take to protect Pleiku *alone* from such attacks in the future. General Johnson mentally figured the size of the perimeter, how many men were needed for static security, how many men to go out into the countryside to patrol. Then he gave Wicker his answer: "Fifteen thousand Americans." For Pleiku alone.) It was exactly what the American mission in Saigon wanted.

The Pleiku hit had come in the middle of the night; when the MACV operations rooms opened up, all the officials, civilian and military, filed in. Titans everywhere, Taylor, Westmoreland, Alexis Johnson. There was so much brass that Alexis Johnson, Taylor's deputy, had so little to do that he wrote the press release, which annoyed the press officer, Barry Zorthian, because Zorthian felt it was poorly done and badly written. Incredible scenes, maps of 1:50,000 of the Pleiku area were pulled down, and there was Taylor with a magnifying glass peering closely at the map, as though looking for the mortar positions. Then a flash of excitement. In walked Mac Bundy, who was usually on the *other* end of the phone in Washington, sympathetic and cool, yet, they always felt, not entirely believing that it was as bad as they said. Now Mac was on their end of the phone. Striding in crisply, asking a few questions, confirming the latest details on the number of men killed. Then it was Bundy who told an aide to get the White House, not Taylor, who was nominally the President's man, but Mac Bundy. "The White House is on the phone, sir." Then sharply, very lucid, Mac took over, wasting no words, very much in control. Retaliation was in order. The attack had been directed specifically at Americans, and not at Vietnamese, thus we had to retaliate. Anything else would signal incorrectly. Clip. Clip. Clip. Let's go.

THE BEST AND THE BRIGHTEST   521

The next day Bundy left Saigon for Pleiku, where he visited the wounded; the scene made a strong impression on him. Those who worked for him and with him were surprised by the intensity of his feeling (as if he had blown his cool); since this sort of thing had been going on for some time, had not Washington realized that there would be killing? Why was he so surprised? It was and would continue to be a rare emotional response; for weeks after when someone questioned what they were doing with the bombing, the words would pour out, boys dying in their tents, we had to do something, we can't just sit by, we had to protect our boys. Even Johnson was fascinated by Bundy's emotional reaction; in the past Johnson had felt Bundy's doubts about Vietnam. He was not like That Other Bundy, as the President called Bill Bundy. The one thing about That Other Bundy—he went through the CIA and his brother Mac didn't. That Other Bundy will take it and ram it in up to the hilt. But Mac won't. Mac spent too much time at Harvard with all those poets and intellectuals while his brother was dealing with men. But after Pleiku it was, Johnson said, like talking to a man next door to a fire who's hollering for help. Later he told Bundy, "Well, they made a believer out of you, didn't they. A little fire will do that." And he went around with some of his other friends in the White House, telling how Bundy at Pleiku reminded him of the preacher's son, very proper and priggish, who had gone to a whorehouse. Later when they asked him he would say: "It's really good . . . I don't know what it is, but I like it . . . It's really good."

At almost the same time that Bundy in Saigon was on the phone to Cyrus Vance in Washington getting Bundy's recommendations to go ahead with a retaliatory raid, Johnson was meeting with the National Security Council, and there it became very clear which way the Administration was headed. Though the subject was not really a prolonged bombing campaign but a one-shot retaliation, there was no doubt that larger issues were also being determined, that it was all coming together and that the great decisions had in effect been made. Johnson, after all, did not use the NSC to determine policy, he considered it too large and bulky and thus too leaky, too many people who talked too much. He used it more as a forum, to inform the rest of the government on which way things were going and signing doubters on (though it had been noted that in the past Adlai Stevenson, who was kept on short rations by both the Kennedy and Johnson Administrations, tended to break the rules by pretending that it was a real meeting and thus arguing too long and too often. Significantly, neither he nor Bill Fulbright was invited to the crucial NSC meetings on the Vietnam escalation in 1965).

Now everyone seemed to agree on a retaliatory strike except Mike Mansfield, who had been invited to the meeting. The Senate Majority Leader had been increasingly unhappy about the prospect of escalation, and now he thought we were edging closer and closer to following in the French footsteps. Did we have to bomb the North, particularly when Kosygin was there? Did we really have to retaliate? Might this not lead to a larger war, possibly a war with China? It might, Mansfield argued, draw China and Russia closer together and heal their growing split. It was certainly going to get us deeper into a war that we all wanted to avoid. Wasn't there something else we could do? Wasn't there some alternative, some negotiation? Even as he finished, the others at the meeting could tell that Johnson had welcomed his dissent; it was a desired part of the scenario because it permitted Johnson to do his performance, which he now did. No, there was no alternative. We had tried to be peaceful, we had tried to disregard provocation in the past, but now it had gone too far. Lyndon Johnson, he said, was not going to be the President of the United States who let Munich happen. Who stood by while aggressors picked on their little neighbors. And he was not going to let these people kill American boys who were out there, boys who were dying in their tents. What would happen to me if I didn't defend our boys; what would the American people think of me, with those boys out there dying in their sleep? It was all flag, and as he spoke the others nodded, and Mansfield nodded, as if he too knew, involuntarily or not, that he had somehow just played the role Johnson had prescribed for him, and that in a sense a curtain was coming down. The decisions had been made, all the questions had been asked, and now the answers were given.

There was one area expert who was present at the last few meetings— Llewellyn Thompson, former ambassador to the Soviet Union and an expert on Russia, and to a far lesser degree on China. He had particularly good credentials with the policy makers because he had given quite accurate advice during the Cuban missile crisis, but he was in no way an expert on Asia or on Vietnam; there was no man with expertise on Hanoi present (an expert on the Soviet Union was tough; but there was no one because of the McCarthy period who was a real expert on Asia—they had been too soft). Thompson himself was wary of the bombing; he had assisted George Ball on some of his memos against such a policy, in particular warning that it might drive the Soviet Union together with the Chinese, and that it was a very dangerous game. Now at the meeting he again expressed his doubts about bombing, but he did say that if we bombed within certain limits, the Soviets would not move against us. Which was all they needed to hear. He also warned against bombing in certain areas which might bring in the Chinese, and along with Ball, he was effective in setting some of the bombing limits. But he did not talk at length about what the North Vietnamese reaction to bombing would be, which was not considered by the White House to be a particularly important question. War meant Russia or China, not North Vietnam. Thompson's advice, which was based on the global balance but not on the particular country involved, would not deter his superiors, and years later he would have a haunting feeling that he should have opposed it more forcefully at the time, somehow weighed in more.

So retaliatory tit-for-tat raids were authorized against the North. The President said that it was a limited strike, but the doors were closing and closing fast. In the *New York Times*, Charles Mohr, the White House correspondent who knew Vietnam well—his honest reporting in the past had precipitated his resignation as a *Time* correspondent in Vietnam—pointed out that the attack was not that unusual. It was not particularly large, a company or less of Vietcong, and there was no noticeable evidence that it was Hanoi and not the Vietcong who had engineered it. Other attacks in the past, Mohr noted, had been just as intense. But his was a lonely voice. Naturally, McNamara carried the ball for the Administration in a press conference:

Q: Mr. Secretary, do you regard this latest incident as perhaps even more serious than the Gulf of Tonkin episode?
A: I think it is quite clear that this was a test of will, a clear challenge of the political purpose of both the U.S. and South Vietnamese governments. It was a test and a challenge, therefore which we couldn't fail to respond to—which neither the South Vietnamese government nor the U.S. government could fail to respond to without misleading the North Vietnamese as to our intent and the strength of our purpose to carry out that intent.
Q: Mr. McNamara, the fact that we struck at South—Southern bases in North Vietnam, are you saying that we know definitely that North Vietnam instigated or participated in this attack on these three places?
A: Captured documents which we have obtained from individuals who have been infiltrated through this corridor plus prisoner-of-war reports that we have obtained in recent months lead us to believe that the volume of infiltration has expanded substantially. The number of men infiltrated in 1964, for example, was twice the number in 1963. This plus other evidence leads us to believe that Hanoi has consciously and purposely stepped up the pressure against the South Vietnamese. And we have every reason to believe, based on our intelligence sources, that the attacks on Pleiku, Tuy Hoa, and Nha Trang was ordered and directed and masterminded directly from Hanoi.

That night the President also spoke. Using what appeared to be imitation Kennedy rhetoric, he said: "We love peace. We shall do all we can in order to preserve it for ourselves and all mankind. But we love liberty the more and we shall take up any challenge, we shall answer any threat. We shall pay any price to make certain that freedom shall not perish from this earth." Which was pretty strong and heady stuff for an attack which was basically little different from any other Vietcong attack over the last four years of the war. As for the increased infiltration, that was all peripheral, the discussions in recent months had not centered on infiltration, rather it had centered on diminishing ARVN and South Vietnamese capacity and will to resist (they had been aware of one North Vietnamese regiment which had crossed over from the

North into the South and which sat poised in the mountains just waiting, but which had not gone into any action).

Even as Johnson and McNamara were speaking, Bundy was winging home from Saigon with his report. It was an important moment; he had been uncommitted in a fluctuating bureaucracy and now the anticipation among the top people was that he was signing on, not just for retaliatory bombing but for a real program. If so, the doors were closing for good. On the way back he worked on the memo with McNaughton. There are, in the annals of Vietnam, thousands and thousands of memos and documents, as the Pentagon Papers would later show. But in an Administration where business was done by phone, they were at best small markers of a long and complicated and sad trail; very few of them had any meaning themselves or were influential at the time they were written—perhaps Nassam 288, which was the only statement of U.S. purposes and objectives, perhaps the Taylor-Rostow report. And the McGeorge Bundy memo from Pleiku. It had effect, it moved people, it changed people at the time. It was by itself a landmark showing how far a bad policy had gone. Starting with the false premise of an irrational China policy, all the brilliant rationalists had built on that, made all the great rational judgments based on one major false original assumption. It was as if someone had ordered the greatest house in the world, using the finest architect, the best stonemasons in the world, marble shipped from Italy, choicest redwood for the walls, the best interior decorator, but had by mistake overlooked one little thing: the site chosen was in a bog.

So it was with Vietnam; they had come all the way down the pike, and now with Bundy, the definitive rationalist, signing on, it would show more clearly than anything in the aborted quality of his arguments. That was one part of it, but more important at the moment was its political impact within the bureaucracy; here was a man with a brilliant sense of which way power was moving and a great capacity to move along with it. So it was a crucial holdout signing on, and in addition, a man who himself was regarded as something of a weather vane. There was one other factor as well: the intensity, almost passion, of the document, the force of it, so unusual in paper work in general and for Mac Bundy in particular. As the Xeroxes of the Bundy memo went to the top level and second level of players, particularly in the Ball group, there was a sinking feeling that it was all over, that the Bundy memo told it all, Mac had come down with the hawks and had come down very hard. Mac Bundy, so quick and facile, so superior, so quick to put down illogic in others, seemed in his Pleiku memo to be a mockery of himself. It was filled with judgments he had little background to make. But most of all was his estimate of the chances for the success of what he was advocating, and the reasons for doing it:

8. We cannot assert that a policy of sustained reprisal will succeed in changing the course of the contest in Vietnam. It may fail and we cannot estimate the odds of suc-

cess with any accuracy—they may be somewhere between 25% and 75%. What we can say is that *even if it fails, the policy will be worth it. At a minimum it will damp down the charge that we did not do all that we could have done, and this charge will be important in many countries, including our own* [italics added]. Beyond that, a reprisal policy—to the extent that it demonstrates U.S. willingness to employ this new norm in counter-insurgency—will set a higher price for the future upon all adventures of guerrilla warfare, and it should therefore somewhat increase our ability to deter such adventures. We must recognize, however, that that ability will be gravely weakened if there is failure for any reason in Vietnam.

In a way the Bundy memo reflected one of the problems of the people in the Kennedy-Johnson Administrations; they always thought that no one else was quite as smart as they were, that they could play games, and that no one else knew the score. They were, it was a failing of the group, too smart by half; for example, the idea that by bombing they would refute the charge that they had not done everything possible for Vietnam; clearly, by bombing and not sending troops they would be doing far less than the maximum, and the military and the Vietnamese knew it; of course there would be cries to do more, to go a little further.

The memo began:

The situation in Vietnam is deteriorating, and without new U.S. action defeat appears inevitable—probably not in a matter of weeks, or perhaps even months, but within the next year or so. There is still time to turn it around, but not much.

The stakes in Vietnam are extremely high. The American investment is very large, and American responsibility is a fact of life which is palpable in the atmosphere of Asia, and even elsewhere. The international prestige of the U.S. and a substantial part of our influence are directly at risk in Vietnam. There is no way of unloading the burden on the Vietnamese themselves, and there is no way of negotiating ourselves out of Vietnam, which offers any serious promise at present. It is possible that at some future time a neutral non-Communist force may emerge, perhaps under Buddhist leadership, but no such force currently exists, and any negotiated U.S. withdrawal today would mean surrender on the instalment plan.

The policy of graduated and continuing reprisal outlined in Annex A is the most promising course available, in my judgment. That judgment is shared by all who accompanied me from Washington, and I think by all members of the Country Team.

The events of the last twenty-four hours have produced a practicable point of departure for this policy of reprisal, and for removal of U.S. dependents. They may also have catalyzed the formation of a new Vietnamese government. If so the situation may be at a turning point.

The prospect in Vietnam is grim. The energy and persistence of the Vietcong are astonishing. They can appear anywhere—and at almost any time. They have accepted extraordinary losses and they come back for more. They show skill in their sneak attacks and ferocity when cornered. Yet this weary country does not want them to win. . . .

One final word. At its very best the struggle in Vietnam will be long. It seems to us important that the fundamental fact be made clear to our people and to the people of Vietnam. Too often in the past we have conveyed the impression that we expect an early solution when those who live with this war know that no early solution is possible. It is our belief that the people of the U.S. have the necessary will to accept and to execute a policy that rests upon the reality that there is no short cut to success in South Vietnam.

What followed then was the Annex, the recommendations for a sustained bombing campaign,

a policy in which air and naval action against the North is justified by and related to the whole Vietcong campaign of violence and terror in the South. . . . [This would be retaliation] against *any* [italics his] VC act of violence to persons or property.

2. In practice, we may wish at the outset to relate our reprisals to those acts of relatively high visibility such as the Pleiku incident. Later, we might retaliate against the assassination of a province chief, but not necessarily the murder of a hamlet official; we might retaliate against a grenade thrown into a crowded café in Saigon, but not necessarily to a shot fired into a small shop in the countryside. . . .

The reprisal policy, he said, should begin at a low level and be increased only gradually, to be decreased if the Vietcong behaved. It foresaw a visible rise in morale in the South if we undertook a sustained bombing campaign, which came to be true. Thus Bundy alone among the bombing advocates actually realized what he had anticipated, though it was an enormous price for a very limited objective.

He had weighed in. He was, above all, the operational functional man, more interested in functions and role than long-range examination and reflection, a doer rather than a thinker; his instinct was to do the nearest and most rational thing as quickly as possible. If anyone was the exact opposite of Chester Bowles (by now ambassador to India), it was Mac Bundy, a marvelous bureaucrat, brilliant at technique, at moving things. They make a move, we make a move. Perhaps he might have gone the other way, and had he opposed the use of force, which would have gone against all his instincts, he might, with Ball, have turned it around. But it would have been a bitter and bloody battle, and it would have been out of character, for he was not, like Ball, a loner, not a man to lay his body down on the railroad tracks for something like this, an almost lost cause, and an almost lost cause in Asia, a land which existed largely not to interfere with the more serious business of Europe. He was a man with a great instinct for power, and he loved it; he responded to where power was moving, trying at the same time to get people to do intelligent, restrained things in an intelligent, restrained manner.

Besides, the idea and the meaning of failure to him and many of the men around him was an almost alien thing. He was so confident in himself, in his tradition and what he represented, that he had no concept about what failure might really mean, the full extent of it; it never really entered the calculations. He and the others had, in fact, all achieved success; they had won awards, climbed in business and academe, each position had brought them higher. They had of course paid the price along the way. Pragmatism had again and again confronted morality, and morality had from time to time been sliced, but it had always been for the greater good of the career. It was the American way, ever upward; success justified the price, longer and longer hours invested, the long day became a badge of honor, and the long day brought the greater title. Success was worth it, and after all, success in the American way was to do well. But the price was ultimately quite terrible. Washington was the company town in the company country where success mattered, and in the end they could not give up those positions and those titles, not for anything. These were the only things they had left that set them apart; they had no other values, no other identity than their success and their titles. The new American modern man was no longer a whole man; it was John McNaughton able to argue against his interior beliefs on Vietnam in order to hold power, McNamara able to escalate in Vietnam knowing that he was holding the JCS back on nuclear weapons, men able to excise Vietnam from their moral framework. So they could not resign; no one decision, not even a war, could make them give up their positions.

In 1964 Stevenson and his friend Clayton Fritchey were talking about government in general and began to wonder how many Cabinet officers had resigned during this century. Fritchey decided to look it up, and then asked Stevenson what his guess was. Stevenson said he had no idea. "One," said Fritchey. "Who?" asked Stevenson. "William Jennings Bryan," answered Fritchey. In Saigon at almost the same time Arthur Sylvester, McNamara's press officer, was arguing with a young *New York Times* reporter named Jack Langguth over the government's lack of credibility in its Vietnam statements. Sylvester said that although it was unfortunate, there were times when a government official had to lie, but that he, Sylvester, as a former newsman, had a genuine objection to lying. Langguth answered that if you had a real objection to lying, you would quit, and the failure to resign meant that you had a soft job where you could exercise power, and that your principles were secondary. Sylvester looked at him almost shocked. "If you believe that, you're stupid and naïve, and you didn't seem that way at lunch earlier today."

MAC BUNDY AND THE OTHERS HAD ALL BEEN PARTNER TO SO PRECIOUS little failure in their lives that there was always a sense that no matter what, it could be avoided, deflected, and this as much as anything else was the bane of George Ball's existence in those weeks. In the debate Ball kept concentrating on the fact that they had no real contingency plans for failure; he warned them how large the price might be, and he kept suggesting that they stop and think, and then, rather than flirt with the enormity of greater input and greater failure, they cut their losses. Ball sensed that if they reached a higher plateau of violence with no tangible benefits, they would be forced to go even higher. Nor was Ball the only one frightened by the way they were plunging ahead, and in early March of 1965, Emmett John Hughes, a former White House aide under Eisenhower, a man who had always been at loggerheads with Dulles and who was now terrified that the Johnson Administration was taking a course in Southeast Asia that Dulles had wanted and Ike had avoided, went to see Bundy, an old friend. Hughes, who like Bundy was a member of the insiders' club, was worried about how much control there was, and he would find little reassurance at the White House. He talked for some time with Bundy, and his questions clearly reflected the enormity of his doubts. "We're just not as pessimistic as you are," Bundy told him. But what, Hughes asked, if the North Vietnamese retaliate by matching the American air escalation with their own ground escalation? Hughes would long remember the answer and the cool smile: "We just don't think that's going to happen." Just suppose it happens, Hughes persisted, just make an assumption of the worst thing that could happen. "We can't assume what we don't believe," Bundy answered, chilling Hughes so much that five years later he could recall every word of the conversation.

At almost the same time Phil Geyelin, a White House correspondent who knew Southeast Asia well, found himself troubled by the same kind of doubts about the direction of American policy and he turned to William Bundy. Did we really know where we were headed? he asked. Did we really know what we would do if the bombing failed, if the other side decided to match our escalation with its own? But Bundy reassured him; he said he had never been so confident about any undertaking before. Vietnam was no Bay of Pigs, Bill Bundy emphasized; he had never seen anything so thoroughly staffed, so well planned. It reeked of expertise and professionalism, it all gave one a great sense of confidence.

LYNDON JOHNSON HAD TO DECIDE. THE PRESSURES WERE ENORMOUS both ways, there was going to be no easy way out. A few friends like Dick Russell were warning him not to go ahead, that it would never work; Russell had an intuitive sense that it was all going to be more difficult and complicated than the experts were saying, but his doubts were written off as essentially conservative and isolationist, and it was easily rationalized that Russell, like Fulbright, did not care about colored people. Besides, Johnson had bettered Russell in the Senate and now here was Johnson surrounded by truly brilliant men (years later when there were free fire zones in the South—areas where virtually uncontrolled air and artillery could be used—which led to vast refugee resettlement, Russell would pass on his doubts about the wisdom of this as policy to the White House, saying, "I don't know those Asian people, but they tell me they worship their ancestors and so I wouldn't play with their land if I were you. You know whenever the Corps of Engineers has some dam to dedicate in Georgia I make a point of being out of state, because those people don't seem to like the economic improvements as much as they dislike being moved off their ancestral land"). But even Russell was telling the President that he had to make a decision, that he had better move, get off the dime, and Russell would support the flag.

Men who knew Johnson well thought of him as a man on a toboggan course in that period. Starting the previous November and then month by month as the trap tightened, he had become increasingly restless, irritable, frustrated, more and more frenetic, more and more difficult to work with. He was trapped and he knew it, and more than anyone else around him he knew that he was risking his great domestic dreams; it was primarily his risk, not theirs. The foreign policy advisers were not that privy to or that interested in his domestic dreams, and his domestic advisers were not that privy to the dangers ahead in the foreign policy. As a politician Johnson was not a great symbolic figure who initiated deep moral stirrings in the American soul, a man to go forth and lead a country by image, but quite the reverse, and he knew this better than most. His image and his reputation and his posture were against him; at his ablest he was a shrewd infighter. Despite the bombast he was a surprisingly cautious man (in guiding the Senate against McCarthy he had been the epitome of caution, so cautious as to not receive any credit for it, which was probably what he wanted, it was not an issue to be out in front on). He was very good at measuring his resources, shrewdly assessing what was needed for a particular goal: was it there, was it available, was the price of accomplishing it too high? He had advised against going into Dienbienphu in 1954, not because he thought there was anything particularly wrong with intervention, but because he felt that immediately after the Korean War the country simply could not absorb and support another Asian land war; indeed, it was the very psychology of exhaustion with the Korean War which had put Eisenhower into office.

Now he was facing fateful decisions on Vietnam just as he was getting ready to start the Great Society. With his careful assessment of the country, he was sure the resources were there, that the country was finally ready to do something about its long-ignored social problems. The time was right for an assault on them, and he, Lyndon Johnson, would lead that assault, cure them, go down in history as a Roosevelt-like figure. He was keenly aware of these resources, and in late 1964 and early 1965 he began to use the phrase "sixty months of prosperity" as a litany, not just as party propaganda to get credit for the Democrats, but as a way of reminding the country that it had been having it good, very good, that it was secure and affluent, that it now had to turn its attention to the needs of others. Yet he knew he would not have the resources for both the domestic programs and a real war, and as a need for the latter became more and more apparent, he became restless and irritable, even by Johnsonian standards irascible, turning violently on the men around him. Those who knew him well and had worked long for him knew the symptoms only too well; it was, they knew, part of the insecurity of the man, and they talked of it often and guardedly among themselves, since they all were subject to the same abuse. Unable to bear the truth about himself if it was unpleasant, he would transfer his feelings and his anger at himself to others, lashing out at Lady Bird, or George Reedy, or Bill Moyers, or particularly poor Jack Valenti, but really lashing out at himself. And so in early 1965 this great elemental man, seeing his great hopes ahead and sensing also that they might be outside his reach, was almost in a frenzy to push his legislation through, a restless, obsessed man, driving himself and those around him harder and harder, fighting a civil war within himself.

He knew it would not be easy, that the bombing was a tricky business, not as tricky as ground troops, there was, after all, an element of control in bombing ("If they [the Air Force] hit people I'll bust their asses," he said at the start) but tricky nonetheless. And yet, and yet. "If I don't go in now and they show later I should have gone, then they'll be all over me in Congress. They won't be talking about my civil rights bill, or education or beautification. No sir, they'll push Vietnam up my ass every time. Vietnam. Vietnam. Vietnam. Right up my ass." Cornered, and having what he would consider the Kennedy precedent to stand in Vietnam, a precedent which Kennedy set, but probably never entirely believed, and with all the Kennedy luminaries telling him to go ahead, even Rusk's uneasiness having been resolved ("He would look around him," said Tom Wicker later, "and see in Bob McNamara that it was technologically feasible, in McGeorge Bundy that it was intellectually respectable, and in Dean Rusk that it was historically necessary"), he went forward. Of course he would; after all, it could be done. He was a can-do man surrounded by other can-do men. If we set our minds to something, we did not fail. If Europeans were wary of this war, if the French had failed, and thus were warning the Americans off, it was not because they had lived more history and seen more of the folly of war, it was because they had become cynical, they had lost the capacity to believe in themselves, they were decadent. We were the first team.

So it all came down to Lyndon Johnson, reluctant, uneasy, but not a man to be backed down. Lyndon would not cut and run, if it came to that; no one was going to push Lyndon Johnson around. Lyndon Johnson knew something about people like this, like the Mexicans back home, they were all right, the Mexicans, but "if you didn't watch they'll come right into your yard and take it over if you let them. And the next day they'll be right there on your porch, barefoot and weighing one hundred and thirty pounds, and they'll take that too. But if you say to 'em right at the start, 'Hold on, just wait a minute,' they'll know they're dealing with someone who'll stand up. And after that you can get along fine." Well, no one would push Lyndon Johnson of Texas around. This was Lyndon Johnson representing the United States of America, pledged to follow in the tradition of Great Britain and Winston Churchill— Lyndon Johnson, who, unlike Jack Kennedy, was a believer, not a cynic about the big things. Honor. Force. Commitments. Who believed in the omnipotence of American power, the concept of the frontier and using force to make sure you were clearly understood, believing that white men, and in particular Americans, were just a bit superior, believing in effect all those John Wayne movies, a cliché in which real life had styled itself on image (paint the portrait of Johnson as a tall tough Texan in the saddle, he had told Pierre Salinger, although he was not a good rider). And in the Dominican crisis he sent word through McGeorge Bundy for Colonel Francisco Caamano Deno, the rebel leader: "Tell that son of a bitch that unlike the young man who came before me I am not afraid to use what's on my hip."

For *machismo* was no small part of it. He had always been haunted by the idea that he would be judged as being insufficiently manly for the job, that he would lack courage at a crucial moment. More than a little insecure himself, he very much wanted to be seen as a man; it was a conscious thing. He was very much aware of *machismo* in himself and those around him, and at a moment like this he wanted the respect of men who were tough, real men, and they would turn out to be the hawks. He had always unconsciously divided the people around him between men and boys. Men were activists, doers, who conquered business empires, who acted instead of talked, who made it in the world of other men and had the respect of other men. Boys were the talkers and the writers and the intellectuals, who sat around thinking and criticizing and doubting instead of doing. There were good boys, like Horace Busby and for a time Dick Goodwin, who used their talent for him, and there were snot noses, and kids who were to be found at the State Department or in the editorial rooms of the Washington *Post* or the *New York Times* using their talents against him. Bill Moyers was a boy who was halfway to becoming a man, a writer who was moving into operational activities. Hubert Humphrey, Vice-President or no, was still a boy, better than most liberals, but too prone to talk instead of act, not a person that other *men* would respect in a room when it got down to the hard cutting; real men just wouldn't turn to Hubert, he didn't have the weight, and so when Humphrey voiced his doubts on Vietnam he was simply excluded from the action until he muffled his dissent.

Now, as Johnson weighed the advice he was getting on Vietnam, it was the boys who were most skeptical, and the men who were most sure and confident and hawkish and who had Johnson's respect. Hearing that one member of his Administration was becoming a dove on Vietnam, Johnson said, "Hell, he has to squat to piss." The *men* had, after all, done things in their lifetimes, and they had the respect of other men. Doubt itself, he thought, was an almost feminine quality, doubts were for women; once, on another issue, when Lady Bird raised her doubts, Johnson had said of course she was doubtful, it was like a woman to be uncertain. Thus as Vietnam came to the edge of decision, the sides were unfair, given Johnson's make-up. The doubters were not the people he respected; the men who were activists were hawks, and he took sustenance and reassurance that the real men were for going ahead. Of the doves, only George Ball really had his respect. Ball might be a dove, but there was nothing soft about him. He had made it in a tough and savage world of the big law firms, and his approach was tough and skeptical. He did not talk about doing good or put Johnson off by discussing the moral thing to do, rather he too was interested in the exercise of power and a real world that Johnson could understand. He was a doer, an activist, and Johnson would tell him again and again, even as Ball dissented, "You're one of these can-do fellows too, George."

Thus the dice were loaded; the advocates of force were by the very nature of Johnson's personality taken more seriously, the doubters were seen by their very doubts as being lesser men. So he would go ahead, despite his own inner instincts, that the rosy predictions were in fact not likely to be so rosy, that it was likely to be tougher and darker, that George Ball's doubts had a real basis. The thrust to go forward was just too great. Everyone else seemed so convinced of America's invincibility. Even Ball, arguing at the time that it was the right moment to cut our losses, sensed this feeling of American invincibility and will, and would write that by negotiating out, the United States could become a "wiser and more mature nation." But those lessons would have to come the hard way; there were too few restraints. All the training of two decades had been quite the reverse. They had come to the end of one path. They were cornered by bad policies on Asia which they had not so much authored as refused to challenge, both in the fifties when out of power, and in the sixties when in power. And so now they bombed. They did this in place of combat troops, and they believed that it would not last long, perhaps a few months.

A few days later, after the bombing campaign had begun, a White House reporter came across Bundy in the White House barbershop. Bundy was sitting there being lathered, and since he could not easily escape, the reporter thought it was a good time to ask Bundy something that had been bothering him since the incident. "Mac," he said, "what was the difference between Pleiku and the other incidents?"

Bundy paused and then answered, "Pleikus are like streetcars" (i.e., there's one along every ten minutes).

IF ANYTHING, DOUBTS ABOUT PLEIKU AND THE BOMBING, DOUBTS expressed clearly and forcefully, helped remove one other dovish voice from further participation, and that was the Vice-President of the United States, a man whom the liberals had eagerly accepted during the convention as *their* representative in the Administration. The Vice-President, it quickly turned out, was not his own man; no Vice-President is, but the Vice-President under Lyndon Johnson was doomed to be even less so. Lyndon Johnson had always viewed Hubert Humphrey as something of a convenience, to be used at times for his own and the country's greater good, but the special kind of respect that Johnson held for either Dick Russell or Robert Kerr was missing. Johnson was simply too powerful, too forceful for the weaker, pleasant Humphrey, and Johnson was very aware of this. The political career of Humphrey before 1964 had a good deal of the taint of Lyndon Johnson to it. It was Johnson who had legitimized Humphrey the outsider into a Senate insider. The Humphrey presidential campaign in 1960 had more than a little Johnsonian touch, a split between the genuine pro-Humphrey people under Joe Rauh, and the stop-Kennedy Humphrey-Johnson people under Jim Rowe; and now Humphrey had finally reached national office entirely because of Lyndon Johnson's decision.

Those around Humphrey, and there were a good many of them, who thought the Johnson-Humphrey relationship was almost completely one-sided, Johnson using Humphrey on Johnson's terms, would not be disabused of their notion by the new relationship; it would soon become clear that Johnson had no intention of protecting Humphrey from that special misery he had suffered as Vice-President, but rather intended to pass it on in even greater doses. Rarely would a high public official undergo the humiliation and virtual emasculation that Humphrey underwent as Vice-President, almost, it seemed, from the very start. In November 1964, two months before taking office, Humphrey had given a speech in New York on education and departed from his text, carried away by his own enthusiasm, giving the impression that perhaps Humphrey would be the architect of the Administration's education policies. Johnson was furious; this was his terrain and Humphrey was told this in no uncertain terms. Just so there would be no mistake about it, Johnson called in the White House reporters who were with him on the Ranch and told them, "Boys, I've just reminded Hubert that I've got his balls in my pocket." There would be additional reminders to come.

Humphrey was an old-fashioned domestic liberal and he had never been a real believer in the Cold War. He had accommodated to some degree, particularly in 1954 when he was frightened by the McCarthy sentiment in the land, and he had sponsored the Communist Control Act, but generally he had been in the Eleanor Roosevelt–ADA soft-line position, pushing disarmament and trying to limit the arms race. Those instincts, that peace was something you worked for politically, were with him in early 1965 as the Administration edged toward war. At the time of Pleiku he was called in for one of the smaller meetings, and he expressed himself forcefully, perhaps too forcefully, it would seem in retrospect, against the bombing, particularly bombing when Kosygin was in Hanoi. There was a certain candor and force to his presentation and he would soon live to regret it; from then on he was kept on extremely short rations by the President. Washington, of course, is a tough and gossipy town; everyone knows who is and who is not going to meetings, who is and who is not in on the inner-memo traffic. When a man is moved outside the flow, it is fatal, everyone else avoids him, fearing the stigma may be contagious; what starts as a partial isolation soon becomes almost total. From the time of his dissent on Pleiku, Humphrey was not invited to meetings, not informed of important memos or the drift of the policy. He was, in effect, frozen out. His staff, already small, would scurry around Washington trying to pick up the play on Vietnam for him. In April, Humphrey's aides heard that there was a National Security Council meeting on Vietnam and wondered if their man would be invited. Humphrey told them to find out, so an aide placed a call to Bromley Smith, who ran the NSC meetings. Was Humphrey invited? A good question, said Smith, but he didn't know, he would ask Mac Bundy, who said he didn't know but he would ask the President, which he did. Johnson was furious and answered Bundy at his scatological best, goddamn it, couldn't he have a secret goddamn meeting without every goddamn person in town knowing about it and wanting to get in.

So Humphrey was stained, and it was not a good stain; every one of the other principals, wanting to keep their effectiveness and credibility with this tempestuous President, knowing his vagaries, became wary of being seen with Humphrey; he had become a cripple and everyone else knew it. When Humphrey's people heard in the early months of 1965 that George Ball was making a major stand against the war, they had thought it might be a good idea if Ball and Humphrey got together, since they were both working in the same general area. So a staff aide of Humphrey's named John Rielly approached George Springsteen, who was Ball's aide, and it would shortly become clear that the Ball people did not want Humphrey involved; his assistance was not, so to speak, an asset. And Humphrey remained cut off and isolated, and in July, when they made their fateful decisions, the men would file out of the NSC room and the White House photographers would take their pictures and everyone would be there, it seemed, including Leonard Marks of USIA, Horace Busby, Dick Goodwin, Jack Valenti. Everyone but the Vice-President of the United States.

It was not just humiliation on Vietnam which was vested upon Humphrey, but it appeared in many other forms as well. There was the time when Johnson was cruising on the Potomac in his presidential yacht, and when he saw Humphrey entertaining reporters on his yacht, Johnson had his captain call up Humphrey's captain demanding to know who was on board. Thereafter, by a new rule, Humphrey could not take out a yacht without first clearing it with Marvin Watson, who was in charge of important matters like that. Nor could Humphrey use one of the many planes available to the White House without his air attaché first writing a memo to Johnson's air attaché requesting the plane; Johnson's air attaché would then pass the memo to Marvin Watson, who would write a memo for Johnson's overnight box requesting the President's approval. Such is the treatment of Vice-Presidents by former Vice-Presidents. All of this eventually had enormous effect on Humphrey. He was not a particularly strong person to begin with, and there was always in him a desire to please everyone around him, often at the expense of intellectual honesty, almost too much enthusiasm, and so now he would get on board. The way to come on board would be to sell the war to his liberal constituents, or failing that, at least to fend them off, to neutralize their liberal voices with his liberal voice. So in late 1965 and early 1966 he made his way back on the team.

In 1966 he was assigned a trip to Asia (again in a particularly humiliating way. It was a two-and-a-half-week trip and he was given twenty-four hours' notice, no chance to prepare, barely a chance to get his various vaccinations). Jack Valenti was sent along as liaison man with the White House, to keep an eye on the Vice-President, to call Johnson every day and to bring the President's instructions to Humphrey, which were, of course, quite simple: optimism, the President wants optimism. The trip was a disaster, too long, too little staffing, too few briefing papers, too little sleep (at one point Humphrey signed an agreement with the Thai government which went way beyond the State Department's own positions in giving the Thais an American military commitment), but the worst part was Humphrey's final statement and report on the mission. Johnson had told Humphrey that he wanted a report which would brand China as *the* aggressor throughout Asia, a report which, in the President's words, would "nail Fulbright, Mansfield and the *New York Times* editorial board to the wall." The report, as Humphrey projected it in front of his staff, in one long and disastrous meeting, would say he had visited all the countries of Southeast Asia and there was only one source of aggression in Asia and it was Peking, and it was the same in Vietnam, Thailand, India, Malaysia and the Philippines. He had known Communists since he was mayor of

Minneapolis and they were all alike and they didn't change. But some of his aides were doubtful at best of the wisdom and accuracy of this particular statement, and one of them, Bowles's disciple James Thomson, who was the son of a China missionary and a young man who had been working for a more realistic policy, strongly dissented. The statement, Thomson said, simply wasn't true. As Thomson dissented, some of the other staff people backed him up; it was in effect the Humphrey staff, having lost their own man, now trying to stand up to the Johnson policies. But Humphrey had not slept for two days and it all came unwound; he lost control and started shouting that Thomson had organized a cabal against him; well, he knew what was going on, he knew about Communists, they came at you from many directions, and sometimes they came at you from behind, like Jim Thomson. It was not his finest moment; his staff was shocked.

Chapter Twenty-four

THE DECISION TO MOUNT A SUSTAINED BOMBING CAMPAIGN was not made until February 13, 1965, two days after the Vietcong had launched yet another attack on the U.S. barracks at Qui Nhon. The significant thing about the bombing campaign, this decision which had taken so long, involved so much planning and in which the principals thought they had been so judicious, was that it had been kept completely separate from the decision on combat troops; it was to be an entity in itself. But in their hearts the military knew better, and this was a crucial lapse. As such, this differed sharply from the decision making in 1954, when the Army staff had cast doubts about U.S. aerial intervention in Indochina.

In 1954 Army Chief of Staff Matthew Ridgway had made one thing abundantly clear to his superiors as the pressure mounted for air strikes to relieve the French garrison at Dienbienphu: that air power and ground power could not be separated. Indeed, he emphasized, and it was an important word—*emphasized*—that if air power was used and failed, as he felt it almost certainly would, then the stakes would be greater, and ground power would be necessitated. He noted that if air power was used, ground troops would have to take Hainan Island and keep the Chinese MIGs off the back of the Seventh Fleet (as in 1965 the use of air power would mean that air bases in the South would be extremely vulnerable to increased and intensified retaliation). In 1965, as the pressure built up for the use of bombing, no one made the comparable case. Ridgway, it would turn out, was the exceptional man. In 1965 each branch of the service did its thing, the Air Force programed air power, the Army ground power, the Navy wanted aircraft-carrier roles. Of the generals there was no towering figure like Ridgway, so secure in his reputation as a combat leader to stand up to a President as overpowering as Johnson and make him live with the price. Earle Wheeler was a good staff officer, intelligent, a good bureaucrat, but he was no Ridgway. The one general who might have had comparable prestige, Max Taylor, was wearing civilian clothes, and his cables during that period were careful to separate bombing from ground troops, the reverse of what Ridgway had done some ten years earlier.

Now, in 1965, the bombing campaign was going ahead under the name of Rolling Thunder; it was, in the minds of most of the civilian principals, designed to make the other side negotiate, and thus avoid combat troops; but in the intelligence community the men most knowledgeable about Vietnam knew that it would not work even to this degree, and that the very incidents which had finally provoked it, the bombings, Pleiku and Qui Nhon, were a sure sign from the North that Hanoi would never capitulate, never negotiate in the face of bombing pressure. Thus the very acts which helped initiate the bombing were evidence from the other side that the avowed purpose of it would not work. But it would, the principals thought, stave off the use of troops. On February 22, nine days after the decision to go ahead on a bombing campaign, General William Childs Westmoreland, the commander of U.S. forces in Vietnam (COMUSMACV, in military parlance, or *Commander US Military Assistance Command, Vietnam*), sent in a request for two U.S. Marine corps to provide security for the U.S. air base at Danang, the base from which more and more raids against the North (and the Vietcong in the South) were being launched.

It was a small request, just two battalions, and the mission was minor too, simply to provide security. But it was the beginning; it was the first time American combat units would arrive as units, and there was a sense among many in Washington and Saigon at the time that it was not the end either in numbers or in the extent of the mission, that both would soon be expanded, and that the man who had ordered the troops knew this better than anyone. And they were right. But it was a very small request, and it had to be done. In Hawaii, Admiral U.S. Grant Sharp of CINCPAC pushed the Westmoreland request with particularly well chosen words, words designed to drive fear into any serious, concerned civilian, that the troops be delivered to Westy as quickly as possible "before the tragedy," as he put it, and Washington quickly acceded, though there were doubts. Slipping in the first troops was an adjustment, an asterisk really, to a decision they had made principally to avoid sending troops, but of course there had to be protection for the airplanes, which no one had talked about at any length during the bombing discussions, that if you bombed you needed airfields, and if you had airfields you needed troops to protect the airfields, and the ARVN wasn't good enough. Nor had anyone pointed out that troops beget troops: that a regiment is very small, a regiment cannot protect itself. Even as they were bombing they were preparing for a new rationale, the protection of our men and matériel, which meant the arrival of our boys, which of course would mean more boys to protect our boys (and later greater bombing of the North to protect our boys, who were of course there originally to protect the airfields). The rationale would provide its own rhythm of escalation, and its growth would make William Westmoreland almost overnight a major player, if not *the* major player. This rationale weighed so heavily on the minds of the principals that three years later, in 1968, when the new thrust of part of the bureaucracy was to end or limit the bombing and when Lyndon Johnson was willing to remove himself from running again, he was nevertheless transfixed by the idea of protecting our boys. During that month of agonizing review he would call in General William Momyer, commander of the 7th Air Force in Vietnam, and ask him if he—and the boys—could live with it. Would it endanger American lives? Momyer answered yes, he could live with it. But Johnson was not satisfied, it was a delicate issue and one which weighed heavily on his conscience, and so once more he would personally summon General Momyer and ask, "Can you live with it?" and once more General Momyer said he could live with it and the boys could live with it, and Lyndon Johnson nodded. But he was still bothered, and a third time he would ask General Momyer if he could live with a bombing halt, and for the third time General Momyer would say yes, he could. These things, set in motion, were much harder to stop and turn around than anyone had imagined.

That airfields would need troops for protection was no surprise to William Westmoreland; he had in fact for some months been quite convinced that American combat units would be needed to save Vietnam from the Communists, and he thought the war was going quite badly. In February and March 1965 he was considerably more pessimistic than his old friend Max Taylor; he thought the war was in the South and thus the answers, and victory, were to be found in the South. He had no confidence at all in the ARVN despite the lip service his command continued to pay toward the optimism invented in earlier and more euphoric days. In fact, he had started the planning on the needs of the combat troops in 1964. The embassy's chief political officer, Max Taylor, had said that the bombing would bring political benefit, and so Westmoreland, who was not a presumptuous man (Max was, after all, astute politically and Westy was not), was quite willing to go along with the Taylor judgment. But he had a feeling deep down that this was a minor decision, a stop-gap measure when the gap had already passed, a gesture to the civilians as much as anything else, and so he continued with his own contingency planning for American ground troops. He was not rushing anyone, not pushing anyone; he knew it was a sensitive problem for civilians. He would recall the night of Pleiku with a certain detached amusement, the excitement of the civilians there ("George McBundy, he was a big hawk then," he would say later); McNamara staying up all night in his office in Washington awaiting the outcome. Rostow, they told him, had gone around with all the control officers that night talking to them excitedly, emotionally. The civilians, he had thought at the time, were taking this all very seriously, and they were much more optimistic about what this might bring. If you knew anything about the military, you knew this was only a token thing, simply showing that the U.S. was getting ready. Rolling up its sleeves to do a job. Not the last time, he thought, that the civilians were naïve about what the military might accomplish.

As early as August 1964, after Tonkin, Westmoreland had asked for security troops for Vietnam and for the beginning of a logistical command. He had wanted one Marine battalion at Danang for security reasons; the 173rd Airborne Brigade (then stationed at Okinawa) in the Tan Son Nhut–Bien Hoa area, also for security; and in addition, he wanted an Army Engineer group and Signal Corps units which would anticipate a larger build-up if necessary. The Army Engineer group included three or four battalions, plus specialized engineering companies, some of them for ports, some for airstrips. Westmoreland was even then trying to get them into the country to prepare the inner logistic base for combat troops eventually coming ashore. Since the engineers weren't provided, in mid-1965, when the combat troops did start arriving, the logistical component was not ready; instead of the petroleum being pumped in by an underwater pipe line already laid down by the engineers, the 55-gallon drums had to be hand-lifted to shore or carried over with a crane shovel.

Westmoreland had also asked for three Hawk antiaircraft battalions for the Danang and Bien Hoa areas, in case the North Vietnamese responded to American air attacks by bombing the South. A brief by-play immediately took place which was to reflect the sharply differing attitudes toward American combat involvement. In Washington, considerable debate ensued over the Hawk battalion, and on November 14, 1964, the Joint Chiefs directed deployment. Ambassador Taylor, however, recommended against it, fearing that it would begin Americanizing the war. When, on November 25, CINCPAC recommended landing the Hawks, it appeared that they would arrive after all, but then, in early December, Taylor was back in Washington again recommending that they hold back the Hawk battalion and divert it to Okinawa; once again deployment was stopped. Now with the approval of the Marine battalion landing teams, the Hawk battalion was finally approved for Danang. At the same time, in mid-August 1964, when Westmoreland made his recommendations for new security troops, he also told Admiral Sharp at CINCPAC in a cable that although the United States knew that the air strikes were a reaction to a specific provocation, in the eyes of the North Vietnamese they were overt attacks. If, he said, the other side responded, it would respond on the ground. "Even if they don't take action now, they will later on, in response to escalation on our part and they are preparing the capability for it." Then he listed the three possibilities for North Vietnamese reaction. The first was an overt attack across the DMZ, which he said was unlikely because of the exposure to major air attacks. The second was an increased pattern of infiltration, and a major step-up of Vietcong activity in the South. This, he said, was likely, but probably not enough to satisfy Hanoi's desire for reprisal. The third, he said, was infiltration of North Vietnamese divisions. This could lead to a sudden attack on Danang or Hué. The Vietnamese general staff, he said, thought this was most likely. For the moment, Westmoreland said, there was no specific intelligence that they were infiltrating divisions, but he certainly gave them the capability.

It was a very important cable, this one from Westmoreland to CINCPAC, because it showed that he knew that there would be a North Vietnamese reaction to bombing. It was not something the mission pushed upon Washington, it did not want to scare Washington out of the war, but it was something that the American military were aware of but not frightened by. For all the evidence that the Vietcong gave of their combat toughness, and for all the abundant evidence of the ferocity and professionalism (and size) of the North Vietnamese army, there was a certain Caucasian arrogance about the Vietnamese ability, a belief that when pitted against American troops, the Vietnamese would have to cave in, that American troops with their fire power, with their air support, their helicopters, would simply be too much. The arrival of the first team would do it. The principals simply could not understand the leavening influence of the terrain, the jungle, the paddies, on their modern fire power, thus stripping away the greatest advantage the Americans had, nullifying all the hardware, making even the helicopters a limited weapon (and cruelest of all ironies, coming up with a basic infantryman's weapon, the Chinese-made AK-47, which worked better under extremely difficult conditions and jammed less frequently than the basic weapon carried by the Americans). Thus, with technology stripped away, were the Americans that impressive? Would they be braver, more willing to die than their enemies, who were leaner, less expectant of what life was going to give them, easily as well led, and above all *Vietnamese*?

This came later. In the beginning the belief in our superiority was a part of Westmoreland's attitude, and it was even more a part of the key general who was one of his chief advisers during those crucial months, Bill Depuy, one of those men who played a major role all through Vietnam and were virtually unknown to the public. Depuy was one of the Army intellectuals. Very bright, considered by most civilians in the Pentagon the brightest general they had ever met. He was not like other generals in his background. Unlike them, he made for a long time a point of living off-post in Washington, in the nice Cleveland Park area, far from the incestuous inner world of Army generals and Army wives talking of who was doing what to whom; but a better residence from which to meet important civilians and influence them. He had been in the CIA for some time, and he had been brought to Vietnam by Dick Stilwell, another of the Army intellectuals who had served in the CIA. Depuy had risen rapidly, he had made it with Westmoreland, and quickly become his most trusted adviser on strategy. He was a formidable figure, tiny but cocky and imperious as if to make up for that lack of height (when he finally got a division, in Vietnam, the 1st Infantry, a pick division, he made a fetish of firing his battalion commanders and company commanders, replacing them with his own men—public relief of command it was, and it was very controversial. Army Chief of Staff Harold Johnson, a conservative traditionalist, thought it was criminal; but it was considered part of Depuy's style, his toughness: *Don't mess with Depuy*). He was a skilled bureaucrat, an effective military politician and he was extraordinarily important in the early planning of the American ground strategy (search and destroy was as much his strategy as it was Westmoreland's).

In late 1964 he was probably the most pessimistic of the generals about the capacity of the ARVN to hold on without American troops, but he was also one of those most confident about the capacity of American troops to fight there. John Vann would later recall that when Depuy took over the 1st Division, Vann and a few senior Vietnamese officers tried to advise him a little about the background of the fighting and the Vietcong. But Depuy was not interested, no one who had been associated with the past, flawed as it was, could teach him anything. He told the old-timers in effect, Just stay out of my way and I'll show you how it's done. He believed that massive fire power and American mobility were the answer, that the enemy simply could not stand up in the face of it. Eventually, like others before him, he would learn how tough the enemy was, and by the end of his tour as a general his strategy was a good deal less aggressive. He had a tendency to establish contact and then pull back his troops and pound the area with air and artillery, a tactic which lowered his own losses, increased civilian casualties and led to vastly inflated casualty claims. This attitude—the awe of the new technology, the new mobility—existed in Washington as well as Saigon. McNamara still believed that the new technology could affect the war in a decisive way, and so did Rostow. Rostow was in fact particularly enthusiastic about it, and Lou Heren, the correspondent for the London *Times*, would recall being at a dinner with Rostow when the key decisions were being made in 1965, and Rostow spouting both his enthusiasm and his ratios. Normally, explained Rostow, the ideal ratio against guerrillas was 10 to 1, a figure which the United States would not be able to meet. But there were factors of fire power and of mobility, and each was given a factor of 3. Thus one needed only a ratio of 4 to 1. Heren, who had spent long years covering the war in Malaya, explained that it was not a war but a police action which the British had fought there; had there been bombings and use of tanks, the British would have lost the population, and thus lost the war. Heren would remember Rostow sneering at him. Heren was old-fashioned, he said, too much like the now departed Hilsman. He did not understand the new strategy, the new mobility. That atmosphere prevailed in many quarters, a belief in American industrial power and technological genius which had emerged during World War II. Later there would be a phrase for it. Fulbright, who was appalled by it, would call it "the arrogance of power." We had power and the North Vietnamese did not; besides, they were small and yellow.

In February 1965, as the bombing started, Westmoreland was ready and eager to get on with the job of getting troops in, a job he had, like any top general, readied himself for and a job which turned him from an adviser to a commander, a change which he naturally welcomed and which would change the balance once and for all in Washington, where the government was still more divided than it seemed, and where the sending of combat troops was still an idea so chilling that it was deemed the best way to handle it was never to mention it. A *commander*. A commander changed the balance automatically, a commander who said he needed this many men, had to have them, could not vouch for the safety of the men under his command otherwise, who said he could not do the job otherwise. An ambassador you could argue with, a member of the Joint Chiefs you could argue with and turn down. An Undersecretary of State was important, but if rejected, there was no political damage. But a commander was something else, he was your man in combat who was responsible for your boys, and if turned down, it might be politically explosive (Westmoreland never received command for the entire theater, in part because of the military's own bureaucracy, in part because Lyndon Johnson had not forgotten about Douglas MacArthur, aware of a commander who becomes too big, too famous, who challenges his Commander in Chief). So a commander changed the balance; and if a President wanted to make sure that he did not have to send troops, then he had to be very careful in his choice of commander and in his instructions to that commander.

THE BALANCE CHANGED FIRST IN SAIGON, WHERE TWO DISTINGUISHED generals, old friends, had worked side by side in 1964, even though one of them, Max Taylor, was in civilian clothes. But civilian clothes or no, there was never any doubt in 1964 who was the senior U.S. official in Saigon; it was Max Taylor, with no visible stars, friend and confidant of two Presidents, former

Chairman of the JCS. And though Taylor was extremely sensitive about not dominating Westmoreland, careful to consult him on all decisions, it was Taylor who controlled the mission, and most important of all, controlled its estimates. And though in 1961 he had rather cavalierly suggested the sending of combat troops, with their mission singularly poorly defined (on the apparent assumption that once there, they would simply stand as a symbol and not have to fight anyone), he had, in the year he spent in Vietnam as ambassador, become increasingly nervous about the role of combat troops, knowing this time that if they arrived they would have to fight, and that this would be a cycle hard to stop. Now, even as he was endorsing the bombing, he was trying to stop the troops, and despite an old and abiding friendship he was by February 1965 in considerable conflict with Westmoreland.

It was symbolic that Taylor, who had been the top civilian and who saw himself as controlling the U.S. decisions in Vietnam, would day by day in March and April lose control while Westmoreland, CINCPAC and the JCS began to make more and more decisions; the thrust and initiative went to them, and as Taylor declined in influence, Westmoreland rose. It was symbolic, for it told a larger story of how the civilians, all of whom were sworn to control events and to control the military, had lost control, except in effect to slow down and partially limit the military, and how the play had gone over to the military. For in those months, despite the efforts of Max Taylor, who, having been a major advocate of bombing, would surface as a major brake against ground forces, there would be a struggle over both the number of troops and the mission for them, and the latter, almost more important than the former, was gradually expanded in three phases, from security (the simple protection of air bases) to an enclave theory (which would put U.S. forces in coastal bases and allow them a certain limited initiative against the enemy), until finally the aggressive Westmoreland-Depuy strategy of "search and destroy" evolved in mid-1965. As far as Washington was concerned, it was something they slipped into more than they chose; they thought they were going to have time to make clear, well-planned choices, to decide how many men and what type of strategy they would follow, but events got ahead of them. The pressures from Saigon for more and more men would exceed Washington's capacity to slow it down and think coolly, and so the decisions evolved rather than were made, and Washington slipped into a ground combat war.

But it was not something that the military in Saigon slipped into; the planning of troops, the need for them and how to use them was something that had long been in the contingency planning stage, and now, slowly, MACV was moving toward it, careful not to ask for too much too soon lest it scare the White House; in fact, CINCPAC was far more aggressive than Westmoreland in the early days; Westy was asking for small units and the JCS was asking for three divisions, a figure far larger than the commander dared ask for, fearing that it might blow the whole thing. In April the military arm of MACV was asked to do an estimate for Westmoreland on the enemy capacity for reinforcement; when the assignment was given, no one knew what the answer would be. But when Colonel William Crossen, one of the top intelligence officers, put it together he was appalled: the number of men that Hanoi could send down the trails without seriously damaging its defenses at home was quite astonishing. The North was very small but turned out to have a very large army. When Crossen came up with his final figure he could not believe it, so he checked it again, being even more conservative in the use of enemy figures, and still he was staggered by what he found; the other side had an amazing capacity and capability of reinforcing. When he brought the study to Westmoreland's staff and showed the figure to a general there, he looked at it and said that it was impossible. Not impossible at all, answered Crossen, checked and double-checked. "Jesus," said the general, "if we tell this to the people in Washington we'll be out of the war tomorrow. We'll have to revise it downward." So Crossen's figures were duly scaled down considerably, which was a good example of how the Army system worked, the staff intuitively protecting the commander from things he didn't want to see and didn't want to hear, never coming up with information which might challenge what a commander wanted to do at a given moment. Because the Westmoreland staff in February, March and April of 1965 knew that he wanted to get in the ball game with combat troops, it did everything carefully, never getting ahead of itself. The design was in private, if the truth were to be known, rather grand, but Lyndon Johnson was a great salami slicer, and no one was smarter than Westmoreland at knowing how much salami to order at a given time, how much he would be allowed to carry home.

It all unfolded as if on cue. Westmoreland had dispatched his deputy, General John L. Throckmorton, to Danang to survey new security requirements for the expanded air base. Not surprisingly, General Throckmorton found the Vietnamese unequal to the task (the very same generals a few months earlier, if questioned about the capacity of the Vietnamese to secure bases, would have replied that of course they could have handled it) and recommended that the entire Marine Expeditionary Brigade be sent to Danang. At first the military had intended to call them the Marine Expeditionary Force, but the civilians in the embassy, somewhat more sensitive to the nuances of the country, had suggested that since the French had been known as the French Expeditionary Forces, it might be wiser to call the American force the Marine *Amphibious* Force. Westmoreland, somewhat more cautiously, cut the request back to two battalion landing teams instead of three. Thus, if approved, it would mean 3,500 more Americans in Vietnam; there were already about 20,000 Americans in the country, but none in a combat battalion unit. They would be used for security, and that only.

It was at this point that Taylor voiced the first of a series of objections. On February 22 he cabled back to Rusk, his reservations beginning:

As I analyze the pros and cons of placing any considerable number of Marines in areas beyond those presently assigned I develop grave reservations as to wisdom and necessity of so doing. Such action would be step in reversing long-standing policy of avoiding commitment of ground combat forces in South Vietnam. Once this policy is breached, it will be very difficult to hold the line. If Da Nang needs better protection, so do Bien Hoa, Tan Son Nhut, Nha Trang . . .

Then, he noted, the sending of U.S. troops would almost surely see a decrease in responsibility on the part of the Vietnamese and encourage the instinct to let the Americans carry even more. It would not, he thought, release many ARVN troops for other duties. In addition, he was uneasy about the political problems of the war:

White-faced soldier, armed, equipped and trained as he is, not suitable guerrilla fighter for Asian forests and jungles. French tried to adapt their forces to this mission and failed; I doubt that U.S. forces could do much better . . . Finally there would be ever present question of how foreign soldier would distinguish between a VC and a friendly Vietnamese farmer. When I view this array of difficulties I am convinced that we should adhere to our past policy of keeping our ground forces out of direct counterinsurgency roles.

Having outlined all objections as strongly as he could, Taylor then deferred to the commander. Westmoreland was, after all, responsible for the base, and his concern, Taylor said, was "understandable." With these warnings against the inherent dangers, Taylor agreed to the most limited use of a one-battalion landing team limited force. He was the first to see the concomitant problems; one reason that he did was that unlike the civilians, he understood how the military played the game; if you opened the door slightly, the crack would slowly and quietly but inevitably become wider; and he knew also the degree of planning that was going on in Saigon. Once Westmoreland went for troops, it would not be just Westmoreland, it would be CINCPAC and the JCS as well, and it would be very hard to hold the line. He was absolutely correct; at the same time that he was expressing doubts, CINCPAC was signing on enthusiastically to the idea of the Marines going to Danang, implying that Admiral Sharp would not be responsible for the damage if they were not sent, and showing good old-fashioned American ignorance of the complexity of the war, by belittling Taylor's doubts about the capacity of the Marines to fight in a war like this ("the Marines have a distinguished record in counter-guerrilla warfare"). Under pressure like this, and being asked really for very little, Washington, with almost no debate, on February 26 approved two Marine battalion landing teams for Danang (there was a last-minute attempt by John McNaughton to send the 173rd Airborne from Okinawa to Danang, apparently because the sending of the 173rd would seem a less permanent commitment, and because the Marines had a history of being occupying forces in small banana republics and thus there was less stigma attached to the Airborne. For reasons of their own, largely logistical, the military quickly blocked McNaughton).

On March 8, 1965, the first of two Marine battalions started coming ashore at Danang, and though the Vietnamese government had asked that it be done as quietly and inconspicuously as possible, they had waded ashore in full combat dress and had been garlanded with flowers by young Vietnamese girls. They were to protect American facilities, secure the airfield, and as far as engaging the enemy was concerned, all public statements emphasized that they would not engage in day-to-day actions against the Vietcong. But the foot was now in the door, and in a subtle sense the balance of power within the U.S. mission in Saigon had begun to change. Westmoreland was now a new and more powerful figure than Taylor, he had taken the initiative; Taylor was on the defensive, from now on his cables and arguments would be attempts to limit the use of force. And at the same time Westmoreland would become the most important new player. The commander.

IT WAS A ROLE WESTY WAS READY AND PREPARED FOR, BORN TO, eager for. His biographer, Ernest Furgurson, would title his book *Westmoreland: The Inevitable General.* Surely he looked like a general, the jaw jutted out, the features were forceful and handsome, there was no extra poundage; he played tennis in ferociously hot weather to sweat the weight off because he thought a general should look like a general, that troops commanded by a fat sloppy general would give fat sloppy performances. The face was strong and sharp, and finally clean, Westy was something clean. It was not surprising that as the war dragged on and became messier and messier, the Administration and the prowar media turned more and more to Westmoreland as a symbol of the U.S. presence, something clean in a very messy war. It was, in fact, hard to imagine him as anything else, and later it became something of a joke that Westy could never have been anything but a general. "Well, what about as a brand-new baby?" someone suggested. "No," said another friend of his, "can't you see it? The doctor arrives with a spanking new naked baby and he holds the baby out to the proud parents. 'Mr. and Mrs. Westmoreland, I'd like you to meet your son . . . General Westmoreland.' "

Everyone had always thought he would be a general; he had loved uniforms as a young boy, had looked good in them, had been an Eagle Scout, a reputation which had stayed with him during all his Army career, when he always seemed a little straighter, a little more clean-cut than the other officers. Even when he was a cadet, he and his roommates had sat around discussing when he should get married, if he should marry right after graduation or wait, serve for ten years, advance high in rank, and then get married. Wouldn't too early a marriage slow him down on his way to being a general and Chief of Staff of the Army? They had in fact talked long and frequently of his career in those days and they had all decided that Westmoreland would be Chief of Staff of the Army, a job about which they knew nothing except that it was the top job, and thus Westy should have it. And so Westmoreland's friend and classmate Chester V. Clifton, who later became military aide to Kennedy, would refer to Westmoreland in cadet days as Chief, making it a nickname. They did of course have to disguise it, because when people asked why they called him Chief it would be embarrassing to say that he was to be Chief of Staff, so Clifton, when questioned by superiors, said that it was because Westmoreland had some Indian blood.

He was the organization general, superb at managing; it would later be said of him that his logistical build-up in those early months of Vietnam was an act of pure brilliance (no one had gone without a hot breakfast in those difficult days) and that it would be long studied at West Point and other military schools for its textbook excellence. When he was a general and he took a special course at the Harvard Business School he made an unusually good impression on his corporate business contemporaries, better than the generals usually made, and several tried to lure him away from the military for their companies (indeed as the business school made a better impression on him than it did on most generals, so too Westmoreland enthusiastically recommended it to some of his Army contemporaries, who, accepting his advice, went there and were completely bored). His business school classmates had the feeling that he would have gone right up in corporate life, risen to the top at Chase Manhattan; if later there were other generals who had some reservations about him, about his aloofness, his lack of feel for the country and the war, he nonetheless never failed to impress civilian visitors. The higher they were in corporations or institutions, the more effective he was with them; they seemed to understand how his mind worked, each had a natural appreciation of the other's positions and problems.

He was aloof, reserved, a decent man with a high moral tone in the American sense (he would not, as an aide noted, fire a man for incompetence but he would fire one for the suggestion of immorality); one had a sense of Westy's moral tone, and a sense that he was aware of it too. He was a reserved man with few close friends, terrible at small talk, totally committed to his work, his job of being an inspiring commander. He was in fact inspirational-looking, inspirational-acting and inspirational-sounding, and yet, curiously, in Vietnam there was no Westy cult (as later there would be an Abe Abrams cult, a kind of anticult; Abrams gruff, rough, patterning himself after a sort of latter-day U. S. Grant. Abrams came in when the war was very old and tried to hold it down under limited post-Tet resources, and suddenly he got all the good publicity when Westmoreland was getting all the bad publicity and somehow being blamed for Tet. Westmoreland was deeply depressed about it and wanted to make a public statement saying that the gains which were being made under Abrams had been originated during his tour, and friends had to take him aside and tell him that the last thing a very troubled United States Army could stand at that particular moment was a public split between Westmoreland and Abrams).

Westmoreland had trained and studied and prepared for an entire career for this command, but he would, like so many others, be a victim of his own war; in another time, a simpler war, he would have been the ideal general, decent, intelligent but not brilliant, hard-working, courageous, respectful of civilian authority, liked by the men who served under him, ideally trained to fight a great, well-organized war on the plains of Germany. Perhaps his name would have ranked with that of Eisenhower, Bradley, Ridgway, the best of our professional soldiers. But this war would stain him as it stained everything else. As many of his countrymen came to doubt the war, they would come to doubt him; as so many of the civilians who had helped plan the war bailed out on it, thinking it unwinnable and not worth the cost, Westmoreland, his name somehow attached to it more than anything else in his career, the men he commanded still serving there, could not let go, and public antagonism would center on him. Even the men who had once praised his sense of duty, his caution, his decency, turned cool. "A blunt instrument," Bill Bundy would say of him in private.

He was dedicated, and unbelievably hard-working; if sheer attention to detail, long hours of work and right attitudes could have done it, then he would have come home a success, his country proud, an acceptable figure at college campuses as well as American Legion halls. If going by the book could have done it, he would have been a success too, for he was a stickler for the book; it had brought him far. Instead he came home to a country torn apart by the war, and he himself was one more symbol of that division, a painful and bitter reward for a lifetime of service. He was of course always aware of his role as a symbol (he could at times breakfast in his underwear in order to keep his fatigues pressed) and he had an almost mystical sense of himself as a symbol of the mission, keeping morale up, letting the troops know that he, Westmoreland, was with them, it was really slightly MacArthur-like; if no one else was aware of them, cared about them, then he, General Westmoreland, did. He knew what he looked like and that it was an asset to his job: the cap was tilted at just the right angle, the step was always double time. Once when Westy was out driving his own jeep in the boondocks, he saw two nurses in the distance. He stopped the jeep, double-timed over to them, introduced himself, "I'm General Westmoreland," shook hands, had his picture taken with each nurse, double-timed back to the jeep, telling friends that it was good for their morale, adding that he must be the most photographed man in the world because every man in Vietnam had a camera and they had all taken his picture.

The impression he made was a very good one, particularly on civilians. There was nothing of the braggart in him; his estimates on the war were, if anything, a good deal more restrained than many of his civilian superiors. He did not seem like a man who enjoyed killing, there was no stench of death around him, he seemed more like what you would want a citizen army to produce in a great democracy, an intelligent, reasonable, dedicated man. It was the war which was unreasonable yet it was in his tour of command that events like My Lai took place; it was his command and the McNamara command which had produced things like the body count, in a war which turned so much American might loose at an enemy sheltered so often in the population. When Neil Sheehan traveled with Westmoreland on his plane in the summer of 1966 he asked if Westmoreland was not worried by the enormity of civilian casualties which the bombing and shelling were causing in the South. "Yes," said Westmoreland, "but it does deprive the enemy of the population, doesn't it?" It was a significant comment; it meant that for all the Army's distaste for the war, the fire power loosed on both enemy and population, the American command was aware of what it was doing and sanctioned it; messy, yes, but the only way to separate the Vietcong from his strategic base. MACV knew about it, it didn't want to know too much, it would look the other way if possible, but it knew it was all going on out there.

He looked so good, and his presentations were always very good, yet for all of this there was something a little wooden about him. He was a fine physical specimen, and yet he was not a particularly good tennis player, not that good an athlete. No rhythm. There was a sense that his presentations were a little better than his true grasp, as if somehow it had all been memorized just before he walked into the room. He articulated the war well, or at least he seemed to, having been taught by some of the best phrase makers in the business to articulate it, that you had to win the people, that this war was different from all other wars, that it was political, but there was a feeling that he spoke the war better than he felt it, that in a war where so much of it was a sense of nuance and feel, he was particularly without feel. He could say that control of the population was important and that the Vietcong were linked to the people, and yet there was a sense that he did not really understand the root of the war. He believed that if you knocked off the enemy's main battalions, destroyed them, then that would do it, and he never really understood that the enemy's great strength was his political strength, that the main-force units were the visible part of the iceberg, and that above all he had a capacity to replenish, that if a battalion was destroyed it would be painful but they could replace it. A dangerous enemy to choose to fight a war of attrition against.

He liked the Vietnamese and was genuinely committed to their cause, but there was never a real sense or feeling for their frailties, fallibilities, their corruption, their loss of innocence (had they ever been innocent?). He was, finally, too American, too successful in the American and Western sense, too much a sterling product of a success-oriented country to feel the rhythms and nuances of this particularly failed society; he was the finest product of an uncorrupted country where doing good was always rewarded, one worked hard, played by the rules, went by the book, and succeeded. Success. Theirs was a corrupted, cynical society where the bribe, the lie, the decadence had become a way of life, where Vietnamese officers lied frequently and readily to their American counterparts, thinking this was what the Americans wanted, surprised later that the Americans should feel even a minor betrayal in this. Westy gleaming in his decency, the Vietnamese never quite comprehending it. Westy at the Cercle Sportif, playing his last tennis game, at the end lining up the little Vietnamese urchins who had served as ball boys, street-tough from some of the meanest streets in the world, unlikely candidates for Eagle Scouts, learning the black-market rate *before* they learned arithmetic, knowing even before they reached their teens the full glory of East-West decadence. Westy lining them up as if in company formation, telling an American who had played with him to translate. "You have been my ball boys." Nods of their heads. "You have served well. You have been faithful." More nods of heads. "I would like to reward you." Nods. Expectant smiles. The tip. "Here is your reward. You may have all my tennis balls." Looks of immense disappointment.

It was typical. The Americans, particularly the military, were so straight and Westy was the classic example; he was so American, like all Americans in Vietnam he wanted the Vietnamese to be Americans, he saw them in American terms, he could never seem to see them as themselves. He was not really at ease with them, though he wanted to be, and a friend would remember one of Westy's first field trips when he was still deputy commander, a trip to Chau Doc province, which seemed to sum up Westmoreland's frustration and inability to penetrate the society: Westy having lunch with the very sophisticated province chief, who spoke classic Sorbonne French and no English and who had laid on a great feast. Midway through the meal, about the third serving of rice, it became clear that Westmoreland had nothing to say to this man, that he wanted almost desperately to talk with him, but there was no common bond, no real curiosity about the society. Finally the conversation going like this—Westy: "I notice in your country your people eat a good deal of rice." Translated. Province chief: *"Oui, oui."* Westy: "In my country, our people eat a good deal of bread." Translated. Province chief a little puzzled and a little worried. *"Oui, oui."* Westy: "In my country, we call bread 'the staff of life.'" Translated. Province chief nods, very puzzled and very worried—is this American general about to spring a trap, is he subtly edging the conversation toward the subject of corruption? Is he suggesting that the province chief is allowing the landlords to tax the peasants working the paddies too heavily? Westy: "I guess in your country your people could say that rice is the staff of life." Translated. Province chief heaves a sigh of relief. Agrees readily. Westy: a supremely conventional man in a supremely unconventional war.

He was a general who obeyed his orders; Johnson had chosen him in part because he had sensed in Westmoreland a man who would not play games or try to circumvent him, and in that sense he had chosen well. (Johnson subsequently did not worry too much about Westmoreland turning on him; he knew that Westy was straight, and more, that he was extremely ambitious. When an aide once mentioned the possibility that Westy might go public with the war, Johnson quickly deflected it. "No, he won't," the President said, "because I'm the one person who has what he wants." By that he meant future promotion. Then the President suddenly added, "It's the same with Hubert." Johnson, the aide thought, was always more at ease with ambitious men, he could understand them, know their price; it was men with a sharp limit on their ambitions who were a problem for him.) The general was very honest, he shunned a political role. He never protected himself in his cables, and he tried to do the job the civilians set for him; his greatest failing was in believing it could be done. He was never aware of just how much doubt there was about the war in Washington among the civilians; everyone seemed to have signed on, and thus to Westmoreland there was a sense of a clear mandate, he was not aware of the extent of misgivings, signature by signature. When he finally came back and spoke to the Congress, he did it at the request of his Commander in Chief. It was something he was not that eager for, and he had turned down a similar but somewhat vaguer request from McNamara a year earlier (he had written his speech for the Congress himself, and when a civilian friend looked at the opening paragraph he suggested that he change it, since it began "I stand here today where General MacArthur stood . . ." Typically, of course, there was no element of chance even to that speech: Pentagon janitors checking the building very early in the morning of his address were stunned to find the main auditorium absolutely empty except for one man, General William Childs Westmoreland, booming away, loudspeakers all go, his forthcoming speech blaring out. Time after time.) He had played by the rules even when they had all turned away from the war, and he did not go public with complaints, though he had them. Johnson had chosen well in that sense; whatever hurts there were, were private ones. He would not feed the right wing, the jingoists, although occasionally some of the hurt showed through in talking about the civilians. Bob McNamara was someone who told him not to worry about resources, we were the richest country in the world. So it had not ended for him as auspiciously as it had begun. After Tet even Rostow, the last believer, was heard around the White House to have a change in tone. Rostow, who had been so proud of talking about *Westy*, Westy wanted this and Westy said this, and Westy feels, was heard in those weeks after Tet to say that General Westmoreland felt, and General Westmoreland believed.

HE HAD HAD AN ENVIABLE BOYHOOD AND CAREER. THE SON OF UPPER-middle-class people in South Carolina; goals set, goals achieved, values confirmed. A classic American story. Career admired. A low quotient of materialism, the goals, the goals were loftier, to serve, to protect. The son of people who belonged, who had been on that soil for 150 years. Ten of his ancestors had fought in the Civil War. His father had attended the Citadel, probably the South's best-known military school, but had been expelled for what was boyish enthusiasm, and thus had never served himself. He had become a businessman, a banker, married a Childs, a well-known Columbia family.

William Childs Westmoreland was born on March 26, 1914, in Saxon, three miles west of Spartanburg. Westmoreland's father was soon made manager of a major textile mill, an important job in the local social hierarchy; it meant a big two-story house with a simple cabin in back for the Negro servants. The Westmorelands lived in sharp contrast to the stark poverty of the mill workers; Westy as a young boy was allowed to play with his schoolmates who were the children of mill workers, but his younger sister, in keeping with local class and caste, was not. The Westmorelands were well connected in the hierarchy of that time. Childs, as he was known, knew the right people, went to the right church, with the right Sunday school teacher, James Byrnes, then a congressman, later a senator and Secretary of State, a family friend who would keep an eye out for this well brought up, serious young man. The young Westmoreland, who liked soldier suits as a boy, went into the Boy Scouts and did particularly well. Even then he seemed to love uniforms. As he won merit badges he was always careful to make sure that his mother sewed them onto the uniform with just the right spacing. He moved ahead quickly as a scout, First Class and then Eagle, and in 1929, when there was a World Scout Jamboree in Europe, Westy went, though it cost $395, a good deal of money in those days; a special court of honor had to be set up in South Carolina to qualify him as an Eagle Scout so he could go. When he returned he was interviewed in the local paper with a photograph and the caption "Spartanburg's Own."

He went on to Spartanburg High, the diligent young man, always well dressed, always very correct, his parents always proud of how many of their friends would tell them what a fine boy he was. The model boy. Studious but not brilliant, but on the basis of application, grades in the 90s, physically sound and dedicated but not a particularly gifted athlete. Inevitably class president. Upon graduation he decided to go to the Citadel (which he almost became the head of in 1970; when it appeared that he might leave the job of Chief of Staff, there was considerable talk that he would head the Citadel for a year or two and then perhaps run for governor of South Carolina). He did well at the Citadel, finishing 33rd in a class of 169 members, but impressing others with more important qualities, his leadership ability, evident even then. Others deferred to him. Even then he liked to drill, he liked the military austerity and discipline; he liked the ordered world, he was to be more at ease in it than the freer, open, less ordered world of the civilian; in the military you knew what was expected of you, others knew what was expected of them.

After his first year there he decided that he did want a military career, so he went to see his old friend Jimmy Byrnes about an appointment to Annapolis; the standing offer from Byrnes had been: "Just let me know when you're ready for that appointment, young man." Byrnes suggested that West Point offered a better and fuller life than Annapolis, and so West Point it was.

There for the first time in his life he became Westy, and he seemed to stand out, the dedication, the energy, the bearing; within a few months his classmates were discussing whether or not he would be First Captain of his class. It was 1931, the height of the Depression, which had hit the country but not his family. He was younger than most of his classmates, many of whom were college graduates, now turning to the Academy because there were no civilian jobs. He did well as a plebe, finishing 71st among 328 in his class. Again, not brilliant, but intelligent and very hard-working. He liked West Point; the values inherent in the discipline and the sacrifice came easily to him and he sensed he would do well in his career (indeed, even on summer vacation he would put in extra hours practicing parade-ground commands in isolated South Carolina forests). Those years also meant that the Depression, which would sharply touch so many young men of that era, would have little effect on him; West Point was a particularly sheltered place. If not the most brilliant member of his class, he had other qualities, bearing, leadership—other men would look to him to lead. He had the capacity to impress both his superiors and his contemporaries. This was the model young man, with a certain maturity to him. That Southern manner was disarming: he had ambition without seeming ambitious. So Westy became First Captain of his class, the Point's highest honor, which in itself seemed to guarantee a brighter career. He finished with an overall academic standing of 112 out of 276 for his four years, but he ranked eighth in his class in tactics. He wanted to join the new Army Air Corps upon graduation, but his eyes were too weak; he had studied too hard in keeping his grades up, and so, because he was good in math, he settled for the field artillery.

The years between the wars were slow ones, slow advancement, slow in challenge, though the pace would quicken as World War II approached. Even then Westmoreland was the kind of young officer that the older officers' wives coveted for their daughters. But he was also serious, painstakingly creating his own charts for artillery guides (only to find that though they were accurate, researchers at Fort Sill had beaten him with similar charts produced by slide rules). He was a young officer that more senior men kept their eye on, and when the war finally came he moved ahead quickly; by September 1942, at twenty-eight, he was a lieutenant colonel, commander of an artillery battalion, ready and anxious to get into the middle of the war, superbly trained for what was ahead, wanting to play his part. One of those men who never feared, who can only go forward, who sensed his own destiny.

Two months later he got his first chance in the North African campaign with the 9th Division, pushing his big guns into action at the Kasserine Pass and catching the Germans by surprise, making the Germans feel that the Allied forces were larger in number than they in fact were. He gained a Presidential Unit citation for his 34th Field Artillery Battalion, and throughout the North African campaign there was a new subsurface reputation. Hot unit, hot commander; Westy, it was said, could really move his unit. But Westy was not satisfied. He wanted more action, and he wanted to be with the hot new mobile units, the Airborne, the exciting units which were going to go where the action was the heaviest. Westmoreland had tried to get into Airborne earlier in his career, and he had struck up a friendship with Colonel James Gavin, obviously a comer and a leading proponent of airborne tactics. With the 82nd Airborne leading the invasion into Sicily in July 1943, Westy made a move to go Airborne. He drove up to General Ridgway's headquarters, introduced himself, said he had heard what the Airborne was going to do, and he wanted to offer the general the best artillery support he could get, adding that in addition to his artillery pieces, four dozen trucks, scarce as to be almost sacred, a great sweetener, came with the deal. Ridgway, needing more wheels for his division, immediately asked his division artillery commander, a particularly sharp young brigadier named Maxwell Taylor, to go and take a look at this new unit with its 155-mm. howitzers which he was about to acquire. Taylor, who felt himself an expert on the use of 155s, was visibly impressed with the sharpness of Westy's unit and went back to tell Ridgway that they had made a very good deal. This was, among other things, the beginning of the Westmoreland-Taylor friendship.

Westmoreland's unit, attached to the 82nd, moved rapidly across Sicily with the Airborne troops until the 82nd was pulled out for more traditional infantry, but his reputation as an aggressive commander with a sharp unit grew. He was awarded the Legion of Merit for his part in Africa and Sicily. He and his unit then went to England to prepare for the coming Normandy invasion. Taylor, now a major general and commander of the elite 101st Airborne, asked for Westmoreland, offering him a job as division artillery executive officer and a colonel's eagles. If there was any doubt about his future, it was ended with that request. But the 9th Division was unwilling to give him up. He was slated for the same job in the 9th, where he again excelled, became chief of staff although only a bird colonel, and gained a Bronze Star for co-ordination of other units in the bridgehead at Remagen.

He stayed chief of staff of the 9th throughout the rest of the war, and then at the end he was advised by the commander, General Louis Craig, that his career was very bright, but that it was time to switch to the infantry, where the real future for the very best still resided. He was wary at first, thinking that too much careerism might be implicit, but he soon accepted command of an infantry regiment, and shortly afterward was made commander of the 71st Division, being largely in charge of taking the division home. Still, he was only thirty years old, he had commanded a division, and as his West Point classmates might have predicted, he had not bothered to marry, it might have slowed him down.

He was barely back home and on his way to a Pentagon assignment when he got a phone call from his old friend Jim Gavin, now commander of the 82nd Airborne and one of the most celebrated officers in the Army, a dashing, romantic figure. "Slim Jim" Gavin, who had led the jump on D-Day into Normandy, now offered Westmoreland one of three parachute regiments in the 82nd. Westmoreland wanted it, but, he reminded Gavin, he had never jumped. So he went to jump school at Fort Bragg, and returned as a regimental commander. It was the Army system very much at work; he was a much sought after officer. There were always too few men of that caliber and too many slots, so everyone in the Army was on the lookout for excellence, and the word would go up and down who were the special ones. A fine commander made himself look even better by collecting and using other, younger marked men in his unit, culling out the best, using the back-channel grapevine to pick the winners. Gavin was a winner and now he was picking a winner. It helped Westmoreland and it helped Gavin too.

Now, never having jumped in combat, Westmoreland was commanding some of the most combat-toughened men in the Army, men who built their very special mystique because they jumped out of airplanes, and very few of their fellow troopers and almost none of their fellow countrymen did. (There is the classic Airborne story about a general inspecting Airborne troops. "And do you like to jump out of planes, soldier?" asks the general. "No, sir," answers the trooper. "Then why are you here?" "Because I like to be around men who do," answers the trooper.)

Westmoreland was soon made chief of staff of the division, at Gavin's request, a particularly flattering recommendation; indeed it was soon said that when Gavin left the division, there would be no trouble finding his successor, since there was a young light colonel named Westmoreland who could run the division as well as Gavin. Westmoreland had made it, chief of staff of the 82nd at the age of thirty-two. There was even time now to get married to an Army brat named Kitsy Van Dusen (who friends found had a leavening influence on Westmoreland). At the 82nd he impressed his superiors with the dedication, the organization, the skill, the attention to detail, the enormous industry, the valued—in the Army, and business—capacity to anticipate demands. To his contemporaries he was a cold one, you did not get close to Westy, you kept your distance. He seemed to have no confidants; the system was his confidant.

He was marked for great things; when as chief of staff of the 82nd he received a letter suggesting that his next assignment be the Command and General Staff School at Fort Leavenworth, a plum assignment for most officers his age, a reassurance that they were on their way, Westmoreland was irritated. He thought he was beyond that, that he was something special, which he was, for his commanding general, Williston Palmer, said not to worry, that his career was being guided on a different level, above all the usual mechanics. When Westmoreland finally went to Leavenworth it was not as a student, but as an instructor; he would teach there and at the Army War College at Carlisle Barracks. They were good assignments but irritating to him because the Korean War had started and he wanted to get there for the action. He finally did, in July 1952, as commander of the 187th Regimental Combat Team; it was once again a plum and a sign that he was special. During the Korean War the Pentagon was flooded with requests for Westmoreland, every division seemed to want this letter-perfect soldier who had been sponsored by both Taylor and Gavin. The command he got was the choicest one; the 187th was the only Airborne unit in Korea, an elite team, which meant that its commander had ultrahigh visibility. Yet Korea was not a particularly harsh war to him, he did not see that much action, and he came out of Korea with his first star at the age of thirty-eight.

From Korea he went back to the Pentagon, this time as Deputy Assistant Chief of Staff for Manpower Control, from there to Harvard Business School, and in 1955 to Secretary of the General Staff under the new Chief of Staff,

Max Taylor. (It was as if history were repeating itself; Taylor had held the same job under George Marshall.) It was a very difficult job, serving essentially as secretary and chief protector of the Chief, making sure he knew what he should know, that he see whom he should see, that he was protected if necessary, that his time was not wasted. If Taylor was cold and austere, so was his Secretary. Later, when the revolt of the colonels broke out, Westmoreland assured Taylor that he would clean it up for him and did, in the view of the colonels, a little too quickly and antiseptically. They felt that Westmoreland had played the game very skillfully during the growing rebellion: had it succeeded, he was in deeply enough to go along; had it failed, he was not sufficiently involved not to be absolved. So there was a feeling among some of them that he had been almost too ruthless in crushing it and wiping out the traces (it was the coldness which some of them remembered, the lack of a phone call saying, in effect, we know what you were doing and that you were authorized to do it—lie low and we'll take care of you).

He handled the difficult assignment with his usual excellence and in 1958, when Taylor was reactivating his old division, the 101st, Major General Westmoreland, the youngest major general in the Army, was given the command, another plum, plus a word from Taylor that the officers of Taylor's generation were already plotting the career of men like Westmoreland. He did well at Fort Campbell with the 101st, was superb at public relations, so good in fact that it was part of Tennessee and Kentucky gossip at that time that he might well have political ambitions. He also pushed very hard at efficiency, trying to translate it into percentages. He had always liked figures and statistics (Westmoreland, says a friend, is not much interested in sociology or personality; he is much more interested in facts and figures; if he had to describe your personality he would probably do it in percentages). He launched a program called Overdrive to gain greater efficiency at the post; the results of it a year later would have delighted McNamara had he then been at Defense, and would show why McNamara and Westmoreland got along so well for such a long time. Overdrive, it seemed, had brought an increase of 420 percent in valid suggestions from men and civilians on the post; a 24 percent drop in combat troops doing administrative work; and a 12 percent reduction in rations ordered for the same post population. It was also at Campbell that a practice jump saw a last-minute wind foul the planes and result in the death of six paratroopers; the next day Westmoreland was the first to jump.

After Fort Campbell he was given another dream assignment, Superintendent of West Point, a slot in the past held by MacArthur and Taylor. He stayed there for three years, and was credited with vast improvement in managerial techniques (Taylor, his predecessor there, had expanded the curriculum). At West Point he again had ultrahigh visibility and he impressed everyone. The appearance—to look that good, that straight and *soldierly*—was not without its immense benefits; and Westmoreland was far from unaware of the peripheral impact, particularly upon civilians. He knew that it was money in the bank, that they were in awe of him, and he was not above using it. More than other generals he had always sought out political figures where he was stationed, gotten to know them, to let them know he would work with them, to impress and reassure them. In 1962, when President Kennedy was going to visit West Point, Westmoreland was not particularly pleased when he looked at the preliminary schedule for the trip because it did not provide enough time for the general to be with the President. Over a period of days Westy's aides very carefully and thoroughly renegotiated the entire schedule, doubling the amount of time that Westmoreland would spend with the President, which had its effect because Kennedy came away from the visit deeply impressed with Westmoreland. For a time in 1962 when Kennedy was looking for a new Chief of Staff of the Army, he wanted to reach down and pick Westmoreland until he was finally advised by others that you simply did not make a very junior major general Chief of Staff. At least not in peacetime.

In 1963 Westmoreland left the Point and was given the XVIII Airborne Corps (which gave him command of the 101st and the 82nd). He was clearly one of the three top generals in the Army, a future candidate for Chief of Staff, or for any other special command which might arise. In fact, Westmoreland had been the dark-horse candidate for the command in Vietnam as far back as 1961, when they had finally turned to Harkins. Some of the civilians around Kennedy thought he appeared to be a better general and that Kennedy should not let seniority be a bar to excellence; Taylor, however, wanted Harkins. So in 1964, with the war getting worse and Harkins clearly having lost the respect and confidence of his civilian superiors, the question arose as to who would succeed him. This time the military would go with its best, and the choices were the elite of the Army. The senior man was Harold Johnson, then serving as Deputy Chief of Staff for Military Operations (and soon to be Chief of Staff), intelligent, spare, a man with little political tact or grace; the youngest was General Bruce Palmer, considered then probably the brightest general in the Army, sixth in his class at West Point (and soon to handle the Dominican crisis); Westmoreland; and Abe Abrams, the tough, crusty tank commander who was considered one of the great officers of World War II, a favorite of Patton's.

Johnson and McNamara were both impressed by Westmoreland. McNamara liked his reputation for efficiency, for being straightforward. Westmoreland could phrase things in terms McNamara understood, which did not hurt. Johnson in particular was pleased by Westmoreland's reputation; he had liked the general when they met at West Point, and Johnson was impressed that Westmoreland was straight from West Point, perhaps he would be better prepared to train the Vietnamese army (that hope still burned, the myth that the problem with the ARVN was a lack of training; Americans had been training the Vietnamese army for a decade, and still held to the hope that more training was the solution). There was another quality that Johnson liked about Westmoreland and that was that Westy was a Southerner. Johnson, surrounded by Easterners, felt more comfortable with Westmoreland's Southern accent. But it was Taylor, who had known Westmoreland for so long, who swung the balance (and who did not really understand the war at that point; he was convinced that Westmoreland's airborne experience would be helpful; nothing, in fact, was ever more meaningless in Vietnam than the costly, clumsy airborne assaults which the ARVN periodically launched). So it was Westmoreland who was chosen, a good, hard-working man, supremely conventional, supremely confident, classically managerial in style, not a man of subtlety. Rather the corporate general, chosen for the most complex war this country had ever fought. It would be a summation of the letter-perfect career.

On his way to Vietnam he stopped off at West Point to make a farewell speech to the cadets, the men who had arrived at the Point at the same time he did, and he delivered an unusually personal speech, as if knowing, which he probably did, that many of them would soon serve in his command in Vietnam. He told them he considered himself and his fellow West Point men a special breed, with a calling comparable to that of the ministry, bearing a "sacred trust to provide the dedicated leadership and service to our nation, which is so essential to our national security. I certainly view this, and I am sure you view it as a very high calling, and a noble cause. I feel it is up to a West Pointer to dedicate his personal life and his conscience to this idea. This has been the West Point tradition over the years. I must say this country can be thankful if this is the case." But outside the Academy, he warned, "you're going to be dealing with just ordinary people . . . all people aren't honest. Many have low, if any, sense of duty. Many citizens go to extremes to avoid any kind of military service to their country. I feel that West Pointers must be different, and that is why as a group they have been universally and uniquely successful throughout history." He warned that not all the problems they faced would be solvable, that life was not easy, but then, in an almost classic exposition of the can-do philosophy, he added, "In my view the positive approach is the key to success . . . and it's the one that has a strong influence over people. Men welcome leadership. They like action and they relish accomplishment . . . speculation, knowledge is not the chief aim of man—it is action . . . all mankind feel themselves weak, beset with infirmities, and surrounded with danger. The acutest minds are the most conscious of difficulties and dangers. They want above all things a leader with the boldness, decision, and energy that with shame, they do not find in themselves. He then who would command among his fellows, must tell them more in energy of will than in power of intellect. He has to have both, . . . but energy of will is more important. . . ." Then this man, who was the embodiment of the book soldier, who seemed to be able to control his own destiny and everything that he set his mind to, ended with a quotation from Kipling:

> "If you can talk with crowds and keep your virtue
> Or walk with kings—nor lose the common touch,
> If neither foes nor loving friends can hurt you
> If all men count with you, but none too much;
> If you can fill the unforgiving minute
> With sixty seconds' worth of distance run,
> Yours is the Earth and everything that's in it,
> And—which is more—you'll be a Man, my son!"

If he was conventional and not brilliant, he had one failing: he did not feel at ease with other unconventional men. His staff in Saigon would not be brilliant; it would in fact reflect him and his limitations. He was conventional; it would be conventional. He did not feel the nuance of the war; it did not feel the nuance of the war. It was to an uncommon degree a reflection of him, and it was not by chance; even the generals around Westy *looked* like generals. In 1967 when one of the brightest generals in Vietnam, Fred Weyand, was to be given a full field force, in effect a corps command, Westmoreland told him to go ahead and choose any senior civilian he wanted as an adviser. Weyand thought about it for quite a while and said he wanted John Paul Vann (the same Vann who had left the Army in protest over the Harkins reporting system, who had returned to Vietnam as the lowest-ranking AID civilian and had worked his way back up and was considered by many to be the single most knowledgeable American there). "I don't know about Vann," said Westmoreland, "better think it over. Vann's a troublemaker. A very difficult man to get along with." Weyand thought on it for a while and still requested Vann. (Vann would have a profound influence on Weyand's thinking, in effect saying that the search-and-destroy strategy played into Hanoi's hands, and that the troops should be kept closer to the population centers. This resulted in a major split between Westmoreland and Weyand on use of troops in 1967, but it also perhaps helped save the U.S. mission from an even greater defeat at the time of Tet. It was Vann who first noticed that the enemy was up to something unusual and seemed to be massing, and who prevailed upon Weyand to hold back on sending troops to the far regions. Weyand held back despite pressure from Saigon for search-and-destroy operations in the exterior reaches of his zone. When the other side struck, Weyand's forces were not nearly as scattered as they might have been.)

So he went to Vietnam, apparently exuding confidence; the U.S. mission which had been staggering and near its knees seemed to regain a certain confidence. Westy was here and he was the best. The first team was on its way. He would avoid the mistakes of the past, the Harkins mistakes, the overoptimism, the self-delusion, and for a time Westmoreland would recommend to friends books which were extremely critical of Harkins and his reporting system. (Indeed, at his farewell speech at West Point, he had warned against "snow jobs . . . In connection with my forthcoming assignment, that is one of the real problem areas—to get the facts from the Vietnamese as to what is going on in that strife-torn country. Because the Vietnamese, as soldiers under your command, are inclined to tell you what you want to hear, and not what the actual facts are. . . .") But though he had started realistically, Vietnam enveloped him as it had other Western generals; he too showed his frailty, he too became more and more frustrated by the war, and he too turned to those who would give him the good news. He too began to see in the press, which at first he had handled so well, an almost sinister opponent. And so in early 1967, Joe McGinniss, then just a young reporter for the Philadelphia *Inquirer*, would spend a day traveling with Westmoreland to the coastal town of Phan Thiet. There a young American officer startled McGinniss by giving an extraordinarily candid briefing on how bad the situation was, how incompetent the ARVN was. Westmoreland had demanded the briefing and the young American had been uneasy about giving it, apologizing for being so frank with a reporter present, but finally it had come pouring out: the ARVN soldiers were cowards, they refused to fight, they abused the population, in their most recent battle they had all fled, all but one man. That one man had stood and fought and almost single-handedly staved off a Vietcong attack. When the officer had finished his briefing, still apologizing for being so candid, Westmoreland turned to McGinniss and said, "Now you see how distorted the press image of this war is. This is a perfect example—a great act of bravery and not a single mention of it in the *New York Times*." But all of that would come later, the gnawing frustration; for in the beginning his very arrival, his presence in Vietnam had seemed to give more oxygen to the mission: from now on things would be done correctly. By the book. But he was a man trained for great wars, with his own vision of great wars. Not a man for small and frustrating wars. A man born to command and with a vision. "He wants," wrote Peter Arnett of the AP, the best reporter of the war, "to be CINCWorld."

Chapter Twenty-five

I N MARCH 1965 THE STRUGGLE BEGAN OVER THE SENDING OF combat troops, a struggle which saw Westmoreland and Taylor divided, CINCPAC and the JCS lined up with the advocates of force, and with General Harold Johnson, Chief of Staff of the Army, playing a crucial role, eventually siding with the advocates. The battle would touch on the use of troops, number of troops, and equally important, strategy. Starting in March, the strategy evolved from security to an agreement to follow a Taylor-devised enclave strategy, and finally, by June, to a much more vigorous Westmoreland-Depuy search-and-destroy strategy which would help remove all restraints on the use of American ground forces. It was an evolution which entailed surprisingly little foresight and planning, or definition of roles and strategies on the part of the civilians. One step followed another, each step being an attempt to hold the line, each leading them in deeper, all of it slipping away. In this period Taylor was the man who opposed the use of combat troops, but events worked against him. (Not by chance did Ball quote Emerson on events being in the saddle and riding mankind. For no man would it be more true than Max Taylor. He would try to hold the line on major combat-troop commitments, and in so doing, concede smaller victories to those who wanted greater force, until step by step he was pulled along and the entire debate went beyond him; he, like others, was overtaken by events.)

THE TRIP OF GENERAL HAROLD K. JOHNSON TO VIETNAM WAS important. He was sent specifically by Lyndon Johnson, who had given him a real dressing-down. The President had let loose, right in front of members of the general's staff. All he heard from his generals, President Johnson said, was "Bomb, bomb, bomb. That's all you know. Well, I want to know why there's nothing else. You generals have all been educated at the taxpayers' expense, and you're not giving me any ideas and any solutions for this damn little piss-ant country. Now, I don't need ten generals to come in here ten times and tell me to bomb. I want some solutions. I want some answers." So General Johnson had hied himself to Vietnam, arriving there on March 5 all fired up, hot for solutions. He spent a week looking over the entire situation, conferring at length with both Westmoreland and Taylor, and found that there was a considerable difference in their estimates of future needs. Westmoreland already wanted combat troops, and he wanted to use them aggressively; Taylor was more conservative, he was wary of how well combat troops might work, and he was reluctant to take too much of the burden away from the Vietnamese. If a division were to be used, he wanted to use it more cautiously, perhaps first in enclaves along the coast, where the troops would have an easy exit to the sea, and where they would have less difficulty with lines of communication than troops stationed in the highlands. They would fight in their own defense and do some limited patrolling, thus releasing the ARVN for other duties, but they would not assume the burden of the war. The use of a division in the coastal region would mean extended lines of communication, and it might be more open-ended in terms of numbers and mission. Taylor opposed using a division for either purpose at the moment, he told both Washington and General Johnson, but if it had to come to a choice, he favored the coastal enclave theory as simpler, safer and less costly. (A year later, when Taylor's old Airborne rival, Jim Gavin, who had opposed the war, surfaced with the idea of winding down the war by moving to an enclave strategy, the Administration chose Taylor as the weapon with which to knock Gavin down, which Taylor did, Gavin and the general public never knowing that Taylor had proposed roughly the same strategy.)

But Westmoreland insisted on troops. The situation, he said, was not quite desperate, although perilously near it. He was sure that the Vietcong had not even begun to use its full strength, that it was sitting back preparing a major campaign, and he doubted the ARVN capacity to withstand it. He needed troops, and he wanted the right to maneuver them. Since Westmoreland was the commander, he convinced General Johnson, a man who had many doubts about another land war in Asia, to go along with him, and on his return the Army Chief recommended that an entire American division be sent (and to the highlands, for a mission which would bring greater results). The Harold Johnson recommendations, which would change the nature of the commitment, were so closely held that the highest official at CIA would have to smuggle illicit copies from friends at the White House.

A division which Westmoreland might have gotten at the time, mid-March. But the Joint Chiefs, always more ambitious, always committed to greater force, had been pushing for three divisions (including one Korean division); the Chiefs wanted to be sure that if force was used, there was enough of it. The JCS recommendation stopped temporarily at McNamara, because neither he nor Lyndon Johnson wanted three divisions; but the three-division idea was not dead and had replaced Harold Johnson's one division, thus wiping it out. The rest of the Chief of Staff's recommendations reinforcing ARVN, doing the same things with more vigor, were passed on, leaving Westmoreland with a feeling that had the JCS held back, he would have had his one division, which made him extremely careful about how big a slice of salami he would ask for in the future.

Yet on March 17 he asked for a Marine battalion landing team for the town of Phu Bai, near Hué; Westy wanted to build a larger base to serve as helicopter field and take the burden of choppers away from the already overcrowded Danang base. Taylor gave his concurrence, but warned again that this was simply a reminder that there would be more requests for troops, that once in, it would not be easy to stop.

During March, day by day and then week by week, the play was slowly changing. The civilians became increasingly passive in their positions, the military increasingly active, the civilians no longer taking the initiative but sitting back, being overwhelmed by the requests and demands of the military, different generals demanding different things. The civilians were on the defensive, trying to weigh the accuracy and legitimacy of the requests from the military. The JCS wanted a lot of force, and an aggressive policy, three divisions, but then, they always asked for too much. Taylor was far more cautious; he was not saying no, he was casting doubts about the ability of U.S. forces to fight (doubts which his chief political superior Lyndon Johnson did not particularly share, would in fact consider a form of reverse racism, as indeed the Administration would later accuse Fulbright of racism, in believing that Asians were not as valuable as Caucasians). Taylor was trying to hold it down, and he was doing it in part in a very dangerous way; that is, he was challenging not the basic assumption of the war or the commitment but the assessment of Westmoreland of how serious the situation was; he was saying in effect it simply wasn't that bad. This meant that if the situation deteriorated any further, he would have to sign on or have his arguments completely neutralized. Since the long-range rhythms of the country, growing Vietcong strength and steady ARVN deterioration were on the side of Westmoreland, the future, so to speak, was his. In addition to Westmoreland and the JCS, there was also CINCPAC, constantly calling for more force, more troops. The question soon, then, would be not whether or not to send combat troops, but how many and under what mission and ground rules.

TAYLOR RETURNED TO WASHINGTON AT THE END OF MARCH FOR A series of meetings which would ostensibly determine strategy. What was significant about these meetings was the timing. After six weeks of Operation Rolling Thunder, the massive bombing of the North, it had become obvious that the bombing was not going to bring Hanoi either to its senses or its knees, and that as a political weapon against the North it had probably failed, which meant that there would be increasing pressures from the Chiefs both to expand it into a *military* weapon and, now that they were this far in, for more ground forces. It was becoming clearer and clearer that the move which was supposed to have prevented sending troops was not going to affect Hanoi's decision making, except perhaps to make them escalate. Since Taylor knew that Westmoreland would be submitting a major request for troops, he had already changed his position. From what was an essentially blanket opposition to the use of combat troops and a reluctant approval of even a security mission, he had continued to be eroded. He knew better than most what the military were aiming for, and that the tempo was being speeded up. Now he was arguing not against U.S. troops but for a much more restrained use, for the enclave strategy, for testing out the troops in the enclave strategy, which allowed an easy U.S. exit and which kept the U.S. troop ratio down. The Plimsoll line was very much on his mind. What was it, he asked friends, the point at which for every American you added, you in effect added nothing but simply subtracted one ARVN. Was it 75,000 or 100,000, or perhaps as high as 125,000? At which point did it become an American war? What point would signify the end of the counterinsurgency program, of which he had been the major architect?

Back in the United States, Taylor met with McNamara and the Joint Chiefs on March 29. The Chiefs were pushing the three-division plan, which would send a Marine division to Danang and an Army division to the highlands, with the third (Korean) division to go to an as yet undetermined place. The Chiefs had already decided on that, and they seemed to have McNamara's tentative approval. But Taylor said no, he thought it was open-ended and felt uneasy about sending troops into the far reaches of the country. That would mean letting the ARVN sign off; besides, that much force was not yet necessary. McNamara, always more at ease with Taylor than with the other generals, was visibly impressed; the other Chiefs, who had always been dubious about which side Taylor was on and had not wanted him to become Chairman of the Joint Chiefs because they felt that he was not one of them, were particularly uneasy about the possibility of getting into Vietnam and using too little force, another Korea, another crippling war. They saw in Taylor the kind of general who would allow the civilians to get away with it.

Taylor further told McNamara and the Chiefs that he was worried about the political effects of combat troops. Anti-Americanism was just beneath the surface and could be used by the enemy against us. In addition, he was worried about the absorptive capacity of the country—how many Americans could it take, and also the logistical limitations. McNamara said he could understand that, but he was concerned about the force ratios, which were getting worse and worse (the Chiefs, who had alerted Westmoreland on the effectiveness of this on McNamara's thinking, had done their work well). As Taylor argued, trying to hold the line and slow down the entire process, General Wheeler was making the exact opposite case, that it was quite bad, and saying that it was important to start making decisions so that they could go with logistical planning, otherwise events might move outside their control. At that point McNamara said that he still thought we should go ahead with troops, but we should be very wary of the political problems caused by the troops, and the absorptive capacity of the country. Taylor had slightly held the line, and after the meeting some of the generals were particularly bitter because they felt that Taylor was no longer in the chain of command at all, he was a civilian (only an ambassador, and ambassadors had never outweighed generals), but he was having it both ways, he was still being counted as a general. They sensed in the meeting with McNamara that they were losing it again, they had worked hard to get him to move and accept their position. That goddamn Taylor, one of them thought, as he walked out of the meeting, he can really get away with it, he really knows how to talk. Like a damn politician. Max always *looks* so good, he thought.

At the same time Westmoreland had dispatched his own man, General Bill Depuy, with his own plan to Washington. His mission, Westmoreland stated, was to keep South Vietnam from going to the Communists. It was clear that while the bombing might bring some results, it would take a long time, and it would not affect many aspects of the war in the South. With the ARVN continuing to deteriorate, the military situation was critical. Westmoreland wanted seventeen maneuver battalions, and he wanted them for the Central Highlands, where he feared the Vietcong might cut the country in half, or at the least capture a provincial capital and hold it, using it for propaganda benefits. Having been told by the Chiefs that force ratios were effective with McNamara, Westmoreland dwelled on them. The ratio, because of the decline in ARVN, was now down to 1.7–1. If events went as predicted they would soon be down to 1.6–1; however, using his projections, that decline could be turned around (an American Marine battalion with its heavy gear and air support Westmoreland estimated as the equal to three ARVN battalions, and an American airborne battalion, lighter in equipment, as the equal of two ARVN battalions). Westmoreland wanted the equivalent of two full divisions, and he wanted to use them in the Highlands: a full division in the Pleiku–Qui Nhon axis, and a brigade each at An Khe, Pleiku and Kontum. The seventeen battalions would magically become thirty-eight ARVN battalions and this would mean that the force ratio in II Corps, which he considered critical, would go from a dangerous 1.9–1 to a healthy 2.9–1. Nor did he want his troops in enclaves; it was, he thought, too negative a military philosophy to bring in *American* units with the idea of a Dunkirk uppermost in everyone's mind. The idea that they were only there to prevent defeat seemed negative. If the Americans were to come and to have effect, they must fight. If the Americans, better equipped, trained tougher than the ARVN, came and did not fight, this would not help the war effort, it might lower ARVN morale. In addition, the enclave theory put the Americans into too much contact with the population. He wanted to send the troops to the highlands and to engage them and get the maximum benefit from their presence.

On April 1 Taylor made the case against a wide-open search-and-destroy strategy and against the highlands, and for the enclave, and essentially against sending any more troops immediately. There was no desperate crisis in Saigon, he said, and they were not on a crisis footing. Rather there was time to take the American units which had already arrived and experiment with them, see how well they fought, see what the other side's reaction was. Taylor reminded everyone that to go ahead with the larger force requests was to change a long-standing policy against the use of American troops. And perhaps it wasn't necessary. There was time to find out. There could be more experimentation with the missions of the Marines already in the country. He himself did not feel it necessary to repeat his doubts about American combat troops in Asia. They would control the land they stood on, nothing more. Those words would be remembered by other civilians long afterward. And he carried the day; the President was not eager for more troops; if there was a chance to slow it down, then he was willing. Rusk too was uneasy about the whole thing, uneasy about getting involved in a ground war, though similarly, being a great chain-of-command man, a great one to go with the man on the spot, a respecter of military expertise, very uneasy about not giving a commander what he wanted. McNamara was willing to wait, telling the JCS to go ahead with the planning of the three-division force.

So Taylor temporarily held the line, but he also gave up something in the process; in order to buy time, he conceded something on missions. It would no longer be a question of security of bases. The President bought that; they all agreed on it. While they would not give Westmoreland the seventeen battalions he wanted but only two more Marine battalions (and a Marine air squadron), Westmoreland could expand their mission. The Marines were no longer just to sit on the defensive and guard their perimeter; instead, they were to be more aggressive and more active, under guidelines to be worked out by McNamara and Rusk. Thus Taylor, who had been uneasy even with the idea of a security mission for American troops, had, in fending off a search-and-destroy strategy, surrendered the security mission and moved to the enclave strategy. Johnson and the others were all relieved to be able to delay the decisions, although, as in the case of the original Taylor-Rostow mission in 1961, while they had the illusion of holding the line, they had in fact opened it up even wider; they were, step by step, losing control to the military and this was one more crucial step.

This was not a particularly happy session. They were perilously near sending combat troops, with the knowledge that the bombing would not work as they had hoped, and that they were going to have to do more. It would, said Bill Bundy, take two or three months before they would hear from Hanoi on negotiations, an estimate based on Bundy's belief that it would take that long for the United States to show clear evidence that it intended to win and had the resources to win in Vietnam (thus the contradiction: at that time they were still talking about a *minimal* use of force in a limited enclave strategy, yet they wanted maximum response from Hanoi). There was unanimous agreement that the United States had to show that it would win in the South before Hanoi would be willing to talk; Hanoi, they all thought, believed things were going its way. It would take more might, raising the bombing pressure and bringing U.S. troops there. The coming of U.S. troops would show our seriousness. The question, then, was how much pressure the United States could bring to bear on Hanoi without reaching what they called the flash point, the flash point being the point at which the Chinese Communists would enter the war with their own troops. There was a general agreement that the flash point was the destruction of the MIGs and the airfield at Phuc Yen. But, added Bill Bundy, the North would not give in unless we hit them close to the flash point. "The flash point" was an important phrase; it was the point to which they could escalate without really going to war. War was the Chinese coming in and events getting out of hand. What they were doing was below the flash point; thus it was not war. (Almost immediately after they finished the meeting McCone, who was very hawkish in person, though fair in representing the views of the more dubious experts in the Agency, argued that it was all a dark alley, that by changing the mission of U.S. troops to more offensive actions, they would simply bring more requests for more troops without changing the basic nature of the war. The war would remain, under the existing ground rules, unwinnable, since it would not change the basic balance and since Hanoi could simply send down more men.)

There was one other important thing the President and his aides decided on April 1: although they were changing the nature of the American commitment and the mission of the Marines, there was to be no announcement of it.

Quite the reverse; everyone was to minimize any change, to say that the policy had not changed. The President had enough problems with his domestic programs without being hit from the other side about going to war. Let it all take its time. This was crucial. They all understood, and the word did not slip out for another two months, at a State Department briefing when a State Department briefing officer, Bob McCloskey, came upon the fact that the mission had indeed changed. Johnson was predictably furious. James Reston of the *Times* was later to write that Lyndon Johnson escalated the war by stealth; he could not have been more right.

The next day Taylor met at the State Department with Rusk, McGeorge Bundy, Bill Bundy and Leonard Unger, U.S. ambassador to Laos. Rusk began by saying he was sure that Taylor now understood the political pressures on the President from both directions. Now, as for the new strategy, Rusk said, the Marines could be used in local counterinsurgency, and they could be used as strike reaction forces. They should have an active and aggressive posture. They should carry the fight to the enemy. On the other hand, Rusk emphasized he did not want to lose the ability to describe the mission as defensive.

Later, when he had returned to Saigon, Taylor summed up for himself his impressions of the Washington meetings. He had gone back to Washington to clarify three problems: the tempo of the bombing campaign, Rolling Thunder; the introduction of combat troops to close the manpower gap, and finally, in his own words, "the political trap on how do we end the war." Taylor felt he had received clear guidance on the first two questions. On the third he was not so sure. "We had," he dictated to his secretary, "two cards to play. The first was to stop the bombing. The second was to withdraw our forces from the South. There was some inclination to play the two cards separately, but the ambassador [Taylor] did not agree with this idea, and he thought the President also did not. We had thought of ways to permit the Communists a way out without abject surrender . . ."

But Taylor's confidence that he had been able to hold the line with the enclave theory (he believed there would be two months to experiment with the four Marine battalions, operating within a fifty-mile radius, all nicely laid out) was soon shattered. Disappointed over the loss of his two divisions, Westmoreland renewed an old request about something which had always bothered him, the area around Bien Hoa and Saigon, where two major airfields stood as vulnerable to Vietcong attacks as Danang. In addition, he was anxious to have maneuver forces as mobile as the Airborne around Saigon, and he was anxious to have the precedent of a major elite Army unit brought into the country. So he renewed his request, asking for a brigade to Bien Hoa, and an Army brigade to Qui Nhon. Again the rationale was security, but again the visions went far beyond that. The request went in on April 10; almost immediately the JCS approved it and passed it on to McNamara; on April 13 McNamara approved the brigade for the Bien Hoa area (but not for Qui Nhon, again the illusion of holding the line).

On April 15 Taylor learned of the move and was shocked; it was clear now that his influence was waning and the pressure was too great (the decision to send the brigade, he cabled back to Rusk, "shows a far greater willingness to get into a ground war than I had discerned in Washington during my recent trip"). Now there would always be too many needs, too many generals demanding troops, pushing contingency plans. The line would be harder and harder to hold, the President more and more uneasy in what was becoming his new and as yet unannounced role, war President, more and more having to meet the demands of his generals, dealing with their requirements, rather than those of his civilians. The generals would have his ear more, simply because he would be more and more responsible to the boys out there. For the military pressures were mounting, and mounting quickly. Taylor thought that he had held the line against the three divisions during his visit to Washington, but not everyone thought so. One of the decisions had called for an increase in the deployment of logistical troops for Westmoreland's command. Taylor had interpreted this as a beefing up of the logistical base for the troops *already* in the country. But the Chiefs were shrewder; when they did not get the three-division force, they had been told by McNamara to go ahead and start the planning for three divisions, and now they decided to use the increase in logistical troops as a way of initiating the three-division force. The logistical troops, by their interpretation, were to be the advance party of the three-division force. They asked McNamara if they were correct in this interpretation of the logistical troops. He answered that they were, and told them to go ahead with the planning. Thus on April 6 Admiral Sharp was informed by the JCS that after meeting with McNamara they had received the following directive: "This will confirm my understanding that the Joint Staff is preparing a detailed plan and time schedule for the actions necessary to introduce a two-to-three division force into South Vietnam at the earliest practicable date." This was the first signal of what was to come soon; Admiral Sharp, already anxious to get moving and get troops into the country, responded quickly. He called a meeting in Honolulu for April 9 and 10 to do the definitive planning for the logistical troops which would soon form the base for the three divisions at Qui Nhon and Nha Trang. Taylor cabled back that it was not his understanding that the logistical troops were an advance guard for the three divisions, but no one was paying much attention to him; he was in fact already complaining to Washington about being cut out of important cable traffic. So even here Taylor's ability to hold the line was only partial.

There was a momentum to the military and it was carrying everything along with it; Admiral Sharp was becoming increasingly irritated with Taylor's hesitance, and was beginning to push harder in his own cables to undermine Taylor. Taylor, for instance, had been very uneasy about the Marines coming ashore. He had been reporting back the Saigon government's sensitivity to a greater American presence, and he now centered his reservations on the question of how much armament the Marines would bring with them. He mentioned specifically the 8-inch howitzers; the government of Saigon did not like them, and there was, he reported, the danger that these howitzers could deliver an atomic warhead. This was too much for the already irritated Sharp, and on April 14 he cabled Westmoreland:

How anyone can get excited about an eight inch howitzer delivering an atomic warhead I fail to understand. The F-100 can deliver an atomic warhead, the B-57, the F-4 can deliver them . . . All these have been in the country for a long time. So it is really rather ludicrous to make anything of an eight inch howitzer being able to deliver an atomic warhead.

Sharp was also telling Westmoreland, still somewhat uncertain what his instructions were regarding the troops he was getting, that as far as Sharp could determine from the JCS, Westy's job was to get on "with killing Cong."

At almost the same time the President began to meet with some members of the Congress to explain his problems and let them know that he might have to send some American boys to Vietnam. A small number, it seemed. At one meeting the figure sounded like 40,000 or 50,000, but for Gaylord Nelson, one of the senators present, it was nonetheless disquieting. He had not liked the drift at all, and that night as he drove home with his old friend Hubert Humphrey, he told Humphrey that it looked bad, the nation was being pulled into a big war.

"You know, Gaylord," said Humphrey, "there are people at State and the Pentagon who want to send *three hundred thousand* men out there." Humphrey paused. "But the President will never get sucked into anything like that."

THE FORCES PUSHING AGAINST LYNDON JOHNSON AS HE CAME CLOSER and closer to a decision seemed terribly imbalanced. On the one side were the Chiefs and the Saigon generals, wanting troops, sure of themselves, speaking for the Cold War, for patriotism, and joined with them were his principal national security advisers, all believers in the use of force. Those committed to peace were not as well organized, not as impressive, and seemingly not as potent politically; if anything, in making their case to him, they seemed to unveil their weaknesses more than their strengths. One incident revealed how frail the peace people seemed to Johnson. On the first weekend in April the Americans for Democratic Action were holding their annual convention, and a group of the leadership asked to see the President, specifically to protest the bombing. The meeting was granted and about a dozen ADA officials went over to see the President. Some of the ADA people were quite impassioned; the bombing of the North, they said, simply had to stop. It was wrong, it was against everything America stood for. Johnson himself tried as best he could to deflect the criticism. He was under great pressure from the military to use more force, he said; he had tried to negotiate, but Hanoi continued to be the aggressor. He read at great length from a speech that he intended to give on the Mekong River development project; he was, he said, trying to do there what he was doing here at home. But he was not able to assuage their feeling. It was a sharp and tough exchange. The ADA people were particularly worried about McNamara's role, and several of them criticized the growing power of the Secretary of Defense, whom they visualized as being a major hawk. Johnson moved to set them at ease. "Why are you people always complaining about McNamara?" he asked. "Why, Mac Bundy here"—pointing to Bundy—"is a much bigger hawk than McNamara." But even the ADA people did not seem to be particularly unified; there were divisions within the group, and John Roche, a Brandeis professor who was the outgoing chairman, seemed quite sympathetic to the Johnson position. As the group was leaving, it passed through the White House press room, and Joe Rauh, one of the ADA officials, told the waiting reporters that the exchanges had been sharp ones, that the ADA had expressed its opposition to the bombing in very strong terms. At that point Roche tried to soften Rauh's statement, and the two clashed over the wording, Roche wanting a more subdued description.

The whole incident immediately convinced Johnson that he could handle the liberals, that they had no real muscle, that they were divided among themselves. Even as he said good-bye to the ADA representatives, he showed in the Joint Chiefs, plus McNamara and Rusk, for one of the pressing meetings on the use of ground troops. Because he liked to begin each meeting by referring to the one which preceded it, the President now reached into the wastebasket and scooped up the notes which the ADA people had brought to the meeting and written to each other during it. Then, mimicking his previous guests to perfection, he began to read the notes to the assembled Chiefs, pausing, showing great relish in ridiculing each, adjusting his voice as necessary, taking particular pleasure in one that Rauh had written: "Why doesn't he take the issue of Vietnam to the United Nations?" That one in particular broke them up. Then, the liberals dispensed with, they got down to more serious things, such as the forthcoming decisions on ground troops.

Nor was Johnson's instinct to use force tempered in April by the experience in the Dominican Republic. When the frail political legitimacy of the Dominican government began to fall apart, and when leftist rebels began to make a challenge, Johnson moved quickly to stop another Cuba. Presidents in the past had been soft on Cuba and had paid for it. No one would accuse Lyndon

Johnson of that. So despite the fact that the reports from the Dominican were remarkably unclear, with the American ambassador filing wildly exaggerated estimates on the amount of violence taking place, and totally unconfirmed reports on the extent of Communist subversion, Johnson moved swiftly. He would use force. No one at a high level in the Administration dissented, or suggested that the United States had no legal justification for moving in with force, or indeed that it did not even know what was happening. Force it was, overkill, not just the Marines, but the Airborne as well, 22,000 troops, and they went in, and whatever the uprising was—the Administration seemed unclear about that—it was put down. American muscle had determined the outcome. Oh, there had been protests from the left, and from people nervous about things like this, but Johnson had paid no attention and it had worked out—or seemed to work out. So if the same liberals were making the same soft sounds on Vietnam, why pay attention? People forgot about these things if they worked out, and there was no doubt what would happen when real men walked into one of these fourth-rate countries and set things right. So there was, out of the Dominican, an impression confirmed that if you just stood tall, why, things would come your way, though of course the difference between the depth and root of the insurgency in Vietnam and the sheer political frustration and chaos of the Dominican was very, very great. But the Dominican, whatever else, did not discourage Lyndon Johnson from the use of force. Nor, of course, the men around him.

THE PRESIDENT WAS INCREASINGLY CONCERNED ABOUT THE SITUATION in Vietnam, but he was less wary of the French experience than Taylor or Ball; he was more confident of what *Americans* could do. In addition, and this was to be important later as the question of enclave strategy versus search-and-destroy strategy arose, he was not a man to sponsor a defensive strategy, to send American boys overseas, to see American boys killed, and then yet be involved in a long, unrewarding war. He was not a man for that kind of war, a man to be charged with a no-win policy. The political trap of the Korean War was real to him: he knew what it was like to be attacked for failing to win a war, for getting in with a no-win policy. If Americans were going to be there, they had better be aggressive. Clean it all up and get home. Show Ho what Americans could do, and get him to the table. Consequently, when Taylor appeared almost querulous about Westmoreland's April 10 request, McNaughton immediately explained that "highest authority" thought the situation was deteriorating, that something new was needed in the South, which included using the 173rd for security and for combat operations, as Westmoreland wanted. Taylor still thought it precipitous; he had cabled earlier saying that it went ahead of the planning agreed upon during his visit to Washington; then on April 17 he moved to block the deployment, which he could do by not clearing it with the Vietnamese government; he said he would not move to clear it with the government until he got further and more specific instructions from Washington. What he wanted, he said, was a sixty-day experimental period with forces already in the country; he was wary of what he called "hasty and ill-conceived proposals for deployment of more forces." He was still trying to hold them off, but the pressure was building, and his position was preserved only by greater and greater concessions.

Which became very clear within a week as many of the principals gathered in Honolulu to go over strategy and troop commitments for the immediate future. Time was now running out on them. They had in the past done everything to prevent sending ground troops to Vietnam; since 1954 that had been a primary objective; now, eleven years later, it was all coming to an end. They had bombed in order not to send troops, in order to make Hanoi talk, but it was clear that the bombing was having very little effect (McCone of the CIA was reporting that it wasn't really hurting Hanoi at all). Rather the result might be the opposite; there were now reports of at least one North Vietnamese regiment in the country and a second poised on the border. There were indications that more might be coming down the trails. The bombing had failed, just as the counterinsurgency commitment had failed. The erosion of the anti–ground-troops position could be seen through the changes in Taylor; he was at once committed to winning the war (or saving South Vietnam), remaining a player in good standing with the other players, loyalty to the traditions of the U.S. Army, and at the same time keeping the U.S. ground forces out and preventing a repeat of the French experience. As the pressure increased, his position would change degree by degree, his resistance to U.S. troops diminishing.

Honolulu marked the end of an outlook on Vietnam. In the last four weeks Johnson had been slipping from being a peacetime President to a wartime one; more and more under the influence and pressure of the JCS; the civilians more and more on the defensive, trying to halve the requests of the JCS (which simply meant that the military would double whatever it really wanted), trying to limit the missions. Now at Honolulu this would become ever more clear. It was the crucial meeting to decide needs and strategies. It was attended by McNamara, Bill Bundy, McNaughton, Earle Wheeler, Admiral Sharp, Taylor and Westmoreland, and the military was now numerically beginning to dominate.

Now, for the first time, Westmoreland was the dominating figure. He was no longer the number-two man from Saigon, there to sit behind Taylor looking strong and supportive, there to say that the military situation wasn't quite as bad as the political, there to say that the ARVN reserve forces were depleted. The bombing, which he had always doubted, had failed (although they were all too polite to say so; they said instead that it would not work within the proper time limit). Now it was his turn to play, and they would find that he was a forceful player who knew what he wanted, how much to ask for and how much not to ask for. At this meeting he would ask for troops and give in on strategy. It was in that sense Westmoreland's conference. It was as if the change in President Johnson's mind, the realization that more dramatic and aggressive measures were needed, had turned it to him. Since Westmoreland had in the past argued that the war was really in the South, that the North was a peripheral part, they had not turned to him, because if they had, it would have meant troops. Now that the bombing had failed, they had to listen to him. If Hanoi was to give up the war, he claimed, it would have to be beaten in the South; if Hanoi thought that victory was close in the South, it would be more than willing to bear the bombing. Thus the problem was on the ground, and success would only come on the ground. Otherwise it was an endless, open-ended war, which would see, despite the greater American role and input, an eventual South Vietnamese collapse and loss, or at best a long and bitter conflict which would barely stave off defeat.

Westmoreland did not specify how many ground troops were needed; he was not eager to scare off the civilians, and he did not talk at length about what the North Vietnamese reaction would be (that was not his job, to forecast Hanoi's intentions. He knew it had the capability, but the discussion of intentions, that was for the intelligence community). He was pleased to find that McNamara was now more sympathetic to the use of troops, and this was what the President seemed to want. As for the bombing, it was helpful and we should continue to keep the pressure up; but it would not do the job alone. Taylor in particular said that it was important not to attack the North Vietnamese assets within what was now called the Hanoi-Haiphong doughnut. This, he said, would be killing the hostage. There would, however, have to be more ground troops; Westmoreland said it was basic to any kind of success, and there was complete agreement on this, that the ARVN could not do it; it was having a hard time filling up depleted units rather than creating new ones. The strategy, they agreed, was the Taylor enclave strategy. Essentially experimental. Sharp, Wheeler and Westmoreland wanted a grander, more aggressive strategy, but this was not the time to argue that. The thing to do was to get the troops in-country first, and then worry about strategy and use later.

So Westmoreland got almost all he wanted in terms of numbers. He had gone into the Honolulu meeting with 33,500 Americans in the country. At Honolulu, 40,000 more were committed, with others discussed and put on the preparation list. Westmoreland would get his Army brigade for Bien Hoa by May 1, his first Army troops. He would get three more Marine battalions, plus three tactical fighter squadrons, for Chu Lai, where an airstrip was being built. He would get an Army brigade for the Qui Nhon-Nha Trang area by June 15, and he would get all the necessary logistical complement necessary. In addition, the United States would go ahead with plans for an Australian battalion to Vung Tau, and a Korean regimental combat team for Quang Ngai. This meant that the United States would have thirteen maneuver battalions and 82,000 men in-country, plus four Third Country battalions and 7,250 men. The men at Honolulu also discussed the need for, but did not yet recommend, further troop commitments. This included an Army airmobile division (nine battalions), which Westmoreland had always wanted and which despite the general agreement on the enclave strategy would go to the Central Highlands, as well as the remainder of the Marine expeditionary force, which was two battalions, and an Army corps headquarters; further, the Koreans would come up with a full division, consisting of six battalions. All this amounted to seventeen additional maneuver battalions, which would have brought the total for Westmoreland to thirty-four battalions. The planning and logistical problems of getting the divisions ready and pointed toward Vietnam was to go ahead. It was all moving Westy's way.

The strategy was of course still Taylor's. It was less than what the military wanted, and it seemed to go along with what the President wanted, a little more than the past, but not yet a ground war. Taylor had a feeling that he had held the line again, and again the reverse was true. Those at the conference were agreed that the war would last longer than had previously been expected. In the past they had thought of the bombing producing results within six months, and when congressional critics such as Ernest Gruening had questioned the President about it, he had asked for six months. Six months to get them to the table. Everything cooled off by Christmas. Now they were prepared for more pessimistic estimates. McNaughton's notes on the conference said that it would take more than six months, "perhaps a year or two to demonstrate Vietcong failure in the South." This was the old American optimism and arrogance; the French had fought there inconclusively for eight years with an enormous expeditionary force, but the Americans fighting from defensive enclaves would do it in a year, maybe a little more. The phrasing here, summing up the meeting, was quite similar to Taylor's cable of April 17: the idea was to use the enclaves to take the initiative away from the enemy, otherwise, he had cabled, ground war might "drag into 1966 and even beyond." (On April 24 Taylor sent an "Eyes Only" cable to McNamara, where he said he wanted to modify his position as agreed upon in Hawaii. Where it had said that it might take a year or two to affect Hanoi's will, Taylor wanted it to read "this process will probably take months—how many is impossible to estimate . . ." He was thus, in fact, becoming a little more optimistic.) After the meeting was over, selected correspondents from both the *New York Times* and the Washington *Post* were called in and given a deliberate leak. The judgment of the military, said the official spokesman, was that it would not be a

short war after all. In fact, it might last as long as six months. The North
would not be able to withstand the American pressure that long.

THE CONFERENCE WAS OVER, AND THE FIRST MAJOR STEP TOWARD
combat troops had been taken. It was true that essentially the strategy was
still to be enclave, and in that sense Taylor had held the line, but it was a frail
line indeed. The strategy was agreed upon without direct Vietcong or North
Vietnamese military ground pressure (which, when it came, given the extraordinary weakness of the ARVN, would mean even greater pressure to use the
American troops as aggressively as possible). It was a "victory strategy," in
their own words. It did not call for victory in the classic military sense; it was
a victory strategy because it would deny victory to the other side. The
Vietcong, denied these vital enclaves, would realize that they could not win,
and would thus sue for a negotiated peace. It was, in effect, brilliant planning
which defied common sense. (Indeed, a few months earlier Mac Bundy had
shown a member of his staff some of the planning for the escalation, particularly the bombing, and the aide had been impressed by how thorough it all
was, lots of details. Bundy asked the aide what he thought, and he answered
that though he didn't know anything about the military calculations, "the
thing that bothers me is that no matter what we do to them, they live there
and we don't, and they know that someday we'll have to go away and thus
they know they can outlast us." Bundy considered the answer for a moment.
"That's a good point," he said.) Now we would bring victory by fighting from
enclaves. It was an extraordinary strategy because it meant that the Vietcong,
having the United States pinned down in tiny enclaves, would be able to
squeeze tighter and tighter on the rest of the country, take the rice and agricultural products, recruit at will, and yet somehow tire of a war with the
United States, as they had not tired of a war with France. It was also a policy
ill conceived for that particular President, because Lyndon Johnson, once
committed, was not a man for half measures, for a stalled, drawn-out war, for
a war policy that his critics could quite correctly seize on as a no-win policy.
So it was one more half measure, one more item in the long list of self-delusion on Vietnam. We would once again try to do something on the cheap, and
yet, even though it was at a bargain-basement price, we would be conveying
to Hanoi the intensity of our will and commitment, and they would thus
quickly come to their senses. Perhaps the greatest illusion was the idea that
we cared more for what was going on than they did, that we would pay a
higher price, that they would feel the threshold of pain before we did. It was
of course an obvious lie; but the principals had, in their desire not to come to
real decisions, painted themselves into a corner where lie followed lie.

So nothing had been solved at the Honolulu conference, but it was the last time that Max Taylor was a major player, his farewell in fact. When it was all over, Taylor, the man who had been the architect of the counterinsurgency, of the small war in 1961, and who in 1964 and 1965 had opposed the use of combat troops, had in fact played exactly the role he did not intend to play. He had, by fighting to limit the troop escalation step by step, helped them to slide into it. The gap from each step to the next step always seemed relatively small, each step that had been exacted while he held back had simply made the next step a little easier, never too great. He had been a conduit, not a brake.

THEY HAD COME TO THEIR ESSENTIAL AGREEMENT IN HONOLULU ON April 20. The next morning John McCone, informed of their decision, told the NSC that it simply meant that Hanoi would increase its infiltration and step up the war. Thus more Americans. Thus more North Vietnamese. Thus a higher level of violence.

When George Ball heard of the decisions at Honolulu, he was appalled; he sensed that they were crossing a point of no return and he was disturbed about their lack of awareness of what was happening. On that afternoon he again made a major appeal to hold the line. The request to go to 80,000 confirmed what he had always feared, the beginning of the long slide toward an American combat commitment without a real recognition or admission by the men themselves that this was so. Eighty thousand, he knew, might not long remain the ceiling. It was not a figure to frighten the President, but it was an extremely dangerous precedent. If they could go to about 80,000 without great pressure from the Vietcong, what would be next? And what were the guidelines to be, what was the strategy? At what point would they stop? That afternoon he pointed out that the figure of 80,000 represented a quantum jump of 150 percent. Nor would it, he said, induce Hanoi to quit, and cited the opinion of McCone given that morning, that Hanoi would now substantially increase the rate of infiltration into the South. It was, he said, time to pause, to wait and to look, and to try and do some political soundings. The bombing, he noted, had hardly turned out to be the decisive act predicted for it. We had been bombing the North for ten weeks, a total of 2,800 sorties, going from 122 per week to 604 in the last week, an awesome show of bombing; this had slightly improved Saigon's morale, and probably hurt the Vietcong morale. But there was, and he was obstinate about this, no evidence that it had caused Hanoi to slow down the infiltration. Rather the reverse was becoming evident. We were, he said, at a threshold. It was time not to send more men, to rush ahead without a clear strategy, without a clear definition of what we were getting into. Instead, it was a time to pause, to re-examine Hanoi's position. There was, he thought, much that was acceptable in Hanoi's recently announced four points for negotiation. It was time to make a major effort to see what the possibilities of negotiation were, but it was, he realized even at the time, the wrong proposal at the wrong time. No one was interested in such a solution because we would have been negotiating from weakness (nor, of course, would there have been much interest in negotiation had we been in a strong position, then we would have wanted to win). We could not negotiate until we had committed enough of our own resources to turn the tide; at that time, however, having invested much more, the price we wanted to extract from negotiations would have risen.

Ball found himself very much alone; in a sense McCone seemed to be arguing from the same position, but McCone wanted to use more force. Taylor seemed to be arguing from the same position, but he was unwilling to face the reality of what it meant, withdrawal. And Bill Bundy felt the same way, saw the dangers, but he, too, was unwilling to do the unthinkable, to cut our losses. Bill Bundy was an even more divided man than Taylor at this point. As a CIA man he had dealt with Indochina and he knew better than most the French chapter of that story; he was very uneasy about committing American troops, of what this might do to the population. At the same time he was a believer in using force, and he was a good bureaucrat and an ambitious one, and he knew which way the play was going. So at this point the idea of American troops was an unnerving one, and like Taylor he was worried about the Plimsoll line: would it come at 75,000, or 80,000, and during this debate Bill Bundy seemed to be making the case against sending combat troops, the weakness of the society, the hazards of following in the French footsteps. And Ball, who had been searching for allies, who had believed one more man would turn it, thought: Here is my man, my one ally. When they went back to State together, Ball suggested to Bundy that they work together on a major paper on how to extricate the United States from the growing quagmire. It was a crucial moment. Bundy desisted. He saw all the problems, he had all the doubts, he told Ball, but he did not go *that* far, he was not prepared to reverse twenty-five years of American policy. We couldn't let Vietnam go down the drain . . . So he left Ball there and it became a Ball paper, not a Ball-Bundy paper. But Ball was far from alone in believing that the combat-troop commitment was just about to start, that it would be impossible to control and that the North Vietnamese would match our commitment and match us in endurance. Yet it was a lonely time for Ball.

There was in the meetings occasional support from Bill Bundy, but then he would always slip away. Taylor was not really an ally; he was a doubter, but when it came down to the hard edge, he was always on the other side. Rusk was a friend, he never sprang ambushes at the meetings (as McNamara did), but he was an impenetrable man. He had few beliefs but those he had went very deep; if the world was changing, Dean Rusk was not; he had learned his lessons and learned them well. Munich. Mutual security. Containment. The necessity of a democracy to show dictatorships that it could not be bluffed. And a belief that American force could do anything that its leaders set their minds to.

It was not Ball's easiest time and McNamara was the problem for Ball in those days. He was the ripper. On the sidelines, Mac Bundy was the kibitzer, joining in with McNamara to cut at Ball, but it was McNamara who did the ripping. He would not have done it unless he thought it was the role the President wanted him to play, the President in a sense seeming to encourage both Ball and McNamara. So McNamara was forceful and tough, the advocate of escalation. Perhaps he did have doubts, he was certainly not euphoric (he would say years afterward that he was not without doubts, he knew it would not be easy). But his own doubts were reconciled when he was in those meetings; then they were never evident, and he was brilliant and forceful at obliterating others. In those days after Hawaii, Ball would argue that this step opened the door, that they had been, in his words, at the threshold and they were on their way to crossing it. Soon they would lose control, he said; soon we would be sending 200,000 to 250,000 men there. Then they would tear into him, McNamara the leader: It's dirty pool; for Christ's sake, George, we're not talking about anything like that, no one's talking about that many people, we're talking about a dozen, maybe a few more maneuver battalions. McNamara was a ferocious infighter, statistics and force ratios came pouring out of him like a great uncapped faucet. He had total control of his facts and he was quick and nimble with them; there was never a man better with numbers, he could characterize enemy strength and movement and do it statistically.

Poor George had no counterfigures; he would talk in vague doubts, lacking these figures, and leave the meetings occasionally depressed and annoyed. Why did McNamara have such good figures? Why did McNamara have such good staff work and Ball such poor staff work? The next day Ball would angrily dispatch his staff to come up with the figures, to find out how McNamara had gotten them, and the staff would burrow away and occasionally find that one of the reasons that Ball did not have comparable figures was that they did not always exist. McNamara had invented them, he dissembled even within the bureaucracy, though, of course, always for a good cause. It was part of his sense of service. He believed in what he did, and thus the morality of it was assured, and everything else fell into place. It was all right to lie and dissemble for the right causes. It was part of service, loyalty to the President, not to the nation, not to colleagues, it was a very special bureaucratic-corporate definition of integrity; you could do almost anything you wanted as long as it served your superior.

IF THEY WERE AT THE THRESHOLD, THE CROSSING WOULD COME sooner than any of them thought. The Vietcong had passed the winter resting, building up their forces, expanding their logistical base to go with their bigger, more formidable units. In early May the Vietcong began their spring offensive. They struck the capital of Phuoc Long province in regimental strength. It was a ferocious, audacious attack; in addition to the sheer bravery and intensity which had marked the Vietcong in the past, there was now an added element of the size of the units. In the past the Vietcong had usually been outnumbered and outgunned by the ARVN and had usually won simply because its units were better led and better motivated. Now, in addition to being better units man for man, they were turning out to have units as large and as well armed, the weapons they had captured in 1962–1964 were finally being used. The ARVN was no match for them. The Vietcong overran the town, held it for a day and then retreated. The message was ominous: if they could strike here this openly and with this force, they could do it elsewhere in the country. And they soon did.

To Westmoreland and Depuy, who were already convinced of the basic weakness of the ARVN and of the Vietcong capacity, it was clear that the ARVN would not be able to hold the line. The big beefed-up Vietcong battalions and regiments were a formidable infantry force, fighting on their terrain, in a type of war they had virtually invented, and in which they set the rules. (Years later Westmoreland would describe this particular time as the point at which the Vietcong had won the war, but neither side realized it.) Now they were knocking off ARVN battalions with lightning speed, and the results were always the same, the destruction of the ARVN units. What was more ominous for Westmoreland was that this systematic destruction of the ARVN was taking place without the Vietcong using anywhere near its full potential (in early June, after a series of major ARVN defeats, the Vietcong had used only two of its nine regiments in any serious form). What was perhaps even more dangerous was that elements of one North Vietnamese division, the 325th, had clearly entered the country and were poised (but still unused) in the Kontum area, while elements of the 304th were also suspected of being in the northern regions of the South. It looked as if the enemy was moving in for the kill.

In May, Westmoreland's cables became increasingly forceful and pessimistic, warning that the situation was very bad, that the ARVN simply could not hold the line, and warning of the danger of the Vietcong cutting the country in half, something that had long worried the American command, though it was, in fact, a fairly thin threat, since the Vietcong did not hold terrain. No single cable from Westmoreland jarred Washington; rather it was like a gathering cloud, warning Washington that things were going poorly, that Saigon's worst fears were being confirmed. Then at the end of May the Vietcong ambushed an ARVN regiment near Quang Ngai; the ARVN rushed reinforcements to the scene, and these were, in the tradition of this war, also ambushed, a favorite tactic of the other side. The battle lasted for several days; the ARVN force was badly mauled, two battalions completely destroyed, and ARVN commanders showed fear in the face of the enemy.

A few days later, on June 7, Westmoreland asked for a major American troop commitment, and for freedom to use the troops as he saw fit. He was asking for immediate U.S. reinforcements totaling thirty-five battalions; in addition, he named nine other battalions that he might soon want. This became known within the bureaucracy as Westmoreland's forty-four-battalion request. His request was endorsed by Admiral Sharp at CINCPAC, and the feeling in Washington appeared to be immediately favorable. Four days after he made the request, Westmoreland was told by the Chiefs that the President was close to approving most of what he wanted. Then on June 17 Taylor also signed on; he told Washington that the situation in Saigon was every bit as serious as Westmoreland was claiming, which removed the last real restraint. Only tactical reservations had held them back, in particular Taylor's feeling that things weren't that bad, but now there was a consensus. Everyone was lining up behind U.S. troops, including the most influential civilian-military official. They had in fact made decision after decision in the last few months slipping into the combat troop commitment; they had closed off the only real alternative, which was negotiation from a position of weakness. Now they were crossing the Rubicon. The Westmoreland package would take them to 200,000, and it would be open-ended. There was of course some hope that the 200,000 might do it. The President hoped so.

On June 22 General Wheeler, at the President's request, cabled Westmoreland asking him if the forty-four battalions would be enough to convince the other side that it could not win. Westmoreland, always a good deal more cautious about the job ahead than the civilians, said that he did not think anything would affect the Hanoi-Vietcong position in the next six months, but that this would establish a favorable balance of power by the end of the year, and thus reverse the then favorable Vietcong balance. For the United States to take the initiative, he added, further forces would be needed in 1966, and beyond that. What he was saying was not that different from what George Ball was saying: it was getting big and it might get bigger. For almost immediately after Westmoreland's request, Ball made his last pitch. He knew now that he had in effect lost: he was now trying to fight a delaying action. Instead of our going to 200,000 as recommended, he wanted to hold the line at 100,000, with an understanding that this was the ceiling, and to use the troops for a three-month trial period. But he knew he was on the defensive, that he was taking what were by now compromised positions. Nonetheless, he again warned that we were underestimating the enemy and his endurance. A half-million Americans would not do the job, he warned; rather, the enemy would simply match our level of violence. As for optimism by generals, the French generals had always exuded optimism, and it had done them no good. But it was all getting out of control now, and Ball knew it.

The issues were no longer whether to send combat troops, or essentially what mission they would be employed in (Westmoreland was asking for freedom to maneuver them as he chose, and being a commander, that would almost automatically be his prerogative). At this point the issues were whether or not to go on a wartime footing (as the Chiefs wanted), to call up the reserves, to bring the war openly into the budget on special financing, and thus in an open and honest way let the public know what was ahead. In particular the question of the reserves was one which dominated the decisions in late June and July. But in any real sense the question of combat troops on the mainland of Asia had already been answered. They had inched their way across the Rubicon without even admitting it. The job of their public spokesmen had been to avoid clarifying the changes in the policy, to misinform the public rather than inform it.

THE LAST DAYS OF MAY AND THE EARLY DAYS OF JUNE WERE NOT A time that George Reedy would later recall with very great pleasure. They were in fact a nightmare for him. He was Lyndon Johnson's press secretary and he was caught between growing pressure from the White House correspondents to find out what was going on about Vietnam, a sense that the rules were changing, and an almost total blackout on the subject by Johnson and an almost neurotic desire by the President to keep it that way, for of course, given the nature of Johnson, the more things changed and the worse they got, the less he wanted written about them. Reedy was in fact caught directly between the clash of those two most distinct and separate forces at work in the Johnson Administration, the private men making secret decisions on Vietnam as though they were part of a closed society, and the traditional open American society, represented by the American press. The result was a constant horror for Reedy, a daily humiliation for a very sensitive man from which he would not easily recover. Each day the reporters would surge forward, not unlike picadors in a bullfight, with their prickly questions on Vietnam, and each day Reedy would try to turn them aside, and each day there would be a little more blood, primarily Reedy's, on the White House press-room floor. Reedy, a former wire-service man, a thoughtful man (who would later write one of the era's most reflective books on the Presidency), had prided himself on his candor. Now he watched his own reputation for honesty diminish daily. If being assaulted by twenty reporters each day was not sufficient torture, there was more: Lyndon Johnson was beating on him too, Johnson was blaming Reedy for each negative story in the press which hinted at the imperfections of Vietnam. Why couldn't Reedy be like Pierre Salinger? Pierre got Kennedy good positive stories (Johnson forgetting his own anger with Pierre when he failed to get a Kennedy-style press for Johnson). Why couldn't Reedy be a *creative* press officer? To make sure that Reedy might not be too creative, however, Johnson deliberately kept him as far as possible from any meetings and any information on Vietnam. Those were orders; neither he nor any member of his staff was to know about Vietnam. If he did not know, he could not leak, and thus he could truthfully stand before the reporters and say he knew nothing. Vietnam was a military operation, and if there was any news it would come from Arthur Sylvester at the Pentagon (who of course was under orders to say nothing). The White House reporters, playing that particularly savage game, knowing that Reedy had no access to power, treated him accordingly with mounting disrespect. He was becoming something of a joke to them, and they wrote that he was on his way to becoming the greatest "No comment" press secretary in White House history. His job seemed increasingly to be a dartboard for an angry and irritable press.

At the State Department, similar scenes were unfolding day after day. In particular, a struggle of remarkable proportions was taking place between John Finney of the *New York Times* and Robert McCloskey, the State Department briefing officer. Finney was not particularly well known outside his profession, but within it he has a flawless and enviable reputation; he is the very model of what a reporter ought to be. Before covering the State Department, he was the *Times*'s man on science, almost a pioneer journalist covering the relationship between politics and science; to both that assignment and his subsequent covering of State he brought a kind of relentless intelligence and integrity, and he was, above all, dogged. Now in late May, with the arrival of the Marines in Vietnam, he began to question their mission, he was old enough, he would say later, to know that if the Marines were there, sooner or later they were going to fight. His antagonist was his friend McCloskey, who was a special favorite of the men who covered State. He had a reputation for being straight, honest and professional, and many reporters considered him the best briefing officer in Washington. His credibility with reporters was very high because he had a reputation for working hard to give accurate information on State Department policy, whether good policy or bad.

For days the State Department press corps, led in large part by Finney but with other reporters chiming in, had been asking what were essentially the same questions, again and again, doggedly, knowing somehow that something was going on, determined to keep the pressure up. "Bob," the scenario would go, "is there a new mission for the Marines?" "Bob, does this imply a change of American policy?" "Bob, will the Marines go into combat as units if the Vietnamese request them?" Back would come the answers, sounding frailer and more tired all the time: No, they were there to protect American personnel and American property; no, there was no change of mission. The pressure, the repetition, were at the heart of it, and of course it worked. The more pressure they put on, the more McCloskey felt that he had to respond honestly, so while the questions kept coming, McCloskey was very quietly trying to gather information on what the policy really was (the principals were still trying to hold the new decisions as closely as possible; and most high members of the government were as poorly informed as the American public as to what was happening). McCloskey and his superior, James Greenfield, the Assistant Secretary of State for Public Affairs, had been trying to get their superiors to announce as honestly as possible what the new policies were (Greenfield felt strongly that if American troops were going into combat, the American public should not learn about it after the fact from military spokesmen in Vietnam), but nothing had been decided at the higher level, though a contingency statement was drawn up at one point. Meanwhile McCloskey was on the phone a good deal, talking to friends at State and Defense, trying to find out exactly what the new rules of engagement were. He was, in effect, becoming a reporter.

On June 7 he went before the daily briefing and fended off the questions in the normal way. Later that day he was able to put together the pieces in his own mind about what the new American policy was. The next day he decided to speak openly about it; he knew he was acting on his own and taking an enormous risk—in effect, putting his job on the line—and that his protection from above might be minimal. He knew exactly what was at stake, but he also felt very strongly that it was the right thing to do, that if there was any kind of right to know, it extended to decisions on how American troops were used. It was, on McCloskey's part, a personal act of courage.

Thus at the briefing on June 8, when the questions came, McCloskey was ready. The way in which the people of the United States found out that the policy had changed was instructive:

Q: Let me ask one other question. What you are saying means that the decision has been made in Washington as a matter of policy that if Westmoreland receives a request for U.S. forces in Viet-Nam to give combat support to Vietnamese forces he has the power to make the decision?

A: That is correct.

Q: Could you give us any understanding, Bob, as to when Westmoreland got this additional authority?

A: I couldn't be specific but it is something that has developed over the past several weeks.

Q: Is this from a legal point of view, a delegation of the President's authority or what is the formal point of view?

A: Well, yes. The President as Commander in Chief in turn delegates authority to military commanders, and in this case, General Westmoreland.

It was a very big story, and within minutes the wire services were carrying it. At the White House, where the AP and UPI tickers were lodged, the press corps and Lyndon Johnson saw the stories at almost the same time. Johnson went into one of his wildest rages. Perhaps in his mind he always had known this would happen, but it was as if he believed he could change things by the force of his will: if he willed them not to happen, they would not happen; if he denied that events were taking place, they would not take place. Now even that illusion had been shattered and he was shouting and screaming at Reedy, at anybody who walked near him. Who the goddamn hell leaked this? Who the hell was McCloskey? McCloskey—where the hell did he come from? Some kid at State. Well, his ass was going to be briefing people in Africa very goddamn soon. Who the hell authorized the leak? Find out if Rusk or Ball or someone at State authorized that leak, and get them over here. It was goddamn well treason. Jesus Christ, couldn't a President of the United States make a decision in secret without some kid at State named McCloskey giving it out? Couldn't you have secrets any more? Why had Reedy let it happen? Another White House aide, hoping to see Johnson on a domestic matter, was warned by friends: don't bring it up today, bring it up tomorrow or next week, next month, next year, but not today, he's murderous today.

At State the storm was beginning to erupt, and it looked as if McCloskey would have to go. But one man protected him: he was called upstairs by Dean Rusk, who was very gentle with him. Rusk thought it was very unfortunate that McCloskey found himself in the situation that he did, but Rusk could understand it. Anyway, Rusk would try to straighten it out. And so Rusk went over to the White House, which was of course pouring out the most vehement of denials of the story, and offered his protection to McCloskey, and the next day he called McCloskey in and told him not to worry about it, that it would all take care of itself. So McCloskey remained at his job, but within the month George Reedy was replaced by Bill Moyers as White House press secretary.

Chapter Twenty-six

LYNDON JOHNSON HAD BEEN FRENETIC AND IRASCIBLE IN THE previous months, as if he had found himself suspended between his ambitions and his desires and the grim promise of Vietnam; and the more there seemed to be a possibility of a choice, the more difficult and touchy he had been. Now as he slowly made his decisions he seemed to take strength from them and from the people around him. He became quieter, less frenetic, more deliberate in his decisions. If he took sustenance from those around him who urged escalation, then similarly, as if almost by chance, he just managed to see less of those who had doubts or seemed to have doubts; he gave signals of what he wanted to hear and what he did not. (One reason why he did not seem to like McCone—they did not get on very well and McCone would make a quick exit—was that McCone, even though he was more hawkish than Johnson, more hard-line in his attitudes, had insisted in those days in February, March and April on telling the President the very blunt truth.) It was not just the very top men, McNamara, Bundy, Rusk, Wheeler, McNaughton, who reassured him, it was his other friends as well who were telling him to go ahead. These men were all liberals, committed to the good things in life, to decency and humane values. They were for civil rights and for peace; they did not talk about keeping the niggers in their place, or lobbing grenades into the Kremlin men's room; they were good men, urbane, modern, if they were for a war, it would be a good war. So Johnson saw around him confirmation of the soundness, the wisdom and the decency of what he was doing, even among his most

trusted friends, like Abe Fortas. Particularly Abe Fortas. He was a private adviser, unusually close to Johnson, making the transition from enormously successful attorney to Supreme Court Justice in those very months that Johnson
was making the transition from peacetime President to wartime President.
Few people were as influential with Johnson as Fortas, who was loyal to no
other politician in Washington; he had been the lawyer who helped turn Congressman Johnson into Senator Johnson. If there were those on Johnson's staff
who did not think that Fortas was a man of any real political sensitivity, nonetheless he was the kind of man Johnson admired: he was a liberal without
being a do-gooder, a man of force who got things done without showing softness. Johnson had autographed a photo to Fortas: "To Abe, who makes the
most of the horsepower God gave him." Which was very Johnsonian. And
now during the crucial months before he went to the Supreme Court and
even after, Fortas was in constant contact with the President, Johnson
phoning him almost every night and replaying the day's events, listening to
Fortas' wisdom. Fortas was a tower of strength, a pillar of hawkishness, a man
of few doubts about the wisdom of going forward, and Fortas would remind
Johnson that no President had ever lost a war, that the political consequences
of withdrawal were terrible. Fortas was the classic hard-line liberal, though of
course he knew little of Southeast Asia and little of this country as well, but
that did not bother him, he was a hawk and proud of it. (When the final decisions were in and Max Frankel of the *New York Times* wrote a long summary story of the decision making, he would describe the fact that Justice
Fortas had played a role, and the phrase he would use was that Johnson had
also consulted with "Justice Fortas, who is not a dove." Proofreaders being
what they are, the story came out as "Justice Fortas, who is a dove." The next
day Fortas called Frankel to tell him the story was very good and to mention
that he was a hawk, not a dove, just for future reference.)

There was of course a special irony in this because Fortas had gone to the
Court, where he was not supposed to be involved in politics or consult with
the executive branch at all, and he had by means of a classic Johnsonian maneuver replaced Arthur Goldberg, who had left the Court precisely because
he was somewhat restless with the judiciary and the lack of political action
there. Goldberg had been making noises about his own restlessness just before
the death of Stevenson, and after Stevenson's death, John Kenneth Galbraith
would return to his home to find a message to call the President. Galbraith,
shrewd in the ways of both power and Lyndon Johnson, realized immediately
what Johnson was after, a good Kennedy liberal name for window dressing to
succeed Stevenson at the UN; it was not an assignment Galbraith sought, a
forum of limitless debate where everyone else tended to speak almost as
much as Galbraith, but he realized that if he turned it down, he had better
have another name for the President. Thus Galbraith thought of the itchy

Goldberg and passed on the name to Johnson, noting that Goldberg seemed to want more action. The President was delighted, it was even better than Galbraith; it cleared Goldberg from the Jewish seat of the Court and opened it up for Fortas, and at the same time, by sending Goldberg to New York, created a potential rival to Senator Robert Kennedy. Within minutes Goldberg was summoned to the White House. Arthur, the President said, the next man who sits in this seat is the man who brings peace in Vietnam. Goldberg nodded. It's the most important job there is, it demands the best man available and I want you to help your President. I want you to go to the UN and make peace. Which was followed with a long and full enunciation of Goldberg's unique qualifications to bring peace, with Goldberg still nodding.

So he left the Court to go to the United Nations, where he did not bring peace, where he found that he had effectively pulled himself out of the action and the decision making, where he was being used to make the case for a policy about which he had constantly mounting doubts, where he would destroy much of his hard-earned and justly deserved reputation as a humane liberal, and where, most galling of all, he would watch the man who replaced him on the Court play a genuine role on the decision making in Vietnam. (However, in July, Goldberg would argue vehemently against calling up the reserves, and when Johnson decided against doing it, against going on a real wartime footing, Goldberg would take some satisfaction that he had played a role here. Probably the reverse is true, that Johnson never intended to call up the reserves, and was delighted to have the case made against the obvious signs of war, such as a reserve call-up.)

So JOHNSON MADE HIS DECISION; IT WAS, HE THOUGHT, A PERSONAL challenge from Ho. If Ho wanted a challenge, a test of will, then he had come to the right man. Lyndon Johnson of Texas would not be pushed around, he would not try to negotiate with Ho and those others, as he said, walking in the streets of Saigon. He was a man to stand tall when the pressure was there. To be counted. He would show Ho his mettle, show the toughness of this country, and then they could talk. Rusk agreed; this was one democracy that was not going to show itself weak, it had the right leader (later during the Glassboro meetings with the Soviet leadership, Karl Mundt, as conservative a senator as could be found, was appalled to find that the Soviet Union's Kosygin did not have the kind of power to go to war that Johnson seemed to have). Johnson would not shirk from this test of wills. Besides, it was above all a political decision and a domestic one at that; it was a question of how he read the country, and when he found doubters on his own staff, some of the younger people, he would tell them, You boys don't understand, you don't know the relationship between the Congress and Asia. It was an emotional thing; they had never seen it because during their political lifetime it had been bottled up, but it was still there. He would lose his presidential possibilities, he said, if Ho was running through the streets of Saigon. Listen, he added, Truman and Acheson had never been effective from the time of the fall of China. Lyndon Johnson had a mandate for the moment. But this way if he failed on Vietnam it would be gone quickly. McNamara and Bundy seemed to be saying it could be done quickly, perhaps in six months, perhaps a little more. And the test cases were also quick. The Cuban missile crisis had gone quickly and that was a dry run for it, and the Dominican Republic, hell, he had sent a few troops in there and he had put out the fire in a few days. Hardly a shot fired. Look what had happened in the Dominican, when American boys had gone ashore. So this one would be quick too. Just give him six months. Of course, six months later he would be unmovable, too deeply involved in something that was going badly to talk rationally. It was one more sad aspect of Lyndon Johnson that there was the quality of the bully, and the reverse quality as well; he was, at his best, most open, most candid, most easy to reach, most accessible when things were going well, but when things went poorly, as they were bound to on Vietnam, he became impossible to reach and talk to. His greatest flexibility and rationality on the subject came before he had dispatched the first bombers and the first troops; from then on it would all be downhill. Doubters would no longer be friendly doubters, they would be critics and soon enemies; and worse, soon after that, traitors. There was no way to reach him, to enter his chamber, to gain his ear, other than to pledge total loyalty. Only one man would be able to change him, to dissent and retain his respect—and even that was a tenuous balancing act which virtually destroyed one of his oldest friendships, and that was Clark Clifford in 1968.

So, cornered, he would go ahead. He was not just reading their country, which was small, Asian, fourth-rate, bereft of bombers and helicopters; he was above all a political animal and he was reading his *own* country and in that he may have misread it; he read the politics of the past rather than the *potential* politics of the country, which his very victory of 1964 illuminated. (He had won as a peace candidate, and it is likely that had a new China policy been openly debated, with Johnson in favor of it and Goldwater opposing, it might have enlarged his margin; at the least it would have had little negative effect, probably would not have cut into his margin in any appreciable sense, and would have liberated him from one of the dominating myths of the past. But as the issue had been dormant by both liberal and conservative consent for a decade—the liberals giving consent, the conservatives owning the policy—there was no desire to change it.) The Democrats, who had been hurt by the issue in the past, were quite content to keep it bottled up. As was Johnson, a good and traditional liberal who was also a man of the fifties and of

Texas in the fifties, where McCarthyism had been particularly virulent, an era of potentially monolithic Communism, where the fewer questions about how monolithic it was, the better.

Those fears and suspicions of the Communists had never entirely left him; he was capable of wanting conciliation with the Soviet Union and holding the most basic kind of distrust of the Russians. The fact that the Vietcong attack took place while Kosygin was in Hanoi had a particularly negative effect on Lyndon Johnson. The Russians were not to be trusted, he would repeat to aides, they broke treaties and lied. Andrei Gromyko had come right in and lied to Jack Kennedy during the missile crisis; that had made a deep impression on Johnson. He would kid the White House people, particularly Bundy, about their friendships with Ambassador Dobrynin, teasing Bundy, "He's trying to slip Dobrynin in here just like he slipped Gromyko in here," and then adding, quite seriously, "You can never know about a man like Dobrynin." You had to watch those Russians. The Kosygin visit to Hanoi was, in his view, somehow quite sinister, despite the warnings at State that it might be the North Vietnamese's way of showing the Soviets that they would not be controlled. It played on his darker vision of the Russians and convinced him that Kosygin was out there stirring up something.

The forces at work in the fifties were very real to him. If Jack Kennedy was a man who knew more about where the sixties were headed but whose intellect preceded his courage, who stepped forward gingerly, then Johnson was far more a man of the past. He reacted to what he thought the country was; the country which had twice defeated Stevenson for the Presidency, where the powerful people on the Hill seemed primarily to be hawks, where the dominant figures of journalism were proud survivors of the worst of the Cold War, and where American universities had also given willingly, too willingly, in fact, of their talents and support to the Cold War. He did not see the new generation coming up, that the changing demography would become a major political factor, that there were new forces coming up quickly which were right below the surface, forces loosed by change, media change, economic change, demographic change, birth control and sexual change, change wrought here by change in the Communist world, the self-evident split between the Russians and the Chinese. All of this would challenge the existing order in politics, journalism, the universities. The new forces would coalesce with forces which had been around since the Stevenson days and which would have a major political impact. It would turn out that the Cold War generation's control was very shaky indeed, and that the entry of the new forces into American political life would be very much accelerated by Johnson's own entry into the war. They would never, even under the best and sunniest days of the Great Society, be people and forces much at ease with him, it was all moving too quickly for that, but his very entry into the Vietnam war would catalyze them and give them muscle previously missing. The forces of peace in 1965 were thin and scattered, timid in challenging the accepted Cold War attitudes; three years later they were massive and audacious, powerful enough to unseat one President, to bring a tie vote in the Senate on a weapons system (the ABM), an unheard-of thing, and powerful enough to make military spending a major domestic issue.

That would all come later; perhaps another politician might have sensed it, if not clearly identifying the change. But Lyndon Johnson did not sense it, rather he sensed he had position on everybody else, he had control of the center, he had moved all opponents to the extreme. He had handled the Congress, signed it on without really signing it on; he had handled the press by slicing the salami in pieces so thin that they were never able to pin him down, and he had handled Ho by making it seem as if Ho were attacking him at Tonkin. He was using force but using it discreetly, and he was also handling the military. They were moving toward war, but in such imperceptible degrees that neither the Congress nor the press could ever show a quantum jump. All the decisions were being cleverly hidden; he was cutting it thin to hold off opposition.

If there were no decisions which were crystallized and hard, then they could not leak, and if they could not leak, then the opposition could not point to them. Which was why he was not about to call up the reserves, because the use of the reserves would blow it all. It would be self-evident that we were really going to war, and that we would in fact have to pay a price. Which went against all the Administration planning: this would be a war without a price, a silent, politically invisible war. The military wanted to call up the reserves, and their planning always included a reserve call-up, usually in the nature of 200,000 men (certain specialized units such as engineer battalions and prisoner-of-war specialty units), and Johnson did not discourage them. He seemed to be telling them that yes, they would get the reserves, that this beautiful military machine which Bob McNamara had put together would not be raped for that little fourth-rate country. And he seemed to encourage McNamara to think that there would be a reserve call-up, encouraging him to fight for them and ask for them, so that in that final climactic week in July, McNamara went before one of the larger NSC meetings arguing for the reserves, and then at the end Johnson said no, there would not be a reserve call-up, he would not go that far. But having held the line against McNamara, having let him build the case so strongly in front of his peers, he realized he had set an ambush, and as they walked out of the room Johnson turned to one of his aides, winked, pointed to McNamara and asked, "Think we'll get a resignation out of him?" But then, because he realized he might have hurt McNamara, that he might have felt that he had been misled, he sent a helicopter by and the McNamaras were taken to Camp David for dinner. A social evening, after all. No one left with hurt feelings. Knock them down and then pick them up.

He was against a call-up of the reserves for other reasons as well. It would, he thought, telegraph the wrong signals to the adversaries, particularly China and the Soviet Union (frighten them into the idea that this was a real war) and Hanoi, which might decide that it was going to be a long war (he did not intend to go into a long war, and he felt if you called up the reserves you had to be prepared to go the distance and you might force your adversary to do the same). He also felt that it would frighten the country, and he had just run as a peace candidate; similarly, he felt it would be too much of a sign that the military were in charge and that the civilians would turn over too much responsibility to the military. Finally, and above all, he feared that it would cost him the Great Society, that his enemies in Congress would seize on the war as a means of denying him his social legislation. It was his oft-repeated theme, that his enemies were lying in wait to steal his Great Society. Oh no, they wouldn't confront it directly, they were afraid of being against the poor, but they would seize on the war as a means of crippling him. He was always a man who could believe in two very sharply conflicting sides of a question, and he could, right in the middle of a hard-line discussion, change and say that he, Lyndon Johnson, had the most to lose if we went to war. He would interrupt his pro-war monologue and switch sides, saying that they might throw him out of office, he might lose the Great Society. Those people out there, he would say, don't want to go to war. They don't want a war in Vietnam, they want the good things in life. And then, mercurially, he was back, planning for the war, talking about slipping his hand up Ho Chi Minh's leg before Ho even knew it.

But the decision against the reserves was convenient, it postponed the sense of reality of war, and it perpetuated both the illusion of control and of centrism within the bureaucracy. Of moderation, of Lyndon in the center, being pushed by the military but carefully weighing the alternatives, of not giving in to the military. It also meant a delay on the realization of the scope of the war, and that was crucial.

For in all those weeks of debating about what to do, looking at options, of trying to decide what the necessary level of force was, of trying at first to stave off the inevitable, the use of combat troops, and then giving in to it, the principals never defined either the mission or the number of troops. It seems incredible in retrospect, but it is true. There was never a clear figure and clear definition of what the strategy would be. There was eventually grandiose talk of giving Westmoreland everything he needed—and Westy was told by McNamara that he could have whatever he needed; this was, after all, the richest country in the world—but even Westmoreland knew there were restraints, he had to negotiate for the troops, slice by slice with McNamara, he knew that if he asked for too much too quickly he might not get it (just as later McNamara would reluctantly give increments that he didn't want because otherwise he would be denying a commander his necessary troops; each finally would have a deterrent against the other). The Joint Chiefs talked of a million men, but it was never really defined. And in the chambers of the President, in the days through July, it was a figure which was never defined, though there was a certain gentlemen's agreement that it would be, at a maximum, about 300,000. Anything above that was out of the question, and it was unfair on the part of Ball, for instance, to claim, as he did in June and July, that it would go higher, to half a million. There was of course a dual advantage in not defining the number of men and the mission: first, it permitted the principals themselves to keep the illusion that they were not going to war, and it permitted them not to come to terms with budget needs and the political needs. Thus, if the mission was not defined it did not exist, and if the number of troops was not set it could always be controlled. Second, if the figure was not decided upon and crystallized within the inner circle, it could not leak out to the press and to the Congress, where all kinds of enemies lurked and would seize upon it to beat him and to beat his Great Society program. If you carried the figure in your own mind, no one could pry it out; all they had were those thin, and sometimes not so thin, slices of increments that slipped out, and even those you could and would dissemble about.

So the failure to define the figure was an aid against the press and the Congress, but it was also eventually to prove a problem within, because both the size and the strategy were never defined. Westmoreland would start the war believing it was an open-ended commitment, never accurately filled in on the extent of the reservations of some of his civilian superiors; the civilians would start knowing that the military wanted big things, but believing first that the military always exaggerated its requests for manpower and for more money and that it was a bloated figure. They never came to a real agreement, and they deliberately fuzzed their mission and their objective and the price. Six years later McGeorge Bundy, whose job it was to ask questions for a President who could not always ask the right questions himself, would go before the Council on Foreign Relations and make a startling admission about the mission and the lack of precise objectives. The Administration, Bundy recounted, did not tell the military what to do and how to do it; there was in his words a "premium put on imprecision," and the political and military leaders did not speak candidly to each other. In fact, if the military and political leaders had been totally candid with each other in 1965 about the length and cost of the war instead of coming to a consensus, as Johnson wanted, there would have been vast and perhaps unbridgeable differences, Bundy said. It was a startling admission, because it was specifically Bundy's job to make sure that differences like these did not exist. They existed, of course, not because they could not be uncovered but because it was a deliberate policy not to surface with real figures and real estimates which might show that they were headed toward a real war. The men around Johnson served him poorly, but they served him poorly because he wanted them to.

There were brief moments when the reality seemed to flash through. Once during the early-June discussions the President turned to General Wheeler and said, "Bus, what do you think it will take to do the job?" And Wheeler answered, "It all depends on what your definition of the job is, Mr. President. If you intend to drive the last Vietcong out of Vietnam it will take seven hundred, eight hundred thousand, a million men and about seven years." He paused to see if anyone picked him up. "But if your definition of the job is to prevent the Communists from taking over the country, that is, stopping them from doing it, then you're talking about different gradations and different levels. So tell us what the job is and we'll answer it." But no one said anything; it was not the kind of thing they picked people up on, and so the conversation slipped over to the other subjects, vague discussions of strategy, the difference between an enclave strategy and a security mission, and they did not define the mission.

Later during the June discussions, again a figure came up. Clark Clifford, who sat in both as a friend of the President's and as a member of the intelligence advisory board, and who was neither hawkish nor dovish in those days (mostly being a shrewd old lawyer, dubious; his reputation as a hawk would come, when once we were committed and he opposed a bombing halt), was present at a meeting when he heard General Wheeler mention a figure and then add that with six or seven years at that figure, we could win. The figure sounded like 750,000 to Clifford, so when it was his turn to speak, he got up and began: "The way I understand it, we're talking about a figure of seven hundred and fifty thousand troops and a war that will go on for five or six years and I'd like to ask General Wheeler a question."

The President immediately interrupted him: "No one's using a figure like that."

Clifford turned to Wheeler, and Wheeler nodded his head and said yes, he had indeed used a figure like that.

Johnson, irritated, said it was ridiculous. No one envisioned a figure like that.

At which point Clifford asked to continue and said, "Even if it *is* the figure and it works, my question is, What then?"

Wheeler looked a little puzzled. "I don't understand the question."

So Clifford repeated it: if we won, after all that time, with all that investment, "What do we do? Are we still involved? Do we still have to stay there?"

And Wheeler answered yes, we would have to keep a major force there, for perhaps as long as twenty or thirty years. Whereupon the conversation again went in different directions and the question of the figure was dropped.

In July, during the final ten days of decision, Clifford remained dubious, and once during the final session at Camp David before the President made his decision, they went around the table one by one signing on to the inevitable. Finally they came to Clifford. It was not just his words but his manner which surprised the others there. He leaned back, thought and then seemed to pound the table as he spoke, speaking so forcefully that later one witness was not able to remember whether he had or had not hit the table. "They won't let us do it," he said. "Whatever we do, they will match it. The North Vietnamese and then the Chinese will not let us do it. If we send men, the North Vietnamese will send men. And then the Chinese." He said we should negotiate with the other side if possible. And then Clifford, an old-style man who delights in almost purple oratory, paused and said, almost melodramatically, "I see catastrophe ahead for my country."

THE SENSE OF THE FRAGILITY OF IT ALL, THE DELICACY OF WHAT happened when American troops entered, was evident at almost the same time in Saigon. There Eugene Black was visiting, having accepted a job from Johnson to be head of Johnson's Mekong River Redevelopment Commission, and Black had been given a long briefing by Westmoreland. The briefing was very pessimistic indeed; he told of the almost total collapse of the ARVN forces. The 173rd Airborne and the Marines were already in the country, Westmoreland said. He had asked for 100,000 more combat troops, and he thought he would get them. But even if they arrived, the important thing to remember, Westmoreland said, was that we must not take this war away from the Vietnamese. If we did, we would be in the same position as the French, and it would be hopeless. Black then asked what the cutoff point would be. Westmoreland paused for a moment and said 175,000; that would be the figure. Over that figure and they would give up the war, and it would get worse and worse.

At the end of the briefing Black thanked him for the tough-mindedness of his briefing and said that the general had been very helpful. Now was there anything that Black could do for Westmoreland back in Washington? Yes, said Westmoreland, tell everyone in Washington that if I get the troops I ask for and all the breaks that I could possibly have the right to ask for, it will take six or seven years to turn it around. It will be a slow and hard thing. It was, thought someone who was present at the Westmoreland-Black meeting, almost a Greek thing, that Westmoreland knew that 175,000 would be the cutoff figure, and yet when it didn't work out, he was carried along by the force of the thing, demanding more and more troops.

Even while Johnson was going through what was in effect the count-down meeting with his top officials, McNamara was in Saigon during the weekend of July 17, clearing everything with Westmoreland, checking out the number of troops, trying to sense what might be needed in the future, and what the mission would be. Westmoreland's request for a troop commitment which would go to 200,000 was already in, and while McNamara was in Saigon he learned in a cable from his deputy, Cy Vance, that the President was going ahead with the thirty-four battalions (which with the Korean and Australian battalions would bring it to a total of forty-four battalions). Thus at a minimum the U.S. troop level would be 175,000, and if the Koreans did not have the troops, then we would go their part too, bringing it to 200,000. (Curiously, in his memoirs Johnson does not tell the story this way; instead he makes it appear that he waited for McNamara's return and McNamara's request for the additional forces before going ahead, thus putting more of the burden on the Secretary of Defense.) McNamara did return to Washington on July 20 and did report immediately to the President saying that the President had three options. The first was to withdraw under conditions which would be humiliating, the second to continue at the present level of about 75,000, which would mean that the United States might be faced with equally harsh decisions in the near future, or finally a sharp increase in the U.S. military pressure against the Vietcong in the South. This last was, he said, "the course involving the best odds of the best outcome with the most acceptable cost to the United States."

But in any real sense, that decision had already been reached. The only loose ends left were the questions of how public to go with the decisions and whether to call up the reserves (McNamara forcefully argued for a reserve call-up of 235,000 men). On his return McNamara prepared a draft press release which announced that 100,000 more Americans were going, but that was not what the President wanted and it was sidetracked. There was some talk of putting together a major speech outlining the gist of the decisions: that we were entering a major war, that it might be a long war, and that it would demand great American tenacity and endurance. At Defense some of the young civilians had been uneasy with the covert way the decision making had been going, and it was agreed that a speech should be written. The speech put the blame mostly on China for her aggressive policies, and it ended: "They are watching us to see whether we have the determination and resolution to stick with it. They are betting that we don't have it. We are, finally, being tested. The enemy is looking for the answer to how long we will resist. We have that answer in the words of a distinguished American, who recently died, 'till hell freezes over.'" The author of the speech was Daniel Ellsberg.

But it was not what the President was looking for; he was afraid of being too overt with his policy of scaring the Congress and the press. Instead he decided that he would make public only 50,000 of the agreed-upon 100,000 to 125,000. (That week Ellsberg ran into Douglas Kiker of the *Herald Tribune*, who had just spent two hours with the President, and Johnson had assured Kiker that it was all a bunch of rumors, this talk of changing policy, this gossip about a new strategy and combat troops. Just filling out a few units, the President said.) It was in fact the real beginning of the credibility gap; and Johnson was a part of it and so were all his top advisers. They knew they had decided on the larger figure, that it was a quantum jump, and that they were being party to a major deception of the American people, that many more far-reaching decisions had been made than they were admitting. (In his memoirs this is a particularly tricky question for the President. He admits that they had made decisions involving up to 200,000 men, and notes briefly that the commanders said that they could get by with 50,000 for the immediate needs.)

It was all over; the only thing left was the actual notification of the bureaucracy (the charade of a National Security Council meeting) and of congressional leaders. The first came on July 27. There Johnson had McNamara, just back from Vietnam, summarize the situation, growing Communist strength, steady government deterioration. Then Johnson took over. He had five choices. One was to blast the North off the map with bombers. Another was simply to pack up and go home. The third choice was to stay the way we were, perhaps lose more territory and suffer more casualties. "You wouldn't want your boy to be out there crying for help and not get it," he said. The fourth was to go to the Congress for great sums of money, to call up the reserves and go on a wartime footing. But, he said, if we did that, went to that kind of a land war, then North Vietnam would turn to China and Russia and get greater aid (one thing he did not mention was that he was uncertain what treaties Hanoi had with Peking and Moscow and was afraid that an actual declaration of war might involve them immediately and directly). "For that reason I don't want to be overly dramatic and cause tensions," he said. "I think we can get our people to support us without having to be too provocative and warlike."

So he said the fifth choice was really very much the fourth: to expand the war without going on a wartime footing, to give the commanders what they needed. He had, he said, decided that this was the correct one, the centrist, moderate one: only Lyndon Johnson could go to war and be centrist and moderate. Then he turned to them and asked if anyone there had objections. He asked the principals one by one. The key moment was when he came to General Wheeler and stood looking directly at him for a moment. "Do you, General Wheeler, agree?" Wheeler nodded his agreement. It was, said someone who was present, an extraordinary moment, like watching a lion tamer dealing with some of the great lions. Everyone in the room knew Wheeler objected, that the Chiefs wanted more, that they wanted a wartime footing and a call-up of the reserves; the thing they feared most was a partial war and a partial commitment. But Wheeler was boxed in; he had the choice of opposing and displeasing his Commander in Chief and being overruled, anyway, or going along. He went along. It was the beginning of what was to be a very difficult war for him, of being caught again and again between his civilian authorities and the other Chiefs (whose views he shared but was always able to contain himself). It was for him an endless series of frustrations, and only his brilliant political negotiations kept the Chiefs together and prevented several resignations at different points. He came out of it an exhausted and depleted man, his health ruined by major heart attacks, and the questions which he had faced at that July meeting still unanswered.

The congressional leaders came later that evening. Johnson had been extremely careful in past meetings with them to make sure that if both Mansfield and Fulbright were there, they would be called upon for their views last. Call the hawkish ones first. Thus the easy ones like McCormack and the hawkish ones like Dirksen would already be on board, he would seem to have a majority already going with him, and then he would ask Mansfield and Fulbright last what they thought. This time he did not even bother to invite Fulbright; their friendship had declined rapidly in recent weeks in part because of Vietnam and in part because of the Dominican Republic. With the congressional leaders Johnson again made the same pitch he had given earlier to the NSC, then he went around and summoned their views. One by one they signed on. Finally he turned to Mansfield. The Senate Majority Leader had all along expressed doubts; he knew too much about the French experience to want to see a U.S. entry. His own sense of the problem was that things were worse than we realized and that an American presence would work against us. He strongly opposed sending troops. He thought there was growing discontent in the country about the war, and that it would divide rather than unite the country. He hoped deeply and desperately that there was some other course of action, but if this was the President's decision, he would support him loyally.

The next day at his press conference Johnson announced that we would increase the number of men from 75,000 to 125,000. We were sending combat troops. The "lesson of history" dictated that the United States use its might to resist aggression. He said:

"We did not choose to be the guardians at the gate, but there is no one else.

"Nor would surrender in Vietnam bring peace, because we learned from Hitler at Munich that success only feeds the appetite of aggression. The battle would be renewed in one country and then another country, bring with it perhaps even larger and crueler conflict, as we have learned from the lessons of history."

As for troops, he had asked Westmoreland what he needed to meet what was called "this mounting aggression. He has told me. We will meet his needs."

Later in the press conference a reporter asked if the sending of additional troops implied any change in the policy of relying mainly on South Vietnamese troops and using American troops to guard installations and act as emergency backup.

Johnson answered: "It does not imply any change in policy whatever. It does not imply change of objective." On the contrary, it was the beginning of an entirely new policy which would see what was the South Vietnamese war become primarily an American war. That would become evident in the forthcoming months.

The next day the President's decision was hailed by most people. Taxicab drivers and barbers were interviewed, and like Speaker McCormack, they said they supported their President, he knew best. The most interesting story that day, however, was written by Hanson Baldwin, the *New York Times*'s special military correspondent, a man who was close to most of the senior generals and admirals. Baldwin had in the past been faithfully passing on and advocating their belief that it would take time, and perhaps one million men. Now on a day when, to the average civilian at least, the military appeared to have won out, Baldwin was reporting shock and dismay among the nation's top officers, including the JCS. They had expected a good deal more—a reserve call-up, a wartime footing. Instead it was going to be one more tricky war, with civilians making the decisions, keeping the military out of the decision making. The Baldwin story was important because it reflected that even from the start it was going to be an aborted war.

But the decision had been made and there was seemingly a consensus, but it had only developed because no one was being particularly candid with anyone else. Despite the veneer of having been consulted, the Congress had not been consulted; despite Johnson's signing on of General Wheeler, the military were restless; and the exact decisions were being kept as cloudy as possible so that the President could still get his domestic proposals through the Congress. It was a consensus, all right, but a very frail one indeed.

Westmoreland would get everything he wanted. Well, almost everything. That was the decision. Of course, right from the start there was a decision against the reserves, which meant that there had to be considerable juggling of the units already ticketed for Vietnam, and some units would arrive later than expected. But still, he would get anything he wanted. He wanted a lot, of course. He saw it as a major war, a real war, their first-line units against our first-line units, a long struggle, perhaps two or three bitter years of fighting, and then a trailing down. But he was prepared for it on his side. And the troops would be his: he knew he would have to negotiate for them, that McNamara would control the purse strings, and that the Administration did not want to be too exact about figures at a given time, for fear of scaring the enemy as well as the Congress and the public, which nevertheless would dutifully rally to the war. And so it would be done in slices. When McNamara returned in late July, he had not only brought back the battalion request, but he had also brought back the estimate that Westmoreland would probably need another 100,000 for 1966; thus the unofficial, private consensus figure was about 300,000. It was not a figure which would last long, large as it was, for it was based on the optimum possibility, that the other side would not make a major reinforcement if we upped the ante. That hope would turn out to be one of the most short-lived of the war as the North, which had been sending men down the trails since early 1965, began to escalate as we escalated, matching our commitment with theirs.

In August the American troops were streaming into the country, and by September it was clear that the original estimate of 175,000 for 1965 would probably go as high as 210,000. Still there was a sense that we were in control. One of the great illusions of the war for both the French and the Americans was that they could control the rate of the war; in reality the other side always did. It could escalate or de-escalate the tempo by deciding how many of its own men to send into battle at a given time.

Chapter Twenty-seven

In 1954 GENERAL RIDGWAY HAD CAREFULLY PROGRAMED EX-
actly what would be needed to fight the Vietminh and to help the French.
The cost for one year would be an estimated $3.5 billion. Eisenhower there-
upon called in his economic advisers and his Secretary of the Treasury,
George Humphrey. "George, what would all this do to the budget?" he asked.
Humphrey thought for a few moments and then gave a quick answer: "It'll
mean a deficit, Mr. President." In a way, thought one man present at the
meeting, any idea of intervening in Indochina died at that moment.

War had not become any less costly in the ensuing eleven years, particularly a war whose principal architects felt it could all be accomplished by expensive technology and modern military machinery, a war part of whose purpose was to spare Western, if not Asian, lives, a war in which the most
expensive new helicopters replaced tanks. So the cost of the war would soon
become one more public relations problem for the President. The full dimen-
sions of the American commitment could be kept partially secret from the
press and the Congress and the allies. But eventually someone had to pay for
it, and in the very process of the payment, some of the plans, projections and
realities would have to become public. Early in 1965 the Joint Chiefs were
pushing for special funding for the war, knowing that it would be expensive;
and knowing that the more open the Administration was about funding the
war, the more open it was likely to be in admitting to the nation that it was, in
fact, at war. The Chiefs wanted a wartime footing which included traditional

wartime budgetary procedures—invariably meaning higher taxes—and they lost that fight in July 1965 when Johnson decided to go ahead and make it open-ended, without really announcing how open the end was. As a result even at that point, when one might have expected, by checking defense expenditure projections, to find an honest assessment of what the war would be, the reverse was true. In his attempt to keep the planning for the war as closely held as possible, Lyndon Johnson would not give accurate economic projections, would not ask for a necessary tax raise, and would in fact have *his own* military planners be less than candid with *his own* economic planners, a lack of candor so convincing that his economic advisers later felt that McNamara had seriously misled them about projections and estimates. The reasons for Johnson's unwillingness to be straightforward about the financing were familiar. He was hoping that the worst would not come true, that it would remain a short war, and he feared that if the true economic cost of the war became visible to the naked eye, he would lose his Great Society programs. The result was that his economic planning was a living lie, and his Administration took us into economic chaos: the Great Society programs were passed but never funded on any large scale; the war itself ran into severe budgetary problems (the decision in 1968 to put a ceiling on the American troops was as much economic as political); and the most important, the failure to finance the war honestly, would inspire a virulent inflationary spiral which helped defeat Johnson himself. Seven years after the commitment of combat troops, that inflation was still very much alive and was forcing a successor Administration into radical, desperate economic measures in order to restore some financial balance.

The economy in the spring of 1965 had already reached the point of overheating, and some of the President's economic advisers were becoming worried about inflationary dangers, even without the prospect of a major war. After years of high unemployment, the level had dropped close to the target of 4 percent. Now, with a war in sight, the advisers were even more uneasy. Johnson and McNamara were implying that it would not be a big war, but there were already rumblings in the early fall of 1965 from people on the Hill that this was likely to become a very big war. The rumbling came from men like John Stennis and Mendel Rivers, who estimated that the cost for fiscal 1966, which ended in June 1966, would be about $10 billion. The Administration was denying this, but for the moment Johnson had fairly good credibility. He had claimed in the past year that he intended to cut back defense spending, and although Rivers and others contradicted him, lo and behold, the President *had* cut defense spending. So for the moment his reputation was reasonably good. Later it would turn out that Stennis and Rivers knew quite well what they were talking about, since they were tapped into the best of the back-channel military messages through their close liaisons with Westmoreland and the Chiefs. Thus they had a very good idea of what Westmoreland was asking for and what McNamara had promised him. Which made it a big war. Based on this, they were claiming that it would cost about $10 billion for the year ending July 1966. That figure was of course far above the estimates coming from the White House (in his July messages Johnson had talked about a projected figure of only $2 billion more than previously estimated Defense funds).

The projections coming from the Hill upset Gardner Ackley, chairman of the Council of Economic Advisers. He did not really believe them, but he wanted guidance from the White House, and assurance that his own forecast was accurate. With his own estimates projected at a maximum cost of $3 billion to $5 billion, Ackley wanted to say in a forthcoming speech that anyone using the figure of $10 billion was operating on a figment of his imagination. Encouraged by the Administration to answer these critics, Ackley decided to clear the speech with McNamara, who assured him that the cost would be relatively low, nowhere near $10 billion. So Ackley went ahead, and unfortunately the figure finally was about $8 billion, far closer to the Stennis-Rivers estimates than to the McNamara estimates.

But that was a marginal miscalculation compared to what was in store. The Council of Economic Advisers became more and more uneasy about the direction of the war; they felt they had been looking quite good recently as economic advisers and they wanted to keep it that way. The economy was going full blast, everyone seemed to have more money than ever, prosperity was everywhere—even the very poor were about to be let into the mainstream of American life—and *Time* magazine had just put John Maynard Keynes on its cover. So the Council was up and the members wanted to stay up; they thought the time had come to slow the economy down, to turn down, or turn off, the faucet, particularly because of the problems at Defense. With an overheated economy already on hand, and a war and major domestic legislation just ahead, they felt it was time to move for a tax increase. On December 10, 1965, they sent a message to the President to that effect, basing their demand for more taxes on the growing needs for the war and the additional domestic requirements. In Ackley's opinion there was a sense of urgency at the time; he believed that this was the kind of thing which could easily get away from you. In addition, he felt that war estimates were always faulty, the needs always greater than the projections.

The President seemed somewhat receptive to the idea of the tax increase, but did not seem to share Ackley's sense of urgency. Ackley was telling the President he could not have three things: the war, the Great Society and no inflation. If he wanted all three, then he would need a tax increase. But if this was obvious to Ackley, it was not so obvious to Lyndon Johnson. The President feared that if he went to the Congress for the tax increase he might blow the whole thing. The Congress, Johnson told friends, would give him the war, but not the Great Society. So the President, who had sliced everything so thin, decided he would slice this one too: he would hold back on the real estimates of the war for a year—perhaps major expenditures would not be necessary after all, perhaps Hanoi would have folded—meanwhile he would push very hard to get the Great Society legislation through by early 1966, and then, once it was passed, he would concentrate on the war. Thus by the time the extent of the involvement in Vietnam was fully apparent, the Great Society would already be a fact. "I don't know much about economics," he told friends, "but I do know the Congress. And I can get the Great Society through right now—this is a golden time. We've got a good Congress and I'm the right President and I can do it. But if I talk about the cost of the war, the Great Society won't go through and the tax bill won't go through. Old Wilbur Mills will sit down there and he'll thank me kindly and send me back my Great Society, and then he'll tell me that they'll be glad to spend whatever we need for the war."

He knew he was cornered and he decided to negotiate what he wanted through, piece by piece, as stealthily as possible. Now there were three sets of players, each acting independently of each other: the military, who wanted major financing for what they had been told was a major war; Johnson's domestic aides, who were pushing for the Great Society and who knew relatively little about the extent of the military planning (they were encouraged by the President to know as little as possible); and Johnson's economic planners, who sensed the potential of the conflicts involved but did not know the extent to which decisions on military forces had already been made. The key man in all this was McNamara. The Great Society projections were relatively public, and the rest of the budget was a stable thing. It was the military projections which were based on secret information and private decisions—secret, it turned out, even to the President's own economists.

In December 1965 McNamara began drawing up the plans for the military budget for fiscal 1967, a budget which would run from the middle of 1966 to the middle of 1967 and which would go to the Congress in January 1966. By this time he had already consulted with Westmoreland and had his darkest fears confirmed—Hanoi was reinforcing at a faster rate than we were; it would be a large war, and quite likely a long one. Westmoreland's July 1965 estimates that we would need only 300,000 troops by the end of 1966 had been discarded; the approved figure was now 400,000 Americans by the end of 1966, and a probable figure of 600,000 by the end of 1967. Yet in making the budget, McNamara made the arbitrary assumption that the war would be over by June 30, 1967. It was in direct contradiction to the estimates he was getting from Westmoreland (and in direct contradiction to his own private estimates for Johnson at the time) but it was a plausible assumption for planning. (McNamara wanted the cutoff date left in because in Korea we had fought an open-ended war; consequently too much military equipment had been bought, and he wanted to control that. He was telling the President at this point that he could not guarantee the length of the war, but it would be the most economically fought war in history. That he would guarantee—he would really ride herd on the military.) McNamara placed the cost of the war at $10 billion for the budget. Thus Johnson would be able to propose significant increases in Great Society programs, plus the war, and thanks to the normally rising revenues natural to a growing economy, still show only a minor deficit. It looked like the work of a great economist, but it was really only a shell game. The economic experts and critics who sensed that there was a built-in dilemma looked at the budget searching for the hole and found to their surprise that the hole did not exist, it was all acceptable.

The problem, they knew, was the war, but there was Bob McNamara promising to keep it at $10 billion; and he told the President, but he did not tell the public or the Congress, that he was putting the cost of the war between $15 billion and $17 billion. For the first time there were now memos on this in the bureaucracy, though not for the public; they were private memos, of course, and they were sent over to the Council of Economic Advisers with the notation "For internal use only." Since the Council was already becoming very skeptical about the whole thing, Arthur Okun, one of its members, noted alongside: "But not to be swallowed." At this point the Council began meeting with McNamara and pushing him hard to get a more exact estimate of the cost, and also to get him to push for a tax increase. But they found McNamara, usually so sure, usually so filled with certitudes, very reluctant to come down with a hard figure for the cost of the war, and he gave three figures: high, low and medium. The high was $17 billion (or $7 billion over the original estimate), the medium was $15 billion, the low was $11 billion. Eventually the figure came to $21 billion, which meant that even his own medium private re-estimate for the increase was off more than 100 percent, and his estimate as far as the general public was concerned was off even more. He was not, it would turn out, quite so good a manager as he had claimed, nor his machine quite so efficient, though this did not necessarily make him any more modest. Indeed, a few months later, in discussing the forthcoming budget, he would say, "Never before has this country been able to field and support in combat so large a force in so short a time over so great a distance, without calling up the reserves, and without applying price, wage and material controls to our civilian economy."

It was at this point, in March 1966, under increasing pressure from the Council to go for a tax increase—a modest one, 3 or 4 percent—that the President took his first tentative step. Tentative is the word. He was still worried about his domestic programs and he was wary of blowing the whole thing.

Though he knew by now that the military costs were going to be greater than the estimates in the budget revealed, he kept this to himself. Instead he summoned key businessmen and members of the House Ways and Means Committee in separate meetings and asked them if he should go for a tax increase. He did not, and this was crucial, tell them how much the war was going to cost. Thus they were asked to give estimates and projections on something as important as a tax increase based on totally erroneous information. It was an extraordinary bit of manipulation; indeed, said Ed Dale, the economic correspondent of the *New York Times* in Washington, it was the single most irresponsible act by an American President in the fifteen years that he had covered Washington. Naturally, acting on this limited information, both the businessmen and the congressmen told Johnson not to go for the tax increase; this in turn permitted the President to go back to his economic advisers and tell them that he had discussed a tax increase with the congressional leaders and that they were all totally opposed, he could get no votes for it. One part of the government was lying to another part. Thus was the fatal decision made not to go for a tax increase, a decision made in early 1966 which resulted in the subsequent runaway inflation. Instead of being marginal, the deficit for fiscal 1967 turned out to be a whopping $9.8 billion.

At the same time in early 1966 McNamara kept meeting with the Council of Economic Advisers, and the Council kept pressing him to go for a tax increase. McNamara, however, kept pleading that he did not want to—in fact, could not—go along. He did not have a firm figure on the war, he said, and they would have to trust him. In addition, he insisted the Congress would hang him if he went up there, hang him twice. They would hang him on the war, and hang him on the financing of it. Of course the real reason he did not want to go and testify, it soon became clear, was that open testimony on how deep we were in and how much deeper we were going, would have been the same thing as a formal announcement on the size and duration of the war. Which was the last thing the Administration wanted at that point. So in the early months of 1966, when the planning and budgeting were being done, the Administration did not go for a tax increase. Nor did it admit that the cutoff date of July 1, 1967, was an illusion. It did give up the idea within the Administration itself early in 1966. Much later, in November 1966, McNamara admitted publicly that the cutoff date had been dropped and that since the war would continue to go on, the financing would have to be greatly increased. The Korean analogy was quietly abandoned. When he did make the announcement, Ed Dale of the *Times* wrote an analysis of the decision, and noted that doubling of spending on the war; the article naturally angered McNamara, who felt that it cast doubt upon his reputation as a war manager. So he called Dale to say, with no small amount of irritation, that they had abandoned that assumption early on. Very early on, he said. And Dale answered, "Yes, sir, I know you did, and I know why you did, but you didn't tell us publicly until now." A minor point, of course.

As it became increasingly obvious that the war in the budget and the war in reality were two separate things, doubters and critics began to surface. In mid-1966 the economist Eliot Janeway, asked by senators to comment on the funding of the war, estimated that instead of the monthly drain of $800 million proclaimed by the Administration, the real drain was closer to $2 billion a month, and might go up to $3 billion. This did not endear Janeway to the President, who set out to silence future critics of his arithmetic. In May 1967 Ralph Lazarus, president of the Federated Department Stores and a member of the Business Council, held a press conference and publicly criticized Johnson's war budget (he estimated that government spending on the war for the next fiscal year would be $5 billion higher than the government estimate of $21.9 billion). He was immediately telephoned by no less an economic authority than Justice Abe Fortas, who asked Lazarus to tone down his estimates because they were inaccurate; indeed, Lazarus had upset the President very much with his erroneous projections. Unfortunately, the cost turned out to be $27 billion, which meant that Lazarus was right on the nose. Similarly, the deficit for the year was about $23 billion, closely paralleling the cost of the war.

IN EFFECT, THE ADMINISTRATION WAS GOING TO WAR WITHOUT really coming to terms with it; they were paying for the war without announcing it or admitting it. Faking it. They would barely get through the first year, but even the first year would see the start of the inflation, and it would become more virulent month by month, finally almost a living part of the economy, and the political impact of the inflation became almost as serious a political issue in 1968 as the war itself.

The Administration had slipped by in fiscal 1966, and by fiscal 1967 the deficit was almost $10 billion, but the deficit for fiscal 1968 would be even worse. In late 1966 the Council of Economic Advisers continued to put pressure on Johnson for a tax increase, and by January 1967 they found him far more amenable to their demand, largely because he already had most of his Great Society legislation through Congress, and he had less to lose and felt himself less vulnerable. In the January 1967 Budget Message he proposed the income-tax surcharge but with no date, and then in July the Council of Economic Advisers told him to go for it. In August he sent a message to the Congress. Wilbur Mills read it, made some suggestions, held some hearings, and took his time with it. In mid-1967 Johnson was not the awesome figure of 1965 who could force anything through the Congress as quickly as he wanted; instead he was already a somewhat wounded figure. Now that Johnson was ready for the tax increase, the Congress was not. It took a great deal of negotiating between the Congress and the White House before the bill was passed in July of 1968. It was, of course, all too late: the deficit for fiscal 1968 was $27 billion; as managers of the economy, the Administration's top officials were turning out to be something less than their press clippings implied. The inflation was full-blown, the country was bitterly divided (tensions between blue-collar whites and blacks were made worse by the inflation). Cities, hospitals and schools found themselves caught in destructive, hopeless labor disputes growing out of the inflation. The irony of it all was that the cost of the war itself was not enough to destroy the economy; it never cost more than 3.5 percent of the gross national product, and there were never any real shortages. It was not the war which destroyed the economy, but the essentially dishonest way in which it was handled. In late 1967 General Westmoreland made a request for additional troops. When it came in, the White House sent it to the Council of Economic Advisers for a reading on what the economic realities were. It was the first time Johnson had ever done it, and the Council was very pleased to render its quite negative findings, though there was a general feeling that it was all very late.

Similarly, in late 1967 Tom Wicker of the *New York Times* went to see Robert McNamara. When the subject of the economic miscalculation of the war came up during the interview, McNamara dismissed it in a casual way which shocked Wicker. "Do you really think that if I had estimated the cost of the war correctly, Congress would have given any more for schools and housing?" he asked. Implicit in what he was saying, as far as Wicker was concerned, was that Congress would have given anything necessary for the war and very little for domestic legislation, so they might just as well lie. Wicker left totally appalled by the conversation.

Epilogue

THE WHOLE BASIS OF THE ESCALATION, OF USING GROUND forces, was that it would be brief. At least as far as Lyndon Johnson was concerned, but not as far as William Childs Westmoreland was concerned. In the summer of 1965, dissenting senators going to the White House, uneasy with the number of the troops there, and the rumors that more, many more were on their way, were assured by the President that they need not worry. They should just sit still for six months; all we wanted was negotiations, and these would come by Christmas. All we had to do was show them some of our muscle and give them a sense of our determination. Just six months.

If that were true, then the forbidden word in the White House speeches in the summer of 1965 was "negotiations." It was considered a particularly dangerous word, since it would show our weakness, our lack of intent; it would undermine the already weak fabric of Saigon and it would encourage Hanoi to go against Hanoi's best interests and continue the war. When Richard Goodwin slipped "negotiations" into a speech for the President at Johns Hopkins, he found himself assaulted in a White House corridor shortly afterward by Abe Fortas, and accused of softness. Senator Frank Church, making a major speech on negotiations, soon went to a White House dinner with a large group of senators and found himself under personal attack. The President, looking straight at him, began to attack those who were soft and faint-hearted. There was once another senator from Idaho who thought he knew more about war and peace than the President, Johnson said—an obvious reference to Bill Borah's isolationism. Church was mildly offended by the personal references, but after dinner it was even worse. Johnson singled out Church, backed him into a corner and went at him heatedly, launching into a tirade on Vietnam. It was a violent discussion, and Church thought the President seemed almost high; it was all very explosive, nostril to nostril, and twice Lady Bird, sensing the dangers, tried to separate them, but the President moved her away. Church held his ground and it went on for almost an hour. The next day another senator saw Gene McCarthy and asked how the dinner had gone. "Oh, it wasn't too bad," McCarthy replied, "but if Frank Church had just surrendered sooner we could have all gone home half an hour earlier."

So negotiation was blocked out; the decisions were made, and the troops were on their way. Not just American troops, it turned out, but North Vietnamese troops as well. Though top officials of the American government would later claim that they had bombed and sent American combat troops because the North Vietnamese were escalating, this was patently untrue. By early 1965, a regiment of the North Vietnamese army had been identified as being in the South, and another was believed on its way, but no North Vietnamese had entered battle—that would come long afterward, after the Americans had bombed the North and sent in their combat troops. But with the arrival of American combat troops in the summer of 1965, Hanoi moved to match the American escalation. First-line units of the North Vietnamese army, one of the great infantries of the world, began to move down the trails, ready to neutralize the American build-up. They would not fight in the guerrilla style which had marked hostilities in the past, and they would not fight in the populous regions of the Delta. Rather, they would wait in the highlands, fight in rugged terrain favorable to them, and meet American main-force units there. More often than not, they chose both the time and place of battle. Thus as American forces would provide a shield to the ARVN, the NVA regular forces would provide a comparable shield for the Vietcong; the American force was being neutralized even as it arrived.

In mid-November 1965, regiments of the North Vietnamese army stumbled into units of the elite First Cav (the new heliborne division). The result was a bloody and ferocious battle in difficult terrain, which came to be known as the battle of the Ia Drang Valley. It was the first real testing of American men and arms in Vietnam. Official American estimates were that 1,200 of the enemy had been killed, against 200 American losses. To General Westmoreland and his deputy, General William Depuy, it was viewed as a considerable American victory; it proved the effectiveness and the validity of the new airmobile concept: that we could strike at the enemy in his base-camp areas, that we could overcome normal logistical limitations with our new technology; a range and a mobility that had been denied to the French was now available to us. So a strategy of attrition was possible. It was a battle which encouraged the American military in their preconceptions and their instincts, that the aggressive use of American force and strike power against the enemy in his distant base-camps could eventually destroy his forces and his will. It was a point at which General Depuy, then extremely influential on Westmoreland's staff, was still talking about the threshold of pain. It was something he believed in, that the enemy had a threshold, and that if we hit him hard enough he would cry out; at this very point, in fact, the North Vietnamese were testing out *our* threshold of pain. They would find that ours was a good deal lower than theirs, that we could not accept heavy casualties as they could. Thus Ia Drang was in a way a kind of closing of the door as far as strategy was concerned. We were convinced that we had dealt the other side a grievous blow and we were now ready to deal him more.

But there were others who took a somewhat different view of the battle. John Vann, the Army colonel who had resigned in protest of the Harkins policies, and who was now back in Vietnam as a lowly civilian official, conducted his own private investigation of the battle, and based on his considerable knowledge of enemy tactics, decided that the battle represented something very different from what Westmoreland and Depuy thought. Vann came to the conclusion that the North Vietnamese had deliberately been taking unusually high casualties in order to see where the Americans were vulnerable; in the process they had come up with the answer. The way to offset U.S. might (which was clearly technological and not based on individual bravery or superiority soldier against soldier) was to close with the Americans as tightly as possible, within thirty meters. This neutralized the American air and artillery power. Over a period of time they were able to match American losses on a ratio which was acceptable to them; after all, they were willing to accept far higher casualties in this war.

However different the interpretations of events, the battle of Ia Drang had proven beyond doubt one other factor. It had shown graphically that Hanoi would resist the American escalation with an escalation of its own. In the past, despite the prophecies of the intelligence community, the likelihood that North Vietnamese troops would come into the South had been played down. But by the early fall it was clear that Hanoi was taking its regular units, breaking them down into small sizes, and infiltrating them quickly into the South. In July 1965, when the Americans had decided to send a total of between 175,000 and 200,000 combat troops to Vietnam by the end of the year (with an additional 100,000 ticketed for 1966), the estimate had been that there were still no more than two NVA regiments in the South; by November there were six confirmed North Vietnamese regiments, two more probable and one possible in the South. The bombing, as a weapon of interdiction, had failed. As for affecting Hanoi's will, the bombing and the arrival of American

troops had affected it, but not the way the American principals had anticipated; Hanoi was now determined to send men down even more quickly than
the Americans could bring theirs in. If the full implications of this were lost
on Westmoreland, he nonetheless sensed the immediate one, that the manpower advantage he hoped to have in 1966 was already lost. On November 23
he reported to his superiors:

The VC/PAVN build-up rate is predicated to be double that of U.S. Phase II forces
[these were essentially his 1966 forces]. Whereas we will add an average of 7 maneuver battalions per quarter, the enemy will add 15. This development has already reduced the November battalion-equivalent ratio from an anticipated 3.2 to 1, to 2.8 to
1, and it will be further reduced to 2.5 to 1 by the end of the year. If the trend continues, the December 1966 battalion-equivalent ratio, even with the addition of Phase
II (300,000 men) will be 2.1 to 1.

In the past all the estimates and predictions that the other side would meet
force with force had deliberately been filtered out or diluted; at best the enemy's response was said to be unpredictable, and if anything, the use of American force would bring not counterforce, but negotiations. Now that illusion
was gone; the real world was tougher than the world of doctored war games
and high-level meetings. At the time that Westmoreland made his assessment,
McNamara was in Paris for a NATO meeting; he immediately flew to Saigon,
met with Westmoreland, and negotiated troop levels with the commander. At
the end of November, when McNamara returned to Washington, he recommended to the President that projected force levels be increased to the point
where the American build-up would reach 400,000 by the end of 1965, and
possibly 600,000 by the end of 1967. It was clearly not going to be a short,
limited war any more.

This counterescalation did not bother Westmoreland. He was not euphoric
but he was confident: American force would do it. It would not be easy, but if
we set our mind to it, then it could be done. We would have to pay the price.
(His views throughout were quite similar to Rusk's.) He thought he had a totality of Washington's backing and he prepared for a long war. His MACV
planners in very late 1965 and early 1966 were absolutely confident that the
troop commitment would go to either 640,000 or 648,000 and there was, in
addition, a contingency plan by which it could go as high as 750,000, a figure
that MACV called *the balloon* and considered very much in the ballpark.
MACV was confident; there had been tentative agreement, it thought, from
Defense, and the President had never said no to any request. Westmoreland
was indeed the favored child. In Saigon, Frank McCulloch, the bureau chief
of *Time*, was repeatedly filing that MACV felt that it would get a minimum of
640,000; in Washington, his colleagues working for the same magazine and
covering Defense, not privy to the kind of informal atmosphere which existed

in Saigon, working through weaker sources, kept knocking the figure down, saying nothing like that was in the works. It was in the works, all right, but it was not a figure which Washington wished to give out; only four or five men knew of it in Washington and they weren't talking. Similarly, four or five men knew of it in Saigon and a few of them were talking. Saigon, Lyndon Johnson would always find to his annoyance, was always leakier than Washington.

If MACV was candid with *Time* magazine, which supported the war, it was somewhat less so with Senate Majority Leader Mike Mansfield, who arrived in Saigon in November 1965. Mansfield was traveling with his specialist on Vietnam, Frank Vallejo, and both were extremely uneasy about the policy, and in particular the open-ended quality of it. The sky was the limit, they feared, and Westmoreland was not, Mansfield felt, particularly helpful. Mansfield asked Westmoreland what kind of troop figure he was going for, and Westmoreland kept hedging, no answer was really forthcoming, he kept talking about the fact that he couldn't handle what he already had, he had ships backed up in the harbor. The more Mansfield pushed, the less he found out, and he went back with Vallejo, convinced that if it had been a small number, Westmoreland would have been more candid. This, plus his own uneasiness about the style of open-ended policy, prompted him to write a report predicting that we would end up with 500,000 troops there. All his worst fears about American involvement in Indochina were being realized, step by step.

There were, of course, some indications that the war was changing, that it was sliding from a small combat-troop war to a big one. In late November in Saigon, after a meeting of the mission council, Barry Zorthian, the embassy public affairs officer, told a few select reporters that the strategy had gone from holding the country and preventing the other side from winning, to winning ourselves. Victory. Westmoreland, he said, had a schedule which went as high as 750,000 men. "The name of the game has changed," Zorthian said. "Now we're going to win." One of the reporters he spoke to was Stanley Karnow of the Washington *Post*, who had an uneasy feeling that they had changed policies and objectives in midstream, that this was akin to crossing the 38th parallel in Korea, and that it might have consequences. Of course, there was a certain inevitability to it; a man like Lyndon Johnson would not invest that much for a tie game; Johnson always liked to talk in poker terms and analogies; the more you put into the pot, the more you had to take out as a winner.

If McNamara had learned some of the bitter truth during the November visit, he managed to conceal it admirably. During the trip he had gone to Danang to inspect what the Marines were doing there. While at Danang he had been given a very thorough briefing by a Marine colonel on the situation. The Marines were doing very well in pacification, it seemed. Wherever they appeared and fought, the Vietcong immediately moved back. There was, however, a problem. Once the Marines seemed to have pacified an area, they moved on, and there was a tendency of the Vietcong to come back, and do just as well as before. The result was a danger of spreading the American troops too thin.

That night when McNamara was back in Saigon, he asked Sander Vanocur of NBC, who had hitched a ride with him, what he thought of the day. Vanocur replied that he was very depressed. McNamara, surprised, asked why, and Vanocur answered that we were going to be spread too thin, that it seemed to him a bottomless pit. "Every pit has its bottom, Mr. Vanocur," said the Secretary.

FOR THOSE WHO HAD EXPECTED THE OTHER SIDE TO OBLIGE BY FOLDing quickly, the contrary evidence was now in. For McNamara, who had already been primed by McNaughton for some time on the dangers of counterescalation, the new implications were quite obvious. Since he knew there was no easy way out, he had become a frustrated and divided man. As a weapon of interdiction the bombing had failed, and as a weapon to push Hanoi to the table it had failed; yet he had no other answers and had to recommend a steadily ascending rate of bombing—the rate of sorties went up from 2,500 a month to 10,000 a month in the next year, all of it futile. So by the end of 1965 he was already trapped. While he was negotiating with Westmoreland for more and more troops, though he sensed the hopelessness of the troop escalation, he was at the same time becoming a leading advocate of negotiations within the government. But even now he could not speak openly about what he really felt, how dark he thought it might all be; he could not lose credibility and say that he had miscalculated, that all his forecasts were wrong. That would cost him his credibility, and his effectiveness; he would be known as a dove and he would soon be out. So when he pushed for negotiations at the tail end of 1965, he sold it in a particularly disingenuous way—we could have a bombing pause and try to negotiate, and then, after we had shown that the other side was unwilling to be conciliatory, we would have far greater national support. Worse, because he was committed to force and to the war, he could only offer Hanoi what amounted to surrender. So he was pushing negotiations, but they were doomed negotiations on hopeless terms, and yet in the very effort to bring about negotiations, he was diminishing his credibility with the President.

Some of the particular dilemma of his and the American position, however, had already been seen by his trusted deputy John McNaughton. McNaughton had long feared that the North Vietnamese would respond the way they had, and along with George Ball, he was probably the least surprised member of the upper level of the government. In addition he was picking up other sounds, which bothered him, and this was the changing rationale of the military. At a dinner party in January 1966 he told Henry Brandon that in August 1965 General Wheeler had said that the American aim was victory, and therefore we were putting more men into Vietnam. Now, McNaughton said, Wheeler was using a different rationale—he was saying that unless more men were sent, then American casualties would rise. Thus McNaughton realized that the Americans were in a special kind of trap. In mid-January 1966 he wrote a memo for McNamara:

. . . *The dilemma.* We are in a dilemma. It is that the situation may be "polar." That is, it may be that while going for victory we have the strength for compromise, but if we go for compromise, we have the strength only for defeat—this because a revealed lowering of sights from victory to compromise (a) will unhinge the GVN and (b) will give the DRV the "smell of blood." . . .

McNaughton was clearly influencing McNamara, as were events. When McNamara first came back from meeting with Westy he had rather positively recommended the boost to 400,000 Americans. But two months later, in late January 1966, discussing the same subject, he was more cautious, and seemingly more pessimistic. He wrote:

. . . Our intelligence estimate is that the present Communist policy is to continue to prosecute the war vigorously in the South. They continue to believe that the war will be a long one, that time is their ally, and that their own staying power is superior to ours. They recognize that the U.S. reinforcements of 1965 signify a determination to avoid defeat, and that more U.S. troops can be expected. Even though the Communists will continue to suffer heavily from GVN and U.S. ground and air action, we expect them, upon learning of any U.S. intentions to augment its forces, to boost their own commitment and to test U.S. capabilities and will to persevere at a higher level of conflict and casualties . . .

If the U.S. were willing to commit enough forces—perhaps 600,000 men or more—we could ultimately prevent the DRV/VC from sustaining the conflict at a significant level. When this point was reached, however, the question of Chinese intervention would become critical. . . .

It follows, therefore, that the odds are about even that, even with the recommended deployments, we will be faced in early 1967 with a military standoff at a much higher level, with pacification hardly under way, and with requirements for the deployment of still more U.S. forces.

So McNamara was boxed in, seeing the darkness, recommending more troops as a means of bringing negotiations which were, given the U.S. attitude, hopeless. The real point of it all was that the civilians in Washington, those men who above all else felt they controlled events, had, by the end of 1965, completely lost control. They no longer determined policies, and they did not even know it. One set of reins belonged to Hanoi, the other set to

Westmoreland. The future increments were now being determined in Hanoi by the Politburo there, and in Saigon by Westmoreland and his staff. If Westmoreland had enough troops, then Hanoi would send more; if Hanoi sent more, then Westmoreland would want more. The cycle was out of their hands; nor had they set any real limits on Westmoreland as far as his use of troops in-country was concerned (that is, inside South Vietnam as opposed to attacking neighboring sanctuaries). He was the General, he would use them as he saw fit. His projections were for a long war, larger and larger units fighting, a higher and higher rate of combat, the enemy eventually becoming exhausted. But the Commander in Chief of the enemy forces did not have to run for re-election in 1968.

The strategy of attrition would prove politically deadly for Lyndon Johnson, and yet he had slipped into it. He and the men around him did not spend weeks of painful debate measuring both our and the enemy's resources, deciding on the best way to commit American troops, how to get the most for our men. There was in fact remarkably little discussion of the strategy. It had begun as security, had gone to enclave, and then, without the enclave ever being tested, under the pressure of events, they had gone to what would be search and destroy. It was again an almost blind decision to go with the man on the spot, Westmoreland. It was what he wanted, it was what he would get and so to an extraordinary degree Westmoreland received in-country (as opposed to hitting Cambodian sanctuaries) freedom to maneuver his troops. They were his, to do with whatever he wanted. And out of this came search and destroy, as well as the policy of attrition, a policy which would become one of the most controversial and fiercely debated decisions of the war, a decision that was virtually not even a decision; it was, like so much of the war, simply something that had happened. It was Westmoreland's instincts for the use of power, to use it massively and conventionally, and this with Depuy's aid had produced the policy of search and destroy. Westmoreland was after all a conventional man; his background was conventional war, and both his instincts and responses were conventional. Here, almost within sight—his intelligence was getting better and better—were these very big enemy units. The ideal way to shorten this war, to finish it off quickly, was to go after the big units, this enormous prize just within reach. Just smash their big units, teach them it was all over, and they would have to go to the peace table. Westmoreland knew all about the political infrastructure, how the enemy operated through a very clever and complicated political mechanism, and that this was the root of the war; it gave the other side its most precious asset, its capacity to replenish losses, but the conventional instinct, the temptation to go after the big units was too much. It was, he thought, the best thing he could do for Vietnam, handle this burden for them which they clearly were not able to handle themselves. The U.S. forces would be fighting away from the population, and this would lessen racial tension. It was a strategy which appealed to the American military mind, the use of large force and large units, quicker, less frustrating. He was always particularly optimistic about the results of the operations in the base-camp areas, Cedar Falls and Junction City; to him they presaged victory, and it was the sad truth that he, like those before him, underestimated the capacity of the enemy to replenish (indeed, when the Tet offensive came, the troops came from those very base camps which Westmoreland thought he had cleaned out).

So instead of a limited shield philosophy, we would take over the war. And out of this, the search-and-destroy policy, came the policy of attrition which would prove so costly to Lyndon Johnson. The political implications of such a policy were immense, but he did not think them out, nor did his Secretary of State Dean Rusk nor his Special Assistant for National Security, Mac Bundy. It was perhaps the worst possible policy for the United States of America: it meant inflicting attrition upon the North, which had merely to send 100,000 soldiers south each year to neutralize the American fighting machine. Since the birth rate for the North was particularly high, with between 200,000 young men coming into the draft-age group each year, it was very easy for them to replenish their own manpower (the attrition strategy might have made sense if you could have gone for the whole package, applied total military pressure to the entire country, but the American strategy was filled with limitations as far as that went). So even on the birth rate, the strategy of attrition (which always was based on the belief that the other side had a lower threshold of pain) was fallacious. Add to it the fact that one side was a nation with the nationalist element of unity, and the Communist element of control, that the bombing helped unite its people, that its leadership was able and popular, that its people were lean and tough and *believed* in their mission, which was to unify the country and drive the foreigners out, that there were no free newspapers, no television sets, no congressional dissent, and that this war was not only the top priority, it was the only priority they had.

Against this was a democracy fighting a dubious war some 12,000 miles away from home. The democracy had long-overdue social and political programs at home, and there was such uneasiness about a war in Asia that its political leader felt obliged to sneak the country into the war, rather than confronting the Congress and the press openly with his decision. The Congress and the press would continue to be free, and doubts about so complicated a war would not subside, they would grow. Television would certainly bring the war home for the first time. The country was undergoing vast economic and political and social changes which would be accelerated by the war itself.

It was, in retrospect, an unlikely match for a war of attrition, and reflecting upon it, one high civilian said later that he longed to take the two men most involved in the strategy, who had such vastly different and conflicting problems and demands, and introduce them to each other: General Westmoreland, meet President Johnson. It was, finally, the problem of limited war which had been so fashionable in the early Kennedy days, the difficulty being that you might be a great power of 200 million people fighting limited war against a very small Asian nation of 17 million, except that unlike you, they decided, as happened in this case, to fight *total* war.

Yet the number of men for whom all these factors had real meaning was very small; the Administration's policy of hiding the extent of the war, and the extent of its forthcoming commitments, was still successful in early 1966. It was not, as far as the general public was concerned, going to be a large war. The troop figure was consistently hedged so that opponents of the war did not have a firm target. The burden was still seen as being on Hanoi; we were only trying to get them to a conference table. By the time the general public realized the extent of the war, the depth and totality of it all, then the rationale in Washington would change, it would become Support of our boys out there. At first the critics were told that they should not be critics because it was not really going to be a war and it would be brief, anyway; then, when it became clear that it was a war, they were told not to be critics because it hurt our boys and helped the other side.

All of which would work for a while. Johnson had successfully co-opted the Congress and to a large degree the press. Time was working against him, but this would only be clear later. In the spring of 1965 the protests against Vietnam had begun on the campuses. In the beginning the Administration was not particularly worried about the challenge; Johnson controlled the vital center, and the campuses were not considered major centers of political activity. Yet these questions should be answered, so Mac Bundy was sent off to a televised teach-in to debate the professors, and the Administration was supremely confident about the outcome. Bundy was at the height of his reputation, the unchallenged political-intellectual of Washington, and no one there dared challenge him, for the response would be swift and sharp. But the capital was not the country; what was admired, respected and feared in Washington was not necessarily what was admired, respected and feared in the country, so the teach-in was an omen. In a surprisingly brittle performance he debated Hans Morgenthau, and Edmund Clubb, one of the exiled China scholars. Clubb quoted Lord Salisbury on the dangers of adding to a failed policy. Bundy finally seemed to be saying: We are we, we are here, we hold power and we know more about it than you do. It was not a convincing performance; rather than easing doubts, it seemed to reveal the frailty of the Administration's policy. The teach-in did not end debate, it encouraged it. It also marked the beginning of the turn in Bundy's reputation; up until then, serious laymen in the country had heard how bright he was, but in this rare public appearance he struck them as merely arrogant and shallow.

IN THE FALL OF 1965 RUSK, WHO HAD BEEN LESS THAN EAGER FOR the commitment than most of the others, began to show signs of the toughness, and indeed rigidity, which would later, as the months and years passed, distinguish him from some of the other architects. He was not eager to seek negotiations, and he was uneasy with those on our side who seemed too anxious to talk, afraid they would send the wrong signal, show the Communists our eagerness and our weakness. He felt that the danger in a democracy was that people were spoiled and expected pleasures and were unused to sacrifice; one had to guard against that and he of course would be the guardian. When Adlai Stevenson in 1964 had made his first tentative approach about negotiating with Hanoi to U Thant, it was Rusk who helped keep the discussion of the peace move extremely limited (so limited that his deputy for Asia, Bill Bundy, did not learn of it until the very last moment and was extremely upset). Then, in December 1965, when McNamara began to push for a bombing pause, it was Rusk who was dubious. We should not, he thought, seem too eager for peace; since we had gone to war, we should use our force of arms properly and the other side would have to come to terms with us. A nation as great and as powerful as the United States did not seek war, did not go to war readily, but if it did, then it must be careful not to give away its goals, undermine its own military. There was a consistency to Rusk: he had been the least eager to get in because he had never seen the task as easy, and had few illusions about air power and the quick use of force. In fact, his positions from start to finish, right through to Tet, were remarkably similar to those of the Army generals. His view of the war was a serious one; if we went in we had to be prepared for a long haul, and we had better be ready for it; we had better not flash the wrong signals as soon as we started. Perhaps Rusk, more than any other man around the President, understood Lyndon Johnson, knew that once committed, Johnson would see it through, and that he would want allies, not doubters.

Rusk believed in mutual security, that this was the way to peace; South Vietnam was now linked to mutual security. Thus it must stand; Vietnam had an importance far beyond its own existence. The doubts of the men under him in State did not penetrate his confidence; he was sure of what Americans had to do and sure that they could do it. More than anyone else, more than the military people themselves, he believed what the military said they could do; he took their reports and their estimates perilously close to face value. He told the men under him at State that their job was to wait and watch for the signals from Hanoi, which would give the signal, not the United States. When the signals came, it would be a sign that they were ready to begin; then and only then State's job would begin. "You look for that signal and you tell me when they give it," he told aides. His fault, a deputy thought, was not insincerity, it was the totality of his sincerity. He still believed that the world was the way he had found it as a young man in the thirties, and that good was on our side. Automatically. Because we were a democracy.

His job and State's, then, was to wait. If you were in, you were in. What was it he had told McNamara at the time of the B-52 raids? In for a dime, in for a dollar. So we were in for more than a dollar. And he was different from those around him because they were such rationalists and such optimists, whereas Rusk was always less optimistic, less the rationalist; the others believed that if things did not pan out, they could always turn them around, since they were in control. This was one other reason Rusk was different—he knew his man better.

THERE WERE MANY LYNDON JOHNSONS, THIS COMPLICATED, DIFficult, sensitive man, and among them were a Johnson when things were going well and a Johnson when things were going poorly. Most of the Kennedy men, new to him, working with him since Dallas, had only seen Johnson at his best. Moving into the postassassination vacuum with a certain majesty, he had behaved with sensitivity and subtlety, and that challenge had evoked from him the very best of his qualities. Similarly, during the planning on Vietnam, during the time he had been, as a new President, faced with this most terrible dilemma, he had been cautious and reflective. If there was bluster it was largely bluster on the outside; on the inside he was careful, thoughtful, did his homework and could under certain conditions be reasoned with.

But when things went badly, he did not respond that well, and he did not, to the men around him, seem so reasonable. There would be a steady exodus from the White House during 1966 and 1967 of many of the men, both hawks and doves, who had tried to reason with him and tried to affect him on Vietnam (in May 1967 McNaughton, noting this phenomenon, wrote in a memo to McNamara: "I fear that 'natural selection' in this environment will lead the Administration itself to become more and more homogenized—Mac Bundy, George Ball, Bill Moyers are gone. Who next?" The answer, of course, was McNamara himself). In the late fall of 1965 Johnson learned the hard way that the slide rules and the computers did not work, that the projections were all wrong, that Vietnam was in fact a tar baby and that he was in for a long difficult haul—his commander and Secretary of Defense were projecting 400,000 men by the end of 1966, and 600,000 by the end of 1967, and even so, as 1968 rolled around, no guarantees. At that time Lyndon Johnson began to change. He began to sulk, he was not so open, not so accessible, and it was not so easy to talk with him about the problems and difficulties involved in Vietnam. McNamara's access was in direct proportion to his optimism; as he became more pessimistic, the President became reluctant to see him alone. Johnson did not need other people's problems and their murky forecasts; he had enough of those himself. What he needed was their support and their loyalty. He was, sadly, open-minded when things went well, and increasingly close-minded when things went poorly, as they now were about to do. In the past, during all those long agonizing hours in 1964 and 1965 when they discussed the problems of Vietnam, they had all been reasonable men discussing reasonable solutions, and in their assumptions was the idea that Ho Chi Minh was reasonable too. But now it would turn out that Ho was not reasonable, not by American terms, anyway, and the war was not reasonable, and suddenly Lyndon Johnson was not very reasonable either. He was a good enough politician to know what had gone wrong and what he was in for and what it meant to his dreams, but he could not turn back, he could not admit that he had made a mistake. *He could not lose* and thus he had to plunge forward. It was a terrible thing, he was caught and he knew it, and he knew he could juggle the figures only so long before the things he knew became obvious to the public at large. The more he realized this, the more he had to keep it in, keep it hidden, knowing that if he ever evinced doubts himself, if he admitted the truth to himself, it would somehow become reality and those around him would also know, and then he would have to follow through on his convictions. So he fought the truth, there were very rarely moments when he would admit that it was a miscalculation, that he had forgotten, when they had brought him the slide rules and the computers which said that two plus two equals four, that the most basic rule of politics is that human beings never react the way you expect them to. Then he would talk with some fatalism about the trap he had built for himself, with an almost plaintive cry for some sort of help. But these moments were rare indeed, very private, and more often than not they would soon be replaced by wild rages against any critic who might voice the most gentle doubt of the policy and the direction in which it was taking the country.

So instead of leading, he was immobilized, surrounded, seeing critics everywhere. Critics became enemies; enemies became traitors; and the press, which a year earlier had been so friendly, was now filled with enemies baying at his heels. The Senate was beginning to rise up; he knew that and he knew why—it was that damn Fulbright. He knew what Fulbright was up to, he said; even a blind hog can find an acorn once in a while. So by early 1966, attitudes in the White House had become frozen. One could stay viable only by proclaiming faith and swallowing doubts. The price was high; it was very hard to bring doubts and reality to Johnson without losing access. The reasonable had become unreasonable; the rational, irrational. The deeper we were in, the more the outcry in the country, in the Senate and in the press, the more Johnson hunkered down, isolated himself from reality. What had begun as a credibility gap became something far more perilous, a reality gap. He had a sense that everything he had wanted for his domestic program, his offering to history, was slipping away, and the knowledge of this made him angrier and touchier than ever; if you could not control events, you could at least try and control the version of them. Thus the press as an enemy. Critics of the war became his critics; since he was patriotic, clearly they were not. He had FBI dossiers on war critics, congressmen and journalists, and he would launch into long, irrational tirades against them: he knew what was behind their doubts, the Communists were behind them—yes, the *Communists*, the Russians; he kept an eye on who was going to social receptions at the Soviet embassy and he knew that a flurry of social activity at the Communist embassies always resulted in a flurry of dovish speeches in the Senate. Why, some of the children of those dove senators were dating children of Russian embassy officials. And he knew which ones. In fact, he would say, some of those dovish Senate speeches were being written at the Russian embassy; he knew all about it, he knew which ones, he often saw these speeches before the senators themselves did.

Yet if he had a sense of the darkness ahead in the ground war, he also took a negative view of negotiations; negotiations meant defeat. He had not been particularly eager for the first bombing pause in late 1965, and the results, in his mind, had justified his doubts (one reason he would turn to Clark Clifford to replace the doubting and disintegrating McNamara in late 1967 was that Clifford had seemingly shown his hawkish credentials by opposing the bombing halt in 1965). Nothing but a propaganda benefit for the other side, nothing but more pressure against him, making it harder and harder to renew the bombing. So in the future when there was talk of other bombing halts, he would react with anger and irritation. Oh yes, a bombing halt, he would say, I'll tell you what happens when there's a bombing halt: I halt and then Ho Chi Minh shoves his trucks right up my ass. That's your bombing halt.

So he was entrapped. By early 1966 he was into the war and he knew it; if there was anything particularly frustrating, it was the inequity of it all. Ho did not have enemies nipping at his heels the way Lyndon Johnson did. It was an unfair fight. Yet he was locked into it, and of course it became his war, he personalized it, his boys flying his bombers, his boys getting killed in their sleep. His entire public career, more than thirty years of remarkable service, had all come down to this one issue, a war, of all things, this one roll of the dice, and everything was an extension of him. Westmoreland was an extension of him and his ego, his general. In the past, Dean Acheson had warned him that the one thing a President should never do is let his ego get between him and his office. By 1966 Lyndon Johnson had let this happen, and Vietnam was the issue which had made it happen.

If he was not the same man, then the men around him were not the same men either. In early 1966 Bundy was very uneasy with Johnson. Their relationship, which had never been a natural one, had deteriorated. Bundy was upset by Johnson's disorderly way of running things, by his tendency—when

Kennedy would have let Bundy lock up an issue—to turn, after all the normal players had made their case, to people like Fortas and Clifford for last-minute consultation, and though Bundy had been an advocate of escalation, he was enough of a rationalist to understand immediately that Hanoi's counterescalation meant that events were likely to be messy and irrational. And he knew that with Rusk there, the chance of State was now slim. On Johnson's part there was a feeling that Bundy was somehow, no matter how hard he tried to control it, supercilious ("A smart kid, that's all," Johnson later said of him), plus a gnawing belief that when things went well in foreign affairs the credit would be given to Bundy, and when things went poorly they would be blamed on Johnson. In March 1966, when Bundy was offered the job as president of the Ford Foundation, James Reston at the *Times* found out about it. Bundy, knowing Johnson and fearing his response if there was a story in the *Times*, pleaded with Reston not to run it. The news item was printed and soon there was a story out of Austin, leaked there, that Bundy was indeed accepting, going to Ford. (A few weeks later, at a reception in the White House for young White House fellows, Lady Bird Johnson approached a young man and asked him to tell her what his job was.

"Well, I don't really know," he said. "I used to work for McGeorge Bundy, but now I don't know."

"Oh," said Lady Bird, "Lyndon and I are so sorry about Mac's going. We're going to miss Mac like a big front tooth.")

If Bundy had doubts about Vietnam, and friends thought that in 1966 and 1967 increasingly he did, then they remained interior ones. Johnson, letting Bundy go, knew that he would not become a critic, that he would be available for any and all errands, that he was anxious enough to return and serve, to play by the rules. Which he did; his doubts were very pragmatic ones, whether Vietnam was worth the time and resources it was absorbing and the division it was creating. Yet they remained closely guarded doubts. There was that quality to him—ferocious pride, belief in self, inability to admit mistakes that kept him from being able to react to the war in a human sense. It was as if the greater his doubts and reservations, the more he had to show that he did not have doubts and reservations, and the more confident and arrogant he seemed (debating at Harvard during the 1968 post-Tet meetings, sessions at which he had been an important force to limit the escalation, he would begin by announcing that he would not defend those policies "because I have a brother who is paid to do that," a statement which appalled most of his audience). In the months after he left office he seemed at his worst—glib, smug, insensitive. In March of 1966, right after he left office, he went on the *Today* show, a rare public appearance, and as he walked into the NBC studio early in the morning he was met by a young staff aide named Robert Cunniff, who showed him the make-up room, asked him how he wanted his coffee, and told

Bundy he would be on in about fifteen minutes. Then, further trying to put Bundy at his ease, realizing that many people, even the famous and powerful, are often nervous in television studios, Cunniff tried to make small talk. In some ways it must be a great relief to be out of Washington, Cunniff said, to be away from the terrible decisions involved with Bundy's last job.

"Just what do you mean?" asked Bundy, and there was a small tightening of the mouth.

"Oh," said Cunniff, not realizing what he was getting into, "you know, you must be relieved, getting away from the terrible pressures of the war, making decisions on it."

"Oh, yes," said Bundy, "you people up here in New York take that all very seriously, don't you?"

And Cunniff, who was stunned by the answer, looked quickly to see if it was a put-on, but the face was very cold and Cunniff realized that McGeorge Bundy was not joking.

THERE WAS NO DEARTH OF APPLICANTS FOR THE BUNDY JOB. ROBERT Komer, a Bundy assistant, deemed himself available and qualified and moved his things into Bundy's office. Bill Moyers, anxious to have experience in foreign affairs, was a quiet candidate, knowing the President well, and knowing that you did not necessarily get what you pushed for with Lyndon Johnson. Carl Kaysen, another Bundy deputy, was an insider's choice. And then there was the possibility of Walt Rostow, Bundy's former deputy and now the head of Policy Planning. Komer had his problems; he was an Easterner, and the kind of Easterner that Johnson reacted to, bouncy, ebullient, almost preppy, one had somehow a sense of Komer in white bucks on his way to a fraternity meeting, and he was linked to the Georgetown boys that Johnson disliked. Moyers had his problems; he was young and from Texas and the only degree he possessed was in divinity, and in a White House already sensitive to the charge of too many Texans in high places, the idea of a young biblical Texan handling foreign policy did not go over well. Besides, Moyers had shown a lack of enthusiasm for the war in the past and that did not help him. Kaysen was too reserved, too cerebral.

Gradually the emphasis began to shift to Rostow. The key link here was Jack Valenti, the self-conscious, self-made intellectual, feverishly loyal to Johnson, desperately anxious to improve Johnson's public image (and naturally, with his sycophancy, detracting from it). Valenti, with his desire to improve Johnson's intellectual reputation, was impressed by Rostow, with his enthusiasm, his endless number of theories for almost any subject and situation, his capacity to bring the past into the present with a historical footnote, to make his points thus seem more valid, more historical. (Typically, in April

1966, during one of the periodic Buddhist crises, he wrote that "right now with the latest Buddhist communiqué, we are faced with a classic revolutionary situation—like Paris in 1789 and St. Petersburg in 1917 . . . If I rightly remember, the Russian Constituent Assembly gathered in June 1917; in July, Lenin's first coup aborted; in the face of defeat in the field and Kerensky's weakness, Lenin took over in November. This is about what would happen in Saigon if we were not there; but we are there. And right now we have to try to find the ways to make that fact count.") Comforting words for a President, but even more comforting was his upbeat spirit, his sheer enthusiasm for the President and his policies, particularly the war policies. Rostow had started giving memos for the President to Valenti; Johnson was impressed and encouraged them, and the two got on well together.

One thing in Rostow's favor was his enthusiasm for the war. At a time when many others were becoming increasingly uneasy about the course of American policies in Vietnam, Rostow was quite the reverse; he did not see failure, he saw inevitable victory and believed himself a prophet of events. So Rostow was a good man to have in a White House under attack—he would not turn tail, he would hunker down with the best of them. Which was precisely why a good many of his colleagues from Washington and Cambridge began a quiet, discreet campaign, not so much *for* the other candidates as against Rostow. As Jack Kennedy had once said somewhat ruefully of Rostow: Walt had ten ideas, nine of which would lead to disaster, but one of them was worth having. So it was important, the President added, to have a filter between Rostow and the President. Now it looked like he would be right next to the President. Phone calls were made, doubts about him expressed, enthusiasm for others emphasized. But it did not work against Rostow; if anything, it enhanced his chances and increased his attractiveness. If some of the Kennedy insiders were against him, this was not necessarily a demerit; if Rostow was a little outside the Kennedy circle, his loyalty more likely to be first and foremost to Lyndon Johnson, then so much the better. When Rostow got the job, Johnson told one Kennedy intimate, "I'm getting Walt Rostow as my intellectual. He's not your intellectual. He's not Bundy's intellectual. He's not Galbraith's intellectual. He's not Schlesinger's intellectual. He's going to be *my* goddamn intellectual and I'm going to have him by the short hairs."

So it was that Walt Rostow moved to the White House and for the second time became a major figure on Vietnam. In the past he had been an advocate and an enthusiast of the war, but he had not been taken altogether seriously; his ideas on the bombing were adapted only when there was nowhere else to go. Now he was to move into an important role, the man who was the Special Adviser to the President on National Security, who screened what the President heard and whom he saw, and who gave a special tonal quality to incoming information, an emphasis here and a de-emphasis there, the last man to talk to the judge after all the other lawyers had left the courtroom each day. Whereas Bundy had been careful not to emphasize his own feelings, Rostow had fewer reservations on many issues, particularly Vietnam. It was not deliberate, and indeed much of it was unconscious; he was a believer and a supporter and his enthusiasm showed through. To a President coming increasingly under attack, he was strong and supportive, someone whose own enthusiasm never wavered, who could always find the positive point in the darkest of days. Thus as the policy came under increasing challenge in 1966 and 1967 Rostow helped hold the line; as the President became increasingly isolated, Rostow isolated him more. He was firm and steadfast, and helped load the dice in 1966 and 1967 and 1968 against members of the inner circle having their own doubts. To a Johnson isolated and under attack, Rostow was, said one of his aides, "like Rasputin to a tsar under siege."

IN A WAY GEORGE BALL HAD BEEN COUNTING ON THE 1966 OFF-YEAR elections to help him make his case and turn back the American commitment. By mid-1965 he realized he had lost the first part of his battle; from then on he changed tactics. He moved to a fall-back position—to limit the involvement, to hold the line as much as possible, to keep the United States from any miscalculation which would bring in the Chinese. The latter tactic proved particularly effective with Rusk, but it also hurt Ball in the long run; some of his warnings about Chinese entry (that prolonged bombing of the North would lead to war with Peking in six to nine months) proved false. He was opposing the war, yet kept his legitimacy inside, and he was playing what was essentially a delicate game. He wanted to dissent on the war without provoking emotional resentment on the part of the President or on the part of Rusk. Yet he wanted to make his oppposition clear enough to the President, so that if Johnson needed to change Cabinet officers after the midterm election, Ball would be the clear choice. To George Ball, good policies and good politics went together.

He thought that the signs of the war as a major miscalculation would be obvious by mid-1966, and that it would be self-evident that we were bogged down there. Thus the President, in order to prepare himself for the 1968 elections, would have to cut back on Vietnam and rid himself of its architects, which would mean the likely promotion of Ball. He told friends that he thought the President might lose between forty and fifty seats in the 1966 election, largely because of Vietnam. If this happened he would have to react politically. On this judgment Ball was premature, and curiously enough, like Rusk, he was guilty for the first time of using Korea as his precedent. In Korea the stalemate quality of the war had been visible early; but Vietnam was not like other wars, and the kind of frustration which a war of attrition would

produce was not yet evident. In the fall of 1966 American troops were still arriving, it did not yet seem like a war where half a million Americans would be
involved unsuccessfully, and there was still a general confidence that the war
was winnable, a willingness to accept the prophecies offered from Saigon and
Washington. The real malaise which the war was to produce was still a year
off. The Administration's credibility—that is, its version of the war—had not
yet been shattered. Johnson's capacity to slice the salami so thin had worked,
but the victim in a way would be Johnson; for this premature success, this absence of political reaction, gave him the impression that he could deal with
doves, that the population, caught in a war, would rally to the side of its President. The people of the United States were giving the President of the United
States the wrong signal because the President had given the people the wrong
signal. Someone with a sense of what was coming in Vietnam, a higher level
of violence and then a higher stalemate, might have predicted the dilemma
for Lyndon Johnson in 1968; but for the moment the war was a hidden issue.
(One politician did correctly see the future, and that was Richard Nixon.
Campaigning for the Republicans in 1966, he told reporters that there was a
very good chance Johnson was impaled by the war, and if so he would be extremely vulnerable in 1968, and his own party would turn on him. So Nixon
saw a chance for his own political resuscitation. Knowing that the party did
not want to go to its right wing after the Goldwater debacle and that the liberal wing had vulnerable candidates, Nixon busied himself in 1966 speaking
all over the country for Republican congressional candidates, building up due
bills among them and among local Republican chairmen, due bills which he
intended to cash in during 1968 in what struck him as what would be a less
than futile run against Lyndon Johnson.) But the 1966 election results did not
show any resentment against the war and Ball's dissent was premature;
whether, in fact, it might have changed Johnson, even if there had been evidence of dwindling public support, is debatable. Perhaps even with the loss of
forty seats, Johnson might have hunkered down just a bit more.

So Ball eventually slipped out of the Administration in September 30, 1966,
to be replaced by Nicholas Katzenbach (a typical Johnson move; Johnson
wanted Katzenbach out of Justice so he could place Ramsey Clark there, and
by moving Katzenbach to the number-two job at State, he was hopefully
tying up Robert Kennedy just a little bit more. Thus when in 1967 Robert
Kennedy came back from Paris, having possibly heard of a peace feeler there,
Johnson could tell Kennedy, critical of State, that it was *Kennedy's* State Department). Later after Ball left, friends like Galbraith and Schlesinger talked
with him about resigning, using his departure as something of a protest
against the policies and the direction. But Ball shrugged it off; a resignation
would be a gesture of singular futility in this case, he said, particularly with
this President. It would mean a one-day splash in the newspapers, one head-

line perhaps, and then business as usual, with the President just a little more antagonistic than before to their common viewpoint.

Of the original architects, only one man was undergoing great change, and yet continued to stay in the government to fight for his newer definition of reality—though in a deeply compromised way—and that was Robert McNamara (Bundy had some doubts and from time to time he would pass messages to the President, but his role was in no way comparable to that of McNamara). In a way McNamara was better prepared for the new darkness, since John McNaughton had been preparing him for more than a year on the likelihood of the North Vietnamese responding and stalemating the Americans. The NVA build-up in the South had proven to McNamara, first, that the other side would respond despite the pressure of bombing, and second, that the bombing was hardly an effective way of stopping infiltration. So by March 1966 he was in touch with a group of Cambridge scientists and intellectuals who were trying to design an electronic barrier for Vietnam as a means of stopping infiltration. The link between the Cambridge people and McNamara was Adrian Fisher, a Harvard Law School professor and a close friend of McNaughton's, and the scientists working on the barrier included men like Jerome Wiesner and George Kistiakowsky. The ostensible reason was to stop supplies from coming into the South, but the real reason was to take the rationale for bombing away from the military. McNamara discussed the proposal with the scientists, trying to find out what they would need for specifications and to develop plans for it. Between $300,000 and $500,000, they answered. "All right," he said, "go ahead, but remember one thing. We're talking in very specific terms. This is to stop infiltration, not the bombing. I don't want any talk about bombing." Which they understood, of course, and which the Joint Chiefs understood as well, and they had very little enthusiasm, estimating that the construction and defense of such a barrier would require seven or eight divisions. So they dragged their feet, and they kept putting the price up, until in one classic confrontation McNamara, the same McNamara who was always after the Chiefs to cut costs, to save money, exploded and said, "Get on with it, for God's sakes, it's only money!"

So McNamara, too, was caught in a trap of his own making. Even as he was feeding men and matériel into the pipelines, he doubted more and more their effectiveness, and he was becoming in effect a critic of his own role. If he had had doubts about the bombing by January 1966, they would grow even more during the next few months in the controversy over the bombing of Hanoi and Haiphong's petroleum reserves and oil-storage facilities. The Chiefs, increasingly frustrated with the limits placed on them by the civilians, had been pushing for these targets for some time, and wanted them included in the May bombing lists. Now they had a new and powerful advocate within the White House in Rostow, who not only believed in bombing but had a particular affection for the bombing of electric grids and petroleum resources. Rostow argued that the bombing of petroleum storage had sharply affected the German war machine in World War II (a dubious proposition according to other students of the bombing): "With an understanding that simple analogies are dangerous, I nevertheless feel it is quite possible the military effects of a systematic and sustained bombing of POL [petroleum, oil and lubricants] in North Vietnam may be more prompt and direct than conventional intelligence analysis would suggest. . . ." Rostow was right that the intelligence community would not understand the real effectiveness and significance of hitting POL; the CIA estimated in early June that bombing POL would have little effect.

Despite this the President gave the okay, and on June 29 the strikes were launched. At first it appeared that the raids were extraordinarily successful, with all of the Hanoi storage and 80 percent of the Haiphong facility destroyed. McNamara had gone along with the POL raids; it was the last major escalation that he recommended. What became clear in the months that followed was that the air campaign against POL, although seemingly successful, had, like the previous bombing campaigns, failed. The North Vietnamese had learned to adjust to American power, and dispersed their reserves to areas invulnerable to American attack. So at an extremely high cost in American men and planes, we destroyed the surface storage while the North Vietnamese were able to pressure the Soviets into larger and larger petroleum commitments. For McNamara, it helped seal his doubts; he later criticized the Air Force and the Navy for the gap between the optimistic estimates of what the raids could do and what the actual results were. It meant that he would push harder and harder for the barrier, and that he would begin to work to limit bombing. In effect from then on, and particularly in the fall of 1966, he was something of a dissenter, but a dissenter operating under considerable limits. For one thing, Rusk was not given to the same doubts, and thus the Secretary of State was to the right of him. In addition, if he was fighting from within, he was accepting the assumptions of his opponents, fighting them on a tactical level, not on a deeper one; this made him particularly vulnerable to the counter proposals of Westmoreland and the Chiefs. He began to give up combat troops to hold down on the bombings, dissembling to a degree within the bureaucracy so it would not be too obvious within the government that he was a dove. As such, his half measures always failed.

In October 1966, with the military asking for troop increases which would bring the American commitment to a minimum of 570,000, McNamara went to Saigon again. This time his sense of pessimism was very real; he was convinced that the other side would match us, that in effect Hanoi was now waging its own special kind of attrition, psychological attrition, against us, slowing down the pace of the war slightly, believing that time was on their side. He was affected considerably by reports by one of his own people there, Daniel Ellsberg, whose own gloom was growing and who told McNamara that most of the official optimism was false. On the way back to Washington McNamara talked with aides about the developments, and he seemed very down: things were, he said, worse than a year before. With him was Robert Komer, once the White House aide who had been sent to Vietnam by Johnson to head pacification, a man constantly enthusiastic and upbeat (Komer was liked by journalists, who were amused by his constant optimism. "Do you really believe all that stuff you put out and send back to Washington?" one reporter asked him. "The difference between you and me," he explained, a lovely insight into the semantics of Saigon, "is that I was sent out here to report on the *progress* in the war"). Komer disagreed with McNamara and insisted that the war was certainly no worse than a year before. McNamara asked Ellsberg whether it was better or worse than a year before. "Pretty much the same," Ellsberg answered.

"You see," said Komer, "at least it's no worse."

"But it is worse," insisted McNamara, "because if things are the same, then they're worse, because we've invested so much more of our resources." (On that same plane ride McNamara asked Ellsberg for an extra copy of his report, entitled "Visit to an Insecure Province," and then asked him, in the interests of not straining civilian-military relationships, if he would mind *not* showing it to General Earle Wheeler.)

McNAMARA BEGAN TO BE INCREASINGLY APPALLED BY THE WAR ITself, what we were doing with our power, the pain inflicted on the civilians. He paid particular attention to stories about the destruction caused by the bombing. When Harrison Salisbury of the *Times* visited Hanoi at the end of 1966, his articles were violently attacked by the Administration, particularly Defense Department spokesmen, but McNamara was fascinated by them and followed them closely. He and Robert Kennedy had remained close friends and in 1966 they began to feed each other's dissent, McNamara confirming to Kennedy that the war was not going well, Kennedy confirming McNamara's impressions of what the war was doing to this country. He was an intriguing man in this period; almost as if there were a split personality caught between two loyalties, and more, caught between two eras. In those days he could still be part of the planning of the bombing, but be a very different man in the evening, going to dinner parties, raising a glass to someone like Moyers with the toast "Bless the doves—we need more of them." He was able to head the war machine, give the Montreal speech, and then regret giving it. It was as if there were a Kennedy-McNamara who said one thing to Kennedy-type people, and a Johnson-McNamara who said another to Johnson-type people. He was able to come back in October 1966 and report to Johnson that things did not look good in Vietnam ("I see no reasonable way to bring the war to an end soon"), commenting on how tough and resilient the enemy was, and then conclude that the United States should press on harder militarily and get into a better military position which would make a war of long duration less attractive to the enemy. The word swept through Washington about his unhappiness; some thought he was being disloyal to Johnson, others began to think he was coming apart. In late 1966 he ran into Emmett Hughes of *Newsweek*, who had just written a hand-wringing piece on Vietnam, and McNamara was very sympathetic about the piece, it certainly wasn't a good situation, was it? "I never thought it would go on like this. I didn't think these people had the capacity to fight this way. If I had thought they could take this punishment and fight this well, could enjoy fighting like this, I would have thought differently at the start . . ." Washington watched his dilemma, the split personality, with fascination. A brilliant Defense Secretary, went the Washington line, but no taste for being a War Secretary. His whole ethical and moral structure made him at ease in the job at Defense, but when he became a War Secretary his values were threatened and he could not come to terms with his new role. It was, he sometimes said, the system which had produced the war; yet he was one of the men who was supposed to control the system.

In despair and frustration over the war, in 1967 he ordered a massive study of all the papers on Vietnam, going back to the 1940s, a study which became known as the Pentagon Papers. When it was handed in he read parts of it. "You know," he told a friend, "they could hang people for what's in there." His own behavior seemed increasingly erratic as the pressures on him mounted, and close friends worried about his health. In 1967 when there was a possibility of peace negotiations being worked out through the British, Kosygin was in London and a bombing pause had gone into effect. Acting on his talks with the British, Ambassador David Bruce recommended strongly that we not resume the bombing until Kosygin had left London. Bruce pleaded to State that if it valued the alliance at all, it must observe the British request. Rusk, a great chain-of-command man, accepted the Bruce thesis and pushed it. McNamara argued forcefully against it and tore into it at the meetings, but Bruce and Rusk held the day. A few minutes after the last discussion, McNamara was on the phone to Bruce, congratulating him on his victory, how well he had presented his case, and how proud McNamara was of him. At first Bruce was touched by McNamara's warmth and courtesy, but later he was appalled when he learned that McNamara had been his principal adversary, and the story spread through both American and British diplomatic circles in London.

IF BY 1966, AND INCREASINGLY IN 1967, McNAMARA WAS BEGINNING to move away from the policy, then Rusk was, if anything, more steadfast than ever. He not only believed in the policy, he had a sense of profound constitutional consequences if the President, already at loggerheads with one of his chief advisers, was separated from the other. If Rusk too dissented, if that gossipy town even thought he was a critic, then in Rusk's opinion the country would be in a constitutional crisis. There must be no blue sky between the President and the Secretary of State, he told aides. Besides, he believed the war could and should be won. So he became a rock, unflinching and unchanging, and absorbing, as deliberately as he could, as much of the reaction to the war as possible. The abuse he took was enormous; he who had been the least anxious of the principal advisers to become involved but who had never argued against it, now became the public symbol of it, a target of public scorn, his statements mocked, so that he would once say in exasperation that he was not the village idiot; he knew that Ho was not Hitler, but nonetheless, there was an obligation to stand. In a pay phone booth in his own State Department someone in 1967 scratched the graffito: "Dean Rusk is a recorded announcement." As he became a rock, so his own Department was immobilized; the best people in State, increasingly unhappy about the policy, felt they could make no challenge to it, and that they had become parrots, that and nothing more, and departmental morale sank to a new low.

For Rusk, the job of the Secretary of State seemed to be to absorb pain. That and nothing more. Though there was much to challenge the military on —particularly the political mindlessness of the attrition strategy—State's challenges were few, infrequent, mild and usually on minor matters. Occasionally there would be quick flashes of the hurt, as when he talked about the journalists who covered the war—which side were they on, were they for their country or against it? Years later, when the ordeal was over, he would tell friends that he did not know how he had lasted through it—if he had not been able to have that drink at the end of the day he could not have survived. There were moments when he did not conceal the anger and the rage, though they were few. Tom Wicker of the *Times* was at a dinner party with Rusk at the Algerian embassy one night in 1966 at a time when there had been a Buddhist crisis in Hué, when suddenly Rusk turned to him and started screaming —there was no other word for it: Why can't the *New York Times* get things right? Why does it always print lies? Which side is it on? Wicker, whose own relations with Rusk had always been pleasant, was stunned by the anger and ferocity of the attack, and it was minutes before he could even understand what Rusk was talking about—a report in the *Times* that day saying that Buddhist dissidents had taken over the Hué radio station. Rusk had read the story and had been so upset by it that he had personally called the American consulate in Hué, where of course the American officials had denied the report, and on the basis of this he had proceeded to lecture Wicker on the perfidy of American journalism. The entire episode, particularly the sudden savagery of Rusk's attack—after all, it is not fun to be assaulted by the Secretary of State of the United States of America over coffee and cognac—stayed with Wicker, and six months later when he was in Vietnam he dropped by the American consulate in Hué and asked a young man on the staff there about the Buddhist crisis. Oh yes, said the young man, the Buddhists had captured the radio station, and Wicker, thinking of Rusk and his obvious sincerity, had decided then that the real problem was that they had created an elaborate machine to lie to them, only to become prisoners of their own lies.

But generally Rusk bore the brunt of it well. He did not complain. He was a proud man and at times it seemed as if he took sustenance from the criticism. In the great clubs of New York and Washington his old friends, his sponsors, men like Lovett and McCloy, were worried about Dean being the target of all the nation's anger. One day McCloy stopped Lovett and said that he wished Dean would fight back, answer his critics or yell for help—they would like to get in the fight and help him. But Lovett, who knew Rusk well, said that Dean would never do that, he was too proud. Yet proud or not, at the end the taste, which should have been so good—eight years at the job that he and every other serious young man coveted—was sour, and he was exhausted financially, physically and spiritually. At the small farewell party for him given by some State Department reporters, the atmosphere was suitably pleasant; these men who had covered Rusk for that long recognized in him qualities of grace, decency and modesty which were not always obvious from a distance. And Rusk, who had always held together so well, finally broke. He went over to British correspondent Louis Heren and asked why the British had not sent any troops to Vietnam. Rusk knew of course well enough, as they had all known from the start, that this was a war that no one else had wanted, that except for a genuine effort by the Australians and a semimercenary effort by the Koreans, it was virtually a unilateral war. As gently as possible, Heren began to stumble through the usual rationalizations when Rusk, whose own allegiance, whose own lessons of mutual security were derived from England, suddenly cut him off. "All we needed was one regiment. The Black Watch would have done. Just one regiment, but you wouldn't. Well, don't expect us to save you again. They can invade Sussex and we wouldn't do a damn thing about it."

MANY OF THE PEOPLE AROUND LYNDON JOHNSON, AND MANY OF THE people at State had been relatively pleased when Walt Rostow replaced McGeorge Bundy. In contrast to Bundy's cold, haughty style, Rostow was warm, pleasant, humble, almost angelic, eager to share his enthusiasm, his optimism, with all around. He had time for everyone, he was polite to everyone, there was no element of put-down to him. The real Johnson loyalists were particularly pleased because they had not liked the Bundy-Johnson relationship, and here was Rostow, bearing the same credentials as Bundy, with far more serious books to his credit, a man far more pleasant to work with, and who was joyously, unabashedly pro-Johnson. It was not fake enthusiasm, it was genuine; Johnson had rescued Rostow from the Siberia of Policy Planning, and Rostow was properly grateful, but more important, Rostow genuinely admired Lyndon Johnson. They saw eye to eye on both domestic and foreign affairs, and Rostow thought Johnson the smartest, toughest man he had ever dealt with. As for Johnson, if he had liked about Bill Bundy his willingness to run it in up to the hilt, then Rostow was a man after his own heart.

But the enthusiasm of others for Rostow soon floundered on Rostow's own enthusiasm. He became the President's national security adviser at a time when criticism and opposition to the war were beginning to crystallize, and he eventually served the purpose of shielding the President from criticism and from reality. He deflected others' pessimism and rewarded those who were optimistic. It was not contrived, it was the way he was. Perhaps, too, it was a symptom of the war: a President in a hopeless war did not need, could not accept a chief adviser wringing his hands, an adviser who seemed to reflect the gathering doubts. Maybe the job required a positive thinker. There was no more positive thinker in Washington than Walt Whitman Rostow.

His optimism was almost a physiological thing, organically part of him. He always believed in the war and in particular in the bombing. He believed early in what the bombing would do, that it was something quick and dramatic and that the other side would have to give in. Year after year, as the failure of the bombing became apparent, it did not faze him; just a little more bombing. And enthusiastic himself, he was anxious to pass on his enthusiasm. He headed the Psychological Strategy Committee, which met at the White House to think of psy war, a strategy which, it turned out, would be largely aimed at the American people. If any of the incoming reports indicated any kind of progress, Rostow immediately authorized a leak. Business Week got computer data charts of attacks by Vietcong (if they were down); the Christian Science Monitor got computerized population-control data from the Hamlet Evaluation Survey; the Los Angeles Times received data on the searches of junks and hamlets secured. He could always see the bright side of any situation, and in that sense he became legend. In the thousands of items flooding in from Saigon as part of the information glut he could find the few positive ones, pounce on them and bring them to his boss, as for instance one morning in 1967 when he told the President that never had the Boy Scouts of Vietnam gone out to clean up the rubble as they had just done in Danang. He made his predictions and nothing bothered him. He could grab Dan Ellsberg in July 1965 and excitedly pass on the news about the bombing (which to most experts in the CIA had already proven itself a failure): "Dan, it looks very good. The Vietcong are going to collapse within weeks. Not months but weeks. What we hear is that they're already coming apart under the bombing." They did not come apart in a few weeks, but neither did Rostow, and Ellsberg went off to Vietnam, where for two years he became something of an authority on the failure of the Vietcong to collapse. Two years later, tired, depressed, and thoroughly pessimistic about the lost cause in Vietnam, he returned to Washington, where he found Rostow just as upbeat as ever.

"Dan," said Rostow, "it looks very good. The other side is near collapse. In my opinion, victory is very near."

Ellsberg, sick at heart with this very kind of high-level optimism which contrasted with everything he had seen in the field, turned away from Rostow, saying he just did not want to talk about it.

"No," said Rostow, "you don't understand. Victory is very near. I'll show you the charts. The charts are very good."

"Walt," said Ellsberg, "I don't want to hear it. Victory is not near. Victory is very far away. I've just come back from Vietnam. I've been there for two years. I don't want to talk about it. I don't want to see any charts . . ."

"But, Dan, the charts are very good . . ."

He had a great capacity not to see what he did not choose to see; in Washington at a dinner given for Everett Martin, a distinguished *Newsweek* reporter expelled from Vietnam for the pessimism of his reporting in late 1967, Rostow managed to pass the entire evening without ever acknowledging that Martin had been in Vietnam. Within the bureaucracy the word went out among those who briefed him that if they wanted to get his attention they had to bait their news with sugar, get the positive information in first, and then before he could turn off, quickly slip in the darker evidence. (Once in 1967 after a somewhat pessimistic briefing by John Vann, Rostow, slightly shaken, said, "But you do admit that it'll all be over in six months." "Oh," said Vann somewhat airily, "I think we can hold out longer than that.")

With the White House under siege, with increasing evidence that the American military commitment to Vietnam had been stalemated, Rostow fought back; in the White House basements, aides culled through the reams of information coming in from Saigon and picked the items which they knew Rostow was following, particularly the good ones. They would send this up to Rostow, and he would package it and pass it on to the President, usually with covering notes which said things such as—this would give confirmation to the statement which the President had so wisely made to the congressional leadership the day before. The notes were similar—there were little touches of flattery: The record of your success indicates . . . Your place in history will bring you . . . The theme was the greatness of the cause and the immortality of Lyndon Johnson. Later, as McNamara's doubts became more evident, there would be references to the need to stop McNamara's wickedness, and when Clark Clifford replaced McNamara and began to fight the policy, there were verbal references to the need to "combat Cliffordism."

He fought evidence which was contrary. He encouraged George Carver, the CIA man who was assigned to brief the White House, to be more optimistic, and by 1967 there was a major split within the CIA. Most of the pure intelligence analysts were much more gloomy than Carver (in fact, in savvy Washington circles it was said that there were two CIAs: a George Carver CIA, which was the CIA at the top, generally optimistic in its reporting to Rostow; and the rest of the CIA, which was far more pessimistic. Rostow himself, drawing on his experience as a World War II intelligence officer, was not above reanalyzing and challenging some CIA reports and somehow making them, upon revision, more optimistic than they had been. He fought elements of the government which he considered unworthy and disloyal. When officers at State put out a weekly summary called the "Evening Reading Items," a one-page sheet which attempted to show how American moves in Vietnam looked to Hanoi (showing in effect that we were more aggressive than we thought we were and reflecting Hanoi's determination to keep coming), Rostow was appalled. He hated the sheet and got into bitter conflicts with State over its right even to publish it. It's very pessimistic, he would argue, and it's all supposition. All supposition. Nothing hard in it. But the State Department people argued back that the President had to see it, we had to know how we looked to the other side.

He also played a form of gamesmanship with Rusk and McNamara, particularly McNamara. He would pore over the voluminous amount of incoming military information, make his selections, and come up with one or two positive pieces of news. Then he would call Rusk and McNamara, very cheerful, very upbeat: Have you seen the new captured documents? They're terrific! Have you seen the stuff about the battle at An Xuyen? Great victory. A civil guard company stood off a VC regiment. The body count in Chau Doc is marvelous! . . . It was always minuscule stuff in a broad vast war with hundreds of other items far more pessimistic, but it kept McNamara and Rusk busy wasting long hours culling the material themselves so they would be prepared for his calls. Thus valuable time was wasted and the great men of the government went through material checking out platoon ambushes lest they be ambushed themselves. And Lyndon Johnson, already isolated because of the war and because of his office, was kept even more remote.

By the nature of his office, a President is separated from his natural constituency and from the art of his profession, politics. The office restricts his movements, his access to events and reality, since few want to bring the President bad news. If a politician is a senator, a friend can sometimes tell him the honest truth in a gentle manner. If he is a President there is no such equality, no way of gently and honestly bearing bad tidings. Respect for the office demands that bad news be filtered down. At first Johnson was isolated involuntarily by the nature of the job, but then as the war progressed, the isolation became voluntary. He saw enemies everywhere. He became a figure of scorn. A scurrilous play, *MacBird*, was written about him and enjoyed remarkable critical success. He became a cartoonists' delight: he bombed Vietnam and wept crocodile tears, and the tears turned out to be maps of Vietnam; he showed his famous abdominal scar and the scar turned out to be a map of Vietnam.

The liberal intellectual community, crucial to the success of a Democratic liberal President, was turning on him. The first signs had come in 1965 when he gave a major Festival of the Arts—what he hoped would be an intellectual ratification of his great electoral triumph. Instead it turned out to be an intellectual rejection of his Vietnam policies. Some of the writers and artists invited wanted to boycott, others wanted to come and picket and read protests. "Half of those people," Johnson said, "are trying to insult me by staying away and half of them are trying to insult me by coming." But the art festival was the beginning: rather than crowning his legislative victories, it symbolized the intellectual community's rejection of the war. More radical voices, fueled by the war, came to prominence, and in so doing, moved the traditional liberal intellectual center over to the left. The liberals had to move to the radical position on the war or lose influence. The Fulbright hearings came in early 1966, and further legitimized opposition; gradually opposition became increasingly centrist and respectable. Opposition mounted on the campuses; Norman Mailer in 1966 could dedicate a book of essays to Lyndon Johnson with grati tude for having made young Americans cheer at the mention of Mailer's name.

With liberal pressure mounting, with Robert Kennedy making the first uneasy gestures toward opposition, Johnson turned ever more inward. He dared not venture out; isolation begot isolation. When in mid-1967 he decided to defend his policies, the site and the group he chose was significant—the annual Junior Chamber of Commerce meeting. If a liberal Democratic President, needing a friendly and respectful audience, had to choose the Jaycees, then he was in trouble (as was his protégé Hubert Humphrey; Mrs. Humphrey, questioned about antagonism of American youth to her husband in 1968, answered that it was not true that the Vice-President was not keeping up with youth—the Humphreys, she said, kept in touch with many of the Jaycees). Someone like Martin Luther King, Jr., could not be a friend on civil rights and a critic on the war; he became in effect an enemy, he had to be kept away. (Of course the price for those who stayed friendly to Johnson was quite considerable, it moved them increasingly away from their own people and their own constituencies. At one Negro meeting in March 1967, Whitney Young of the Urban League defended the war and ended up in a bitter confrontation with Dr. King; Young told King that his criticism of the war was unwise, it would antagonize the President and they wouldn't get anything from him. King, genuinely angry, told him, "Whitney, what you're saying may get you a foundation grant, but it won't get you into the kingdom of truth.")

The protests turned uglier and more personal, neoviolent, and then violent. Attitudes and passions long concealed by the two-party system were now unleashed. More and more trusted staff people left, including some of Johnson's own people—Reedy, Moyers and even Valenti. The departure of Moyers in 1966 was considered crucial; though he had been the White House press officer and thus a spokesman for the war, he was known on the inside as a doubter, and he had worked to make other doubters available to the President. When Moyers left, feeling himself locked in by the growing inflexibility around him, James Reston wrote that he was a casualty of the war, that he had been wounded at Credibility Gap. Johnson himself was furious when Moyers left. He hated it when anyone left him, anyway, but Moyers was special, he was the proxy son. Johnson raged after he departed—that boy had been using Johnson all this time, out there having dinner with the Kennedys, advancing his own career. Well, Lyndon Johnson wasn't stupid, he knew what Moyers had been doing, he read the clips, and why was it that his press secretary's image kept getting better and better, but Johnson's image got worse and worse?

As the temper in the country grew uglier, the White House became more of a fortress, and security arrangements became more and more stringent. Johnson, aware of the mood and the criticism of him, the highly personal nature of it, told friends, "The only difference between the Kennedy assassination and mine is that I am alive and it has been more torturous." Inside the fortress Johnson's aides pleaded with him to go out more, to leave the office; they wrote memos saying that even if demonstrators attacked or humiliated him, it would rebound to his credit, and that it was extremely unwise for him to stay locked up in the White House. But the Secret Service people would have none of it; it was far too dangerous, they said, they had never seen the anger and the instability in the country focused as it was on the Chief Executive. They would not permit it.

Nor could Johnson plead effectively for his war. Wars are supposed to unite nations, to rally divided spirits, and Johnson had counted on this in his private political estimates. But this war was different; rather than concealing or healing normal divisions in the society, it widened them, and gaps became chasms. Presidential aides, looking for comforting precedents, had gone back to the World War II speeches of Franklin Roosevelt and were startled by how bloodthirsty it all seemed; the Jap was to be smashed like the animal he really was. In contrast, Johnson had to be restrained, he had to announce every few minutes that he did not intend to overthrow Hanoi. Nor could he bring a Medal of Honor winner to the White House for a speech without acerbic editorial reaction. He was boxed in. He could not unleash the dogs of war without creating dreams of winning; it was impossible to unleash them partway. The pressures now seemed to come from both sides, Westmoreland and CINCPAC asking for more troops and greater bombing targets, the civilians asking for greater controls. Limited war was not limited in the pain and dilemmas it brought to a President. In late 1966 the military began to build up pressure for the bombing of Hanoi and Haiphong, blocking the harbor, taking apart the industrial capacity of both cities. The military brought with it evidence that this way the war would be won quicker; that, though drastic, in the long run this would save lives. Doing the hard thing was often doing the right thing. As a way of dramatizing this last point, one of the senior officers brought along projections for what the invasion of the Japanese mainland might have cost the Americans in lives had we not used the atomic bomb. They even had the figure: 750,000 lives saved. Johnson was fascinated and asked the senior military how they had arrived at the figure. The answer was quite simple, they said: some of their bright young men at the Pentagon had fed the right information from previous landings and battles into a computer, and thus come up with the figure. The President seemed duly impressed and asked to meet the young men who had made the projection. When they were eventually ushered into his office, the President feigned interest in their methodology for a while and then told them, "I have one more problem for your computer—will you feed into it how long it will take five hundred thousand angry Americans to climb that White House wall out there and lynch their President if he does something like that?" Which ended for a time the plan to bomb Hanoi and Haiphong.

But this did not abate the military pressure, which continued to grow. In April 1967, with support for the war fast dwindling, he brought General Westmoreland home to speak before the Congress and the Associated Press Managing Editors Convention. But the Westmoreland appearances did not ease the pressures against him; if anything, the criticism of Johnson for using Westmoreland, for bringing the military into politics, mounted. Nor did Westmoreland reassure the President in private messages. At this point Westmoreland had 470,000 Americans, and he was asking for an increase which would bring the total to 680,000 men by June 1968, or at the very least a minimum increase of about 95,000, to 565,000. But even with this increase his forecasts were not optimistic. Without the top figure, he told Johnson, the war would not be lost, but progress would be slowed down; this, he said, was not encouraging but realistic. Then Westmoreland noted that every time we took an action, the other side made a countermove. At this point the President asked him, "When we add divisions, can't the enemy add divisions? If so, where does it all end?" Westmoreland answered that the NVA had eight divisions in the country and had the capacity to go to twelve, but if they did, the problems of support would be considerable. He did note, however, that if we added more men, so would the enemy. But we had finally reached the crossover point, Westmoreland insisted, a crucial point in his war of attrition: we were killing men more quickly than they could add them. Even so, the President was not entirely put at ease. "At what point does the enemy ask for [Chinese] volunteers?" he asked. Westmoreland answered, "That's a good question."

Johnson then asked his commander what would happen if we stayed at the already high figure of 470,000 men. It would be a meat-grinder war in which we could kill a large number of the enemy but in the end do little better than hold our own, Westmoreland said. The limitations of troops (this country already regarded it as too unlimited a war) meant that he could only chase after enemy main-force units in fire-brigade style. He foresaw the war then going on in the current fashion for five more years. If the American force was increased to 565,000, Westmoreland saw the war going on for three years; with the full increment of 210,000 it could go on for two years—which would take Johnson into 1970. General Wheeler was there (anxious for Westmoreland to get the troops as a means of also getting a reserve call-up) and the President asked him what would happen if Westmoreland did not get the full 210,000. Wheeler answered that the momentum the Americans had would die, and in some areas the enemy would recapture the initiative; it did not mean that we would lose the war, but it would certainly be a longer one. For Lyndon Johnson, a year away from an election, already besieged, already sensing the growing restlessness in the country, hearing these rather dark predictions of his generals, it was hardly a happy occasion.

TWO YEARS TOO LATE THE CIVILIANS WERE FINALLY LEARNING HOW open-ended they had made the war, and how little they had determined the strategy. Ten days later John McNaughton wrote in a memo to McNamara:

I am afraid there is the fatal flaw in the strategy in the draft. It is that the strategy falls into the trap that has ensnared us for the past three years. It actually *gives* the troops while only *praying* for their proper use and for constructive diplomatic action. Limiting the present decision to an 80,000 add-on does the very important business of postponing the issue of a Reserve call-up (and all of its horrible baggage) but postpone it is all that it does—probably to a worse time, 1968. Providing the 80,000 troops is tantamount to acceding to the whole Westmoreland-Sharp request. This being the case, they will "accept" the 80,000. But six months from now, in will come messages like the "470,000–570,000" messages, saying that the requirement remains at 201,000 or more. Since no pressure will have been put on anyone, the military war will have gone on as before and no diplomatic progress will have been made. It follows that the "philosophy" of the war should be fought out now so that everyone will not be proceeding on their own premises, and getting us in deeper and deeper; at the very least, the President should give General Westmoreland his limit (as President Truman did to General MacArthur). That is, if General Westmoreland is to get 550,000 men, he should be told "that will be all and we mean it."

The government was now clearly divided, and the President was caught in the middle. The Chiefs and Westmoreland wanted an ever larger war and ever greater force, but this time McNamara was in effect able to hold the line. Westmoreland would not get the minimal 70,000 he wanted; rather, there would be a compromise and he would get about 50,000, bringing the U.S. troops to a ceiling of 525,000.

It was a special irony that the burden of making the case against the war now fell to the civilians at Defense. Nominally the reaction should have come from the White House, from aides to the President anxious to protect their man from false estimates from the military; or from State, a place supposedly sensitive to the political dilemmas of the war. But Rostow made the White House staff supportive, a hotbed of cheerleaders, and at State, Rusk kept his people from analyzing failures (thus the erratic behavior of Bill Bundy in all those years; he jumped around from position to position, he seemed to be saying that we were doing the right things, but we weren't doing them well enough; he was never able to use his intelligence and that of his staff on the real issues. His intelligence went in one direction, but his responsibility to his superior, Rusk, turned him in another. As a result he became increasingly irritable and harsh to those under him).

By mid-1967 McNamara was moving to try and cap the war, particularly the bombing. In October 1966, for the first time, he had let Systems Analysis loose on the issue of the war, asking them to check on projected increases the Chiefs wanted for bombing in 1967. The willingness to bring in Systems Analysis was significant not so much as an attempt to prove that the war was not working, but as a willingness to surface more and more as a critic. He knew that the use of Systems Analysis would anger the military and cause him political problems, that it would be evidence of his own pessimism, but at this point he was willing to take additional heat in order to get the facts. The Systems Analysis people of course recommended against the bombing. They reported that the bombing did not cause Hanoi great problems, that these losses were readily made up by the Soviet Union and that thus an increase in bombing placed a greater burden not on North Vietnam, but on the United States. For example, CINCPAC's expanded bombing requirements would generate 230 aircraft losses in 1967 and cost us $1.1 billion while doing only negligible damage to the other side. (At the end of 1967 Systems Analysis would do another estimate on the war and find that despite the bombing, the GNP of North Vietnam had managed to go up in 1965 and 1966, and had fallen off only in 1967, and that North Vietnam's allies had given Hanoi over the war years $1.6 billion in economic and military aid—that is, four times what it had lost through bombing. "If economic criteria were the only consideration, NVN would show a substantial net gain from the bombing, primarily in military equipment," it reported.)

But by 1967 McNamara had not yet made the case against the bombing. He had made an early appeal for limiting the bombing, and his appeal, pressed at a very high level in the government, had resulted in a ferocious argument—sharp and furious. Word of it did not leak out, because it had been held at such a high level, and because McNamara himself was so close-mouthed about it and operated so close to his vest. But John McNaughton later told friends that had it gone through, there would have been at least two senior military resignations.

McNamara lost that first round, but he had decided to continue fighting. He wanted to win within the bureaucracy because that was the battlefield he knew best. He wanted above all to make the case that the bombing could not win the war, that it was a subsidiary part of it at best, and that the limits were greater than the effectiveness. He thought of using the material in a press conference but decided that was too limited a forum; he thought of giving a single speech but decided that the complexity of his points might be lost; it was too much for a one-shot presentation. So while he was looking for a forum, he prepared his case. He pushed the CIA very hard for judgments on how effective the bombing had been and received in return what were considered some of the best reports ever done by the Agency. In August, when the Stennis committee, primed by frustrated and unhappy generals, was holding hearings on the air war, McNamara was asked to testify. It was exactly what he wanted. He knew about committee hearings by now, and how to make points and make news. He worked mostly by himself with very few aides right up until the last minute, deliberately not clearing his presentation with the White House, knowing that clearance would not come through.

In testifying, he recognized the impact of what he was doing and saying. He did not attack previous bombing; rather, what he sought was to remove bombing as a means of attaining victory. He knew it would infuriate the President, and it did; afterward he was summoned to the White House to receive a full blast of presidential anger. It was a rare moment for McNamara; he, the compleat corporate man, had broken the corporate rules, and he had acted as an individual, as a man with his own rights and privileges. In a way he lost; eventually the fifty-seven targets which the JCS wanted and which the Stennis committee had criticized him for not authorizing were cleared by the President with, of course, no appreciable change in the war. But he had written into the record a powerful official argument against the bombing and this would have greater effect in the coming year. In doing this, he paid the price; he separated himself from the military publicly, and he undermined his long-range usefulness. From then on the President made sure that Earle Wheeler was at the Tuesday lunches. A few months later the President, wanting to make some minor point on the war to a senator, suggested that the senator go by and see Bob McNamara. And then he caught himself: "No, don't go see Bob—he's gone dovish on me."

But a dovish Secretary of Defense in control of a military empire was a political problem for Johnson. It meant that his own house was divided, almost openly so after the Stennis hearings. McNamara annoyed the Chiefs, caused problems on the Hill, and was a constant reminder to Johnson himself that perhaps it did not work, that it was all lies. By mid-1967 Johnson had turned on McNamara (it was not enough that McNamara's earlier 1965 projections had been wrong; what was worse was that he was now trying to act on a new set of calculations); the President still described his Defense Secretary as brilliant, but there was a new sarcastic touch to it. In mid-1967, when McNamara proposed limiting the bombing, gradually reducing it in scale as a means of getting negotiations started, Johnson took the proposals, handed them to an aide, and said, "You've never seen such a lot of shit." Clearly, McNamara was no longer an asset; he was a man caught between conflicting loyalties, and Johnson was aware of his very close relationship with Robert Kennedy. Nineteen sixty-eight being a political year, Lyndon Johnson was not about to enter a campaign with a vital member of his official family publicly dissenting on the most important issue. Without checking with McNamara, Johnson announced in November 1967 that his Secretary of Defense was going to the World Bank. The move came as a surprise to the Secretary and he did not know whether or not he had been fired. The answer was that he had been.

But not everyone had gone dovish on the President, neither General Westmoreland nor another important member of the team in Saigon, Ambassador Ellsworth Bunker. When this kindly, gentle New England patriarch with perhaps the most enviable and least assailable reputation in American government—everyone spoke well of Ellsworth Bunker—had arrived there in 1967, the doves had all felt a surge of optimism. Bunker's record for sensitivity and integrity were impeccable; at State a certain excitement had been kindled by Bunker's appointment. But Bunker, who had been so open-minded in the Dominican crisis, was very different in Saigon; the American flag was planted now, American boys were dying, and though he was freed of the mistakes of the past, he felt the need to justify the past American investment. So he bought all the military estimates and assumptions; he was the bane of some of the younger men on his staff who worked desperately to bring him together with doubters, to tell him that the whole thing was hopeless and that we were stalemated. But Bunker was confident, and in the next five years he became one of the two or three most important and resilient players, in particular standing behind Thieu and Ky at the time of Tet, when most people were ready to write them off. So in 1967 if the military were optimistic, Bunker was optimistic. When members of his staff and journalists brought him unfavorable estimates, he turned away. He could not understand why they were so pessimistic, he said, when generals as able as Bruce Palmer were optimistic. Why, Bruce Palmer was one of the finest and most intelligent officers in the U.S. Army, they had worked together in the Dominican crisis, and General Palmer had assured him that things were going well in Vietnam. So how dare these young reporters be pessimistic? It was something he simply could not understand. Indeed, at one dinner party for journalists in late October 1967, Bunker began to talk confidently about how well things were going, and how bright the immediate future looked; what he really wanted was to set the ARVN free in Laos, a plan close to the hearts of the American military. When he answered that, a reporter sitting next to him began to laugh. "Why are you laughing?" Bunker asked. "Because if you send them into Laos they'll get their asses whipped, sir," the reporter answered. Bunker looked somewhat offended and said that this was not what he understood from his talks with our generals; some four years later he finally got his chance and sent the ARVN into Laos, and sure enough, they got their asses whipped. But even that did not faze Ellsworth Bunker, and he continued as the most consistent, influential and rigid hawk in the country, and he would continue to stay on in Vietnam, a friendly and gentle visage on a deteriorating policy.

Yet for all the optimism of men like Bunker and Westmoreland, talk of stalemate, of the war being unwinnable, continued to appear, driving the President into spirals of rage. What was all this goddamn talk about stalemate? What stalemate? What the hell did a bunch of journalists know about war? Yet, curiously, the source was his own military machine. Some of his generals were sick of what was to them the half-hearted quality of the whole thing, the attempt to win on the cheap. General Wallace Greene told some reporters at a background briefing that the war was in fact stalemated in Vietnam, that we needed mobilization and were paying too light a price. We needed to get on with the job. Six hundred thousand men would do it. "In 1964 I told them it would take four hundred thousand men and they all thought I was crazy," he said. "I was wrong. We needed six hundred thousand men."

At almost the same time a young Army officer was sent over to the Pentagon to attend a briefing of the Air Force Chief of Staff, John McConnell. It was the normal daily briefing, and in the figures the substance became clear: great personal risks on the part of American airmen for very small gains. Just like yesterday and the day before. Day after day of risk to make toothpicks on the Ho Chi Minh Trail; no absence of danger but a real absence of targets. This time the frustration showed and McConnell just sat there after the briefing ended, holding his head in his hands, saying, "I can't tell you how I feel . . . I'm so sick of it . . . I have never been so goddamn frustrated by it all . . . I'm so sick of it . . ."

If Saigon was headed by men who had no doubts, who exuded confidence, and Washington and the United States were filled with men beginning to turn on the war, then there was only one thing to do: bring Saigon to Washington. In 1967, as a means of generating new enthusiasm for his policies, the President brought Westmoreland and Bunker back to America for major speeches designed to polish up the war's image and remove those mounting doubts. But the visits had little effect; Westmoreland's appearances simply inspired more protest, more charges that the President was manipulating the military for political gains. For Bunker and Westmoreland it was perhaps the first glimpse of how serious the President's domestic problems were. The protests against the war were no longer voiced by some small strident minority; there was a deep and growing frustration of vast segments of American society. But that society had little link to the special world of Saigon, where so many of the decisions which affected American life were now being made. American domestic problems did not matter to the officials in Saigon; the idea that American society might actually turn on the war was alien. So Saigon was the separate organism: upbeat, confident, optimistic. For the New Year's Eve party at the American embassy, the invitations read: "Come see the light at the end of the tunnel."

Whose light at the end of the tunnel? If Lyndon Johnson knew increasingly in his gut that it had all gone wrong, that the other side had not folded, then he had one thing working for him: the other side's victories were never clear, never tangible. The NVA and the Vietcong were resilient, but their successes never showed; they did not hold terrain, they faded into the night, their strength was never visible. Even the NBC and CBS camera teams, frustrated by the fact that they usually arrived at a battle after the other side had already slipped away, had a title for the film of most battles: "The wily VC got away again." So if the enemy and his gains were invisible, it was hard for domestic American critics to make the case against the war, to make the case for the success of the enemy. Instead it was the word of General Westmoreland against the word of a bunch of snot-nosed kids.

The Tet offensive changed all that. For the first time the patience, durability and resilience of the enemy became clear to millions of Americans. In the past, the Vietcong and NVA had always fought in distant jungle or paddy areas, striking quickly and slipping into the night, their toughness rarely brought home to the American people. In the Tet offensive they deliberately changed that. For the first time they fought in the cities, which meant that

day after day American newspapermen, and more important, television cam-
eramen, could reflect their ability, above all their failure to collapse according
to American timetables. The credibility of the American strategy of attrition
died during the Tet offensive; so too did the credibility of the man who was
by now Johnson's most important political ally, General Westmoreland. If
Westmoreland's credibility was gone, then so too was Johnson's. The Tet
offensive had stripped Johnson naked on the war, his credibility and that of
his Administration were destroyed. Indeed, Johnson and Rostow made it even
easier for Hanoi; almost as soon as the offensive started they moved to combat
the full force of a military push with words, a technique which had, after all,
worked in the past. The Tet offensive began in earnest on January 31 and it
would be felt for weeks; but within two days of its beginning, on February 2,
Johnson held a press conference saying that the offensive was a failure, that
the Administration had known all about it, in fact the Administration had the
full order of Hanoi's battle. It was demonstrably untrue, and the public was
aware of it. Rostow had been warned by aides before the press conference
not to do this, not to commit the Administration's credibility into one more
battle, that it might backfire, but he did not listen and the President went
ahead. Thus, in the following days as the sheer fury of the offensive mounted,
as the frailty of the defenses became more evident, the Administration simply
looked more foolish, as evidenced by a February 6 Art Buchwald column,
datelined Little Big Horn, Dakota:

Gen. George Armstrong Custer said today in an exclusive interview with this correspondent that the battle of Little Big Horn had just turned the corner and he could
now see the light at the end of the tunnel. "We have the Sioux on the run," Gen.
Custer told me. "Of course we will have some cleaning up to do, but the Redskins are
hurting badly and it will only be a matter of time before they give in."

So with Johnson's involuntary co-operation, Hanoi had managed to make
the White House look particularly foolish; now the President faced an election year suddenly more vulnerable than ever . . .

THE PROTECTION OF THE PRESIDENT IN AN ELECTION YEAR OF COURSE
had been an unwritten, unspoken goal among his principal aides. Even Westmoreland, in wanting larger troop commitments, had seen it as a way of expe-
diting the war, and thus helping the President. In Saigon in the fall of 1967
Robert Komer, the chief of pacification, bumptious, audacious, anxious to
show everyone in town how close he was to the President (six photographs of
Lyndon Johnson on his office wall, a Saigon record), had gone around dinner
parties telling reporters that he had assured the President that the war would
not be an election issue in 1968. It was not one of his better predictions.

The President was in fact extremely exposed. The war had become the one issue of his Presidency; it had burned up not just his credibility but his resources as well. He had initiated the Great Society but never really built it; he had been so preoccupied with handling the war that the precious time and energy needed to change the bureaucracy, to apply the almost daily pressure to make the Great Society work, those qualities were simply not forthcoming. As far as the Great Society was concerned he was a father, but finally an absentee father. Nor had he been a very good practicing politician; he had let the Democratic party disintegrate, had not kept in touch with its principal figures, in part because of lack of time, in part because a genuine rapport might have necessitated listening to their growing doubts about the war. So he was isolated from even moderately loyal politicians. Inflation was rampant, and inflation certainly was not easing racial tensions as the country hurtled through racial change. It made vulnerable blue-collar workers feel even more vulnerable, even more resentful of the increasing protest going on around them. Nor was Johnson's position with blacks solidified; he had pushed more and broader civil rights legislation through the Congress than any President in history, and had endeared himself to a generation of older, middle-class blacks. But that was not a visible thing; what was visible was the potent anger of younger, more militant blacks, restless not only with Johnson's leadership, but with their own traditional black leadership, and they were busy linking the peace movement with what had once been the civil rights movement. The country in late 1967 seemed to be more and more in disarray; protest seemed to beget protest. Lyndon Johnson, who above all loved to control events, even little events, had lost control of the country, and he had immobilized himself on the one issue that might allow him to regain it. In 1963 Paul Kattenburg, the young State Department expert on Vietnam, had returned from Saigon to tell Roger Hilsman that Vietnam was poison, and it would poison everything it touched. Now, four and a half years later, the poison was very deep in the bloodstream.

Part of the frustration and bitterness, of course, was the feeling in the liberal community—the political segment most aggravated and most offended by the war—that it was powerless, that Lyndon Johnson was a liberal Democrat and could not be beaten, that they had no real political alternative. For the mythology lived; one could not unseat the sitting President of his own party. Eventually, however, despite the protests of older liberals (some of whom wanted to fight Johnson only on the platform at the forthcoming convention), younger liberals went looking for a candidate. They had only one choice, they thought, and that was to take the issue to the country and make the challenge to the President within the party. Robert Kennedy was the logical choice, but he was torn by the idea. Part of him wanted to go and was outside the system; part of him was still a traditionalist and believed what his ad-

visers said, that you could not challenge the system. In the end he turned it
down. Then they went to George McGovern, who was sympathetic and interested, but he faced a re-election race in South Dakota and that posed a problem. But if no one else would make it, then he told them to come back. So
they turned to Gene McCarthy of Minnesota, and he accepted. There comes
a time, he told reporters, when an honorable man simply has to raise the flag.
"What will you do if elected?" a reporter asked, and borrowing from Eisenhower in 1952, he answered, "I will go to the Pentagon."

But if a Robert Kennedy challenge frightened Johnson, one by Gene
McCarthy did not; he did not seem a formidable candidate, he had a reputation for being a little lazy. Johnson saw McCarthy enter the race and viewed
it as one more way of demonstrating how frail the left really was.

But even as McCarthy was making his lonely way through the small towns
of New Hampshire, General Vo Nguyen Giap was moving his men down the
trails for what would be called the Tet offensive. It began on January 31,
1968; day after day as the battle continued it became clear that the optimism
from Saigon had been premature, that the enemy was tough and durable, that
journalistic critics had been more correct in their estimates about the war
than the government spokesmen. The Tet offensive destroyed Westmoreland's credibility; what crumbled in Saigon now crumbled in Washington and
crumbled in New Hampshire. The people of this country were already sick of
the war and dubious of the estimates of the government; reading as they did
in early March that the generals in Saigon wanted to send an additional
200,000 men, it seemed to symbolize the hopelessness and endlessness of the
war. American politics and the war were finally coming together. In New
Hampshire, Gene McCarthy took more than 42 percent of the vote, pushed
Robert Kennedy into the race, and a race by Kennedy was no longer a joke to
the President. It was a serious threat.

Nor was the President entirely in control of his own house. He had purged
McNamara because he was no longer on the team and because he was a walking reminder of failure, but McNamara's successor, Clark Clifford, was turning out to be even more difficult. Clifford was the prototype of the rich man's
Washington lobbyist, the supersmooth, urbane lawyer who knows where
every body is buried, the former high official who works for the government
just long enough to know where the weak spots are; to Johnson he seemed a
reassuring replacement for the idealistic, tormented McNamara. But Clifford
was proving to be a new kind of high official for Lyndon Johnson; whatever
else, he was not the corporate man. Instead he had a great sense of his own
value, and did not believe that anyone hired Clark Clifford except to gain the
full benefit of Clark Clifford's services. A great lawyer is paid for telling a rich
and powerful client the truth, no matter how unpalatable. (The story is told of
Clifford's being called by a company president who explained a complicated

problem and then asked for Clifford's advice. Clifford told him not to say or do anything. Then he sent a bill for $10,000. A few days later the president called back protesting the size of the bill, and also asked why he should keep quiet. "Because I told you to," Clifford answered and sent him another bill, for an additional $5,000.) He knew that if he went to work for the President he would be making a considerable financial sacrifice, so he fully intended to weigh in with the best of his wisdom, not simply to lend his name to a dying cause for the sake of being congenial. Earlier he had edged away from being the head of CIA under Kennedy and had rejected tentative offers by Johnson to become Attorney General and Undersecretary of State. When he took office at Defense he was already bothered by the growing domestic turbulence over the war and his own feeling that perhaps it was indeed hopeless. Also, he had just finished a tour of Asia for the President during which he and Max Taylor worked to drum up additional troops for the war from Asian allies. Their report at the end of the trip had been properly supportive, but Clifford was bothered by the fact that the other Asian nations showed no great interest in sending additional men. Oh yes, they thought standing in Vietnam was a marvelous idea, and they certainly gave us their blessing, but it just so happened that they had very little in the way of resources. The threatened dominoes, Clifford discovered, did not seem to take the threat as seriously as we did. Since he was a man of compelling common sense, this offended his sense of reality and proportion.

In addition, he was privy to the forces that McNamara had unleashed at Defense in the last year and a half, the dovishness now prevalent there. John McNaughton was dead, in an airplane crash, but his replacement, Paul Warnke, was a Washington lawyer with no previous experience in foreign affairs, and thus marvelously irreverent and iconoclastic toward all the myths of the period. He was, in fact, a heretic by the era's standards. (Once asked by a reporter when his own doubts about Vietnam had begun, Warnke said, "At the beginning, in 1961. I could never understand why a smart politician like Jack Kennedy was always talking about being against insurgencies when we should obviously have tried to be for them.") Warnke was more open in dealing with his subordinates than McNaughton had been, and the young civilian defense intellectuals therefore felt themselves encouraged in their doubts. These were unlikely doves; they were all men who had entered the Defense Department convinced that the world hinged on the great struggle between the United States and the Soviet Union. They had been among the most militant Cold Warriors of the period, but now the evidence in the decade was going the other way, and they were for tempering the arms race and limiting the Pentagon's power. Nor were they professional bureaucrats; most were men with Ph.D.s who could go back to universities and thus did not feel that their careers depended upon subservience to existing myths. So a curious struggle developed as the battle began over the limits of war: State, which was supposed to set the political limits, had no doubts because of Rusk and neither did the military under the Chiefs, and they became allies against the civilians at Defense. (Daniel Ellsberg symbolized the conversion—or reconversion—of the Defense intellectuals, though of course there were others. But Ellsberg seemed to dramatize the great currents of an era. At Harvard he had seemed at first the normal humanist student; serving as president of the literary magazine, more humanist and aesthete than warrior. But he had gone from Harvard to the Marine Corps and had drifted, during the years of the fifties, into the world of defense studies and theories, believing that the competition between the United States and the Soviet Union was the key to the survival of all values. He had ended up in Washington in the Kennedy years, one of the bright stars in John McNaughton's constellation of young intellectuals, and he had done some of the early planning on the war. In 1965 he went on assignment to Vietnam and gradually turned against the war; year by year both his doubts and his outspokenness had grown. In 1969 he publicly criticized President Nixon's policies on Vietnam, statements which expedited his departure from Rand, and which were picked up in the *New York Times*. An old friend named John Smail read in the *Times* of Ellsberg's statements and wrote asking: "Are you the Dan Ellsberg I used to know in college?" Ellsberg answered back, in what was an epitaph for many in that era, "I haven't been for a long time, but I am again.")

The Defense civilians had in the past year turned up increasing evidence on the futility of our commitment. Studies made by Systems Analysis showed that the bombing did not work, that for much of the war, North Vietnam's GNP had risen at the prewar rate of 6 percent. If the bombing was failing, so, too, claimed the civilians at Defense, was the strategy of attrition. We had, despite three years of ferocious fighting, barely touched their manpower pool. Defense estimates showed that no more than 40 percent of the males between seventeen and thirty-five had served in the Army, that more than 200,000 North Vietnamese became of draft age every year, and that only about 100,000 had been sent off to the war. Indeed, their main-force army had grown during the war from 250,000 to about 475,000. The war of attrition had barely touched them; we were not keeping up with their birth rate.

All of this had a profound effect on Clifford. Being a good politician and a Democratic party loyalist (he was the principal architect of Harry Truman's election in 1948, which was one additional reason why Johnson had now chosen him), he also knew the political limits of what was going on. He wanted, friends thought, to turn Johnson around on the war; perhaps, separated from the war, Johnson could run again. But whatever else, Clark Clifford did not intend to see his own reputation destroyed by either Lyndon Johnson or Vietnam. So in the months of February and March 1968 as the Tet battle raged, as the Joint Chiefs reopened the old Westmoreland request for 206,000 more troops, Clifford fought ferociously to turn the tide, to limit the number of troops and to reduce the bombing. In that battle he was usually alone. Rusk, Taylor, Bill Bundy, Rostow were no help. Nick Katzenbach, Undersecretary of State, worked quietly to help him, but he was limited with Rusk as his superior. Nor did Clifford find the President receptive or pleased by this lonely struggle. Their relationship, once so warm and easy, turned cool and distant. The President did not seek his advice, and Clifford's phone did not ring. He was even cut off from important cable traffic by the White House in ensuing months. But he posed a special problem: when McNamara had gone soft on the war, that could be ascribed to McNamara's idealism, his distaste for blood, his friendship for the Kennedys. But none of this could be said of Clark Clifford; he was no Kennedy enthusiast, no kook, there was nothing soft about him. Slowly, cautiously, painfully, Clifford forced Johnson to turn and look honestly at the war; it was an act of friendship for which Johnson could never forgive him.

And slowly Clifford found allies. Not men in government so much as men outside it, men who had Johnson's respect. In late March, Johnson summoned his Senior Advisory Group on Vietnam, a blue-chip Establishment group. These were the great names of the Cold War: McCloy, Acheson, Arthur Dean, Mac Bundy, Douglas Dillon, Robert Murphy. And over a period of two days they quietly let him know that the Establishment—yes, Wall Street—had turned on the war; it was hurting us more than it was helping us, it had all gotten out of hand, and it was time to bring it back to proportion. It was hurting the economy, dividing the country, turning the youth against the country's best traditions. Great universities, their universities, were being destroyed. It was time to turn it around, to restore some balance. At one of the briefings of the Wise Men it was Arthur Goldberg, much mocked by some of the others, who almost single-handedly destroyed the military demand for 205,000 more troops. The briefing began with the military officer saying that the other side had suffered 45,000 deaths during the Tet offensive.

Goldberg then asked what our own killed-to-wounded ratios were.

Seven to one, the officer answered, because we save a lot of men with helicopters.

What, asked Goldberg, was the enemy strength as of February 1, when Tet started?

Between 160,000 and 175,000, the briefer answered.

What is their killed-to-wounded ratio? Goldberg asked.

We use a figure of three and a half to one, the officer said.

Well, if that's true, then they have no effective forces left in the field, Goldberg said. What followed was a long and very devastating silence.

Acheson had told the President earlier that the Joint Chiefs did not know what they were talking about, and the switch in this group, which was saying in effect that the war had to be de-escalated, had a profound effect on the President. Did they know things he didn't know? He demanded to be briefed by the same three officials who had briefed them on the war. Events, and pressure, it was clear, were closing in. He was cornered now. Even in the last days he had fought off those who wanted to stop the bombing, telling Arthur Goldberg angrily, "Let's get one thing clear. I am not going to stop the bombing. I have heard every argument on the subject and I am not interested in further discussion. I have made up my mind, I am not going to do it." He had in late March given particularly belligerent speeches, but now he was caught and he knew it. The Wise Men, as they were called, were telling him what the polls and the newspapers had told him; that the country had turned on the war.

New Hampshire had not been an isolated test. The next primary was in Wisconsin, and the President was entered there as well. The early reports from Wisconsin were very bad. No workers, no volunteers, no enthusiasm. Cabinet members went to Wisconsin in the President's behalf, and drew small crowds. The President himself could not speak in his own behalf—it was too much of a security problem. The polls were bad and getting worse. One night in mid-March there was a sign which the President, hoping against hope, noticed and which he thought might mean there was some change—an upswing. A meeting in one town seemed jammed and enthusiastic. It was actually a small room, but the way the television camera flashed around it made the hall seem like the Roman Coliseum. The President, watching the meeting, called Larry O'Brien, his political operative, to congratulate him and say that it all looked very good. O'Brien, hearing the enthusiasm and excitement in the President's voice, tones and emotions missing now almost four years, thought Johnson was being a little carried away, so O'Brien cautioned him. "Mr. President, it was a good meeting and we had a few hundred people here, but it was in Clem Zablocki's area and he worked hard and the union people worked hard, but it doesn't mean much. To tell you the truth, we're in real trouble here." Later he would tell Johnson not to expect more than 35 percent of the Wisconsin vote, and that it might even be below 30. Lyndon Johnson knew then that he was beaten. He knew he was locked in; he could not do what he wanted on Vietnam and run for re-election. Rather than absorb one more defeat, he withdrew from the race on the eve of the Wisconsin primary and announced that he was pulling back on the bombing. The war was finally turning around; it was time for de-escalation. For Lyndon Johnson it was all over.

In November 1968, after the election, a group of executives from a New York publishing firm went to the White House to talk with Walt Rostow about publishing his memoirs. The three were important men from the house and the prospect of Rostow's book was tempting—big figures were in the air. The meeting was pleasant, and Rostow was very friendly. There was some small talk, some reminiscence about the war and the past, and at one point Rostow mentioned that he did not think that the war had been a factor in the 1968 campaign, and he turned and asked his visitors what they thought. One of them, James Silberman, said that he could not vouch for other states, but in the state he lived in, New York, it most certainly had been an issue, most likely the decisive issue. Silberman noticed that Rostow immediately changed the subject, and also that he did not direct any more questions his way. In fact, when the meeting broke up a few minutes later the editors noticed that Rostow shook hands pleasantly with two of them and completely ignored Silberman.

LYNDON JOHNSON HAD LOST IT ALL, AND SO HAD THE REST OF THEM; they had, for all their brilliance and hubris and sense of themselves, been unwilling to look to and learn from the past and they had been swept forward by their belief in the importance of anti-Communism (and the dangers of not paying sufficient homage to it) and by the sense of power and glory, omnipotence and omniscience of America in this century. They *were* America, and they had been ready for what the world offered, the challenges posed. In a way Lyndon Johnson had known better, he had entertained no small amount of doubt about the course he was taking, but he saw, given his own instincts, his own reading of American politics, his own belief in how he had to look to others, no way of getting off. He and the men around him wanted to be defined as being strong and tough; but strength and toughness and courage were exterior qualities which would be demonstrated by going to a clean and hopefully antiseptic war with a small nation, rather than the interior and more lonely kind of strength and courage of telling the truth to America and perhaps incurring a good deal of domestic political risk. What was it Jack Kennedy had said about Adlai Stevenson during the Cuban missile crisis when he had mocked Stevenson's softness—that you had to admire the way Stevenson was willing to fight for his convictions when everyone else in the room was against him. The irony of that statement was missing for Kennedy and it was missing for Johnson as well.

Nor had they, leaders of a democracy, bothered to involve the people of their country in the course they had chosen: they knew the right path and they knew how much could be revealed, step by step along the way. They had manipulated the public, the Congress and the press from the start, told half truths, about why we were going in, how deeply we were going in, how much we were spending, and how long we were in for. When their predictions turned out to be hopelessly inaccurate, and when the public and the

Congress, annoyed at being manipulated, soured on the war, then the architects had been aggrieved. They had turned on those very symbols of the democratic society they had once manipulated, criticizing them for their lack of fiber, stamina and lack of belief. Why weren't the journalists more supportive? How could you make public policy with television cameras everywhere? The day after he withdrew from re-election in 1968 Lyndon Johnson flew to Chicago for a convention of broadcasters and he had placed the blame for the failure squarely on their shoulders, their fault being that the cameras had revealed just how empty it all was. A good war televises well; a bad war televises poorly. Maxwell Taylor was the key military figure in all the estimates, and his projections—that the war would be short, that the bombing would be a major asset—had proven to be false, but he had never adjusted his views to those failures; there was no sense of remorse, nor concern on why they had failed to estimate correctly. Rather, even in his memoirs, the blame was placed on those elements of the society which had undermined support for the war; when his book was finished, friends, looking at the galleys, cautioned him to tone down criticism of the press. What was singularly missing from all the memoirs of the period—save from a brief interview with Dean Rusk after the publication of the Pentagon Papers—was an iota of public admission that they had miscalculated. The faults, it seemed, were not theirs, the fault was with this country which was not worthy of them.

So they lost it all. There was a sense of irony here, as if each player had lost, not just a major part of his personal reputation, but much of what he had truly believed in and wanted, much of what he had manipulated for in the first place. Johnson of course had never wanted to go to war, he had become a war President reluctantly, in large part because he feared that otherwise he would lose the Great Society. He had instead gotten the war, but the Great Society was stillborn, it lacked his time, his resources, his second term to bring it to any genuine effectiveness. Which he was bitterly aware of. (In 1969 when a former Pentagon official named Townsend Hoopes wrote a book on how Clark Clifford had turned the war policy around, Johnson was furious with the book. "Hoopees! Hoopees! Who the hell is Hoopees? Here I take four million people out of poverty and all I ever hear about is Hoopees.") The one thing he could not admit was that he had miscalculated on Vietnam, that Clifford had subsequently turned him around, and that the war had driven him out of office. The knowledge that this was true led to the suspension of his friendship with Clifford for several years, and the closer anyone came to telling the truth, the more Johnson bellowed in anger. He had, it seemed, in his version of events always been in control; everything had worked out as he intended it to.

For McNamara, the great dream had been of controlling the Pentagon and the arms race, but the war had ruined all that. War Secretaries do not limit the power of the military, and to a large degree he had lost control. The war absorbed so much of his time, his energy, his credibility, that he had little to give to the kind of controls he might have wanted. It was not by accident that his name would come more to symbolize the idea of technological warfare than it would civilian control of military.

McGeorge Bundy was a rationalist in an era which saw the limits of rationalism and which rekindled the need for political humanism; the man of operations and processes in an Administration which seemed to undermine the limits of the processes without moral guidelines. But above all he was a man of the Establishment, the right people deciding on the right policies in the right way, he believed in the capacity and the right of an elite to govern on its terms. The war changed all that; it not only tarnished his personal reputation so that his endorsement of an idea or a candidate had to be done covertly, but it saw a major challenge to the right of the elite to rule. In the Senate, the leading doves believed they had been wiser than the executive branch, and they were beefing up their staffs and playing a larger role in foreign policy. Too, the years had made all the other political groups in the country aware of just how little a part they played in foreign policy, and by the end of the decade the outlanders, Negroes, women, workers, were determined to play a greater role; they had reached the moat and were pressing on.

Dean Rusk had believed not so much in the class as in the policies, mutual security, strong political and military involvement everywhere in the world to stop totalitarians. The war, of course, had brought on a new sense of the limits of power, and with that a growing attitude about the need for the United States to roll back its commitments, which Rusk and others deemed to be a new isolationism. If anything, to a new generation of Americans the war had blurred the differences between the democracies and the totalitarian states. Thus the war, rather than setting the precedent of what the United States had done in the past and would continue to do in the future in the world, had symbolized to growing numbers of Americans what the United States must never do again. It reversed all the traditional directions of American foreign policy, and for Rusk this was a far more bitter thing than the personal abuse which he had suffered.

Max Taylor had always believed in the liberal society and the citizen-democratic Army, a professional army respected by its citizenry, the best kind of extension of a healthy society. The Army would contain the finest young men of the society, well-educated civilized young officers, and this very fact would temper old civilian suspicions and alienations. The war of course had ravaged the Army; the kind of officer Taylor sought for the Army suffered because of it and was increasingly driven out of service. A bad war means a bad system; the wrong officers are promoted for the wrong reasons, the best officers, often unable to go along with the expected norm, the fake body count, the excessive use of force, wither along the way. And the gap between the Army and the society as a whole did not close, it widened; there was a growing sense of antimilitary feeling in the country, and the Army was of course selected as a scapegoat.

The Democratic party too was damaged. It had been hiding from its past at the very beginning of the Kennedy era, unwilling to come to terms with China and what had happened there, and in large part it had gotten into trouble in Vietnam because it accepted the Dulles policies in Asia. But Dulles policies or no, it was the Democrats who had brought us into Vietnam, and the sense of alienation between the party and not just the young but millions of other nominal Democrats was very large. American life was changing very quickly and the party was adjusting very slowly; it seemed increasingly an outmoded corroded institution, its principal spokesmen figures of the past.

Such as Hubert Humphrey, who was one more victim of the war. He had of course always wanted to be the Democratic nominee for the Presidency and he had finally received the nomination one terrible night in Chicago, but by that time it was no longer worth anything (there was a certain irony in this too, because he had sought it so long and feverishly and promiscuously as to be unworthy of it). He was nominated in Chicago on a night when police hacked the heads of the young, and Humphrey's only response was to kiss the television set. He had gained the nomination and in so doing lost most of what was left of his reputation.

But it was Lyndon Johnson who had lost the most. He had always known this, even in the turbulent days of 1964 and 1965 when the decisions on the war seemed to press on him; even then he was more dubious than those around him, knowing that of them, he had the most to lose. And he lost it, so much of his reputation, so much of his dreams. He could not go to the 1968 Democratic convention, it was all too painful and explosive; nor did he attend the 1972 convention either. There at Miami Beach the Democrats had hung huge portraits of their heroes of the past in the main hall, photos of Presidents and national candidates. But Lyndon Johnson's photo was not among them, rather it could be found in a smaller room where photos of past congressional leaders hung. He had always dreamed of being the greatest domestic President in this century, and he had become, without being able to stop it, a war President, and not a very good one at that.

A Final Word

IN THE DAYS, WEEKS AND MONTHS AFTER HIS WITHDRAWAL FROM the race and his decision to cut back on the bombing, Lyndon Johnson was immobilized on the war and so was his Administration. He had been most at ease with a consensus policy, a policy in which all the very great men agreed on the essential wisdom of one centrist idea, and now this consensus was openly and finally shattered, his government totally and irreconcilably divided, and he simply could not come to terms with the division. Events had forced him to set a limit on the American escalation, which he had done reluctantly, though his own generals had warned that even at the current rate of commitment of more than 500,000 Americans, the war might drag on indefinitely. So he had at once limited the war, but he could not make the next step which might see the liquidation of it politically. Perhaps there was simply too much of his own ego involved in it. So the policy on the war was in a kind of suspension.

Clifford at Defense and Harriman in Paris, as the summer of 1968 passed into the fall, were pushing very hard for the kind of political decisions which would see diminishing importance placed on the wishes of the Saigon government, with the United States, if need be, ready to by-pass Saigon. Similarly, in Saigon, Ellsworth Bunker was emerging as a singularly strong proponent of the Thieu regime who felt that in the wake of the Tet offensive we had to strengthen rather than weaken Saigon, and he was arguing forcefully that at this late date we could not let go of Thieu, that the regime was legitimate, and more, viable. Bunker, a man with an awesome reputation of his own, was a strong and forceful player, and in a divided bureaucracy his word was crucial. He was picking up the support of both Rusk and Rostow, thereby effectively neutralizing the work of Clifford and Harriman. In March and April, Clifford had won the first round; now the second round, whether or not to keep going on the disengagement of Americans whether Saigon liked it or not, was going to Bunker. This did not stop Clifford from fighting; he was arguing that we had to continue to de-escalate, that it was important not just to limit the commitment but to end it, that Saigon was not in any true sense an ally, that its legitimacy was dubious, that reality was that the United States had overreached itself in Vietnam and now we had to admit it and adjust to it. But Johnson was unable to resolve his new dilemma. With Saigon dragging its feet on negotiations, Clifford prodded everyone along during the fall and publicly criticized the Thieu regime. He was clearly trying to set a new policy for the Administration and move into the vacuum, letting Saigon know that if it wanted any kind of deal at all, it would have to bend as the United States was now bending. Clearly, Clifford was hoping that the President would follow his lead, but Johnson was too deep into the war and he was not that anxious to admit that this ally, for whom he and his country had sacrificed so much (an ally which had in effect cost him his Presidency), was not a worthy ally, not a real government in a real country. In effect, Clifford was arguing the same things that George Ball had advocated four years earlier, but with so many more chips already in the poker game that it was too painful for Johnson to accept the argument of cutting his losses. He could not split off from Saigon, and Saigon was of course holding back on negotiations precisely because it sensed that Nixon would be elected and that he would be easier to deal with than Humphrey (in his memoirs, Johnson would lament Thieu's obstreperous behavior at this point, saying that it was the first time Saigon had failed to come through for him; which it was, though of course it was the first time he had asked them for anything).

Johnson stayed strictly neutral during the campaign. Though Humphrey was in a sense his political protégé, the President seemed less than anxious to do him any special favors, in part because the issue of the war was in his mind so transcending that he did not want to play politics with it, and in part, friends of his sensed, because he had interior doubts about Humphrey's capacity to run the country, at least by Johnsonian standards—was Humphrey tough enough?

IT WAS A VIEW OF THE CAMPAIGN NOT UNLIKE THAT OF RICHARD Nixon, who had feared a race against Johnson and the White House but who seemed to relax now that his opponent was Hubert Humphrey. It was like running against Johnson without Johnson. Humphrey bore the burden of the Johnson years without the strengths; he had the visible stamp of Johnson, he carried the albatross of the war and the divisions that the war had brought to his party; he seemed, in all, a palpably weak candidate. So Nixon decided to run a do-nothing, say-nothing campaign. The Democrats were divided on Vietnam, the Republicans were not; Vietnam was a problem for the Democrats, not for the Republicans. He did not spell out his policies, in large part because he had none. He contented himself with telling audiences that he had a plan to end the war, even touching his breast pocket as if the plan were right there in the jacket—implying that to say what was in it might jeopardize secrecy. The truth was that he had no plan at all. Throughout the campaign his unwillingness to develop a serious substantive policy on Vietnam, which was, after all, the issue tearing the country apart, was the bane of some of his younger staff members. They were repeatedly pushing him to deal with the war, what it meant, why it had gone wrong, but they found him singularly unresponsive. To the degree that he showed his feelings on the war, particularly early in the campaign, he seemed as hawkish as the Administration. He talked about his belief that the war would be brought to a successful conclusion and that the Tet offensive, which had been launched in January 1968, was simply a last-ditch effort by an exhausted enemy. His staff soon convinced him to ease off on his support for the Administration, helped, as it were, by the ferocity with which the NVA and the Vietcong were fighting during the Tet offensive. But the issue for him was not the compelling tragedy it was for so many other Americans, something that you had to come to terms with on its own merits, something where the failure had to be traced and explained to a troubled and divided country; rather it was an issue like others, something to maneuver on, to watch Johnson, Humphrey and Wallace on.

As the Tet offensive dragged on, as dovish and antiwar sentiment mounted in the country even among conservative Republicans (John McCone, Nixon's staff discovered, thought the United States had to get out of Vietnam. What about loss of prestige? McCone was asked. Well, there would be loss of prestige but it was worse for the United States to stay), the staff moved Nixon to giving what was a reasonably dovish speech on Vietnam. It was prepared by a talented young writer named Richard Whalen who thought the war a hopeless mistake. The speech was scheduled for delivery in early April, but by that time Johnson had withdrawn on Vietnam, so Nixon felt himself under considerably less pressure and canceled it. From then on, though the country was locked in paroxysms of anguish on the war, Nixon sat it out, and at one strategy meeting when Whalen implored his candidate to be candid about Vietnam, insisting that the American people had been seriously lied to and knew they had been lied to, and that Nixon had to challenge the Administration on the war, Nixon listened to Whalen impassively. But there was no response and Whalen thought to himself: "I might just as well be talking to Humphrey. Nixon looks just the way Humphrey must look when his people tell him to break with Johnson." Discouraged by this attitude, Whalen left the Nixon campaign staff shortly after the Republican convention, but no matter—the Democrats were overwhelmed by problems and the candidate had few of his own. He was convinced that he had Humphrey boxed in on the war; he had a good pipe line to what the Humphrey camp was thinking on the war—pushing the candidate to ask for a bombing halt—and Nixon let Johnson know that he, Nixon, was against the bombing halt. Thus the capacity to split the Democratic party.

In late September the polls showed Nixon leading Humphrey 45 to 30; if he was concerned about anything it was the strength of Wallace, and he was wary of seeming too liberal, too dovish, and thus losing his Southern support. So the campaign was in one sense a repeat of the Tom Dewey campaign, though with far greater technological skill. If Nixon avoided confrontation with the public and with reporters, he nonetheless seemed, by means of carefully controlled televised confrontations with his own supporters, to be meeting people, he seemed to be candid. Meanwhile Humphrey, despite the efforts of his staff to separate him from Johnson, was unable to make the break; he was able to take draft copies of a plan for a new and more independent Vietnam to the President and then unable to show them to the President. "Hubert," said Larry O'Brien, head of the Democratic party, in August, "paid a high price for being a good boy." But then, very late in the campaign, and under constant prodding by his staff and his audiences, Humphrey began slowly, painfully, timidly to dissociate himself from Johnson and the war. Suddenly his campaign came alive, money came in. The final vote in November was extremely close: a 15 percent edge in the polls had dwindled to less than 1 percent, Nixon winning 31.77 million to 31.27 million. In part because of his silence and his failure to come to terms with such an awesome issue, Nixon had helped turn a potential landslide into a cliffhanger.

SO HE WAS PRESIDENT AND HE HAD ENJOYED A FREE RIDE ON Vietnam. He had not announced what his thoughts were on the subject, nor would he be in any hurry to. To Republican doves who had supported him during the campaign he had appeared optimistic about the chances for an end. He had told some of them during the campaign that if he was elected he would end the war within six months. After his election that still seemed to be the timetable; in April 1969 Representative Pete McCloskey of California, who would later challenge Nixon on the war, and Representative Don Riegle of Michigan, who would aid McCloskey in the campaign, went to see Henry Kissinger to plead that the Administration keep its promise and end the war shortly. Kissinger replied that a breakthrough was imminent. "Be patient," he said. "Give us another sixty to ninety days. Please stay silent for the time being." But the first signs of what the Administration's policy would be had already come from Kissinger himself. Even before Nixon took office, Kissinger, who was the vital national security assistant, had gone around Washington telling friends that the most serious mistake the Johnson Administration had made was the public criticism by Clifford and Harriman of Saigon. In contrast, said Kissinger, the Nixon Administration would move to strengthen the Thieu regime. To many dovish Washington officials who viewed Clifford's attempt to separate Washington from Saigon as the wisest thing the Johnson Administration had done, and felt that it had, if anything, not gone far enough, what Kissinger was saying was ominous. If Nixon was going to strengthen Saigon, then there would be no real change forthcoming in the political objective of the United States and in what the Administration was offering Hanoi. We might lower our troop level there, but the war would continue the same. Though we would probably cut back on American troops in Vietnam (not out of fondness for the other side, but because American political realities demanded it), we were not offering the other side anything new politically.

The answer on the Nixon policies came in November. With antiwar sentiment mounting again, with larger and larger antiwar moratoriums being held, Nixon finally moved. He did not speak to the protesters, he spoke beyond them, to what had become known as Middle America or Silent America, telling them that they were the good Americans who loved their country and their flag, and he summoned them now to support him. He wanted peace, but peace with honor; all Americans would want him to honor the commitment to a great ally. In the speech he seemed to be debating Ho. What was important about the speech was its tone. The rhetoric was harsh and rigid, and there was talk about their atrocities (just a few days earlier Seymour Hersh, a free-lance writer, had uncovered the first evidence of the massive American massacre of women and children at My Lai). The rhetoric seemed more like that of the previous Administration than an Administration which intended to end the war; indeed, a few days later Dean Rusk said at a Washington dinner that he was a member of the loyal opposition, but after Nixon's speech he was more loyal than opposed.

At the same time that Nixon invoked the support of Middle America he also unleashed his Vice-President, Spiro Agnew, to attack the media and war critics, Agnew in effect becoming Nixon's Nixon. The idea was simple: to freeze critics of the war and the President, to put them on the defensive. Support of the President was patriotic; criticism of him and his policies was not. Eventually Agnew's role became even clearer—to purge the Congress of dissident doves, that is, to remove from the Congress those men most opposed to a war that Nixon was supposed to be ending. By this time Nixon's policy became clear: it would be Vietnamization, we would pull back American troops, probably to 250,000 by 1970, and perhaps to as few as 75,000 by 1972. There would be fewer and fewer Americans on the ground, and greater and greater reliance on American air power. What could be more tempting than to cut back on American troops and casualties and still get the same end result which Lyndon Johnson had sent more than 500,000 men in quest of? So he was dealing with the war without really coming to terms with it; it was the compromise of a by now embattled President who knew he had to get American troops out but who still believed in their essential mission. So now he sought peace with honor. "What President Nixon means by peace," wrote Don Oberdorfer in the Washington *Post*, "is what other people mean by victory."

ABOUT THE SAME TIME HENRY KISSINGER, WHO HAD EMERGED AS the top foreign policy adviser of the Administration (in part because he, like Nixon, was hard-line on Vietnam, whereas both William Rogers, the Secretary of State, and Mel Laird, the Secretary of Defense, had been ready to liquidate the war in the early months of the Administration), was asked by a group of visiting Asians if the Nixon Administration was going to repeat the mistakes of the Johnson Administration in Vietnam. "No," answered Kissinger, who was noted in Washington for having the best sense of humor in the Administration, "we will not repeat their mistakes. We will not send 500,000 men." He paused. "We will make our own mistakes and they will be completely our own." There was appreciative laughter and much enjoyment of the movement. One thing though—Kissinger was wrong. To an extraordinary degree the Nixon men repeated the mistakes and miscalculations of the Johnson Administration, which prompted Russell Baker to describe it all as "the reign of President Lyndon B. Nixonger." For step by step, they repeated the mistakes of the past.

They soon became believers in their policy, and thus began to listen only to others who were believers (they began to believe, in addition, that only they were privy to the truth in reports from Saigon, that the secret messages from the Saigon embassy, rather than being the words of committed, embattled men, were the words of cool, objective observers). Doubters were soon filtered out; the Kissinger staff soon lost most of the talented Asian experts that had come in with him at the start of the Administration. Optimistic assessments of American goals, of what the incursion into Cambodia would do, of what the invasion of Laos would do—always speeding the timetable of withdrawal and victory—were passed on to the public, always to be mocked by ARVN failure and NVA resilience. More important, Nixon saw South Vietnam as a real country with a real President and a real army, rich in political legitimacy, and most important, capable of performing the role demanded of it by American aims and rhetoric. So there was no tempering of rhetoric to the reality of failure and miscalculation in the South; Nixon himself spoke of the fact that America had never lost a war, precisely the kind of speech a President needed to avoid if he wanted to disengage. Similarly, if there was an overestimation of the South Vietnamese, there was a comparable underestimation of the capacity, resilience, determination and toughness of the other side. Even in 1972, when Hanoi launched a major offensive, Kissinger called in favored Washington correspondents to be sure that they downplayed the importance of the offensive; like so many French and American spokesmen before him he saw it as the last gasp—"One last throw of the dice," Kissinger called it.

But the Nixon Administration, like the Johnson Administration before it, did not control events, and did not control the rate of the war; and though it could give Thieu air power, it could not give him what he really needed, which was a genuine, indigenous political legitimacy. While Thieu's regime was as thin and frail as ever, the North Vietnamese were imbued with a total sense of confidence. Time was on their side, they were the legitimate heirs of a revolution, nothing confirmed their legitimacy more than American bombs falling on the country. Eventually, they knew, the Americans would have to leave. What was it a fully confident Pham Van Dong had told Harrison Salisbury of the *New York Times* in December 1966 in Hanoi: "And how long do you Americans want to fight, Mr. Salisbury . . . one year? Two years? Three years? Five years? Ten years? Twenty years? We will be glad to accommodate you." And the war went on. American air power served its limited purpose; it could, at great cost, keep the South Vietnamese from being routed. Administration sources praised progress in pacification, but there was no real pacification; the 1972 NVA offensive ravaged any frail gains, and Nixon, in frustration, approved an even fiercer bombing campaign against the North, lifting many of the restraints which had marked the Johnson years. In world eyes the bombing, in the name of a losing cause, made the United States look, if anything, even crueler. Peace seemed nowhere near in the summer of 1972, unless the President abruptly changed his policies, and so the American dilemma remained. Time was on the side of the enemy, and we were in a position of not being able to win, not being able to get out, not being able to get our prisoners home, only being able to lash out and bomb. The inability of the Americans to impose their will on Vietnam had been answered in 1968, yet the leadership of this country had not been able to adjust our goals to that failure. And so the war went on, tearing at this country; a sense of numbness seemed to replace an earlier anger. There was, Americans were finding, no light at the end of the tunnel, only greater darkness.

Author's Note

I BEGAN WORK ON THIS BOOK IN JANUARY 1969. I HAD JUST COME from covering the domestic turbulence created by the war during the 1968 campaign and I had seen the Johnson Administration and its legatee defeated largely because of the one issue. At that point I was looking for a new assignment, and my colleague at *Harper's*, Midge Decter, suggested that I do a piece on McGeorge Bundy, who was after all the most glistening of the Kennedy-Johnson intellectuals. It would be a way not only of looking at him—very little was known about what he really did and stood for—but also of looking at that entire era. I thought it was a good idea, since the Kennedy intellectuals had been praised as the best and the brightest men of a generation and yet they were the architects of a war which I and many others thought the worst tragedy to befall this country since the Civil War; indeed I felt then and still feel that the real consequences of the war have not even begun to be felt. So I began the piece on Bundy, which turned out to be much broader than a profile of a man, in effect the embryonic profile of an era. The Bundy article took me three months of legwork. The subject himself was not noticeably cooperative while doing it, nor particularly enthusiastic about the final product. When the article was finished I had a feeling of having just started, though it was very long for a magazine piece, 20,000 words. I realized I had only begun to scratch the surface and I wanted to find out the full reasons why it had all happened, I wanted to know the full context of the decisions, as well as how they were made. Why had they crossed the Rubicon? They were intelligent men, rational men, and seemingly intelligent, rational men would have known the obvious, how unlikely bombing was to work, and how dangerous it was to send combat troops, and that if we sent American units we would be following the French. (When I began work on the book I did not realize how pessimistic the intelligence people both at State and CIA had been about the proposed venture. At key points in 1964 and 1965 when journalistic reporting from Saigon had been particularly pessimistic, it was the argument of those in government, like Bill Bundy, that if outsiders could only see the secret cable traffic they would know how well things were going and how well they were likely to go. Quite the reverse was true; if the Senate Foreign Relations Committee, the press and the public had known of the extent of the intelligence community's doubts, there would have been a genuine uproar about going to war.)

So I set out to study the men and their decisions. What was it about the men, their attitudes, the country, its institutions and above all the era which had allowed this tragedy to take place? The question which intrigued me the most was *why,* why had it happened. So it became very quickly not a book about Vietnam, but a book about America, and in particular about power and success in America, what the country was, who the leadership was, how they got ahead, what their perceptions were about themselves, about the country and about their mission. The men intrigued me because they were fascinating; they had been heralded as the ablest men to serve this country in this century—certainly their biographies seemed to confirm that judgment—and yet very little had been written about them; the existing journalistic definition of them and what they represented was strikingly similar to their own definition of themselves. So I felt that if I could learn something about them, I would learn something about the country, the era and about power in America. (When I began my legwork, friends of some of the principals told me that it was a mistake to dwell too much on individuals, that the thrust of something like the pressure for this war went beyond individual men. Perhaps, perhaps, but in 1961 no group of men would have argued more vehemently against that very conception, the inability of able, rational men to control irrational events, than the group of men taking power.)

THE BOOK IS LARGELY THE PRODUCT OF MY OWN INTERVIEWS. FOR more than two and a half years I worked full time interviewing people who might be knowledgeable about the men, the events, the decisions. On the decisions themselves it was people primarily in the second, third and fourth tier of government who were helpful in piecing together the play and the

action, although finally several of the principals themselves began to cooper-
ate. Gradually, as I got into the book, I began to work backward in time, trying
to find out how the earliest decisions on Vietnam had been made, how the
trap was set long before anyone realized it was a trap. In all I did some five
hundred interviews for the book, seeing some people as many as ten times,
checking and cross-checking as carefully as I could. The interviews produced
about two thousand pages of single-spaced notes for the book. In addition, I
carefully read the literature of the Kennedy-Johnson period (the Kennedy
literature either totally admiring or bitterly hostile, the Johnson literature
more critical and analytical; it was clearly easier to stand back and analyze
Lyndon Johnson than it was Jack Kennedy). I went through the magazines
and newspapers of the period, and I also read on the fall of China, on the
earlier decisions on Vietnam, and then went back to some of the literature on
the early days of the Cold War, trying to judge the decisions in the context
of the era, with the perceptions which existed then. I had begun the writing
on the book in the late spring of 1971; shortly afterward the Pentagon Papers
were published: if anything, they confirmed the direction in which I was
going and they were rich in the bureaucratic by-play of the era. They were
a very real aid; they set out time and place and direction during those years.
They were for me invaluable and for anyone else trying to trace the origins
and the decisions on Vietnam (the clarity of John McNaughton's insights into
the American dilemma by January 1966 when he realizes that the United
States is locked in a hopeless war is by itself absolutely fascinating). In addition, long before the papers were published, Dan Ellsberg himself had been
extremely generous with his time in helping to analyze what had happened
during the crucial years of 1964 and 1965.

ORIGINALLY I HAD INTENDED TO LIST AT THE END OF THE BOOK THE
names of all the people I had interviewed. However, I recently changed my
mind because of circumstances: the political climate is somewhat sensitive
these days, and the relationship of reporter to source is very much under
attack. The right of a reporter to withhold the name of a source, and equally
important, the substance of an interview, is very much under challenge, and
the latest Supreme Court decision has cast considerable doubt about what
were assumed to be journalistic rights. Even on this book my rights as a
reporter have been diminished; I was subpoenaed by a grand jury in the
Ellsberg case, although I made it clear to the government that I knew nothing
of the passing of the papers. My freedom as a reporter was impaired by the
very subpoena of the grand jury and the need to appear there. I will therefore
list no names here.

EARLIER ON IN THE BOOK I DISCUSSED THE REPORTERS WHO WERE IN Vietnam during the 1962–64 period, saying that while their political and military assessments had been quite accurate (an accuracy ironically acknowledged by the Pentagon's own analysts in the Pentagon Papers history), I felt that they too had failed in part, particularly in comparison with the young State Department China officers of an earlier period, with whom they were in some ways comparable. To a considerable degree I was writing about myself. Some of us who have been critics of the war for a long time were probably ahead of the society as a whole and our profession as a whole, but in our hearts I think we wish we had done a better job. My own attitudes on Vietnam developed over a period of time. In September 1962 I arrived in Saigon as a reporter for the *New York Times*, believing at first in the value of the effort, not questioning the reality of a country called South Vietnam. It was a small war then, the Americans were only advisers, and it seemed to be a test of two political systems in a political war. I thought our system the better, our values exportable, and thought perhaps with luck and skill our side might win, but events soon disabused me. The American optimism of the period was clearly mindless; the Vietcong were infinitely stronger and more subtle than the government, their sense of the people far truer. For dissenting this much from the requisite optimism we became of course prime targets of the Administration and the embassy. At first my journalistic colleagues and I traced most of the faults to the Diem regime itself; however, the more I reported, the longer I stayed and the deeper I probed, the more I felt that despite the self-evident failings of the Ngo family regime, the sickness went far deeper, that all the failings of the American-Diem side grew out of the French Indochina war, in which the other side had captured the nationalism of the country and become a genuinely revolutionary force. In coming to this conclusion I was affected primarily by two men, my colleague Neil Sheehan, then with UPI, and my friend and colleague Bernard Fall. Thus, instead of believing that there was a right way of handling our involvement in Vietnam, in the fall of 1963 I came to the conclusion that it was doomed and that we were on the wrong side of history. My first book on Vietnam, *The Making of a Quagmire*, written in 1964 and published in April 1965, was extremely pessimistic and cast grave doubts about escalation; the North, I wrote, was essentially invulnerable to bombing, and combat troops would bring the same political problems encountered by the French. I felt then that after the long years of supporting the Diem regime, we owed it to the Vietnamese to stay a little longer and continue the mission as long as they felt they could continue the fight, that the signs would have to come first from them (when those signs did come, in late 1964, they became the justification not for withdrawal and cutting back, as George Ball was then pleading in the government, but rather for the American government to switch policies and take over the war). I watched the escalation with mounting disbelief and sadness. It seems the saddest story possible, with one more sad chapter following another. Like almost everyone else I know who has been involved in Vietnam, I am haunted by it by the fact that somehow I was not better, that somehow it was all able to happen.

IN A BOOK LIKE THIS, WHICH TOOK SO LONG TO WRITE, I AM INdebted to many people. I am particularly grateful to my three editors then at *Harper's Magazine*, Willie Morris, Bob Kotlowitz and Midge Decter. In the years I worked there they were a writer's delight. They had the capacity to invoke the best in you; they encouraged you to reach for more and the editing was intelligent and careful; in addition, they all encouraged me to take on this book. John Cowles, the publisher of *Harper's*, was particularly generous to me and the other writers on the staff. James Silberman at Random House has been strong in support of this book, and wise in his sense of conception of it. Bill Polk and Peter Diamandopoulos at the Adlai Stevenson Institute have been extremely generous; after I resigned from *Harper's* in the spring of 1971 they were quick to offer me a fellowship, and in addition to enjoying the particularly warm and pleasant association of the Institute and its fellows, I am grateful on a more basic level—without their help I could not have finished the book on the projected schedule. Edmund Gullion, dean of the Fletcher School of Diplomacy and an old friend from Congo days, was also quick to offer me a place on his staff after the *Harper's* bust and I taught there in the summer of 1971 mostly on the subject of Vietnam, though the dean and I could not disagree more about the subject.

I have mentioned that Dan Ellsberg was generous with his time. There are two others whose professional help I would like to acknowledge. James Thomson, a lecturer in American–East Asian relations at Harvard and now curator of the Nieman Fellows as well, was particularly helpful in making the crucial connection for me between what had happened to the China experts and the impact of this upon the bureaucracy during the Kennedy-Johnson years. In effect, he opened doors which, when I began the book, I did not know existed. He was also extremely generous in showing me his own work on the subject, and his article for the *Atlantic Monthly* on the anatomy of decision making on Vietnam is by far the best single analysis of what happened. With Leslie Gelb, who edited the study which became known as the Pentagon Papers, I had many fruitful discussions about the era. He made available to me his own as yet unpublished chapters on the Roosevelt and Truman era, which were of great value. I am very appreciative of his kindness, particularly in the light of the fact that what I was writing was in effect competitive with his own work.

Among others who have helped me are Richard Merritt, who was quick and fast in checking factual material; Barbara Willson at Random House, firm, tenacious and very effective in editing what was a very long manuscript which came in piece by piece; Julia Kayan, Elaine Cohen and Ann Lowe were also generous with their time at Random House; my lawyer Marshall Perlin was generous and conscientious when I was subpoenaed. Karen Witte was kind enough to Xerox much of the manuscript for me—no small job; Jean Halloran and Avery Rome, both of them *Harper's* exiles, typed the manuscript and occasionally edited it as they typed. Others who were helpful were the staff at Claridge's in Washington, my favorite hotel where I often stayed during long weeks of interviewing; Sam Sylvia of Nantucket was particularly generous on a personal level; and Rhonas A. McGhee of Washington made helpful suggestions from time to time.

BESIDES LISTING THE USUAL BIBLIOGRAPHY, I WOULD LIKE TO mention some of the sources which were particularly valuable and upon which I was more than normally dependent. They include Milton Viorst's article on Dean Rusk, originally published in *Esquire* and then reprinted in his collection *Hustlers and Heroes*; John Finney's magazine article "The Long Trial of John Paton Davies," *New York Times Magazine*, August 31, 1969; E. J. Kahn's profile of Averell Harriman in *The New Yorker*, May 3 and May 10, 1952; Pat Furgurson's biography of Westmoreland, entitled *Westmoreland: The Inevitable General*, which saved my doing a good deal of legwork on the general's boyhood; the books on Lyndon Johnson by Hugh Sidey, Rowland Evans and Robert Novak, and also Phil Geyelin's book; Joe Goulden's book on the Tonkin Gulf incident; Chalmers Roberts' article on the decision not to intervene in Indochina in 1954, "The Day We Didn't Go to War," *The Reporter*, September 14, 1956; Leslie Gelb's chapters from his as yet unpublished book on the origins of the war in Vietnam dealing specifically with the Truman and Roosevelt eras; Don Oberdorfer for what happened in the latter stages of the Johnson Administration in his book *Tet*, and Townsend Hoopes's book *The Limits of Intervention* on the same general period. Ed Dale of the *New York Times* suggested that I spend some time finding out about the economic policies of the Administration during the escalation and was helpful in trying to guide me through it. In addition, the interviews given for the Kennedy Library by Robert Lovett, Henry Luce, Joe Rauh, Dean Acheson, George Kennan and John Seigenthaler were unusually valuable, particularly the Luce interview. It dealt with his 1960 dinner with Joseph Kennedy when they discussed how Jack Kennedy should run as a presidential candidate, and it closely parallels material that Luce gave to John Jessup for Jessup's book on him.

Bibliography

BOOKS ON JOHN F. KENNEDY HIMSELF, AS WELL AS THE KENNEDY CIR-
CLE AND THE KENNEDY STYLE AND CULTURE:

ABEL, ELIE, *The Missile Crisis*. Philadelphia, Lippincott, 1966.
BOWLES, CHESTER, *Promises to Keep: My Years in Public Life 1941–1969*.
    New York, Harper, 1971.
BRADLEE, BENJAMIN, *That Special Grace*. Philadelphia, Lippincott, 1964.
BURNS, JAMES MACGREGOR, *John Kennedy: A Political Profile*. New York,
    Harcourt, 1959.
DOYLE, EDWARD P., ed., *As We Knew Adlai*. New York, Harper, 1966.
FAY, PAUL B. JR., *The Pleasure of His Company*. New York, Harper, 1966.
GALBRAITH, JOHN K., *Ambassador's Journal: A Personal Account of the Ken-
    nedy Years*. Boston, Houghton Mifflin, 1969.
——, *The Triumph*. Boston, Houghton Mifflin, 1968.
HILSMAN, ROGER, *To Move a Nation*. Garden City, N.Y., Doubleday, 1967.
JESSUP, JOHN K., ed., *Ideas of Henry Luce*. New York, Atheneum, 1969.
LANSDALE, EDWARD GEARY, *In the Midst of War: An American's Mission to
    Southeast Asia*. New York, Harper, 1972.
MCNAMARA, ROBERT S., *The Essence of Security: Reflections in Office*. New
    York, Harper, 1968.
MORISON, ELTING, ed., *The American Style*. New York, Harper, 1958.
ROSTOW, WALT W., *The Stages of Economic Growth*. 2nd ed. New York,
    Cambridge University Press, 1971.

SALINGER, PIERRE, *With Kennedy.* Garden City, N.Y., Doubleday, 1966.

SCHLESINGER, ARTHUR M., JR., *Kennedy or Nixon: Does It Make a Difference?* New York, Macmillan, 1960.

———, *A Thousand Days: John F. Kennedy in the White House.* Boston, Houghton Mifflin, 1965.

SORENSEN, THEODORE, *Kennedy.* New York, Harper, 1965.

STEIN, JEAN and PLIMPTON, GEORGE, *American Journey: The Times of Robert F. Kennedy.* New York, Harcourt, 1970.

TANZER, LESTER, ed., *The Kennedy Circle.* Washington, D.C., Luce, 1961.

TAYLOR, MAXWELL, *The Uncertain Trumpet.* New York, Harper, 1960.

WALTON, RICHARD J., *The Remnants of Power: The Tragic Last Years of Adlai Stevenson.* New York, Coward-McCann, 1968.

WHALEN, RICHARD J., *The Founding Father: The Story of Joseph P. Kennedy.* New York, New American Library, 1964.

WHITE, THEODORE H., *The Making of the President 1960.* New York, Atheneum, 1961.

WISE, DAVID, and ROSS, THOMAS B., *The Invisible Government.* New York, Random House, 1964.

JOHNSON AND THE JOHNSON PEOPLE AND STYLE:

ANDERSON, PATRICK, *The President's Men: White House Assistants from FDR through LBJ.* Garden City, N.Y., Doubleday, 1968.

BRAMMER, WILLIAM, *The Gay Place.* Boston, Houghton Mifflin, 1961.

EVANS, ROWLAND, and NOVAK, ROBERT, *Lyndon B. Johnson: The Exercise of Power.* New York, New American Library, 1966.

FURGURSON, ERNEST B., *Westmoreland: The Inevitable General.* Boston, Little, Brown, 1968.

GOLDMAN, ERIC F., *The Tragedy of Lyndon Johnson.* New York, Knopf, 1969.

HAYES, HAROLD, ed., *Smiling Through the Apocalypse: Esquire's History of the Sixties.* New York, McCall's, 1970.

JOHNSON, HAYNES BONNER, and GWERZTMAN, BERNARD M., *Fulbright: The Dissenter.* Garden City, N.Y., Doubleday, 1968.

JOHNSON, LYNDON B., *The Vantage Point: Perspectives of the Presidency.* New York, Holt, 1971.

JOHNSON, SAM HOUSTON, *My Brother Lyndon Johnson.* New York, Cowles, 1970.

McPHERSON, HARRY, *A Political Education.* Boston, Little, Brown, 1972.

O'NEILL, WILLIAM L., *Coming Apart.* Chicago, Quadrangle, 1971.

REEDY, GEORGE E., *The Twilight of the Presidency.* New York, Norton, 1970.

SIDEY, HUGH, *A Very Personal Presidency: Lyndon Johnson in the White House.* New York, Atheneum, 1968.

STEINBERG, ALFRED, *Sam Johnson's Boy*. New York, Macmillan, 1968.

TREWHITT, HENRY L., *McNamara: His Ordeal in the Pentagon*. New York, Harper, 1971.

VIORST, MILTON, *Hustlers and Heroes: An American Political Panorama*. New York, Simon & Schuster, 1971.

WHITE, THEODORE H., *The Making of the President 1964*. New York, Atheneum, 1965.

WHITE, WILLIAM S., *The Professional: Lyndon B. Johnson*. Boston, Houghton Mifflin, 1964.

WICKER, TOM, *JFK and LBJ: The Influence of Personality upon Politics*. Baltimore, Penguin, 1968.

THE DECISION MAKING ON VIETNAM:

AUSTIN, ANTHONY, *The President's War*. Philadelphia, Lippincott, 1971.

BRANDON, HENRY, *Anatomy of Error*. Boston, Gambit, 1969.

ELLSBERG, DANIEL, *Papers on the War*. New York, Simon & Schuster, 1972.

GEYELIN, PHILIP, *Lyndon Johnson and the World*. New York, Praeger, 1966.

GOULDEN, JOSEPH C., *Truth Is the First Casualty: The Gulf of Tonkin Affair—Illusion and Reality*. Chicago, Rand, 1969.

GOULDING, PHIL, G., *Confirm or Deny: Informing the People on National Security*. New York, Harper, 1970.

GRAFF, H., *The Tuesday Cabinet*. Englewood Cliffs, N.J., Prentice-Hall, 1970.

HEREN, LOUIS, *No Hail, No Farewell*. New York, Harper, 1970.

HOOPES, TOWNSEND, *The Limits of Intervention*. New York, McKay, 1970.

JANEWAY, ELIOT, *The Economics of Crisis: War, Politics and the Dollar*. New York, Weybright, 1971.

LEACOCOS, JOHN, *Fire in the Outbasket*. New York, World, 1968.

LOORY, STUART H., and KRASLOW, DAVID, *The Secret Search for Peace in Vietnam*. New York, Random House, 1968.

MANNING, ROBERT, and JANEWAY, MICHAEL, *Who We Are: An Atlantic Chronicle of the United States and Vietnam 1966–1969*. Boston, Little, Brown, 1969.

OBERDORFER, DON, *Tet*. Garden City, N.Y., Doubleday, 1971.

The Pentagon Papers, as published by the *New York Times*. Written by Neil Sheehan, Hedrick Smith, E. W. Kenworthy and Fox Butterfield. New York, Bantam, 1971.

The Pentagon Papers, U.S. Department of Defense. The Senator Gravel edition. Boston, Beacon Press, 1971.

STAVINS, RALPH; BARNET, RICHARD J.; and RASKIN, MARCUS G., *Washington Plans an Aggressive War*. New York, Random House, 1971.

TAYLOR, MAXWELL, *Swords and Plowshares*. New York, Norton, 1972.

WEINTAL, EDWARD, and BARTLETT, CHARLES, *Facing the Brink: An Intimate Study of Crisis Diplomacy.* New York, Scribner, 1967.

THE HISTORY OF AMERICAN INVOLVEMENT IN INDOCHINA:

BUTTINGER, JOSEPH, *Vietnam: A Dragon Embattled.* 2 vols. New York, Praeger, 1967.

CAMERON, ALLAN W., ed., *Viet-Nam Crisis: A Documentary History*, Vol. I, *1940–1956.* Ithaca, N.Y., Cornell University Press, 1971.

DE GAULLE, CHARLES, *The Complete War Memoirs of Charles de Gaulle.* New York, Simon & Schuster, 1968.

DEVILLERS, PHILLIPPE, and LACOUTURE, JEAN, *End of a War: Indochina Nineteen Fifty-Four.* New York, Praeger, 1969.

DRAPER, THEODORE, *The Abuse of Power.* New York, Viking, 1967.

FALL, BERNARD B., *Hell in a Very Small Place.* Philadelphia, Lippincott, 1966.

——, *Street Without Joy.* Harrisburg, Pa., Stackpole, 1966.

——, *Two Vietnams: A Political and Military Analysis.* 2nd rev. ed. New York, Praeger, 1967.

GETTLEMAN, MARVIN E., *Vietnam.* New York, New American Library, 1970.

GREENE, GRAHAM, *The Quiet American.* New York, Viking, 1957.

GURTOV, MELVIN, *The First Vietnam Crisis: Chinese Communist Strategy and United States Involvement, 1953–1954.* New York, Columbia University Press, 1967.

HALBERSTAM, DAVID, *The Making of a Quagmire.* New York, Random House, 1965.

HUGHES, EMMET JOHN, *The Ordeal of Power.* New York, Atheneum, 1963.

KALB, MARVIN, and ABEL, ELIE, *The Roots of Involvement: The U.S. in Asia 1784–1971.* New York, Norton, 1971.

LEDERER, WILLIAM, and BURDICK, EUGENE, *The Ugly American.* New York, Norton, 1958.

MCALISTER, JOHN T., JR., *Viet-Nam: The Origins of Revolution.* New York, Knopf, 1969.

MECKLIN, JOHN, *Mission in Torment.* Garden City, N.Y., Doubleday, 1965.

PFEFFER, RICHARD M., ed., *No More Vietnams: The War and the Future of American Foreign Policy.* New York, Harper, 1968.

RIDGWAY, MATTHEW B., *The Korean War.* Garden City, N.Y., Doubleday, 1967.

——, *Soldier.* New York, Harper, 1956.

SCHELL, JONATHAN, *The Village of Ben Suc.* New York, Knopf, 1967.

SCHLESINGER, ARTHUR M., JR., *The Bitter Heritage: Vietnam and American Democracy 1941–1966.* Boston, Houghton Mifflin, 1967.

SHAPLEN, ROBERT, *The Lost Revolution: U.S. in Vietnam 1946–1966.* New York, Harper, 1965.

THE CHINA ERA:

China White Paper: August Nineteen Forty-Nine. United States Department of State. Stanford, Calif., Stanford University Press, 1971. (Reprint of 1949 ed.)

CLUBB, O. EDMUND, *Communism in China As Reported from Hankow in 1932.* New York, Columbia University Press, 1968.

DAVIES, JOHN P., JR., *Foreign and Other Affairs.* New York, Norton, 1964.

FEIS, HERBERT, *The China Tangle.* Princeton, N.J., Princeton University Press, 1953.

SERVICE, JOHN S., *The Amerasia Papers.* Berkeley, University of California Press, 1971.

SEVAREID, ERIC, *Not So Wild a Dream.* New York, Knopf, 1946.

STILWELL, JOSEPH W., *The Stilwell Papers,* arranged and edited by Theodore H. White. New York, Sloane, 1948.

TUCHMAN, BARBARA W., *Stilwell and the American Experience in China 1911–1945.* New York, Macmillan, 1971.

WEDEMEYER, ALBERT C., *Wedemeyer Reports!* New York, Holt, 1958.

THE MC CARTHY PERIOD:

BUCKLEY, WILLIAM F., JR., and BOZELL, L. BRENT, *McCarthy and His Enemies.* New Rochelle, N.Y., Arlington House, 1954.

COOK, FRED J., *The Nightmare Decade.* New York, Random House, 1971.

HARPER, ALAN D., *The Politics of Loyalty.* Westport, Conn., Greenwood, 1969.

THE COLD WAR PERIOD:

ACHESON, DEAN, *Morning and Noon.* Boston, Houghton Mifflin, 1965.

——, *Present at the Creation: My Years in the State Department.* New York, Norton, 1969.

BARNET, RICHARD J., *The Economy of Death.* New York, Atheneum, 1969.

CAMPBELL, JOHN, *The Fudge Factory.* New York, Basic Books, 1971.

FORRESTAL, JAMES, *Forrestal Diaries.* Walter Millis and E. S. Duffield, eds. New York, Viking, 1966.

GARDNER, LLOYD C., *Architects of Illusion: Men and Ideas in American Foreign Policy*. Chicago, Quadrangle, 1970.

HALLE, LOUIS JOSEPH, *The Cold War As History*. New York, Harper, 1967.

KENNAN, GEORGE F., *Memoirs, 1925–1950*. Boston, Little, Brown, 1967.

STEEL, RONALD, *Imperialists and Other Heroes*. New York, Random House, 1971.

STIMSON, HENRY L., and BUNDY, McGEORGE, *On Active Service in Peace and War*. New York, Harper, 1948.

THE NIXON YEARS:

RIEGLE, DON, *O Congress*. Garden City, N.Y., Doubleday, 1972.

WHALEN, RICHARD, *Catch the Falling Flag*. Boston, Houghton Mifflin, 1972.

MILITARY:

JANOWITZ, MORRIS, *The Professional Soldier: A Social and Political Portrait*. Glencoe, Ill., Free Press, 1960.

JUST, WARD, *Military Men*. New York, Knopf, 1970.

RAYMOND, JACK, *Power at the Pentagon*. New York, Harper, 1964.

RODBERG, LEONARD S., and SHEARER, DEREK, eds., *The Pentagon Watchers: Students Report on the National Security State*. Garden City, N.Y., Doubleday, 1971.

Index

Abrams, General Creighton W., Jr., 548–49, 559

Acheson, Dean G., 4, 6, 7, 9, 10, 13, 21–24, 28, 29, 32, 53, 60, 62, 69, 93, 95, 106–8, 114, 116, 118, 120, 138, 174, 192, 253, 295, 307, 309, 323, 324, 329–42, 395, 398, 403, 425, 438, 488–89, 493, 591, 653

Ackley, Gardner, 605

Adenauer, Chancellor Konrad, 431

Agency for International Development (AID), 152, 260

Agnew, Vice-President Spiro, 663

Alexander, Henry, 9

Allen, Richard V., 63

Alperovitz, Gar, 418

Alphand, Ambassador Hervé, 95

Alsop, Joseph, 21, 24, 35, 45, 90, 112, 115–16, 165–66, 206, 332, 435, 499–500

Alsop, Stewart, 21, 28, 332

Americans for Democratic Action (ADA), 30, 96, 534, 572-73

Andreson, Wilbur, 229

Angell, Robert, 240

Auchincloss, Louis, 4, 11, 52

Arnett, Peter, 562

Ayub Khan, 292

Bailey, John, 13

Baines, Joseph, 442

Baines family, 443

Baker, Russell, 87, 133, 444, 447, 664

Baldwin, Hanson, 601

Ball, George W., 20, 63, 161, 173–75, 196, 197, 219, 263, 304, 306, 307, 310, 328, 358, 368, 372, 373, 378, 435, 484, 491–99, 502–6, 512, 515, 516, 519, 527–28, 532, 534, 563, 574, 579–81, 583–84, 616, 622, 628–29, 660

Ballantine, Arthur, 332

Bao Dai, Emperor, 126, 334, 335, 336

Barnett, David, 133

Barnett, Robert, 191

Bartlett, Charles, 28, 70

Bator, Francis, 62

Belin, Mrs. G. Andelot, 48

Bell, David, 283

Bennett, Harry, 229

Benton, William, 15

Berlin, Sir Isaiah, 57

Bernhard, Prince, 402

Bigart, Homer, 94, 191

Bird, Robert, 241

Black, Eugene, 9, 597
Bohlen, Charles E., 74, 81, 111, 324
Bonesteel, Charles, 319
Borah, Senator William, 612
Borodin, Michael, 384
Bosworth, Charles, 229
Boulding, Kenneth, 365
Bowie, Robert, 343
Bowles, Chester, 8, 11–24, 29, 30, 33–
    35, 67, 68–71, 89, 93, 102, 103,
    130–31, 152, 155–56, 173, 188–
    90, 197, 254, 273, 493, 526, 536
Bowles, Samuel, 15
Bradley, General Omar, 55, 549
Brammer, William, 439
Brandeis, Louis, 331
Brandon, Henry, 45, 617
Breech, Ernie, 230, 231
Brewster, Kingman, 44, 46–47, 51
Bricker, John, 119
Brink, Francis, 510–11
Brinkley, David, 69
Brogan, Denis, 123
Brown, George, 452
Brown, Herman, 452
Brown, Holmes, 233
Brown, James, 5
Brown, Mordecai, 287
Browne, Malcolm, 205
Bruce, David K. E., 31, 633
Bruce, Lenny, 427
Bryan, William Jennings, 527
Buchwald, Art, 87, 648
Bundy, Harvey, 48–50, 59
Bundy, Mrs. Harvey, 47, 48, 51
Bundy, McGeorge, 8, 28, 30–32, 40–
    63, 68, 69, 72, 93–94, 99, 103,
    160–61, 164, 174, 196, 210, 218,
    220, 224, 264, 277, 285, 289,
    293, 294, 305, 346, 347, 353,
    361, 370–71, 373, 376, 377, 383,
    393, 397, 407, 408, 411–14, 434,
    435, 444, 460, 462, 492, 494,
    497, 498, 500, 508, 514–34, 540,
    570, 573, 577, 581, 588, 591,
    592, 599, 619, 620, 622, 625–
    630, 635–36, 653, 657
Bundy, William P., 8, 24, 32, 50–52,
    55, 59, 355, 358, 359, 373, 377,
    378–79, 391, 393–98, 403, 404,
    461, 487, 500, 501, 507, 509,
    521, 528, 549, 569, 570, 575,
    580, 621
Bundy family, 51
Bunker, Ambassador Ellsworth, 645–
    46, 647, 659–60
Burns, James MacGregor, 12, 40, 96
Busby, Horace, 531, 535
Butterworth, W. Walton, 113, 334, 335

Byrnes, James F., 553, 554

Caffery, Ambassador Jefferson, 82, 85
Califano, Joseph, 432
Cannon, James, 423
Carey, Joyce, 157
Carroll, Wallace, 476
Carver, George, 638
Case, Everett, 335
Casey, Ralph, 153
Castro, Fidel, 20, 67, 409, 514
Celebrezze, Anthony J., 36
Central Intelligence Agency (CIA),
    19, 39, 55, 62, 70, 87–89, 91,
    100, 103, 124, 125, 148, 152–54,
    179, 182, 205, 251, 252, 256,
    260–65, 268, 277, 286, 288, 289,
    294, 306–7, 349, 354, 358–60,
    363, 389, 393, 394, 397, 398, 408,
    458, 485, 498, 512, 542, 575,
    580, 631, 637, 638, 644, 651
Chambers, Whittaker, 116
Chaplin, Charlie, 103
Chayes, Abram, 19, 294
Ch'en Chia-k'ang, 388
Chennault, General Claire, 112, 115
Chiang Kai-shek, 110, 112, 115, 129,
    151, 168, 319, 321, 325, 334, 340,
    341, 388, 389
Chuong, Ambassador Tran Van, 288
Church, Senator Frank, 611–12
Churchill, Sir Winston, 7, 81, 135,
    191, 431, 531
Clark, Ramsey, 629
Clay, General Lucius, 106, 407
Clifford, Clark, 9, 86, 152, 438, 591,
    596, 624, 625, 638, 650–53, 656,
    659–60, 663
Clifton, Brigadier General Chester V.,
    548
Clubb, O. Edmund, 189, 324, 326–27,
    620
Cohen, Benjamin, 169–70
Collins, Ambassador J. Lawton, 148,
    417
Conant, James Bryant, 56–57, 58
Conein, Lou, 286–87, 289
Connally, Governor John, 223
Conway, John, 154, 222
Cooper, Chester, 62, 361, 397
Cooper, Senator John Sherman, 418,
    419
Cottrell, Sterling, 173
Council of Economic Advisers, 607,
    608, 609, 610
Council of Foreign Relations, 6, 33,
    42, 55, 60, 504, 595
Craig, General Louis, 556
Cronkite, Walter, 272

Crossen, Colonel William, 545
Crowther, Bosley, 427
Crusoe, Lewis, 230, 235
Cummings, Attorney General Homer, 331
Cunniff, Robert, 625–26

Dale, Ed, 608–9
Daley, Mayor Richard J., 27
Davies, John Paton, Jr., 103, 104, 111, 116, 138, 184, 189, 324, 325, 339–40, 379–92
Davis, John, 49
Day, Postmaster J. Edward, 40
Deakin, James, 46
Dean, Arthur H., 653
De Gaulle, Charles, 69, 75, 80, 81, 82, 84, 310, 344, 371, 431, 505–7
De Lattre de Tassigny, Jean, 338
Defense Intelligence Agency, 256
Democratic Policy Study Group, 445
Deno, Colonel Francisco Caamano, 531
Depuy, General William, 520, 541–42, 563, 567, 582, 612, 613, 618
De Silva, Pier, 485, 503
Dewey, Governor Thomas E., 31, 104, 662
Diem, Ngo Dinh, 46, 93, 94, 110, 126, 127–35, 146, 147–152, 167–70, 173, 174, 176–79, 181–83, 186, 191, 198, 200, 201, 204–9, 212, 250, 252, 254–57, 259, 260, 262–68, 270, 272, 275, 277–79, 283, 285, 287–92, 297, 300, 330, 351, 369, 374, 378, 397, 483, 497, 517
Dillon, Douglas, 6, 9, 61, 436, 653
Dilworth, Mayor Richardson, 13
Dirksen, Senator Everett McKinley, 600
Dobrynin, Ambassador Anatoly F., 592
Dodd, Senator Thomas J., 440
Don, General Tran Van, 287, 289, 351
Dong, General Pham Van, 297
Dong, Premier Pham Van, 183 , 665
Douglas, Helen Gahagan, 12
Douglas, James, 332
Douglas, Senator Paul, 445
Douglas, William O., 147, 451
Draper, General William H., 470
Duff, Senator James, 477
Dulles, Allen, 6, 19, 55, 68, 148, 152, 153, 394, 395, 408
Dulles, John Foster, 13, 18, 22, 23, 32, 33, 55, 87, 88, 95, 114, 121, 131, 137–38, 140–49, 189, 198–99, 311–13, 322, 325, 329–31,

342–43, 377, 380, 390, 415, 433, 510, 528
Durbrow, Ambassador Elbridge, 127, 129, 272
Durr, Clifford, 109
Dutton, Fred, 345

Economic Cooperation Administration, 198
Eisenhower, President Dwight D., 10, 26, 30, 31, 38–41, 49, 61, 68, 76, 80, 86–87, 89, 95, 103, 119–21, 123, 125, 127, 128, 136–44, 146, 153, 156, 157, 162, 220, 268, 274, 318, 319, 445, 464, 470–72, 475, 477, 528, 529, 549, 603
Elliott, William Yandell, 33, 55
Ellsberg, Daniel, 22, 45, 167, 216, 242–43, 247, 366, 598–99, 632, 636–37, 652
Emerson, Ralph Waldo, 479, 563
Erikson, Erik, 58
Evans, Rowland, 452

Faas, Horst, 184
Fairbank, John K., 190, 386, 391
Fall, Bernard, 183
Farmer, Thomas, 196
Faubus, Governor Orval E., 29–30, 33
Faure, Premier Edgar, 148
Federal Bureau of Investigation (FBI), 19, 190, 436, 624
Federal Power Commission, 100
Felt, Admiral Harry D., 89–90, 166, 205
Fensterwald, Bernard, Jr., 113
Ferguson, Senator Homer, 338
Finletter, Thomas K., 495
Finley, John, 44
Finney, John, 391
Fisher, Adrian, 342, 630
Fisher, Roger, 364–65
FitzGerald, Desmond, 348–49, 408
Fitzgerald, John F. (Honey Fitz), 96
Ford, Edsel, 229
Ford, Franklin, 58
Ford, Henry II, 221, 223, 224, 229, 230, 233, 236, 239, 423
Ford Foundation, 41, 54, 625
Forrestal, Secretary of the Navy James V., 6, 105, 107, 153, 190, 198, 226, 332, 339, 376
Forrestal, Michael, 62, 73, 74, 93, 190, 208–12, 264, 265, 274, 276, 285, 300, 366–68, 369, 376–77
Fortas, Abe, 433, 438, 451, 589–90, 609, 611, 625
Fosdick, Ray, 335
Foster, William C., 174

Frankel, Max, 589
Frankfurter, Felix, 331
Freeman, Secretary of Agriculture Orville L., 71
Fritchey, Clayton, 527
Frost, Robert, 38
Fulbright, Senator J. William, 21, 29–30, 32, 67, 68, 145, 174, 316, 373, 404, 409, 415–20, 435, 468, 528–29, 535, 543, 565, 600, 623
Furgurson, Ernest B., 547

Galbraith, John Kenneth, 8, 22, 37, 56, 57, 60, 98, 134, 152, 161, 309, 589–90, 629
Gandhi, Mahatma, 386
Gates, Thomas, 10, 86
Gavin, General James, 163, 417, 420, 470, 474, 477, 555–57, 564
Geneva Agreement, 136, 145
Geneva Conference, 143, 211
George, Senator Walter, 113
Geyelin, Phil, 528
Giap, General Vo Nguyen, 124, 171, 650
Gilpatric, Roswell, 34–35, 36, 128, 131, 173, 215, 246, 258, 263, 478
Goldberg, Arthur J., 71, 448, 457, 506, 589–90, 653–54
Goldwater, Senator Barry M., 8, 235, 296, 299, 300, 402, 403, 406, 415, 416, 419, 420–26, 451, 464, 487, 591, 629
Goodpaster, Andy, 320
Goodwin, Richard N., 33–34, 60, 63, 309, 393, 449–50, 531, 535, 611
Graff, Professor Henry, 406, 449
Green, Marshall, 461
Green, Senator Theodore, 338, 416
Greene, Graham, 125, 291
Greene, General Wallace, 437, 438, 483, 489, 490, 646
Greenfield, James, 586
Griffin, Robert Allen, 335, 336
Gromyko, Foreign Minister Andrei, 592
Gross, Congressman H. R., 507
Gruening, Senator Ernest, 404, 577
Guevara, Che, 68, 123, 159–60
Gullion, Edmund A., 94, 260

Hamilton, Fowler, 152
Hamilton, George, 393
Hamilton, James Pierpont Morgan, 320
Hamlett, General Barksdale, 204
Hand, Judge Learned, 114
Harder, Delmar, 230
Harkins, General Paul D., 90, 179, 180, 183–88, 191, 200–5, 209–12, 248, 249, 251, 279, 280, 283, 287–89, 297, 306, 371, 373, 405–6, 408, 441, 466, 559, 561, 562, 613
Harriman, W. Averell, 6, 21, 23, 31, 73–75, 76, 90–93, 103, 155, 170, 175, 188–98, 213, 250, 253, 254, 261–63, 268, 271, 274–77, 283, 293–95, 299, 300, 307, 310, 321, 344, 345, 358, 367, 369, 374–78, 380, 383, 389, 393, 478, 496, 659–60, 663
Harris Poll, 422
Hart, Senator Philip A., 222
Hellman, Lillian, 4, 58
Helms, Richard, 263, 458
Henderson, Deirdre, 22
Heren, Louis, 542–43, 635
Herrick, Captain John, 412, 413
Hersh, Seymour, 663
Herter, Christian, 86
Higgins, Marguerite, 175, 206
Hilsman, Roger, 104, 123, 124, 190–91, 197, 208, 210, 213, 250, 254–58, 259, 261, 264, 265, 271, 274, 283, 287, 292, 363, 369–75, 378, 392, 543, 649
Hiss, Alger, 390, 394
Hiss, Donald, 394
Hitler, Adolf, 53, 79, 317, 226, 634
Hoffa, James, 273
Holborn, Fred, 95
Holmes, Oliver Wendell, 49, 468
Hoopes, Townsend, 156, 656
Hoover, President Herbert, 39, 49, 50
Hoover, J. Edgar, 19, 436, 437
Hopkins, Harry, 80, 82, 112, 191
Hughes, Emmett, 528, 633
Hughes, Thomas, 19, 363
Hull, Cordell, 62, 79, 308
Humphrey, George, 603
Humphrey, Vice-President Hubert H., 13, 14, 17, 19, 22, 29, 145, 223, 425, 445–46, 531, 533–36, 572, 639, 658, 660–62
Hurley, Patrick, 112, 190, 389

Iacocca, Lee, 236
International Control Commission, 86
Irons, Richard, 52, 53
Isaacs, Harold, 318, 386

Jackson, C. D., 156
Jackson, Senator Henry M., 22
Janeway, Eliot, 609
Jenkins, Walter, 437
Jenner, Senator William E., 121
Jessup, Philip, 334–35

Johnson, Alexis, 520
Johnson, General Harold K., 490, 520, 542, 559, 563, 564–65
Johnson, Secretary of Defense Louis, 307
Johnson, President Lyndon Baines, 13, 20, 22, 25, 27–29, 41, 42, 66, 93, 98, 104, 120, 133–35, 140, 141, 144, 145, 158, 168, 178, 209, 218–21, 225, 247, 260, 261, 291–94, 298–99, 302–6 passim, 495–500, 501, 503, 505–23, 528–33, 536, 538, 539, 543, 545, 552, 559–60, 564, 565, 570, 572–77 passim, 658, 659–64, 665
Johnson, Mrs. Lyndon B. (Lady Bird), 433, 506, 530, 532, 612, 625
Johnson, Robert, 355–58, 497
Johnson, Sam, 442, 443
Johnson family, 443
Jorden, William J., 173
Karnow, Stanley, 77, 135, 177, 615
Kattenburg, Paul, 191, 266–67, 268, 277, 369–71, 649
Katzenbach, Nicholas deB., 51, 162, 345, 392, 421, 629, 653
Kaysen, Carl, 62, 65, 72, 294, 309, 393, 470, 626
Kefauver, Senator Estes, 25
Kelleher, Brigadier General Gerald, 185
Kem, Senator James P., 121
Kennan, Ambassador George F., 7–8, 74, 83, 99–100, 103, 107, 111, 194, 198, 324, 339–40, 341, 380, 383, 394–95, 420
Kennedy, Senator Edward M., 214, 435
Kennedy, President John F., 4, 11–44, 54, 59, 61–77, 86, 88, 89, 91, 92, 94–104 passim, 206, 207–12, 214, 220, 223, 224, 227, 241–43, 246–47, 251, 253–55, 259–60, 262, 264, 268–73, 276, 282, 285, 286, 288, 292, 293, 295–302, 305, 309–11, 314, 321, 343–46, 348, 357, 362, 374, 376, 378, 380, 383, 391, 395, 403–9 passim, 592, 620, 625, 627, 632, 640, 651, 655, 658
Kennedy, Jacqueline (Mrs. John F.), 36, 40, 75, 133, 246, 376, 404, 432, 479
Kennedy, Joseph P., Sr., 4–5, 9, 18–19, 30, 59, 74, 97, 98, 99, 191, 196, 299, 376, 383, 407
Kennedy, Rose (Mrs. Joseph P., Sr.), 9, 380
Kennedy, Robert F., 12, 17, 27, 30, 41, 46, 54, 68–70, 74, 77, 123, 152, 153, 191, 216, 218, 224, 237, 246, 247, 265, 272–76, 285, 377, 383, 402–3, 406–7, 433, 434, 454, 458, 464, 465, 470, 477–79, 519, 590, 629, 639, 645, 649–50
Kennedy, Ethel (Mrs. Robert F.), 218, 246, 479
Kennedy family, 16, 19, 51, 218, 224, 434
Kerensky, Alexander F., 627
Kerr, Clark, 428
Kerr, Senator Robert, 100, 454, 533
Keynes, John Maynard, 605
Khanh, General Nguyen, 351–52, 482–83, 484, 509
Khrushchev, Premier Nikita S., 65, 72, 73, 75–77, 90, 101, 121, 195, 297, 344
Kiker, Douglas, 599
Kim, General Tran Van, 287, 351
King, Admiral Ernest, 80
King, Larry, 440
King, Martin Luther, Jr., 13, 60, 422, 519, 639–40
Kipling, Rudyard, 561
Kirk, Admiral Alan, 55
Kirk, Roger, 55
Kissinger, Henry, 56, 63, 242, 364, 393, 662–65
Kistiakowsky, George, 630
Kleberg, Congressman Richard, 451
Kleiman, Robert, 485
Knowland, Senator William, 121, 139, 140
Knox, Frank, 50
Komer, Robert, 62, 161, 298, 413, 626, 632, 648
Kong Le, 88
Kopechne, Mary Jo, 435
Kosygin, Premier Aleksei N., 519–20, 522, 592, 633, 634
Kraft, Joseph, 46
Kraus, Professor Charles, 117
Krock, Arthur, 10, 26
Krulak, Major General Victor, 191, 204, 205, 257, 263, 271, 275–80, 282, 349, 408
Kubrick, Stanley, 427
Ky, Air Marshal Nguyen Cao, 167, 483, 509, 510, 646

Ladd, Lieutenant Colonel Fred, 187–88, 202, 203
La Follette, Senator Robert, 117
Laird, Secretary of Defense Melvin, 664
Langguth, Jack, 483, 527

Lansdale, Brigadier General Edward, 124–29, 148, 150, 161, 164, 207, 278
Lara, Francis, 124
Lasswell, Harold, 443
Lattimore, Owen, 116
Lazarus, Ralph, 609
Le Carpentier, Lieutenant General Marcel, 136, 336
Leclerc, General Jacques Philippe, 84
Lehman, Senator Herbert H., 195
LeMay, General Curtis, 460, 461–62, 483, 489, 490
Lemnitzer, General Lyman L., 68, 89, 255
Lenin, V. I., 627
Leviero, Anthony, 476
Lin Piao, 122
Lincoln, General George (Abe), 319, 320
Lippmann, Walter, 26, 30, 45, 54, 145, 422, 435, 500
Lodge, Ambassador Henry Cabot, 260, 262–65, 267, 271, 272, 282–83, 285, 287–90, 291, 298, 355, 371, 372, 464
Longworth, Mrs. Alice, 237
Lovett, Robert A., 4–10, 11, 32, 35, 36, 50, 106, 220, 221, 226, 228, 309, 323, 328, 343, 635
Lowell, A. Lawrence, 48, 53, 394
Lowell, Amy, 48
Lowell, Augustus, 48
Lowell, John Amory, 48
Lowell, Percival, 48
Lowell family, 47–48
Luce, Claire Booth, 153
Luce, Henry R., 18–19, 33, 111, 343, 447
Ludden, Raymond, 111, 184
Lundy, J. E., 229

MacArthur, General Douglas, 4, 120, 142, 299, 319, 327, 328–29, 342, 471, 543, 549, 552, 558, 643
McCarran, Senator Patrick A., 121, 190
McCarthy, Senator Eugene, 29, 41, 46, 47, 230, 311, 429, 438, 456, 612, 650
McCarthy, Senator Joseph, 12, 57, 105, 113, 116, 117–20, 174, 318, 324, 329, 331, 335, 390, 394, 529
McCarthyism, 7, 12, 14, 21, 26, 60, 97, 99, 103–4, 121, 147, 165, 188, 189, 366, 379, 382, 386, 388, 426, 492, 500, 534, 592
McCloskey, Senator Paul N., Jr., 662
McCloskey, Robert, 570, 585–87

McCloy, John, 9, 24, 50, 319, 635, 653
McConaughy, Walter, 169, 189
McCone, John, 39, 152–54, 155, 258, 263, 276, 294, 306, 512, 569, 575, 579–80, 588, 661
McConnell, General John P., 483, 490, 646–47
McCormack, Congressman John W., 247, 299, 600, 601
McCulloch, Frank, 614
McDonald, Admiral David, 489, 490
McGee, Gale, 440
McGhee, George, 102–3, 160
McGinniss, Joseph, 562
McGovern, Senator George, 650
Macmillan, Prime Minister Harold, 310
McNamara, Robert S., 10, 32, 34, 39, 41, 43, 45, 61, 69, 71–72, 88–90, 93, 144, 173–76, 186, 187, 196, 213–50 passim, 498, 501, 503, 513–19, 523, 524, 527, 530, 540, 542, 553, 558, 565, 566–71, 573, 575, 577, 580, 581, 588, 591, 593–95, 598–608, 610, 614–17, 621–22, 624, 630–34, 642–45, 653, 656
McNaughton, John, 61, 247, 293, 295, 354, 362–69, 396, 400, 448, 460, 461, 487, 488, 501, 503, 507, 515, 519, 524, 527, 546–47, 574, 575, 577, 588, 616–17, 622, 630, 642, 644, 652
McNaughton family, 362
Magsaysay, Ramón, 124, 126
Mailer, Norman, 97, 426, 639
Malcolm X, 428
Manful, Mel, 252
Mannes, Marya, 18
Manning, Robert, 345
Mansfield, Senator Mike, 29, 139, 147, 207–8, 295, 521–22, 535, 600, 615
Mao Tse-tung, 122, 124, 321, 340–42, 387–89, 390
Marcantonio, Congressman Vito, 108
Marks, Leonard, 535
Marquand, John, 51
Marshall, General George C., 6, 7, 9, 35, 79, 80, 105, 106, 108, 112, 113, 118, 309, 318–23, 324, 333, 463–81, 469, 471, 472, 558
Marshall Plan, 7, 197, 198, 339
Martin, Everett, 637
Marx, Karl, 160
Masaryk, Jan, 106
Maybank, Senator Burnett, 113
Mazo, Earl, 24

Meany, George, 222
Mecklin, John, 205, 251, 260, 262, 275, 277
Meiklejohn, Alexander, 385
Mekong River Redevelopment Commission, 597
Mendenhall, Joseph A., 275, 276–77, 282
Metheny, Brigadier General Lyal, 475
Miller, Arjay, 229, 230
Miller, Loye, 447
Mills, Ben Davis, 229
Mills, Congressman Wilbur D., 606, 609
Milton, John, 46
Minh, General Duong Van, 286–87, 289, 351
Minh, Ho Chi, 105, 120, 122, 123, 126, 145, 147, 148, 150, 207, 335, 338, 353, 410, 414, 438, 465, 491, 506, 590–91, 593, 594, 623, 634, 663
Moffat, Abbott Low, 83, 84–85
Mohr, Charles, 423, 523
Momyer, General William, 539
Monnet, Jean, 174, 492
Moore, George, 229
Moore, Jonathan, 261
Moorer, Admiral Thomas, 490
Morgenthau, Hans, 620
Morse, Senator Wayne, 404, 415, 417–18, 420
Morton, Senator Thruston B., 139, 146
Moyers, Bill, 40, 220, 437, 439, 487, 497, 503, 530, 531, 587, 622, 626, 640
Moynihan, Daniel Patrick, 73, 92, 104
Mundt, Senator Karl, 590
Murphy, Robert, 106, 653
Murrow, Edward R., 119
Mus, Paul, 84
Myrdal, Gunnar, 156

Nader, Ralph, 239, 428
National Security Council (NSC), 72, 89, 151, 271, 275, 277, 279, 319, 344, 345, 353, 437, 472, 521, 534, 593, 599
National Youth Administration, 451
Nehru, Jawaharlal, 334, 437
Nelson, Gaylord, 418–19, 572
Nes, David, 372–73
Neustadt, Richard, 62
Ngo family, 131, 168, 182, 260, 262–65, 272, 277, 283, 288, 290, 291
Nhu, Ngo Dinh, 127, 129, 131, 168, 181, 182, 209–10, 252, 261–62, 264–65, 272, 285, 287–91, 369
Nhu, Madame, 131, 208, 288

Nitze, Paul, 395
Nixon, President Richard M., 8, 12, 17, 19, 20, 26, 63, 96–98, 108, 119, 140, 163, 207, 324, 392, 420, 436, 450, 472, 629, 652, 660–65
Nolting, Ambassador Frederick E., Jr., 129–32, 168, 177, 179, 181–83, 188, 198, 209, 211, 212, 251, 252, 259–62, 268, 277, 283
North Atlantic Treaty Organization (NATO), 7, 23, 89, 130, 131, 197, 293, 308, 322–23, 339, 614
Nosavan, General Phoumi, 87–88, 92, 93
Novak, Robert, 452
Nuclear Planning Group, 243

Oberdorfer, Donald, 664
O'Brien, Lawrence, 654, 662
O'Donnell, Kenneth, 154, 247, 300, 487
Ogburn, Charlton, 85
O'Hara, Congressman James, 222
Okun, Arthur, 607
O'Neill, William, 428
Oppenheimer, J. Robert, 103
Owen, David, 53

Palmer, General Bruce, 559, 646
Pao, Ambassador C. J., 383
Parker, Theodore, 48
Parsons, Ambassador Graham, 88, 189
Patterson, Robert, 50, 226
Patton, General George S., 180, 185, 559
Peace Corps, 100, 383
Pearson, Drew, 117
Peers, Colonel Ray, 180
Pentagon Papers, 267, 280, 354, 362, 370, 409, 495, 633, 656
Permissive Action Link (PAL), 244
Phillips, Rufus, 275, 278–79, 282, 284
Phouma, Prince Souvanna, 88, 90, 91
Pike, Douglas, 185
Point Four Program, 7
Popovic, Foreign Minister Koča, 100
Porter, Colonel Daniel, 202, 203
Potter, Phil, 298
Pusey, Nathan, 40, 44, 57, 58
Pushkin, G. M., 91
Putnam, Mr. and Mrs. William, 48
Pye, Professor Lucian, 160

Oliver Quayle poll, 406

Radford, Admiral Arthur W., 137–38, 140–44, 475
Raskin, Marcus, 59–60

Rauh, Joseph, 30, 533, 573
Rayburn, Congressman Samuel T., 41, 100, 133, 405, 444–45, 450, 451–52
Raymond, Jack, 249
Reedy, George, 432–33, 439, 449, 456, 530, 584–85, 587, 640
Rielly, John, 534
Reischauer, Ambassador Edwin O., 189–90
Reith, John, 229
Reston, James, 26, 39, 45, 75–77, 570, 625, 640
Reuther, Walter, 70, 154, 222, 423
Rice, Edward, 190
Richards, James, 139
Richardson, John, 205, 261–62, 264, 265, 288
Ridgway, General Matthew B., 142–45, 162, 169, 172, 242, 329, 417, 466, 467, 470, 472, 473, 537–38, 549, 555–56, 603
Riesman, David, 42–43, 58
Rivers, Congressman L. Mendel, 246, 248, 604, 605
Roberts, William, 117
Robertson, Walter, 149
Roche, Professor John, 573
Rockefeller, Governor Nelson, 8, 46, 73, 97, 192, 195, 196, 305, 322, 343, 344, 420
Rockefeller family, 33
Rockefeller Foundation, 32, 33, 34, 35, 41, 220
Rogers, Secretary of State William, 664
Romney, Governor George, 519
Romulo, Carlos, 336
Rooney, Congressman John, 247
Roosevelt, President Franklin D., 16, 21, 22, 26, 39, 50, 52, 79, 80–82, 104, 105, 109, 191, 309, 321, 331, 332, 344, 450, 451–52, 453, 455, 529, 640
Roosevelt, Eleanor (Mrs. Franklin D.), 12, 14, 22–23, 24, 112, 534
Roosevelt, Franklin D., Jr., 139, 223
Roosevelt, President Theodore, 7, 39, 49, 50, 192, 331, 348
Root, Elihu, 7
Rostow, Walt W., 39, 40, 42, 43, 44, 123, 124, 128, 150–52, 155, 156–62, 164, 167, 169, 171, 172, 177, 181, 182, 353, 356, 357, 414, 502, 524, 540, 553, 626, 630–31, 635–37, 643, 648, 653, 654–55, 659, 660
Rowe, James H., Jr., 533
Rusk, Dean, 6, 7, 9, 28, 32–37, 41, 43, 57, 58, 61, 62–63, 69, 70, 72, 89, 93, 102, 128, 155, 160, 173, 175, 176, 189, 196–97, 213, 220, 255, 260, 261, 264–67, 285, 293, 294, 305, 307–29 *passim*, 590, 614, 619, 621–22, 628, 631, 633–35, 638, 653, 657, 660, 663
Rusk family, 312–14
Russell, Senator Richard, 139–40, 141, 146, 440, 444–45, 454, 528–29, 533

Salinger, Pierre, 71, 296, 531, 585
Salisbury, Harrison, 632, 665
Sarris, Lewis, 257–58, 287
Schlesinger, Arthur M., Jr., 22, 36, 40, 59, 60, 63, 74, 99, 103, 152, 155, 175, 190, 309, 383, 393, 477, 627, 629
Schuman, Robert, 337
Scranton, William W., 464
Seaborg, Glenn, 344
Seigenthaler, John, 407
Serong, Colonel Francis, 276
Service, John Stewart, 111, 184, 189, 324, 379, 383, 392
Sevareid, Eric, 383, 386
Sharp, Admiral U.S. Grant, 538, 540, 546, 571–72, 575, 576, 583, 642
Sharpe, Lauriston, 85
Shattuck, Henry, 54
Sheehan, Neil, 207, 409, 434, 550
Shepard, David, 277
Shoup, General David M., 66–67, 269–70, 417
Shriver, Sargent, 40, 221, 383
Shriver, Eunice (Mrs. Sargent), 75
Sidey, Hugh, 439, 449
Sihanouk, Prince, 300
Smail, John, 652
Smedley, Agnes, 387–88
Smith, Governor Alfred E., 193
Smith, Bromley, 534
Smith, Congressman Howard, 65
Smith, Mr. and Mrs. Stephen, 134
Smith, Ambassador Walter Bedel, 106–7, 138, 319
Snow, Edgar, 386
Solbert, Peter, 55
Sorensen, Theodore, 12, 13, 17, 28, 36, 41, 100
Souphanuvong, 92
South-East Asia Treaty Organization (SEATO), 86, 90, 150, 161, 166, 168, 197
Springsteen, George, 534
Sproul, Dr. Robert Gordon, 225
Staebler, Neil, 221–22

Stalin, Joseph, 81, 107, 114, 190, 191, 387, 388, 389, 390
Stanley, Oliver, 81
Starbird, General Alfred, 216
Stark, Admiral Harold, 79
Steele, John, 447
Stennis, Senator John, 154, 246, 248, 294, 295, 440, 507, 604, 605, 645
Stettinius, Edward, 81
Stevenson, Adlai E., 8, 12, 13, 14, 19, 20, 22, 23, 24, 26–29, 31, 56, 67, 70, 95, 102, 153, 174, 254, 293, 309, 322, 408, 435, 445, 448, 492, 493, 521, 527, 589, 592, 621, 655
Stilwell, General Joseph W., 34, 110, 112, 116, 129, 184, 186, 200, 318, 387, 469
Stilwell, Brigadier General Richard Giles, 251–52, 277, 279, 280, 306, 542
Stimson, Secretary of War Henry L., 4, 6, 7, 48–50, 53, 54, 83, 319, 395
strategic hamlet program, 176, 182, 187–88, 275 ff.
Strauss, Admiral Lewis, 30
Sullivan, William, 91, 285, 375, 377
Sully, François, 252
Surrey, Walter, 391–92
Swidler, Joseph, 100, 101
Sylvester, Arthur, 217, 249, 527, 585
Symington, Senator Stuart, 13, 22

Taft, Senator Robert A., 119, 139, 441
Taft, President William Howard, 49, 331
Talese, Gay, 73
Taussig, Charles, 81
Taylor, General Maxwell D., 40, 67, 123, 152, 156, 162–81, 186, 191, 200, 203–5, 216, 218, 242, 263, 264–74, 280, 283–86, 291, 293, 371, 375, 397, 482–89, 498, 502, 503, 507–11, 520, 524, 538–40, 543–47, 555–60, 563–80, 583, 651, 656, 657
Thant, U, 621
Thi, General Nguyen Chanh, 510
Thieu, President Nguyen Van, 646, 659, 660, 663, 665
Thomas, Congressman J. Parnell, 109
Thompson, Ambassador Llewellyn, 74, 76, 90, 111, 522
Thomson, James, 19, 62, 156, 188–89, 190, 413, 536
Thornton, Charles, 226–29, 230, 231
Throckmorton, General John L., 545
Thuan, Nguyen Dinh, 168

Thurmond, Senator J. Strom, 109, 153
Trueheart, William, 130, 251–52, 258, 259, 261, 283, 369, 371–72, 374
Trujillo, General Rafael, 69
Truman, President Harry S., 6, 10, 31, 39, 78, 108, 109, 153, 160, 192, 309, 321, 327, 330, 332, 334, 338, 425, 446, 453, 455, 591, 643, 652
Truman Doctrine, 108, 120, 333
Tshombe, Moise, 292
Tuchman, Barbara, 110
Twining, General Nathan F., 475

Unger, Ambassador Leonard, 570
United Nations, 13, 23, 28, 31, 84, 237, 294, 310, 319, 320, 325, 328, 408, 410, 448, 501, 573, 590
United Public Workers of America, 394
United States Information Agency (USIA), 251, 260, 275, 277, 352, 535

Valenti, Jack, 405, 437, 439, 491, 530, 535, 626, 640
Vallejo, Frank, 615
Vance, Cyrus, 224, 521, 598
Vandenberg, Senator Arthur, 108, 333
Van Fleet, General James, 251
Vann, Lieutenant Colonel John Paul, 202–5, 248–49, 270, 280, 542, 561, 613, 637
Vanocur, Sander, 46, 296, 616
Vincent, John Carter, 78, 79, 83, 112–13, 114, 332, 335
Vinson, Congressman Carl, 246
Viorst, Milton, 34, 48

Walker, General Walton, 142
Wallace, Governor George, 406, 661
Wallace, Henry, 109, 492
Walsh, Father Edmund, 117
Ward, Barbara, 237, 439
Warnecke, John Carl, 448
Warner, Lloyd, 317
Warnke, Paul, 396, 448, 449, 651
Watson, Marvin, 433
Wavell, General Archibald P., 191
Wedemeyer, General Albert C., 112
Weisl, Edward, 451
Welles, Sumner, 79
Westmoreland, General William C., 145, 405, 465, 466, 470, 475–77, 485, 486, 503, 510, 517, 520, 538–68, 571–72, 575–77, 582–84, 586, 594, 595, 597, 598, 600, 602, 604–6, 611–15, 618, 620, 641–43, 646–48, 653

Weyand, General Frederick C., 561
Whalen, Richard, 661–62
Wheeler, General Earle G., 204, 460, 462, 490, 538, 567, 575, 576, 583, 588, 596, 599–600, 601, 617, 632, 642, 645
White, Harry Dexter, 390
White, Theodore, H., 111, 150, 195–96, 381, 386–89, 487
White, William, 441, 447
Whiting, Allen, 191, 496
Whiz Kids, 229, 230, 231, 247
Wicker, Tom, 124, 296, 520, 530, 610, 634–35
Wiesner, Jerome, 72, 103, 309, 393, 630
Wilkins, Roy, 422
Williams, Governor G. Mennen (Soapy), 31, 70, 222
Wills, Garry, 49
Wilson, Charles E., 472, 473, 475, 476
Wilson, Prime Minister Harold, 402
Wilson, Colonel Wilbur, 202, 203

Wilson, President Woodrow, 39, 331, 495
Wofford, Harris, 13–14, 17, 19, 23, 30
Woodin, Secretary of the Treasury Will, 332
World Bank, 220, 227, 514
Wright, Jim, 229
Wylie, Laurence, 58

Yarborough, Senator Ralph W., 291
Yarborough, Major General William, 180
Yarmolinsky, Professor Adam, 217, 224, 243
Yeuell, Colonel Donovan, 474–75, 476
York, General Robert, 203
Young, Earl, 278–79
Young, Ambassador Kenneth Todd, 131–32, 182, 272
Young, Whitney, 312, 640
Youngblood, Rufus, 298

Zaplocki, Clem, 654
Zorthian, Barry, 352, 520, 615

About the Author

DAVID HALBERSTAM, one of America's most brilliant and respected journalists, first came to national prominence in 1962 and 1963 with his reports from Vietnam for the *New York Times*; these dispatches earned for him the Pulitzer Prize in 1964. He has also received the George Polk Memorial Award for foreign reporting, the Page One Award from the American Newspaper Guild, and with Neil Sheehan and Malcolm Browne, the first Louis M. Lyons Award, given by the Nieman Fellows of Harvard University. *Commentary* called him "the *Times'* most exceptional reporter of recent years"; *Harper's* termed him "at the age of thirty-five . . . a legend in American journalism"; and when sociologists at Columbia University polled 150 American intellectuals on the most important influences on their thinking about Vietnam, they responded by citing the late Bernard Fall and Mr. Halberstam. His own journalistic odyssey has taken him to the smallest daily in Mississippi for a year, to four years on the Nashville *Tennessean*, and to the *Times*, where he served for six years as a foreign correspondent in Leopoldville, Saigon and Warsaw. In 1967 he left the *Times* to work for *Harper's* as a contributing editor, where he remained until 1971. At present he is a fellow of the Adlai Stevenson Institute.

Born in New York City, Mr. Halberstam graduated from Harvard, where he was managing editor of the *Crimson*. His first major book was *The Making of a Quagmire*, a pessimistic and prophetic report on Vietnam published in early 1965, which Graham Greene read with "extreme fascination and respect—a really important book." His other books include *The Unfinished Odyssey of Robert Kennedy*, which the *Times* called "far and away the best book about Senator Kennedy"; *Ho*, described by Harvard University's East Asian Research Center as "an important and incisive essay"; and a novel, *One Very Hot Day*, of which the *Christian Science Monitor* said, "This is one of those books that every American should read."